The Analogy of Love
*Divine and Human Love at the Center
of Christian Theology*

GARY CHARTIER
La Sierra University

IMPRINT ACADEMIC

Copyright © Gary Chartier 2007

The moral rights of the author have been asserted.
No part of this publication may be reproduced in any form without permission,
except for the quotation of brief passages in criticism and discussion.

Published in the United Kingdom by Imprint Academic
PO Box 200, Exeter
Devon, EX5 5YX, United Kingdom

Published in the United States of America by Imprint Academic
Philosophy Documentation Center
PO Box 7147, Charlottesville, VA 22906-7147, United States of America

ISBN 9-781845-400910

Chartier, Gary
The Analogy of Love: Divine and Human Love at the Center of Christian Theology
Includes bibliographic references and index
1. Theology, Doctrinal. 2. God—Love
3. Love—Religious aspects—Christianity. I. Title

A CIP catalogue record for this book is available from the
British Library and the United States Library of Congress.

http://www.imprint-academic.com

For
Helen Chartier,
mother extraordinaire

Contents

	Dedication	iv
	Contents	v
	Acknowledgments	ix
	Preface	xv
1.	Love at the Center	1
	The Meaning of Love	1
	Love and the Architecture of Theology	2
	Love and the Content of Theology	8
	Features of a Love-Centered Theology	14
	Love and Complacency	15
2.	Love Begins Where We Are	19
	Belief and Love	20
	Love, Belief, and Action	21
	Love and Revelation	22
	Love and the Roots of Belief	24
	Love, Faith, and Reason	33
	Confidence and Commitment	35
	The Apparent Absence of God	37
	The Reality of Pointless Harm	39
	Love and the Attractiveness of Christian Belief	49
3.	Whose Nature and Whose Name Are Love	51
	Love as Personal	52
	The Christian Meaning of "God"	55
	The Functions of Trinitarian Doctrine	56
4.	The Power of Love	59
	The Roots of Christian Talk about God as Holy Spirit	60
	Starting with Suffering	60
	Love and the Nature of Divine Power	61
	Love Cherishes the Particular	63
	God's Spirit and the Reception of Revelation	68
	God's Spirit and Prayer	69
	God's Spirit and Spiritual Gifts	74
5.	Love Makes the World	81
	The Loving Creator	82
	Love and the Reality of Creation	83

	Loving God in Creation	85
	Loving the Creator through Science	96
	Loving God's Good Creation	97
	The Contours of Love	102
	Alternative Conceptions of Love for Creation	106
	Divine Command Ethics and God's Love for Creation	112
	Morality and Religion	121
	The Shape of Shalom	122
	The Sabbath and Creative Love	128
6.	Disordered Love	131
	The Abuse of Sin-Language	131
	Inadequate Accounts of Disordered Love	133
	Disordered Love and the God of Love	135
	Sin and Harm	135
	Disordered Love as a Condition	141
	Gender and Disordered Love	144
7.	Love Takes Flesh	149
	Jesus, the Remembered Lover	150
	Jesus' Disclosure and Demonstration of God's Love	156
	The Identity of Jesus and the Love of God	160
	Jesus and Maleness	163
8.	Love Suffers Long	167
	Jesus' Birth and His History	167
	Jesus and God's Suffering Love	170
	Our Story and Jesus' Story	177
	The Cross and the Vulnerable God	179
	The Politics of the Cross	184
	The Representative Particularity of Jesus' Suffering	185
	The Cross and the Reality of Death	185
	Jesus' Descent to the Grave	186
9.	Love Is Alive	187
	The Difference Jesus' New Life Makes	188
	Why Love Affirms Jesus' Life beyond Death	190
10.	Love Bears All Things	197
	Divine Acceptance	198
	Salvation and Meaning	203
	Love, Growth, and Healing	204
	The Dynamics of Human Forgiveness	209
	Judgment as Love's Work	211
	The Activity of Jesus and God's Healing Work	213
	The God of Love and the God of Hell	222
	Love and Double Predestination	224
11.	A Loving and Beloved Community	229
	Rooted in Love	229
	The Church, Jesus, and God's Spirit	231
	Love as the Church's Calling	232
	Love as the Mark of the True Church	243
	The Inclusiveness of the Loving and Beloved Community	246
	Universal Love and Dialogue across Traditions	249
	Loving a Challenging Church	269

12.	Love Hopes All Things	275
	Love's Hope for History	275
	Why Love Hopes Beyond Death	280
	The Significance of Personal Hope Beyond Death	283
	Index	287
	About the Author	295

Acknowledgments

As is surely appropriate for a book in which love plays a central role, *The Analogy of Love* reflects the importance in my life of innumerable conversations and connections.

To my teachers of Christian doctrine, Christian ethics, and the philosophy of religion—Brian Hebblethwaite, Charles Teel, Jr., Fritz Guy, John Hick, Nicholas Lash, and T. Richard Rice—I owe a substantial debt of gratitude for helping me to see how faith might seek understanding. Fritz, in particular, has read substantial portions of this book on at least three separate occasions during the various stages of its evolution.

Other friends have been significant interlocutors during the time this book was being conceived and written. They include Elenor Webb, Annette Bryson, Jeffrey Cassidy, Aena Prakash, Alexander Lian, Andrew Howe, Carole Pateman, Craig R. Kinzer, David B. Hoppe, David R. Larson, Deborah K. Dunn, Donna Carlson, Eva Pascal, Heather Hessel, Joel Sandefur, John W. Webster, Julio C. Muñoz, Kenneth A. Dickey, Lawrence T. Geraty, Linda M. Gilbert, Linn Marie Tonstad, Maria Zlateva, Miralyn Keske, Nabil Abu-Assal, Patricia Cabrera, Roger E. Rustad, Jr., Ronel Harvey, Ruth E. E. Burke, Sel J. Wahng, W. Kent Rogers, and Wonil Kim. Jeffrey, in particular, helped to improve the book with his last-minute review of the proofs.

I first used the material in this book as the basis for a course, Christian Beliefs and Life, which I taught at La Sierra University in the spring of 1992. Enrolled in that class, the first I had ever taught, were Beverly Nation, Chantelle Kite, Eddy Palacios, Greg Hoenes, Guillermo McGregor, Jennifer Cline, John R. Rivera, Jr., and W. Kent Rogers. My dialogue with a number of these students has continued over the intervening years—Kent, in particular, devoted a directed study a decade later to reacting to the book in a later form. I remain grateful for the willingness all of these students exhibited to engage with me in a discussion of difficult and important matters during a quarter many of us found memorable and challenging.

More recently, a group of senior students enrolled in La Sierra University's Honors Program gamely agreed to participate in a quarter-long conversation with me about the book in a course called Religion and the Future. They were often—doubtless rightly—critical; but they were always respectful, curious, and thoughtful. Natalie Marchand, José Vargas, Clayton Koh, Nicole Modell, and Megan Pennington all deserve my thanks for the attention they gave this book. I am also thankful to those who participated in a conversation at a February 1996 meeting of the Pacific Division of Society of Christian Ethics for comments regarding text that appears here as part of Chapter 5, and to Brian Hebblethwaite, David Larson, Nicholas Lash, and Jim Fodor for comments on material incorporated throughout.

In the period since January 1994, I have presented drafts of some portions of this book as homilies at the 8:30 AM worship service at the La Sierra University Church. Among those who have been on-hand have been Adeny Schmidt and Ken Sutter, Dan Smith, Ernestina Garbutt-Parales, Gary and Janet Bradley, Jean Lowry, Kathleen and Robert Dunn, Mary Jo Standing, Paul and Suzanne Mallery, and Rhona Hodgen. Brad Whited, in particular, encouraged me to pursue publication of what is now a portion of Chapter 6.

Participants in the Sabbath School class I teach at the Loma Linda University Church—inherited directly from David Larson and indirectly from Fritz Guy and Jack Provonsha—have joined in lively exchanges regarding ideas contained in these pages, and, in at least one case, a substantial portion of the text. They have included Ardyce and Dick Koobs, Brian Bull, Bruce and Susan Wilcox, Cyril Blaine, Forrest Bailey, George and Shirley Javor, Ignatius Yacoub, Ladan Ask, Larry Arany, Michael Scofield, Sydney Allen, and Torben Thomsen.

Teachers with whom I never studied Christian doctrine or the philosophy of religion have nonetheless shaped my thinking in all sorts of ways for which I am thankful. I would be remiss if I failed to acknowledge Vernon Howe, James W. Beach, Albert E. Smith, Arthur Rosett, Carole Goldberg, Cruz Reynoso, David M. Veglahn, Delmer G. Ross, Edward Ney, Elliot Dorff, Fred Hoyt, Gary Bradley, Gene Gascay, George Hilton, Jack Coogan, Jacques Benzakein, Jerry Kang, Kenneth H. Karst, Lawrence D. White, Niels-Erik Andreasen, Pamela Hieronymi, Peter Arenella, Randall Peerenboom, Rennie B. Schopeflin, Richard Abel, Richard Steinberg, Seana Shiffrin, Stephen Gardbaum, Stephen R. Munzer, Taimie L. Bryant, and W. Rand Norton. Though they were never actually my teachers, Barbara Herman, Barry Graham, Bob Grant, Don Cupitt, Ed Karlow, Eugene Volokh, Juan Velez, Judy Meyers Laue, Kenneth Vine, Lee Wilson, Leon Mashchak, Madelynn Haldeman, Margarete Hilts, Nicholas Sagovsky, Paul J. Landa, Roger Tatum, and Stephen W. Sykes all proved helpful, supportive, and engaging outside the classroom.

A number of thinkers who were never my teachers have been especially influential in shaping my thinking. As I trust the notes at least sometimes make clear, I have learned and continue to learn about things that matter from David Ray Griffin, Keith Ward, Karl Rahner, Stephen R. L. Clark, Robert Merrihew Adams, Nicholas Wolterstorff, John M. Finnis, Austin Farrer, John B. Cobb, Jr., Alasdair Macintyre, Alvin Plantinga, C. F. D. Moule, Charles M. Fried, Chuck Scriven, Colin McGinn, David Brown, Diogenes Allen, E. P. Sanders, Germain Grisez, Hans Küng, Henri Nouwen, Hugh Prather, Iris Murdoch, Jack Provonsha, James William McClendon, Jr., John Caputo, John Macquarrie, John Rawls, John Searle, Karl Barth, Langdon Gilkey, Marcus Borg, M. Scott Peck, N. Tom Wright, Nancey Murphy, Onora O'Neill, Paul J. Griffiths, Richard Swinburne, Robert P. George, Sam Keen, Stanley Hauerwas, T. M. Scanlon, Thomas Nagel, William C. Placher, William Lane Craig, and Wolfhart Pannenberg. Rereading the work of Professor Provonsha, in particular, I am struck by how much I have learned from him. George Newlands, John McIntyre, Vincent Brümmer, Daniel Day Williams, and Clark Pinnock have written about love and theology in ways that sometimes parallel what I have done here; their explorations of this important theme deserve ongoing attention.

The institutional context in which I have functioned during most of the time since 1991 has played a valuable role in fostering and facilitating my work. The respect, gratitude, and affection I owe to John Thomas, dean of the School of Business, are incalculable. Dean Thomas has nurtured my research and provided me with unstinting personal and professional support, and I am honored to own him as my friend. I am also grateful for the assistance and support of Fritz Guy and Lawrence T. Geraty, La Sierra University's presidents during the time this book was "under construction"; Dorothy Minchin-Comm, Ron Graybill, and Arthur Patrick, successive editors of *Adventist Heritage* magazine; Adeny Schmidt, dean of arts and sciences and, subsequently, vice president for academic administration during my time at *Adventist Heritage*; Warren C. Trenchard, provost from 2003; John R. Jones and John W. Webster, deans of the university's School of Religion while this book was gestating; James W. Beach, dean of arts and sciences from 1999; Andy Truong, Bob Beshara, Danette Zurek, Elias Rizkallah, George Ogum, Heather Miller, Jodi Cahill, Juanita Singh, Kristine Webster, Lee H. Reynolds, Luke Robinson, Prudence Pollard, Siddharth Swaminathan, Tadeusz Kugler, and Wally Lighthouse, professional colleagues in the School of Business; Steven G. Daily, university chaplain; Melanie Johnson, assistant to the chaplain; the late Paul J. Landa, professor of the history of Christianity; Vern Carner, director of the La Sierra University Press, David Dudley, director of the university's Counseling Center; Vernell Kaufholtz, assistant to the dean of the School of Business; Cheryl Bauman, student academic advisor at the School of Business; and Marvella Beyer and Suzy Kaspereen, assistants to the deans of the School of Religion.

Libraries play an indispensable role in almost all scholarship, obviously, and mine has been no exception. The La Sierra University Library was my principal base of operations. I am grateful for the help given me by members of its faculty and staff, including Barbara Lear, Chris Cicchetti, Cindy Parkhurst, Gilbert Abella, H. Maynard Lowry, James Glennie, James Walker, Jon Hardt, Kitty Simmons, Sandra Browning, Vera Mae Schwartz, and others. Other area libraries were helpful as well. I drew regularly on the library resources of the University of California at Riverside, which has proven invaluable to my research over the years; I also acknowledge gladly the assistance I received from public services librarians at UCR's Tomás Rivera Library. References to a variety of resources held by the Del E. Webb Memorial Library, Loma Linda University, have found their way into my footnotes at various times. My experiences at the Webb Library are consistently richer than they might otherwise be because of the presence and assistance of Chris Cao, Daryl Swarm, Denise Bell, Elton Jornada, Marilyn Crane, Petr Cimpoereu, Sam Cho, and others; reference librarians whom I do not know have also been helpful to me. The Thompson Library of the Loma Linda University Center for Christian Bioethics has provided me with more than one valuable source, and Genie Sample graciously tolerated my not-always-responsible habits as a patron of the Center's library. I note, too, with thanks the contribution to my research during the last decade and a half made by the Riverside County Public Library, some of whose holdings have also informed my thinking and writing during the last decade and a half.

Anthony Freeman has been a thoughtful, helpful editor. I am grateful for his support for this book and for the freedom he has given to a sometimes-idiosyncratic author.

Thanks also to Adrian Macintyre, Ahmed Jamal, Al Azevedo, Alan Swarm, Albert Sanchez, Alfonso and Hurda Duran, Alina Sanchez and George Bryson, Alma, Ami Saunders, Amy Eva-Wood and David Wood, Ana Gamboa, and Melanie Teel, Andrew Johnston, Andrew Trim, Anees Haddad, Aneva Sanchez, Angelique Aitken, Angie Kwik, Anju Massey, Anne and Darryl Collier-Freed, Anne Marie Pearson, Armond and Pamela Manassian, Arthur Kline, Ashleigh and Fred Clarke, Audrey Judd, Babyloni Anderson, Bailey and Judy Gillespie, Barbara Favorito, Benjamin Rockwell, Bill Hessel, Blair Bradley, Blanca Fromm, Bob and Rosalie Bauman, Bob Griffiths, Brad Abernethy and Jocelyn Downie, Brenda Glennie, Brent Bradley, Brent Kinman, Brian Brock, Bridgette Duggan, Bronwen Larson, Candace and Lennard Jorgenson, Carol Richardson, Carolyn Pearson, Carson Stewart, Catherine Taylor, Charles Jackson, Cheng Ng, Cherie and Glen Rouse, Cheryl Koos and Clark Davis, Chris Drake, Christine Cassidy, Christopher Reeves, Chuck Sandefur, Cliff Clue, Coco Owen, Colleen Beshara, Craig Svonkin, Cruz Reynoso, Crystal K. Coleman, Curtis Hardin and Maxine Park, Damon Kelsay, Daniel Aldana, Daniel and Paula Ardron, Daniel and Michele Pfenninger, Daniel Schramm, Daryl Swarm, David and Kathy Stone, David and Ligia Doran, David and Stephanie Brooks, David Bergland, D. P. Harris, David Pendleton, Deana Pascal, Demetra Andreasen, Dennis de Leon and Milenne Aldana, Dewald Kritzinger, Diana Zlateva, Dmitri Radoyce, Don Cicchetti, Don Hunter, Donna Greschner, Doug Clark, Doug Hackleman, Ed Boyatt, Ed Zackrison, Edward Pflaumer, Edward W. H. Vick, Edwin Karlow, Elissa Kido, Elizabeth Burns-Wainwright, Enoch Hwang, Erik K. Frykman, Eric Merrifield, Ernie Schwab, Esther Kim, Esther Kinzer, Esther Saguar, Frank Knittel, Gary Gilbert, Gary and Suha Huffaker, George Lucas, Gerald Winslow, Gillian Geraty, Gina Foster, Gina Neff, Ginger Hanks-Harwood, Glen and Irene Van Fossen, Glenn and Patricia Foster, Glenn Jeffery, Gloria Hicinbotham, Gloria Nakamura, Greg Cushman and Mirna Cabrera, Greg Frykman, Halcyon Wilson, Heather Ferguson, Helen and Michael Pearson, Helen Pai, Helen Weismeyer, Iain Hodgins, Ian Markham, Ian Smith and Fiona Barnard-Smith, Irene Blair, Iris Landa, Isobel Combes, Ivan Rouse, Ivonne Chand, Jack Coogan, James Carleton-Paget, James Sterling, James W. Walters, Jan Hilton, Jan Holden, Janeen Veglahn, Janelle Albritton, Janelle Jones, Janet Weighall, Janice Mazurek, Jay Ardron, Jay Cook, Jay Razzouk, Jeff Anderson, Jeff Dupee, Jeffry M. Kaatz, Jennifer Benzakein, Jennifer Tyner, Jeremy Bryson, Jerry McIntosh, Jesse Leamon, Jessica Ludescher, Jessie Norton, Jim and Mary Wilson, Jim Butcher, Jim Fodor, Joanie Sanchez, Joann Kristensen, Joanne and Joseph Greene, Jocelyn Gunnarsson, Joel Garbutt-Quistiano, Joel Haldeman, Johana St. Clair, John and Karen Elder, John B. Wyatt III, John Bergland, John Brunt, John D. Ng Wong Hing, Johnny Ramirez, Jon and Marianne Butler, Jon Cicle, Jon Vanderwerff, Jon-Erik Prichard, Jonathan P. Zirkle, Josef Purkart, Joseph Wilson, Julian Lethbridge, Julie Prichard, June Magi, Justin Ramsacker, Justin Sandefur, Karen and Rudy Carillo, Karl Kime, Kathleen Stuart, Kathy Repique, Keith and Ruth Howson, Kelly Bradley, Ken Matthews and Carmen Wisdom, Kendra Haloviak, Kent A. Hansen, Kevin Smith, Kharolynn Pascual, Kimberly Cortner, Kirk Chung, Kit Watts and Penny Shell, Krista Motschiedler, Kulreet Grewal Chaudhary, Lani Norton, Lari Mobley, Larry Downing, Laurell K. Hamilton, Leanne Teruya, Les Camacho, Lesley Ashley, Lilly Salcedo, Lina Soria, Linda Caviness, Lindsey Davis, Lissie Glennie, Lorelei Hermann, Lorna Reid, Lotfy and Nadia Abu-Assal, Lou and Marjorie Venden, Lourdes Morales-Gudmundsson, Lucerne French Snipes, Luke Ford, Marc Benzakein, Marc Maitland, Marcia Guy, Margo Haskins, Marilyn Karlow, Maritza Duran, Mark and Ruth Ranzinger, Marta Teel, Marvin Karlow, Maryann Benzakein, Mazin Thahab, Melissa Cushman, Melody Weaver, Michael Andreasen, Michael Kinnen, Michelle Burke, Mike Miller, Mike Welch, Montcalm Joham, Monte Miller, Monte R. Andress, Murrey Olmstead, Nabil Razzouk, Nate Brandstater, Neil G. Robertson, Nenette Amoguis, Norman Woods, Pam Dietrich, Paul Nelson, Pei Pei Tan, Peta Dunstan, Peter J. Balderstone, Peter Cress, Peter Wendel, Pico Rivera, Randy Isaeff, Rebecca Saunders, Reggie Dablo, Renard Doneskey, Rene Ramos, Richard and Jill Guy, Richard Case, Richard J. Myers, Richard Pershing, Rick Newmyer, Rick Washburn, Rick Williams, Rob and Mina O'Connel, Rob Benzakein, Rob Holland and Angela Jones, Robert Ji-Song Ku, Rod and Leah Stuart, Roger Churches, Roger McFarland, Romaine and Roberta Saunders, Ronel Harvey, Rosalie Lynn, Roy Blaine, Roy Branson, Roy Kryger, Rupert Sheldrake, Russell Willis, Ruth Gascay, Sandra Ingram, Schorschi Decker, Sclorial Tu, Scott Andress, Scott Paden, Seema Agarwal, Seema and Tony Lechner,

Serena and Sigve Tonstad, Shabbir Lakha, Sharilyn Horner, Shelley Price, Sonia Ceballos, Stephan P. Mitchell, Stephen Smith, Steve French, Sue Curtis, Susan Pai, Susan Patt, Sylvia and Wilton Clarke, Tamara Zane, Taylor Ruhl, Ted Hessel, Todd Hart, Todd Trumper, Todd Willmert, Tony Zbaraschuk, Trey Jackson, Vernon Koenig, Victoria DeStefano, Vittorio Trionfi, Walter Mackett, W. G. Nelson, Walt and Darlene Hamerslough, Wendy Wareham, Wilfred Airey, Willard Meier, Willie Sanchez, Winona Howe, and Won K. Yoon.

My parents deserve a great deal of credit for being consistent cheerleaders throughout my professional development. My father, who nourished my intellectual curiosity even as he found theologians an odd lot, did not live to see this book completed. My gracious and lovely mother graced my life with warmth, sweetness, and thoroughly unconditional love until the day I sent this book, dedicated to her, to the publisher. Her good humor and generosity of spirit made her an exceptional person whose life is worth celebrating for lots of reasons quite unrelated to me, but I am pleased to honor her especially for her many tangible and intangible contributions to my life.

Through all of these people and institutions, I hope, God has been at work in my life. I will not presume to trace the movements of divine providence; but I thank God for touching my life (and the lives of those who will, I hope, profit from this research in the future) through all of those whose generosity I have acknowledged, through others I have failed to name, and in divers other—doubtless unfathomable—ways.

Preface

Christian belief matters. Where you put your trust makes a difference. So does the way you understand your world. That's why Christians have always taken their convictions seriously. When contemporary people respond to an account of Christian convictions by asking, "So what?" they're echoing a question the church has tried implicitly to answer whenever it has articulated the beliefs that define its identity.

In what follows, I hope to show why Christian convictions continue to be relevant for people facing the complex challenges of the contemporary world. I believe that the understanding of Christianity I have developed here is important not only for what and how people *think*, but for how they *live*.

This book is an experiment. It is an attempt to spell out what Christian belief would look like if love were self-consciously located at its center, as both an organizing principle and a control on theological formulation. It is thus also an attempt to articulate an account of Christian belief in which—because it seeks to affirm divine love in the face of the great challenge posed for believers in God's love by evil and suffering—divine action is conceived of as consistently persuasive rather than coercive. It is a development of the Christian tradition: I think I can fairly claim to be telling you a good deal about what Christians do in fact believe, and not merely about what I might wish my tradition to say. But it is a *development*, an exploration of a possible tendency or direction within Christianity. It seeks to answer the question, "What would Christians say if Christians took love as seriously as they claim they do?" and "What would they say if they really made love central to their understanding of the character of God?" So while I believe I'm accurately characterizing much that is actually there in the Christian tradition when I describe what "Christians believe," I'm also in many places speaking in the hypothetical mode, even if I don't say so explicitly. Of course, I claim no infallibility as either an exponent or as a critic of my tradition.

In general, I try to offer plausible arguments for the positions I take. But, on occasion, I simply assert. When I do, it's sometimes because I think it should be obvious that what I say follows from arguments I've already offered. Sometimes, though, I simply hope what I say will commend itself because of its inherent attractiveness. And sometimes, alternatively, I'm advancing an account of things I hope the reader will *recognize* as true to the world she inhabits, the God she worships, the tradition (or traditions) with which she identifies, an account that will perhaps integrate insights or perceptions she's already had in a way that prompts her to nod in agreement. I emphasize that, whatever the nature of the support I offer for a given claim, vigorous argument can honor an author's efforts more than thoughtless agreement.

I begin by framing the argument to follow by offering an account of two aspects of a love-centered theology. I consider love as an organizing principle for theology, and love as a constraint on what we can say theologically. Treating love as central to theology is authorized by centuries of Christian tradition, as well as by its fruitfulness and illuminating power: things often look different, interestingly different, if viewed in relation to love. Viewing love as a limit on theological formulation reflects the conviction that God is necessarily conceived of as love, a conclusion for which I offer several interlocking reasons. At the same time, I recognize that a theology focused on love runs the risk of complacency, and I make some suggestions designed to help reader and author alike to avoid that risk.

Before proceeding to the substantive theological issues that form the heart of the book, I articulate an understanding of the nature of religious belief to which love is central. On the one hand, love for our tradition rightly impels us to retain and defend our beliefs. On the other hand, authentic love must be characterized by responsiveness to the *other* as *other*, and this means, in turn, that we must be willing to be surprised by, and to learn from, voices outside our tradition. Adequate judgments about religious belief will reflect, I suggest, our critical reflection on our tradition in response to the challenge of otherness. I conclude Chapter 2 by considering two particular challenges to Christian belief—those posed by the apparent absence of God and the reality of pointless suffering.

In Chapter 3, I consider the Christian characterization of God as personal and as Trinity. Talking about God as personal is not dispensable, I argue, even though we cannot seek irreverently to undertake the study of divine psychology. Speaking of God as personal is, among other things, a way of safeguarding and expressing the conviction that God is love; I seek to spell out several ways in which referring to God as personal conveys a number of key Christian convictions. I suggest that speaking of God as Trinity is *not* an exercise in divine psychology or sociology, but a way of ensuring that we acknowledge that revelation is God's work from beginning to end and that we decline the idolatrous temptation to anchor our talk about God in a single district of experience.

The doctrine of God as Holy Spirit is characteristically addressed between Christology and ecclesiology. I take it up early in the book, in Chapter 4, because I opt to make reflection on divine action central to what I say about God's Spirit. An understanding of the power and activity of God's Spirit is implicit in what I want to say about creation, Jesus, salvation, the church, the course of history, and the last things. I believe that the conviction that God is love necessarily sets the terms within which we must think about the character of divine activity in the world. On the one hand, this means that our account of divine action must be consistent with a satisfactory response to the problem of pointless suffering. On the other hand, however, our account of divine action will not reflect the conviction that God is love unless it is *also* consistent with the belief that God is personal, and thus acts *particularly* in the creaturely world, responding freely and creatively to specific circumstances in the world.

That God is creator is, I think, a conviction with multiple and profound ramifications for a wide range of Christian beliefs. I focus in Chapter 5 on the significance of belief in creation for spirituality, science, and ethics. I suggest that a spirituality of creation will begin with the assumption that, as creator, God is present and active in every district of experience. God and creation are not in competition, I argue, and creation is a fitting focus of our love. I suggest that scientific practice is a kind of spiritual discipline, and the history of science makes clear that belief in creation played a key role in the emergence of modern scientific thinking. And I outline an ethic of love for creation, explain the understanding of basic moral principles and aspects of human welfare central to that ethic, distinguish it from consequentialist and situationist alternatives, and illustrate it with reference to issues including the non-human world and the economy.

Creation provides the context for reflection on sin—understood as disordered love—both because creation is the ground of ethics and because, I maintain, one important aspect of sin is the denial that one is a part of God's good creation. I explain this notion in Chapter 6. I also consider the essential connection between sin and harm, reflect on the social embodiment of sin, and consider the relationship between sin and gender.

Love is central to Christian belief and practice (to the extent that it is) because of the words and actions of Jesus of Nazareth. I explore the identity of Jesus in Chapter 7. My initial focus is on the appropriate role of the church's memory as a source of presumptions regarding Jesus' identity, and on the historical features of his activity that can reasonably be seen as warranting characterizing him as God's revelation. Then, I reflect on the meaning and implications of doing so.

While I address historical issues related to Jesus' evident self-understanding in Chapter 7, my primary concern there is theological. Historical issues related to Jesus are the focus of Chapter 8. I use the motif of *suffering*—understood not only as pain but also as the capacity to be affected by others, to be, in a sense, at their disposal—to organize much of the discussion. I consider Jesus' historical particularity as well as the source of much of his suffering, including his passion and death: his creation of an inclusive community that challenged those committed to maintaining unjust social hierarchies and rigid, exclusive identity-markers. And I reflect on his crucifixion and its implications, including the reality of divine suffering.

Following his death on the cross, Jesus was encountered in person by his disciples. In Chapter 9, I address the remarkable cluster of events that followed Jesus' crucifixion. I begin by offering an overview of the significance of the belief that Jesus' disciples met him alive after his death. Then, I discuss historical evidence that bears on the correctness of their belief.

Humanity suffers from a range of problems—lack of self-worth, meaninglessness, and personal and social sin among them. I consider several aspects of God's response to these problems in Chapter 10. I begin with divine acceptance—which is simply, I maintain, another way to talk about God's unconditional love. After that, I turn to personal growth and healing as well as interpersonal forgiveness, before suggesting that judgment is part of love's work and noting how God's love responds to the threat of meaninglessness. Then, I examine various accounts of the place of God's activity in Jesus in God's healing work in the world. While traditional substitutionary accounts are unsatisfactory, a variety of other aspects of God's healing activity are rooted in Jesus' ministry, death, and life beyond death. Finally, I argue that belief in hell and in double predestination should be rejected as inconsistent with the conviction that God is love.

The conviction that God is love is tangibly embodied in the church, the focus of Chapter 11. In this chapter, I consider the church's identity, worship, teaching, sacraments, institutional character, and participation in dialogue across traditions, all in light of the centrality of love. I conclude with a meditation on the challenges associated with loving the church itself.

Hope for the future—both historical and personal—is crucial to Christian belief. I begin Chapter 12 by exploring the work in which God seeks to see love embodied in history; I offer a qualified defense of the view that we should expect this work to have tangible, positive results. Then, I consider hope for personal life beyond death. I explain why I believe such hope is a reasonable consequence of the conviction that God is love, and I highlight some of its implications for love in the present.

Throughout the book, I refer at various points to the practice of Sabbath. The weekly day of celebration and rest has received increasing attention from writers about both spirituality and theology. I believe it offers useful insight into and support for Christian living, and I seek to highlight its connections with a range of Christian beliefs and practices.

The various tentative proposals I make throughout the book doubtless need more work. But I develop the ideas on which I focus primarily here in order to further the book's central experiment—an attempt to see what a systematic account of Christian belief organized and normed by love could look like in practice—and I hope they will be evaluated accordingly.

A few years ago, an acquaintance asked me if I believed. Our world is complex; and the more we know, the more questions we need to pose. I told him, "I hope." I believe the vision I articulate here is reasonable and attractive, but I cannot *prove* the claims I make. Perhaps I ought to preface many more sentences with "It is plausible that . . ." or "We may reasonably hope that . . ." or something similar. I can at best offer you possibilities to explore. I'm inviting you on a journey. Together, we can hope. And pray. And work. And love.

—GARY CHARTIER
La Sierra University
Riverside, California
February 21, 2007

1

Love at the Center

God is love. We, in turn, can and should love God, each other, ourselves, and the whole grand and glorious creation. These two convictions form the heart of Christian belief. Throughout this book, I want to explore what they might mean, to experiment with the articulation of a vision of Christianity centered on and normed by divine and human love.

I seek in Chapter 1 to explain and defend my approach to doing Christian theology by focusing on two key claims: (1) the twofold theme of divine and human love can serve fruitfully as an organizing center for an account of Christian belief;[1] and (2) the conviction that God is love and that we are called to love can serve as a critical control on our theological reflection and assertion. There are multiple reasons for putting love at the *center* of Christian theology, and doing so will affect how we organize and conduct our reflection on God and God's world. There are also multiple justifications for treating love as our *primary analogy* for God and as a *critical control* on our God-language. However, while love is crucial to good theology, a love-centered theology runs the risk of a certain kind of complacency, which it must self-consciously avoid.

THE MEANING OF LOVE

I operate throughout this book with a relatively intuitive conception of love. While there are different aspects of love, they are linked conceptually and psychologically. Love is, at root, a positive orientation on the other,[2] an orientation that acknowledges the value of the other. I suggest that, when we talk about love, we are talking, at least, about care, delight, identification, loyalty, desire, and respect.

Love as *care* graciously seeks the well-being of the other, for the other's own good. Love as *delight* finds it a good thing—indeed, a wonderful thing—that the other exists; simply knowing of the other's reality can be a source of pleasure, even joy. Love as *identification* acknowledges that the other, while other, is also in some sense part of the self, so that the interests of the self and those of the other are integrated and what affects the other unavoidably affects the self. Love as *loyalty* acknowledges the beloved's need for constancy and dependability, and offers the beloved the gift of reliable presence. Love as *desire* seeks closeness, intimacy, with the other, freely given, and acknowledges the value of the gifts—most fundamentally, but not usually not only, the gift of presence—actually or potentially

---

1. For a parallel claim, see George M. Newlands, *Theology of the Love of God* (London: Collins 1980). See also John McIntyre, *On the Love of God* (London: Collins 1962); Daniel Day Williams, *The Spirit and the Forms of Love* (New York: Harper 1960).

2. Cp. John B. Cobb, Jr., *The Structure of Christian Existence* (Philadelphia: Westminster 1967): love is "any mode of relating to an object as a positive intrinsic value, in which conscious psychic activity is decisively involved" (127; footnote omitted).

offered by the beloved to the lover. Love as *respect*—presupposed by all other kinds of love—recognizes the otherness, the independence, of the other; where the other is another finite person, it takes the form of *equal* respect, acknowledgment of the equality of the other and the self in dignity and worth.[1]

I believe these elements generally characterize, in different ways and in different degrees, the focal instances of love in our experience: love of friends, love of family members, romantic and erotic love, and love of groups and institutions (nations, schools, perhaps even sports teams!).[2] While their relationship, and the degree to which they are present, will vary with different kinds of love, they are all recognizably important for our various creaturely loves.[3] I suggest that they are present, as well, in God's relationship with the finite world. Thus, when I refer throughout this book to God's love for creation, I assume that the love on which I focus includes all of these elements.[4] When I speak of our love our love for God, I understand a love that comprehends most or all of these aspects, at least in some degree. When I refer to our love for each other, the context may suggest the presence of all of these features; but even if it does not, love between persons as I characterize it here should be understood to be, at minimum, love as equal respect.

Love and the Architecture of Christian Belief

Christians have consistently focused on love as the most important divine attribute and the most significant characteristic of flourishing and responsible creaturely life. And love is clearly preferable to several possible alternate accounts of the heart of Christian belief and can take into account some or all of the principal emphases underlying each one.

Love at the Center of the Tradition

It should require little argument to show that love plays an exceptional role in biblical and post-biblical Christian accounts of God's nature and identity and

---

1. Obviously, it would be false to say that God and creatures owe each other *equal* respect. But respect as such is surely a dimension of the God-world relationship. Further, part of what God does in loving the world is to foster equal respect among persons; and in exhibiting the love of equal respect toward other creatures, as in exhibiting other varieties of love, creatures love God. Love as respect rightly marks the relationships between persons and the non-sentient creation, though of course love as *equal* respect does not. There may be contexts in which equal respect *is* an appropriate specification of respect where relationships between persons and non-personal or quasi-personal sentients are concerned, though there may be others in which this makes less sense; love of other kinds will clearly be appropriate in such relationships.

2. With respect to groups and institutions, love as equal respect will focus on their individual members, taking care, among other things, not to ignore their particularity and collapse them into their communities. Where multiple, comparable groups are concerned, it will avoid arbitrary preference for one over another.

3. It has become commonplace to distinguish various shades of love using the Greek words for them—*philia, agape, eros, storge, epithymia*. See, for instance, C. S. Lewis, *The Four Loves* (New York: Harcourt 1960); Paul Tillich, *Love, Power, and Justice: Ontological Analyses and Ethical Applications* (New York: OUP 1954). Cp. Robert Johann, *The Meaning of Love: An Essay Towards a Metaphysics of Intersubjectivity* (Glen Rock, NJ: Deus-Paulist 1966).

4. I assume, too, that divine love is what the best interpersonal love among finite persons seeks to be—unconditional, not contingent on our behavior or performance. Cp. John J. Powell, *Unconditional Love* (Allen, TX: Argus 1978); Hugh Prather and Gayle Prather, *I Will Never Leave You: How Couples Can Achieve the Power of Lasting Love* (New York: Bantam 1996).

of creaturely life before God in the world. Jesus powerfully and provocatively identified the call to love God and love other persons as the greatest of the commandments, pointing to love's centrality for Christian ethics and spirituality. And 1 John points to love as God's definitive characteristic, declaring that "God is love."[1] A stress on the centrality of love is evident throughout the Bible.

As early as Genesis, God is characterized as the God of faithful love. And the "song of Moses," which the Israelites are depicted as singing after their deliverance from the Egyptians, identifies God's liberating work as a product of love. God promises love to those who are faithful to the covenant in the Exodus version of the Ten Commandments. In its worship, Israel acclaims God as one whose love is unending. Nehemiah declares that God is "ready to forgive, gracious and merciful, slow to anger and abounding in steadfast love . . . ." The psalmists find repeated opportunities to acknowledge, praise, and claim God's love. Isaiah portrays God as saying, "For the mountains may depart and the hills be removed, but my steadfast love shall not depart from you, and my covenant of peace shall not be removed, says the Eternal, who has compassion on you." For Jeremiah, to know God is to know One who delights in "steadfast love, justice, and righteousness . . ." and who has loved Israel "with an everlasting love . . . ," one whose steadfast love is abundant and "who does not willingly afflict or grieve anyone." Joel announces that God "is gracious and merciful, slow to anger, and abounding in steadfast love . . . ." The book of Jonah depicts God as welcoming the repentant, as unwilling to condemn, and as the God of the nations as well as the God of Israel.[2]

Jesus identified God as merciful and compassionate, embracing the marginal and the lost with love. John's Gospel declares: "For God so loved the world that he gave his only Son, so that everyone who believes in him may not perish but may have eternal life. Indeed, God did not send the Son into the world to condemn the world, but in order that the world might be saved through him." St. Paul celebrates the supremacy of the divine love revealed and conveyed in Christ and announces that "the love of Christ" prompts him to engage passionately in ministry. Christ, he says, "loved me and gave himself for me." "The love of God" figures in the famous benediction with which he closes 2 Corinthians. Ephesians declares that "the love of Christ . . . surpasses knowledge . . ." and that God "is rich in mercy," loves with a "great love," and intends to display "the immeasurable riches of his grace in kindness toward us in Christ Jesus." The love of Christ becomes a model for marital love in Ephesians. And 1 John stresses the central, fundamental character of divine love. "God's love was revealed among us in this way: God sent his only Son into the world so that we might live through him. In this is love, not that we loved God but that he loved us and sent his Son to be the atoning sacrifice for our sins."[3]

Of course, 1 John is equally insistent on the importance of human as well as divine love. "Beloved, let us love one another, because love is from God; everyone who loves is born of god and knows God. Whoever does not love does not know God, for God is love." And the theme of the value of love between finite persons resonates throughout the Bible. In Leviticus, Moses enjoins the Israelites to

1. Mt. 22:37-39=Mk. 1229-31; 1 Jn. 4:8. Unless I indicate otherwise, I quote biblical passages from the New Revised Standard Version.

2. Gen. 24: 14, 27; 32:10. Ex. 15:13; Ex. 20:6; Neh. 9:17; Ps. 5:7, 6:4, 13:5, 7; 18:50; 21:7; 25:6, 7; 26:3; 31:7, 16, 21; 32:10; 33:5, 18; 40:10-11; 48:9; 51:1; 52:8; 57:10; 59:10, 16-17; 63:3; 69:16; 86:5, 13, 15; 89:1-2, 14, 24, 28, 33; 98:3; 103:8, 11, 17; 106:45; 107:8, 15, 21, 31; 108:4; 109:21; 117:2; 119:64; 130:7; 145:8; Isa. 54:10; cp. Isa. 63:9 ("in his love and in his pity he redeemed them . . . ."); Jer. 9:24; Jer. 31:3; Lam. 3:32-3; Joel 2:13. (I opt to render JHWH as "the Eternal" here and elsewhere.)

3. Lk. 15; cp. Lk. 19:10; Jn. 3:16, 17; Rom. 8:35, 39; 2 Cor. 5:14; Gal. 2:20; 2 Cor. 13:13; cp. 2 Thess. 2:16; Eph. 3:19; Eph. 2:4, 5, 7; Eph. 5:25; 1 Jn. 4:10, 11.

love their neighbors as themselves. Micah announces that what God asks of Israel is simple, characterizing God's expectations in a way that makes clear the value of interpersonal love as the sum and substance of faithfulness: "He has told you, O mortal, what is good; and what does the Eternal require of you but to do justice, and to love kindness, and to walk humbly with your God?"[1] Other aspects of love receive meaningful attention in the First Testament, as well. The book of Ruth preserves for us a story in which friendship occupies a central place. The narratives of David's life make clear the significance of his close friendship with Jonathan.[2] Proverbs stresses the importance of friendship.[3] And the Song of Songs deliciously celebrates erotic love.

Jesus informs his disciples that the love of neighbor includes the love of enemies. He calls them to love their neighbors as themselves, to treat others as they wish others to treat them. His friendship with the Beloved Disciple receives particular attention in the Fourth Gospel, and the Bethany trio of Mary, Martha, and Lazarus are depicted as his close friends. Love figures repeatedly in the Newer Testament authors' injunctions to the early Christian congregations. St. Paul urges the Roman Christians: "love one another with mutual affection . . ." and emphasizes that "love is the fulfilling of the law." And to the Corinthian Christians he pens his powerful poem to love, declaring that love is greater even than faith and hope. To the Galatians, he declares that "the only thing that counts is faith working through love." To the Thessalonians, he underscores what he assumes they already know—that love is a vital expression of Christian responsibility. 1 Peter calls its readers to "love one another deeply from the heart" and to "maintain constant love for one another, for love covers a multitude of sins." Similarly, Hebrews commends "mutual love." Colossians urges "compassion, kindness, humility, meekness, and patience," calls for forgiveness, and challenges the Christians at Colossæ: "Above all, clothe yourselves with love, which binds everything together in perfect harmony." "[L]et us love one another," enjoins 2 John. Jude urges its readers to "keep . . . [themselves] in the love of God . . . ."[4]

The human love to which the biblical authors attend includes creatures' love for God as well as God's love for creatures. In Deuteronomy, Moses enjoins Israel to love God supremely and undividedly. Joshua characterizes love to God as a key responsibility the Israelites are called to fulfill. Hosea declares that God desires "steadfast love and not sacrifice, the knowledge of God rather than burnt offerings," and famously likens Israel's relationship with God to a marriage. Appropriately, given Jesus' injunction to love God wholeheartedly, James stresses the importance of Christians' love for Christ and for God. For 1 John, loving God is crucial, but is expressed in love for other persons—in adhering to God's commands.[5]

The focus on love evident throughout the Bible is echoed in the developing Christian theological tradition. Augustine's theological and philosophical reflections are marked by a repeated focus on love.[6] Duns Scotus saw the enactment and proclamation of love as the central purpose of the God's self-revelation in

1. 1 Jn. 4:7, 8; Lev. 19:18; Micah 6:8.
2. 1 Sam. 18:3-4, 20:1-42; 2 Sam. 1:19-27, esp. 25-6.
3. John E. Johnson, "The Contribution of Proverbs to Ethics" (ThD diss., Dallas Theological Seminary 1984) 180-210.
4. Mt. 5:44=Lk. 6:27; Mt. 19:19; Mt. 7:12=Lk. 6:31; Jn. 13:23, 21:7, 20; Luke 10:38-42; John 11:1-44, 12:1-8; Rom. 12:10; Rom. 13:9; Gal. 5:14; Jas. 2:8; Rom. 12:10; 1 Cor. 13:13; Gal. 5:6; 1 Thess. 4:9; 1 Pet. 1:22; 1 Pet. 4:8; Heb. 13:1; Col. 3:12-14; 2 Jn. 5; Jude 21; note the Trinitarian form of the injunction (Jude 20-21).
5. Deut. 6:5, 11:1; Joshua 22:5; Hosea 6:6; Jas. 1:12, 2:5; 1 Jn. 4:20, 5:2-3; cp. 2 Jn. 6.
6. Mark Baurman, "Grace as Love in the Theology of Augustine" (MA thesis, Graduate Theological Union 1996); Hannah Arendt, *Love and Saint Augustine*, ed. Joanna Vecchiarelli Scott and Judith Chelius Stark (Chicago: U of Chicago P 1996).

Jesus.¹ And love emerges as an important theme in Bernard of Clairvaux, Dante, Jan van Ruusbroec, Thomas Aquinas, Julian of Norwich, John of the Cross, Martin Luther, Francis de Sales, Søren Kierkegaard, John McLeod Campbell, Therese of Lisieux, Walter Rauschenbusch, P. T. Forsyth, Karl Rahner, Thomas Merton, Wolfhart Pannenberg, Dorothee Sölle, and a variety of mediæval and modern theologians from diverse cultural and theological backgrounds.²

Alternatives to Love

The identification of God as love and the attention given to love throughout the Bible and Christian thought makes it seem reasonable and natural to treat

---

1. Seamus Mulholland, "Incarnation in Franciscan Spirituality—Duns Scotus and the Meaning of Love," *Franciscan* Jan. 2000; Joseph Klein, *Die Charitaslehre des Johannes Duns Skotus, die edelste Frucht der Liebesweisheit des franziskanischen Geistes*, Franziskanische Studien 11 (Munster: Aschendorffschen 1926).

2. Bernard of Clairvaux, *On Loving God*, with an analytical commentary by Emero Stiegman, Cistercian Fathers Series 13B (Kalamazoo: Cistercian 1995); Kenelm Foster, *The Mind in Love: Dante's Philosophy*, Aquinas Society of London Aquinas Paper 25 ([London:] Blackfriars 1956); Krijn Elzard Braas, *Mint de Minne: Eros en Agape bij Jan Van Ruusbroec: Een Wetenschappelijke Proeve op het Gebied van de Godgeleerdheid* (Kampen: Kok Pharos 1993); Etienne Gilson, *Wisdom and Love in Saint Thomas Aquinas*, Aquinas Lecture 1951 (Milwaukee: Marquette UP 1951); Francis J. Klauder, *A Philosophy Rooted in Love: The Dominant Themes in the Perennial Philosophy of St. Thomas Aquinas* (Lanham, MD: UP of America 1994); Paul J. Waddell, *The Primacy of Love: An Introduction to the Ethics of Thomas Aquinas* (New York: Paulist 1992); B. J. Diggs, *Love and Being: An Investigation into the Metaphysics of St. Thomas Aquinas* (New York: Vanni 1947); Michael Dauphinais and Matthew Levering, *Knowing the Love of Christ: An Introduction to the Theology of St. Thomas Aquinas* (Notre Dame, IN: U of Notre Dame P 1992); Julian of Norwich, *The Revelation of Divine Love in Sixteen Showings Made to Dame Julian of Norwich*, trans. and intro. M. L. de Mastro (Liguori, MO: Triumph 1994); cp. Margaret Ann Palliser, *Christ, Our Mother of Mercy: Divine Mercy and Compassion in the Theology of the Shewings of Julian of Norwich* (Berlin; New York: de Gruyter 1992); Andre Bord, *Les amours chez Jean de la Croix*, Beauchesne Religions 24 (Paris: Beauchesne 1998); See, *e.g.*, Christa Muller, *Das Lob Gottes bei Luther: vornehmlich nach seinen Auslegungen des Psalters*, Forschungen zur Geschichte und Lehre des Protestantismus 7.1 (München: Kaiser 1934); James S. Langelaan, *The Philosophy and Theology of Love: According to St. Francis de Sales* (Lewiston: Mellen 1994); Michel Terestchenko, *Amour et desespoir: de Francois de Sales a Fenelon* (Paris: Seuil 2000); Chantal Anne, *L'amour dans la pensee de Søren Kierkegaard: pseudonymie et polyonymie: essai* (Paris: L'Harmattan 1993); C. Edward Deyton, *Speaking of Love: Kierkegaard's Plan for Faith* (Lanham, MD: UP of America 1986); Michael Jinkins, *Love Is of the Essence: An Introduction to the Theology of John McLeod Campbell* (Edinburgh: St. Andrew 1993). Isabelle Pretre, *Therese de Lisieux, ou, l'intelligence de l'amour* (Paris: Guibert 1997); Walter Rauschenbusch, *Dare We Be Christians?* (Cleveland: Pilgrim 1993); Leslie McCurdy, *Attributes and Atonement: The Holy Love of God in the Theology of P. T. Forsyth* (Carlisle: Paternoster 1999); Mark Lloyd Taylor, *God is Love: A Study in the Theology of Karl Rahner*, AAR Academy Series 50 (Atlanta: Scholars 1986); Thomas Merton, *Learning to Love: Exploring Solitude and Freedom*, ed. Christina Bochen (San Francisco: Harper 1997); Lou Ann G. Trost, "An Ontology of Power, Love, and Freedom in the Theology of Wolfhart Pannenberg" (PhD diss., Graduate Theological Union 1998); Janet Christine Gear, "Love in the Face of Suffering: A Study of Dorothee Sölle's Prophetic Mysticism" (MA thesis, Pacific School of Religion 1996); Mikhail Georgievich Meerson-Aksenov, *The Trinity of Love in Modern Russian Theology: The Love Paradigm and the Retrieval of Western Mediæval Love Mysticism in Modern Russian Trinitarian Thought: From Solovyov to Bulgakov* (Quincy, IL: Franciscan 1998); Andrea Tafferner, *Gottes- und Nachstenliebe in der deutschsprachigen Theologie des 20. Jahrhunderts*, Innsbrucker theologische Studien 37 (Innsbruck: Tyrolia 1992); Pierre Rousselot, *The Problem of Love in the Middle Ages: A Historical Contribution*, trans. and intro. Alan Vincelette, ed. Pol Vandevelde (Milwaukee: Marquette University Press 2001).

it as the organizing center of theology. In addition, I believe, love is preferable to a variety of other potential organizing principles, and can take appropriate account of the concerns that might make structuring Christian belief in light of these principles attractive.

For many Christians, *sovereignty* has often seemed like the most important divine attribute. What matters most about God is that, as they see it, God is in control. The fundamental truth about God's relation to the world is that the world is at God's disposal, subject to God's power. On this view, we need to learn how to be submissive subjects, and perhaps how to exercise power over inferior creatures. And people who organize their thinking about God around the theme of sovereignty don't seem able to avoid the conclusion that God is responsible for the abuse and disaster that mar our lives.

Or take *holiness*. *Holy* means *different*, *other*. But calling God holy—given the way the word is sometimes used—often seems to imply that God's overwhelming majesty and untarnished goodness create an unbridgeable gap between the divine and the human. A holy god is purportedly an unapproachable god, a god in the business of judging and rejecting the unholy. We can model a holy god of this kind by rejecting people who seem in one way or another impure—contaminated, contaminating. At the same time, we may wallow in the insecurity that belief in an unapproachable God may foster, feeling prone to rejection ourselves. Alternatively (or at the same time), we may use an emphasis on holiness conceived as unapproachability and majesty to bolster our own spiritual self-confidence: flawed we may be, but at least we're insiders, accepted (or tolerated) by a holy God, and so in a position to reject rather than to be rejected.

Righteousness carries similar freight. A righteous God (it might be thought, given the way we often use the word "righteous") identifies and punishes the wicked—who are, likely, all of us. Threatened with the censure of such a deity, we may feel compelled to devote ourselves to cleaning up our acts, to working hard at changing the mind of the divine lawmaker, while perhaps taking time out to make sure others are doing the same.

Creativity seems much a much more attractive center for our thinking about God and ourselves. But sometimes the emphasis on God as creator leaves us with an absentee deity, on permanent vacation while we manage the show. God becomes a kind of architect, one who designs structures for others to inhabit. Such a god will leave us alone, and needn't concern us very much, except, perhaps, as a spur to our own creative work.

Christians have traditionally commended *faith* and *hope* as crucial elements of our lives before God. And many people have found in one or the other an attractive center for Christian belief and practice.

If faith is conceived of as essentially *cognitive*—as the assent to truths endorsed by authority—an understanding of Christianity organized around faith might stress intellectual comprehension as the most important aspect of a person's response to God. On the other hand, if faith is seen as a *trustful response* to God's love, a faith-centered conception of Christian belief might focus on the Christian's inner life—perhaps her private world of prayer—or the transformation brought about in her life by coming to endorse Christian beliefs.

A vision of Christianity organized around the theme of hope might direct our attention to a life beyond death in which we will be compensated for the losses we have experienced in this life. The result may be that we turn our eyes away from the joys and sorrows of ordinary life, viewing our day-to-day existence as less important than the future we anticipate beyond death. Alternatively, a hope-centered vision might foster and express hope in history—hope for the political, economic, cultural, psychological transformation of our world that our work under God might bring about. Inspired by such a vision, we might be liberated to transform our world, but we might also be alienated from our present experience, always waiting for the arrival of the future we anticipate.

Any attractive and sensible account of Christian belief will certainly take God's sovereignty, holiness, righteousness, and creativity seriously. It will celebrate and encourage faith and hope. But each of these themes, I am convinced, is best understood in relation to and in light of God's love and ours.

- God's *sovereignty* is not the sovereignty of coercive dominance but the sovereignty of persuasive love.[1]
- God is *different* from us, *other* than us, and thus *holy*. But one thing that makes God different from us is precisely that God is present and active in all our experience, that though we are more distant from some aspects of reality than others, all things find their home in God. God is other than we are, but this is in part precisely because God is always already present with us in love. It is also in part because God loves faithfully and unconditionally, while we so often do not, because God embraces that which is flawed and imperfect, which we may find it hard to do. God rightly inspires awe. But one of the most awe-inspiring things about God is the beauty of divine love.
- What we do and who we are matter to God. But they matter because God loves us and all creation, not because God wants or needs opportunities to dominate us or to punish us for moral infractions. And when we fail to show comparable love, God's response is to woo and heal and transform, not to reject.
- God's *creativity* is a powerful source of the novel and the beautiful, and our creativity is a wonderful gift to God and to each other. But divine creativity is oriented toward love—toward the initiation of loving relationships and the enrichment of the creation God cherishes. And our own creativity most clearly mirrors God's when it, too, is oriented toward love—toward making our own lives and the lives of other creatures fuller and fostering their welfare.
- *Faith* as *cognitive*—as intellectual understanding—matters. But it is never a means of securing God's love for ourselves. In the same way, faith as *conative and affective*—our trusting response to God's love—is crucially important. But it is best seen as presupposing God's love, and as a way of deepening and more fully experiencing God's all-embracing love.
- *Hope* for a life of love beyond death with God and each other is certainly appropriate. But God loves us and the whole world in the present. Similarly, it is worth hoping—and working—for changes in our world's history. But those changes must themselves be inspired and guided by our love for each other, for ourselves, and for all God's world; what we hope for is precisely the fullness of love. And we can experience the present as loved by God, as an arena in which God's love is active and in which God's loving gifts are to be experienced and lovingly shared, not merely as an antechamber in which we wait for the future.

It matters whether love or something else lies at the heart of our understanding of Christian belief. Seen in relation to love, Christian convictions and practices take on their proper meaning. And love provides us with a standard we can use to assess what we teach—a standard central to the Christian tradition, but a standard that can also inspire ongoing reform of that tradition.

---

1. For the language of "persuasion" (and its cognates) applied to divine activity in the world, see, *e.g.*, Austin Farrer, *Saving Belief: A Discussion of Essentials* (London: Hodder 1964): "divine persuasion . . . is an invisible persuasion, moving natural things to behave naturally" (72); divine providence can be seen "as a persuasion of our mixed and foolish aims toward an end less disastrous than their natural results" (73).

Love and the Content of Christian Belief

Putting love at the center of Christian belief means more than just organizing Christian belief around love, important as that is. It also means taking love seriously as a *norm* for Christian belief. In this section, I explain what might be involved in treating love as a principal control on our God-language.

If we are to use the conviction that God is love as a critical control on our theological reflection and assertion, and if we are to understand divine love as meaningfully similar to human love, we must have good reason for predicating love of God. Seeking to elaborate the underlying logic of at least some strands of the tradition and to justify our ongoing adherence to its position regarding divine love, I offer a set of overlapping arguments for the conviction that that we ought to speak of God as loving. I explain what it might mean to use love as the analogical basis for our God-language, as the central point of contact between human experience and the character and activity of God. And I explain how love can and should function as the central norm for our theology.

Why We Must Speak of God as Loving

If love is to serve as a critical control on our God-language and as our principal analogy for God, we need some warrant for believing that God is loving.[1]

First, we say that God is love because of the way God is characterized in our formative traditions. These traditions are not infallible, and they certainly demand critical reflection and scrutiny, but they record insights from which it is reasonable for our analyses. As I have already emphasized, the Bible is full of declarations that love is central to our understanding of God. To take a classic instance: ". . . love is from God; everyone who loves is born of God and knows God. Whoever does not love does not know God, for God is love. . . . God is love, and those who abide in love abide in God, and God abides in them."[2] Jesus testifies verbally and through the quality of his life to the divine love. To regard Jesus as revelatory of God, to honor the insights of the Jewish and Christian traditions into the character of God, is to give pride of place to love in our characterization of divine activity and the divine nature.

Second, there is an argument from the *inner demands of the Christian life* for speaking and thinking of God as love. We will have no reason, except raw self-interest, to concern ourselves with a god who is not loving. Suppose that divine action were the manifestation of hatred, indifference, or caprice. We would have no good reason to attend to God except in terror and rebellion. That God is love is a crucial assumption we must make in order to find anything like ordinary religious practice meaningful, desirable, or appropriate, to take a genuinely religious interest in God and in relationship with God. Only the God of love is worth worshipping, loving, or trusting. If only for our sanity's sake, we must wager that God is, indeed, love.

Third, there is an argument from *personal experience*. Of course, not all of us have had experiences in which we were conscious of God as gracious and loving. But many Christians (and others) have reported such experiences.[3] Those Christians who have experienced God as love have been formed by the Christian tradition, with its insistence on the reality of divine love. And non-Christians who testify to

---

1. In Chapter 2, I explain how I believe our convictions about God and God's relationship with the world can and should be warranted. The justification for the approach I am taking at this point depends in part on what I say there.

2. 1 Jn. 4:7b-9, 16b.

3. A particularly famous example is Julian of Norwich. See, *e.g.*, *The Works of Julian of Norwich*, http://www.luminarium.org/medlit/julianbib.htm (last visited Feb. 9, 2007).

experiences of God marked by their awareness of divine love have similarly been shaped by their religious traditions. But people's religious traditions don't *create* experiences out of whole cloth—rather, they *condition* them. An experience can conform more or less easily to a pattern mandated for it by tradition; it can reflect traditional expectations. But it can also lead to ruptures and transformations in the community to which the person who undergoes it belongs. Experience can, obviously, surprise us. So experiences of God as gracious and loving can't simply be dismissed as indefensible products of our acculturation. Thus, we have some reason to take them seriously as sources of insight into who God is.[1]

Fourth, there is an argument from *divine omniscience*. Could it be the case that God had no concern for or genuinely intimate awareness of the created world? An uninvolved, unconcerned god would not truly be perfect. As truly infinite and omnipresent, God would be aware of every facet of the creation, would *feel* every facet of the creation. God would necessarily be sympathetic: God would *feel-with* creation. Thus, God could not will harm to the creation, or be indifferent to it, without being indifferent to the state of God's own reality, too. God must identify with the fate of creation, then—if for no other reason than that the life of creation is intimately bound up with the divine life—and must thus necessarily be the God of love.[2]

Fifth, there is an argument rooted in *the meaning of divine goodness*. We must speak of God as *necessarily* good. God can have no question about what is good; and no internal conflict or tension could prevent God from actualizing the good known with infinite divine wisdom.[3] Presuming that love is good—and it is difficult to maintain otherwise without rendering talk of divine goodness virtually meaningless[4]—it follows necessarily that God is loving, and perfectly so. Our talk of God as *good* is analogical: it builds on our use of *good* to characterize human

1. Cp. Caroline Franks-Davis, *The Evidential Force of Religious Experience* (Oxford: Clarendon-OUP 1989).

2. David Ray Griffin, *God and Religion in the Postmodern World: Essays in Postmodern Theology* (Albany: SUNY 1989) 142-4; Keith Ward, *Divine Action* (London: Collins 1989) 26.

3. Keith Ward, *Religion and Creation* (Oxford: Clarendon-OUP 1996) 215-9; Keith Ward, *Rational Theology and the Creativity of God* (Oxford: Blackwell 1982) 135; Richard Swinburne, *The Existence of God*, rev. ed. (Oxford: Clarendon-OUP 1991) 179-83. Thomas Morris challenges the specific arguments offered by Ward and Swinburne, but nonetheless maintains that theists may rightly appeal to their modal intuitions in support of the view that God is necessarily good; see *Anselmian Explorations: Essays in Philosophical Theology* (Notre Dame, IN: U of Notre Dame P 1987) 63-9. Robert Merrihew Adams argues that divine justice and grace, but not the specific forms they take in particular circumstances, are necessary; see Robert Merrihew Adams, *Finite and Infinite Goods: A Framework for Ethics* (New York: OUP 1999) 175-6.

If love is an authentic human excellence, that it must be exhibited by the creative source of all human good. As creator of human goodness, God must be loving. David Braine, *The Reality of Time and the Existence of God: The Project of Proving God's Existence* (Oxford: Clarendon-OUP 1988) 320-32, argues, in effect, that to say that God is the source and origin of all that is is to say that God is thus the source and origin of human goodness. According to Braine, discerning God's "goodness in some way or respect in upholding created persons in dynamic existence precisely as good in this way or respect establishes His goodness in the way or respect concerned not just in this but in all His operations, and indeed in His overall design for Nature as a whole. If there become kinds or facets of goodness in creation known only through Revelation, then from this would follow the presence of this in God also as archetype" (331-2).

4. Cp. Morris's rejection of "the well known claim that it is not possible that God do evil since whatever God does is by definition good." As he notes: "notoriously, the problem with this sort of reasoning is that it evacuates the belief in God's goodness of any determinate and stable content" (59).

actions and states of character. We can give content to our talk of divine goodness by reflecting on the meaning of human goodness. But of the central traits characteristically associated with human goodness, only love can be predicated of God without qualification. Thus, to speak of God as good is to speak of God as loving; otherwise, there would be no meaning to our talk of God as good at all.[1]

These brief arguments obviously need more elaboration if they are to be decisive. But they do give us good reason to take the belief that God is love seriously. Thus, they provide some justification for our treating love as our principal analogy for God and as a decisive constraint on our theology.

What Do We Mean When We Speak of God as Loving?

If love is to serve as a critical control on our God-language, we also require some warrant for believing that our own experiences of loving and being loved provide the content for our talk about God as love.

Christians have favored two approaches to the question of how we can talk appropriately about God. They have spoken of the *analogy of faith* and the *analogy of being*. Talk about God rooted in the analogy of faith builds on Christian revelation. Theology dependent on the analogy of being begins with our understanding of creaturely reality and builds a picture of God as perfectly exemplifying the goodness we encounter in fragmentary form in creatures. It looks to creaturely reality to discern the features that being in the most general sense must exhibit. Then, it abstracts away those characteristics that reflect limitation and imperfection.

Proponents of the analogy of faith as our best clue to the nature and identity of God suggest that special divine revelation is superior to any other means of knowing who God is. And they point out that the God purportedly known through the analogy of being isn't a particularly attractive God—and doesn't look very much like the God of love known in and through Jesus of Nazareth.

The God we meet in Jesus, they suggest, is passionately involved in human life and human history—suffering, speaking, acting. By contrast, they maintain, the God to whom the analogy of being points is static, unmoved, and remote. An alien idea of perfection has been used to filter out just those things that make God the *living* God. Further, they observe, to begin with creaturely reality is to begin with reality that is not only finite but also morally broken. Perhaps we can't tell much about the divine reality by inspecting a creation that is so deeply flawed. And, in any case, *we* who do the inspecting are deeply flawed. If the only control on our God talk is our own best thinking, they note with dismay, then our own self-interest and lack of vision may get in the way of our understanding of God. We may erect an idol in place of the true God. We may cut God down to size. We may even delude ourselves into believing that we can ascend to God on the basis of our own intellectual reflection, congratulating ourselves for having found God, rather than acknowledging that God has already found us.[2]

---

1. Brian Hebblethwaite, "Divine and Human Goodness," *Ethics and Religion in a Pluralistic Age* (Edinburgh: Clark 1997) 65-75.

2. Sometimes, "the analogy of faith" is taken to mean an approach that, while employing the Bible as the only source of our analogical language for God, makes particular elements of the Bible—those in which the Pauline view of grace is elaborated—or Protestant church teachings that affirm the Pauline view of grace decisive for the interpretation of all of the Bible. See Daniel Payton Fuller, "Biblical Theology and the Analogy of Faith," *International Journal of Frontier Missions* 14.2 (April-June 1997): 65-74. The view that grace ought to be central in theological construction and that claims inconsistent with the conviction that grace is central should be rejected, has obvious similarities with the approach I advance here. In this sense, then, my

Those who favor the analogy of being will argue that, if God is creator, the divine nature must be reflected in creation in one way or another. Creation's rootedness in God must, in fact, *be* necessary. Otherwise, creation wouldn't really be creation, and God wouldn't be God. And if this is so, then we can ask certain basic question about the character of the divine reality. What must God be like in order for the world to be God's creation? And, as a divine creation, shouldn't the world somehow reflect God's character?

Further, they will argue, it isn't easy to identify divine revelation. Just because someone claims to have received a divine revelation doesn't mean that she actually has done so. Doesn't there need to be some way of assessing putative claims to revelation? And, if so, wouldn't arguments about what God must necessarily be like prove helpful? If we know that the divine nature *must* be like *this*, then we will be better equipped to distinguish authentic from inauthentic putative revelations. The temptation to self-interest afflicts even those who claim to know God solely through revelation, they will note. Indeed, appealing to revelation may sometimes be, not a means of restraining one's spiritual arrogance, but a way of reinforcing that arrogance: if God has told me what the divine will is, then I am beyond challenge, beyond criticism. Wouldn't some certain knowledge of God, independent of any purported special revelation, serve as a check on excessive self-confidence?

Those who favor the approach to God through the analogy of being might also note that beginning with creation and understanding what it means for anything to *be* at all doesn't require that we view God as static and lifeless. Only if we presuppose a contestable view of divine perfection will this be required. Building our God language on an analysis of the creaturely world doesn't mean thinking of God as without freedom and somehow beyond genuine interaction with creation.

In this book, I employ what I call the *analogy of love*—an approach to God-language that exhibits similarities to both of these models, but which differs from each.[1] A theology to which the analogy of love is central will maintain that we should seek to understand God first and foremost as love, and that we cannot avoid grounding our understanding of God's love in our own experience of loving and being loved.[2] Thus, like one rooted in the analogy of being, a theology rooted in the analogy of love starts with creaturely reality and builds up to an approach evidently parallels that of some proponents of the use of the analogy of faith to norm our talk about God.

1. Cp. Vincent Brümmer, *The Model of Love: A Study in Philosophical Theology* (Cambridge: CUP 1993) and Sallie McFague's discussion of the models of God as lover and friend in *Models of God: Theology for an Ecological, Nuclear Age* (London: SCM 1987). The notion that an approach to God from humanity, understood as in God's image, is an alternative to approaching God through nature and special revelation has some affinity with the understanding of things I defend here; cp. Jack W. Provonsha, *God Is With Us* (Washington, DC: Review 1974) 40-8.

2. See Trevor Hart, "How Do We Define the Nature of God's Love?" *Nothing Greater, Nothing Better: Theological Essays on the Love of God*, ed. Kevin J. Vanhoozer (Grand Rapids: Eerdmans 2001) 94-113. For an incarnational theology, says Hart, God "does not lift us up out of our creatureliness, elevating us to some deified state in which we are able to contemplate divine realities directly . . . . This means, of course, that we cannot ignore or circumvent the familiar and ordinary associations that words and realities taken up into the service of divine revelation have for us." Thus, "[t]o this extent, a theology of the love of God cannot short-circuit or set aside the contributions that human experiences and understandings of love have to offer . . . ." Our conception of divine love "will already be fashioned from the messy stuff of human experience and ideas" (99). Hart goes on to suggest that this affirmation of the creaturely locus of our language about divine love must be qualified by a recognition of the effects of sin on our familiar love-talk and of the reality of divine transcendence.

understanding of divine reality. But it privileges love, which is dynamic, active and interactive, capable of suffering. It therefore *begins* with an understanding of God as living, temporal, involved in our experience. The analogy of love cannot lead us to a god who is utterly detached from creaturely reality.

At the same time, the approach to God via the analogy of love has affinities with the approach to God through the analogy of faith. For the idea that love ought to be central to our understanding of God is not one that simply emerged from a vacuum. It is a central theme in the Christian tradition. It reflects what Christians have identified as God's decisive self-revelation. And the Christian understanding of love has reshaped the understanding and experience of love in our culture. Christian revelation and tradition authorize the appeal to love as a vital analogy for God, and our own experience of love is not isolated from or independent of revelation and tradition.[1]

We cannot develop an account of love in abstraction from the gospel. Our understanding of divine love must reflect what the life of Jesus shows us about who God is.[2] Jesus' agonized cry from the cross should put to rest any suspicions we might have that love is effortless, cheerful, and pain-free. Considering God's self-disclosure in the life of Jesus can expand our vision of love to include suffering and challenge.

But it is not quite correct to say that "it is the Christian story which *alone* is able to identify what for Christians is true love."[3] The claim that God is love is a claim that employs human language. The language of love is not holy language, with an exclusively religious meaning. Indeed, it is so effective as religious language in part precisely because it taps into powerful, common, human experience. For this language to be meaningful when used about God, it must have some prior meaning when applied in the context of our daily lives. It need not mean exactly the same thing when used about God and when used about finite persons. But there must be reasonable continuity between the use of the word to describe human relationships and its employment to characterize God's interaction with the world. After all, there are limits on what can plausibly be said to count as loving: hatred, vindictiveness, hostility, and aggression could not qualify as *love* without stretching the meaning of the word beyond recognition. And we must be able to offer plausible accounts of the dissimilarities between our talk about God as love and our talk about love between finite persons. Otherwise, talk of God as loving will be deprived of significance.

Christianity has profoundly affected the way we think and feel about love. But when the Bible and the Christian tradition speak of God as love, they are not introducing an alien notion. They are qualifying and extending an existing one. And once the Christian vision of love has been brought into focus by Christian revelation and tradition, it can in turn challenge us to ask to what extent the stories

---

1. A focus on love helps us to move past the traditional opposition between the analogy of faith and the analogy of being. It also helps us, I think, to transcend the opposition between historical and ontological interpretations of Christianity. An historical interpretation focuses on the particular, the unexpected; an ontological interpretation emphasizes the constant character of God's activity in the world, and sees Christianity primarily as an explication of generic features of human existence. A focus on love preserves the constancy typical of an ontological approach to Christianity, because love is an essential characteristic of all divine activity. But it also preserves the openness to particularity typical of an historical approach, since love is free and personally responsive.

2. So Douglas John Hall, *Professing the Faith: Christian Theology in a North American Context* (Minneapolis: Fortress 1993) 154.

3. George A. Lindbeck, *The Nature of Doctrine: Religion and Theology in a Postliberal Age* (Philadelphia: Westminster 1984) 83 (italics supplied).

we tell are God's stories or our own, whether the way we identify and characterize God is consistent with the understanding of divine love which Christianity itself has bequeathed us. Our experience of love, which has been shaped to a significant degree by the Christian tradition, and our ongoing, developing understanding of that tradition itself should and do exist in a continuing relationship of mutual correction and refinement. The Christian tradition can help us to understand love more fully and more truly, but our own experience of love can also help us to assess the beliefs and practices of our tradition.

To understand God using the analogy of love is to allow our convictions to be shaped by a complex interplay of the church's narratives and affirmations about God on the one hand and our own experience and reflection on the other. We know something of what love is from our own encounters with those who have loved us and those we have loved. Even as the Christian story expands and refines our talk of love, pruning away the shallow and the naïve, so our own experience of love can challenge doctrinal formulations as beyond the pale of love.

Love as a Critical Principle

As our principal analogy for God, love can and should serve as a critical principle that helps to distinguish good theology from bad. Shaped and extended by our Christian heritage, our experience and understanding of love can inform our understanding of the claim that God is love, and so help us determine which theological proposals are credible. "A religious belief which runs counter to our moral beliefs is to that extent unacceptable."[1] As John Greenleaf Whittier wrote,

> Not mine to look where cherubim
>   And seraphs may not see,
> But nothing can be good in Him
>   Which evil is in me.
> The wrong that pains my soul below
>   I dare not throne above,
> I know not of His hate,—I know
>   His goodness and His love.[2]

If our talk of God as loving *is* meaningful,[3] it clearly excludes some things we might be inclined to say about God. A given claim about the God who is love can be valid only if it is consistent with the claim that God *is* love, when *love* is a meaningful term that makes significant contact with ordinary human experience— ordinarily, when it is consistent with our characteristic use of *love* in the context of

---

1. Stewart R. Sutherland, *God, Jesus and Belief* (Oxford: Blackwell 1984) 16, qtd. James Barr, *Biblical Faith and Natural Theology* (Oxford: Clarendon-OUP 1993) 219.

2. John Greenleaf Whittier, "The Eternal Goodness," *English Poetry* 3: *From Tennyson to Whitman*, Harvard Classics, ed. Charles Eliot, 51 vols. (New York: Collier 1909-14) 43: no. 792; Bartleby.Com 2001 (http://www.bartleby.com/42/792.html; last visited January 19, 2007). For an example of an approach evidently presupposing the appropriateness of an argument from the meaning of goodness to an understanding of the action and character of God, see Robert Merrihew Adams, "Atoning Transactions," *Philosophy and Theological Discourse*, ed. Stephen T. Davis, Claremont Studies in the Philosophy of Religion (New York: St. Martin's 1997) 98: ". . . an unforgiving fastidiousness about the moral character of one's friends is not a virtue, and *therefore* is surely no part of the holiness of God" (italics mine). Thanks to Jack Provonsha for bringing "The Eternal Goodness" to my attention in various places.

3. Though he does not address all the difficulties attendant on analogical talk of God as morally good in ways comparable to those in which creatures may be said to be morally good, Keith Yandell does provide some useful support for the applicability of our language of moral goodness—and so of love—to God in *Philosophy of Religion: A Contemporary Introduction* (London: Routledge 1999) 304-5.

interpersonal relationships. And the norm of love as equal respect seems to be both readily defensible on rational grounds and deeply rooted in the Jewish and Christian traditions. That God is love, and that love for God and love as equal respect for other persons are integral to Christian ethics and spirituality, suggests a twofold theological *criterion of love*:

- one *should not* affirm a proposed belief if doing so is inconsistent with asserting that God is love; loving God; loving one's neighbor as oneself; or understanding God as calling one to love one's neighbor as oneself;[1] *and*
- one *should* affirm a proposed belief if doing so follows from doing any of these other things.

Suppose someone claims, as many slaveholders and their defenders did before the abolition of slavery, that God regards slavery as morally appropriate. Love as equal respect seems to be inconsistent with treating another as property when one would not want to be treated as property oneself. And ignoring the norm of love as equal respect is inconsistent with God's intention and creational design for humanity. But, given this, the criterion of love seems also to require the conclusion that God cannot regard or ever have regarded slavery as appropriate. Thus, it will be consistently more reasonable to believe, in light of this norm, that God has *never* approved of slavery than to credit purported independent evidence of God's approval of slavery.

A person who wants to defend a belief that seems inconsistent with the criterion of love may, of course, argue that the challenged belief *isn't* inconsistent with the criterion. Perhaps we simply can't see how God could do this, or be like that, and still be loving in a way we can recognize, but maybe this says more about us than it does about God. Perhaps ignorance—or willful blindness—keeps us from seeing the compatibility of the challenged belief with the conviction that God is love. Or perhaps we should revise our view of divine love.

Sometimes, of course, we should accept arguments of this sort—though, of course, revising our conception of love too significantly means running the risk of disconnecting our talk of God from our experience, or even rendering it devoid of meaning. Perhaps on occasion we should maintain two convictions despite the profound tension between them. But I suggest that we would ordinarily do well instead to revise an existing belief, or reject a proposed one, if affirming it appears clearly inconsistent with the criterion of love.

Features of a Love-Centered Theology

Suppose we agree that divine and human love ought to be at the center of our theology. What difference will this make for *how* we determine what to say theologically and *what* we do, in fact, say?

- *Our theology will emerge from community*. Love will be the matrix of our reflection. Love will bond us to other lovers, both past and future, so that we are conscious of ourselves as loving and beloved members of a tradition, in conversation with our predecessors and committed to offering something of value to those who follow us. And love will lead us to engage in ongoing communal conversation

---

1. Thanks to Thomas B. Talbott for this point. For Talbott's analysis of salvation, judgment, and human destiny, see Thomas B. Talbott, "On Predestination, Reprobation, and the Love of God," *Reformed Journal* 33.2 (Feb. 1983): 11-5; cp. Thomas B. Talbott, "The Doctrine of Everlasting Punishment," *Faith and Philosophy* 7 (1990): 19-42; Thomas B. Talbott, "Providence, Freedom, and Human Destiny," *Religious Studies* 26 (1990): 227-45; Thomas B. Talbott, *The Inescapable Love of God* (Boca Raton, FL: Universal 1999).

about the things that matter most, the things we love most. Love will be not only the focus of our theological reflection but also its form.

• *Our theology will be relational.* It will emphasize that God and the world both act, and that the world affects God just as God affects the world. It will emphasize, too, that relationality is constitutive of human being, and other kinds of creaturely being as well.

• *Our theology will be praxis-sensitive.* It will incorporate critical reflection on the practice of love. Our seriousness about love can't be a piece of ideology that insulates us from the responsibility actually to *be* loving; we will seek to make love real in our lives. And that means that our theology will be concerned with helping us—as persons and as communities—to be more effective lovers.

• *Our theology will be integrated with spirituality.* One way of thinking about Christian spirituality is seeing it as *living out of the heart of the Christian tradition.* And, given the importance of love for that tradition, this must mean loving God, ourselves, and other creatures. A love-centered theology will foster our formation as loving persons. It will encourage loving actions and loving hearts. It will serve the practical concerns of church and world for thinking that makes us whole and fosters right relation between God and creation. And it will feed both private devotion and public proclamation and celebration.

• *Our theology will be fun.* We sometimes speak of "intellectual *eros.*" We are drawn toward knowledge, understanding, and truth by their inherent attractiveness. A theology that takes love seriously ought to take this aspect of our humanness seriously as well. Knowing is fun, especially knowing about what matters most. So is the process of gaining knowledge. Good theology should respect and respond to these erotic aspects of the process and result of doing theology. It ought to acknowledge that discovering is delightful, and that discoveries are, too.

Love and Complacency

The conviction that God is love should reside at the heart of our theology. But the identification of God as loving and of love as the center of Christian belief can serve to excuse complacency and sentimentality.

A sense of being isolated and valueless lurks around the edges of our consciousness. We long for an embrace secure enough and all-encompassing enough to sustain us when we feel rejected, hopeless, and thoroughly alone. We yearn for a care that sustains us, accompanies us, precedes us along the way—protecting, guiding, nurturing us. If God is love, really love, then God's presence in our world and in our lives is good news indeed.

But is love necessarily good news? Is it the good news we need to hear? Christians have spoken about God as love so often, so indiscriminately, with so many different meanings that highlighting love as the center of Christian belief may sound naïve, trite, or complacent. Making love the central element of Christian belief may appear to be nothing weaker than a reaction to a religious style marked by dogmatism, authoritarianism, and judgment. Thus, one critic complains that "love of the most unjudgmental variety" has become "the norm by which every other quality attributed to the Deity . . . [has been] tested, altered, or discarded." The God once acclaimed as "Father Almighty" is now "the Grandfather All-merciful." So "generations of North American liberal Protestants have by now grown used to a 'Christian God . . . incapable of anger—and they have treated 'him' accordingly: with condescension and often secret contempt."[1] Affirming that "Jesus loves everybody" may seem too often to serve as unnecessary

---

1. Hall, *Professing* 55.

comfort for those in power, those who shirk their responsibility to others, those who do not know just how much they really need love, much less how much they need to love others.[1]

Unconditional love is, in one important sense, nonjudgmental. It embraces the beloved, holds her secure and cherished, without regard to what she does or feels or is. If this is the love of the Grandfather All-merciful, so be it. Given many people's experiences of tyrannical, abusive, or distant fathers, replacing the Father Almighty with the Grandfather All-merciful doesn't seem like such a bad idea. The good news is precisely that God loves sinners, that God loves them whether or not they behave appropriately, that God is faithful when we are faithless. Misconceptions of God that get in the way of appreciating this radical divine love deserve to be rejected and forgotten.

But accepting someone, loving her unconditionally, is not the same thing as endorsing her character or her behavior. Indeed, precisely because I love someone I may be driven to challenge her, to unsettle her, to call her to let go of what prevents her from realizing her potential. I must be concerned to help her avoid self-deception, and so to acknowledge the reality of the others with whom she has to do. Further, truly to love her as *other*, rather than simply because of my own satisfaction in or desire for her, is to be open to otherness, to the reality of that which is *not me*. That means that the beloved cannot be the only focus of my care; I cannot, therefore, regard with indifference how the beloved treats others, for being open to otherness means being open to them as well.[2]

To announce, then, that God loves everyone unconditionally is not to say that God is unconcerned about the ways in which we hurt each other and ourselves. Love will not let me waste my life in the pointless pursuit of prestige, superficial satisfaction, or material gain. Love threatens to unsettle us and unravel our orderly worlds as it challenges our complacency, smugness, and greed. Because God loves the rest of creation, divine love will not let me support exploitative and oppressive structures and ways of life. Love challenges us to be aware of ourselves—of our complacency, our irresponsibility, our acquisitiveness—and thus has the potential to prove deeply unsettling.[3] Further, the very fact that divine love is offered to us unconditionally is a kind of judgment; we may be loath to

1. Hall, *Professing* 504; Hall references Ronald Goetz, "Jesus Loves Everybody," *Christian Century*, Mar. 11, 1992: 274-7. Cp. Douglas John Hall, *When You Pray: Thinking Your Way into God's World* (Valley Forge, PA: Judson 1987) 26-30. His real and appropriate concerns do not keep Hall from emphasizing that "the language of love . . . is at the center of the entire biblical narrative. Every aspect of Christian theology is in the last analysis a midrash on the theme of love: God 'is love.' Jesus Christ is the 'beloved Son,' whom God sent into the world because 'God so loved the world.' Love is the 'fruit of the Spirit.' The whole of Christian ethics—'the law and the prophets'—is summed up in the command to love God and one's neighbor. Love is not only a way of articulating the foundational ontology of . . . [the Christian] tradition, it is *the* way" (*Professing* 323-4).

2. For a weaker version of the same argument, see Bernard Williams, *Morality: An Introduction to Ethics* (Cambridge: CUP 1973) 24-6. Williams suggests that we consider, say, some "stereotype from a gangster movie . . . ," a "ruthless and rather glamorous figure who cares about his mother, his child, even his mistress." Even this less-than-admirable character, Williams observes, "is capable of thinking in terms of others' interests, and his failure to be a moral agent lies (partly) in the fact that he is only intermittently and capriciously disposed to do so." The important thing to note here is that "there is no bottomless gulf between this state and the basic dispositions of morality." Thus, the point of the example is to show "that if we grant a man with even a minimal concern for others, then we do not have to ascribe to him any fundamentally new kind of thought or experience to include him in the world of morality, but only what is recognizably an extension of what he already has."

3. Hall, *Professing* 155.

fered to us unconditionally is a kind of judgment; we may be loath to accept it precisely because to do so would be to acknowledge that our relationships with God are not products of our own achievements[1] and that we are not able to secure the meanings of our own lives. In short, love itself may generate so much tension and conflict that it "can and must sometimes feel like hate."[2]

But love's challenge to us is never grounded in the threat of rejection or retribution or retaliation. Love does not threaten to penalize us with its own withdrawal. There is nothing cheap about such love, with its insistent call to growth in flourishing and responsibility. But the challenge it issues to our complacency is always the challenge of a lover who cherishes us without limit. That is why it remains, finally, good news.

A legitimate concern to avoid complacency need not lead us to treat love as anything but vital. Thus, I will seek in the remainder of this book to articulate an account of Christian theology that is centered on love and that tests theological proposals using the criterion of love. In Chapter 2, I will reflect on the justification of Christian belief. Even here, love makes a difference.

---

1. Hall, *Professing* 154.
2. Hall, *Professing* 154.

2

Love Begins Where We Are

Christians believe in love. We believe in love when we are confident that love is the ultimate truth about the universe, when it is in love that we repose our trust and to love that we pledge our loyalty. And we believe in love when love provides our believing with a context and a goal, when our believing takes place *in* love.

There are several ways in which love is the origin and context of our believing. God's love lies at the root of all our apprehension of and response to God; thus, we begin to love in an atmosphere of love, in the atmosphere that is God. We truly know only that which we love; thus, our knowledge of God depends on our seeking God with loving desire and opening ourselves to God in venturesome trust. We can open ourselves to God only if we experience love as a real possibility; thus, our encounters with each other in love determine whether we will experience trust in God as a genuine option. We come to know God not as isolated individuals but as a result of communal witness; thus, relationship—love—serves as the means by which our convictions are born and nurtured.

Love is central to the substance of Christian belief. And because beliefs have consequences, and love, for Christians, is the most important of those consequences, Christian belief should lead to, and inform, Christian love. God's love grounds our knowledge of God—this is the point of talk about revelation. Christian belief, which seeks to be accountable to divine revelation, is rightly rooted in love of our traditions and, at the same time, love for the others—persons communities, ideas, alternative traditions—we experience as surprising and challenging those traditions. The interaction between love for our traditions and love for the otherness that can challenge those traditions leads to an account of the process of forming, evaluating, retaining, and developing Christian belief that we might call an "epistemology of life." There are positive reasons for a variety of Christian beliefs, but we need not formulate and defend those beliefs on the basis of minimal, universally acceptable assumptions, though we must certainly take appropriate account of objections advanced against them from alternate traditions.

We can and must make choices about the adequacy of our religious beliefs under conditions of uncertainty (though doing so should not be confused with *faith*, which is no substitute for critical reflection). The apparent absence of God and the reality of pointless suffering both make it difficult for some people to believe confidently that love is at the heart of the universe. If God is creator, however, and not an object in the world, experience of God will not take the form of experience of some finite object. And pointless suffering can be understood as a consequence either of divine self-restraint or of the character of creation. A credible response to the problem of suffering will need, of course, to be consistent with the conviction that God is love. Such a response, in turn, will lie at the root of a plausible account of divine action in the world.

Belief and Love

Love is a matter of interpersonal relation. But believing sometimes seems thoroughly individual, if not individualistic—a very private matter, an act of heart and mind and will that is invisible to everyone but the one who believes.

Such a conception of belief seems to emphasize the unique dignity and value of each person, to stress the value of individuals and the importance of individual responsibility: each of us must believe *personally*. And, to be sure, Christianity does emphasize personal responsibility and thus, implicitly, the distinctive worth of every sentient creature. If we are Christians, we have to take individua*lity* seriously. But we don't have to support the ideology of rugged individual*ism*. Christian belief is about love and relationship and connection and union and responsibility. What Christians believe undercuts a conception of created beings as isolated and independent. To believe Christianly is to believe in love.

Love and the Substance of Christian Convictions

The specific things Christians believe give us good reason to affirm our connectedness—our life together in love. First of all, believing in God means affirming that love is at the heart of reality, since God *is* love. And it hardly makes sense to understand love as the ground and goal of the universe, to worship the God who is essentially love, while behaving as if "love" did not name the basic truth about the universe, identify the underlying order of things.

To name God as creator is, among other things, to assert that we live in one world—a *uni*verse, not a *multi*verse—and that all of us are rooted in a single Source. We are united with each other in virtue of creation. And God's ongoing work in the world is best understood as the outpouring of divine love on a world which is loved into being.

In the ministry of Jesus and in God's Spirit's ongoing activity, loves creation and inspires us to love. Jesus' life was marked by a loving commitment to and connection with other persons, and by an ongoing, loving intimacy with the One to whom he prayed. The story of Jesus thus reminds us of God's love. In turn, as the early Christian church enthusiastically affirmed, this love overflows to the entire world. Called by the love of God in Jesus, we are one in God's love. Thus, we emulate that love in a way that recognizes the connectedness which links us with each other.

God's healing activity is potentially of benefit to all of reality, not simply the strand of history directly connected with Jesus. But Jesus' life reveals the God who is present and active everywhere. In Jesus, we see the God to whom *all* creatures are related, whether they acknowledge this fact or not. By highlighting Jesus' universal significance, we underscore the unity, the connectedness, of creation.

And the church both symbolizes and reinforces our connectedness with each other. Talk of the church's universality reminds us that it is—or is meant to be—a completely inclusive community. Our relationships with others, both our contemporaries and those who have preceded us, are central to our lives as Christians.

Thus, what Christians actually do believe makes it difficult to understand Christian believing as the activity of isolated individuals. Each person who believes does so individually. But the *fact* of her believing and the *content* of her believing are inexplicably without reference to community. *What* she confesses as a Christian commits her, if she takes it seriously, to recognizing the fact that she is essentially related to other people, individually and corporately. And it commits her to a common purpose and identity, which she shares with the Christian community.

The Nature of Believing

While as a mental state, a belief is, in principle, only accessible *directly* to the person whose belief it is,[1] it manifests itself in action, action that takes place against a backdrop of interpersonal relationships and social institutions. Christian belief is publicly expressed in worship. In their common celebrations, Christians identify with and own a community. And Christian beliefs are identity-forming convictions, convictions that shape personal self-understanding and guide public action; they are not simply trivial factual assertions or interesting but irrelevant metaphysical postulates. Thus, if they are taken seriously, they will determine the nature of one's public behavior. Further, the self that acts is a self formed in relationship. It is in the course of its various interactions with other people and with its various communities that it acquires the capacity to believe, an understanding of what believing means, and an account of how believing can be justified.

LOVE, BELIEF, AND ACTION

One aspect of our love is the love of the true for its own sake. We seek to understand just because knowledge is good in and of itself. But the love of knowledge is not the only element of Christian love. We love God through gratitude, worship, and prayer. And we love God's creatures through attentive, sensitive appreciation of and care for them in all their particularity. Making Christian convictions one's own is about identifying ourselves as loved and loving persons. It is never a matter *merely* of assenting to a set of propositions.

Thus, to say, "I believe in God" is not simply to maintain that one believes the proposition "there is God." If the word "God" means what Christians believe it does, then the reality of God could not be an issue regarding which one could be indifferent. To believe as a Christian is to *interpret the whole world* in particular ways. It is to *experience one's world* in particular ways. It entails that *one's identity is or should be shaped* in particular ways. And it suggests that one is *prepared to behave* in particular ways. It is to acknowledge oneself as part of a world rooted and grounded in love, a world in which we can and must love, a world about which *love* is the most true thing that can be said. It is to commit oneself to relying on God, to trusting Go, to loving God. (That is why confessions of belief are appropriate elements of the experience of worship and prayer.) One may not, of course, sense all of the implications of Christian belief at once. And weakness of will may interfere with one's efforts to live out the behavioral consequences of that belief. But, in principle, belief in God can and should affect one's entire existence, directing it toward love.

"I believe in God" isn't *just* cognitive, therefore. But it *is* cognitive, just the same. If I say, "I believe in God," and if I am using these words naturally, I am saying something about God, and not just about myself. It makes little sense to say, "I believe in God," if one simply means, for instance, "I'm making a commitment to being a loving person." If that were what one meant by "I believe in God," then reference to God would be superfluous and arbitrary, with no necessary relation to what one really wanted to say. It would make more sense to talk explicitly about one's own loving behavior, rather than cloaking them in confusing and (in fact) irrelevant God-language. If one does not really believe that there

---

1. Contrary to the views of those who wish to equate belief with its manifestation in action or to argue that an exhaustive knowledge of a person's brain physiology would enable us to understand her inner life perfectly. For a pointed critique of the first of these doubtful views, see John R. Searle, *Mind: A Brief Introduction* (New York: OUP 2004) 35-74.

is God, then one would have no reason to mention God at all. One could simply mention one's other reasons for living and believing—for loving—as one had chosen to do.

But, for Christians, God-talk *isn't* pointless. The implication of Christian God-language is that *God*, not merely an ideal, rightly evokes our love. When we love God's creation, we're acting in harmony with the way things really are; we're not just projecting our passion against the void.[1] We are joining with God in an adventure of love, and God's gracious, guiding, sustaining presence accompanies us as we love. At the same time, our love is not required to *substitute* for God's all-encompassing care for all creation; if there is God, then we do not need to be God, assuming the impossible task of loving infinitely. In short, talk about God isn't reducible to talk about myself and my world.

LOVE AND REVELATION

Christian God-language and Christian belief are ultimately rooted in God's own revealing activity. God's revelation is not just the transmission of *information*; it is God's self-gift to us. What God gives us is—God's own self.[2] And wherever or whenever we receive God's self-gift, we do so not only at God's initiative but also through God's empowerment and mediation.

Love seeks communion and communication. A completely hidden god would not be the God of love. Talking about revelation fits appropriately with talk of God as love, for lovers like nothing more than to share themselves with each other, through word and touch and music, through taste and scent and feeling. Love is active, reaching out to share with the beloved. And that is as true of God's love as of ours. If we say that God is personal, and that God is love (claims which are obviously contestable, but which I seek to defend elsewhere in this book), we will find it natural to conclude that God reveals God's own self to us.

Because God is love, God's revelatory activity is dialogical.[3] That is, what God communicates through nature, history, and experience is apprehended by persons who interpret it, integrate it with what they already know, and respond to it. And God, in turn, responds to them. That is part of what it means for God to engage in relationships with creatures that are marked by mutual freedom and love. But this means, in turn, that God's revelation is not perfectly apprehended or communicated. For creatures bring their assumptions, their finitude, their fallibility, and their sin to the task of apprehending what God seeks to communicate, reflecting on it, and conveying it to others. If there were no free creatures, God could ensure that God's character and purposes were perfectly understood. But, since freedom is a presupposition of love, there would, in this case, be no opportunity for love between God and creation or within creation.

The same fact—the historical nature of God's self-disclosure—explains not only why people do not always perfectly understand God's self-disclosure or

---

1. A phrase I owe to Stephen R. Donaldson.
2. So Walter Kasper, *The God of Jesus Christ*, trans. Matthew J. O'Connell (New York: Crossroad 1989) 225. Cp. Pannenberg, *Jesus* 175. Brunner (10-11) makes a somewhat similar point in respect of the experience of salvation: only the fact that God's self-revelation can only be responded to by means of God's own loving action can explain the fact that divine revelation is responded to in trust by some persons and not by others. If it were otherwise, how could salvation really be a gift of love? On this view, God's Spirit effects the trust of those who are saved. But does the contemplated response here really count as a response at all? Brunner avoids the obvious implication—double predestination—only by asserting that we can conclude nothing from the fact that some respond and some do not (416).
3. See David Brown, *The Divine Trinity* (London: Duckworth 1985) 69-98.

convey it perfectly to others, but also why human understanding of God's self-revelation is not uniform, why one tradition might be a better source of insight than another.

Since God is love, God's revealing activity is universal. Because God is creator, because of the universal presence and activity of God's Spirit, God is, in principle, revealed everywhere, throughout the non-human creation, human history, and human experience. This is so even though God can likely reveal more about divine love, more detail about divine purposes, in communities of persons and through human history than through nature.

However, since God's self-disclosure occurs in and through the processes of history, some people will be better positioned than others to discern some aspects of God's character and purposes. Different historical circumstances will present God with different possibilities. God's self-disclosure will occur in and through the images and categories available in the context in which divine self-disclosure is taking place. This means that God's character and purposes, revealed in and through particular cultural forms, will be more or less comprehensible to particular people. Some historical conditions and circumstances will make it easier to grasp some things God is trying to convey than others.

A community's having previously apprehended a particular aspect of God's self-revelation more or less aptly will enable it to understand subsequent facets of the divine self-disclosure more clearly. To be sure, God seeks to communicate with all people in all cultures and environments. But the historical sedimentation of understanding in a given community—reflecting previous free, contingent responses to divine revelation rendered particularly suitable by favorable circumstances—could make that community more effective overall as a receiver and transmitter of particular insights into God's character and purposes.

Christians have identified Jesus of Nazareth as decisively revealing God. Consequently, they have also stressed that the strand of history centered on Jesus—and so including the story of Israel and that of the church—has distinctive revelatory value as a source of understanding in respect of God's character and purposes. While the presence and activity of God's Spirit are universal, God's presence and activity in Jesus provided God's Spirit with a distinctive opportunity to affect the course of human history. The reception of this revelation by the early Christian community marked a decisive historical moment. And that, in turn, created new possibilities for God's Spirit to facilitate the reception of subsidiary revelation.

If we see God's Spirit as present in, with, and under the human spirit, we can characterize God's Spirit as the *medium* of divine self-revelation and the *facilitator* of its reception. God's Spirit grounds and inspires our reception of God's self-revelation. God gives revelation; present and active in the world, including the life of Jesus, *God* is ultimately the *content* of God's own revelation. But God's Spirit also enables us to appropriate this revelation. Jesus reveals the character of God in history; it is God's Spirit who grounds and inspires our *reception* of that revelation.[1] The work of God's Spirit lies behind and within the reception of revelation. And very reception of God's self-communication at one moment creates the capacity for a new phase of divine revelation at the next.

---

1. The affinity of this conception with some ideas of Karl Barth should be obvious. I develop it here in a way that depends on the analysis provided by Wolfhart Pannenberg in *Jesus—God and Man*, trans. Lewis L. Wilkens and Duane A. Priebe (Philadelphia: Westminster 1968) 174-9. See also Gordon Kaufman, *Systematic Theology: A Historicist Perspective* (New York: Scribner 1968) 94-116. On God's Spirit in particular, see Karl Rahner, *Foundations of Christian Faith: An Introduction to the Idea of Christianity* (New York: Crossroad-Seabury 1978): "God's self-communication must always be present in man as the prior condition of possibility for its acceptance" (128; cp. 118-9).

Of course, the presence and activity of God's Spirit are not exclusively dependent on, nor do they presuppose, any particular event of revelation.[1] God can be revealed whether or not people know about or understand or believe any prior divine self-disclosure. Not everyone has encountered God's revelation in Jesus. And even those who *have* been exposed to it may not possess the categories to understand what it means. Those who present it may do so inadequately. Their experiences may make apt belief unattractive or impossible. If basic trust is lacking, a person will find it difficult or impossible to read the world through Christian eyes. And there may be all sorts of other impediments to sensible belief. Beliefs that are themselves true may, for instance, seem to be wrapped up with other beliefs, institutions, or patterns of behavior that appear on other grounds to be untenable. It may seem to require incoherent affirmations, or tolerance for injustice. I'm not saying that these objections to Christian belief can't be met. I'm saying that not everyone *knows* they can't be. Because of their personal experiences or their social, cultural, or historical circumstances, many people cannot be expected to endorse beliefs that are, in fact, true. But, because God's work is as wide as creation, such people's failure to affirm these beliefs is no sign that they have refused to love and trust God.

Love and the Roots of Belief

I propose here what I call an *epistemology of love*. On this view, we are entitled to presume the validity of the beliefs we hold at any given time. We must, however, be open to challenges to those beliefs. We do not address those challenges by evaluating individual beliefs in isolation, however: instead, we must treat them as challenges to our *webs* of belief. We may reject a given challenge entirely, accept it entirely, or accept it in part; but a logical price-tag will be attached to each option, and we will need to adjust our belief-systems accordingly. I identify this proposal as an epistemology of *love* because loving can prepare and enable us to believe appropriately. There are at least three ways in which this is so.

• We rightly begin our reflection on religious questions, and all other questions, with the beliefs we have. Taking these beliefs seriously is a matter of honoring our own experiences and needs, and so of love for ourselves.

• Our convictions are mediated to us through traditions and communities of belief and practice to which we are in one way or another attached. Owning these traditions and adhering to them is a matter of *piety*, of regard for the wisdom and experience and insight of those who have gone before us. Piety is a kind of love—a love for our forebears and for the institutions and traditions they have bequeathed us.

• At the same time, the acceptance of convictions we value and which meet our immediate needs, and loving attachment to tradition and community, can lapse into an idolatrous refusal to be surprised or to criticize. Truly to love is to be sensitive to what is novel, what is different from our expectations, to love what *is* rather than what we imagine *should be*. Love therefore entails a willingness to be surprised by God and to be critical of the beliefs we value and the traditions we love precisely in order to be faithful to the God of surprises.[2]

---

1. Wolfhart Pannenberg, *Systematic Theology* 1, trans. Geoffrey W. Bromiley (Grand Rapids: Eerdmans 1991) 249-50, seems to present us with an unappetizing choice between trivializing God's Spirit's importance—by implying that God's saving work apart from the proclamation of the gospel doesn't involve God's Spirit—or localizing salvation to the stream of history where the story of Jesus is related.

2. On love and/as hermeneutics, see Wendy Farley, *Eros for the Other: Retaining Truth in a Pluralistic World* (University Park, PA: Pennsylvania State UP 1995); Anthony

In this section, I consider these complementary elements of an epistemology of love. I begin by suggesting that, because we may reasonably treat as given the beliefs we have when we reflect on a problem, the burden of proof always rests on someone who wishes to challenge those beliefs. I note that, while we do not require positive reasons for believing, we may, in fact, have such reasons. I examine the significance of epistemic piety and the important role of tradition as a source of our beliefs. And I outline the implications of love for otherness as a counterweight to regard for tradition, noting that intellectual responsibility requires us to consider serious challenges to our beliefs and that the dialogue across traditions required to resolve those challenges is possible.

The Burden of Proof

We acquire our religious convictions in all sorts of ways. Someone may come to believe, for instance, because of a complex of personal experiences,[1] or because Christian convictions seem to meet her deeply felt needs (insofar as need, understood as desire, is a kind of love, an appeal to need may form part of an epistemology of love).[2] One may come to read the world Christianly because one has recognized the pattern of the events that make up one's own story and the world's as the one described in Christian teaching.[3] Christian beliefs may be learned from parents or teachers, or acquired as the result of a growing personal conviction from numerous sources too various and subtle to identify or distinguish.[4]

Precisely for this reason, Christian convictions often seem illegitimate to modern people. Positive arguments in their favor are lacking, critics maintain. These beliefs are irrational, dependent only on blind, arbitrary whim. Whatever we believe, we must provide compelling *positive* arguments for our beliefs before we can justifiably accept them.

This is often a consequence of the way we're taught to understand good thinking in general. We learn to suppose that we must justify all of our beliefs with reference to basic truths that couldn't be rejected by any rational person, or at least to determine that adequate evidence for them is available to us. We're taught to doubt our beliefs until they have been justified in this way. And we're encouraged not to believe any more strongly than the positive evidence will allow. Of course, few people actually get their beliefs—religious or otherwise—primarily by means of arguments. Most of us don't pretend to start from scratch and think through the options neutrally until we arrive at rationally compelling beliefs. But we are often implicitly encouraged to think that this is exactly how we ought to proceed if we want valid beliefs.

C. Thiselton, *Interpreting God and the Postmodern Self: On Meaning, Manipulation and Promise* (Grand Rapids: Eerdmans 1995) 47-78. As Thiselton sums up his approach: "In Christian theology we often describe approaching the biblical text as *listening in reverent expectancy*, while we view approaching another human *self* as considering their unique personal identity and personal history with care, with attentive respect, or with what the New Testament writers call *agape*. This means *creative regard for the Other; it is a love prompted by will, not by prior 'like-mindedness'*" (51; italics Thiselton's).

1. See Langdon Gilkey, *Naming the Whirlwind* (Indianapolis: Bobbs-Merrill 1968); Peter L. Berger, *A Rumor of Angels: Modern Society and the Rediscovery of the Supernatural*, rev. ed. (New York: Anchor 1990).
2. Diogenes Allen defends this proposal in *The Reasonableness of Faith: A Philosophical Essay on the Grounds for Religious Beliefs* (Washington, DC: Corpus 1968).
3. So William C. Placher, *Unapologetic Theology: A Christian Voice in a Pluralistic Conversation* (Atlanta: Westminster/John Knox 1989).
4. See, *e.g.*, John Henry Newman, *An Essay in Aid of a Grammar of Assent*, 5th ed. (London: Burns 1881).

Consequently, religious people have spent a lot of time trying to defend their beliefs on putatively universal premises, and they've often felt forced to modify their convictions or reinterpret them so they can be grounded on what are supposed to be rationally compelling foundations. They may regard themselves as intellectually irresponsible if they haven't identified persuasive positive arguments for their beliefs, and they sometimes imagine that their beliefs are legitimate only if they can show that they *could* have arrived at these beliefs in this way.

However, whatever path we take to our beliefs, religious or otherwise, we are not *required* to demonstrate their truth with positive arguments before we grant them legitimacy.[1] The truth about God is not relative—whether there is God is not a function of whether *I* believe there is. But being rationally *entitled* to hold a particular belief *is* dependent on one's circumstances.[2]

It is obviously difficult to identify premises *everyone* would have to accept in order to meet standards of rationality on which everyone would agree.[3] The law of non-contradiction seems like a reasonable example. So does the proposition, *Not all of reality is under the control of my conscious self.* And perhaps the affirmation that each of one's actions is exhaustively determined by its antecedents is performatively self-contradictory. I have no stake in denying that there are any rationally inescapable truths. Clearly, however, not everyone would agree that even the claims I have identified are rationally necessary. Even if they were, they wouldn't be sufficient to settle many serious intellectual debates. And, in any case, I think, we do not need to meet the challenge of showing how our beliefs follow from unchallengeable premises before regarding them as rationally acceptable.

Instead, when we think about our beliefs, we can appropriately start "in the middle."[4] Normally we do not, for instance, question the essential reliability of our senses, the reality of other people, or the existence of the external world. I believe that other people are thinking, feeling, conscious persons—not robots created to confuse me. If someone claims that positive arguments actually show that what I suppose to be other people are, in fact, only pseudo-people, then I may need to find arguments to refute her. But I do not have to find arguments which prove that other people are real before I am free to trust my conviction that they are.

And that's the case with our beliefs generally. We can begin by trusting them, even though we need to be alert to potential challenges. We remain free to believe what we already do, in fact, believe unless we know of good reasons not

---

1. Thanks to Annette Bryson for the opportunity to discuss this issue. In this portion of Chapter 2, I draw on material I also used, to somewhat different effect, in "Righting Narrative: Robert Chang, Poststructuralism, and the Limits of Critique," *UCLA Asian Pacific American Law Journal* 7.1 (Spring 2001): 105-32. I am grateful to Jerry Kang for his comments regarding that article.

2. I owe this distinction to Jeffrey Stout, *Ethics after Babel: The Languages of Morals and Their Discontents* (Boston: Beacon 1988).

3. I want to emphasize as strongly as possible that I do not intend this as in any way a denial that meaningful discourse about God and the world aims to be accountable to a reality beyond the individual reasoner or her community, and that the norms of language, logic, and ethics are not optional, but necessary; see Nagel, *Word*. The question, once we move beyond concerns with logical inconsistency and performative self-contradiction (cp. David Ray Griffin, *Reenchantment without Supernaturalism: A Process Philosophy of Religion* [Ithaca, NY: Cornell UP 2001] 5, 29-35, for a useful discussion of "hard-core common sense"), is how best to assess truth-claims. My contention is that we can and must do so by beginning with the beliefs we actually have, not that we may maintain those beliefs if doing so involves us, for instance, in self-contradictions.

4. For a good example of such an approach, ably defended, in the context not of religion but of ethics, see Charles Larmore, *The Morals of Modernity* (Cambridge: CUP 1996) 89-117.

to.[1] We need not start from narrow, limited premises and try to reconstruct our beliefs about the external world, other people, and so forth. We can challenge and rebut and modify these beliefs. But we reasonably begin with the beliefs we have, most of which are derived from our traditions and communities.

It's therefore up to someone else who wishes to dislodge these beliefs to do so, if she can offer us appropriately persuasive arguments. In a book first published in 1976, Antony Flew defended what he labeled a "presumption of atheism."[2] I suggest that this is best seen, not as a presumption with which everyone must begin, but rather as a presumption with which—were we to talk about these matters—*he* would be entitled to begin.

If I were to conduct an argument about religious matters with a non-theist, it would be incumbent on me to offer negative arguments against relevant non-theistic metaphysical positions, positive reasons for theistic belief, rebuttals of relevant anti-theistic arguments, or all three. There would, in *this* case, be a presumption of non-theism—how could I reasonably ask my conversation-partner to abandon the view of the world she already holds as a starting point for our discussion?

An atheist is entitled, therefore, to a presumption of atheism from any theists who wish to dispute religious matters with her, just as they are entitled to presume the validity of their beliefs should she opt actively to challenge them. But that's quite different from saying that the theist should accept such a presumption *when assessing her own beliefs.*

Positive Reasons for Believing

The fact that we don't *need* positive arguments if we are to be justified in retaining a variety of our beliefs, religious and otherwise, doesn't mean there *aren't* valid arguments for the Christian beliefs. It doesn't mean, for instance, that evidence for the reality of God isn't to be had, or that it doesn't, can't, or couldn't not play an important role in the processes by which some people come to cognitive Christian belief.[3] Features of our experience as well as facts we know about the world do seem to puncture self-contained descriptions of reality, impelling us to seek its ground in God. Reports of the death of arguments for God's reality have been much exaggerated.[4]

---

1. See Nicholas Wolterstorff, "Can Belief in God be Rational if It Has No Foundations?" *Faith and Rationality: Reason and Belief in God*, ed. Alvin Plantinga and Wolterstorff (Notre Dame, IN: U of Notre Dame P 1985). See also Wolterstorff's *Reason within the Bounds of Religion*, 2d ed. (Grand Rapids: Eerdmans 1984); Clark 1-26; Nancey C. Murphy, *Beyond Liberalism and Fundamentalism: How Modern and Postmodern Philosophy Set the Theological Agenda* (Valley Forge, PA: TPI 1996); Nancey C. Murphy, *Anglo-American Postmodernity: Philosophical Perspectives on Science, Religion, and Ethics* (Boulder, CO: Westview 1997).

2. See Antony Flew, *The Presumption of Atheism and Other Philosophical Essays on God, Freedom, and Immortality* (London: Elek/Pemberton 1976). Flew seems to have concluded more recently that this presumption can be overcome, at least in part—he appears to have endorsed a form of deism, at least tentatively; see "Atheist becomes Theist: An Interview with Former Atheist Antony Flew," *Biola News and Communications*, http://www.biola.edu/antonyflew/ (last visited Jan. 13, 2007); for further details, see http://www.antonyflew.com/ (last visited Jan. 13, 2007).

3. Obviously, such evidence could not be the basis for belief of the other sort, reliance on God's loving acceptance, because such reliance, being a free choice, cannot be evoked in the same way as a conviction.

4. See Richard Swinburne, *The Existence of God*, 2d. ed. (Oxford: Clarendon-OUP 2004); Stephen R. L. Clark, *God, Religion, and Reality* (London: SPCK 1998); Griffin, *Reenchantment* 169-203; Keith Ward, *Rational Theology and the Creativity of God* (Oxford: Blackwell 1984); Alvin Plantinga's frequently cited paper, "Two Dozen (or So)

Consider some questions:
- Why is there order in the world?
- Why does the world have the *particular* order that it does?
- Why is the world's order so fruitful? Why is it productive of complexity, of life, of *us*?

Queries like these continue reasonably to evoke responses that make reference to the purposes and activity of God. It is difficult to explain the character of the universe while ignoring God. In particular, the existence of human beings, dependent as it is on a delicate balance of natural factors, seems to cry out for explanation.[1] At the very least, such arguments prompt us to *ask* ourselves whether it is reasonable to affirm the reality of God.[2] Similarly, experiences in our daily lives of order and trust and moral obligation may raise the question of God and may suggest God as the answer to that question.[3] Lying behind all our individual experiences is the experience of our own finitude and of the mysteriousness of the infinity that is the context for that finitude. This experience can be profoundly religious in character, raising as it does ultimate questions about humanity and the universe; it, too, can point us to God.[4]

Not only philosophers doubtful about the rational justification of religious convictions but also Christian believers suspicious of the arrogance of reason have questioned the validity of an approach to God from the nature of the world and our experience of it. The viability of Christian belief certainly doesn't depend on whether anyone has offered or could offer a successful rational argument for belief in God. But reasoning about God on the basis of human experience and the character of the world has been important not only in Christian history but also in the Bible itself. The prophets, St. Paul, and other biblical writers seem to reason about God in this way.[5] Again, this doesn't itself *prove* anything, but it makes it harder, at any rate, for a Christian to reject reasoning of this kind out of hand.

Love, Community, and Tradition

Whatever the fate of rational arguments for Christian belief, it remains the case that, on the whole, our beliefs are not individual creations. They are mediated

---

Theistic Arguments," *Michael Sudduth's Analytic Philosophy of Religion Website*, http://www.homestead.com/philofreligion/files/Theisticarguments.html (last visited Jan 4, 2007) (Plantinga's lecture notes paralleling the paper, cited here, are available at a variety of locations on the Internet; the paper remains unpublished). The evolutionary argument against naturalism, developed independently by its two principal contemporary advocates, is outlined in Stephen R. L. Clark, *From Athens to Jerusalem: The Love of Wisdom and the Love of God* (Oxford: Clarendon-OUP 1984) 29-30 and Alvin Plantinga, *Warranted Christian Belief* (New York: OUP 2000) 227-40, 281-4; Thomas Nagel, himself an atheist, underscores the difficulties with evolutionary epistemology to which this argument points in *The Last Word* (New York: OUP 1997) 134-7. Elenor Webb's "argument from the avocado" overlaps the argument from design, the æsthetic argument, and the argument from qualia that Robert Merrihew Adams develops in "Flavors, Colors, and God," *The Virtue of Faith and Other Essays in Philosophical Theology* (New York: OUP 1987) 243-62.

1. Cp. John Polkinghorne, *Science and Creation: The Search for Understanding* (London: SPCK 1988) 24-5; Owen Gingerich, *God's Universe* (Cambridge, MA: Belknap-Harvard UP 2006).

2. So Diogenes Allen, *Christian Belief in a Postmodern World* (Louisville: Westminster/Knox 1989).

3. See Gilkey and Berger.

4. Walter Kasper, *The God of Jesus Christ*, trans. Matthew J. O'Connell (New York: Crossroad 1989) 84-7.

5. For the biblical evidence, see James Barr, *Biblical Faith and Natural Theology* (Oxford: Clarendon-OUP 1993).

to us by *traditions* that shape our doing and our thinking through language, behavior patterns, ideas, and symbols. We learn who we are and who we ought to be from those traditions.

A religion is a kind of culture, a culture into which one is inducted by birth or naturalization. One does not construct the elements of the culture oneself; one acquires them through a process of formation and acclimation. If human institutions—languages, traditions, communities—got in the way of our experience of God, "then the best way to prepare someone for the experience of God would seem to be to abandon them, at birth, in some untracked waste far from human habitation."[1] In fact, however, this notion is absurd. None of us begins in a wilderness, free of language, ideas, habits, and customs, and then sets out to discover the truth about the universe. We need tradition and community if we are to understand and love God and God's world.

The fact that a belief is a belief one already holds is a perfectly good reason to retain it, absent successful challenges. But the fact that it has been sifted, assessed, evaluated by its tradition is a further reason to accept it as valid, both as a matter of respect for one's tradition and, more importantly, as a matter of acknowledging the value of the reflection and evaluation of beliefs undertaken by one's predecessors in that tradition—who may well be wiser than oneself.

> The refusal to accept another's word or take for one's basis a theory one cannot oneself demonstrate can only be supposed to be our duty by someone who has quite forgotten what she herself is bound to do in every area of life. We live within a sea of testimony: everything that we ordinarily count upon has been handed on to us; the very possibility of demonstrating anything itself rests on our having been initiated into the techniques and presuppositions of the testifying community. . . .[2]

We can legitimately conclude that not all well-established beliefs are true, and that we must leave ourselves some room for manœuvre not to be tied down to one doctrine merely because people in the past have thought it true. But it does not follow that long-established beliefs and practices have no greater claim on our practical and theoretical allegiance than newly minted ones. They have the signal advantage that they are there, that their ramifications have, to some extent, been explored, that we have some idea of what they really amount to. Old doctrines are not true merely because they are old, any more than new ones are true because they are new: but it is not absurd to suggest that the old ones have our prior allegiance, that they do not need to establish themselves on just the same terms as new theories, that they have, as it were, the benefit of the doubt.[3]

It should not be surprising that the perspective afforded by a particular tradition might contribute to one's insight and understanding. Perhaps only people situated in particular contexts will be able to acquire beliefs that in fact enable them to draw helpful conclusions about the way the world actually is. Getting the right beliefs may sometimes depend on being in the right place at the right time. It may depend on interpreting the relevant data using an appropriate framework, not just collecting them. A particular intellectual or cultural context may help, rather than hindering, the acquisition of beliefs that are *true* irrespective of context. The fact that traditions shape our believing does not make our believing any less valid.

---

1. Nicholas Lash, *Easter in Ordinary: Reflections on Human Experience and the Knowledge of God* (London: SCM 1988) 58.
2. Stephen R. L. Clark, *Civil Peace and Sacred Order*, Limits and Renewals 1 (Oxford: Clarendon-OUP 1989) 7-8.
3. Clark 14.

Love and Otherness

Traditions are valuable gifts. They offer us meaning, identity, security, and support. Being part of a tradition means not having to start the business of being human from scratch. And part of an epistemology of love is certainly being open to the good gifts our traditions have to offer us—especially, perhaps, the unexpected ones our own assumptions and preoccupations may obscure. But human traditions are, precisely, *human* traditions. They are finite and fallible. They are not God. They may deserve love, but they don't deserve worship.

Because traditions give us so much, we may be tempted to treat them as beyond question. We may respond to any challenge to our traditions defensively. Anyone who disagrees with us must be stupid or spiritually deficient. Less obnoxiously, we may rest confidently in our traditions' apparent achievements without ever considering their possible flaws. Or we may respond with a complacent relativism: we see it this way, they see it that way; we'll keep doing things our way, and they can do whatever they like. And even if we don't always value the gifts our traditions give us, they may seem so powerful, so imposing, that we don't feel we can or should challenge them. But none of these stances is consistent with love—not with the love of others, and certainly not with the love of God: "the essence of piety is that we and our favourite thought-worlds stand under judgment, and that Reality is more than we can, in our own strength, conceive."[1]

An integral part of love is paying attention to what is other than ourselves in ways that allow our own egos to leave center-stage. As long as we treat all of reality as if it orbited around ourselves, we will be unable to love. We love when we recognize that the realities we encounter are distinct and different and potentially surprising. We love when, at least sometimes, this recognition evokes delight in what is new and different, a genuine recognition of a beauty to which we may have been oblivious,[2] rather than fear at what unsettles our overconfident perceptions. I love when I desire the other *as other*, rather than seeking to absorb her into myself or proceeding as if she and I were identical. Our loving desire "for truth . . . resides . . . in . . . [the] abyss between what we know and possess and the infinite exteriority of others." This loving desire for truth, for the beautiful reality that is other than ourselves, "exists . . . in the infinite joy of reaching for what cannot be contained or possessed. . . ."[3]

Remember that love is not an alien imposition on Christian belief. Love is at the heart of Christian belief. So being a Christian entails being open to that which is to other. All creation is God's. The whole world is the arena within which God's Spirit moves. God loves the whole world. This means, in turn, that Christians are called to do so as well. They are called, therefore, to be attentive to the possibility of being disturbed and challenged and unsettled and revived by surprising words from within our traditions, from people partially or entirely outside the Christian tradition, or from ourselves. It is obviously not the case that just any novel word is correct. Loving our traditions and appreciating the insights they offer, we may challenge and dispute and engage enthusiastically in conversations in which we remain attached to our beliefs. But we cannot rightly identify those beliefs with the God in whom we believe. Only God is worthy of worship. However attached to our beliefs we are, loving otherness means we must be willing to treat them reflectively, to recognize that they may need to be improved or transformed.[4]

---

1. Clark 10.
2. Farley, *Eros* 85.
3. Farley, *Eros* 200.
4. Thanks to Sarvenaz Sheybany and Jim Harrison for providing the occasion for earlier reflection on these matters.

We cannot complacently assume that, in the absence of challenges from others, our traditions are problem-free. Suppose we truly love the other—the other in our community or outside it whose silence may conceal a challenge to our convictions, the other in ourselves whose doubts we have ignored, or the truth worth discovering of which we simply haven't been aware. Then we will not need to be prompted by anyone else's objections to continue the task of rethinking our beliefs, of loving our tradition precisely in order to contribute to its development. This isn't a matter of hoping, masochistically, that our beliefs will be disconfirmed. It *is* a matter of knowing that an absence of conflict over our beliefs is no sign that they are perfect. Realizing that we are finite creatures, recognizing our fallibility, means expecting surprises and keeping our eyes open to discover them. This is part of loving the truth.

Nor can we decline to surprise others, to offer them different perspectives on their own beliefs.[1] Debates about moral and religious matters are frequently fruitless and counter-productive, but when we *can* be helpful to others by offering them good reasons to rethink their beliefs, it is not unloving to do so.

When we conclude that a difference in belief between ourselves and others is an important one, we may simply be exhibiting insensitivity to the ways in which different beliefs and practices represent responses to circumstances quite different from ours, circumstances that demand reactions correspondingly different from our characteristic ones. Loving otherness means being aware of genuine differences in circumstances and experience that may render alternative understandings and behaviors appropriate. Sometimes, that is, apparent disagreements aren't real disagreements at all. It's not that they do X while we do Y when faced with Z, but rather that we respond to Z by doing Y, while for them X is a response to W. Sometimes, then, loving otherness will mean discovering that an alternative belief or practice isn't really at odds with our own, or that it represents an alternative but appropriate way of responding to a common problem.

On the other hand, though, loving otherness means caring about truth. It means recognizing that we—and others—can be surprised. It means that we're not trapped by our traditions and habits, not completely prevented by them from seeing what they may deliberately or inadvertently conceal.

To care about a truth that transcends what I or we may think does not mean that we have some kind of unmediated access to the mind of God. We can't comprehend Truth with a capital T. But the whole notion that we're fallible makes sense only the on the view that we can, in fact, correct and improve our beliefs, and that others can do so as well.

If that's so, then we must acknowledge the challenge that the beliefs of others pose to our own, and recognize that they, in turn, may grow through encounter with our convictions. We may, indeed, have a gift to offer those with whom we may disagree. Loving otherness means cherishing persons who see the world differently, not only by being willing to be *surprised by* them but by being willing to *surprise* them. For instance: modern, materialistic people in the West have a great deal to learn from traditional cultures—including a more traditional Christianity—about respect for the earth and for other creatures. At the same time, cultures that regard women as inferior to men may have something to learn from Western egalitarians. I want to say more about these matters when I discuss dialogue across religious boundaries. But I think it's important to emphasize now at least that a simple live-and-let-live attitude won't do.

Sometimes, you or I can be the other—alienated from our own perceptions and our own communities. We may adopt perspectives from our traditions uncritically, and even when they seem unfruitful or oppressive we may retain them.

---

1. Cp. Thiselton 13.

Taking love seriously as a foundation of our epistemology will mean letting *our own* experience surprise us. We love ourselves, quite appropriately, when we listen to our own pain, when we wonder whether our own experience is a pointer to the need for our tradition to grow. And we love both our traditions and our fellow adherents when we ask questions about conventional wisdom. Keeping our eyes and ears and hearts open is a way of love that expands our insight and understanding, even if it can lead to potentially uncomfortable conflict.

Responding to the Challenge of Otherness

When we love otherness—our own or that of others or that of truth itself—we will confront challenges to our beliefs. How can we assess them?

When a particular belief we already hold is challenged, or when we consider the possibility of adopting a new belief, we need to examine how well it fits together with all of our other convictions. We need to examine the coherence of the challenged belief with everything else we believe.

Our beliefs form a more-or-less interlocking web,[1] a network of linked convictions. Individual beliefs find meaning and support within the context provided by this network. When evaluating an idea, one seeks to determine how accepting or rejecting it will affect one's total array of convictions. Rather than determining if it can be deduced from or rendered probable with respect to certain other, foundational truths, the thing to do is to examine how well it coheres with the totality of one's existing beliefs. It will be possible to make trade-offs that allow one to justify almost any conclusion. But one *may* find that the revisions in one's belief-system required to fit a particular belief into it simply make one's web of belief too unwieldy. And, in that way, one will have judged the belief in question to be unjustified.

As we engage in conversations with those who disagree with us from inside and outside our tradition (including ourselves), our focus will sometimes be on individual beliefs. But often our concern will be with more extended networks of convictions. An individual belief or practice makes sense within the broader context of a whole tradition. When a question arises about a particular conviction, therefore, the real issue may be the overall adequacy of the tradition rather than the truth of a particular belief. If a belief makes sense in terms of the tradition's account of human existence, and if that account as a whole seems adequate, that may be enough to justify the belief in question. Indeed, the inner logic of a belief system may itself generate new beliefs.[2]

It will rarely be possible to address controversial issues in abstraction from the big picture. So while an *ad hoc* discussion about specific issues can be important, it will often provide a way into a conversation about the adequacy of a tradition's vision of things as a whole. At that point, the point of a conversation will focus on the comprehensive adequacy of the *entire tradition*, its ability elegantly to integrate all of the relevant data into a coherent whole.

Different persons and communities see and experience the world differently, and there are no easily constructed bridges among them.[3] Certainly, one cannot

---

1. See W. V. Quine and J. S. Ullian, *The Web of Belief*, 2d ed. (New York: Random 1978).

2. This seems to be an implication of Brian Hebblethwaite, "The Appeal to Experience in Christology," *Christ, Faith and History: Cambridge Studies in Christology*, ed. Stephen Sykes and John Powell Clayton (Cambridge: CUP 1971) 268-70.

3. This is not to say that there are no bridges at all. See James Wm. McClendon, Jr., and James M. Smith, *Convictions: Defusing Religious Relativism* (Valley Forge, PA: TPI 1994); William Werpehowski, "*Ad Hoc* Apologetics," *Journal of Religion* 66.3 (July

construct such bridges by trying to find premises for one's arguments that "every rational person" will accept—the fact that there are competing definitions of what counts as a rational person is part of the problem.[1] The other ideas in relation to which one evaluates a challenged or potential belief, and the strategies one uses for assessing it, will have been acquired from one's tradition or traditions—or at least reflect their influence. One can criticize one's own tradition. And one can converse across traditional lines. What one cannot do is jettison tradition *as such* and start from scratch.[2] Thus, when we confront the challenge of otherness, we will be engaged in *ad hoc* conversations with people (living, dead, or imagined) whose convictions differ from our own, exploring the implications of our experiences and beliefs. We don't need universally valid arguments, ones that could theoretically compel the assent of absolutely everyone, in order to do that. All we need is to meet the particular objections raised by particular conversation-partners (including our own uncooperative selves).

There is a great deal of common ground that unites people from different traditions. But there doesn't seem to be a universal understanding of human experience or knowledge that can be used to justify our beliefs to *every single* conversation partner. So we don't have to wait around for one before we can feel confident that our beliefs can meet the objections raised by people with whom we discuss our convictions. We don't have to give up our own standpoint in order to have conversations with people from other traditions. We can speak and think and believe in light of our traditions, even though we need to be genuinely open to the possibility of making significant discoveries as a consequence of such encounters.

Our conversations with those who differ with us will take many forms, and they will have many outcomes. Sometimes we may judge that a challenged or potential belief can be affirmed in its current form despite objections, even though an objector remains convinced that her objection is a valid one. Sometimes, by contrast, an objector may be persuaded that our response has invalidated her objection. And sometimes *we* may be convinced that an objection embodies a significant truth that ought to be embodied in our own web of belief. In any case, we can reasonably regard our beliefs as justified to the extent that they do survive the actual challenges they confront, from other people and from ourselves, or are appropriately adjusted in response to those challenges.

Love, Faith, and Reason

Sometimes, the problem of religious belief is framed as the problem of the relationship between "faith" and "reason." But faith and reason, at least as I understand them here, can't be in conflict with each other, not even in principle.

1986): 282-301; Placher 105-74; Paul J. Griffiths, *An Apology for Apologetics: A Study in the Logic of Interreligious Dialogue*, Faith Meets Faith Series (Maryknoll, NY: Orbis 1991).

1. See Alasdair MacIntyre, *Whose Justice? Which Rationality?* (Notre Dame: U of Notre Dame P 1988).

2. This kind of view is often challenged (or celebrated) as itself embodying a kind of relativism: what Christians say is only "true" for them—within the "Christian language-game." This analysis fails to distinguish between the essential context-relativity of *justifying* or *warranting* beliefs, and the universality of the claims being made regarding the *truth* of the beliefs. As Gerard Loughlin, *Telling God's Story: Bible: Church and Narrative Theology* (Cambridge: CUP 1996) summarizes George Lindbeck's position, "the issue turns on holding together a correspondence theory of truth with coherentist and pragmatist criteria of justification . . ." (160n70). On the distinction between justification and truth in the context of a discussion of, among other things, cultural relativity, see also Stout.

Faith is trust, reliance. To have faith in God is to trust God, to rely on God. Implicitly or explicitly, it is to love God, and to regard God as loveable (whether or not one has thematized one's awareness of God). At root, it is to understand oneself as grounded, secure, finally unthreatened by the unavoidable contingency of one's experience, and to experience the universe as a fundamentally friendly place[1]. We can understand faith as an act or as an attitude. As an act, it is a matter of positively relying on another. As an attitude, it is a disposition to rely on another. In neither case is it a matter of believing otherwise unwarranted propositions.

> Anyone can see that faith is the attitude appropriate towards the God of Christians. Supposing we believe that there is such a God, and supposing we are reasonable beings, we shall trust him to do for us what the Gospel promises in his name; and trusting is faith. We shall trust him, if he exists, but we can hardly trust him *to* exist.[2]

Adequately informed Christian faith presupposes rationally warranted Christian belief (though, as I have tried to argue in my elaboration of an epistemology of life, its rational warrant need not be provided by positive argument).

Faith is not how we come to believe this or that religious proposition; faith is what we do once we believe and understand the truth about God. If we already have reasons to regard a religious authority as reliable, then it may well be reasonable to trust this authority, and thus to accept propositions emanating from this authority which one might not otherwise endorse. But trust isn't how we come to accept an authority as authoritative in the first place (unless, of course, we do so on the say-so of another authority we *do* have independent reason to trust, and so on, and so on . . . .)

Faith is not some kind of convenient shortcut to propositional belief. But sometimes it's treated as if it were. So, for instance, a person who finds it hard to accept a remarkable religious claim—say, the claim that Jesus, though crucified, is alive today—may be told, "Have faith!" But faith really won't help here. If I already have good reason to believe that God has communicated something, then it will make sense to trust God in the absence of first-hand knowledge. But the problem is more likely to be whether there is God in the first place, or whether God is responsible for the communication in question.

We can, of course, take a risk, choosing to worship, to pray, to cultivate ourselves as persons before God, to reach out in love to God even though we are uncertain of God's reality, while we remain uncertain just what the nature of ultimate reality might be. Blaise Pascal famously recommended this as a strategy for persons on the edges of authentic Christianity. But if we do this—and all of us may do it, for perfectly good reasons, at one time or another—we must not suppose that acting "as-if" is a route to *warranting* particular propositions about God. Acting as-if may put us in a position to discover the validity and worth of a relationship with the God who is really there, and it may be appropriate without argumentative warrant. But it is not itself a way of bypassing the challenge of determining what the universe is really like.

I can choose to trust the God in whom I already believe. I can choose to take the risk that there is God and to act accordingly. I can choose to put myself in a position in which warrants for belief in God's reality is available and in which I will be disposed to discern these warrants and respond positively to them. But I cannot, *logically* cannot, choose to believe in God, in the sense of directly accepting as true the proposition that there is God. It is not psychologically possible to

---

1. I owe this phrase to Jack Provonsha.
2. Austin Farrer, *God Is Not Dead* (New York: Morehouse 1966) 9-10; cp. Austin Farrer, *Saving Belief: A Discussion of Essentials* (London: Hodder 1964) 15.

choose to believe *in this sense*. And, even if it were, a proposition I accepted as a matter of choice, without warrant, would have no claim on my assent; I would not be rationally entitled to affirm it. It is sensible to talk about making a person's making a trustful choice in relation to God once a person supposes that there is, or might be, God. But it makes no more sense to talk about choosing to believe in the reality of God in the first place than it does to talk about choosing to believe that ordinary lungs will enable one to breathe underwater.

I've stressed that adequately informed Christian faith is a response to warranted Christian belief. But it is possible to have Christian belief without Christian faith and to have Christian faith without Christian belief. One can have belief without faith because one can accept the proposition that there is God while not truly understanding this proposition and responding to it volitionally and affectively. One may acknowledge the reality of God while not responding to God in trustful love. On the other hand, one can also have faith without accurate belief. One can be a centered, grounded person, aware of oneself as both valuable and finite, who experiences and treats the universe as a fundamentally friendly place—while at the same time holding false or wildly inaccurate beliefs about God. (It might make sense to say that one had genuine experience of God, but that this experience was inadequately thematized.) Obviously, one's beliefs will influence one's attitudes. Having the right beliefs makes it more likely that one's attitudes and actions will be appropriate. But it remains true that one can have the kind of faith that matters religiously—one can be a person who responds aright to love—even one is thoroughly mistaken about the way things are.

Confidence and Commitment

I've attempted to outline a way of validating and developing our beliefs that takes reason seriously. We know God through our traditions, through the challenges of positions in tension or conflict with those traditions, and through our felt need for God. But the view I've outlined regarding the rational justification of religious belief may appear inadequate. For reason has too often been understood to require that we believe only what positive evidence justifies us in accepting, and to believe no more strongly than our warrants permit. Thus, it may seem that to make religious belief rational means not taking religious beliefs seriously. There is, some critics may suggest, a disproportion between the commitment reason can license and the commitment Christianity (or any other meaningful religious or moral tradition) requires. The former must always be tentative, partial, probabilistic; the latter must be total. Therefore, so the argument runs, reason is inappropriate in religious matters.

The fact that we begin *with*, rather than having to argue *to*, our tradition helps to address this problem. We don't have to proportion the strength of our beliefs—religious or otherwise—to the strength of the *positive* evidence we have for them. Our beliefs *do* have to be somewhat tentative, in the sense that we know they could always be falsified—this is part of what it means to love otherness. But the recognition that our beliefs *can be* invalidated need not undermine our seriousness about them unless and until they actually *are* falsified.

More importantly, we believe in order to love. However tentative our beliefs, when we are faced with an imperative to action, we can't avoid deciding one way or another—not deciding is itself a decision—if we seek responsibly to love God and God's good creation.[1] Insofar as Christian convictions shape and encourage a particular way of being in the world, one is forced to consider

---

1. Cp. Farrer, *Belief* 13-4.

whether one accepts or rejects those beliefs every time one considers whether to choose Christianly or not.

This kind of deliberation presents me with a forced option. The existential, moral, and political significance of religious convictions renders impracticable a relativism that regards them all as equally valid. It therefore requires us to evaluate competing claims and assess their relative adequacy. A live-and-let-live attitude toward any and all forms of social and cultural life may sound good in the abstract, but it leaves no basis for legitimate conflict with oppression, injustice, or ignorance. We cannot simply claim that the assertion "genocide is wrong" is true for us (whatever that might mean), but not for the Nazis. The diversity of worldviews has unavoidable practical consequences; and these consequences require us to distinguish among competing religious visions.

Shall I respond in delight to the world as God's good creation, or shall I flee from it in order to escape my contingency? Shall I accept other people as God's children, or deny them the acceptance God offers me? Shall I continue in a course of action that may lead me to martyrdom? These are questions which demand yes-or-no answers. And so the fact that religious judgments are subject to revision is beside the point. Of course my convictions *may* be wrong. But they are the ones which seem correct to me now, or I would not call them mine; and, as such, they must contribute to any decision I make. We often have to make all-or-nothing choices in light of our convictions despite the fact that those convictions are not absolutely certain. Sometimes we must choose, and do so using whatever resources are at our disposal.[1]

In fact, we probably shouldn't expect overwhelming evidence for our beliefs or overwhelming clarity in our understanding of them. God works *with the grain* of human history—both personal and communal. God interacts with human beings where they are, trying to get them to understand the character of human existence and the point of divine action in the world using their categories of understanding and their experiences as jumping-off points. God does not communicate with a given community of people using concepts, ideas, and images that make no sense to them.[2] And God does not bypass the structures of nature and history in communicating with us. The reality of creation—of persons and the rest of the world—imposes real limitations on divine-human communication.

Consequently, there's always a gap between what God is trying to say and what we are able to hear.[3] So when we make judgments about our religious beliefs, the data we're interpreting will always be relatively ambiguous. To refuse to hold our beliefs somewhat tentatively would be to assume that our circumstances permit God to communicate perfectly with us, that we understand God in ways unaffected by our prior convictions, experiences, and attitudes. It is not, therefore, simply the possibility of rational assessment that must make us admit that our beliefs could be changed; it is our understanding of how God works in the world, and of the limits our creatureliness and historical particularity impose on our ability to understand and appropriate God's revelation—indeed, our recognition of the fact that we are creatures, and most emphatically not God.

---

1. Cp. Joseph Runzo, *Reason, Relativism and God* (New York: St. Martin's 1986) 222; Gerald O'Collins, *Fundamental Theology* (New York: Paulist 1981) 158-9. Robert C. Roberts addresses a number of the same problems in *Faith, Reason, and History: Rethinking Kierkegaard's Philosophical Fragments* (Macon, GA: Mercer UP 1986) 140-3.

2. So Brown 72 (cp. 69-98).

3. See David Basinger and Randall Basinger, "Inerrancy, Dictation, and the Free Will Defense," *Evangelical Quarterly* 55.3 (July 1983): 177-80; David Basinger, "Inerrancy and Free Will: Some Further Thoughts," *Evangelical Quarterly* 58.4 (Oct. 1985): 351-4. Cp. Austin Farrer, "Infallibility and Historical Revelation," *Interpretation and Belief*, ed. Charles C. Conti (London: SPCK 1976) 151-64.

If we love the truth, and our traditions, and other people, we will be alert to the challenges our beliefs face. We don't need to construct positive arguments for our beliefs before accepting them. The fate of such arguments need not determine the fate of our convictions. And we do not need to go masochistically in search of objections to our convictions. But we do a disservice to God, the truth, and ourselves if we hide from real challenges. Indeed, we have to consider relevant objections to them if we are to be rationally entitled to hold them. I want now to consider two challenges any sensitive religious person in our culture cannot avoid confronting: the apparent absence of God and the reality of pointless suffering.

The Apparent Absence of God

It is sometimes hard to believe in God because God's presence does not seem to be part of our everyday experience. Modern Western people may all feel a bit like the Soviet cosmonauts who came back from space and reported that they hadn't encountered God.

Partly, of course, the fact that we can't put our fingers on God is a sign of the fact that God is *God*. The infinite creator can't be reduced to a slice of finite reality. Anything we can point to, anything that is *here* and not *there*, wouldn't and couldn't be God. But of course there's more to our concern than this. For we would at least like to see some clear signs of God's presence or activity. For some people, the traditional arguments for God's reality successfully highlight such signs. For others, especially vivid experiences seem to point decisively toward the reality of God. But the world seems empty of God's presence for many people.

I suspect, though, that this may be as much a function of our socialization as of anything else. In some cultures, in some communities, in some families, people will learn to read the world as redolent with God's presence;[1] in others, they will not. Some environments will encourage people to ask the ultimate questions to which God may be seen as the definitive answer; other will discourage such questions as meaningless. But even if one's culture—and it is really only modern Western culture which experiences God as absent—or one's family discourages one from reading one's experience as experience of God, one need not conclude that God is really absent. If the Christian doctrine of God is correct, we encounter God in and through every experience we have. But we come to recognize this fact only as we are trained to experience the world in this way, directly or indirectly through the influence of a religious community.

One thing the Christian community can—and should—teach us is that we may experience God as absent because we're not looking for the divine presence in the right place, or that we're simply unsure what we're looking for. The God confessed by Christians is no stranger to or in the world. The world doesn't go about its business uninterrupted except during those odd moments when God decides to do something; rather, God is continually active in the world, in every event.

If God is active in and present to every aspect of creaturely reality, then we ought not to look for God only or primarily in particular districts of our experience. Perhaps, in fact, we regard God as absent because we expect the divine presence to be manifest only in extraordinary, dramatic events. To experience the

---

1. And it is important to note here that the way in which a family or other primary community teaches one to read the world is neither primarily nor exclusively a function of the explicit teaching one receives: the quality of life fostered by the family or primary community is of significantly greater importance. Its capacity to foster or frustrate a sense of meaning and purpose and to encourage or destroy a sense of basic trust are crucial ingredients. See Ray S. Anderson and Dennis Guernsey, *On Being Family: A Socio-Theology of the Family* (Grand Rapids: Eerdmans 1987) 132-6.

world Christianly is not so much to discover new and strange bits of reality (though Christian experience may, of course, *involve* discovering regions of reality previously alien to us) as to learn to read our ordinary experiences correctly as experiences of God's presence.[1]

Some people can doubtless increase the likelihood of intense, "mystical" experiences of God by disciplined preparation over time, while others cannot; aptitude for such experiences may have as much to do with the psychic or physical characteristics of the experients as anything else And awareness of God's gracious and loving presence seems to come unbidden into the lives of many who do not seek it.[2] The right response seems to me to be that of Austin Farrer. Describing a period of adolescent religious turmoil, he writes:

> I thought of myself as set over against deity as one man faces another across a table, except that God was invisible and indefinitely great. And I hoped that he would signify his presence to me by way of colloquy; but neither out of the scripture I read nor in the prayers I tried to make did any mental voice address me. I believe at that time anything would have satisfied me, but nothing came: no 'other' stood beside me, no shadow of presence fell upon me.

Farrer found liberation in a deeper understanding of God's action in the world:

> I would no longer attempt, with the psalmist, 'to set God before my face'. I would see him as the underlying cause of my thinking, especially of those thoughts in which I tried to think of him. I would dare to hope that sometimes my thought would become diaphanous, so that there should be some perception of the divine cause shining through the created effect, as a deep pool, settling into a clear tranquility, permits us to see the spring in the bottom of it from which its waters rise. I would dare to hope that through a second cause the First Cause might be felt, when the second cause in question was itself a spirit, made in the image of the divine Spirit, and perpetually welling up out of his creative act.
>
> Such things, I say, I dared to hope for, and I will not say that my hope was in any way remarkably fulfilled, but I will say that by so viewing my attempted work of prayer, I was rid of the frustration which had baffled me before. And this is why, when Germans set their eyeballs and pronounce the terrific words 'He speaks to thee' (Er redet dich an) I am sure, indeed, that they are saying something, but I am still more sure that they are not speaking to my condition.[3]

No particular, distinguishable kind of event—seeing a vision, hearing a voice, having a special feeling—needs to happen in order for us to encounter God, the creator of everything, who is present to us in the midst of all our individual experiences. If these are the kinds of things we mean when we talk about "religious experience," then it must be insisted that experience of God and "religious experience" are not to be equated. God cannot be localized. Rather, as we learn to see our experience through Christian eyes, we come to experience Gods activity *throughout* our lives.[4] Our experience acquires particular meaning within

---

1. Cp. Lash. See also John Hick, *Faith and Knowledge: A Modern Introduction to the Problem of Religious Knowledge*, 2d ed. (Ithaca, NY: Cornell UP 1966).
2. See John Hick and Michael Goulder, *Why Believe in God?* (London: SCM 1983).
3. Austin Farrer, *The Glass of Vision* (London: Dacre 1948) 7-8.
4. See Lash 242-53. As Lash notes in connection with Schleiermacher's talk about the experience of "absolute dependence" as experience of God: "The word 'God' is inherited from our culture and our history. It is by reflectively and critically appropriating and interpreting the cultural, historical processes which produced us, and in which we find ourselves situated, that we acquire the use of the language or languages by means of which we attempt to give an account of our human experi-

the context provided by the collection of beliefs, practices, images, and ways of talking that we are taught as Christians. Being part of the Christian tradition of belief and practice enables us to see God's presence in the world and in the circumstances of our lives. It is as we critically appropriate the "traditioning" offered us by the Christian community that we come to understand and interpret our experience Christianly; and it is this traditioning that can address the problem of God's apparent absence from our experience. Christian belief does not depend on our having had experiences of God's presence like those Farrer was seeking. Rather, if we have learned to interpret our experience Christianly, we are free to continue to do so until we encounter compelling objections.

The Reality of Pointless Harm

If God is love, why do bad things happen to God's creatures? The fact that creaturely lives seem filled with so much pointless harm rightly serves as the basis for a telling objection to Christian belief. For it seems that either God *could* prevent the pointless harms people suffer, but does not, and that the divine *goodness* thus falls short of perfection, or that God would prevent these harms but *cannot*, and that the divine *power* thus falls short of perfection. In either case, so the argument runs, the reality of a perfectly powerful, perfectly good God is ruled out. And there is no realistic doubt that the reality of evidently pointless harm calls Christian convictions into question.

We need, it seems, to formulate *some* way of understanding God's relationship to the harms we and others experience. In light of what we conclude, we will be able more effectively to construct an account of loving divine action in the world that is credible in the face of evil and suffering. Several accounts of God's relationship to evil are possible.[1] I will consider four here.

• While retaining the belief that God can and does exercise coercive power in the world, and the belief that God is in some sense good, we can deny that calling God *good* means saying that God loves us in anything like the way we love each other. Calling God *good* doesn't mean calling God *loving* by analogy with ourselves.

• Alternatively, while retaining the belief that God can and does exercise coercive power in the world, we can maintain that God is loving while denying that

---

ence. It is from this process of critical remembrance that Schleiermacher acquired his use of the term 'God.' It is only by this process, therefore, that he is able to designate the 'whence' of the feeling of absolute dependence as 'God.' It may not be a very good designation (since we do not know what it means). But we know what we are trying to name when we use it" (127-8). For a helpful anticipation of the same position, see Hebblethwaite, "Appeal" 263-78.

1. See, *e.g.*, Austin M. Farrer, *Love Almighty and Ills Unlimited*, Christian Faith Series (Garden City, NY: Doubleday 1961); Edward H. Madden and Peter H. Hare, *Evil and the Concept of God*, American Lecture Series 706 (Springfield, IL: np 1968); Alvin Plantinga, *God, Freedom, and Evil* (Grand Rapids: Eerdmans 1977); John Hick, *Evil and the God of Love*, rev. ed. (London: Macmillan 1977); Marilyn McCord Adams and Robert Merrihew Adams, eds., *The Problem of Evil*, Oxford Readings in Philosophy (New York: OUP 1990); Wendy Farley, *Tragic Vision and Divine Compassion: A Contemporary Theodicy* (Louisville, KY: Westminster/Knox 1990); David Ray Griffin, *God, Power, and Evil: A Process Theodicy* (Lanham, MD: UP of America 1991); David Ray Griffin, *Evil Revisited: Responses and Reconsiderations* (Albany: SUNY 1991); Marilyn McCord Adams, *Horrendous Evils and the Goodness of God* (Ithaca, NY: Cornell UP 1999); Daniel Howard-Snyder, ed., *The Evidential Argument from Evil* (Bloomington: Indiana UP 1996); Richard Swinburne, *Providence and the Problem of Evil* (Oxford: Clarendon-OUP 1998); Stephen R. L. Clark, *The Mysteries of Religion: An Introduction to Philosophy through Religion*, Philosophical Introductions 3 (Oxford: Blackwell 1986) 144-51; George N. Schlesinger, *New Perspectives on Old-Time Religion* (Oxford: Clarendon-OUP 1988) 42-76.

what seems harmful to us really *is* harmful. We can maintain that every particular instance of harm to a creature serves some justifying end.

• While acknowledging that the harms there are really *are* harmful, and while retaining the belief that God can and does exercise coercive power in the world, we can maintain that God's permitting them is compatible with God's love because the possibility of evil and suffering—rather than the actual occurrence of any particular instance of evil or suffering—is a necessary condition for the achievement of substantial goods.

• We can characterize God's perfect power as persuasive rather than coercive, and so deny that God can *unilaterally* prevent or end all harms.

Redefining God's Goodness

Roy Clouser puts the first position—that we should understand God's goodness as radically different from our own—very starkly:

> ... God is not mandated by his own nature to be as good as we can possibly conceive or wish; his creating and taking on the characteristic of being good to us means he is good in just the ways he promises to be, not in every way we can wish or imagine. Chief among the ways he swears to be good are the covenant promises to forgive those who turn to him and to grant them his love, his fellowship and everlasting life.
>
> But nowhere in Scripture does he promise to be as beneficent as possible to as many people as possible. He does not promise to prevent all suffering or alleviate all pain. Since he never promised any such things, he is not obliged to do them. In short, Scripture never claims that God is maximally perfect in the sense Anselm and other theologians adopted from the ancient Greeks....
>
> The upshot is that *we cannot judge God by the standards that apply to us.* ... God allows Job to suffer. If you or I did that when we could have prevented it, we would be evil. God commands Abraham to sacrifice his son. If you or I did that, we would be evil. God has determined the time and cause for the death of every person. If you or I did that, we would be evil. God says that he "sends a strong delusion" to those who oppose him "to make them believe what is false" (2 Thess 2:11 RSV). If you or I did that, we would be doing something evil. Ditto for God's not preventing all the suffering that results from evil choices, natural disasters, or accidents resulting from heart attacks. But God is not bound by the laws of morality in the ways that bind us, and God's goodness does not consist in doing what we would have to do to be good. Since God is the Creator of the norms of ethics and justice, they do not apply to him except insofar as he has freely bound himself to them by making covenant promises.
>
> The greatness of God's goodness, then, does not consist in his perfectly obeying the norms of justice and morality or in having the most beneficent character we can imagine, but in the fact that although he was not obligated to us at all, he in fact made wonderfully loving and merciful promises to us anyway! Promises aside, he would owe us zilch. But he freely made the promises when under no obligation, and so now has just the obligations he has sworn himself to uphold. So can you see how wildly off it is to suppose that God can't be real if there's suffering in the world? ...
>
> ... [T]he only judgments we're entitled to make about God concern whether he has kept the promises he has made, and those promises are enough to counterbalance the worst sufferings that people can endure.[1]

This response seems very problematic. While we need to avoid assuming that our ideas and concepts apply without qualification to God, "the goodness of

---

1. Roy Clouser, *Knowing with the Heart: Religious Experience and Belief in God* (Downers Grove, IL: IVP 1999) 147-50.

God must bear some positive relation to the sorts of human actions we regard as good. Otherwise, why ascribe *goodness* to God?"[1] We have to think of God as perfectly good, and of perfect goodness as perfect love. Philosophical argument points us toward belief in divine perfection and suggests that love is essential to this perfection. And the Christian tradition and the experience of many Christians—and non-Christians—identify love as definitive, even constitutive, of God.

To deny that talk of *goodness* when applied to God means anything resembling what it means when applied to us is simply to make our talk of God's goodness nonsense, or close to it—conveying no real meaning. Further, the goodness of God could be of no *concern* to us if it were compatible with any conceivable divine action, or with a range of possible divine actions much broader than those that might be thought to flow from love. There are therefore strong arguments both against believing we should deny God's love and in favor of the view that we could have no positive religious interest in a putative deity in whose love we could not trust.

Clouser continually denies that God is *obligated*, except with respect to God's own promises. But this is a red herring. The question is not in what senses God might be said to have obligations. The question is whether the central Christian conviction that God is love is actually true. Clouser could respond that it is, but that its meaning is limited: God's being loving just means that God does what God promises to do. But this is a most Pickwickian sense of love. Characterizations of God as loving in the Bible and in the Christian tradition do not suggest so narrow a limitation of the meaning of divine love. And certainly such a limitation is inconsistent with our ordinary use of "love." The person whose disposition to love extends no farther than faithfulness to her promises but who does not otherwise avoid harming others or ignoring their pain would not ordinarily be regarded as especially loving.

Why should God's freely assuming obligations bind the divine will if God is beyond our norms of morality and goodness? If we undertook certain obligations, no doubt it would be wrong of us to ignore them. But it is unclear why the same should be true of God if, by definition, God is, as Clouser suggests, simply beyond the obligations that place moral limits on *our* actions. Who says God has to keep God's promises? Once God is understood as exempt from moral assessment, we have no reason to believe God is faithful, to trust God to keep promises.

Even supposing we could trust God to be loving in more than this minimal sense, it surely isn't right that the most glorious eschatological future would necessarily justify the occurrence of the suffering we experience. This is so, first of all, because it could plausibly be thought to do so only if the occurrence of each instance of suffering were a necessary condition for the eschatological future or, at least, some valuable component of that future. If I wantonly gouge out your eye, and then explain that my conduct was acceptable because I'm now going to pay you a billion dollars in compensation, I've missed the point. The money and the eye are incommensurable, so that the one can't compensate for the loss of the other in any non-arbitrary sense. And I didn't *have* to gouge your eye out in order to give you the billion dollars—I could simply give you the billion dollars while leaving your eye alone. I wronged you, and the subsequent compensation can't change that. A good state of affairs that follows some harm only makes sense of the harm and justifies it if the *harm itself* is necessary to the occurrence of the

---

1. Paul Helm, *The Providence of God*, Contours of Christian Theology (Downers Grove, IL: IVP 1994) 167; cp. 201.

good outcome or if the *possibility* of the harm is necessary to the occurrence of the good outcome.[1]

This position seeks to blunt the challenge of suffering and evil by qualifying our understanding of God's goodness beyond recognition. So it finally provides no meaningful response to the charge that the reality of pointless harms is inconsistent with the belief that God is love. In effect, it seeks to resolve the problem by *denying* that God is love. It is hardly a satisfactory alternative for anyone who believes that love should be our principal analogy for God.

Denying the Reality of Pointless Harms

Another possibility might simply be to refuse to regard apparent harms as genuinely harmful. To be sure, a great many things *seem* harmful to us, but perhaps their awfulness is merely illusory. Perhaps they are themselves really good, or perhaps they are necessary means to things that are really good.

More specifically, then: this second response could mean that God causes or permits every apparent harm we encounter in order to bring about some specific good for us or someone else. God lets Ralph die in a car accident, say, because it keeps Ralph from meeting his lover, who will reject him, and whose rejection will spur him to a life of violent crime. Or perhaps God fails to deliver people imprisoned at Buchenwald and on the way to the gas chambers to prompt their successors to see the horrors of genocide and to refuse to permit it to happen in the future. Or perhaps God allows Emma to contract bone cancer because confronting her illness will enable her to build strength of character. Maybe God infects a group of soldiers with typhoid fever to prevent them from laying waste to a region of a neighboring country they have invaded.

There are at least two problems with this sort of position. The first is that we don't have any very good reason to think that many of the harms we experience lead in any obvious or direct way to subsequent goods. Sometimes, to be sure, they may, but it is hard to see that they do so as an ordinary matter of course—or, indeed, to see how they could. Much that happens seems simply awful—destructive, hurtful, and pointless. What is and what seems to be may be different. Perhaps every apparently pointless instance of suffering really does bring about some good that makes it worthwhile. Perhaps. But it would take more than the mere possibility that this is so to convince me that my experience of the world's awfulness is in an important way illusory.

The second problem is that, even if this or that harm might lead to a good outcome, this wouldn't be sufficient to justify causing or permitting the harm in order to effect the outcome. If we imagine that God *causes* any of the harms we experience, it is hard not to see this as entailing the conclusion that God in these cases truly *identifies* with these harms. If I choose to accomplish some very good objective—say, providing lots of money to Oxfam—by doing something wrong—say, killing my stingy Uncle Charlie in anticipation of inheriting his millions, which I propose to give away—I've owned the wrongful act of killing him, made it part of my character. Despite the goodness of my objective, I've still identified with the wrong I've done to Uncle Charlie. God couldn't purposefully or instrumentally will harm to creatures—even for ends that arise out of love—without God's love being similarly compromised.

Of course, not all proponents of this view will suppose that God actively causes any of the suffering we experience. Perhaps God actively causes no

---

1. Cp. Keith Ward, *Ethics and Christianity* (London: Allen 1970): "The thought of future happiness may make present pain more bearable, but its occurrence will not make one's suffering more fair" (235).

suffering, but actively *prevents* all and only those harms that will not be proven worthwhile because of the good they will bring about or permit to be realized, while permitting all and only those harms that *will* be proven worthwhile.

But there is still reason to be troubled. While on this version God does not intend or will or identify with any harm to creatures, it still seems as if the divine love is somehow lacking. For it seems that to envision God as loving is to envision divine care as active, as seeking the positive good of each creature and not merely refraining from harming it. It is not clear that God could be said truly to love a particular person if, while able to prevent harm to her, God allowed her to be harmed because of the benefit her suffering might make possible to someone else—a caregiver, perhaps. We would wonder, I think, about the integrity of a parent who permitted a child to be injured on the theory that another child, by nursing her injured sister, would achieve greater maturity. I think—though others may have different intuitions—that a responsible parent would not permit a child to be injured even if she knew (presuming she *could* know) that the injury would redound to the child's *own* benefit. And the actual affects of injuries on those who suffer them gives us little reason to suppose that the harms which occur make the lives of the injured better. A pious agnosticism might allow us to imagine that others may suffer long-term benefits from someone's injury, even if we cannot see such benefits occurring or regard them as likely. But when the well-being of the sufferer herself is in question, it is even harder to see many instances of harm as beneficial.

Further, creaturely freedom means that the consequences of any given injury are not certain. Perhaps someone will respond to her own or another's injury in a positive way, or perhaps she will do so in a negative way. One outcome may be more likely than the other, but neither is certain. And if this is so, there is no guaranteeing that every harm permitted will turn out to serve a worthwhile end, even if it once seemed probable that it would. What *is* certain at any given time is that some harm is occurring. So it would seem as if being loving would often mean preventing the harm, which is certainly bad, rather than permitting it in order to facilitate a possible subsequent good.[1]

To be sure, a proponent of the second view could maintain that creatures are not free in the manner required if the problem of uncertainty is to get under way. In this case, however, she would be claiming, again, that God was responsible for all of the evil actions in the world. As a result, again, she would have difficulty explaining why God was not rightly thought of as identifying with all evil actions.

Further, the enterprise of justifying present harms in the name of future benefits is incoherent when it is based on the assumption that the benefits could outweigh the harms. The problem with talk about weighing and comparing basic aspects of human welfare[2] is that they can't be meaningfully quantified. Even if they could be, they couldn't be measured on a common scale—so that, presuming some simple kind of quantification were possible, four units of friendship could be seen to be equivalent to six units of æsthetic experience or one unit of play. There's no way to compare the instances or aspects of well-being embodied in one state of affairs with those embodied in another. So there's no way to describe the aspects of

---

1. Even if God's omniscience involves knowledge of future free choices, an appeal to divine foreknowledge will not solve the problem I highlight in this paragraph. For what is needed here is not knowledge of what will happen but knowledge of what would happen—what is needed, that is to say, is "middle knowledge," knowledge of the truth of counterfactuals of freedom. I think there is good reason to doubt that middle knowledge is possible. See William Hasker, "Middle Knowledge: A Refutation Revisited," *Faith and Philosophy* 12.2 (April 1995): 223-36; "Anti-Molinism is Undefeated!" *Faith and Philosophy* 17.1 (January 2000): 126-31.

2. Or other sorts of welfare; I have focused on the human case for simplicity's sake, not because it is the only one that matters.

human welfare—or the harms to human welfare—present in a given situation as greater or lesser than those present in another. If this is so, then the quantitative comparison God must be imagined to perform when determining that goods outweigh harms in a given context is simply not possible. Harms are real, quite apart from any contribution they may make directly or indirectly to facilitating participation in the various dimensions of human welfare, and there is no way of combining good things with harms to cancel the harms out.[1]

Suffering as a Necessary Possibility

Perhaps, a third alternative might hold, God takes a "hands-off" attitude, permitting some suffering to occur, because some important objectives can be achieved only if God declines to prevent certain kinds of harms or because it would actually be wrong for God to do so. The position I just considered and rejected holds that God permits harms because *particular harms* are means to good ends of one sort or another. The position I am considering now holds instead that *God's non-intervention* is necessary to the achievement of God's purposes in creation, or that intervention itself would be wrong—because it would violate the freedom or integrity of creation or represent a direct attack on some other good.

For proponents of this position, God is actively seeking to prevent or end all the harms there are—*within the limits necessarily imposed by God's choice to create*. But these limits mean that God cannot prevent or end all harms. On the strongest version of this view:

> Omnipotence is the power to do whatever can be done absolutely, that is, whatever is logically possible . . . . But to overcome the tragic structure of finitude, to free animate beings from all suffering, to determine finite freedom so that it will always love the good and have the courage to pursue it—these things are not possible. The potential for suffering and evil lie in the tragic structure of finitude and cannot be overcome without destroying creation.[2]

Creatures all too often ignore, resist, or reject God's will. And since there are good reasons for God not to prevent suffering coercively, by unilaterally overruling the freedom of creatures or the integrity of created structures and processes, harms happen despite God's will and despite God's active opposition to them.

A proponent of this view need not have any particular theory about why God does this. She might simply maintain that we can reasonably believe that a perfectly loving God has good reason to avoid coercive action,[3] good reason for permitting the occurrence of every instance of suffering that does occur in our world, even if we are unsure what God's reasons often are. Provided that, at the same time, we say that what seem to be the morally evil acts of creatures really are the acts of creatures, that these acts have not been caused by God, we have shown that there is no strictly logical compatibility between the claim that there really is suffering in the world and the claim that God is perfectly good.[4]

---

1. See, *e.g.*, John Finnis, *Natural Law and Natural Rights*, Clarendon Law Series (Oxford: Clarendon-OUP 1980) 113; cp. 95-7, 110-8, 131-2; John Finnis, "Commensuration and Practical Reason," *Incommensurability, Incomparability, and Practical Reason*, ed. Ruth Chang (Cambridge, MA: Harvard UP 1997) 215-33; Robert P. George, "Does the 'Incommensurability Thesis' Imperil Common Sense Moral Judgments?" *In Defense of Natural Law* (Oxford: Clarendon-OUP 1999) 94-100.

2. Farley, *Vision* 124.

3. For a general statement of this sort of position, see Keith E. Yandell, *Philosophy of Religion: A Contemporary Introduction*, Routledge Contemporary Introductions to Philosophy (London: Routledge 1999) 124-64.

4. Cp. a number of the contributions to Howard-Snyder.

This is not an absurd position. Surely the universe is a much more mysterious place than we realize. It is reasonable to suppose that God's purposes vastly transcend ours. On the other hand, though, it is important to preserve an understanding of divine action that is consistent with the conviction that God acts lovingly in relation to each creature. As I already suggested, I think we ought to reject the idea that God causes or permits harms to creatures in order to bring about good outcomes of various sorts. For God to love creatures is for God to love *each* creature and to desire and seek *its* good rather than turning it into a means to be used in behalf of some other creature's good. The harms creatures suffer often *appear* terribly pointless. So it seems important to suggest *some* good that might be served by God's decision not to use coercion—on the view under consideration—to prevent them from taking place. In the absence of some account of this kind, it will be hard—even if not impossible—to avoid the conclusion that the occurrence of these harms flies in the face of the conviction that God is love.

Thus, the most common variant of this position *has* identified goods respected by God's permission of various harms: creaturely freedom, moral and spiritual development, and growth in knowledge, as well, perhaps, as the inherent worth and integrity of the various constituents of the created order. The proponent of this position posits something resembling the view "that there are certain necessary conditions—logically necessary conditions, that is (in other words, it is incoherent to suppose that they could have been avoided)—for the formation of finite, creaturely, persons, intended to live creatively in love and knowledge of one another and their Maker."[1] Because genuine love and moral and spiritual maturation are impossible without freedom, God must allow creatures to choose freely, even though sometimes their free choices will harm other creatures or themselves.

Similarly, for proponents of this sort of view, physical accident is an unavoidable consequence of God's decision to create a material world, a world composed of innumerable interacting systems. And the possibility of physical accident is required for the activity of rational agents. We can only make real choices if we can accurately anticipate the consequences of those choices. We can only act meaningfully if we act within an impersonal, predictable environment that does not vary simply with our moral characters or our whims. We can only come to understand the world through our experience if its behavior is constant enough for us to acquire knowledge about it through generalizations based on what happens to ourselves and others. An impersonal, regular, physical order may also provide people with valuable opportunities for the development of moral virtues as they confront a relatively intractable reality that may surprise, puzzle, and challenge them, and with which they may sometimes collide in destructive ways.[2]

Further, a proponent of the third view might maintain, the physical order is not pliable to our wills because God loves and values all of creation and works in and through each of its elements; thus, God does not make even inanimate creation wholly subservient to the interests of sentients. As a result, when an earthquake happens, the

> will of God expressed in the event is his will for the physical elements in the earth's crust or under it: his will that they should go on being themselves and acting in accordance with their natures.
> ... [God] does not let natural forces have their heads up to the point only at which their free action would conflict with some fixed principle of higher purpose, for example the welfare and safety of mankind, nor does

---

1. Brian Hebblethwaite, *The Essence of Christianity: A Fresh Look at the Nicene Creed* (London: SPCK 1996) 72-3.
2. See Swinburne, *Providence*.

he, when that point is reached, substitute miracle for nature and stop physical forces from indulging in their characteristic behavior.

What would happen to the system of nature if God did habitually overrule, is too terrible to contemplate. Fortunately he does not overrule; he uses, or in some mysterious way persuades. . . .

. . . [A] volcanic eruption, taken in itself, shows the Creative Mind thinking physically, not humanly. For the divine thought identifies itself with nature at every level on which nature operates.

[There are natural disasters] . . . because God makes the world make itself; or rather, since the world is not a single being, he makes the multitude of created forces make the world, in the process of making or being themselves. It is this principle of divine action that gives the world such endless vitality, such vital variety in every part. The price of it is, that the agents God employs in the basic levels of the structure will do what they will do, whether human convenience is served by it or not.[1]

On this view, there is no one-to-one correlation between experiences of harm on the one hand and particular goods on the other. Sometimes we suffer because of others' wicked or foolish conduct. It must be possible for aggressors to act in ways designed to cause us harm if they are to be capable of making free choices. They must be able to make free choices if they are to achieve authentic moral and spiritual maturity, which *is* a genuine good. So while our suffering itself is not intended by God, permitting it is a necessary condition for the exercise of creaturely freedom, which God respects and values.

This position may, indeed, provide an adequate response to the challenge posed for Christian belief by the reality of pointless suffering. It is not, however, free of difficulty.

Suppose there are good reasons for a perfectly loving God capable of acting coercively in the world to avoid doing so as a general rule. Still, an objector might ask why God should not on occasion act coercively to right the world's wrongs. If the only constraint on divine action is the need to respect creaturely freedom and maintain the integrity and predictability of the non-living created order, the critic will suggest that we should expect God to do more. Perhaps God ought not constantly to reorder nature and history, but, an objector might argue, an occasional dramatic display of divine power would be helpful. Because it would be rare, such a display wouldn't necessarily undercut our capacity for free action or the general reliability of physical processes. Even if God would wreak havoc by stopping every murderer's bullet in mid-air, wouldn't divine love *sometimes* open the doors of Stalinist prison camps or deflect blows aimed at children about to be abused?

A proponent of the third position could respond that God does just that on occasion. The critic might reply that attempts to identify God's hand in history are notoriously controversial. She might also ask whether we might not reasonably expect *more frequent* coercive acts on God's part, if these are possible. The defender of the third position might retreat to the view that divine self-restraint must be

---

1. Austin Farrer, *God* 87-91. Farrer imagines an objector who asks "why God rooted the higher forms of existence in lower forms, with all their inevitable stupidity and mutual disregard; or why he gave these lower forms freedom to run themselves, instead of moving them like pawns on a chessboard. . . ." In response, Farrer maintains: "You suggest that God might have made some such higher forms as he has made, without rooting them in the action and being of lower forms. I reply, that we have no power to conceive anything of the kind. And as to your suggestion that natural forces might have been kept in divine leading strings, I can only say that, so far as I know, running oneself one's own way is the same thing as existing. If God had made things to exist, but not to run their own way, he would have made them to exist, and not to exist" (*Belief* 52).

consistent, without exceptions, if creation's freedom is to be respected. And so the debate would continue.

The third alternative response to the problem of suffering is promising, but it leaves on the table questions that deserve further reflection. However we assess it, though, its practical consequences may differ little, if at all, from those of the fourth alternative I am about to consider (a point I underscore in Chapter 4). Each of these views leads us to have relatively similar expectations regarding God's activity in the world.

Rethinking the Nature of Power

Another possible response to the challenge of pointless suffering calls us to rethink what we mean when we describe God as perfect in power.[1] Talk about God as perfect in power often seems to imply that God really has *all* the power there is, that creatures don't have any genuine power of their own. Maybe, though, this isn't the most accurate or helpful way to think about divine power.

To say that something completely lacks power—by which I mean here simply the capacity to exert real influence on some aspect of reality—is really just to say that it doesn't exist at all. If something really exists, it must have some ability to make a difference. Or so I want to argue.

If this view of things is correct, then to say that God is perfect in power means that God has all the power it is possible for God to have. But just how much power it is possible for God to have will depend on what kinds of reality there are *other* than God. Living things are free in various degrees. And though non-living things and structures and systems are not conscious or capable of deliberate, free action, they, too, have a reality of their own—sometimes even a capacity for a kind of spontaneity. They are real, too, and they are thus able to exert influences that are truly their own.[2]

The fourth response to the problem of evil maintains that God doesn't unilaterally override the freedom of creatures or violate the integrity of the created order's processes. On the third view, God's not doing this was a matter of self-restraint, of respect for creaturely freedom and integrity. On the fourth view, it's a matter of what's possible, given that there are actually existing creatures. God is actively seeking to prevent all the harms there are, within the necessary limits imposed by the reality of the creaturely world. But creatures all too often ignore, resist, or reject God's influence. And since God cannot prevent harms coercively, by unilaterally overruling the freedom of creatures or the integrity of created structures and processes, harms happen despite God's will and despite God's active opposition to them.

This position clearly allows us to affirm the goodness of God in the face of suffering without justifying suffering or excusing complacency. But it's understandably troubling to many people. We want to know that God *can* effortlessly overmaster every difficulty we encounter, even if God doesn't do so in fact. And if the freedom of creatures and the integrity of physical processes are *givens* for God, God may not seem worthy of our confidence. We want God to love us. But we want to know that divine love *can* find expression in coercive power. After all, a coercive God can deliver us from the harms that beset us. A coercive God can make sure everything turns out all right in the end. A coercive God can keep us

---

1. For a critical reflection on one cluster of problems associated with this approach, see Gary Chartier, "Non-Human Animals and Process Theodicy," *Religious Studies* 42.1 (2006): 3-26.

2. See Edward Farley, *Divine Empathy: A Theology of God* (Minneapolis: Fortress 1996) 310; Charles Hartshorne, *Omnipotence and Other Theological Mistakes* (Albany: SUNY 1984) 10-26.

safe. And even if God isn't coercive very often, it's nice to know we might be able to count on some divine coercion now and then.

These are serious concerns. For many people, calling God creator means that God has just this kind of coercive power: because God is creator, God can exercise completely coercive power at will. For basic theological and philosophical reasons, as well as because the vision of a coercively powerful God can be a source of profound security, people want to retain it.

The problem, of course, is that if calling God perfect in power really means God can act coercively, we're left with the question why God doesn't do so more often. Now, for instance. The third view I discussed above answers this question by saying, in effect, that God makes a policy decision, a value judgment that it is better not to act coercively. Unavoidably, we are left wondering whether the value judgment God is supposed to have made is really plausible, given the awfulness we and others experience. By contrast, understanding God's power as all the power it is possible for God to have, given the reality of creatures, explains why God doesn't unilaterally eliminate the suffering we confront: it simply isn't possible for God to exercise all power, because there are created centers of power other than God, over against God. God loves unfailingly, but God's will is not always done, and because the creation is *real*, not imaginary, every constituent of it has the capacity to say *no* to God.

While this view helps to underscore reality of God's love in the face of suffering, it obviously raises the question whether we can, indeed, rely on God, given the power that non-divine realities have. And so it, too, may not leave us feeling altogether satisfied.

I don't think, as I've suggested, that we need to decide at this point between the third view and the fourth. For both rightly emphasize the freedom of creatures, and both lead us to expect God to act persuasively, rather than coercively. Provided either is credible—and it seems to me that arguments can be offered for both—the reality of apparently pointless suffering need not be a decisive problem for Christian belief.

The Significance of Suffering and Evil for Belief in God

How we think about God's relationship to evil is important in significant part because it affects how we think about God's activity in the world. And it certainly can *affect* our ability reasonably to affirm the reality of God. Even if we have not resolved the question of evil to our satisfaction, however, we need not regard belief in God as untenable. It is clear, I think, that we must affirm that creatures are genuinely free in relation to God, and we must expect God's activity in the world to be persuasive, rather than coercive. It is not, however, necessary that we be able to defend a full-fledged account of *why* this is the case in order for our belief in God to be rational.

There are, as I have already noted, many different reasons a person's Christian belief can be justified. To be sure, some religious believers derive their conviction that God is from a consideration of the world's ordered goodness. Someone who bases her belief in God on the appearance of purposive order and design in the world must demonstrate how the argument from order to an Orderer is compatible with the existence of so much *dis*order in the world. An argument for the reality of the Christian God based on the perceived "designedness" of the world definitely has to take account of the reality of pointless suffering. At minimum, it has to acknowledge that the fact of such suffering reduces the probability that the world's order points to a designer, or show why the reality of gratuitous harm *doesn't* make it less likely that the world results from God's ordering love. Either way, suffering poses a problem for any argument from design.

But even this problem—which need not, in any case, be decisive—does not arise for anyone whose belief in God is not *founded* exclusively on the argument from design. If you rationally believe in the God of love on the basis of some other sort of argument, because you were taught to do so, or because your experience points toward the reality of God in one way or another, then it follows that there *must* be a solution to the problem of evil, whether or not we can see what it is. If you're justified in believing in God for some reason or reasons other than or in addition to the order of the created world, then the your belief can be valid even if you can't arrive at an immediate satisfactory response to the difficulty posed by the need to reconcile God's goodness with the fact of pointless suffering.[1] To the extent that you *don't* begin from the world's order, the problem you face is to understand *how* a perfectly good, perfectly powerful God is related to the reality of suffering and evil, rather than to determine if the fact of suffering and evil makes belief in God impossible.

Love and the Attractiveness of Christian Belief

Whatever the arguments offered for or against Christianity, it is unlikely that a person who lacks a sense of basic trust,[2] who does not and cannot experience the world as at least potentially love's arena, will find Christian belief plausible.[3] And if Christian belief does not contribute to a sense of basic trust, people are unlikely to find it appealing. The experiences that precede someone's evaluation of Christian belief, and the kinds of experiences fostered in the context of the Christian community are perhaps as important as any other factor in determining how people assess Christian beliefs.

Even if one is *told* that God is loving, one may still experience one's parents and the other authority figures in one's life as distant and dominating. Consequently, one may have little choice but to build one's picture of God from the raw materials provided by one's negative experiences of parents, teachers, and others. One cannot be blamed if one rejects such a god; indeed, one probably ought to do so. There is nothing sinful about failing to believe in an

1. See Nelson Pike, "Hume on Evil," *God and Evil: Readings on the Theological Problem of Evil*, ed. Pike, Contemporary Perspectives in Philosophy (Englewood Cliffs, NJ: Prentice-Hall 1964) 85-102. According to Pike, as "Philo himself has suggested, when the existence of God is accepted prior to any rational consideration of the status of evil in the world, the traditional problem of evil reduces to a noncrucial perplexity of relatively minor importance" (102). I believe that Pike's argument can, in fact, be made stronger than it is. For Pike holds that only if the reality of God is demonstrated necessarily by reason or is accepted "on faith" (in what?) can it be treated as axiomatic in the way I have suggested here. In fact, however, probabilistic arguments for God's reality will yield similar results *unless* the features of experience to which they appeal are ones directly affected by evil. Forms of the teleological argument will have to take evil into account, for the appeal to order cannot be made in the absence of an explanation for what seems very much like disorder in our world (*e.g.*, that which produces suffering). But the ontological argument, for instance, includes no terms regarding which the existence or non-existence of evil would make any difference. If the reality of a perfect God is possible, and, if possible, then necessary, it is irrelevant whether any given finite existent or collection of finite existents is good or evil. And even the fact of evil is *relevant* to versions of the teleological argument only—as Pike notes—insofar as they purport to justify belief in a *loving* God; the teleological argument could still provide reason for belief in an intelligent, purposeful designer even if it left open the question of the designer's goodness.

2. On basic trust, see, *e.g.*, Wolfhart Pannenberg, *Anthropology in Theological Perspective*, trans. Matthew J. O'Connell (Philadelphia: Westminster 1985) 220-42.

3. I owe this point to Heather Hessel.

authoritarian, oppressive god, or in a seemingly distant, uncaring, and uninvolved absentee proprietor. Concrete relationships and communities are an important source of confidence that basic trust is possible and desirable. We need to be sensitive to the fact that people who do not believe in God may find it *impossible* to do so, because basic trust seems so false to their experience of the world.

Of course, coming to understand that the God revealed in Jesus is the source and ground of the universe can re-orient one's perception of one's world, perhaps making basic trust seem like an option for the first time. In fact, it is surely one of the central tasks of the Christian community to nurture a sense of basic trust. But if one lacks that sense—which often means that one has had no genuine opportunity to experience community—it is improbable that one will acquire or retain the conviction that there is God. That is why community (including both political community as well as the community that is the Church) and relationships of all kinds (especially with parents, spouses, and friends) can contribute so significantly to the development of people's Christian beliefs.[1]

Just because one does not acquire or retain Christian convictions does not, of course, mean that one cannot be accepted by God and touched by divine love— divine action is surely not limited to places where people understand God correctly, or none of us would experience God's love. But whether one does or does not identify with the Christian community, lack of basic trust is a problem that hampers any attempt to live a flourishing and fulfilled human life. So we need to find ways to make community happen in the church and beyond, and to enable the formation and maintenance of stable, intimate relationships. That is an important part of what it means for us to make belief in God attractive. If the character of reality can ultimately be understood by referring to the God of the gospel, then the good news of God's love is true whether or not we say it is. Our fragmented and broken lives can hardly *prove* that God's love is a reality. But by fostering a sense of acceptance and trust, we can give people new ways of seeing what might otherwise appear to be a bleak and unfriendly world. And we can give them real evidence that basic trust is a genuine possibility they can experience—in part through their relationships with us.

I hope throughout this book to show, directly and indirectly, that Christian convictions *can* foster basic trust. In Chapter 3, I will explore what it means to talk about God as personal and the ways in which the doctrine of God's Trinity can be seen to safeguard the understanding that God's revelation is love's work and that we can and should love God, rather than any idol.

1. Cp. Lash 199-218.

3

Whose Nature and Whose Name Are Love

To believe in *God*—as opposed to the various tribal gods of nation, church, family, and self that pretend to deserve our absolute loyalty—is to believe that there is a fundamental unity at the heart of things. It is to recognize the reality of a center of meaning and value that calls into question all the claims to ultimacy staked by the varied objects of our experience and provides a reference point around which our disparate values can be organized.[1]

Talk about God is inseparable from talk about what is really real and really valuable, what is really worth loving. It is talk about the character of reality as a whole. Thus, to say that God is trustworthy is to assert that a stance of *basic trust*—the conviction that the universe is ultimately a friendly place—is appropriate. To say that God is love is to identify love—mutual care and delight and desire—as the *heart of* reality, and as an *ideal for* reality, as a basic guideline for relationships with persons, communities, and the world.

I don't mean, of course, that God is *the same as* created reality as a whole; that's pantheism. As free and personal, God could not be *identical* with the world. But Christians believe that God is at the root of everything that happens in the world, that God designs, sustains, shapes, and inspires created reality. Thus, even though there is fragmentation and chaos in the world, Christians believe, God continues to guide and heal. And because the world is God's creation, and because God is perfect, the elements of the creaturely world must mirror God's perfection in ways appropriate to their own particular characters (even if also in ways affected by the distortions that result from brokenness and moral failure).

Christians confess God as personal—not as a matter of arcane divine psychology but as a way of spelling out what it means to speak of God as, most centrally, free and loving. There are all sorts of gods to believe in, of course, and which ones we identify as ultimate can make a considerable difference in our lives. Christians don't subscribe to a generic view of God. Christians identify God as disclosed in and through Jesus of Nazareth, though of course the sources of the Christian understanding God include not only that decisive revelation but also history, reason, tradition, science, and personal experience. The disclosure of God in Jesus gave rise to the Christian doctrine of God as Trinity—of mutually corrective emphases as shaping Christian discourse about God, and of God as at work in the process of revelation from start to finish.

---

1. My indebtedness to H. Richard Niebuhr, *Radical Monotheism and Western Culture, with Supplementary Essays* (New York: Harper 1960) should be obvious here.

Love as Personal

To say that God is love is to say that God is personal. Impersonal mechanism is not as fundamental to reality as personal freedom. God is not an abstract "supreme value"—God is purposive love.[1]

Christian belief in God as personal doesn't involve any fantastic claims about the possibility of insight into God's "inner life." It certainly doesn't require Christians to suppose that *God* is personal in just the same sense in which *we* are personal. Instead, I think, it means that reality is in some sense *meaningful* and *orderly*; that its meaning and order are products of *freedom* and *purpose*; that this freedom is *responsive*; that this freedom is *love*'s freedom, and that it is therefore empathic and at work both benevolently and desiringly in the world; that it fosters communion and seeks creation's welfare through loving, interactive *communication*; that this loving freedom, as free, cannot be controlled and manipulated; and that because of this loving freedom, there is reason to *hope* for both ourselves and other persons and for our world. That is, to say that God is personal is to confess something like the following:

• When we trust God, we are trusting in the creative ingenuity of free divine love to weave a coherent quilt of meaning from the sometimes seemingly ragged threads of our lives. Despite the very real and often destructive chaos that is evident throughout cosmic, human, and personal history, our existence is meaningful. That is, it finds its place within a broader, enveloping context from which it acquires significance. While it contains random elements, it is not

---

1. Edward Farley, *Divine Empathy: A Theology of God* (Minneapolis: Fortress 1996) argues that it is not possible to reach the conclusion that God is personal or "a person" (he focuses more on the problems of the latter than on those besetting the former) on the basis of the experience of redemption, which provides, on his view, the raw materials from which the doctrine of God is best constructed. He maintains that to speak of the ultimate source of redemption as "a 'person' is to mythologize it" and to treat ultimate reality as "a specific entity," as also to apply a characteristic of one dimension on which redemption operates—agency—to what which redeems. Further, "the act of worship [does not] require God as a personal entity" (132). Arguments against speaking of God as "a person" do not, it seems to me, tell against characterizations of God as personal: personal language is better than impersonal language for God. There may well be rational arguments for this conclusion (cp. Rahner and Braine, below); certainly, the contingency of the world's order counts in favor of the view that it is the result of free choice. But even within the sphere of personal experience with which Farley is concerned, his arguments don't seem decisive. To the extent that worship involves thanksgiving, it seems to suggest, at any rate, free divine action. To speak of God as "reconciling love" (130) in the context of redemption seems to require that God be more than an impersonal process binding alienated finite persons together. And that which lies behind the experience of "being-founded" that lies at the center of individual, "agential" redemption, on Farley's view, "evokes metaphors of care, concern, and intimate relation." Thus, Farley himself maintains, "[t]he real in the sense of founding is already in some sense a personalized cipher" (128). And "[i]n interhuman redemption God is the infinite Thou who presses alienated relation beyond guilt, resentment, penalty, and vengeance to reconciliation" (243); obviously, Farley's use of "Thou" is metaphorical here, but insofar as this metaphorical language is appropriate in one sphere of redemption, it might follow that it should be applicable to the God who is at the root of redemption in all its aspects. In his earlier study of soteriology, he maintains that if that which is the source of being-founded "addresses the passion of the interhuman, it would seem to be in some sense a personal other"; "in founding . . . the desired eternal horizon is disclosed as the transmundane power and meaning of being which is both good and personal"; God is "the personal and good ground of things . . . ." Edward Farley, *Good and Evil: Interpreting a Human Condition* (Minneapolis: Fortress 1990) 151.

pointless or *completely* random. Something underlies our connections with each other and with the cosmos, something that fosters order, complexity, and the emergence of value at the cosmic, historical, and individual levels. (This is not, of course, the same thing as saying that we can discern what the relevant patterns or trajectories *are*.) Someone might object that it seems overly anthropomorphic to speak of God as having "purposes," if these are understood as psychological states. But to say that there is some sense of order, that there is something that seeks what can meaningfully be described as a *goal*, that the ongoing life of the cosmos is not mechanical and blind, may be as close as we need to come—when we're s peaking *functionally*—to the affirmation of divine purpose.

• That which impels cosmic and human history toward order and value is not simply a *process* or a static *abstraction* or *ideal*. The world is not lured toward order and value by the outworking of a deterministic process with necessary phases and an inescapable outcome or by ideals that somehow exist on their own. On the other hand, the emergence of order and value does not occur simply by chance. Rather, the presence of order and value in the world reflects the use *freely* chosen divine means to achieve *freely* chosen divine ends. It can best be explained with references to *purposes* rather than merely *processes*.

• These purposes are, in a sense, contingent. Value is not an arbitrary posit of the divine will, but many different values could be realized in the universe. To speak of God as *free* is, among other things, a way of underscoring that things could be other than they are and still valuable, still worthwhile.

• God *responds*. This means that God selects methods and goals in light of what we do. The divine ordering of nature and history is continually being revised in light of the choices made by creatures. But the divine responsiveness is more than a matter of action; it is also a matter of evaluation and feeling. God's experience of the world is different because of what we do and undergo. God responds with care and concern when we are harmed and with joy when we flourish. And, indeed, God feels what we feel—whether we feel delight or agony.

• God is *empathic*, feeling-with creation when it suffers and when it enjoys, and desirous—seeking communion with creatures. Predicating these attributes of God as such is part of what it means to speak of God as personal. But they don't simply apply to God *in se*; they have implications for our reading of the ordering of history and nature. The purpose of this ordering is love, and its character is loving. That means, first, that the order we discern in the world is not designed merely to embody some abstract beauty. Rather, it is designed to foster the harmonious flourishing of creation. Second, this order is designed for loving communion: it is designed to bring us into loving relationship with God and with each other. Third, the ascription of empathy to God is a characterization of a fundamental way in which God works in the world, bringing empathic awareness of every aspect of creation appropriately to bear on every other aspect.[1]

• To speak of God as personal is to speak of God as *communicating*, as revelatory. It is to expect that we will be able to gain some insight into God's nature and purposes, that God is not a nameless, hidden It. It is also to expect that, whatever understanding we gain, we gain at God's own initiative.

• Talk about God as personal is a way of saying that God *transcends manipulation and control*. Things and processes can be manipulated, but persons always

---

1. Farley, *Empathy* 286-315.

elude our attempts to pin them down.¹ Thus, talk of God in personal terms ensures that God is not an object that could be controlled.²

- To affirm that God is personal is finally to endorse a "cosmic optimism."³ It suggests the appropriateness of affirming, on the basis of the divine benevolence and the divine desire for *friendship* with creation, that, in the famous words of Julian of Norwich, "all shall be well, and all shall be well, and all manner of things shall be well." We do not and cannot specify the content of Christian hope with great precision. But speaking of God as personal means, at any rate, that we can reasonably look toward a future marked by genuine fulfillment for persons and for the whole creation.

But even if talk of God as personal is *meaningful*, we can ask whether it is *warranted*. Deity must be more than humanity magnified; theology is not just talking about humanity with a loud voice.⁴ Nevertheless, while we have—and could have—no access to the inner divine life, it is appropriate for us to speak of God as personal. The narratives that identify God as confessed by Christians point to free initiative and love as essential divine characteristics, and these cannot be predicated of any sub-personal reality.⁵ And God's self-disclosure in Jesus of Nazareth suggests that human personality is an especially appropriate vehicle for divine revelation. If personal life is required as the means of God's self-communication, then it stands to reason that God is not less than personal.

The conclusion that God is personal is also suggested by the idea of God as creator. The source of creaturely reality can hardly be inferior to that reality. The personal must be rooted in the personal.

> The ground of a reality ... must possess in itself beforehand and in absolute fullness and purity this reality which is grounded by it, because otherwise this ground could not be the ground of what is grounded, and because otherwise the ground would ultimately be empty nothingness which, if the term is really taken seriously, would say nothing and could ground nothing.⁶

That we are personal suggests that God is too, at least in an analogical sense.⁷

---

1. Walter Kasper, *The God of Jesus Christ*, trans. Matthew J. O'Connell (New York: Crossroad 1989) 156-7.
2. That this freedom from manipulability is an essential aspect of personhood has been repeatedly stressed by Wolfhart Pannenberg.
3. The phrase is John Hick's.
4. I owe this metaphor to Karl Barth.
5. Cp. Nicholas Lash, *Easter in Ordinary: Reflections on Human Experience and the Knowledge of God* (London: SCM 1988): "We address God as 'you,' and speak of God as 'him,' rather than as 'it,' not because God is 'a person' (which he certainly is not, for he is not *an* anything), but because our Christian experience of the manner of God's action requires us to acknowledge ourselves to be not merely produced but addressed, not merely made but loved, and speaking and loving are *personal* characteristics" (276).
6. Karl Rahner, *Foundations of Christian Faith: An Introduction to the Idea of Christianity* (New York: Crossroad-Seabury 1978) 74. David Braine makes this point with greater analytical rigor in *The Reality of Time and The Existence of God: The Project of Proving God's Existence* (Oxford: Clarendon-OUP 1988) 266-96. Braine develops his argument around the theme of causation, arguing for the causal dependence of the personal on the personal in debate with Humean accounts of causal powers.
7. Cp. Robert Merrihew Adams, *Finite and Infinite Goods: A Framework for Ethics* (New York: OUP 1999) 42: "most of the excellences that are most important to us, and of whose value we are most confident, are excellences of persons or of qualities or actions or works or lives or stories of persons. So if excellence consists in resembling or imaging a being that is the Good itself, nothing is more important to the role of the Good itself than that persons and their properties should be able to resemble

To say that God is personal is *not*, of course, to say that God is just like a finite personal reality—just like any of us, for instance. We know what persons are from inspecting ourselves—finite centers of consciousness and action, situated over against each other in relationships that limit and define them. But God is infinite, and so by definition not limited. Our ordinary categories of understanding can be used only metaphorically with reference to God. Any reality I could describe accurately in human language would not be God at all, but at best an idol of one sort or another.

And in a sense, of course, we only know idols. That is to say, we only encounter God in and through images and concepts drawn from our experience of life in the world—resources ultimately inadequate to characterize the limitless creator. It is easy, of course, to cut God down to size by identifying the divine reality with fallible, human pictures of God. But if we are to respond to God *as God*, we have no choice but constantly to qualify and correct our understandings of God and the words in which we express them, refusing to bind God to any formulation in human language.

Thus, when we use personal language of God, we must do so intensely aware of its limitations. To ascribe freedom and purposiveness to God, for instance, is not to suppose that divine purposes are comprehensible to us. To use of God the language of personal dialogue and encounter, the language of love, is not to imagine that the infinite creator exists over against creatures as other creatures do. It is simply to safeguard—using the most powerful and fruitful metaphor available to us—our conviction that God is love, that God is free, and that God cannot be controlled or manipulated by us.

The Christian Meaning of "God"

The Christian meaning of God is *love*. The word "god" functions more like "The President of the United States" than like "Barack Obama." The various sorts of gods are as different as George W. Bush and Abraham Lincoln. The specifically Christian identification of God—through the story of Israel, Jesus, and the Church, as well as through rational reflection and our analysis of nature and experience—tells us which God we're dealing with. God is to be known everywhere; a god who could be localized wouldn't be God. But God's self-disclosure in the story of Israel and the life of Jesus sharpens our understanding of who God is. This understanding gives rise to the Christian doctrine of God as Trinity.

Divine revelation is rooted in, expressive of, and constrained by love. The doctrine of God's Trinity is a reminder that all of our discourse about God must be accountable to what we know about God a God who is infinite, whom we can and should love in place of all the idols that might seek to claim our attention, a God who can be loved in the order of creation, in the spontaneity of God's Spirit's movement in our experience, and through the life of Jesus. At the same time, it highlights the reality that divine revelation is love's work throughout.[1]

The Origins of Trinitarian Belief

The immediate historical origin of the doctrine of God as Trinity was evidently the early Christians' attempt to make sense of their experience of Jesus and the Holy Spirit. They were convinced that God was revealed in Jesus of Nazareth. And they experienced God's Spirit at work in their individual and corporate lives.

---

or image it. that is obviously likelier to be possible if the Good itself is a person or importantly like a person."

1. For the usage, "God's Trinity," see Lash, *Easter* 267.

First-century Judaism and Græco-Roman philosophical monotheism affirmed that God was *one*. This notion was a powerful antidote to conceptions of the universe reflected in stories of warring and factious pantheons. It implied that reality could be trusted to be consistent. It liberated people from the fear of arbitrary upsets brought about by petty divine tyranny.

Belief in divine unity mattered, therefore. But so did God's revelation in Jesus and the work of God's Spirit in the church. The doctrine of God as Trinity reflected the early Christians' efforts to discern a way to affirm the belief in divine unity they presupposed on the basis of the twin traditions that informed their thinking—but do so in light of the significance of Jesus and God's Spirit for their worship, theology, and practice. Two alternative responses to this problem emerged: God was understood by analogy with communities of persons or with individual persons.

The Character of Trinitarian Belief

The first approach, typically associated with Eastern Christianity, views human persons-in-community as providing the most useful analogy for what God is like. "Father" (a term Jesus had used in his prayer-life), "Son" (a term likely used by Jesus,[1] and certainly for him by the first Christians), and "Holy Spirit" were terms to be used for God conceived of as a divine community of love given and received. This view preserved divine unity by maintaining the existence of a necessary oneness of purpose and nature among the "persons" of the Trinity. The other, Western Christian, view took the individual self as the best available model of God. On this view, "Father." "Son," and "Holy Spirit" named different, simultaneously present aspects of the one divine being or dimensions of the one divine activity.

The Eastern, "social," model for the Trinity can be a richly inspiring resource for reflection on the nature of humanness and of reality as a whole—stressing the significance of relationship for who we are as human persons and identifying community as the normative human experience. It is fascinating and suggestive, but it may require us to say more about the nature of the divine reality than our language permits us to. It has the potential to lead to fruitless speculation about the functional differentiation of the Trinitarian "persons"—and to the obvious question of the significance and necessity of such differentiation. And to the extent that it uses the word "person" in its contemporary sense to refer to the Trinitarian persons, it may run the risk of underwriting excessive confidence in our ability to describe God with ordinary language.

The typically Western, "individual," model has the advantage of simplicity and economy. It does not pretend to tell us anything occult about the inner life of God. And it rightly recognizes that an infinite and omnipotent God can surely be and act in a variety of ways simultaneously. If we employ it, however, we need to be certain that we don't think and speak as if God were rather like ourselves, only larger and friendlier. We need to be careful to preserve our recognition that God and the world are *different*.

THE FUNCTIONS OF TRINITARIAN DOCTRINE

There are multiple ways in which Trinitarian language can appropriately shape our talk about God. Here, I focus on two: its role in ensuring that we love God, rather than various idols, and its function as a reminder that God's self-communication is love's work.

---

1. See, e.g., Matt. 11:27.

The Universality of Divine Love

We can see the doctrine of God's Trinity as way of ensuring that our vision of God will be appropriately comprehensive, that the reach of our love will be universal—as a safeguard against idolatry.[1] It can function in this way by pointing us to varieties of divine activity and different regions where we ought to look if we are to understand who God is and what God is up to in the world.

To see God as Trinity is to acknowledge we meet one God as the creator who cannot be identified with any aspect of the creation; in history—especially the story of Jesus, but also the history of Israel and the church, and our own personal histories; and at the heart of personal experience. It is to acknowledge that we need to look in all of these places if we want to understand who God is and what God is doing in the world: we have to take the whole of God's creating, revealing, and healing activity into account. In short, the doctrine of God's Trinity is an expression of the insight that nothing less than God deserves our ultimate loyalty or our final love, that if we want to understand and respond aright to God, we cannot love anything less than God with absolute allegiance. If we want to love God, rather than an idol, we will understand that God cannot be localized, and so that no one district of experience can serve as the sole anchor for our God-language.

Thus, the doctrine of God as Trinity is not a short cut that might enable us to bypass the difficult and demanding business of continually rethinking our conceptions of God. It does not provide us with speculative, esoteric knowledge of God's own life. Rather, it tells us that the only way to avoid exchanging God for an idol is to allow the pressure exerted by the distinct points of reference for our talk about God perpetually to correct our language about God.

The Revelation of Divine Love

Love is the ground and goal of God's self-revelation. So we can also understand Trinitarian language as calling attention to God's role as the ground and mediator of this loving self-disclosure, its content, and the facilitator of its reception. The love of God is active in each moment of revelation, and speaking of God as Trinity can serve to underscore revelation's triune pattern.[2]

First, then, it is God, who is love, who *reveals*. God is not absent from the creation; God is love; and a lover cannot be a stranger. So God communicates with us. God freely chooses to act in ways that will bring into being a community of free and responsive, potentially loving creatures and as a result of which these creatures will know God as love and respond in love to God. By bringing into being creatures capable of understanding their world, God makes creaturely apprehension of the divine nature and will possible. And through God's work in nature and history, creatures are enabled to gain a clearer understanding of who God is and what divine love is doing in God's world. God takes the initiative.

Second, it is love *that* God reveals. God's revelation discloses the love at the heart of the universe. Love is not only the *source* but also the *content* of God's self-revelation.

Third, love is the *means by which* God reveals. It is through God's own presence in the world that we come to know God. No creaturely reality is simply

---

1. See Lash, *Easter* 254-85; Nicholas Lash, *Believing Three Ways in One God: A Reading of the Apostles' Creed* (Notre Dame, IN: U of Notre Dame P 1993) 30-3; cp. James Wm. McClendon, Jr., *Systematic Theology 2: Doctrine* (Nashville: Abingdon 1994) 322.

2. This account of the meaning of Trinitarian belief is obviously directly dependent on that of Karl Barth. Augustine famously suggested that we could speak of the relations of the "persons" of the divine Trinity on analogy with the relations among lover, beloved, and love. See also Hans Urs von Balthasar, *Love Alone: The Way of Revelation* (New York: Continuum 1970).

identical with the infinite God, supremely transcendent and supremely immanent. But creation is made to accommodate, express, incarnate God. And so God is present in the world: in nature as well as in history, in the history of Israel as well as the history of all people, decisively in the history of Jesus of Nazareth. God gives, not merely good gifts at a remove, but God's own self. And God is at the root of our *reception* of the divine love. When we discern, apprehend, appropriate God's loving self-gift to us, we do not do so in a vacuum. Our existential and intellectual engagement with and internalization of what God gives us in love is fostered and facilitated by divine inspiration. We are not divine puppets; we *respond* in love to God. But our response is undergirded and conditioned by the active love of God.

Speaking of God as Trinity, then, can be a way of underscoring the fact that God's communication with us is always love's work. The God who is love reveals love in and through love. The doctrine of God's Trinity can thus be read as at least in part a reminder of God's universal presence and universal love, of the fact that from start to finish God's love is at the heart of our experience of and response to that love.

Talk about God's Spirit, in particular, is concerned, at least, with the personal, powerful activity of divine love in nature and history. Properly understood, God's Spirit's power is love's power—persuasive rather than coercive, and aimed at love, at fostering the welfare of creation and loving relationships among creatures, and between creatures and God. In the next chapter, I want to look at how we might want to think about God's Spirit and divine love's activity in the world.

4

The Power of Love

Love makes a difference. To talk about God as love, and so as personal, is to talk about more than a powerful but essentially blind force, like an ocean. It is to say that God is responsive to and concerned about particular creatures—that God achieves and realizes particular purposes in the world as well as ordering the world's basic structures.

To be sure, the sheer fact that someone else loves me makes her present to me in a way she would not otherwise be. Simply to know that I am loved is to find myself empowered and liberated. Realizing that we are cherished by God can be a very powerful experience on its own.

But a lover's love is more than just her inner orientation on her beloved. It is embodied in what she does. Anyone who has ever loved knows that loving means wanting, at least some of the time, to do things for the beloved just to meet her or his needs. If God loves us, then God, too, must desire our well-being *for our sake*. That means God must be at work in our lives, and so in our world, to free and empower and delight and heal us. And since our circumstances are varied and particular, and since there is not one best option for any situation, God's care for us must be free, responsive, particular.

It would be hard to know what make of the claim that God was love if God did not actively seek our good in this way. That is why Christians look for God's love not only in the creative power behind the world's existence and order, not only in the story of Israel, Jesus, and the church, but also in God's Spirit's ongoing activity in nature and history. God's Spirit is the source of "all life, all freedom, all creativity and vitality, and in each fresh particular beauty, each unexpected attainment of relationship and community."[1]

God's Spirit is God as powerfully active. But what kind of power does love possess? And how is it possible to think of a love that is actually able to make a difference in the world when the world often seems so devoid of love? In this chapter, I attempt to articulate an understanding of God's Spirit's particular action in the world in light of the reality of the suffering and evil that so often call love's reality—God's reality—into question.

Talk about God's Spirit's action in the world reflects not only the experience of the early Christians but also that of the people Israel. Both the early Christians and the Hebrews saw God's Spirit as active throughout creation and in the

---

1. Nicholas Lash, *Easter in Ordinary: Reflections on Human Experience and the Knowledge of God* (London: SCM 1988) 267. Emil Brunner highlights the inherent difficulty in formulating a coherent understanding of the Holy Spirit in his *Dogmatics* 3: *The Christian Doctrine of the Church, Faith, and the Consummation*, trans. David Cairns with T. H. L. Parker (Philadelphia: Westminster 1962) 8-9. This difficulty is only underscored by the fact that Brunner himself devotes only fifteen pages of this volume to the doctrine of God's Spirit and situates it within his discussion of the doctrine of the church.

particular events of history. God must be concerned with particular events if divine love is personally engaged with individual creatures. But the reality of suffering raises a challenge for talk about the God of love as active in the world.

As I've indicated, I believe that it might be possible credibly to defend two of the four attempts to see how belief in divine love might be consistent with the experience of pointless suffering which I canvassed in Chapter 2. Both of these accounts of God's relationship with evil affect how we might talk about divine action in the world, but neither rules out belief that God is constantly and particularly active throughout creation. And they tend to yield similar understandings of a loving God's action.

Divine power is love's power. Creation is real, not imaginary, and God's work within creation is persuasive, rather than coercive. Jesus' suffering highlights the reality and freedom of creation. The character of creation is such that loving divine action is possible: creation is more like an organism than a machine, and creatures are capable of free action and able to respond to divine influence. The fact that the God of love is active in the world should be a source of confidence. But it should not lead to an arrogant or infantile identification of God's purposes with our own. We characteristically lack insight into God's intentions in the world.

Active in our lives as multiple levels, God's Spirit fosters our appropriation, our reception, of the divine self-disclosure (as I suggested more briefly in Chapter 3), though without canceling the freedom of sinful, fallible creatures to distort and misunderstand what divine revelation seeks to communicate. The Spirit is also active in our acts of prayer and in divine responses to our prayers, though we must avoid the assumption that, because God is love, God will respond to our prayers like a benevolent Santa Claus. And God's Spirit is the giver of "spiritual gifts" in a variety of ways. Love is actively present in the world.

The Roots of Christian Talk about God as Holy Spirit

The first Christians developed their understanding of God's Spirit by drawing on material in the First Testament and in the writings produced by intertestamental Judaism that spoke of the activity of God's Spirit.[1] Jewish scripture and commentary had referred divine activity in nature, history, and human hearts to God's Spirit. And it was to the activity of God's Spirit that the early Christians ascribed their empowerment for ministry—including their ability to heal, their insights into God's purposes, and the historical developments that facilitated their success in sharing their vision of God's work in the world. They saw God's Spirit as continuing the ministry of Jesus by animating the church.[2] While the early Christians focused on the church as the locus of God's Spirit's activity, the First Testament and the Christian tradition alike speak of the whole cosmos as the arena in which God's Spirit works.

Starting with Suffering

When we have to think about the nature of God's Spirit's action in the world, we are often puzzled. Disease, disaster, oppression, and injustice pose a

---

1. On the relevant First Testament and intertestamental material, see Alasdair I. C. Heron, *The Holy Spirit* (Philadelphia: Westminster 1983) 3-38; C. F. D. Moule, *The Holy Spirit* (Grand Rapids: Eerdmans 1978) 7-21; Eduard Schweizer, *The Holy Spirit* (Philadelphia: Fortress 1980) 10-45.

2. Huw Parri Owen, *Christian Theism: A Study in Its Basic Principles* (Edinburgh: Clark 1984) 53-8. David Brown offers a provocative interpretation of experiences of God's Spirit in the early church in *The Divine Trinity* (London: Duckworth 1985) 159-87.

dreadful and terrifying challenge to the claim that God is love. The problem, of course, is that while we sometimes experience liberation and empowerment, healing and joy, there are all too many times when we do not. We are abused or ignored. People we love are struck down by disease or wounded by prejudice. We find ourselves trapped in behavior patterns that ravage our own lives and those of others. The simple and obvious question is: where is God's love in all this?

A parent or a lover would take enormous risks to save a loved one from harm. Can talk of divine love make any sense at all in the face of suffering? If God is perfectly good and perfectly powerful, why divine action does not simply eliminate the pointless harms that populate the world and distort and destroy our lives?

Ironically, then, the claim that God is *love* is what generates the problem of evil for Christians. If we want to say that God is *love*, we are faced unavoidably with the problem of understanding God's relationship to suffering and evil. And so we need to think clearly about what our responses to this problem might mean for our understanding of God's action in the world.

Though they differ theoretically, the third and fourth possible responses to the problem of evil I outlined in Chapter 2 lead to similar expectations regarding God's Spirit's action in the world. On some versions of the third view, God might occasionally act coercively rather than persuasively. On other versions, God might always *choose* to act persuasively. For the fourth view, some manifestations of God's intentions in the world will be more obvious and more dramatic than others. This won't be because God has made an exception to a general rule against non-coercive divine action—it's not a chosen rule, on this view, but simply part of how reality is—and has exercised coercive power. It will be because some creatures in some circumstances have been more responsive to God's persuasive love. Both views, then, will recognize variety in God's activity in the world, at least as seen in its evident effects on creatures. But on both, there will be good reasons to expect divine activity to be persuasive. Because of the similarity in the practical results of adopting the third and fourth views, we need not decide between them here.

LOVE AND THE NATURE OF DIVINE POWER

"[L]ove . . . implies a certain kind of power. . . . Christian talk about God ought to start with love, not power, and introduce the language of power only in the context of love and only in a way that keeps challenging and subverting it by way of reminder of how easily it might be misunderstood."[1] The conviction that God acts in the world persuasively rather than coercively provides us with a plausible way of acknowledging the reality of pointless suffering while affirming God's love. On either the third or the fourth view of God's relationship with evil and suffering, this conviction seems to be required if we are to take our experience of harm and suffering seriously while still proclaiming and believing that God is love.

Certainly, it would hardly be surprising to find love working in a way that didn't involve overriding creaturely freedom, given what we know about how love behaves generally. The lover does not seek to elicit the beloved's response by putting a gun to his head or to ensure his compliance through hypnosis. Indeed, the cost of coercion would be the impossibility of love itself. The love that love seeks is a free response of the self; but coercion, hypnosis, and other strategies that eradicate freedom ensure that the beloved does not truly give himself. The absence of freedom frustrates love's achievement of its own objectives. So there is good reason to expect that divine love, just because it is love, would not ordinarily seek to coerce free creatures.

---

1. William C. Placher, *Narratives of a Vulnerable God: Christ, Theology, and Scripture* (Louisville: Westminster/Knox 1994) 17.

Divine Power and the Reality of Creation

Anything we say about divine power must be understood within the context provided by, among other things, the conviction that God is the world's loving creator. Creation is the paradigm case of divine action. In creation, God's infinite wisdom and love shape a free creation that is not God, that is *other* than God. The doctrine of creation shows us divine power used, not to dominate, but to empower a finite reality whose flourishing and love God desires.

God didn't have to form a world containing free creatures. But a world with no sentients would immeasurably poorer. And, even if such a world were possible, there would be no point in creating one containing sentients whose behavior was programmed in advance. Pre-programmed creatures couldn't respond authentically to God's love: God would know that they were simply reacting to stimuli guaranteed to produce the right results. Creaturely love—including love for God—and creativity wouldn't mean anything. Creatures wouldn't introduce anything new into the universe. *If this were the sort of world God had made, then, for God, there would be no difference between creating a universe and just imagining one.*

Arguably, to be real is to have some capacity to exert influence on others. Absent that capacity, something wouldn't exist at all. But the notion that God exercises all power unilaterally implies that creaturely entities don't really have any power, and so *aren't* real. (Rather than distinct creatures, they would perhaps better be thought of as constituents of God's own being. Somewhat ironically, a position according to which God has all the power seems hard to distinguish from pantheism.[1]) If creation is real, then, this suggests that God's will is not always done, that God doesn't unilaterally determine all states of affairs in the world, that divine power is persuasive, rather than coercive.[2]

Divine Power and the Life of Jesus

God's revelation in the life of Jesus of Nazareth reflects the divine vulnerability inherent in all divine creative activity.

> Jesus did not ... ultimately envisage God as a God who was sovereignly in charge of all things, if by that is meant exercising, if he wishes, absolute control over the actions and fate of all things and creatures.... [T]he fundamental springs of Jesus' understanding of God lie in his vision of a God who enters the world as a merciful, loving, forgiving reality, who is in the world healing and overcoming darkness and evil, who—simply—loves his enemies.[3]

Vulnerable, forsaken, hurting, Jesus put God's persuasive power on display. When Jesus dies on the cross, the myth of God as absolute monarch dies with him. That God should be manifest in the life of a crucified carpenter was a scandalous thought to a lot of people in the ancient Mediterranean world. A famous "cartoon" from the second century depicts a Christian worshipping a crucified jackass. The message is clear: anyone who had been crucified couldn't be much of an object of worship. The idea that God could be revealed in a crucified man turned inherited conceptions of power and status on their heads.[4] God-the-

---

1. Or, perhaps (to use a label sometimes applied to Hegel's view of the God-world relationship), *acosmism*.

2. For a relatively popular presentation of this position, see Charles Hartshorne, *Omnipotence and Other Theological Mistakes* (Albany: SUNY 1984) 10-26; *A Natural Theology for Our Time* (La Salle, IL: Open 1967) 80-2; David Ray Griffin, *God, Power, and Evil: A Process Theodicy* (Lanham, MD: UP of America 1991) 251-310.

3. See John K. Riches, *Jesus and the Transformation of Judaism* (New York: Seabury 1982) 166.

4. Migliore 57.

absolute monarch could have solved the problem of human brokenness and alienation through the use of force. God's response to the human condition in and through the cross suggests a very different picture of how divine love is realized in the world. God's activity within the constraints set by the reality of creation is a key to understanding the nature of divine action.[1]

LOVE CHERISHES THE PARTICULAR

The God we see in the crucified Jesus is the God who persuades rather than coerces, the vulnerable God of love. But the image of the cross might seem to suggest that God is simply passive in the face of the world's pointless harms. To affirm that God is love is, however, to affirm that God is present and active in the world, seeking the well-being of all creation.

The Spirit's work in the world—love's work—must be concerned with specific creatures and events. Authentic love must be *particular*. That is, God's loving action must reflect a divine response to a given situation in the world that is appropriate to that situation. Talk of such particular divine action is essential if God is to be conceived of in personal—loving—terms and if our own lives are to be meaningfully regarded as objects of God's care. Freedom and responsiveness are crucial to love, and divine action can exhibit such freedom and responsiveness only if it is particular.[2] If God loves each element of the vast universe, then love's work in the world must attend to the needs of every constituent of creation.

God must be able to act freely and distinctively, sensitively addressing the particulars of each unique creaturely situation, if talk of divine action is really to mean anything at all. The notion of general or uniform action is ultimately vacuous.[3] Only if I think God is up to something in particular in the world can I choose to participate in the flow of divine action.[4] And only if God is capable of free action in the world that responds to the world's distortions is there hope for social and personal healing.[5]

The power of the God who is love is not like human power as we ordinarily experience it, then: not male power, not authoritarian monarchical power. But the fact that God isn't really a Renaissance emperor—and therefore doesn't always act

  1. Cp. Peter Baelz, *Does God Answer Prayer?* (London: Darton 1982) 26-8.
  2. Keith Ward, *Divine Action* (London: Collins 1990) 137-8.
  3. Such, at least, is the claim of Austin Farrer, *Faith and Speculation: An Essay in Philosophical Theology* (London: Black 1967): "We can talk about the general action of a law, either civil or natural; but this is to speak by metaphor. A law does not act; a multitude of agents, whether physical agents or *agents de police*, act in conformity with it. Or gain, a real action may have a general effect, as when I scatter water from a watering-can. But the action is particular. . . . If God acts in this world, he acts particularly . . ." (61). Peter Baelz, *Prayer and Providence* (London: SCM 1968) seems right to argue that "God's benevolence and general providence are, religiously speaking, still inadequate. In fact for the believer there can be no satisfaction with a general providence which is not also a special providence. His own existential needs raise the specifically religious question, and a satisfying religious answer must meet these needs. That is, the providence of God must be such as to extend to the individual in his particular situation" (126). See also H. H. Farmer, *The World and God: A Study of Prayer, Providence and Miracle in Christian Experience*, Library of Constructive Theology (London: Nisbet 1935) 124-6.
  4. So Farrer, *Faith* 61.
  5. Alexander J. McKelway, *The Freedom of God and Human Liberation* (London: SCM 1990) 22. McKelway goes on: "The universal tendency to deny real freedom in favour of a bondage to self-interest will defeat every theology of liberation unless it has before it a God who is free *from* his creation so that he can be free *for* it by breaking into and through the inevitabilities that control human existence." Cp. McKelway 44.

like we might expect—doesn't mean that God isn't personally active in the world. But God's work in the world is love's work.

Whether we opt for the third or the fourth response to the problem of suffering, we must say, in broad terms, that God does what God can to prevent and minimize all the suffering that mars our world—but that what God can do reflects the reality of the world God has made and is making. To say that the world is *real* is to say that it is free, which means in turn that it cannot be guaranteed always to fulfill God's will. As Austin Farrer maintains in the course of articulating his version of the third position:

> It is not silly, childish or superstitious to suppose that God attends to your prayer or your conduct like a parent watching an infant when the parent has nothing else to do. It is merely to credit God with being God. What is silly, childish and superstitious is to imagine that, in giving you the undivided attention of his heart, your creator will forget his other creatures; that he will be ready to disregard their interests, or the very laws of their being, while he arranges little providences for you, all leading to lollipops.[1]

God's will is often not done in the world, whatever our prayers and faithful actions. But despite the creaturely world's resistance, God continues to work, to persuade all creation with and toward love.

God's Action in a Scientific World

Free, particular, loving divine action in a creation that is itself free must be mediated through the structures and processes of the created world. But we sometimes find it hard to make sense of the idea of God's action being mediated in this way. We tend to balk because we wonder how we could conceive of divine action in our contemporary, "scientific" world. We sometimes wonder how, if the world is a generally orderly and coherent system, we can imagine God acting freely and particularly within it.

God's creation is real, and so free. The world's constituents spend their time going about the business of being themselves. Usually, they do so in relatively predictable ways. The world, especially that aspect of the world with which the physical sciences are concerned, is a basically orderly place.

On the other hand, we needn't believe, that the world's integrity makes it immune to divine persuasion. If the world were a strictly determined system, there wouldn't—by definition—be any "free play" in the course of events. God could plan everything out in advance; but then, of course, we would be back to our earlier problem: there wouldn't be a real world left. There wouldn't by any room for particular, responsive divine action in the ongoing life of the world, because

---

1. Austin Farrer, *Saving Belief: A Discussion of Essentials* (London: Hodder 1964) 45. Subsequently he argues that God "does not violate [the action or organization of nature's elements] . . . by the higher levels or organization and higher modes of action he superimposes. Now in the political sphere [to which Farrer has just made an analogy] a hundred per cent success for public order or for economic planning is unthinkable, so long as individual freedom is given its rights. So in the natural world a hundred per cent success for animal bodies is unthinkable, if the cellular, chemical and atomic systems of which they are composed are to retain their rights, and go on being themselves in their own way at every level." The wonder of the physical creation, he says, "is that at every level the constituent elements run themselves, and, by their mutual interaction, run the world. God not only makes the world, he makes it make itself; or rather, he causes its innumerable constituents to make it. And this in spite of the fact that the constituents are not for the most part intelligent. . . . All they can do is blind away at being themselves, and fulfil the repetitive pattern of their existence." (51-2). Cp. Nancey C. Murphy and George F. R. Ellis, *On the Moral Nature of the Universe: Theology, Cosmology, and Ethics* (Minneapolis: Fortress 1996).

everything would be done by God. And, of course, there wouldn't be any room for *creaturely* action, either. If everything that happened in the world were the product of universal necessity, then my putative actions—since they're part of "everything"—would be the product of universal necessity. And so they wouldn't be actions at all. They would simply be outcroppings of the universal cosmic process.

Fortunately, there's no decisive reason to think that we live in a strictly determined world. The evidence, in fact, is that reality is non-deterministic from the sub-atomic level on up. Of course, sub-atomic randomness isn't the same thing as conscious, purposive free choice. But the fact that there seem to be non-deterministic events in nature suggests that the universe isn't the giant machine people sometimes thought it was during the past few centuries. And there continue to be good arguments in support of the belief that our choices, too, aren't necessitated by our genes or our environments, that *we* make distinctive contributions to our personal and communal histories.[1]

If there isn't a tightly closed natural web of events, then there may be room in the world for God to act particularly in relation to specific personal, communal, and natural situations.[2] Without overriding the natural order, God can lure, inspire, and persuade free creatures—creatures capable of responding freely in all sorts of desirable and undesirable ways to the divine initiative.[3] And there may be, and

---

1. See John Searle, *Rationality in Action* (Cambridge: Bradford-MIT 2001) 269-98; Carl Ginet, *On Action* (Cambridge: CUP 1989); David Ray Griffin, *Unsnarling the World-Knot: Consciousness, Freedom, and the Mind-Body Problem* (Berkeley: U of California P 1998); Thomas Pink, *Free Will: A Very Short Introduction* (Oxford: OUP 2004); Robert Kane, *The Significance of Free Will* (New York: OUP 1998); Austin Farrer, *The Freedom of the Will*, Gifford Lectures 1957 (London: Black 1958); Joseph Boyle, Jr., Germain Grisez, and Olaf Tollefsen, *Free Choice: A Self-Referential Argument* (Notre Dame, IN: U of Notre Dame P 1976); Richard Swinburne, *The Evolution of the Soul* (Oxford: Clarendon-OUP 1985); John Thorp, *Free Will: A Defense against Neurophysiological Determinism* (London: Routledge 1980).

2. Cp. Karl Rahner, *Foundations of Christian Faith: An Introduction to the Idea of Christianity*, trans. William V. Dych (New York: Crossroad-Seabury 1978) 87.

3. The topic of particular providence is helpfully addressed in Timothy Gorringe, *God's Theatre: A Theology of Providence* (London: SCM 1991); Baelz, *Answer* 29-37; Baelz, *Prayer*; Farrer, *Faith*; Diogenes Allen, *Christian Belief in a Postmodern World* (Louisville: Westminster/Knox 1989) 165-81; Farmer; Arthur Peacocke, *Theology for a Scientific Age: Being and Becoming, Natural and Divine*, Signposts in Theology (Oxford: Blackwell 1990) 159-63; Thomas F. Tracy, ed., *The God who Acts: Philosophical and Theological Explorations* (University Park, PA: Pennsylvania State UP 1994); Langdon Gilkey, *Reaping the Whirlwind: A Christian Interpretation of History* (New York: Crossroad-Seabury 1976) 303-6; Brian Hebblethwaite and Edward Henderson, eds., *Divine Action: Studies Inspired by the Philosophical Theology of Austin Farrer* (Edinburgh: Clark 1990); Ward 119-69; Michael J. Langford, *Providence* (London: SCM 1981); Nancey C. Murphy, *Beyond Liberalism and Fundamentalism: How Modern and Postmodern Philosophy Set the Theological Agenda* (Valley Forge, PA: TPI 1996) 135-53; Brian Hebblethwaite, "Providence and Divine Action," *Religious Studies* 14 (1978): 223-36; John Polkinghorne, *Science and Providence* (London: SPCK 1989); Paul Tillich, *Systematic Theology*, 3 vols. (Chicago, IL: U of Chicago P 1951-63) 1: 263-9; Vincent Brümmer, *What Are We Doing When We Pray? A Philosophical Inquiry* (London: SCM 1984) 60-73; Vincent Brümmer, "Farrer, Wiles and the Causal Joint," *Modern Theology* 8.1 (Jan. 1992) 1-14; John R. Lucas, *Freedom and Grace* (London: SPCK 1976); John B. Cobb, Jr. "Natural Causality and Divine Action," *God's Activity in the World: The Contemporary Problem*, ed. Owen C. Thomas, AAR Studies in Religion 31 (Chico, CA: Scholars 1983) 101-16 (reprinted from *Idealistic Studies* 3 [1973]: 307-22); Brian Hebblethwaite, *Evil, Suffering and Religion* (London: SPCK 2000); Gordon Kaufman, "On the Meaning of 'Act of God'," Thomas 137-61; Gordon Kaufman, *Systematic Theology: A Historicist Perspective* (New York: Scribner 1968) 299-313; Philip Clayton, *God*

likely is, some degree of free play in the rest of the world as well, so that the instability present in certain kinds of unstable and highly dynamic systems[1] may enable God to affect the development of those systems without "faking or forcing the natural story."[2]

What science tells us about the world doesn't make God's persuasive action impossible. The implausibility of universal determinism makes it unlikely that scientific laws can be expected to explain everything that occurs; instead, such laws simply describe certain natural regularities in isolation from any factors—the choices of free agents, for instance—except ones clearly specified.[3]

Science, at any rate, does not establish either that any sort of divine action is impossible or that we could never be confident it had occurred. Whatever we say about the scientific assessment of any particular claim regarding divine activity, however, we must think of God's way with the world as the way of persuasive love, mediated in and through the processes of the created order and the free actions of creatures.

The Character of God's Loving Action

More specifically, I think, a plausible account of God's action in the world will include the following elements:

• Such action must, first of all, be *mediated* action. God must be seen as acting in and through the finite elements of the created order. And God's will in the world is achieved as free creatures respond appropriately to divine inspiration and sub-personal creaturely realities react fittingly to divine persuasion.[4]

• Because it is mediated, divine action is, in principle, *hidden* from finite view. God's providential work occurs in and through the processes of the created world, so, it shouldn't surprise us that it isn't easy to identify.[5]

• Particular divine actions will be *consistent with each other*. They will find their meaning and justification in light of the "big picture." And, as part of that big picture, they cohere with their context. They make sense as part of the overall narrative of cosmic and human history. Every event is conditioned by what precedes it, and itself conditions whatever follows it, even though no strict necessity requires that a given event yield a certain outcome.[6]

My body, my memory, and my social context all limit the possibilities of action open to me in various ways, and render some available options more attractive than others.[7] Thus, any human action will be linked in a meaningful way with the diverse range of influences that help to shape it. Telling a coherent story about my action requires appropriate reference to these influences. Respecting the continuities in each agent's story, including the agent's own self-chosen purposes,

---

and Contemporary Science (Edinburgh: Edinburgh UP 1997) 188-269; David Ray Griffin, *A Process Christology* (Lanham, MD: UP of America 1990) 206-16.

1. See Ward 113-5.
2. The phrase is Farrer's.
3. Cp. Allen 165-71; Richard Swinburne, *The Concept of Miracle* (New York: St. Martin's 1970) 23-32; Ward 170-89; David Basinger and Randall Basinger, *Philosophy and Miracle: The Contemporary Debate*, Problems in Contemporary Philosophy 2 (Lewistown, NY: Mellen 1986) 31-58; William J. Abraham, *Divine Revelation and the Limits of Historical Criticism* (Oxford: OUP 1982).
4. Cp. Tillich 1: 266-7; Ward 133; Hebblethwaite, *Evil*.
5. See Farrer, *Faith* 62-7; Ward 75.
6. Cp. Kaufman, "Meaning"; Kaufman, *Theology* 299-313.
7. Thomas F. Tracy, "Narrative Theology and the Acts of God," Hebblethwaite and Henderson 173-96.

God can contribute "to the orienting conditions"[1] of our actions—the natural, social, and personal conditions of which we must take account when we act—and offers novel possibilities where appropriate. "God does not enact our actions, but God does shape the processes by which we shape ourselves."[2]

God's Purposes and Ours

It is all too easy to equate our own purposes with God's. We are tempted to pretend that we can read God's purposes off of the data of our history in relatively straightforward fashion. But the "person for whom the paradigm of divine action is the Cross of Christ, knows in [her or] his heart of hearts that the pattern of divine action is unlikely closely to coincide with the patterns perceived, the projects formulated, by our limited, fearful and deeply egocentric and ethnocentric vision . . . ."[3] We cannot pretend to be so confident about what God is up to in the world that we are tempted to conceive of God as simply the underwriter of our own agendas.

Belief in God's loving work in the world entails the conviction that God is present and active in uniquely appropriate ways in our lives. The conviction that God is love implies that God is responsive to particular circumstances. And it encourages the conviction that human history is meaningful, that God is at work to tie together the various strands of our personal and communal stories into a significant unity, a unity marked by the ultimate flourishing of everyone. But the belief that God acts particularly is a deduction from the premise that God is love; it is not based on the judgment that we know what God is doing in any particular case. It does not encourage the conviction that we can actually *discern* the way in which any given circumstance contributes to this goal.[4]

The attempt to read a divine purpose out of every event can result in arrogance, if we identify God's plans with ours. But it can also lead to unnecessary frustration and anger with God, if we assume that God's hand lies behind every tragedy we experience. And it can tend to make us irresponsible, if we simply wait indefinitely for God to resolve our problems, ignoring opportunities to take the initiative to address the challenges we face because we do not discern an overt

---

1. Tracy, "Theology" 190; cp. 192-3. Among the media for divine influence in our lives, Tracy notes "the liturgical life of the community . . . and in special episodes of religious experiences or in deep structures of religious consciousness," as well as "a wide range of episodes from ordinary life that shape what sort of person one becomes, *e.g.*, in insights into the needs or character or experience of others, in the courage to take risks for the sake of justice or love, in moments of joy and wonder or of exhaustion and despair, in nagging dissatisfactions with the character of our attachments, in a drive to deepened self-knowledge and richer relationship with others, in an expansive desire for fullness of life, and so on" (191).

2. Tracy, "Theology" 195-6; see also Allen 176-8. Cp. Cobb, "Causality": "For God to exercise real influence upon me does restrict me in the sense that I must take account of that influence. But it does not determine *how* I take account of it. Instead, it provides a context of decision in which my range of choices are [sic] extended and made more significant" (115). For a more recent articulation of Cobb's view of particular providence, see "The Relativization of the Trinity," *Trinity in Process: A Relational Theology of God*, ed. Joseph A. Bracken and Marjorie Hewitt Suchocki (New York: Continuum 1997) 13-20.

3. Nicholas Lash, "'These Things Were Here and But the Beholder Wanting,'" *Theology on Dover Beach* (London: Darton 1979) 152. Cp. Tillich 1: 268-9.

4. Cp. Kaufman: "The purpose that informs an act is an interior connection between the various phases of events known to the agent who is performing it, and it is seldom directly visible to external observers, especially to those who can see only a tiny fraction of the total act in question." ("Meaning" 151).

divine response to our needs. We need, I think, to grant our inability to tell exactly what God is up to.

God's Spirit is active in every event, seeking to realize particular purposes. But we know that the divine will is too often not done. And, even when it is, we frequently cannot be certain what God's will *is*. We believe that God wills justice and creation's flourishing, and, in light of this belief, we can make some judgments about divine action. At least tentatively, we can identify large-scale historical patterns that involve the realization of what we understand God to intend as reflecting the effectiveness of God's persuasive providence.[1] "A Christian has his accepted works of the divine hand, which give him his types of Providence in action. In view of these he appreciates the ever-new works of God."[2] But we cannot always be sure, even with respect to communal, national, or global events, whether justice is done or flourishing achieved. And we will unavoidably be even less certain whether this is so with respect to the events of our individual lives. We lack perspective, insight, and relevant information.

Because God is love, God's relationship with each creature and with each event will be particular. But because God's Spirit's power is the power of loving persuasion, we must acknowledge that, all too often, God's will is not done in the world. But because of the freedom, flexibility, and responsiveness of creation, we can be confident that God's will *can* be done, God's purposes achieved, in our lives and in the life of the whole creation.

God's Spirit and the Reception of Revelation

Love seeks not only to speak but to be understood. That is why Christians have seen God's Spirit at work not only in God's self-disclosure to us in creation and history and reason and tradition and experience, but also in the reception and transmission of revelation.

Any time we appropriate God's revelation, God's Spirit is at work in our lives to ensure that we understand correctly what God seeks to communicate to us and that we apply the understanding God seeks us to gain correctly to our lives. Revelation is, as I have stressed, God's work, love's work, from beginning to end. But Christians have talked, in particular, about God's work facilitating the reception of revelation with respect to the preparation of the books that make up the Bible. Here, they have spoken of *inspiration*.

An account of divine action consistent with a suitable response to the problem of evil has clear implications for our view of inspiration. The fact of sin is exceptionally good evidence against the view that God's will is perfectly accomplished under any and every circumstance. And even where sin is not directly an issue, finitude and fallibility still often keep people from realizing God's will.

Thus, to believe that God was present and active in the lives of the biblical writers, and in their activities as writers, is not to believe that God's Spirit overrode or canceled the operation of their cognitive faculties, removed them from their cultural contexts, or bypassed their normal thought processes to reconfigure their categories of understanding. God met them where they were. God's Spirit worked in and through their distinctive personal and cultural circumstances, and their reception of divine self-revelation unavoidably bears the impress of their distinctive circumstances.[3]

1. Cp. Griffin, *Christology* 206-17.
2. Farrer, *Faith* 64. Thanks to Alexander Lian for the opportunity to discuss these matters.
3. Cp. William J. Abraham, *The Divine Inspiration of Holy Scripture* (Oxford: OUP 1981); John Barton, *People of the Book? The Bible in Christianity* (London: SPCK 1988);

There is no *a priori* argument that could show that God's will was not done perfectly by the writers of the Bible. It is logically possible that, although the biblical authors were, like other human beings, both fallible and sinful, their understandings of God, humanity, and nature never prevented them from conveying just what God wanted. But what is *not* logically possible is that God could have *guaranteed* that they would do so, given their freedom. Creaturely freedom can and must play an integral part in our defense of divine goodness in the face of evil. The same considerations that make an appeal to freedom in this context appropriate must render belief in divinely ensured biblical inerrancy untenable.[1]

After all, if God could guarantee that the divine will was perfectly done by free human authors of the Bible, God could also, presumably, guarantee that other human choices were perfectly free and nonetheless perfectly embodied the divine will. And this would leave us with the inescapable question: Why didn't God do this consistently, and so eliminate all evils? If God does not override the freedom of creatures in general to ensure their conformity with the divine will, then we have good reason for believing that God did not do so in relation to the biblical writers in particular.

This realization must lead us to take seriously the embeddedness of the biblical materials in history, and so their inseparability from the cultural contexts in which they were produced, as well as their writers' individual histories and experiences. Further, insofar as we regard God as having successfully communicated with humankind in and through the Bible, then—given what we believe about God—an important hermeneutical principle follows. "[I]f a tentative interpretation of divine discourse has the implication, so far as one can tell, that God would have said or suggested something false or something conducing to what is incompatible with love, that alone is sufficient ground for rejecting the proposed interpretation."[2]

In any case, however, God's Spirit's work takes place in a real world of free creatures. To talk about inspiration is to acknowledge that God cares about preserving and extending the insights gained by human communities in response to divine revelation. It is to emphasize that God continues to be active in our appropriation of revelation, rather than simply retreating in deistic fashion to let events run their course. But belief in God's Spirit's inspiration does not provide us with a foolproof safeguard against the effects of human sin and fallibility on the mediation of God's intentions to the world. Instead, it points to God's Spirit's ceaseless attempts to enable us better to respond to God's unfailing love.

God's Spirit and Prayer

We respond in love to God's creation and God's activity in the world in more than one way. Prayer is an especially important response, in which we

---

David Brown, "God and Symbolic Action," Hebblethwaite and Henderson; L. William Countryman, *Biblical Authority or Biblical Tyranny?* (Philadelphia: Trinity; Cambridge, MA: Cowley 1994); Austin Farrer, *The Glass of Vision*, Bampton Lectures 1948 (London: Dacre 1948); Henry Habberly Price, "Paranormal Cognition, Symbolism, and Inspiration," *Essays in the Philosophy of Religion* (Oxford: Clarendon-OUP 1972) 21-36.

1. See David Basinger and Randall Basinger, "Inerrancy, Dictation, and the Free Will Defense," *Evangelical Quarterly* 55.3 (July 1983): 177-80; David Basinger, "Inerrancy and Free Will: Some Further Thoughts," *Evangelical Quarterly* 58.4 (Oct. 1985): 351-4. Cp. Austin Farrer, "Infallibility and Historical Revelation," *Interpretation and Belief*, ed. Charles C. Conti (London: SPCK 1976) 151-64.

2. Nicholas P. Wolterstorff, *Divine Discourse: Philosophical Reflections on the Claim that God Speaks* (Cambridge: CUP 1995) 226. For caveats—organized around the question, "Has Scripture become a wax nose?"—see Wolterstorff 223-39.

attend directly and lovingly to God. Prayer expresses and deepens our loving engagement with God.

Traditionally, Christian prayer has been understood as prayer *with* Jesus, *to* "the Father," *in* "the Holy Spirit." The Christian enters into the relationship with of trust and dependence with the God Jesus adored and trusted as "Father," a relationship modeled by Jesus; behind the believer's prayerful address to God is the hidden, self-effacing activity of God's Spirit.[1] Our address to God in prayer is evoked by divine action. We who pray are *products* of divine action. We *imitate* and *participate in* divine action by modeling our prayer lives and our spirituality after that of Jesus. Prayer turns out to exhibit a kind of special case of what seems to be the necessary structure of God's self-revelation to humankind. God is involved not only in revelation but also—through God's Spirit—in its reception.

The way we think about God's Spirit as active in the world is especially important as we try to understand certain kinds of prayer. We confess, we praise God's glory, we share our inner experiences with God as we might with human friends. And these kinds of prayers don't obviously presuppose specific accounts of divine action. But at least two other kinds of prayers do: prayers in which we *thank* God for things, and prayers in which we *ask* God for things.[2]

Thanksgiving and Divine Action

When I pray a prayer of thanks, I am noting with delight the fact that things would be different than they are had God acted otherwise. Not all prayers of thanks are responses to special divine acts. I can thank God for a sunset, for instance, without supposing that it was arranged exclusively or primarily for my benefit. As a well-fed Westerner, at least, I can thank God for a meal without assuming that any startling, divinely arranged coincidence lies behind its arrival on my table. I am dependent for my food on God through a whole chain of secondary causes—natural processes, social structures, predictable personal decisions. Because God is at the root of everything that is, we can thank God for sustaining us and the world in being, and for shaping the natural structures that make all sorts of good things in life possible.[3]

But the situation becomes more complicated when I thank God for things that aren't simply regular features of the natural and social environment—my reconciliation with an estranged friend, for instance. The difficulty here is simply that God's will, as we know, is often not done. God is not in the business of determining coercively how things will go. God doesn't simply choose that everything which *does* occur *should* occur. So why should I hold God any more responsible for my friend's change of heart (and mine) than for anything else that happens, good or bad?

God's providential action takes place in and through the elements of the created world, and thus is affected by the integrity and freedom of creatures. We cannot precisely discern the trajectory of God's providential action, though we can identify it with greater clarity in retrospect through its effects. But we know that God is love, and therefore at work for the good. Thus, we may suppose that God's

---

1. See Leonard Hodgson, *The Doctrine of the Trinity* (New York: Scribner 1944) 39, 41.
2. The best recent discussion of prayer is Marjorie Suchocki, *In God's Presence: Theological Reflections on Prayer* (St. Louis, MO: Chalice 1996). For a general treatment of the issue of petitionary prayer—not sufficiently engaged with what I take to be the central problem, but suggestive nonetheless—see Timothy Gorringe, *God's Theatre: A Theology of Providence* (London: SCM 1991) 88-103.
3. Cp. Rahner, *Foundations* 88-9.

persuasive providence has contributed to shaping any situation we have reason to think is a good one.[1]

Indeed, anything which takes place in the created order and which is in accordance with God's purposes can be ascribed to God. Divine creative agency is a necessary condition of every event. But we typically view someone as responsible for an event—when some action of hers is a necessary condition for the event's occurrence—if she intended the event to happen, rather than simply recognizing it as a foreseen but unintended by-product of her action. God must know regarding any divine decision that it makes possible some events and renders others impossible. And because God is creator, no event is explicable without reference to God. God is therefore aware of the possible consequences of every divine decision, and intends that the good consequences should take place. Thus, God intends that every good event which *does* happen *should* happen. So we can be thankful to God for any event we believe is good.[2]

Petition and Divine Action

We do not, of course, only thank God for events that have already occurred; we also sometimes ask God that particular future events occur. Asking God for things in prayer may seem to be an odd sort of thing to do. The possibility of particular divine action means that God *can* respond to our prayers. In this sense, prayer could clearly make a difference. But why God *should* do so is another question. When I pray, an objector might argue, what I want is either likely to make my life (or the world) better or likely to make my life (or the world) worse. But if things would be better if my prayer were answered than if any alternatives were realized, then God should do what I ask (within the constraints set by the reality of creation) whether or not I ask for it, since God—being good—must be seeking to bring about as much good as possible. On the other hand, if things would be worse were God to answer my prayer than they would be were God to do something else, then God shouldn't grant my request, since my own limited and doubtless egocentric perspective shouldn't be allowed to determine what God does.[3]

This challenge is, at root, a challenge to the very possibility of free divine action. It implies that whatever God does, God does necessarily, because God's love means God must always seek the best possible state of affairs in any given situation. But it isn't at all clear that the value of states of affairs can be compared in the way this challenge suggests. If there isn't one unit of value, to which all other measures of value can be reduced, then no rank ordering of states of affairs can be rationally necessary if each comprises several different aspects of human welfare.

One could define the maximally best state of affairs for human beings—of any human being—only if there were some single and clearly defined purpose for all human lives or if all aspects of human welfare could be assessed in terms of some single, underlying measure of value. But there are diverse sorts of good persons and good lives and good experiences, all legitimate if proper attention is paid to all the other dimensions of well-being that claim our attention. And there is no reason to suppose that there exists one unit of value against which all other putative values can be assessed. Economists may treat the price of something as its value, but, unless you believe that this provides you with an exhaustive account of the nature of goodness, you won't suppose that their model can be used to determine the way the universe ought to work.

1. On the notion of mediated particular providence as applied specifically to prayer, see Gorringe 34-46; Baelz, *Answer* 29-37; Baelz, *Prayer*; Brümmer, *Inquiry*.
2. Brümmer, "Farrer" 9-11.
3. Keith Ward (159), on whose own thinking I draw in this section, attributes this formulation of the problem to Origen.

Trying to add up the different aspects of welfare realized in a given event "is *senseless* . . . in the way that it is senseless to try to sum together the size of this page, the number six, and the mass of this book."[1] So it is not possible to compare states of affairs based on quantitative measurements of the dimensions of well-being realized in each. And if we cannot, then we needn't criticize God for choosing one set of goods over another in response to a prayer in the way this objection seems to imply one can. Most or all possible situations will involve multiple values which can legitimately be weighted in different ways. So the options God confronts in determining whether or not to answer a prayer will not necessarily be strictly comparable.[2]

Further, the fact that I want something, that I *choose* it, is one of the things that give it value.[3] God values our own freedom and creativity, and it may be that sometimes God gives us what we ask for because we have asked for it (though we may suppose that, after the fashion of a loving parent, God often wisely refuses to grant irresponsible requests). And the fact that I *ask* for something—recognizing both my dependence on God and the contingency of the divine answer (I'm asking for a gift, not demanding a right)—may sometimes make a difference in determining whether it is really desirable for God to give it to me. My attitude toward God and toward the situation obviously makes a difference in determining the appropriateness of the gift and its value to me. "Our asking, and thus our acknowledgment of our reliance upon God both in general and for the fulfilment of a specific desire, will change God's assessment of what is the best possible thing to do."[4]

The Special Problem of Intercession

Though the same general principles apply, intercessory prayer presents a special problem: even if may sometimes be good for God to help *me* only if I ask, what about asking God for something on behalf of someone else? Suppose I pray for the healing of a friend's cancer—or a friend's marriage. Why should my prayer for another person make a difference in the course of such events? It seems problematic to say that, say, missioner Adams was saved from hostile villagers because, just as they were about to attack, her home congregation was praying for her, while missioner Zitkowski, faced by the same villagers, died because a worship leader back home forgot to mention *her* to the congregation. God's Spirit must be supposed to work on behalf of all of us, including those for whom no one prays.

---

1. See John Finnis, *Natural Law and Natural Rights*, Clarendon Law Series (Oxford: Clarendon-OUP 1980) 113; cp. 95-7, 110-8, 131-2, for Finnis's critique of consequentialism because of, among other things, its assumption that the good can be maximized.

2. These sorts of considerations form the basis for a response to the claim by David A. Pailin, *Probing the Foundations: A Study in Theistic Reconstruction* (Kampen: Pharos 1994), that "God, as perfect, can[not] coherently be held to have any freedom to choose how to respond to each accidental situation." Pailin's argument is that "if God be held always (as perfect, *necessarily* always) to respond to each situation by seeking to secure the maximum increase in value, it is questionable whether God can be held to have the freedom of personal creativity as well as the total awareness of each circumstance and of what is best for each future actual entity when this is considered in relation to the future of all others" (225). Expressions like "maximum increase in value" and "what is best for each future actual entity" lack determinate content. The incommensurability of goods means that a variety of options will be open to God in each case without the divine perfection's being compromised.

3. See Ward 160-1.

4. Ward 161. Note that Ward is elsewhere—rightly—suspicious that there is ever a "best possible thing to do."

Intercessory prayer may be seen, like many other varieties of petitionary prayer, as an alignment of oneself with God's (apparent) purposes in whatever circumstances one is praying about. Thus, for instance, "God, please heal Dex's lung cancer" means, in part, "God, you know I care about Dex, and I know you care about him, too, and I hope for the success of whatever you are doing to bring healing into his life."

But "God, please heal Dex's lung cancer" typically means more than *just* that. Intercessory prayer clearly reflects a desire that God do something in response to a request from a creature. Despite the seeming problem of arbitrariness, I think we can make some sense of this possibility. Our intercessory prayers, like our other petitionary prayers, may make available to God resources that would not otherwise have been at God's disposal. In our praying, we may give God opportunities to benefit others that would not have obtained otherwise.

An intercessory prayer is, implicitly, a request that God empower *me* to make an appropriate difference in the situation about which I'm praying. It may be a way of opening myself to God's love, and thus rendering myself better able to be a mediator of God's healing presence to the world. We effectively offer God our cooperation in aiding those for whom we pray, insofar as we have the ability to affect their lives. Thus, the more people who pray intercessory prayers, the better, for each may be able to contribute something to God's work in the world.[1]

In addition, our intercessory prayers are themselves realities of which others—including those for whom we pray and those in a position to aid or harm them—must take account. In and through God, we are all connected. Even if unconsciously, everyone must respond to every event in the world in one way or another. Our praying subtly changes the background against which everyone's choices must be made.[2] And in so doing, of course, it creates new possibilities for divine action.[3] This action will, like all other kinds of divine activity, be constrained by creation's integrity and freedom. And the extent to which our prayers can make a difference for others will vary from situation to situation. But it is clear that our prayers *can* make *some* difference.

---

1. So Brümmer, *Inquiry* 58.

2. See Henry Habberly Price, "Petitionary Prayer and Telepathy," *Essays* 37-55; Suchocki, *Presence*; Marjorie H. Suchocki, *God–Christ–Church: A Practical Guide to Process Theology*, rev. ed. (New York: Crossroad 1992) 219-22. Prices argues that our minds are able to influence the world and each other in ways none of us really understands very well, and there is evidence that our minds connect us with each other, even if—typically—only at the unconscious level. If there are mental links among persons, then petitionary prayer of all sorts could advantage of these connections. Prayer could open up access to these connections, allowing God to touch others through them without doing anything miraculous. In particular, there may be times when only *our* praying will open up particular links with others, links that are distinctively ours, to God's healing and empowering influence. Prayer may take advantage, on occasion, of particular resonances that exist between us and other people. Prayer on behalf of someone with whom I have such a resonant relationship may allow God to make use of the special channel that binds me to that other person. It might, for instance, enable God to empower me as I touch my friend in the mysterious ways our mental links make possible, and thus bless her in and through my action.

The best current empirical analyses of the relevant sorts of phenomena are offered by Dean Radin; see *The Conscious Universe: The Scientific Truth of Psychic Phenomena* (San Francisco: Harper 1997) and *Entangled Minds: Extrasensory Experiences in a Quantum Reality* (New York: Paraview 2006). For a careful philosophical examination, see David Ray Griffin, *Parapsychology, Philosophy, and Spirituality: A Postmodern Exploration*, SUNY Series in Constructive Postmodern Thought (Albany: SUNY 1997).

3. Cp. Tillich 1: 267.

We cannot ask God to do magic tricks for our benefit or for the welfare of our friends. But we can contribute through our intercessory prayers to God's healing work in the world.

God's Spirit and Spiritual Gifts

Love gives. God's love empowers creatures for their own good and for the good of others. The idea that God's Spirit enables members of the Christian community to perform a variety of diverse but interconnected tasks is an inspiring and empowering one. This notion, the notion of spiritual gifts, occurs on several occasions in the Newer Testament. Its readers are invited to see God at work in a variety of ways, to identify God's action as lying at the root of a variety of human capacities and activities that contribute to the life of the Christian church, including assistance, compassion, evangelism, exhortation, faith, giving, leadership, ministry, service, teaching, wisdom, apostleship, the discernment of spirits, healing, prophecy, knowledge, speaking in and interpreting tongues, and the ability to perform "deeds of power."

The process of selecting pastors or appointing local church officers often seems mundane and prosaic. How does it help to talk about the capacities that enable people to fulfill the tasks associated with these positions as *spiritual* gifts? Are these gifts identical with our natural talents? Such questions are especially puzzling because of our increasing awareness of the role of interacting genetic, developmental, familial, and socio-cultural factors in shaping our abilities, and the evident absence from our experience of extraordinary, immediate divine acts that leave us gifted in ways we were not before. What is the difference between the spiritual gifts the Newer Testament and the Christian tradition maintain are conferred on Christians by the Holy Spirit and the endowments received from our ancestors and our environment or developed by means of our own choices? And does the answer matter?

The Significance of Gift-Language

To speak of *gifts* when describing these endowments matters for several reasons. Viewing our capacities as gifts affects not only how we understand and use them but also how we understand ourselves.

The gift is among the most evocative metaphors available to us spiritually, morally, existentially.[1] For Christians, all of life, every aspect of ordered existence, is a gift. The presents we give each other are simply symbols, sacraments, of all the varied gifts we receive and offer—sometimes fitfully, sometimes with mixed motives, but sometimes in love and with power.

To say that something—anything—is a gift is to say both that it is a given, and that someone gave it. This is, first of all, to emphasize that a gift is something I did not produce. It is not the result of my achievement or my performance or my activity. It just *is*. Thus, I cannot take credit for it. I do not deserve acclaim for it. The givenness of the gift means that it cannot warrant pride or arrogance.

Not only is a gift a *given*; it is received from *another*. It is thus an occasion for gratitude. If it was given to me by someone, then I must recognize and appreciate and celebrate the giver's generosity. Further, a gift plays a role in a relationship with the giver. Identifying a trait as a divine gift may underscore divine care for one's life—perhaps, in some cases, particular concern for one as an individual.

Recognizing the divine generosity that lies at the root of a gift can highlight one's special responsibility to use the gift in service to God. When, as in 1

---

1. See Stephen H. Webb, *The Gifting God: A Trinitarian Ethics of Excess* (New York: OUP 1996).

Tim., a gift is seen as conferred directly through the activity of the community, its authority and one's dependence on it may also be accentuated.

Acknowledging that one's capacities are rooted in God's action, and so in God's love, can also highlight the distinctive potential contribution of one's gifts to God's ongoing activity in history. It may thus be a source of confidence and power—not only for individuals but for the church as a whole. The presence of spiritual gifts in the church may be understood as a sign that there is something distinctive that the church is in a position to do.

The sense that one's contribution is distinctive may suggest that one's role, though *significant*, is *limited*, and finds its meaning in relation to the correlative roles of others. If God is the giver, then divine purposes can be seen to underlie the distribution of gifts, and God can be understood as creating an interdependent community marked by mutual giving.[1] Further, just as the givenness of gifts means that they cannot warrant pride, so their function in preserving, extending, and enriching the community may imply that one need feel no regret at the lack of a given gift. Gifts are not given for our individual benefit alone, but for service to God's world.

If God gives spiritual gifts, then perhaps we can *expect* these gifts to be made available. To believe that these gifts come from God is to believe that we can appropriately ask God for them, and that God will seek to provide them to meet our needs. Gift-language thus serves as a source of confidence in the provision of opportunities to touch the world effectively with God's love.

This cluster of ideas—gift as trust and source of responsibility, gift as relational bond, gift as the product of something other than the recipient's will, gift as intended for service, gift as an element of communal interdependence, gift-giving as a basis for hope—gives the idea of *spiritual gift* its distinctive character. It helps to explain why the use of gift-language matters as we try to understand the traits we might want to characterize as spiritual gifts. Accepting spiritual gifts as gifts means accepting the interdependence that unites us with the other members of the church, and of the wider society, in relationships of mutual giving. It also means recognizing and celebrating the unique contributions our gifts enable us to make to others. Acknowledging spiritual gifts—and others we wouldn't normally label the same way, as well—*as gifts* leads naturally to gratitude toward God and, in turn, to generosity toward others.

To be sure, we should not overestimate the importance of talking about gifts as opposed to talents. Obviously, if each of us were the product of an utterly blind evolutionary process, our personal endowments could and should still be regarded as *givens*. Nature and culture—not our own self-creating wills—would still equip us with our capacities. And so we would still not be free to regard them simply as prized possessions to be hoarded. They would not warrant ascriptions of merit to us.[2] A significant part of the moral and existential core of gift-talk would remain even without reference to any action by God. But Christians have wanted to say more than this. As I have already noted, Christian talk about spiritual gifts highlights the responsibilities that flow from our endowments and their place in our relationships with God.

---

1. This seems to be St. Paul's point in 1 Corinthians.
2. Thus, John Rawls has used the fact that natural endowments are not the products of our efforts to justify his contention that they do not confer on us any inherent rights to access to power, wealth, self-respect, and other goods. See, *e.g.*, *A Theory of Justice*, rev. ed. (Cambridge, MA: Belknap-Harvard UP 1999).

Spiritual Gifts and Divine Action

It is clear that gift-language *functions* in a particular way, that it encourages particular attitudes or behaviors. But it does so because it also embodies an *assumption*—that our gifts are attributable to God. The understanding of divine action I have developed here suggests a model of how God might give us spiritual gifts and thus of the relationship between such gifts and natural talents.

Creation is the primary form of divine action. God exercises enormous influence simply as the designer of the basic patterns, structures, and processes that underlie the world's operation. In addition, the fact that, as creator, God can anticipate the possibility of particular events in the world as a consequence of divine creative activity makes God responsible for those events which God not only anticipates but intends.

Therefore, even if, as deism unpersuasively maintains, God simply established the initial conditions for the operation of a world which proceeded along its course undisturbed, we could still reasonably speak of capacities for such activities as leadership, teaching, and exhortation as divine gifts. Anticipating the possibility that we would come into being and that we would possess particular endowments makes God responsible for these endowments as creator, provided God intends our possession of these gifts. On this basis alone, we can speak of natural talents as, at the same time, divine gifts.[1]

Special Providence as a Source of Spiritual Gifts

I believe we can say more than this, however. We can see God at work not only in the establishment of the initial conditions of the universe but also in its ongoing development, not only in the creation of human life but in the formation of particular genetic patterns over time. We can see God's Spirit's gentle but relentless persuasion in the growth of societies and cultures and in the birth and ongoing life of particular relationships. Thus, we can see God's influence at work in and through those processes by means of which particular persons are formed and equipped for service. We can see the divine intention expressed in and through those events as a consequence of which we acquire our genetic endowments—at every level from the molecular to the societal and beyond. And we can see God's Spirit at work in and through those processes by which we are formed—in the broadest sense—environmentally. In none of these cases will the divine intention probably be realized perfectly: sin and fallibility will take their respective tolls, and the reality of creation what God's Spirit can accomplish in any given situation. Still, at all times and in all circumstances, God's Spirit will be at work to shape our capacities.

Creation is an ongoing process that includes what God does through us as well as what God does in the non-human world. And since God is always at work in and through every event in the world, creation includes everything we do. God's providential action takes place *in and through* ours; it is not, of course, simply identical with ours. But, with that qualifier, we can surely say that God creates in and through the social relationships and developmental processes that shape our gifts, as well as through our genes.[2] Our natural talents are also our spiritual gifts.

---

1. So Brümmer, "Farrer."
2. Cp. Nicholas Lash, *Believing Three Ways in One God: A Reading of the Apostles' Creed* (Notre Dame, IN: U of Notre Dame P 1993) 51-3. "Does not God make cities as well as stars? Is God's self-gift, the Spirit's presence, less intimately and immediately constitutive of promises and symphonies than of plutonium and silt? ... Does not God make cities as well as stars, symphonies as well as silt?"

Spiritual Gifts as Fostered by Christian Belief and Christian Community

It would be possible simply to *define* a spiritual gift as an endowment arising from God's Spirit's work, intended for the service of God's world, and used as part of God's providence for this purpose. And this would capture most of what needs saying about the relationship between natural talents and spiritual gifts. But it needs to be qualified in light of a dynamic understanding of human nature. There is no reason to suppose that all human capacities are simply fixed in rigid fashion. And so Christian belief and Christian community can make a distinctive contribution to who we are.

As a result, we can make some sense of the way in which spiritual gifts might be thought to be related particularly to the church, as they seem to be in the Newer Testament. Life in the church will contribute to the shaping and re-shaping of a person's character, to the formation of a distinct structure of existence—the Christian structure of existence.[1] Her identity and the way she sees and feels and thinks and acts will be affected, to one degree or another, by her immersion in the church. What she is inclined to do, what tasks she can perform joyfully—and thus effectively—will be different from what they would be if she were rooted in some other concrete community, or in no concrete community at all. Her awareness of options, and the attractiveness of those options, will be different because she is a Christian. She may be able to hear and respond to a divine call to which she would otherwise have been deaf. God's Spirit may give a person a gift, then, by leading her into a community in which who she *is* is transformed. (This is not to deny the obvious point that God can give gifts to people who belong to other communities, or none, or that a person's membership in some other community may facilitate God's fostering of the development of particular gifts.)

Immersion in the church's story, its practices, its doctrines, its common life can awaken new feelings and perspectives that condition the development of new gifts or bring dormant gifts to life. But God's Spirit can also give us spiritual gifts through the church because the *institutional structure* of the church includes settings in which particular dispositions for service are fostered and particular opportunities for service are provided.

What God can do in the world is a function of the opportunities creaturely circumstances present to God. It is unlikely that God could lead a pre-Newtonian mathematician to articulate the essence of quantum cosmology, or that God could make someone with my physique and skill-set a professional basketball player. Some circumstances will present God with opportunities that others will not. Mother Theresa, for instance, probably would not have heard a call to serve the poor of India had she been a wife and mother rather than a nun. A church-based health care, development, or educational institution can foster the development of new gifts or the transformation of existing capacities in order to facilitate their contribution to the church's work in the world. The opportunity to occupy a church office may have a similar effect. A person's connection with the church may provide God with a chance to gift her in a distinctive way.

Belonging to the church will affect our inclinations and awaken our capacities. It will also change what we do because what we do will *mean* something new. The *objective* significance of a thing, an act, or an event depends upon its connection with other contemporary, past, or future things or acts or events. We know very little about a lawyer's life, for instance, if we know only that she defends or prosecutes murder defendants. Who the defendants are, why she assists or confronts them in the courtroom, what will happen to them if they are

---

1. See John B. Cobb, Jr., *The Structure of Christian Existence* (Philadelphia: Westminster 1967).

convicted—a whole host of factors contribute to the meaning of a single act: typing a brief on a narrow point of law, rising to lodge an objection, questioning a witness. Similarly, the *subjective* meaning of an act to the actor will depend on how the actor relates what she does to a broader context, to an array of relevant circumstances. The subjective meaning of a thing or an event to a given perceiver will depend on how she relates what she perceives to other realities that give it significance. Meanings are not fixed by circumstances in isolation.

Thus, superficially similar acts done inside and outside the church may have different meanings, and thus be different acts.[1] I may drive a truckload of food to a refugee camp in order to keep people alive so they can fight in the coming revolution; to curry favor with a demanding God; to express my gratitude for divine love; to express my love for vulnerable and infinitely valuable children of God; to fulfill my contract with Oxfam; to pay off a karmic debt; to poison the refugees living at the camp; or, no doubt, for a variety of other reasons. That I locate my actions within the Christian story may mean, then, that their significance varies markedly from what it might be in another setting. Their place in a particular story, together with my motives for doing them, may render them distinctive and different from similar acts performed by someone else. The point is not, of course, that God cannot touch the world with love through the things Muslims or secular humanists do, but only that what they do may not always be the same in meaning as what Christians do even if it is the same in immediate, overt content. This is another reason, then, that Christian's gifts may be special and new.

When we develop and exercise gifts in the church, *we* must choose, at least in part, what to do. God cannot and does not choose for us. God can make no one a preacher, a teacher, an administrator, or anything else against that person's will. But God can woo a person into the church, where she may develop new capacities. God can call her into circumstances where existing talents—themselves God's gifts—can be offered up in service to God. And the very disposition with which she chooses has been affected since the first moment of her life by God's activity: the energy and the inclination to respond to God's many calls themselves reflect God's ongoing, loving presence and influence.

The capacities and endowments of those outside the church are, of course, also God's gifts. Biological, developmental, relational, and cultural factors mediate God's gifts—truly but imperfectly—to all people. "*Every* generous act of giving, with every perfect gift, is from above, coming down from the Father of lights . . . ."[2] The divine Word is spoken of as the "true light, which enlightens *everyone* . . . ."[3] Generosity, insight, and all other good gifts come from God. But, if we find it useful to do so, we can speak of the gifts exercised within the church as *spiritual* gifts as a kind of shorthand, to acknowledge their origin and purpose, and because within the church their ground and goal are understood and proclaimed.

- Those to whom these gifts are given are *aware* that their lives and capacities are God's gifts, and they acknowledge their gifts as given to further God's purposes in the world.
- People who identify with the church therefore choose to use their gifts to further God's purposes in particular ways.
- To the extent that the church has particularly valuable insights into God's purposes, it may be able to provide particular assistance to its members in furthering those purposes.

---

1. Stewart R. Sutherland makes this point nicely (the refugee camp example is his) in his contribution to *The Philosophical Frontiers of Christian Theology: Essays Presented to D. M. MacKinnon*, ed. Brian Hebblethwaite and Sutherland (Cambridge: CUP 1982).
2. Jas. 1:17a; my italics.
3. Jn. 1:9a; my italics.

Some of these gifts look relatively ordinary: the gift of leadership or teaching, say. Others are truly remarkable, apparently involving capacities, quite beyond those of ordinary persons, to know or understand or to touch the lives of others—special insight into God's purposes or the needs of others, for instance, or the ability to heal diseases of mind and body.[1] If God seeks to heal and perfect the world, then divine power will certainly seek to evoke such gifts for the benefit of creation. Persuasive divine providence cannot give just any gift to just any recipient. How receptive a person is to God's influence will affect what spiritual gifts she receives; so will her heredity, her environment, and her own choices to develop in certain ways. The church's shared memory, beginning at least as early as the letters of St. Paul and continuing today, gives evidence that God does impart remarkable gifts to people who are open to such gifts and who are equipped to receive and exercise them. Because they are God's gifts to people—finite, fallible, sinful people—spiritual gifts will not always be used wisely, much less flawlessly or infallibly. But God gives them nonetheless as a gift of love, to enrich the lives of the recipients and of those persons and communities whom they, in turn, can love.[2]

Spiritual gifts may be rooted in biology, psychological development, relationships, or social or cultural forces. They may be evoked or occasioned or fostered by the Christian story, Christians' active sharing of their convictions, or the claims and needs of the institutional church. Whatever their source, they are, like the capacities of those outside the church, God's gifts. Grounded in God's unbounded love, unlimited presence, and ceaseless activity, these gifts enable us to give what we ourselves receive: inspiring, healing, and transforming love in all its forms.

God's Spirit's gifts are rooted in God's creative work. And while God's Spirit works throughout every dimension of reality, the formation of the whole creation is the paradigmatic instance of divine activity. The created order provides the context within which particular divine actions take place, and the shaping of that order is, in turn, the sum of God's individual interactions with all the particular aspects of finite reality. It is to God's work as creator that I turn in Chapter 5.

---

1. See Bruce G. Epperly, *God's Touch: Faith, Wholeness, and the Healing Miracles of Jesus* (Louisville, KY: Westminster/Knox 2001).
2. Cp. John B. Cobb, Jr., "The Relativization of the Trinity," *Trinity in Process: A Relational Theology of God*, ed. Joseph A. Bracken and Marjorie Hewitt Suchocki (New York: Continuum 1997) 13-20.

5

Love Makes the World

Creation can be seen as an act and as a consequence of divine love. Christian spirituality is a matter of loving God for and in creation. The heart of Christian ethics is responding lovingly to the claims of God's good creation and building loving relationships among God's creatures. Celebrating the Sabbath can be an acknowledgment of God's love in creation and as an opportunity to experience that love anew.[1]

That God is creator is the most fundamental affirmation Christians make. This affirmation entails the conclusion that creation is real, not imaginary, and good—worth loving and capable of love. God is other than creation, but we can encounter God in and through our encounters with God's world. Avoiding idolatry doesn't mean not loving creation—it means loving creatures appropriately, without treating any finite reality, including any religious practice or institution, as if it were absolute in value.[2] God and creation are not in competition; and, indeed, we love God as we love creation, whether or not we realize that's what

---

1. See Lynne M. Baab, *Sabbath Keeping: Finding Freedom in the Rhythms of Rest* (Downers Grove, IL: IVP 2005); Donna Schaper, *Sabbath Keeping* (Cambridge, MA: Cowley 1999); Wayne Muller, *Sabbath: Restoring the Sacred Rhythm of Rest* (New York: Bantam 1999); Marva J. Dawn, *Keeping the Sabbath Wholly: Ceasing, Resting, Embracing, Feasting* (Grand Rapids: Eerdmans 1988); Tilden Edwards, *Sabbath Time: Understanding and Practice for Contemporary Christians* (New York: Seabury 1982); Charles Scriven, *Jubilee of the World: The Sabbath as a Day of Gladness* (Nashville: Southern 1978); Kenneth L. Strand, ed., *The Sabbath in Scripture and History* (Washington, DC: Review 1982); Sakae Kubo, *God Meets Man: A Theology of the Sabbath and Second Advent* (Nashville: Southern 1978); Roy Branson, ed., *Festival of the Sabbath* (Washington, DC: Association of Adventist Forums 1985); Karl Barth, *Church Dogmatics*, 4 vols. in 13, ed. Geoffrey W. Bromiley, Thomas F. Torrance, et al., trans. G. T. Thompson et al. (Edinburgh: Clark 1936-69) 3.1: 98-9, 313-38; 3.4: 47-72; Niels-Erik A. Andreasen, *The Christian Use of Time* (Nashville: Abingdon 1978), *The Old Testament Sabbath: A Tradition-Historical Investigation*, SBL Diss. Ser. 7 (Missoula, MT: Scholars 1972); Niels-Erik A. Andreasen, *Rest and Redemption*, Andrews U Monographs (Berrien Springs, MI: Andrews UP 1978); John Brunt, *A Day for Healing: The Meaning of Jesus' Sabbath Miracles* (Washington, DC: Review 1981); Herbert W. Richardson, *Toward an American Theology* (New York: Harper 1967) 108-60; Samuele Bacchiocchi, *Divine Rest for Human Restlessness: A Theological Study of the Good News of the Sabbath for Today*, Biblical Perspectives 2 (Berrien Springs, MI: Bacchiocchi 1980); Abraham J. Heschel, *The Sabbath: Its Meaning for Modern Man* (New York: Farrar 1951). Thanks to Roy Branson, Fritz Guy, Sakae Kubo, and Charles Sandefur for many of these sources.

2. Cp. Nicholas Lash, *Believing Three Ways in One God: A Reading of the Apostles' Creed* (Notre Dame, IN: U of Notre Dame P 1993): "[b]eing . . . weaned from our idolatry is not . . . a question of 'detachment', if by this we mean coming to suppose that noting really matters. On the contrary, it is a question of being brought, like blind people towards eyesight, into some clearer, more accurate and honest understanding of the way things are and might be made to be" (21-2).

we're doing. And this means that those who love us are responding in love to God, whether they know it or not.

The practice of science is a spiritual discipline, a way in which we restrain ourselves and let ourselves be surprised by a world that is other than ourselves. In this way, and because in it we celebrate God's creative artistry, science is a means of loving God. It should not be altogether surprising, then—even if it is ironic in light of later developments—that the doctrine of creation lies behind the emergence of modern science.

The created world is inherently loveable. Moral goodness is a matter of loving creation properly. Both healing creation and developing its inherent potential are important and morally appropriate. Satisfactory moral principles do not impede love—they channel it. As regards interactions between human persons, there are two primary principles that do this: the Golden Rule and the Pauline Principle (though of course more specific guidelines can be derived from these norms). These principles follow necessarily from the character of God's creation. An understanding of Christian love framed with reference to these principles is preferable to views which understand Christian ethics as a species of consequentialism or which deny the possibility that there could be exceptionless moral norms. It is also preferable to a view that sees morality as rooted in arbitrary divine commands.

Love for creation means loving the particular others to whom we are connected by special relational ties. But it also means treating the non-human world with respect and showing care at multiple levels for the vulnerable. The Sabbath provides a weekly opportunity to celebrate the divine love we experience in creation and to affirm and renew our love for the creation and the creator.

The Loving Creator

To believe in creation is to believe that we are here because of God. Put in the language of logic, the activity of God is a *necessary condition* of our existing. There are lots of ways of understanding this claim. Some Christians believe that God brought the ancestors of today's plant and animal species into being directly, while other Christians believe God created and continues creating through the processes described by evolutionary biology. Some Christians speak of creation *out of nothing*, others of creation *out of chaos*.[1] The good news is that we don't need to resolve these disputes in order to see the truth of Christian belief in God as creator, or to grasp its meaning.

For most Christians, the ground of belief in God as creator will be simple: they have learned in the school of Christian worship and discipleship to read the

1. On the relationship between Christianity and science in general, and conflicts regarding the nature of creation in particular, see, *e.g.*, Darrell R. Falk, *Coming to Peace with Science: Bridging the Worlds between Faith and Biology* (Downers Grove, IL: IVP 2004); Howard J. Van Till, ed., *Portraits of Creation* (Grand Rapids: Eerdmans 1988); John C. Polkinghorne, *Science and Creation: The Search for Understanding* (London: SPCK 1988); E. L. Mascall, *Christian Theology and Natural Science: Some Questions on Their Relations*, Bampton Lectures 1956 (New York: Ronald 1956) 32-6, 91-8, 132-66, 254-316; Edward Farley, *Divine Empathy: A Theology of God* (Minneapolis: Fortress 1996) 235-51 (specifying dependence and independence, mystery and intelligibility, and goodness and the tragic as characteristics of implications of the idea of creation). On creation out of chaos, see, *e.g.*, Charles Hartshorne, *Omnipotence and Other Theological Mistakes* (Albany: SUNY 1984). For a vigorous defense of creation *ex nihilo*, see Robert C. Neville, *God the Creator: On the Transcendence and Presence of God* (Chicago: U of Chicago P 1968). How one sorts out these issues will depend in significant degree on the account of divine action one finds the most persuasive.

world as God's good creation. They have been taught that the world has its origin in God, just as they have been taught so many other things they know. For Christians, part of loving God is responding in gratitude to divine love for the goodness of the world, learning to love the One whose presence and activity can be discerned at every point in the world. To love God, instead of an idol, is precisely to love the One who is behind and beyond the world. A local deity wouldn't, couldn't, be God. The scope of God's presence and activity must be as wide as possible if God is to be the focus of our worship and loyalty and the ground of our confidence. Thus, there is an existential demand that we speak of God as creator.[1]

Belief in God as creator is part of the Christian story and, perhaps even more fundamentally, part of the inner logic of Christian belief in God. But of course there are other routes to the conviction that God is creator. We can, for instance, point to the world's order as evidence for the reality of the God who is the source of order. But what matters is not *how* but *whether* we discern God at the root of the world's order and beauty and goodness. To be sure, we know who God the creator is especially through a particular strand of history that centers in Jesus of Nazareth. But the God who is revealed in Jesus is the One who made and is present to the entire world; the One who inspires not only the history of Israel and the church but all other history as well; the One who creates by raising mountains, designing genes, and empowering and inspiring artists and construction workers and politicians. This God, who is always at work to bring freshness and novelty and goodness into being, is the God who loves in creation, the God whom we love in creation, the God who creates love, and the God whose creation we love.[2]

The reality God creates includes dimensions difficult or impossible for us to test and probe. There are realms of existence quite outside our experience and control, quite beyond the reach of meditative technique as much as of microscopic or telescopic analysis. Dimensions of reality radically different than that which we experience in our ordinary lives are likely to be nearly incomprehensible. We can talk about them in poetic images and symbols, we can specify what they are not, but, given our limited cognitive resources, we should not expect to be able to describe them with precision. Believing in creation means recognizing the vastness and complexity of God's world.[3]

LOVE AND THE REALITY OF CREATION

Love means that the created world is *real*. God couldn't have a loving relationship with creation if it were a figment of the divine imagination, or a puppet completely controlled by God: love inherently involves the recognition of otherness. Creation is love's work, God's gift. God didn't need to make this world. God might have been satisfied with a world free of conscious creatures capable of spontaneous and loving action. To believe in creation is therefore to believe that God takes delight in the novelty and the unique excellences of creatures like us and the others that populate our world, and desires to share a beautiful universe with them. Thus, creation emerges from love: God loves the beauty and

---

1. Cp. Farley, *Empathy* 235-51.
2. The best available theological discussion of the meaning of the idea of creation remains Langdon Gilkey, *Maker of Heaven and Earth: The Christian Doctrine of Creation in the Light of Modern Knowledge* (Garden City, NY: Anchor-Doubleday 1965). More recent contributions include Norman Young, *Creator, Creation and Faith* (Philadelphia: Westminster 1976) and Jürgen Moltmann, *God in Creation: An Ecological Doctrine of Creation*, Gifford Lectures 1984-5 (London: SCM 1985).
3. A point Fritz Guy has helped me to see more clearly.

goodness creation brings into being, and God desires the love, the friendship, of creatures, the rich delight of interacting with the created world.[1]

That creation is love's work tells us that the world is *real*, that it is *other* than God, in some meaningful sense *distinguishable* from God. God can *interact* with creatures in loving friendship only if the world is real, and therefore free. If the world lacked freedom, if creation were a cosmic puppet show orchestrated by a hidden divine puppeteer, there wouldn't be any real creation. The world would simply be part of God, or else an illusion. There wouldn't be any difference between *that* sort of creation and one that existed only in God's imagination. No real relationship of love could exist between God and this kind of world. Imaginary creatures, divine marionettes, couldn't offer love to God; love is always something that comes from *another*. To talk about creation, then, is to talk about the reality of the world; and to talk about the reality of the world is to affirm its freedom. And, because the world is free, God fosters creation's flourishing not unilaterally, but through the activity of creatures. Creatures are not passive media through which divine providence works. They are God's partners in the creative process.[2]

That the world is a reality other than God, a reality with an integrity all its own, seems to be one meaning of the Sabbath. On the Sabbath, we delight in creation, because an independent creation, a world with its own integrity, is good. In particular, our own creative activity as human beings—creative activity which is among the media of God's own creative activity—is good.[3]

God never fails to be active in the world, sustaining and guiding it. So when Genesis speaks of God's rest, this is best understood as a figurative reference to God's affirmation of the world *as world*. Because of the presence of free creatures, the world exhibits a capacity for creative self-development. God does not, metaphorically speaking, bemoan this independence and integrity; rather, God delights in it—which implies that it must be essentially good.[4]

Creation rightly evokes our love and God's. The world is other than God. God isn't the same thing as the world—not even all of the world taken together, in its richness and complexity.[5] God isn't the world, and the world isn't God. Because the world isn't God, it is free to be itself—and it is worthy of divine and human love *as what it is*. Because it isn't God, it doesn't have ultimate value, so it cannot rightly demand *unqualified love*. Neither the entire world nor any part of it can claim our love absolutely, in totalitarian fashion. Belief in God puts an end to the tyranny of the idols: myself, my family, my university, my country, my species, my planet. All of these are good, but none of them can claim ultimate allegiance. They're all valuable, but I don't have to be dominated by any of them.

Belief in God the creator means we can love in freedom. Acknowledging the reality of the creator means freedom from bondage to any element of creation, including ourselves. Recognizing that no creature has absolute value, that no *thing* has the right to make ultimate claims on us, is a liberating notion. It frees us to love ourselves and our world without feeling overwhelmed. No element of creation can claim absolute allegiance. No human project—including my own, of course—can demand unquestioning loyalty. Belief in God the creator is thus the

---

1. So Ninian Smart and Steven Konstantine, *Christian Systematic Theology in a World Perspective*, World Christian Theology Series 1 (Philadelphia: Fortress 1991) 201-3.

2. See, *e.g.*, Smart and Konstantine 239-42.

3. For one account of what it might mean to speak of creation as good, see Farley, *Empathy* 247-8.

4. This point is made forcefully, if in perhaps too extreme a fashion, by Jacques Ellul, "The Seventh Day," *What I Believe*, trans. Geoffrey W. Bromiley (Grand Rapids: Eerdmans 1989).

5. This, of course, is the claim of pantheism.

basis for our criticism of any structure, relationship, or commitment that seeks to dominate us as if it were God. If I'm a creature, and not God, then I don't have to do everything. If I'm not the center of value in the universe, then I'm free to listen and attend to the claims of other creatures—to love them. And, on the other hand, if other creatures aren't absolute in value, then I needn't simply become their puppet.[1] I deserve love (at minimum, love as respect), as do they. But I don't deserve unquestioning loyalty, and neither do they.

Loving God in Creation

We love God in and through our love for God's creation.[2] And naming God as creator means delighting appreciatively in God's world. So there's an integral link between creation and spirituality. We love creation because it is inherently, intrinsically good. The spiritual life isn't about being suspicious of the created world—it's about attending to it in love. Spirituality happens in (and only in) the created world. But, on the other hand, it involves recognizing the created world for what it is—as less than ultimate—and, in particular, recognizing oneself as limited and constrained by other elements of created reality.[3]

God's Presence in, to, and with Creation

If we believe in God, and not some local, tribal idol, then we believe that God is intimately present to and with every facet of created reality. And so we must believe that we can encounter God in every region of our experience.

The doctrine of creation stresses the connection between God and the world; but it also emphasizes the *difference* between God and the world: God is not another bit of the world that could conceivably be encountered somewhere in the universe, rather in the way that unwary explorers once stumbled on Australia.[4] As the creator of the universe, God transcends it entirely.

God can't be encountered as an isolated, distinguishable reality. The Mystery who is the world's source must be approached *through* the created world. Our minds can't comprehend God—otherwise we would be God, which we manifestly aren't. Rather, we experience God in and through our experience of the world. Our experience of God the creator lies behind all of our other experiences.

The Non-Competitive Relationship between God and Creation

Thus, there can be no real *competition* between God and the created order for our loyalty. Because God is the world's transcendent creator, not a constituent of the world along with others, capable of soliciting our attention in distinction from them, we do not have to choose to love *either* God *or* the created world. We can love God precisely *as* we love the elements of the created order.

Many people, however, seem to think there's a basic, unavoidable conflict between loving other people and devotion to God. For them, God "is the only

---

1. Thus, Stanley Hauerwas seems to me to be quite right when he observes that the doctrine of creation involves not only metaphysical but moral claims. See *The Peaceable Kingdom: A Primer in Christian Ethics* (London: SCM 1983).

2. My principal resource here is Nicholas Lash, *Easter in Ordinary: Reflections on Human Experience and the Knowledge of God* (Notre Dame, IN: U of Notre Dame P 1988). See also Nicholas Lash, "Human Experience and the Knowledge of God," *Theology on the Way to Emmaus* (London: SCM 1986).

3. In this section, I draw on some material I used previously in "Loving Friends and Loving God," *Spectrum* 27.4 (Aut. 1999): 11-22.

4. This is a comparison frequently made by Karl Rahner.

thing worthy of love."[1] Every other reality is less important, less valuable. Prayer and devotional practices are the only genuinely worthwhile activities. We are wasting time and emotional energy when we focus our attention on other people—time and energy we could instead give to God. Other creatures are at best distractions from God, who is our only true Beloved.

Francis de Sales argued that friendship "is the most dangerous of all types of love."[2] One can devote one's limited time and emotional energy to the love of God or to the love of persons. For the true Christian, he implies, the choice between the two must be clear.[3] And in the widely read devotional manual, *The Imitation of Christ*, Thomas à Kempis declared: "If thou wouldst learn to put away from thee every created thing, Jesus would freely take up His abode with thee."[4] Except "a man be freed from all creatures," Thomas asserts, "he will not be able to reach freely after Divine things."[5] Indeed, he attributes to God the words: "Thou oughtest to be separated from thy acquaintances and dear friends . . . ."[6]

Convictions like those encouraged St. Francis de Sales to fear friendship and inspired Thomas à Kempis to inveigh against social interaction, have undoubtedly been popular throughout the history of Christianity. Ultimately, however, I believe they are wrong. They rest on a misunderstanding of God's relation to the world—a misunderstanding according to which relationships with other creatures are sources of spiritual distraction and God and creatures compete for our love. It is the doctrine of creation that makes clear why this conception is doubtful.

The conviction that God is creator means that God is present to and active in every aspect of created reality. At every moment of our lives, therefore, we are interacting with God.

The understanding of God's relationship with the world embodied in the doctrine of creation is significantly different from pantheism. Pantheism identifies God and the world. The doctrine of creation conceives of God as intimately present to and with the creation, but, unlike pantheism, it does not entail the view that God and the world are the same thing, that God-talk is just another way of describing the world (a way, perhaps, that focuses on the world as an orderly and meaningful whole).

As well as highlighting God's presence in the world, the Christian doctrine of creation also points to the difference between God and creation. Creation is *finite*, limited, constrained. By contrast, God is infinite. God isn't a thing, an object, a bit of finite reality. As the universe's infinite creator, God is different from each of the things that make up the universe, and from the universe in its totality. If God were a creature—if God were finite, limited—God might inhabit only one district of experience or another. God might be present in some places or times or feelings more than others. But limiting God in this way would run counter to the central Christian conviction that God is the infinite creator of all finite reality.

---

1. Simone Weil, "Forms of the Implicit Love of God," *Waiting for God*, trans. Emma Craufurd (New York: Putnam 1951) 212; cp. 210: "There is no final good here below."
2. St. Francis de Sales, *Introduction to the Devout Life*, trans. John K. Ryan (New York: Image-Doubleday 1972) 17, qtd. Margaret R. Miles, *Practicing Christianity: Critical Perspectives for an Embodied Spirituality* (New York: Crossroad 1988) 151.
3. Miles 151.
4. Thomas à Kempis, *The Imitation of Christ*, trans. William Benham, Harvard Classics 7 (New York: Collier 1909) 2.7. Thomas à Kempis urges his reader: "choose for thy companions God and His Angels only, and flee from the notice of men" (1.7). And he maintains that the "greatest saints used to avoid as far as they could the company of men, and chose to live in secret with God" (1.20).
5. Kempis 3.31.
6. Kempis 3.53.

We can encounter God anywhere and in any context. God doesn't live in church. Having pious feelings isn't the only way to be sensitive to God's presence (indeed, it may not even be an especially good way). And turning away from particular things in the world won't enable us to know or love God better. For we can turn away from one finite thing only to another finite thing. And God is not a finite thing at all. Refusing to engage with other people isn't a way to have unmediated experience of God—which is impossible. Not attending to other finite things is just a way of focusing only on oneself instead of on the rest of the world. It's an expression of moral and spiritual solipsism, not a path to spiritual maturity.[1]

Creatures *per se* don't get in the way of our relationships with God. If they did, it would be because God, too, was a finite reality. But God's infinity means that we can—indeed, must—meet God in and through our experiences of things in the creaturely world,[2] not as another reality alongside finite things. We are particular. We are finite. And so there's no way for us to understand or relate to God while bypassing the creaturely world. "Creation is not a hurdle on the road to God, it is the road itself."[3]

A god who could be another creature's rival for our affections—even a *successful* rival—wouldn't really be God at all.[4] "God is not an object beside objects and hence cannot be reached by renunciation of objects. God . . . is not to be found by subtraction and [is] not to be loved by reduction."[5] The Creator is not a competitor with any aspect of creation for our attention and love.

Idolatry and Love for Creation

If we believe that God and creation are in competition for our affection, we may brand creaturely loves as idolatrous. Many of us learned as children and adolescents to beware of idolatry. The parents and teachers who issued these warnings probably didn't think we'd be tempted to identify God with metallic statues. But they did fear that we'd become too attached to other things and people.

If we learn lessons like these too well, passion for personal connection can become a source of guilt. We can become suspicious of delight in and desire for other people. We can begin to fear that God may punish us for loving too much, or that God may call us to sacrifice our loves just because they are intense. We may even envision a malicious deity playing spiritual games with us, testing us by calling us, like Abraham, to give up those who matter to us most to keep God "number one" in our lives.

A renewed appreciation for the actual significance of Christian concern with idolatry can help us avoid the guilt and anxiety that sometimes follow from the view that God and creation compete for our love. We can't treat any finite thing, any creature, as if it were infinite—as if it were God—without falsifying the nature of reality. If we are to treat each bit of finite reality appropriately, then we

---

1. Martin Buber, "The Question to the Single One," *Between Man and Man*, trans. Ronald Gregor Smith (New York: Macmillan 1948) 52.
2. John E. Smith, *Experience and God* (New York: Oxford UP 1968): "[E]very alleged experience of God would also be experience of something else at the same time. If this is so, no singular experience would stand in analogy with a sensible experience of an object as evidence that God exists" (52). Cp. Karl Rahner, *Foundations of Christian Faith: An Introduction to the Idea of Christianity*, trans. William V. Dych (New York: Crossroad-Seabury 1978): "If there is any immediacy to God at all, that is, if we really can have something to do with God in his own self, this immediacy cannot depend on the fact that the non-divine absolutely disappears" (83).
3. Buber 52; cp. 54.
4. Buber 57.
5. Buber 58.

can't allow any single constituent of the creation to trump the claims of all the others. Only if we give ultimate loyalty solely to God, to the infinite reality transcending every particular object in the world, will we be able to put every finite reality in perspective and give each one its due. That's why Christians ought to avoid idolatry.[1]

Being loyal to God *does* clearly mean, then, that one can't act as if a friend, a car, a house, an institution, a nation, even a planet is the only thing that really matters. Loyalty to God relativizes all of our particular loyalties. It puts each one in its proper place. Loving God means that we cannot view any finite reality as *ultimate* in importance.

It *doesn't* mean, however, that we can't or shouldn't care deeply, intensely, about particular people and communities and things. Indeed, love for God manifests itself precisely in our love for and attachment to particular, valuable finite realities.[2] But we need to take seriously the claims not only of those realities that are central to our own particular projects, but also of those on which we haven't chosen to focus, but which may matter profoundly to others.

It is not our job to replace God. We are not responsible for the universe. To act as if we were would itself be an especially pitiful and futile kind of idolatry. We can and should have particular, finite projects of our own, causes and relationships that matter to us deeply. And, obviously, if we care about some things we will be able to devote less attention to others.[3] But we can avoid idolatry as long as we don't treat the things and people *we* care about primarily as the only things and people worth caring about at all.

Idolatry is a fundamentally moral concept. Avoiding idolatry means being morally responsible by respecting each element of the creation for what it is. Idolatry is wrong, not so much because idolatrous behavior doesn't give God what *God* is due, but because it doesn't give the creation what *it* is due. "God does not stand in line waiting his turn at the wicket, not even at the head of the line. Rather, he brings this or that neighbour to the head of the line, and demands our best attention for him. And at another moment, perhaps, he closes the wicket, sends the whole line away, and demands to inspect our books."[4]

We refuse to engage in idolatry by choosing to live morally responsible lives, *not* by forsaking life in the world. If we don't attempt to be God, there's no reason our particular commitments should come into significant conflict with our general loyalty to the good of creation most of the time. But rejecting idolatry means that when conflicts do occur we must be willing let our particular loves take their proper places in relation to the other elements of created reality.

Idolizing someone else is bad for her or him as well as for others whose legitimate claims we may ignore because of our idolatry. Acting as if a creature is a source of absolute good imposes a crushing burden on her or him. Being treated as the center of the universe imposes an enormous responsibility for the idolater's well-being on the idolized person, one she or he is quite incapable of bearing. In

---

1. The notion of "radical monotheism"—the Christian alternative to idolatry—as an essentially moral and political concept is ably developed in H. Richard Niebuhr, *Radical Monotheism and Western Culture, with Supplementary Essays* (New York: Harper 1970); see also Paul Tillich, *Systematic Theology*, 3 vols. (Chicago: U of Chicago P 1951-63) 1: 13; Langdon Gilkey, *Shantung Compound: The Story of Men and Women under Pressure* (New York: Harper 1966) 230-5; Edward Farley, *Good and Evil: Interpreting a Human Condition* (Minneapolis: Fortress 1990) 115-292.
2. Cp. Robert Merrihew Adams, *Finite and Infinite Goods: A Framework for Ethics* (New York: OUP 1999), *e.g.*, 193-6.
3. Cp. Adams 200.
4. Oliver O'Donovan, *Resurrection and Moral Order: An Outline for Evangelical Ethics* (Grand Rapids: Eerdmans; Leicester: IVP 1986) 232-3.

turn, the idolater may use this sense of responsibility as a basis for trying to control the idolized person. And that it tempts the idolater to manipulation and control isn't the only thing that makes idolatry bad for the idolater. Enchanted by the idolized person, she or he may give up freedom, agency, responsibility. She or he may find the failure of the idol to deliver the ultimate satisfaction for which she or he seeks profoundly disappointing. Recognizing persons as infinitely precious and cherishable, but nonetheless incapable of substituting for God, incapable of trumping absolutely the claims of other creatures, is the only way to relate to them properly. Idolatry is a bad idea. But passionate desire, devotion, and care aren't idolatrous: they are appropriate responses to the immeasurably precious creatures human beings are. Idolatry is wrong because of what it takes away from the idolater, the idolized person, and from others.[1]

Understood correctly, then, we should avoid idolatry for the sake of the creaturely world. Loving other people, loving them intensely, needn't be idolatrous. It doesn't have to keep us from loving God. We don't have to ration our love for the people we care about to make sure we've got enough left over for God. We can love God precisely as we love other people (and non-human creatures). God is not in competition with the world, or any part of the world, for our loyalty. Any reality to which we could be loyal only as we turned away from things in the creaturely world wouldn't be God at all; it would be an especially demonic idol.

Loving Creation and Idolizing Religious Practices

The practical upshot of the notion that God and creation are in competition for our loyalty often seems to be that we should engage in worship and the devotional life to the detriment, if necessary, of our relationships with other people. Religious practice should become our all-consuming focus.

Sheldon Vanauken's compellingly beautiful book, *A Severe Mercy*, provides an especially poignant example of how such beliefs can play out in contemporary lives. The book centers on the love between "Van" and his wife, Jean, or "Davy," who shared an intense, passionate love for each other that began in an idyllic, pre-World War II South. After the war, Van and Davy, now married, moved to England, where Van undertook graduate study at Oxford. The influence of C. S. Lewis led the two to become Christians, and they began to live out their convictions as part of a tight-knit group of Christian friends.

When they returned to the United States, the Vanaukens settled in Virginia, where Van began teaching at Lynchburg College. They ministered to Van's students and joined enthusiastically in the life of a local congregation. Then, slowly, a subtle rift began to develop between them. While both believed that Christianity must suffuse their life together, Davy desired God with a single-minded passion that Van feared was progressively impairing her relationship with him.

> When Davy wasn't reading the Bible to prepare for her class, she was reading it for her soul's sake. She was always reading it, or reading Brother Lawrence and other devotional works. I wanted to protest that it was too much; but how could I do that? It's not possible for one Christian to say to another: You love God too much. Nor to say: You are holier than necessary. I couldn't even *think* such thoughts. They would have been dangerous. . . . I merely *felt* a sort of helpless protest. I didn't quite like to see her poring over Isaiah or St. John. I

---

1. See Diogenes Allen, *Love: Christian Romance, Marriage, Friendship* (Cambridge, MA: Cowley 1987).

think I'd have smiled to see her curled up with an Agatha Christie. I knew that everything had to be different now we were Christians—but *this* different?[1]

Van felt as if he and Davy had lost something. "What I wanted, emotionally if not intellectually, was the old Davy back along with the old love of life and beauty and poetry for their own sakes." But this desire "seemingly could not be reconciled with my intellectual commitment to Christ. Even less could it be reconciled with Davy's wholeness, both mind and heart, of devotion."[2]

For Davy Vanauken, finding God seems to have meant letting go of everything else. Loving God meant focusing on worship and the practice of the devotional life almost to the exclusion of everything else. And even though Van felt vaguely jealous of her relationship with God, he seemed convinced that in principle she was right: her single-minded pursuit of God was apparently incompatible with the light-hearted, enthusiastic involvement in the ordinary world that had previously marked her life. But the notion that living before God is a *replacement* for living in the world rests on a misunderstanding of the function of religious practice and the nature of humanity's experience of God.

Worship, prayer, reflection, and other kinds of religious activities are important. They require time. They demand self-discipline. Finding the time for them may mean saying "no" on occasion, to activities with other people. But opting out on this or that shared activity should not mean opting out of ordinary human life to focus exclusively on God.

Participation in the life of a religious community can be very valuable—but not as a uniquely important way of relating with God. Prayer can focus our moral identities and enable us to accept, express, and live out our delight in and dependence on God. However, engaging in overtly religious activities isn't, in any privileged sense, the way we love God. We can't confuse engaging in such activities with being in proper relation to God. We relate to God—appropriately or inappropriately—during every instant of our lives, and each moment provides every one of us with a fresh opportunity to respond in love to God.

Further, our relationships with God are just as much *ours*—limited by our histories and identities and contexts and assumptions—when we do "religious" things as when we do anything else. Churches are human institutions. Doctrines are human constructs. Liturgical rituals are human creations. Religious feelings are inexplicable without reference to human biology and psychology and sociology. God is present and active in and through all these things. They're still *human* realities, though. They're still parts of the world. Meeting God in these ways doesn't enable us to bypass the limitations of creaturely existence. Those limitations affect our relationships with God in explicitly religious contexts just like they do in all the other parts of our lives. The only way to know or experience God without limits is to *be* God.

Worship services and private spiritual practices matter. But they don't enable us to love God in some way that other activities can't. Instead, they help us to own our identities as parts of God's good creation so we can live flourishing, fulfilled, responsible, and joyful lives *in God's world*. Religious practices help us keep our day-to-day experience in perspective; understood correctly, they can't and shouldn't *replace* our day-to-day life in the world. A god who demands us of us that we forsake the good creation for the world of religious practice is not the creator, but an idol.[3]

When "religion" distracts us from our creaturely loves instead of sustaining and enriching them, it may become an idol itself. The person who is so absorbed

1. Sheldon Vanauken, *A Severe Mercy* (San Francisco: Harper 1977) 136-7.
2. Vanauken 139.
3. Cp. Adams 185-7.

by church work, worship, even prayer that she neglects her loved ones may be as idolatrous as the person who allows her concern for hearth and home to keep her from getting involved in the wider world. Similarly, when a religious institution, claiming the sanction of God for what it does, prohibits or discourages relationships with "deviants" or outsiders, it may unwittingly be assuming the status of an idol for its members.[1]

Private spirituality as much as public worship can become a focus of inordinate devotion. The self can make idolatrous demands just like a religious community. And forsaking human connection in the name of a distorted spirituality may not only express but also foster the idolatry of self or church. Relationships with others challenge us to refine our idiosyncratic, individual conceptions of God. In those relationships, we learn to revise our views of God, ourselves, and the world. Alone, we no longer benefit from the implicit and explicit correction our relationships with others make available. And so, ironically, choosing solitary religious practice in place of relationship is as likely to lead to distortion in our relationships with God as it is to enable us to experience greater intimacy with God.[2] By opting for "religion" over interpersonal relationships, we may come inadvertently to idolize ourselves by absolutizing our own religious experiences.

Identifying God and religion—equating God's will with the pretensions of a religious institution or love for God with public or private religious activities—is a subtle but insidious way of limiting God to a narrow stretch of reality, and thus of treating that stretch of reality as if it were the only one that really mattered. But when we give any aspect of finite reality ultimate authority in our lives, we're guilty of idolatry—even if, in this case, an especially genteel and respectable form of idolatry. Recognizing God's status as the world's transcendent creator makes us reject the idolatrous claims of religion as much as it makes us expose the arrogant illusions of states and ethnic groups.[3]

Properly understood, then, belief in God as creator provides no justification for a neurotic piety that perennially assaults our creaturely loves. It calls into question any attempt to make any of these loves, or all of them together, the *only* thing that matters in our lives. But it also rejects idolatrous conceptions of God according to which the world and its creator are in competition for our love. In particular, it judges as inadequate a surreptitious equation of loving God with being religious which implies that the Christian can or should give herself to explicitly religious practices *instead* of living enthusiastically and vibrantly as a part of God's good creation.

Creaturely Loves as Forms of Love for God

Because God is the world's transcendent creator, we can experience and respond to the divine presence under any circumstances. So we do not have to choose between loving God and loving creation. Indeed, we love God precisely as we love the created world. In particular, we love God as we love other people. Thus, creaturely loves can be forms of love for God.[4]

---

1. Cp. Adams 210-3; Luke T. Johnson, *Faith's Freedom: A Classic Spirituality for Contemporary Christians* (Minneapolis: Fortress 1990) 65.
2. Cp. Lash, *Easter* 102.
3. Adams 210-3.
4. In this section, I am especially indebted to Karl Rahner, "Reflections on the Unity of the Love of Neighbour and the Love of God," *Theological Investigations 6: Concerning Vatican Council II*, trans. Karl-H. and Boniface Kruger (London: Darton; New York: Seabury 1974) 231-49. See also *The Love of Jesus and the Love of Neighbor*, trans. Robert Barr (Middlegreen, Slough: St. Paul 1983).

One reason this is so is that love between persons is fundamental to who we are. Every genuinely moral choice is an implicit expression of love for God. For to accept a moral limitation on my being is to accept my status as a creature.¹ With every moral choice I confront comes the requirement that I make or reaffirm a fundamental decision about my own identity. Am I God? Am I valueless? Or am I a part of God's good creation?² Each of us faces this question in every situation. Every time I make a choice about some concrete, particular thing in the world, I am also deciding who I am. Even when not directly confronting another person, even when I am alone, I have to ask if my choices take the reality and value of others—and myself—into adequate account. Our encounters with other people pose the basic moral and spiritual question with particular force and clarity: will we exist with others in relationships of love or will we sacrifice them—or ourselves—in relationships of abuse, domination, or neglect? Will we be open to the world or will we refuse to acknowledge any reality beyond ourselves?³

That relationships of love with other created persons can involve all the aspects of our personalities gives these relationships particular moral significance. Our bodies are involved, along with our ability freely to shape our lives over time and to define our identities by combining the disparate moments of our pasts into coherent narratives; our capacity to hope for—and dread—the future; our moments of disillusionment and moral despair; and our recognition of our finitude and mortality.

Personal relationships call up, challenge, and engage every aspect of our humanness.⁴ Thus, interpersonal love fundamentally reflects who we are.⁵ When we love, therefore, we decisively express our basic orientation to the world—and thus to God. Love for another person—whether as partner, a lover, a family member, or a friend (in this section, and, later, when I turn to a related theme, I'll often use the word "friend" and its cognates for simplicity's sake)—embodies and expresses the decision to accept oneself as a part of God's good creation in several ways.⁶

---

1. Cp. Karl Rahner, "Atheism and Implicit Christianity," *Theological Investigations 9: Writings of 1965-67 1*, trans. Graham Harrison (New York: Herder 1972) 153; Keith Ward, *Images of Eternity: Concepts of God in Five Religious Traditions* (Oxford: Oneworld 1993) 177-8; John Baillie, *The Sense of the Presence of God*, Gifford Lectures 1961-2 (London: OUP 1962) 79-87.

2. Cp. Karl Rahner, "Anonymous and Explicit Faith," *Theological Investigations 16: Experience of the Spirit: Source of Theology*, trans. David Morland (New York: Crossroad-Seabury 1979): a person "accepts God when he freely accepts himself in his own unlimited transcendence. He does this when he genuinely follows his conscience with free consent, because by such an action he affirms as well the condition of possibility of such a radical option which is implicitly bound up with this decision, i.e. he affirms God" (55-6).

3. See Rahner, "Unity" 239-44; cp. Tillich, *Theology*: ". . . there is one limit to man's attempt to draw all content into himself—the other self. . . . One can destroy . . . [the other self] as a self, but one cannot assimilate it as a content of one's own centeredness" (3: 40). See also Rahner, "The 'Commandment' of Love in Relation to the Other Commandments," *Theological Investigations 5: Later Writings*, trans. Karl-H. Kruger (London: Darton; New York: Seabury 1966) 456: the "commandment" of love "does not command man to do something or other but simply commands him to fulfill himself, and charges man with himself, i.e. himself as the possibility of love in the acceptance of the love in which God does not give something but gives himself."

4. Rahner, "Unity" 242.

5. Rahner, "Unity" 243.

6. My analysis here depends on Lash, *Easter* 242-6.

It does so, first, because it is grounded in love as *respect for otherness*.[1] The other is different from me. And so, no matter how much I love her or him, no matter how much our interests may converge, now matter how much we may identify with each other, I must recognize that she is still free, that she can surprise me, that our desires may not always coincide. To take her seriously as a genuine other, free and responsible, is to grant her the space to be who she is.

This is always difficult. Too often, we view other people as extensions of ourselves, as means to the fulfillment of our own desires and needs. Respecting the otherness of someone to whom I am close is especially hard. If one is close to another person, one cannot but *need* her or him. One's need can make it especially difficult to grant legitimacy to the other's desire to be herself. It may be very easy to convince oneself that it is both necessary and appropriate that she should merge her identity with one's own—and thus to deny her difference from oneself. It is a minor miracle to grant real freedom to a person to whom one is close.[2]

But of course love is so powerful, so profoundly moving, precisely because it comes from an *other*. Someone who does not stand over against me cannot really *love* me. The inner logic of love between two people requires the maintenance of otherness, the respect for difference, between them. But despite this pressure exerted by the relationship itself, allowing a person to whom one is close truly to be herself can prove to be a delicate moral task.

To love someone is to be faithful to him even as he grows and changes in the exercise of his freedom This might be an easy task if his interests and one's own, his personality and one's own, his identity and one's own, were simply the same. But the reality of the other's difference from oneself challenges one to be loyal despite change and conflict. That—despite one's distinction from him—he is in an important sense a part of oneself only complicates matters further. By defining who one is with reference to who the other is, by making him part of oneself even as he differs from oneself, one accepts a potentially threatening vulnerability.

To take a close relationship seriously is to accept the responsibility to be loyal precisely to someone to whom one is vulnerable. The claim on one's loyalty of a friend, lover, parent, child, or partner constrains one's options. Accepting this claim means that one must consistently define one's own projects with reference to hers, even when—precisely when—they are not identical with one's own. In opting for fidelity, one accepts oneself as limited, as finite—as a creature.

Another important moral and spiritual dimension of close interpersonal relationships is the essentially *graced* quality of the lives which include such relationships. Accepting close relationships as gifts; accepting another's ongoing, particular self-gifts; and accepting oneself as another's gift are all ways in which one owns oneself as a part of God's good creation.

As a Christian, I will believe that God has been at work in and through the events leading to the formation of my close interpersonal relationships. In this sense, certainly, each such relationship is a gift of grace. But it is possible to accept and respond to the experience of grace in such a relationship whatever one believes about divine providence. That a close relationship cannot be planned or controlled confronts us directly with its character as a gift of grace. Close

---

1. On this point, see Weil 200-8. Weil's view appears to be that only God's loving action could empower friends to respect each other *as other*; when they do so, therefore, they give evidence of openness to God's work in their lives. Paul Tillich offers a nuanced analysis of the balance between identity and difference in love relationships (including friendship) as he reflects on the tension between *philia* and *eros* in *Love, Power, and Justice: Ontological Analyses and Ethical Applications* (New York: Oxford UP 1953) 24-34.

2. So Weil 202.

interpersonal connections come into being when we least expect them. The factors that predispose us to enter them are often unconscious; we are often close to particular people for social, cultural, and psychological reasons we are quite unable to articulate. Seemingly random circumstances bring people together and give them opportunities to discover each other. Thus, our close relationships are, to a significant degree, beyond our conscious control.

Still, whatever may predispose one person to be close to another, each of us is always free to reject an explicitly or implicitly proffered relationship with another. When someone to whom I want to be close chooses to be close to me, I have received a gift. She has not been *compelled* to be close to me by her genes or her environment or divine predestination (despite the fact, again, that God is active in the development of every close relationship—as, indeed, in all the other processes in the created world). She hasn't chosen in a vacuum, certainly; many factors constrain all of our choices. But she *has* chosen, nonetheless, to give me the gift of herself. Indeed, she must continue to choose to be faithful as a parent or cousin, partner or friend. In this way, too, close relationships are gifts of grace. This graced quality is not simply an accident; it is intrinsic to the value of any close relationship. We cannot have the experience of such a relationship without the experience of grace.

Becoming and remaining close to another person reflects the recognition that our lives are better—more fulfilled, marked by greater flourishing—when we *share* ourselves with others than when we *isolate* ourselves. To acknowledge the value of a close relationship with another is to accept that I need someone else if I want to experience a certain quality of life. And after a close relationship has come into being, and I have bonded my life with that of the other, I also need her if I am to be the person I am, to retain the identity I have achieved in relationship with her. In this sense, I am dependent on her.

As one weaves one's life together with another person, one becomes dependent on her in other ways as well. A close relationship itself is a gift. But gifts of various kinds may also accompany or result from it. Gifts of time, money, expertise, and emotional support may all express another's love. Receiving these gifts joyfully may sometimes be easy—but not always. Fearful of domination and abuse, we may flee dependence. But accepting gifts is part of what it means to be close to another person. To let someone know that she has something valuable to give by accepting her gift is a gift in its own right. The people to whom we're close need to know that what they offer us is significant, that it matters. And when we grant the reality of our dependence by accepting their gifts, we affirm again our status as God's creatures.

To be close to another person is to make her part of oneself. Who one is, then, depends on who she is. One is always vulnerable, of course, to forces outside one's control. In a close relationship with another person, though, one explicitly owns and accepts one's vulnerability. One chooses it. One agrees that one's identity will be affected by the actions of another. Realizing that her love has shaped and continues to shape who one is, one accepts that one's identity is the other's gift. It is contingent on her choices and on what befalls her. "A friend is a part of my own being. If he is no longer there, then I have somehow died with him."[1] The other's gift thus includes, in a sense, the gift of myself. To receive this gift of grace thankfully, instead of shunning it as a source of enervating dependence, is also to choose life as a part of the good creation.

Accepting that one is dependent on the people to whom one is close doesn't mean that one has to settle for oppressive and manipulative relationships. Not all dependence is good. But there's finally no getting away from dependence *as such*.

1. Ladislaus Boros, *Meeting God in Man* (London: Herder 1968) 57; cp. Lash, *Easter* 245.

Genuine *independence*—freedom from everyone and everything else—is illusory, and the quest for such independence is self-destructive. In close relationships, we can and should own and celebrate the dependence that is always essential to who we are. In this way, too, we recognize our contingency and vulnerability.

Coming to terms in the context of close interpersonal relationships with our dependence, we accept ourselves as parts of God's good creation. Accepting this dependence is thus another way in which, because we are close to others, we orient ourselves appropriately in relation to God.[1]

A close relationship represents a response to the value discerned in the other or in an actual or potential relationship with the other. I don't mean that we seek—or should seek—to be close only to the virtuous or the beautiful. But everything that *is* at all is valuable. The simple fact of existing is valuable. Being is good. The only perfectly bad thing would be something that didn't exist at all. And particular lives embody particular excellences. Of course, the good that every finite thing embodies is limited—that's just what finitude means. And the goods realized in human lives are distorted by, among other things, humanity's moral imperfection and brokenness. The fact remains, though, that, whenever I participate in a close relationship with another, I am responding the qualities of the other, or of my currently existing or possible relationship with the other, as in some sense good. Close relationships are morally significant, then, because in them we respond to the claims of a goodness external to ourselves.

In close interpersonal relationships, then, we learn to grant the claims of otherness on ourselves. We respect the otherness of each person to whom we're close, thus learning to relativize ourselves and our projects while maintaining the delicate balance between attachment and distance that is crucial to any close relationship. We are faithful, whatever our conflicting feelings. We admit that our close relationship—and, in them, we ourselves—are gifts. And we recognize in the people with whom we're bonded the claims of goodness, claims that are not subject to our manipulating wills. In short, close relationships presents us with the challenge to learn who we are anew as parts of God's good creation. The claim of a person to whom I'm close is an especially insistent call to let go of who I have been and, in ways subtle and not subtle, to reorder my perception of my world and myself, to come to perceive and experience God's good creation more adequately.[2]

To engage seriously in the practice of intimate connection is to accept ourselves as *parts* of God's good creation. It is to grant, practically if not always explicitly, that we are finite, contingent, vulnerable. It is to deny the possibility that we could ever exist on our own, and thus to affirm that we are *creatures*. In owning ourselves as creatures, in accepting ourselves as such, we experience again and again an essential element of the conversion that is necessary if we are to relate appropriately to God. For in close relationships we accept that we are not divine. We recognize our dependence, even as we celebrate the goodness of the grace on which we are dependent.[3] Thus, we orient ourselves aright in relation to God.[4]

As a recognition of one's own creatureliness and of the goodness of God's creation, every moral act is an expression of love for God. But love between persons is especially definitive and paradigmatic for one's identity, expressing as it does the fundamental orientation of the self, its fundamental openness. We affirm

1. Cp. Lash, *Believing* 54: "What we call Christianity is supposed to be a kind of school the purpose of whose pedagogy is to foster the conditions in which dependence might be relearned as friendship . . . ."
2. Cp. Johnson 70-1.
3. Lash, *Easter* 246.
4. Cp. Johnson 82-3.

who we are in love. A close, non-idolatrous relationship represents a choice of a basic orientation of openness to the world, and thus of love to God.

In close relationships, we can reach out in love to God by accepting ourselves as God's creatures. But we can also do so in a variety of other ways. We can appreciate God's goodness as it is reflected in the qualities of those we love. And we can deepen our intimacy with God by sharing God's love for them.

To delight in and desire other people is in an important sense to care about God. For, precisely in virtue of what it is we love about them, creatures reflect the image of God. It is not that one cares about other people only because one also cares about God; one could be completely unaware of the reality of God and still respond appropriately to God's goodness as one encounters it in other people. But in responding to their goodness, one is forming a motivational structure marked by love for goodness—and so for God—whether one realizes it or not.[1]

As one shares God's delight in creation, including, in particular, the people with whom one is close, one grows progressively more like God—one of whose central characteristics for Christians has always been love for creation. Further, by analogy with human friendship, we can see that sharing God's love for the people to whom we're close intensifies our relationships with God. While shared activities do not *constitute* a friendship, they deepen, enrich, and solidify it. Becoming a friend means, among other things, learning to enjoy what one's friends enjoy. Coming to love other people more, then, is parting of what learning to be God's friend must involve. Again, this will hold whether or not one is consciously aware of God's presence or not.[2]

Owning a close relationship with another person reflects one's acceptance of oneself as a part of God's good creation. In such a relationship, one forms and expresses an appreciation for God's goodness and embodies God's love in the world. Loving other people is a form of love for God. "To love love-*in*-someone is, by the courtesy of heaven, to love love and so to love God. It is to turn our eyes towards, to choose and desire the truth of all truth, the beauty of all beauty; to look and to hope in and to love and serve and know the Father, the Son, and the Holy Spirit, from whom and for whom everything in heaven and earth exists, even the cold, flabby, and fantasy-ridden hearts of human beings."[3]

Loving the Creator through Science

Scientific investigation is an element in our spiritual formation, because it requires us to recognize ourselves as limited by the reality we investigate. The practice of science is thus a kind of spiritual discipline, an exercise in piety.[4]

To say that God is creator is not to say we know most or all of the details of how God's good creation is structured or how it behaves. We need to recognize how different much, perhaps most, of it must be from the kind of reality we ordinarily experience, and therefore realize the limitations of the reality typically available to our senses. Loving God the creator means expecting and respecting the surprising otherness of what God has made and is making. It means practicing intellectual humility.

Scientific inquiry involves just this kind of humility. For it involves the willingness to make our judgments and hypotheses about the physical world

---

1. Adams 187-96.
2. Adams 196-8.
3. Rowan Williams, *Open to Judgement: Sermons and Addresses* (London: Darton 1994) 156.
4. See, *e.g.*, Stephen R. L. Clark, *The Mysteries of Religion: An Introduction to Philosophy through Religion*, Philosophical Introductions 3 (Oxford: Blackwell 1986) 69-71.

accountable to that world. Thus, to engage in science is to step aside from prejudice and the inclinations of the ego and to allow oneself to be surprised by what one discovers.

A Christian theology sensitive to the doctrine of creation can therefore endorse the scientific enterprise as spiritually significant. But this is by no means the only connection between the doctrine of creation and the process of scientific research. The idea of creation has been profoundly important for the development of the practice of science.[1]

Early scientific thinkers, influenced by belief in creation, realized that, because the creation—the messy, finite, material created order—was good, then it was worth investigating. It was *other* than God; it wasn't sacred, inherently mysterious, necessarily taboo, so exploring its inner workings was appropriate, not a violation of religious principle. And because God was the creator of *everything*, divine revelation could be discerned in physical as well as in spiritual reality.

As the product of divine wisdom and purpose, the creation was understood to be ordered and intelligible. But, as a gift of divine freedom, its nature couldn't be rationally deduced. God didn't have to create *this* world; God was free to create another, quite different world. And, in any case, God's ways wouldn't likely be very evident *a priori*. To understand what God was up to in creation would require human beings to put away their preconceptions and attend to what was actually the case, just as they had to do in any other situation in which they reflected on the work of the free and living God.

As a result, the processes and structures characteristic of the physical world had to be examined in all their particularity. It wasn't sufficient for the scientist to sit in her armchair and think about the logical connections between things, attempting to formulate philosophical arguments that might explain the order of nature. Instead, she would have to roll up her sleeves and get "out in the field" in order to investigate the way things really worked.

The acceptance of these implications of the idea of God as creator contributed in an important way to the development of the modern scientific enterprise. While science and religion have regularly been inhospitable to each other in recent centuries, the way in which science developed testifies to the importance of a basic religious idea for the disciplined investigation of the physical world.

Loving God's Good Creation

Christian ethics means love: loving attentiveness to creation and appropriate kinds of loving relationships—marked by devotion, friendship, compassion, or respect, as the case may be—among creatures. Love for creation issues appropriately in both the healing of creation and in participation in its development.

The Loveableness of Creation

Creation is loveable: the beauty of being is the basic moral reality. We can discern in the sometimes fragile, always irreplaceable beauty of each constituent of creation a claim to attentive care.[2] The beauty of being demands respect. Acknowledging the reality of what is other than oneself, responding to it by

---

1. I am relying here on Gilkey, *Maker* 117-37; for much more detail, see Christopher Kaiser, *Creation and the History of Science*, History of Christian Theology 3 (Grand Rapids: Eerdmans 1991). Cp. Mascall 91-8.

2. Helen Oppenheimer, *The Hope of Happiness: A Sketch for a Christian Humanism* (London: SCM 1983).

cherishing every other in its particularity, is the heart of love, and so the heart of Christian ethics.[1]

> Freed from the illusion of egocentricity, one is made aware of the mystery and beauty of concrete, actually existing others.... Eros for the other awakens us to beauty and then ripens into ethical existence. The pain of compassion derives from the more primordial beauty of what is harmed. It is always specific, aroused by concrete others—whether encountered face to face or indirectly. This integration of compassion and eros emphasizes that ethical existence arises out of concrete suffering; it is not based in anonymous law, duty, or principle, although it requires these things. Responsibility for others, self-forgetfulness, even self-sacrifice are rooted in an *eros* for life and are subject to distortion to the degree this lineage is broken.[2]

God loves, and each constituent of reality claims *our* love as well, because "[b]eings, simply in their existence, are lovely and valuable."[3]

Plants and planets, mesas and mountains, rivers and skies all rightly evoke love—whether the love of delight, or passion, or care, or respect. But other sentients are especially important. Another living creature *matters* just because she or he is a thinking, feeling, doing, knowing, suffering, creating *other*. To love rightly is to see such a creature through God's eyes, discerning her or his

> unconditional significance.... A person whom I love is somehow revealed to me. I no longer see him through the miasma of his mere relevance to my wants or mere usefulness for my plans and purposes. And when he ceases thereby to be a mere adjunct to my life, I, as it were, break through to him.[4]
>
> ... To love a thing is to see a thing as existing in its own right—to go out to its existence.... [And] the insight into its existence which makes us rejoice

---

1. Love as sensitive acknowledgment of otherness is a key theme in the work of Iris Murdoch, notably *The Sovereignty of Good*, Studies in Ethics and the Philosophy of Religion (London: Routledge 1970). The most succinct expression of Murdoch's conception of the moral life as a basis for Christian ethics can be found in Diogenes Allen, *Love: Christian Romance, Marriage, Friendship* (Cambridge, MA: Cowley 1987) 8-33. Cp. Emmanuel Levinas, "Substitution," trans. Alphonso Lingis, *The Levinas Reader*, ed. Seán Hand (Oxford: Blackwell 1989) 88-125 (this essay is a portion of Levinas's *Otherwise than Being or Beyond Essence*, trans. Alphonso Lingis [The Hague: Nijhoff 1981]); Wendy M. Farley, *Eros for the Other: Retaining Truth in a Pluralistic World* (University Park, PA: Pennsylvania State UP 1995); Knud Løgstrup, *The Ethical Demand* (Notre Dame, IN: U of Notre Dame P 1997); Zygmunt Bauman, *Postmodern Ethics* (Oxford; Cambridge, MA: Blackwell 1993); Zygmunt Bauman, *Life in Fragments: Essays in Postmodern Morality* (Oxford; Cambridge, MA: Blackwell 1995); Zygmunt Bauman, "Postscript: 'To Die for ...', or Death and Morality," *Mortality, Immortality and Other Life Strategies* (Stanford, CA: Stanford UP 1992) 200-10; John D. Caputo, *Against Ethics: Contributions to a Poetics of Obligation with Constant Reference to Deconstruction*, Studies in Continental Thought (Bloomington: Indiana UP 1993); John D. Caputo, *Demythologizing Heidegger*, Indiana Series in the Philosophy of Religion (Bloomington: Indiana UP 1993); Edith Wyschogrod, *Saints and Postmodernism: Revisioning Moral Philosophy*, Religion and Postmodernism (Chicago: U of Chicago P 1990); Robert Gibbs, *Why Ethics? Signs of Responsibilities* (Princeton: Princeton UP 2000); Dwight Furrow, *Against Theory: Continental and Analytic Challenges in Moral Philosophy* (New York: Routledge 1995).

2. Farley, *Eros* 85, 86.

3. Farley, *Eros* 79.

4. J. R. Jones, "Love as Perception of Meaning," *Religion and Understanding*, ed. D. Z. Phillips (New York: Macmillan 1967) 149.

in its existence is at the same time an insight into its suffering, its defencelessness, its profound vulnerability. . . .[1]

Creation as the Ground of Ethics

God's revelation in the life of Jesus underscores the rootedness of ethics in creation.[2] Jesus voices and embodies a divine "no" to human sin and loss. In light of Jesus' story, we can see that God has no intention of leaving creation to flounder.[3] And God's self-revelation in and through a human life highlights God's positive evaluation of humanness. Though distorted, humanness is not evil at root; and we know this because it is a fit medium for God's self-expression. To identify Jesus as God's revelation is to underscore God's involvement with and love for the whole creation, and to see creation as inherently valuable—including those aspects of the creation God has made and is making through us.

Jesus' life beyond death points to the end of human history, and says here again that what is created is valuable—worth loving. Persons are not evanescent sprites who vanish in death. They are capable of life in love beyond death with God and with each other.[4]

If the God of love lies behind the world, and if God's disposition toward the world—revealed in Jesus—is love, then the world must be *fundamentally* loveable.[5] Divine love is not arbitrary: being is beautiful. To be sure, creatures can distort or destroy the created order; and not every event in creation will serve every creature's egocentric agenda. However, *at root*, creation is good: an ordered world, containing free creatures and processes, is a good thing; the basic structures and processes of that world are good, even though capable of distortion; and the creation is capable of experiencing a rich and flourishing maturity, a maturity God is at work in the world to realize.

To say that the whole world is God's good creation is to talk about what God creates though *us* as well as what God creates through other creatures. The creative activity of God's creatures, human and otherwise, is both good in itself and a source of further goodness in the world. As God's partners, creatures are able to contribute to the shaping of a novel and unique history all their own.[6] This uniqueness and novelty is part of what it means for there to be a genuine creation. The possibility of creaturely creativity is not simply a means of ensuring creation's goodness; it is also one of the things that *make* creation good.

Important biblical images and narratives highlight the significance of this way of looking at creation. Both Ezekiel and the Apocalypse envision human history as concluding in a city. In a city, human civilization and culture are on display. That humanity's ultimate destiny takes this form in the Bible highlights the fact that culture is part of God's good creation.[7]

To be sure, the biblical writers sometimes speak critically of "the world." But when they do so, they are not talking about the created world as such. They have in mind "the totality of sin-infected creation. Wherever human sinfulness

---

1. Jones 149-50; italics in original. Selective quotation enables me to twist Jones's meaning here a bit; I think the seeing to which Jones refers here is integral to love, but I don't think it is simply identical with love.
2. See O'Donovan.
3. O'Donovan 13-4, 31.
4. O'Donovan 15.
5. See Gilkey, *Maker* 269-78.
6. Gilkey, *Maker* 200-207
7. See Albert M. Wolters, *Creation Regained: Biblical Basics for a Reformational Worldview* (Grand Rapids: Eerdmans 1985) 41; Samuele Bacchiocchi, *Advent Hope for Human Hopelessness* (Berrien Springs, MI: Biblical Perspectives 1986).

bends or twists or distorts God's good creation, *there* we find the 'world.'"[1] The created world as such is good. Evil is a parasite on an essentially good world. The distinction between good and evil is not identical with some other distinction—between the religious and the non-religious, the sacred and the secular, the holy and the profane.

Sin is fundamentally the denial that one is part of God's good creation. While some Christians have sought to escape sin by separating themselves from creation—by denying themselves sexuality and delectable food and the products of culture, for instance—they've looked in the wrong place for evil. The tension between goodness and brokenness is one that runs through every facet of our lives. Fleeing the world of human culture, or trying to escape from the body, is not a way of escaping from sin. Fleeing from the created world is, in fact, a denial of our nature as embodied selves. Thus, it is really nothing more than an especially sophisticated form of sin. Not only can we not escape sin by fleeing from creation—we can sin precisely by doing so.

There is no part of the universe that is not part of God's creation. So there is no part that is *essentially* evil, and no part which can be understood apart from God. This means that there is no room for Christian hang-ups about sexuality.[2] Even when exploitative distortions of sexuality occur, they provide no excuse for refusing sex as God's good gift. And there is nothing wrong with being finite, contingent, and vulnerable. To deny our vulnerability is to seek to be more absolute than God, who delights and suffers with creation.[3] Only by accepting our vulnerability can we experience genuine human flourishing; only in this way can we receive the rich gifts of friendship and love, or appreciate any other element of the created order.

Similarly, if what God makes through creatures is part of the good creation, then politics, the family, education, work, sport, literature, love, and the arts—including film, television, architecture, music, theatre, painting, and sculpture—must be understood as among the ways in which God enriches the universe through us, as among God's good gifts.[4] God is at work in and through human culture—the explicitly religious aspects, but also everywhere else.[5]

Love for Creation as Healing and Development

Love for creation means relishing and participating in the ongoing, dynamic *development* of creation: this development is valuable in its own right. To affirm the worth of the culture and other aspects of the ongoing creation to which we contribute directly is precisely not to instrumentalize them by treating their value as dependent on their contribution to other things God might be up to in the world. But because creation is marred by the presence of suffering, frustration, and loss, love for creation also means participating in God's work of *healing*.

The metaphor of healing points to an aspect of God's work that is distinct from creation's development. But it is not anti-creational; rather, it highlights the fact that there is nothing fundamentally wrong with being created. God doesn't

---

1. Wolters 53 (my italics).
2. Cp. L. William Countryman, *Dirt, Greed and Sex: Sexual Ethics in the New Testament and Their Implications for Today* (London: SCM 1988).
3. So John Barton, *Love Unknown: Meditations on the Death and Resurrection of Jesus* (Louisville, KY: Westminster/Knox 1990) 33-7. As Barton puts it, "to believe in Jesus as the embodiment of God is to change radically what we mean by God. The God revealed in Jesus is not a detached God, but one whose own freedom is his boundless ability to commit himself to the needs of the world he has made" (36).
4. See Wolters 72-95.
5. See Wolters 64-9.

heal the created world to make it something other than it really is; God heals the created world to enable it to realize its potential.[1] Loving creation—in connection with development or healing—means helping the created world to be itself, to be the best it can be, not turning creation into something it isn't.

Indeed, to talk about God's work in the world as a work of *healing* is to stress that the goodness of creation, and so its need for development, must be understood as logically prior to its brokenness, and thus its need for healing. While our participation in the development of creation is preceded and conditioned by human sin, it is not itself *essentially* a remedy for, much less a product of, moral brokenness: it is a reflection of the inner dynamism toward increasing complexity, flourishing, fulfillment, and diversification that is an essential aspect of God's good creation. It is distinct from, though related to, the healing divine work designed to counteract the effects of sin and brokenness. Consider the relationship between the processes of development and healing in the life of a child infected with

> a serious chronic disease for which there is no known cure, . . . [who] grows up an invalid, the disease wasting . . . [her or his] body away. It is clear that there are two clearly distinguishable processes going on in . . . [her or his] body as . . . [she or he] approaches adolescence: one is the process of maturation and growth, which continues in spite of the sickness and which is natural, normal, and good; the other is the progress of the disease, which distorts and impairs the healthy functioning of the body. Now suppose further that the child has reached adolescence when a cure is found for the sickness, and . . . [she or he] slowly begins to recover its health. As the child approaches adulthood there is now a third process at work in its body: the process of healing, which counteracts and nullifies the action of the disease and which has no other purpose than to bring the youth to healthy adulthood, in which only the normal processes of a sound body will take place.[2]

The healing process and the child's natural development are both important,[3] but they are distinct. And the point of the healing process is to make the child's natural development possible, not to serve as a substitute for it. In the same way, God's healing work in the world reflects the logically prior essential worth of the created order. The development of creation's inherent potential is valuable in its own right—more valuable than the healing process, in the same way that the development of one's mind is more important than the removal of a brain tumor which might ultimately stunt or end that development.

Jesus' ministry reflects concern with both care for creation as such and with the healing of its brokenness. His healings reflected his commitment to the priority of the created order—he cared about people's bodies, and so about their lives in the world—and his commitment to its healing.[4] His parables about the way in which to live while awaiting the complete arrival of God's Realm can be understood as calls to tend creation in various ways.[5] Implicit in his ministry was a call to contribute to the well-being of creation.

We cannot assume that, because the world is God's good creation, it isn't in need of healing; nor can we deny creation's essential goodness. But the prior, fundamental, normative reality is always God's good creation, whose value is highlighted by God's revelation in Jesus. We love the creation through our work

---

1. Cp. Wolters 57-71; Gilkey, *Maker* 278-85.
2. Wolters 39; see also 63-4.
3. Wolters 58.
4. Wolters 61-3.
5. Wolters 63-4.

of healing, but also through our work of developing creation and by enjoying the opportunities for flourishing provided by God's good gifts.[1]

The Contours of Love

Love's attention to others in their particularity requires understanding the various aspects of human well-being. Appropriately attentive love involves ordering love reasonably, and so avoiding unfairness and direct attacks on human welfare. The Pauline Principle and the Golden Rule help to specify the meaning of love for other persons and oneself.

Love as Concerned with Human Welfare

We can love ourselves and other persons[2] only if we have some idea of what constitutes human welfare.[3] Determining what makes for human well-being isn't always easy. Enjoyment is a pointer to welfare, but not a perfect one. And human needs, dispositions, and circumstances are sufficiently diverse that generalizing about the character of human welfare can be a challenge. Nonetheless, we can plausibly identify several distinct, irreducible aspects of human well-being.

The fact that someone enjoys something is decent, though hardly decisive, evidence that it contributes to human welfare. But to talk about enjoyment is, of course, to begin the conversation, not to end it. After all—while abstract conceptions of human well-being cannot be blind us to what's good for a particular person—people can sometimes be mistaken about what will foster their own welfare. The fact that something is enjoyable is typically not what makes it a constituent of human welfare. Many self-destructive behaviors are enjoyable. Many actions and character traits that involve unreasonableness as regards the legitimate claims of other creatures—human and non-human—may be enjoyable as well. Further, participating in some aspects of human welfare may be inherently worthwhile even though, for any number of reasons, they're not subjectively enjoyable.

Something can be enjoyable because experiencing it involves experiencing *sensory* pleasure. It can also be enjoyable because it evokes a positive *emotional* response. It's important to distinguish between pleasurable *sensations* that we week

---

1. Nicholas P. Wolterstorff, *Until Justice and Peace Embrace*, Kuyper Lectures 1981 (Grand Rapids: Eerdmans 1984) 72.

2. The same will, of course, be true, *mutatis mutandis*, where other morally considerable creatures are concerned.

3. For what follows, see Germain G. Grisez and Russell Shaw, *Beyond the New Morality: The Responsibilities of Freedom*, 3d. ed. (Notre Dame, IN: U of Notre Dame P 1988); Germain G. Grisez and Russell Shaw, *Fulfillment in Christ: A Summary of Christian Moral Principles* (Notre Dame, IN: U of Notre Dame P 1991); Germain G. Grisez, *The Way of the Lord Jesus* 1: *Christian Moral Principles* (Chicago: Franciscan Herald 1983); John M. Finnis, *Natural Law and Natural Rights*, Clarendon Law Series (Oxford: Clarendon-OUP 1980); John M. Finnis, Joseph M. Boyle, Jr., and Germain G. Grisez, *Nuclear Deterrence, Morality, and Realism* (Oxford: Clarendon-OUP 1987) 177-296; John M. Finnis, *Fundamentals of Ethics* (Oxford: Clarendon-OUP 1983); John M. Finnis, *Aquinas: Moral, Political, and Legal Theory*, Founders of Modern Political and Social Thought 1 (Oxford: Clarendon-OUP 1998). It will be clear to anyone who knows their work how much I have learned from the so-called "new classical natural law" theorists, though it will also be apparent that I do not share all of their conclusions. I engage more directly with aspects of their work in "Toward a Consistent Natural Law Ethics of False Assertion," *American Journal of Jurisprudence* 51 (2006): 43-64 and "Natural Law, Same-Sex Marriage, and the Politics of Virtue," *UCLA Law Review* 48.6 (Aug. 2001): 1593-1632, as well as in "Consumption, Development Aid, and Natural Law," forthcoming in the *Washington and Lee Journal of Civil Rights and Social Justice*.

for their own sakes and *emotions*, which are complex combinations of thoughts and sensations that are or embody fallible cognitive judgments about what things signify and how important they are.¹

For example: the sensory pleasure associated with consuming chocolate is valuable in its own right, worth seeking for its own sake. By contrast, the feelings associated with being in love are pointers to what the person experiencing these feelings judges as the value of another person, and of a close relationship with that person. Experiencing certain sensations is one reason for consuming chocolate; in general, it's the most important point of doing so. But having the sensations associated with the hormones that can accompany romantic passion isn't the *point* of loving someone.² The point of loving is not the sensory experience of being in love, and one can perfectly well *be* in love with someone whether or not one *feels* the sensations often associated with being in love. Those sensations signify our response to a person, a relationship, we experience as inherently valuable. Similarly, when I am afraid, the sensations of fear I experience are not what I'm afraid of—I'm afraid of whatever it is that's triggered the fear.

Determining what conduces to human welfare is difficult not only because of the complications associated with the real but limited value of enjoyment as a pointer to what makes for human welfare, but also because human beings are diverse. There are many particular human *natures*, each of which shares some, but typically not all, characteristics with others. And of course, our natures are dependent not only on biological but on psychic and social phenomena. God forms our natures through these as much as through our genes and our hormones.³ Social structures, institutions, and practices, all of which help to determine who we are, are God's creations through us—just, as, say, the Grand Canyon is God's creation through the movement of water and other processes and elements of the physical world.⁴ They're part of nature, too. So there's room for a lot of variety.

Despite the diversity, though, there's overlap. So we can confidently draw some general conclusions in light of thoughtful reflection on human welfare (to which, again, consideration about enjoyment can make a real, though limited, contribution). It will be helpful to pay attention to the ways in which we actually make decisions: when we do, we seem to regard some things as giving us reasons for action that don't need justification in terms of yet further reasons.⁵ Humans are likely to share enough characteristics that we can offer a plausible list of the basic aspects of human welfare. It might include life, knowledge, practical reasonableness, friendship, æsthetic experience, play, sensory pleasure, entertainment, self-integration, and religion.⁶ While other things may be good for us, too, I suspect it will be apparent on inspection that these other things are either

---

1. Cp. Martha C. Nussbaum, *Upheavals of Thought: The Intelligence of Emotions* (Cambridge: CUP 2001) 19-88.
2. Robert Solomon makes the point very aptly in *About Love: Reinventing Romance for Our Time* (New York: Simon 1988) 76-81.
3. Cp. Wolters 35-43.
4. This is not to suggest that such structures, institutions, and practices are the only possible outgrowths of creaturely nature. Different kinds of institutions, for instance, might be equally valid responses to the human need for security from violence. These structures are not arbitrary: they represent responses to a "givenness" in reality. But their particular forms are not strictly necessary either (see Wolterstorff 62-3; cp. Wolters 22-3 for what seems to be a different view).
5. Finnis, *Law* 59-99; Finnis, *Ethics* 51; Grisez, *Way* 122.
6. Badness may be a matter either of *damage* to one or more of these goods, or of sensory *pain*, the purposeful infliction of which is wrong apart from whatever damage might be done to a basic aspect of human welfare by an act which inflicts it.

combinations or aspects of these basic dimensions of human welfare, realities dependent on them, or else signs of or pointers to their existence.

No life can include all of the aspects of human welfare. And participating in some of these aspects richly and intensely makes it impossible to experience others as completely, if at all. But that doesn't mean that any of these aspects of human welfare isn't important. It makes sense to opt for *real* aspects of human welfare rather than unreal, imaginary substitutes. And it makes sense, too, to acknowledge the value of even those dimensions of human well-being in which one doesn't oneself participate. Their value still deserves to be recognized; it's unreasonable to attack them, verbally or through one's non-verbal actions, to treat them as if they really weren't valuable after all.

Each basic dimension of human welfare is distinguishable from the others. And each *instance* of every basic aspect of well-being is distinguishable from the others. No one of these dimensions of human welfare is worthwhile just as a means to one or more of the others. And none can be reduced to any of the others or to something else, like happiness. They are *intrinsically* valuable, worthwhile in and of themselves, whether our feelings tell us they are or not. While they can be reliably expected to contribute to our happiness, our happiness them isn't what *makes* them worthwhile; happiness *just is* our satisfaction at experiencing what we apprehend as an aspect of well-being—it's not a separate dimension of human welfare itself.[1]

Because none of these aspects of human welfare is reducible to any of the others, or comprehensible as just a means to one or more of the others, quantitative comparison between classes or instances of these dimensions of well-being are impossible. Even in principle, we cannot quantify instances of play, say, or æsthetic experience, or speculative knowledge. But if we could find some means of assigning a numerical value to the quantity of knowledge embodied in a given book, or the quantity of æsthetic experience in which one could participate by attending a given concert, there would be no intelligible way to compare the two. It is impossible—*logically* impossible—meaningfully to declare that the well-being realized in and through one concert is equivalent to or interchangeable with the well-being realized in and through another concert, or a particular football game, or a given laboratory exercise. We can't make moral choices by quantifying basic aspects of human welfare and comparing the quantities present in various alternative sets of circumstances. Any kind of moral strategy that involves comparisons of states of affairs as better or worse overall can't succeed *in principle*.

Specifications of Love

The incommensurability of states of affairs means that any attempt to subordinate one aspect of welfare to another (or one instance of well-being to another) will be unreasonable. For each dimension of welfare really is valuable, so it will be unreasonable to treat it as if it had no value. But it is not quantitatively (or lexically) comparable to any other. Thus, to treat one as trumping or outweighing any of the others would be unreasonable, too. For on what basis could one talk about the trumping or outweighing, given the impossibility of comparing, and so of ranking or ordering? As a result, attacking any of the aspects of human welfare—directly or as a means to some other goal—will be unreasonable. It makes no sense to argue that the intended end of an action can justify the means used to reach that end even if the means involves purposeful harm to one or more basic dimensions of human welfare. This would be reasonable only if one aspect (or an instance of one aspect) could be inherently more valuable than to another.

---

1. Finnis, *Law* 95-7.

In addition, to choose to attack a basic aspect of human welfare will be to misshape one's identity, to make unreasonably denying the value of a fundamental constituent of well-being part of who one is. Thus, for instance, to intend the death of another is to make *killing* an aspect of one's identity.

> If one intends to kill another, he accepts the identity of killer as an aspect of his moral self. If he is to be a killer through his own self-determination, he must regard himself in any situation as the lord of life and death. . . . Others' natural attitudes toward their own lives must be regarded as an irrational fact, not as a starting point for reasonable community.[1]

I cannot secretly do away with my stingy Uncle Charlie—who has made me the sole beneficiary of his estate—just because I plan to disburse the money to various good causes while keeping none of it myself. To do so is to act directly against Uncle Charlie's life—a basic aspect of his well-being. The harm my act would cause would not be an unintended by-product of my action; it would rather be a necessary part of my plan. The proposal I adopt when I put poison in his coffee necessarily involves willing harm to a basic aspect of human welfare.

Suppose someone says that, overall, the world would be a better place if I poison Uncle Charlie and give his money away to good causes than if I don't poison him. The problem here should be obvious. Basic aspects of human welfare are incommensurable: they can't be reduced to some common coin or interchanged with each other. This means that there's no intelligible, meaningful, non-arbitrary way of weighing them against each other; thus the good (perhaps) achieved (indirectly) by my action *cannot* outweigh the harm done to Uncle Charlie, any more than the number of words on this page can outweigh the speed of light in megameters per hour.[2]

These considerations point to a crucial element of love: the principle that it is wrong to cause harm *purposefully* or *instrumentally*. This principle means that it is wrong to act *directly* against a basic aspect of human welfare (or nourish hostility toward it). Thinking of St. Paul's vehement denial that he would regard it as acceptable to do evil to bring about good consequences, we may call this the Pauline Principle.[3] The other basic moral principle is the requirement of fairness, captured in Judaism, Christianity, and other traditions by the Golden Rule: one's choices should not involve arbitrary preferences among persons.[4] This, too, is a basic demand of reason. For "intelligence and reasonableness can find no basis in the mere fact that A is A and is not B (that I am I and am not you) for evaluating his (our) well-being differently."[5] The Pauline Principle and the Golden Rule are

---

1. Germain G. Grisez, "Toward a Consistent Natural-Law Ethics of Killing," *American Journal of Jurisprudence* 15 (1970): 76.
2. My contentions in this and the preceding two paragraphs depend on arguments offered by the new classical natural lawyers.
3. See Rom. 6:1—"Should we continue in sin in order that grace may abound? By no means!" I owe the phrase "Pauline Principle" to Donagan and to John Finnis, *Fundamentals of Ethics* (Oxford: Clarendon-OUP 1986) 75, 109-11.
4. Cp. Lev. 19:18, Mt. 19:19, Jas. 2:8. Germain G. Grisez and Russell Shaw, *Beyond the New Morality: The Responsibilities of Freedom*, 3d. ed. (Notre Dame, IN: U of Notre Dame P 1988) formulate this principle as follows: "Do not, in response to feelings, act or refrain from acting toward someone on the basis of a preference, unless the preference is required by human goods" (119).
5. Finnis, *Law* 107; John Finnis, "Commensuration and Practical Reason," *Incommensurability, Incomparability, and Practical Reason*, ed. Ruth Chang (Cambridge, MA: Harvard UP 1997) 227-9. While the principle of fairness certainly provides what Finnis terms "reasonable scope for self-preference" (*Law* 107), the norm of moral equality does not preclude and may (as in fulfillment of some open-ended promises to intimates) require self-sacrificial giving on behalf of someone else. Paul Tillich's notion of redemptive or

not alternatives to love or constraints on love: they are specifications of what it means truly to love persons (including oneself).

A creational vision of persons acknowledging all of the basic constituents of human welfare, adhering in relations with other persons to the two primary moral principles I've elaborated,[1] and respecting and caring for the non-human world parallels the biblical vision of harmonious, flourishing peace, or shalom. The Hebrew prophets used "shalom" to describe the well-being of God's good creation. To "dwell in shalom is to *enjoy* living before God, to *enjoy* living in one's physical surroundings, to *enjoy* living with one's fellows, to *enjoy* living with oneself."[2] Shalom is love enacted throughout creation.

Alternative Conceptions of Love for Creation

Love that respects the basic aspects of human welfare and adheres to the Golden Rule and the Pauline Principle contrasts with a variety of alternative construals of morality. It rules out inadequate accounts of what it means to love—as bringing about the best overall state of affairs in any situation, or as ignoring the Pauline Principle and the Golden Rule in favor of whatever a situation might be thought to entail.

Love of the Undifferentiated Whole

Consequentialism is the view that we are required to maximize the overall good, that we seek "the greatest good of the greatest number."[3] It enjoins love

---

"creative" justice provides one way of linking justice with self-giving love of this sort; see Tillich, *Love* 64-6. Of course, creative justice is to be expected of those capable of exhibiting it; cp. Mary Daly's criticism of Tillich's notion in *Pure Lust: Elemental Feminist Philosophy* (Boston: Beacon 1984) 276-7.

1. Finnis and Grisez suggest that there are various moral principles (or "modes of responsibility") in addition to the Golden Rule and the Pauline Principle (they offer different versions of the relevant list at different points). These norms include a proposed prohibition on acting out of or nurturing hostility, which I believe can be seen plausibly as forming part of the Pauline Principle. I am doubtful that the other proposed norms are binding in the ways and to the degree Finnis and Grisez suggest that they are; thus my suggestion that there are two basic moral principles for interactions among finite persons like us. Other principles may, of course, be appropriate as regards human interactions with the non-human world, though some variant of the Golden Rule may be applicable to relationships with higher mammals, and the Pauline Principle will surely apply to interactions with non-human sentients.

2. Wolterstorff 70. Wolterstorff articulately criticizes the view that true happiness is found in the intellectual contemplation of God: personal relationships, embodiment, and embeddedness in the natural world all count for something as well (124-6). Roger Scruton develops an understanding of happiness as the basis for a non-utilitarian morality in *Sexual Desire: A Philosophical Investigation* (London: Weidenfeld 1986) 326-37.

3. On the difficulties faced by consequentialist approaches, see Alasdair MacIntyre, *After Virtue: A Study in Moral Theory*, rev. ed. (Notre Dame, IN: U of Notre Dame P 1984) 61-3, 67-8, 185; Finnis, *Law* 111-9; Finnis, *Ethics* 80-108; Finnis, Boyle, and Grisez 177-296; Grisez and Shaw, *Morality*; Nel Noddings, *Caring: A Feminine Approach to Ethics and Moral Education* (Berkeley: U of California P 1984) 86-7, 151-4; Bernard A. O. Williams, *Morality: An Introduction to Ethics* (Cambridge: CUP 1993); Bernard A. O. Williams, "A Critique of Utilitarianism," *Utilitarianism: For and Against*, by John J. C. Smart and Williams (Cambridge: CUP 1973) 77-150; Gilbert C. Meilaender, *Faith and Faithfulness: Basic Themes in Christian Ethics* (Notre Dame, IN: U of Notre Dame P 1991) 89-113; Alan Donagan, *The Theory of Morality* (Chicago: U of Chicago P 1977) 172-209; Germain G. Grisez, "Against Consequentialism," *American Journal of Jurisprudence* 23 (1978) 21-72; Stephen R. L. Clark, "Natural Integrity and Biotechnology," *Human Lives: Critical Essays on*

for society, the world, the universe as an essentially undifferentiated whole. Classical utilitarianism—the oldest variety of consequentialism—maintains that all kinds of happiness can be added up quantitatively; that possible courses of action can be compared based on the amount of happiness each is likely to generate throughout the universe; and that a moral actor should in each situation make the choice, of those open to her, that will bring about the most happiness.[1] Newer sorts of consequentialism have given other definitions of the imagined overall good, but have argued, like classical utilitarianism, for the wrongness of declining to maximize the good, however defined.

Classical utilitarianism is mistaken in treating happiness as the substrate underlying the other dimensions of human welfare. It is similarly mistaken in supposing that happiness could be quantified in such a way that the happiness-producing potential of different states of affairs could be compared in straightforward fashion. It seems not to recognize the qualitative differences between kinds of satisfaction.[2] And it is mistaken in supposing that subjective satisfaction with something either constitutes its real value or provides irrefutable evidence of its value.

Any position that enjoins maximization of the overall good—globally or in a given situation—will encounter the problem of the incommensurability of the basic aspects of human welfare (and of individual instances of these aspects). Once the consequentialist acknowledges the absurdity of thinking that happiness is a mental state we seek when we pursue actual particular aspects of human welfare, and that maximizing the overall good is the same as maximizing happiness, she will need some other quantity to maximize; otherwise there will be no way to make sense of talk about the overall good. But because of the incommensurability of the various dimensions of human welfare, it is impossible to quantize or quantitatively rank aggregates of different kinds of human welfare, or different instances of the same aspect of human well-being. Thus, the kind of maximizing that consequentialism seems to require is *impossible*.

Basic aspects of human welfare are both inherently valuable and incommensurable. These features of the fundamental dimensions of well-being entail the Pauline Principle, which requires us not to inflict harm purposefully or instrumentally. Consequentialism treats this principle as irrelevant: we should always seek the greatest overall good (assuming this is a coherent notion), no matter what harms we choose to effect along the way. And we should understand ourselves as responsible for any outcomes that might be seen to follow from any of our choices, whether we intend the outcomes or not.

Thus, the consequentialist will say, if my refusal to bomb a city during a war leads to prolonged hostilities, and thus to the deaths of more civilians and military personnel, then I am responsible for those deaths. I should choose to bomb, therefore, because my doing so will bring about, or at least make possible, the survival of those people who will die if hostilities continue.

The consequentialist can offer no good reason for the view that I am responsible for the deaths of those noncombatants who will, as she supposes, be killed if the conflict continues. I do not intend their deaths or plan for them.

Consequentialist Bioethics, ed. Jacqueline A. Laing and David S. Oderberg (London: Palgrave 1997) 58-76; David S. Oderberg, *Moral Theory: A Non-Consequentialist Approach* (Oxford: Blackwell 2000) 65-76, 97-101, 132-33. For a critical philosophical assessment of a related movement in social theory, see Martha C. Nussbaum, "Flawed Foundations: The Philosophical Critique of (a Particular Type of) Economics," *University of Chicago Law Review* 64 (Fall 1997): 1197-1214.

1. To be sure, it doesn't follow that the actor's focus is on bringing about the most happiness: she might focus consciously on something else entirely, per various kinds of "indirect" utilitarianism.
2. See Finnis, *Law* 95-7, 110-8, 131-2; *Ethics*.

Even if it could be shown that my not attacking a civilian population center was a necessary condition for subsequent noncombatant deaths, it would not follow that I brought those deaths about in a morally relevant way. The claim that I did, that I am responsible for any outcome I can foresee will follow from a choice I make, is not an argument for consequentialism; it is simply a restatement of one of consequentialism's premises.

And the consequentialist's proposal obviously calls for violation of the Pauline Principle. I choose to harm those present in the city when I bomb it as a means to reduce conflict. I have identified with the harm, and I have acted unreasonably—since any violation of the Pauline Principle is unreasonable. For the consequentialist's proposal to make sense, she would need to show that basic aspects of human welfare aren't inherently valuable or that they aren't incommensurable; otherwise, the Pauline Principle stands. The same kinds of considerations will apply any time I purposefully effect a harm, whether as an intrinsically worthwhile purpose or as a means to some other goal: I violate the Pauline Principle, and so deliberately choose against love for those I intend to harm.

Consequentialism is inconsistent with the Pauline Principle. And the incommensurability of the basic aspects of human welfare means that the kind of maximization it commends is impossible. It also seems ill-equipped to acknowledge the value of self-integration or the claims of special moral relationships.

Self-integration—making a coherent whole out of one's life—receives short shrift from consequentialism.[1] The consequentialist must always evaluate people's projects and commitments in light of whatever might be imagined as contributing most effectively to the welfare of the entire universe. Thus, it seems unavoidably to hold that the moral decision-maker must always sit lightly to her projects and commitments. Forging a coherent life-plan, with goals that matter deeply and projects that are pursued consistently over time, will be difficult if the well-being of the universe as a whole can always exercise a veto over one's day-to-day choices.

Consequentialism also fails to acknowledge the particular duties we have to others in virtue of our promises to and covenants with them and their distinctive vulnerabilities to us. It is concerned only with the welfare of the group *viewed as a whole*; it deliberately brackets concern for particular persons and sub-groups. Thus, it is insensitive to the special relations that bind us to particular persons, institutions, communities, and things. It fails to exhibit the concern with each personal and impersonal constituent of the world *in its particularity* that seems to be an appropriate expression of love in view of the reality and loveableness of each creature. And this is true whether love means the ecstasy of passion or the quiet decency of respect.

Consequentialism is sometimes cashed in Christian terms: Christians may be told, "Perform the most loving possible act," with the most loving possible act, in turn, understood as the one that leads to the putatively best overall consequences. Joseph Fletcher, for instance, wholeheartedly endorsed the identification of Christian love with consequentialism.[2]

Fletcher's commitment to consequentialism is evident in his discussion of a variety of cases. When Jesus is anointed at Bethany, the "disciples say that love must work in coalition with utilitarian distribution, spreading the benefits as much as possible. Jesus is cast into the role of defending Leo Tolstoy's doctrine that love wears blinders, sees only the neighbor there. If we take the story as it stands, Jesus was wrong and the disciples were right."[3] If one can carry only a single man from a burning building, and "the choice is between your own father

---

1. Williams, "Critique" makes this point with particular force.
2. See Joseph Fletcher, *Situation Ethics: The New Morality* (London: SCM 1966) 95.
3. Fletcher 97.

and a medical genius who has discovered a cure for a common fatal disease, you carry out the genius if you understand agape. This is the agapeic calculus."[1] Dropping nuclear bombs on Hiroshima and Nagasaki might prove to have been a product of the calculus of love.[2]

Baptizing consequentialism and articulating it using the language of Christian love doesn't make it any more viable as a moral theory. Certainly, it isn't a necessary expression of love. Consequentialism is just one of a number of specific, contestable, conceptions of what love is and requires. The question is precisely, *Who will we love through our actions?* A proponent of the moral position I defend here will answer: *We will love those in relation to whom we will act fairly and whom we will not choose to harm purposefully or instrumentally*. The consequentialist's answer, in effect, is: *We will love everyone as part of an undifferentiated whole*. The disagreement is not about who favors love and who doesn't; it's about what love *means*. And, if the Golden Rule and the Pauline Principle specify what love means, then consequentialist judgments will often appear as *failures* of love; it is *precisely out of love*, for instance, that American leaders should have refused to rain down death on noncombatants in Hiroshima and Nagasaki.

There is real tone-deafness in Fletcher's analysis of Jesus' treatment of the woman who anoints him at Bethany. The only alternative to consequentialism he seems able to envision is one in which love means doing whatever the person who happens, at random, to be in front of me seems to need. But surely it makes more sense here to see Jesus responding out of a sense of particular concern and care for this woman, concern that emerges from her unique vulnerability to him and his unique opportunity to make a difference in her life because of that vulnerability and, perhaps, bonds between them reflective of a unique relational history.

Might not the same kind of point be made with respect to the prospective rescuees from a burning building? Might not my father reasonably expect a degree of care from me that the scientist might not? Choosing to care for a vulnerable woman or for an endangered parent is hardly a matter of not being loving. Rather, it represents a different vision of love from the one Fletcher defends.

Special relationships *channel* and *focus* love. And they generate reasonable expectations of care and loyalty. Often, at least, part of what it *means* to love someone else is precisely to give her or him an assurance of constancy. Marital love and close friendship are obvious examples, but there may be other special relationships in which it is important for someone to know she or he can count on me, no matter what. Suppose the other knows that whether I can be relied on to keep my covenant with her or him depends on whether doing so can be expected to make the universe as a whole better. If so, she or he can hardly experience the security and freedom my commitment is supposed to engender in the first place.

> If a person genuinely means to attach an exception-making criterion to his promises or to his marriage vow, if he means to live by a rule of practice which states that the marriage covenant holds, that promises should be kept except when by a direct appeal to what Christian love requires it would be better not to keep them, he had better say so, since the one he promises or his marriage partner . . . will not understand it that way.[3]

Consequentialist proposals seem to ignore the distinction between what I do and what I allow someone else to do, and the difference between an outcome I bring about purposefully and one that's a by-product or side effect of my pursuit of another goal. And they ignore the value of self-integration, by undermining

---

1. Fletcher 115.
2. These examples are drawn from Fletcher.
3. Paul Ramsey, "The Biblical Norm of Righteousness," *Interpretation* 24.4 (Oct. 1970): 426. See also Ramsey's *Deeds and Rules in Christian Ethics* (New York: Scribner 1967).

the coherence of my life story; the value of fairness, by disregarding the claims of those (including those with whom I am linked by special relationships) they suggest I ought to harm or disregard for the good of others; and the value of friendship, by treating all relationships as, in effect, on par with each other.

Love for God's good creation is best seen as love for the *particular* other, love that respects distinctive responsibilities, commitments, and vocations that give shape to our lives, rather than as an undifferentiated universal benevolence. Consequentialism attempts to be an expression of love. But I think the deep-seated problems with consequentialism, and the winsomeness of the alternative conception of Christian love I have tried to articulate, point us in another direction.

Situation Ethics as a Misconstrual of Love

To say that love is the heart of Christian ethics has sometimes been interpreted as a claim that that neither moral generalizations nor moral absolutes have any validity. Moral decisions must be made on a case-by-case basis. Fletcher, the prime exponent of so-called "situation ethics," seems often to have understood his position in consequentialist terms. But a commitment to situation ethics often reflects the view that *all* principles, including the consequentialist injunction to maximize the good, are untenable. All one can do when making moral decisions is to discern the unique requirements of each situation and act accordingly.

Loving reality means being prepared to accept its surprises. Really loving, really paying attention to what is other than ourselves, requires us to let go of our assumptions, to abandon the *a priori* schemes we use to organize our lives and our social worlds. Love acknowledges that the generalizations we find it easy to make may be wrong, dreadfully wrong.

The world is a terribly complex place. Sometimes its variety and intricacy threaten to overwhelm us. So it is natural that we should find tidy rules appealing. Generalizations make an unmanageable reality seem more orderly. Large organizations, especially, seem to find it impossible not to establish and implement inflexible rules designed rather less than adequately for a wide variety of particular cases. Bureaucracies often encourage unswerving adherence to such rules even when, in individual instances, they clearly seem inapplicable. Churches often create and apply rules inflexibly, and often enough they attribute their own penchant for inflexibility to God.

Such an attitude can breed frustration. A generalization is typically adequate at best in a majority of cases. Acting in accordance with an underlying moral principle often demands much more flexibility than such a rule can provide. A bureaucratic norm designed to protect teenagers from harming themselves in one way or another, for instance, may be applied without exceptions, in a way that unduly restricts the freedom of adolescents who exhibit good judgment and self-control. Especially when we are impelled by love, we cannot avoid attending to the particularities that may seem to render general rules inapplicable, or we will fail to love the actual people we confront in particular situations.

It is important, however, not to assume too quickly that an ethic of love has no place for absolutes, for exceptionless moral requirements. This was a popular claim a generation ago, of course. Proponents of situation ethics argued that there was no way to know what we ought to do, what love really required, without looking at individual situations, and that, when we did look at individual situations, we would discover the appropriateness of a variety of exceptions to traditional moral norms.

But this conclusion is not the inevitable outcome of paying careful, loving attention to the particular features of each situation and each creature affected by our actions. It's certainly not obvious or self-evident, even if it is sometimes supported by what are thought to be unquestionable platitudes about the impossibility of reducing complex situations to tidy patterns. Why, exactly, might it not be the case that any situation with certain features, *whatever* the other features might be, should rightly evoke the same moral response?

It's important to emphasize that to say that there are *some* absolutes isn't the same thing as saying that there are, or should be, *many* of them. Flexibility is important; there are lots of appropriate ways to love God and God's world. Many different choices in similar or identical circumstances will often be *fair*, for instance. But the Golden Rule *itself* isn't optional. And while fairness often allows for flexibility, sometimes it doesn't. For instance: while most promises are implicitly or explicitly qualified in various ways, in some cases we deliberately make promises that rule out exceptions; I think it's fair to say that many people's vows to avoid sexual contact with people other than their spouses are like this. A smaller number of people regard their marriage vows themselves in this way. Since promise-keeping is a demand of fairness, in these cases we will confront exceptionless requirements that follow from the Golden Rule.[1]

The Pauline Principle is also a source of exceptionless requirements. It precludes *purposeful* (and thus instrumental) attacks on basic aspects of human welfare under any circumstances. (It is perfectly consistent with conduct in which we do not cause harm purposefully or instrumentally, but in which we—fairly—bring harm about as a by-product.) Whenever someone proposes precisely to harm a fundamental dimension of human welfare—purposefully or instrumentally—her proposal is unreasonable.

If I propose to bomb a civilian population center to end a war, or to kill a defenseless prisoner to avert a crime wave, whatever else may be true, I'm acting unreasonably. Nothing else about my situation could make it the case that my action turned out to be reasonable after all. For my unreasonableness, if I carry out my proposal, will consist in making a choice that either treats a basic aspect of human welfare as if it weren't inherently valuable, or else seeks to treat it as somehow less important than another aspect (or an instance of the same aspect). Both of these options don't make sense; they're rationally indefensible. So there can never be a good reason to violate the Pauline Principle, understood as a prohibition on any direct attack on a basic aspect of human well-being. Thus, I don't need to know any more about a proposal than that acting on it would violate the Pauline Principle to know that it could not, ever, be acceptable. The other features of the situation in which the proposal is considered simply aren't relevant. It appears, then, that an ethic of love can incorporate exceptionless moral norms.

Adherence to the Pauline Principle will often not be at issue. In many cases, we must simply ensure that we follow the Golden Rule—that we make decisions we could live with were our roles and those of the people affected by our decisions reversed. While the requirement of fairness is itself an absolute, there will often be many ways in which it is possible to act fairly. But fairness sometimes makes absolute requirements. Some proposals for action will be ruled out absolutely by the Pauline Principle. Sometimes, the Golden Rule's demand of fairness will require one to fulfill a promissory obligation or honor a special relational responsibility at potentially great cost. But when we adhere to these principles, we are not ignoring love, opting for law in place of love, or anything of the sort. Rather, love itself—love for those we decline to harm intentionally, love for those to whom we have promised our fidelity—demands that we acknowledge that there are some things we simply may not, or must, do.

1. For accounts of exceptionless promises of fidelity, see, *e.g.*, John J. Powell, *Unconditional Love* (Allen, TX: Argus 1978); Hugh Prather and Gayle Prather, *I Will Never Leave You: How Couples Can Achieve the Power of Lasting Love* (New York: Bantam 1996).

Divine Command Ethics and God's Love for Creation

The account of moral requirements I have sought to articulate in this chapter is a creation-based account. On this view, moral requirements have the character they do because of the way God has made and is making us and the world, together with the basic, inescapable requirements of reason.

A creation-based account of ethics holds that value is inherent in the created order.[1] Thus, in bringing certain kinds of creatures into being, God made a necessary choice that the moral order would be of one sort and not another. God could have made other sorts of creatures, to whom different sorts of responses were appropriate. But inherent in the project of making the sorts of creatures God chose to create is the unavoidable decision to make creatures whose well-being necessarily claims our love and God's and which is definable in particular ways.[2]

The understanding of Christian ethics as rooted in the loveable goodness of creation seems reflected in the teachings of Jesus, who

> conceived the Law not as a set of conditions to be fulfilled if a man was to have access to divine power but rather as a divine gift to man which might enable him to find fulfillment. Thus he does not simply insist that these are the commandments of God, which therefore must be fulfilled, whether intelligible or no. . . . Rather he points men to the central matter which is that the intention of these ordinances is that they should enable all men to live as they would individually desire to do. . . . Where there is obscurity or controversy it is this central principle which must decide . . . .
> Jesus' legal teaching, that is to say, seeks to realize the intention of the creator in ordering and caring for the world, rather than simply advocating obedience to law because it is the *Law of God*.[3]

Nonetheless, some Christians believe that God freely creates moral norms independently of the character of creation.[4] In this section, I note some difficulties

---

1. See Carlton D. Fischer, "Because God Says So," *Christian Theism and the Problems of Philosophy*, ed. Michael D. Beaty, Library of Religious Philosophy 5 (Notre Dame, IN: U of Notre Dame P 1990) 355-77 for an articulate and helpful defense of a similar position. In particular, see 363: ". . . what is or isn't good for us is determined by our design. . . . [God] creates *us*, but with *us* comes the standard, the operating manual. It is up to God what *we* are *like*, but once we are as we are, it is not up to God to decide what is good for us. . . ."

2. For a general critique of the notion that the creation is not itself the ground of the moral order, see O'Donovan 31-52.

3. John Riches, *Jesus and the Transformation of Judaism* (New York: Seabury 1982) 130-1. Riches (216n54) contrasts Jesus' attitude with that attributed to Rabbi Johanan ben Zakkai, who is supposed to have said regarding purity regulations: "The dead body does not really defile; the water does not really purify; but God has said, I have ordained an ordinance, I have decreed a decree; it is not permitted to you to transgress my decree" (Num. R. Hukkat, 19.8). Riches cites Matt. 7:12 and Mk 2:27 (nn55-6) as examples of Jesus' teaching which substantiate the view he defends, and adduces in further (n57) support Robert J. Banks, *Jesus and the Law in the Synoptic Tradition* (Cambridge: CUP 1975) 113-4 and Hans Hübner, *Das Gesetz in der Synoptischen Tradition: Thesen zur progressiven Judaisierung and Qumranisierung der Synoptischen Tradition* (Witten: Luther 1973) 113-4.

4. Adams offers by far the most impressive and sophisticated defense of divine command ethics today, brimming with good sense. He does not regard judgments about *excellence* as contingent on divine commands. Goodness, he suggests, consists in resemblance to God, and resemblance relations are necessary. Obligations, however, *do* depend on divine commands, at least to a significant degree (though something may be *bad* without *prohibited*). Though Adams has not convinced me that most obligations are, in fact, rooted in contingent divine commands, *Finite and Infinite Goods* is clear, well argued, and wise, a source of useful insights into a wide range of moral challenges and philosophical puzzles.

with this view, sometimes labeled "voluntarism" because it takes God's will (*voluntas*) to be more basic than God's knowledge—or God's love.

If God *loves* creation, then it follows that creation is loveable and that God wouldn't pointlessly restrain the freedom of creatures by imposing moral demands on them that didn't foster their well-being. And if the basic aspects of human welfare couldn't *not* be valuable, given the kinds of creatures we are, and if the Golden Rule and the Pauline Principle are necessary requirements of reasonable action, we seem to have a straightforward account of morality that makes no reference to divine commands. The divine command view of what makes things right or wrong, contributory or non-contributory to human well-being, is inconsistent with the conviction that God is love. It depicts a god who is fundamentally arbitrary. And it risks evacuating talk of God's love of any content.

God as Arbitrary Will?

On the divine command view, God is the last of the mediæval emperors, who can decide arbitrarily to do anything at all. The moral order is God's contingent and arbitrary creation.

This view seems to hark back to the typical relationship between a parent and a six-year-old: "Why do I have to?" "Because I said so." God's naked power becomes the only real explanation for any value or requirement. Today, torturing innocent children might be wrong; tomorrow, God could opt to make it an obligatory sign of Christian loyalty.

It won't do any good to respond to the charge that this approach leads to counterintuitive conclusions by saying that God is faithful, and therefore wouldn't behave arbitrarily. For why *should* God be truthful or consistent in interacting with us? If faithfulness has any value, on the view I am criticizing, it has such value only because God happened to decide it did. And God could just easily decide it didn't. So there's no reason, on this view, to regard God's actions as predictable, patterned, or ordered.

Not surprisingly, the view that there is no standard for thought or action beyond God's arbitrary will helped to generate modern nihilism and atheistic existentialism. The proponent of the view that moral norms are rooted in arbitrary divine commands must maintain that norms couldn't obtain without such commands. And if this is so, there must be no good arguments for moral norms that don't finally make reference to divine commands. Thus, people's doubts about God led to doubts about morality: absent a commanding divine will, there seemed to be no reason to take morality seriously. Ironically, at the same time, the picture of God advanced by proponents of the view that morality had its source in divine commands came to provide the model for radical human freedom endorsed by nihilism and atheistic existentialism. Possessed of this kind of freedom, the nihilist self purports to *decide*, rather than discovering, what is and isn't valuable, just like the God of divine command theories. The nihilist self is really the arbitrary God writ small.[1]

Adams's differentiation between the right and the good, with only the former understood as contingent (in part) on the divine will, reduces the gap between his position and mine quite substantially. It is also important to emphasize that as regards both epistemological and substantive moral questions, someone following Adams's approach and someone opting for mine could often reach comparable conclusions.

1. See Michael Allen Gillespie, *Nihilism before Nietzsche* (Chicago: U of Chicago P 1995). Stephen Clark suggests, along related lines, that to take the view that there is "indeed no reason, apart from God's arbitrary will, for God to command this or that" is, in effect, to endorse "the Arian heresy," for which God's *Logos*, the order of things, is an arbitrary divine creation (Clark, *Mysteries* 98).

Making God's will rather than God's reason, knowledge, or love the ground of ethics led to nihilism. It can also lead to deep-seated resentment against God and traditional Christianity. Part of the process of becoming mature is differentiating oneself from one's parents. The slow process of maturation involves discovering that there are reasons for what may seem like arbitrary parental commands, and discovering one's capacity to assess those reasons. Parents who love their children want them to be themselves, want them to make their own decisions. It's as important to good parents that their children's decisions be genuinely made by the children themselves as that the decisions be wise and responsible ones.[1]

Like good parents, God is in the business of making persons—God's creative and healing activity testifies to that. But it isn't really very surprising that, if God were pictured as a cosmic parent in relation to whom one was always a toddler, from whom one never had any independence, the idea of God would become a frustrating and oppressive one in many people's minds. A god who infantilizes is hardly attractive.[2] I suspect that libeling God as an arbitrary dictator is responsible for much of the contemporary reaction against theistic religion.

Reasons for Obeying Divine Commands

If divine commands ground our moral obligations, then it seems as if we are left in the uncomfortable position of being unable to explain why these commands themselves are worth obeying.

The divine command theorist could, of course, answer that this is simply a matter of divine power: God is to be obeyed because God is bigger and stronger than we are. Or she might suppose that God will favor us if we obey divine commands. But neither of these seems like an especially attractive motive. Acting on the basis of these sorts of reasons is apt to make our moral practice inauthentic. And it doesn't really comport very well with the way I think we actually experience our moral obligations.

When we act morally, we experience ourselves as being *claimed* by something—by the need of another, say, or by the possibility of some previously resisted variety of human flourishing. Each of these things seems to provide us with reason on its own to act in particular ways; it seems odd to introduce the threat of divine sanction or the hope of divine favor into the picture. Indeed, doing so seems to change the meaning of our moral actions—and to remove the genuinely moral element from them. Fear and the desire to please are motives concerned exclusively with the actor, rather than with the others affected by the actor's choices, or with the relationship between the actor and those others. And acting out of either motive doesn't look too much like the image of moral action we find in the central biblical and Christian tradition.

Another possibility is that we should obey divine commands out of gratitude. But this won't do, either. To say that we *should* be grateful is to presuppose something like a debt owed to another. But the notion of a debt, of *owing*, is itself an essentially moral one. To urge gratitude as a motive for obeying the divine volition is, in effect, to say that we *ought* to be grateful. But why should we? Either because gratitude is commanded by God—in which case we're trapped in an infinite regress—or because gratitude is required by the nature of things and not in virtue of a divine command, in which case a divine command theory begins to appear at least incomplete as an account of the basis of moral obligation.

---

1. The aptness of this example in connection with this point has been suggested to me by Fritz Guy.
2. For a further criticism of the thinking that lies behind infantilizing models, see Noddings 43-4, 97-8.

Of course, the divine command theorist could say that gratitude isn't an obligation, but an instinctive emotional response. A grateful person just naturally tries to make her benefactor happy. This is no doubt often true, but it obviously doesn't account for the *force* we associate with moral obligations. If gratitude isn't itself obligatory, then it must simply be an option: if you feel grateful, that's fine, but if you don't, that's just an interesting fact about your psyche. And if it's optional, then only someone who wants to express her gratitude will have a reason to obey a divine command. Those who feel grateful will seek to avoid murder because it is prohibited by God; those who don't feel grateful will have no particular reason to do so. But we clearly don't experience moral obligation as simply a matter of acting on the basis of contingent desires. To say that something is obligatory is to say that I have a reason to do it *whatever* I happen to desire. If moral obligation is a matter of responding in gratitude to divine commands, and gratitude itself is optional, then following the commands themselves must be optional, and being moral must be optional.

An account of the moral life based on gratitude also misses the fact that gratitude is a bad motive for moral or spiritual performance. The right reason to act morally is because morality reflects the way reality really is. The fact that God wants us to live morally is not, *per se*, the reason we ought to do so; rather, God wants us to live morally because doing so makes sense. The view that we ought to live morally out of gratitude obscures the fact that the way we ought to live depends on the way our creator has made us.

An account focused on gratitude seems further to trade on the manipulability to which guilt feelings can give rise. To say that morality should be motivated by gratitude is effectively to say that we should spend our time trying to erase infinite debts to God.[1] The view that the moral life is grounded in gratitude seems to envision God as saying, rather like the stereotypical invalid mother, "Of course, I wouldn't *ask* you to do anything for me. I know that, if you love me, you'll do whatever you have to . . . ." But the God revealed in Jesus *cancels* debts. The goal of God's work in the world is not to make us servants—especially ones driven by our own guilt-laced gratitude—but, to use the Bible's language, *children and heirs, friends*. The notion that Christian living is based on gratitude appears to miss that fact. Gratitude to God is important, valuable, even obligatory, but it doesn't provide an appropriate basis for the moral life.

Divine Command Views and the Trivialization of God's Love

A further problem for divine command theories of ethics depends on the fact that such theories seem to make it difficult to talk about God's love.

Think for a moment about what it might mean to say that God loves the world, or you, or me, or anything else.[2] Part of love as care and respect is regard for the beloved's good. If we say that God loves the world, we might ordinarily think we were saying, among other things, that God seeks the welfare of

---

1. Cp. John Barton's observation about appeals to gratitude in the context of atonement theory: "I have enough sins already, without Christ dying in order to provide me with the opportunity to commit another and infinite one, the sin of ingratitude for the sufferings he bore. Such interpretations of Christ crucified merely lock us yet more firmly inside the religious hall of mirrors, beyond any possibility of escape" (30).

2. Cp. Gary D. Bradcock, "The Concept of Love: Divine and Human," *Nothing Greater, Nothing Better: Theological Essays on the Love of God*, ed. Kevin J. Vanhoozer (Grand Rapids: Eerdmans 2001): the "view that God loves specific human beings, not because of any good in them, but purely because that is what . . . [God] chooses to do, represents, if not a denial of the doctrine of creation, at least an unhelpful disjunction between it and the doctrine of redemption" (35).

creatures. The notion that God seeks the well-being of creatures is easy enough to understand on the assumption that human welfare is what it is in virtue of the way God made us. But suppose, now, that what counts as human welfare is not a function of our created characteristics, but rather an arbitrary creation of the divine will. Then it is unclear what it might mean to say that God loved the world. After all, God would be, *ex hypothesi*, free to decide that anything at all counted as human welfare.

If anything at all could count as human welfare, then anything God did could count as *seeking* human welfare. So anything at all God did could count as loving creation. If no account of creaturely well-being can be given independent of God's arbitrary decrees, then the notion that God loves the world is evacuated of all content. "God loves the world" would simply mean: God does whatever God does.

A proponent of divine command ethics might respond by arguing that what does or doesn't constitute *human welfare* is objectively given, but that *moral requirements* are nonetheless determined by God's arbitrary choice. But this response isn't altogether satisfactory.

The objector has conceded that the basic elements of human welfare are objectively valuable. And this means, roughly, that they serve as reasons for action—for God, and presumably also for rational creatures—apart from divine commands. But the basic moral principles—the Golden Rule and the Pauline Principle—provide reasons for action, too. There's not a huge gulf between the basic dimensions of human well-being and the basic moral principles: they're both action-guiding. Once the proponent of divine command ethics concedes that there can be some sources of objective reasons for action, it is unclear why there couldn't be others. Why would we need to explain moral norms as contingent divine creations when they could be understood, like the basic aspects of human well-being, as simple consequences of the way we're made?

There are positive arguments for the two basic moral principles: they flow from the inherent value and incommensurability of the basic aspects of welfare, and the general equivalence of persons. If the arguments I have already offered are correct, these principles obtain in virtue of the nature of rational action and the created characteristics of human persons.

The features of reality that make the two basic moral principles appropriate would necessarily affect the content of any commands issued by God. If the basic aspects of human well-being are *objectively valuable*, then any divine command would need to treat them as worthy of respect. And if they are fundamentally different from each other and irreducible to any imagined substrate, then any divine command would need to treat them as incommensurable. Thus, any putative divine command would need to take the Pauline Principle as given. Similarly, if human beings are generically equivalent in important respects, any such command would need to take the Golden Rule as given.

If the divine command theorist denies that the two basic principles are rationally defensible, she will need to mount persuasive arguments against these plausible principles, which are, after all, rooted not only in reason but also in the Bible and the Christian tradition. And, even if she successfully undermines them, she will still need to refute plausible arguments offered on behalf of alternative principles or patterns of moral action,[1] as well as ones offered in defense of the

---

1. See Alan Gewirth, *Reason and Morality* (Chicago: U of Chicago P 1978); Alan Gewirth, *The Community of Rights* (Chicago: U of Chicago P 1996); Alan Gewirth, *Self-Fulfillment* (Princeton: Princeton UP 1998); Thomas Nagel, *The Possibility of Altruism* (New York: Oxford 1970); Thomas Nagel, *The View from Nowhere* (New York: Oxford 1986); Thomas Nagel, *The Last Word* (New York: OUP 1997) 101-25; T. M. Scanlon,

view that, even though there are no general moral principles, situations *do* impose requirements on moral actors.¹ If she can show that no arguments for plausible moral principles are successful, then she will be free to argue that only divine commands explain the force of moral requirements—but at the cost of making those requirements appear arbitrary and making God look like a tyrant.

On the other hand, if she agrees that the Golden Rule and the Pauline Principle *are* rationally defensible and that these principles outline the contours of what is morally required,² she seems to have a problem. For, if they are defensible, then divine commands will either require, permit, and forbid the same behavior required, permitted, and forbidden by these principles, or they will not. If they do, then it seems that the divine commands are superfluous. But if they do not, then it seems that God would be demanding that people act irrationally, in a manner inconsistent with their created characteristics.

Perhaps a divine command theorist might respond by accepting that the Golden Rule and the Pauline Principle obtained objectively. She might accept, too, that it would be inconsistent with divine love and divine reason to command or permit anything contravening these principles, or to prohibit anything required by them. At this point, she would have given up most of what might be thought to make a divine command theory interesting: divine commands would not be invoked to explain many moral requirements, and certainly not the most central ones. But the divine command theorist might suggest that divine commands could still reduce the range of actions *permissible* for human beings. Some things that might otherwise be appropriate for human beings to do would be prohibited, and some things that might otherwise be optional would be required. We can call the relevant sorts of divine injunctions *option-restricting commands*.³

The problem here for the divine command theorist, it seems to me, is to explain why it would be consistent with divine love for God to issue commands restricting the range of permissible human behavior beyond the constraints imposed by the Golden Rule and the Pauline Principle. Such commands would restrict the range of personal autonomy and reduce the variety of the aspects of

---

What We Owe to Each Other (Cambridge, MA: Harvard UP 1998); Donagan; David Wiggins, *Ethics: Twelve Lectures on the Philosophy of Morality* (Cambridge, MA: Harvard UP 2006); David McNaughton, *Moral Vision: An Introduction to Ethics* (Oxford: Blackwell 1988); Alasdair MacIntyre, *Virtue*; Alasdair MacIntyre, *Whose Justice? Which Rationality?* (Notre Dame: U of Notre Dame P 1988); Alasdair MacIntyre, *Three Rival Versions of Moral Enquiry* (Notre Dame: U of Notre Dame P 1990); Alasdair MacIntyre, *Dependent Rational Animals: Why Human Beings Need the Virtues* (Chicago: Open 1999); Henry S. Richardson, *Practical Reasoning about Final Ends* (Cambridge: CUP 1994); Martha C. Nussbaum, *Women and Human Development: The Capabilities Approach* (New York: CUP 2000). Cp. Martha C. Nussbaum, "Still Worthy of Praise," *Harvard Law Review* 111 (1998): 1776-95 (a critique of Richard Posner's skepticism about normative moral theory).

1. For this view, see Jonathan Dancy, *Moral Reasons* (Oxford: Blackwell 1993).
2. Or that other moral principles or patterns of moral action obtain objectively, or that situations impose objective moral requirements.
3. Adams rejects the notion "that our overriding, fully moral obligation is constituted by what *would* be commanded by a supremely good God, whether there is one or not." A key reason for his rejection of this analysis is that he does "not believe that there is a unique set of commands that would be issued by any supremely good God. . . . Some commands, surely, could not issue from a perfectly good being; but there are some things that such a deity might command or might not command." By way of example he offers putative divine commands regarding "religious ceremonies," but also suggests the possibility of "a diversity of principles regarding euthanasia that could have been commanded by a supremely good God; perhaps different weightings of the importance of preventing suffering as compared with other values at stake would be possible for such a deity" (255-6). The question, of course, is why God would issue option-restricting commands at all in these cases.

human welfare in which a person might otherwise be free to participate. On the view that God issues option-restricting commands, God has made creatures with genuine freedom, but then goes on to restrict their freedom unnecessarily. It seems as if issuing option-restricting commands wouldn't be an expression of love on God's part. Suppose various choices regarding participation in this or that dimension of human well-being are all consistent with the Golden Rule and the Pauline Principle. Why not let a thousand flowers bloom and permit people to make any of these choices?

With respect to option-restricting commands, it seems as if the divine command theorist once again faces a dilemma. If issuing such a command were necessary, then its necessity would have to be a function of something other than an arbitrary divine edict. Otherwise, it wouldn't make sense to talk about necessity. On the other hand, if issuing such a command isn't necessary, then it's hard to see that issuing an option-restricting command would be an expression of divine love. Restricting the range of otherwise legitimate options open to moral actors doesn't seem overly loving. On the imagined divine command theorist's view, God could refrain from restricting freedom, but instead chooses to constrain it.

Only, I think, if there is some overarching reason that makes limiting the range of personal choice necessary or highly desirable does issuing an option-restricting command seem consistent with divine love. Such commands might be necessary as solutions to coordination problems.

Divine Commands, Coordination, and Vocation

The less arbitrary the divine command theorist makes divine commands appear, the less they seem to be commands and the more they appear to be requirements of reason. In general, it seems as if the divine command theorist can blunt charges of divine arbitrariness only to the extent that her theory ceases to be a theory of divine commands and becomes something else.

But under some, special circumstances, this need not be the case. Regarding God as loving means that God would not and could not issue arbitrary commands restricting human freedom. But divine commands may sometimes be unavoidable with respect to what we can call "coordination problems."[1] To offer a trivial example of a coordination problem: it doesn't obviously matter in any meaningful way whether each of us drives on the left or the right side of a given road. It matters a great deal, however, that there be some established norm that coordinates my actions and those of other drivers.

A coordination problem arises when there is no decisive reason to prefer one arrangement of tasks, activities, or responsibilities, but in which *some* authoritative choice among the possible arrangements is necessary so that those affected will support each other's efforts, or at least avoid impeding them. A battlefield commander may have no clear warrant for dispatching each of three patrol groups in a particular direction, but she may nonetheless rightly believe that the three must proceed in *different* directions if they are to be most effective.

It is easy to see how divine commands might be necessary in cases of this sort. Suppose coordinated activity on behalf of some good end is necessary, but there is no intrinsic reason to prefer one arrangement of possible responses to another. In this case, a divine choice—contingent, and thus in a narrow sense arbitrary in its particularity, but obviously *necessary* in another sense—could helpfully and appropriately resolve the coordination problem.

This is one way to understand some contingent instances of divine *vocation*, the assignment to particular people of tasks, projects, or relationships that are

---

1. I owe this phrase to Finnis, *Law*; see, *e.g.*, 232-3.

distinctively their own. A divine command imposing a vocation could be oppressive: ordinarily, if God were simply to place a demand on a person under circumstances in which the person could appropriately have behaved in a number of different ways, God's action would seem tyrannical. Typically, if one has a vocation, the vocation will flow necessarily from one's circumstances and characteristics. But when it is *essential* that a coordination problem be resolved, perhaps God might offer a contingent vocation to pursue a particular path in a manner consistent with creaturely autonomy and divine concern for the flourishing of creation. If *someone* needs to perform each of several interrelated tasks, and the odds are good that absent some divine coordinating activity the whole array of tasks will not be performed, a contingent divine vocation could be an appropriate means of enabling each of the persons involved to participate in loving creation in a situationally appropriate way.[1]

Of course, a contingent vocation will be effective only if God communicates it clearly. And since it is not plausible to regard moral actors as constantly confronting coordination problems to be resolved by divine vocations, agents cannot reasonably be expected to anticipate that they will receive vocations for this purpose. Thus, they will not typically have good reason to seek contingent vocations (as opposed to ones that simply emerge from their circumstances).[2] Further, following a vocation will make sense as a contribution to a solution to a coordination problem only if a significant fraction of those whose activities need to be coordinated are aware of and responsive to relevant vocations.

Voluntarism and Divine Love

The belief that value and goodness are arbitrary, determined independently of the created order, is often used to support a powerful conception of God's love.[3] According to this conception, God's acceptance is bestowed on creatures

---

1. Adams criticizes the view that "if we have the values of actions and demands, we do not need the actual social requirements to explain the nature of moral obligation" (245). He asserts that "it matters that the demand is actually made. It is a question here of what good demands other persons do in fact make of me, not just of what good demands they could make" (246). But I want to suggest that the demands we confront come as much from people's circumstances as from their requests. A person in need demands my help in virtue of her need, apart from whether she ever issues a command or a plea. See, e.g., Murdoch; Bauman, *Ethics*.

Adams's recognition that some divine commands follow necessarily from God's love means that the key difference between his position and mine may turn out to be simply a different judgment regarding the relative quantities of the obligations flowing ineluctably from the divine love and those created *ex nihilo*, as it were, by the divine will. But interesting differences do continue to obtain. Adams believes slavery "is evil, a violation of persons," "an aspect of moral horror," and "an evil institution, even in societies where no one believes so" (369). However, that "no one in a society has any thought that a practice such as slavery is wrong" provides us with "some reason to suppose that . . . [the members of the society] have not received a divine command against it, since receiving a command implies a real possibility of being aware of it. And this would be reason for me to say that they were not violating a moral duty, even though the practice was an evil" (370). Could a member of a slaveholding society to come to the conclusion that slavery was a great evil without at the same time coming to the conclusion that it was prohibited? Does not the prohibition follow from the *nature* of slavery itself? I take it the key point here is Adams's apparent belief that one can be obligated only by a requirement of which one is, or should be, aware.

2. Adams's discussion of vocation (292-317) is superb and insightful.

3. Cp. Ronald M. Green, *Religion and Moral Reason* (New York: OUP 1988): if radical proponents of divine command views "have sometimes ended by portraying God as totally unfettered by human moral constraints, they have paradoxically done so to preserve God's most lofty moral attributes of mercy and grace" (128).

without reference to their worth.[1] And this notion can seem moving and exciting and liberating. For it can help to free us from the deep-seated worry that, because our performance is always, in various ways, inadequate, and because our being itself is imperfect, we will never merit God's acceptance. People who feel ashamed—as most people do at one point or another—about what they do or who they are can find voluntarism very comforting when it's framed this way. If divine love is given without regard to our performance or the perfection of our being, we can rest confidently in God's acceptance.

But one needn't be a voluntarist to find good reason for the kind of security voluntarist accounts of divine love purport to offer. For as long as being *as such* is valuable because it *is*, rather than because of what it does; as long as the beauty and vulnerability of created being rightly evoke a response of delight and desire and care; as long as it is the case that God necessarily suffers and enjoys whenever creatures suffer and enjoy, there will always be decisive reasons for God to love us quite apart from our performance. To say that creation is inherently loveable is not to maintain in any way that God's love for us is predicated on our performance or the perfection of our being.

And, of course, the sense of security putatively fostered by the voluntarist conception of God's love cannot itself be terribly secure. For, first of all, what God bestows arbitrarily God can also remove arbitrarily. And, second, if no divine response to any creature as such is more appropriate than any other, God could perfectly well manifest divine love by torturing or ignoring creatures. To be sure, if creatures have no inherent value, then it's possible to imagine God behaving toward them in the way we conventionally call "loving." But then "loving" wouldn't mean anything. As I've already suggested, if nothing is inherently good for creatures, then even the idea of love becomes, literally, meaningless. Any action at all can count as loving, as long as what is good or loving depends solely on God's will. To say, "God loves the world," just becomes another way of saying, "God does whatever God does."

We can affirm the reality of genuine divine love without being voluntarists. And voluntarism tends, in fact, to undermine the confidence it is supposed to engender. Thus, its purported support for confidence in God's love would provide us with no reason to endorse voluntarism even if there were not a variety of reasons to reject it. A creation-based account of value and obligation can accommodate concerns about divine love that animate voluntarism, while avoiding difficulties related to love that seem likely to plague the voluntarist. And this provides a further reason to accept an understanding of value and obligation consistent with the view that God truly loves creation.

The Appeal to Divine Commands as a Means of "Saving the Appearances"

Many moral precepts that some contemporary people might regard as arbitrary divine commands did not seem to their original proponents to be arcane and incomprehensible pronouncements defensible only with reference to the divine will. Rather, these moral convictions depended on overarching world views that included clear accounts of the nature of humanness and of the cosmos within which human beings found their place. Moral "abominations," for instance, were decried because of their significance within "a broader context of cosmological and social assumptions and categories."[2]

---

1. Adams (150-76) offers a superb assessment of this notion, with which I am generally in agreement.
2. Jeffrey Stout, *Ethics after Babel: The Languages of Morals and Their Discontents* (Boston: Beacon 1988) 159.

Earlier generations were able to offer rational defenses of prohibitions which now seem to require justification with reference to arbitrary divine commands because they were able to demonstrate the relationship between these prohibitions and their underlying frameworks of practice and understanding. Our difficulty today is that our views of the cosmos, human beings, and society have changed radically; but our sense of what is and is not morally reprehensible has not always changed with them.[1]

Thus, it becomes increasingly more difficult to justify some proscriptions which once seemed almost self-evident. In the absence of coherent accounts of reality that rendered these proscriptions comprehensible, it is hard to view contemporary attempts to base the moral life on arbitrary divine commands as anything other than unpersuasive strategies serving simply to "save the appearances" of a traditional morality, to rescue the husk long after the substance has vanished.

If the social structures that provide human beings with order and meaning are in transition, and aspects of human nature with them, people may despair of finding any secure and stable source of moral judgments within the natural order. Thus, they may look to arbitrary divine edicts—presumably unaffected by social change—as sources of stability. "Man's finitude and sinfulness entail that he can have no knowledge of God but what he receives by grace, and man is held to possess by nature no criteria by which he can judge what God says, or is alleged to say. . . . The reasons for obeying God have to be in terms of his power and his numinous holiness rather than of his goodness."[2]

It is understandable enough that, in a time of never-ending transition, people might identify certain norms as divine commands and strive to enforce them, for the sake of stability, whether or not they appeared to be rooted in love for creation.[3] But doing so does not represent an adequate response to a loving creator. It is no compliment to picture God as an arbitrary tyrant. If God loves creation, then the most credible approach to ethics will see moral requirements as grounded in the character of created being.

Morality and Religion

If morality means loving creation rather submitting to arbitrary divine commands, does that mean that religion generally and Christian convictions specifically are morally irrelevant? Not at all.

Morality is linked with religion because it is a matter of responding lovingly to God's good creation. It is, after all, God's creation whose flourishing we frustrate when we sin. As creator, God is responsible for morality in the same way that the manufacturer of an automobile is responsible for determining proper maintenance procedures for the automobile.[4]

Morality is also a religious matter because religious belief can assist us in discerning the morally good. Identifying the good depends on understanding the character of creation and the nature of responsible action in relation to other persons and the non-human world. But our capacity to understand is limited and our reasoning and our perceptions are flawed. The Christian story can help us to discern more clearly what choices and character traits will appropriately embody love for the good creation. The story of Jesus' life, for instance, helps to form in our

---

1. Stout 159.
2. Alasdair MacIntyre, *A Short History of Ethics* (New York: Macmillan 1966) 119.
3. See Green 129: "contemporary defenders of forms of revelation that defy reason and common sense are challenged to ask whether they have not, in some essential way, departed from . . . [the Jewish and Christian] faith tradition."
4. So Fischer.

characters the disposition to reconciliation, even at sacrificial cost. Belief in life beyond death helps to underscore the profound value of personhood. And so on.

The fact that the church facilitates our moral living also helps to connect specifically Christian religious belief with morality. The church is a "community of moral discernment"[1] in which we are taught Christian "language" (which includes a moral dimension). In the church, a morally rich tradition and its attendant practices, images, concepts, etc., are handed on from generation to generation. Further, the church provides us with a context in which persons can wrestle with each other as they seek to find solutions to moral challenges. In the church, people whose vision of reality has also been shaped by the good news of God's love can juxtapose their judgments and perceptions, so that they can all come to understand more adequately what God is doing in the world. The church can hold us accountable for living up to the Christian convictions we profess. Of course, the church's judgment is anything but perfect, but the conversations church life makes possible can facilitate our growth in understanding what it means to love creation and in embodying that love.

God is important for morality in another way. The ontological status of moral norms is a matter of continuing debate. We talk, vaguely enough, about such norms supervening on, or being determined by, non-moral facts. But it is often clear neither *what* it is that supervenes nor whether we might be said to apprehend moral norms under any circumstances, since it is difficult to see how something could be in some way apprehensible without having the capacity to exert causal influence.[2] (This is, of course, a problem for non-moral—logical, mathematical, epistemic—norms as well.) Someone who believes in God need not believe that morality is rooted in the divine will to understand God as accounting for the ontological objectivity of moral norms. Rather, like their mathematical and logical counterparts, the truth-makers for moral propositions can be understood as necessary aspects of the *being* of God.[3] As such, they would be real—and, not only real, but accessible to us epistemically (among other things, they could presumably be perceived in the same manner in which we might be thought to perceive God generally).[4] In this way, too, therefore, God makes a difference with respect to the choices we make as we love in the world.

The Shape of Shalom

An ethic based on love for creation will recognize the distinctive value of particular persons. It will acknowledge the important fact that special relationships are among the ways in which our lives are ordered in God's world, and—in fact—that these relationships contribute unavoidably to making us the distinctive persons we are. It will recognize the claims of other such groups—the claims of our local communities, of our countries, of our globe. It will take into account the interests of the non-human creation, both animate and inanimate. And it will be concerned with vulnerable members of the human community.

---

1. So James Gustafson.
2. See, *e.g.*, Stephen Clark's discussion of this implication of moral realism in *God, Religion, and Reality* (London: SPCK 1998) 94-5.
3. See Keith Ward, *Ethics and Christianity* (London: Allen 1970); David Ray Griffin, *Reenchantment without Supernaturalism: A Process Philosophy of Religion* (Ithaca, NY: Cornell UP 2001) 299-301
4. See Griffin 52-93.

Love in Community

A Christian vision of human fulfillment rooted in the idea of shalom will not attend to individual enjoyment or fulfillment in abstraction from the wider context of relationships within which persons are formed: relationships with God, relationships with other persons, relationships with communities and institutions, and relationships with our natural environment. It is a pointless abstraction to talk about personal enjoyment apart from these relationships. We can appropriately give different constituents of creation different kinds of consideration, but we will not forget that all of creation is interconnected.

A creational ethic will build on the realization that we experience life's greatest riches in relationships and communities. Thus, it will encourage particular, one-on-one relations in which the full intensity of interpersonal communion can be experienced.[1] And it will involve concern for the wider human community. The enjoyment of human community is surely frustrated by poverty, oppression, or war. And God's shalom is served when we give money or time to fight poverty, when we work to change structures that deprive people of power over their own lives, and when we promote reconciliation, and thus avert conflict.

Loving the Non-Human World

Commitment to creation as the basis for ethics need not lead to the view that all elements of reality are strictly equal in valuable: pebbles, plants, and people aren't the same, and they shouldn't be treated as if they were. But the doctrine of creation does nudge us to attend to each for what it is. No element of reality is without value, and the idea of creation encourages us to seek that value and affirm it within the wider context of the created order. No element of creation has *ultimate* value; but each element can nonetheless have *inherent* value.

Trees and trilobites don't simply exist just for our benefit. Their purpose *to be themselves*, and they ought to be respected accordingly. Recognizing that they have more than merely instrumental value also frees us to grant their beauty, their capacity to evoke delight, for which they deserve our affirmation and respect. That will mean preserving natural wonders like the Grand Canyon for their own sakes. And it will mean establishing respectful alliances with non-human creatures, ones in which our interests and theirs are both served. Thus, some such creatures may prove to be loyal friends and companions, provide us with food (milk, cheese, or honey, say) or clothing (wool, for instance), or help us understand the rest of the world better. But a commitment to shalom will mean not imprisoning non-human animals (say, in puppy mills) or killing or harming them to provide ourselves with food or clothing or to facilitate scientific research.[2]

---

1. See, *e.g.*, Gilbert C. Meilaender, *Friendship: A Study in Theological Ethics* (Notre Dame, IN: U of Notre Dame P 1981); Mary Elizabeth Hunt, *Fierce Tenderness: A Feminist Theology of Friendship* (New York: Crossroad 1990); Marilyn Friedman, *What Are Friends For? Feminist Perspectives on Personal Relationships and Moral Theory* (Ithaca, NY: Cornell UP 1993).

2. See Stephen R. L. Clark, *The Moral Status of Animals* (Oxford: Clarendon-OUP 1984); Stephen R. L. Clark, *Animals and Their Moral Standing* (London: Routledge 1998); Mark Rowlands, *Animals Like Us*, Practical Ethics 3 (London: Verso 2003); Stephen F. Sapontzis, *Morals, Reasons, and Animals* (Philadelphia: Temple UP 1987); Tom Regan, *The Case for Animal Rights*, 2d. ed. (Berkeley, CA: U of California P 2004). In "Consumers, Boycotts, and Non-Human Animals," *Buffalo Environmental Law Journal* 12 (Spring 2005): 123-94, I examine the ways in which implications about human diets are sometimes drawn from judgments about the moral standing of animals.

Loving Vulnerable People

Loving creation means making political and personal choices marked by respect and care for vulnerable people. In turn, this will mean adopting a two-sided attitude toward material possessions.

On the one hand, there can be no place in Christianity for a pious asceticism that rejects material things as inherently inferior to "spiritual" (understood as immaterial) things. Creation—both physical and cultural—is good. It is to be celebrated as God's good gift. There is no excuse for trying to be more spiritual than God, who values *matter* enough to be present and active in it. This appreciation for creation should lead us to delight in the created world and in the things God has made and is making through human beings. Loving others and loving ourselves means welcoming and enjoying the non-human world and the products of human culture.

On the other hand, love for creation—for ourselves, for our friends and families, for earth's ecosystems, and for the poor—means avoiding the excesses of the "health and wealth gospel" that sees the acquisition of unlimited personal wealth as a sign of Christian maturity.

A drive for financial success can become an attempt to deny our contingency, to reject our status as creatures. Money and possessions can seem—falsely—to liberate us from the insecurities we all face.[1] Thus, focusing on our possessions can be a means of denying our status as creatures.

Of course, this strategy doesn't work. In fact, taking our acquisition of created things too seriously threatens to undermine our ability to enjoy God's good creation. Someone supposedly once asked a billionaire how much money would make him happy. His reply was classic: "Just a few dollars more." If we never learn to say "enough," then we will be trapped in an endless cycle of acquisition. Our relationships will suffer. Our health will suffer. Even our capacity to get anything out of what we already possess will suffer. After a point, more possessions just don't give us enough to compensate for their extra cost. A Ferrari might be nice, but would it really give me that much more than a Toyota Prius?

The fact that material possessions don't and can't meet our deepest needs, but that we are tempted to treat them as if they did and could, is one important reason for us to be generous. Generosity is the practical antidote to the dominance of money. There's no point in renouncing created things as if they were bad; they're not. But by giving them to others we loosen our grip on them sufficiently to ensure that enrich rather than impoverishing our lives.

Secondly, seriousness about creation must mean respect for all constituents of the created order—all other persons and non-human creatures as well. This means that we cannot indulge in a lifestyle that depletes the earth's resources beyond repair. As the home of a vast array of living things, our planet deserves to be cared for, not raped. Our consumer choices can reflect this concern, as we buy durable, recyclable goods, opt for efficient means of transportation, and challenge industries that kill or torture non-human creatures or waste non-renewable resources.

Not only must we avoid attacking the non-human world, but we also need to see ourselves as essentially related. We are linked with concentric circles of people, from our families and close friends to associates on the job and in church to local communities to nations to the world itself. We are responsible for all of the others with whom we are essentially related. This means that we need to give generously not only to our friends, families, and local communities, but also to those who need our help around the world. It also means that we must be

---

1. See M. Douglas Meeks, *God the Economist: The Doctrine of God and Political Economy* (Minneapolis: Fortress 1989) 167-70.

willing to accept higher taxes when necessary so that our society can care for the basic needs of its members and assist others beyond its borders.¹ We must seek a way of life that is just and sustainable. As long as *sustainable* means *sustainable for everyone*, the two requirements turn out to be the same. A sustainable lifestyle will be one that allows all of creation to flourish, that allows each person to experience a fulfilling and enjoyable life, and that shows respect for the non-human creation.

There is no way to specify in advance just what each person's obligations in this regard will be. There are a few things about which we can, however, be reasonably confident. We have responsibilities to strangers as well as to family members, friends, and neighbors. The needs of others call us out of our preoccupation with ourselves. The Golden Rule doesn't preclude caring primarily for ourselves or for those close to us. But it suggests that those we don't know matter, and deserve our consideration, just like those we do know, even if we may nonarbitrarily prefer those with whom we have special relationships. No finite individual is God; none of us is responsible for doing everything. But each of us can and should do something.

Specific circumstances, as well as responsibilities to particular persons and for particular projects, will affect our duties to impoverished strangers, as will specific vocations. Some vocations may channel our time, energy, and resources into particular aspects of the human good: improving the world as a whole may not play a large role in some people's nonetheless good lives. On the other hand, some vocations may call people to exemplary lives of voluntary poverty that challenge others to change the ways in which they think about and use resources. In any case, whatever the limitations created by individual vocations, commitments, and circumstances, particular projects and responsibilities, and the need for fairness,

---

1. On the relevant moral requirements, see Liam Murphy, *Moral Demands in Nonideal Theory* (New York: OUP 2000); Martha C. Nussbaum, *Frontiers of Justice: Disability, Nationality, Species Membership* (Cambridge, MA: Harvard UP 2006); Henry Shue, *Basic Rights: Subsistence, Affluence, and US Foreign Policy*, 2d. ed. (Princeton: Princeton UP 1996); Onora O'Neill, *Faces of Hunger: An Essay on Poverty, Justice, and Development* (London: Allen 1986) 152-62; Onora O'Neill, *Towards Justice and Virtue: A Constructive Account of Practical Reasoning* (Cambridge: CUP 1996) 196-200; Scanlon 224; Luke T. Johnson, *Sharing Possessions: Mandate and Symbol of Faith* (Philadelphia: Fortress 1981) 132-9; Charles Fried, *Right and Wrong* (Cambridge, MA: Harvard UP 1978); Gewirth, *Rights*; Gewirth, *Self-Fulfillment*; Finnis, *Law* 173-7; Gary Chartier, "Peoples or Persons? Revising Rawls on Global Justice," *Boston College International and Comparative Law Review* 27.1 (Winter 2004): 1-97; Chartier, "Consumption"; Robert L. Goodin, *Protecting the Vulnerable: A Reanalysis of Our Social Responsibilities* (Chicago: U of Chicago P 1985); Meilaender, *Faith*; Adams. On strategies for living well while spending less, see Janet Luhrs, *The Simple Living Guide: A Sourcebook for Less Stressful, More Joyful Living* (New York: Broadway 1997); Georgene Lockwood, *Complete Idiot's Guide to Simple Living* (Indianapolis: Alpha-Macmillan 2000); Jeff Davidson, *The Joy of Simple Living: Over 1,500 Simple Ways to Make Your Life Easy and Content—At Home and At Work* (New York: Rodale 1999); Elaine St. James, *Living the Simple Life: A Guide to Scaling Down and Enjoying More* (New York: Hyperion 1998); Duane Elgin, *Voluntary Simplicity: Toward a Way of Life That Is Outwardly Simple, Inwardly Rich* (New York: Morrow 1981); Doris Jantzen Longacre, *Living More with Less*, intro. Ronald Sider (Scottdale, PA: Herald 1980); Doris Jantzen Longacre, comp., *The More-with-Less Cookbook*, intro. Mary Emma Showalter Eby (Scottdale, PA: Herald 1976); Juliet Schor, *The Overworked American: The Unexpected Decline of Leisure* (New York: Basic 1991); Juliet Schor, *The Overspent American: Upscaling, Downshifting, and the New Consumer* (New York: Basic 1998); Juliet Schor, *A Sustainable Economy for the Twenty-First Century* (New York: Seven Stories 1998); Juliet Schor et al., *Do Americans Shop Too Much?* (Boston: Beacon 2000). Schor, Elgin, and others are featured as commentators in *Affluenza* (Oley, PA: Bullfrog Films 1998).

many people can and should give substantially to organizations devoted to sustainable development and the relief of suffering.

Meeting this challenge will be easier, of course, if we opt for sustainability in our own lives—if we choose lifestyles that don't deplete the earth's resources and that make efficient use of what we have, if we say no to mindless consumption. For instance:

- For people who are comfortable in relative proximity to others, co-housing—in which some facilities are common and others individual—may make it easier to avoid financial pressures.
- Even those uncomfortable about co-housing can opt for smaller houses on smaller lots or for condominiums or townhomes rather than detached homes.
- In places with satisfactory train systems, public transit can provide an inexpensive and resource-efficient alternative to automobile use.
- High-end thrift shops can enable people to look good without spending a great deal on clothing.
- Used furniture, appliances, automobiles, and electronic goods may meet our needs for beauty and functionality very effectively, and at significantly lower prices than their new counterparts.
- Vegetarianism is not only environmentally friendly, healthy, and a useful means of highlighting the wrongness of the killing of animals but also less expensive than meat-eating.
- Limiting family sizes obviously reduces expenses dramatically.

And creative people will obviously think of a variety of other ways of living well without spending compulsively.

Again, the point is not, of course, that the material world is anything but good. The profusion of consumer goods can add to the richness and variety and beauty of our lives. Options are worth celebrating, and the good creation is worth enjoying. But it's no fun to be trapped into thinking that we constantly need more *stuff*, that our value depends on what we own. And by spending less on the acquisition of stuff, we can contribute with less stress to the work of fostering sustainable development at home and around the world.

The point is also not to become neurotic about money. Our very seriousness about economic justice could make us as obsessed with possessions as if we were caught up in the rat race. Our concern for our possessions can be destructively dominant in our lives if we're worried about giving them away just like it can if we're worried about getting more of them.[1] The important thing is to learn to be relaxed and open about material things. This realization will free us to treat them as parts of the good creation which can add to our lives, but which we can and must use also to touch the lives of others and which we must employ in a way that reflects our love for the whole creation.

A cultural commitment to sustainability and responsibility toward those who are vulnerable is crucial. And absent appropriate steps by governments, individuals must take responsibility for expressing their care for others more directly—often through non-governmental organizations. But economic injustice is not primarily a matter of individual responsibility or irresponsibility; it is first and foremost about social structures and processes, law and political power. We are primarily responsible for exercising our responsibility for others collectively: public authorities can address the problem of global poverty more effectively than can individuals.

Thus, loving creation means supporting and actively contributing to the development of policies that promote not only more wealth but also a also a just,

---

1. See Jacques Ellul, *Money and Power*, trans. LaVonne Neff (Grand Rapids: Eerdmans 1984).

inclusive, non-subordinative community in which everyone's needs are met and decision-making is not subject to the will of those with economic power.[1] Christian respect for particular persons means that a just economic order cannot rightly be sought or enforced using the power of an authoritarian state: Stalinism and Maoism are clearly out. There are good reasons to be suspicious of protectionist measures that arbitrarily privilege some over others, often embody xenophobic attitudes, and frequently harm consumers as well as producers. And it seems doubtful that top-down state planners will often be better than markets at determining production levels and distribution patterns. But Christian sensitivity to the reality of sin means that we can hardly trust the good will of individual managers and entrepreneurs and philanthropists alone to empower the impoverished people of our planet. The action of local, national, and international communities is essential. Thus, love for creation may mean endorsing a range of justice-oriented policies.[2]

- Absent special needs, circumstances, or responsibilities, each member of the community owes it to other members to work.
- The community is responsible for ensuring that all of its members enjoy access to health care, education, culture, food, clothing, shelter, and communication and transportation facilities.
- Enterprises must accept direct, public responsibilities to local, national, and international communities.
- Members of the public must be involved in the ownership of large and mid-sized enterprises, and the public as well as ordinary workers must be involved in decision-making at the board level and below.[3]
- Economic power should be decentralized as much as possible, so that individual workers and work-groups as well as local communities can participate effectively in the formulation of the economic decisions that affect their lives.
- Politics and culture must be insulated from the corrosive effects of economic power--being wealthy can't and shouldn't mean being able to control the political process or the processes of cultural production.
- Workplace decisions about employment and promotion need to be made in ways that afford everyone affected with due process—employment at-will, for instance, at least after brief probationary periods, violates human dignity.
- Workplace cultures and policies must reflect respect for the equal worth and fundamental dignity of all workers and consumers.
- Public authorities must regulate business activities to ensure the protection of the nonhuman world and of the health, safety, and well-being of workers and the public.

1. See Michael Walzer, *Spheres of Justice: A Defense of Pluralism and Equality* (New York: Basic 1983).
2. For proposals regarding the details, see, *e.g.*, Gary Dorrien, *Soul in Society: The Making and Renewal of Social Christianity* (Minneapolis: Fortress 1995); Gary Chartier, "Toward a New Employer-Worker Compact," *Employee Rights and Employment Policy Journal* 9.1 (2005): 51-119; Alec Nove, *The Economics of Feasible Socialism Revisited*, 2d. ed. (New York: Harper 1991); John Roemer, *A Future for Socialism* (Cambridge, MA: Harvard UP 1994); James A. Yunker, *Economic Justice: The Market Socialist Vision* (Lanham, MD: Rowman 1997).
3. On industrial democracy, see, *e.g.*, Carole Pateman, *Participation and Democratic Theory* (Cambridge: CUP 1970); cp. her introduction to Ronald M. Mason, *Participatory and Workplace Democracy: A Theoretical Development in Critique of Liberalism* (Carbondale: Southern Illinois UP 1982).

We can certainly differ about the policy choices needed to improve life on our troubled planet. But it is clear that policy shifts have an important role to play in fostering a community of solidarity, mutual empowerment, and love, and so in expressing our love for God's good creation and enacting God's love for the world.

The Sabbath and Creative Love

The Sabbath is a weekly reminder that God's creative activity is at the heart of the Christian life. On the Sabbath, we remember our creator in a very concrete way: we rest.

Rest is an appropriate response to God's creative action because we owe our being to God. We're not responsible for the universe, and our Sabbath rest symbolizes an attitude of rest that ought to underlie all of our activities. Frantic worry about determining the course of events is inappropriate if the world is in God's hands, not ours.

Creation also gives rise to Sabbath rest in another way. The Sabbath represents an experience of community and freedom from domination. In Deut. 5, the Sabbath is justified on the grounds that it is to be a memorial of God's liberation of Israel from Egypt. It is apparent from the context that the Sabbath could serve as such a memorial because on it the people Israel would experience in an especially pronounced way the freedom from slavery they had won in the Exodus. Just as the Israelites had been freed from drudgery in Egypt, so now they were to avoid any kind of work on the Sabbath.[1] And this freedom from work was to be enjoyed not only by adult male citizens—the dominant class in ancient Israel as in most other societies—but also by women and children, slaves and foreigners.

Viewed in this way, the Sabbath doubtless served as a social leveler in Israel when faithfully observed, as it has the potential to do now.[2] On the Sabbath, distinctions based on work—and thus on socio-economic class—would have been minimized. And, of course, it's often difficult to return completely to "normal" after one has experienced alternative possibilities of social organization. So it's likely that when people experienced equality on the Sabbath, some of that sense of equality must have been retained during the week.

I think we can plausibly see this experience of liberating Sabbath rest as reflective of a creation ethic. Ex. 20, with its focus on creation, isn't necessarily saying something different from Deut. 5. Because human beings have been created in God's image, they are more than beasts of burden.[3] It is their created natures which make their liberation appropriate and the flourishing of which their liberation can foster.

On this view, the Sabbath is a time to experience rest from the struggle for value through achievement, as well as rest from interpersonal hierarchy—and so to experience the equality that is ours in virtue of the way God made us, and the inherent worth that is a consequence of the simple fact of our being. In this way, too, Sabbath rest is an affirmation of creation.

---

1. See Paul Lafargue, *The Right to be Lazy*, trans. Charles H. Kerr (Chicago: Kerr 1975). (Lafargue was the son-in-law of Karl Marx.) For a more recent analysis of issues related to work in contemporary society, see Juliet Schor, *The Overworked American: The Unexpected Decline of Leisure* (New York: Basic 1991); cp. Fritz Guy, "A Time for Being: Or, Why Karl Marx Should Have Gone to Sabbath School," *Insight* 14 (Feb. 1, 1983): 11-2, one of the principal sources of this analysis.

2. See Niels-Erik A. Andreasen, "Jubilee of Freedom and Equality," *Festival of the Sabbath*, ed. Roy Branson (Washington, DC: Association of Adventist Forums 1985) 97-106.

3. So Abraham Joshua Heschel.

Rest is also important because it is intimately related to our *celebration* of God's creative work. We rest on the Sabbath because the creation is fundamentally good, whatever its flaws. We rest, that is, because we do not need to work in order to ensure creation's basic goodness. That goodness is assured in virtue of the fact that the creation is God's loving gift. We can celebrate that fact; and Sabbath time gives us opportunity to do so. In our worship, we experience and express delight at the goodness of the creation.

We don't always delight in the creation, of course, or celebrate it. Our love for God and God's creation are sometimes painfully and profoundly distorted. In Chapter 6, I examine how disordered love can disrupt and destroy our lives.

6

Disordered Love

All too frequently, our love is disordered or misdirected. Christians have traditionally used the label *sin* to talk about the disorders to which our loves can be subject. In this chapter, I want to examine the dynamics of disordered love.

At the individual level, sin is the failure to treat oneself as a part of God's good creation. Many people find talk of sin troubling, no doubt particularly in light of inadequate conceptions of sin. Linking sin with our status and value as creatures is one important way of underscoring the connection between sin and our relationship with God; another is emphasizing that God suffers with creation, so that harm to creation is necessarily also a cause of divine suffering. Sin has both individual and social dimensions; as embodied in social life, it is both a consequence and a cause of individual sin, and is responsible for much that is destructive and ugly in our world.

All sinful conduct is harmful, but not all harmful conduct is sinful, because people can be ignorant of relevant facts or norms. Ignorance of applicable norms can cause someone to feel guilty for conduct that is not, in fact, sinful, as the case of Huckleberry Finn makes clear.

Disordered love has a social dimension as well as interpersonal and individual ones. This social dimension at least helps to explain the propagation of disordered love through history and its status as a condition influencing our behavior before we are able to make reflective moral choices. While it thus helps to warrant talk of original *sin*, it does not justify belief in original *guilt*. Disordered love gives rise to exclusion and subordination based on gender, which in turn brings about alternative, gendered styles of disordered love.

The Abuse of Sin-Language

It's perhaps worth beginning by noting that talk about sin is a major turn-off. The word raises people's hackles. An evangelist once lured people to a meeting by announcing that he would be giving a talk entitled "Escape from behind the Iron Curtain." When his sermon got under way, he informed those who had expected a thrilling tale of flight from Eastern Europe that his topic was actually "Escape from behind the Iron Curtain *of Sin.*"[1] He probably knew that all the people in town sufficiently interested in a discussion of sin to attend a talk about it could have held a convention in a phone booth. Sin isn't a very popular theme. And when we consider how talk about sin has functioned in people's lives in the Christian world, it's easy to see why.

Christians have sometimes felt that intense feelings of guilt were necessary for anyone genuinely to experience divine love and acceptance. So they have

---

1. I owe this example to Stanley Chartier.

sometimes self-destructively fostered these painful feelings in themselves and others. Further, church leaders who have consciously or unconsciously realized the power of guilt have used it to manipulate people. Consequently, the Christian church has too often been involved in manufacturing guilt—to "enrich" the experience of God's love or to dominate its members. And other social institutions have also exploited feelings of indebtedness to enable them to ensure that people behaved in desired ways.[1]

A further problem with talk about sin is that so often creation hasn't been seen as the ground of Christian morality.[2] Instead, sin has been treated as a matter of violating arbitrary divine edicts not actually rooted in the nature of creation. God has been understood as a harsh, demanding, patriarchal father issuing unchallengeable commands.

The experience of family is a key source of the metaphors that back up our understanding of the moral and spiritual life.[3] It's not surprising that a model of sin as violating paternal commands would prove so widespread; after all, our experiences of (often-patriarchal) families are pervasive. It's also hardly surprising that this model would prove so powerful: those experiences are often so emotionally freighted. The fear of parental disapproval, intensified and magnified, provides the raw material for our fear of divine disapproval; the fear of losing parental love as a result of disobedience often provides the raw material for our feelings of guilt.

The association of these feelings with sin-language makes religiously based moral sanctions very effective. But the temptation to use this language in oppressive ways because of its effectiveness is very great for anyone in authority. And the use of these metaphors in relation to God is often a source of resentment and hostility. If God is the Big Daddy in the Sky, the obedient Christian is a dependent infant unable to think for herself.[4] Not only can this approach undercut our attentive love to God's creation; it can also dispose us to respond to God with fear or hatred rather than love. It doesn't picture God as loving, and it has the potential to stand in the way of real love between creatures, and between creatures and God. A love-centered Christian theology should find it doubtful at best.

Because of the ways in which sin-language has been abused, it's hard to use the word "sin" effectively. The reaction to moralistic control on the part of church authorities has been so great that the connotations of the word are basically positive in many sectors of our culture. Domination through guilt-manipulation has turned out to be a sham. People have concluded that the church's traditional talk about sin serves primarily not to protect people from the effects of destructive behavior but to prevent them from enjoying valuable and worthwhile pleasures. "Sinful" has, in fact, become almost a synonym for "extremely pleasurable"—as in, "This chocolate is *sinfully* delicious." Presumably related to this transformation in meaning is the curious association of sin and immorality with *sex* in some people's minds, as if human sexuality were somehow a context within which sin were more likely to appear than any other, or as if harms done to people in the context of sex were worse than harms done in other contexts.

---

1. See Albert O. Plé, *Duty or Pleasure? A New Appraisal of Christian Ethics*, trans. Matthew J. O'Connell (New York: Paragon 1987) 3-79; Wolfhart Pannenberg, *Christian Spirituality* (Philadelphia: Westminster 1983); Richard K. Fenn, *The Secularization of Sin: An Investigation of the Daedalus Complex* (Louisville, KY: Westminster/Knox 1991) 171-91.

2. Cp. Jack W. Provonsha, "Creation," *A Righteous Remnant: Adventist Themes for Personal and Social Ethics*, ed. Charles Teel, Jr. (Loma Linda, CA: Loma Linda U Center for Christian Bioethics 1995).

3. Cp. George Lakoff, *Moral Politics: What Conservatives Know That Liberals Don't* (Chicago: U of Chicago P 1997).

4. See Plé 45-79.

In the minds of many contemporary people, the church is in the business of hiding the really good things from us by calling them sins. Now that we have discovered how oppressive the church has been, they conclude, we should turn sin-language on its head. Thus, the word *sinful* becomes an adjective that points to all the really good things in life. Now that everyone knows that sin is just the creation of an authoritarian hierarchy, according to this line of reasoning, it's an appropriate form of revenge to mock that hierarchy by using the very instrument its members employed to control people—but with a completely inverted meaning. Inverting the meaning of sin-language also serves to limit its ability to carry the emotional weight that has permitted it to function oppressively.

I think that the critique which lies behind the contemporary inversion of and protest against traditional sin-language is largely correct. Sin-language has been abused. But the reality to which it points still needs to be addressed. For sin-language has to do with a key feature of the Christian vision: Christianity asserts that our loving is disordered, that the disorders to which our loves are subject fracture our relationships with God and with each other. It also asserts that God continues to act to heal our spiritual wounds. To understand Christian belief, then, it is crucial to understand what those wounds are like.

Inadequate Accounts of Disordered Love

There have been all sorts of definitions of sin. Humanity's fatal spiritual flaw has been identified as a manifestation of everything from sexuality to self-love to an unwillingness to obey divine commandments. Obviously, some of these definitions have more merit than others.

- Sexuality is immensely powerful, and it can impel us to love rightly or destructively. There's nothing inherently wrong with it; rather, it is a great gift with enormous potential for good.
- Loving oneself unfairly at the expense of others can be a source of great harm. But identifying self-love as the root of sin can imply that the self, which God loves, isn't lovely and loveable (is God's love, then, simply irrational or arbitrary?). Defining sin as self-love also obscures the fact that many people— including those who assert their own interests aggressively in competition with others—really don't love themselves; their behavior often seems designed to compensate for the fact that they don't see themselves as loved or loveable. It also obscures the fact that many people *don't* prefer themselves unfairly to others or assert their own claims and interests without reference to those of others; their problem is not that they see themselves as too important but that they don't see themselves as important enough.
- Traditional legal metaphors suggest that sin is a matter of offending or disobeying God: as the creator of the moral law, on this view, God is offended when human beings violate it. This model's account of sin paints God, anthropomorphically, as an offended patriarch or a cosmic bureaucrat more interested in maintaining power than in seeking the well-being of creation. In any case, the moral law is a consequence of the way creation *is*, not a separate, free-floating creation; morality is about love for God and for creation.

It's clear that we need another account of sin, one focused on love.

Disordered Love and the God of Love

Our disordered love for creation is both an influence on and a reflection of disorder in our loving relationship with God. Sin happens when I fail to accept myself as a part of God's good creation. But it has to be understood with reference to God as well as to creation: it is rooted in a misapprehension of myself in relation to God, and, to the extent that it causes creatures to suffer, it causes God to do so as well.

Why Moral Failure Is Also Sin

Sin-talk isn't simply talk about moral failure with some religious flavoring thrown in for good measure. Talk about sin *is* talk about moral failure, but when we're talking about sin, rather than about ethics, we're talking not so much about what *constitutes* moral failure or how we might *identify* it as about its meaning and its underlying dynamics.

What makes something appropriate or sinful is its loving responsiveness to God's good creation, and, through creation, to God. Sin can involve harm to oneself, to other persons or groups, or to the non-human world. In any case, it will harm God's good creation—if it didn't, it wouldn't be sinful: sin is *first of all* about our love for creation. But it also affects the God who loves creation, and it reflects the distortion of our love for God.

The life of Jesus—and, in particular, his cross—highlights God's solidarity with a vulnerable and hurting creation. Whenever we harm creation, God suffers. For God identifies and suffers with the created world. The harm sin does to God is inextricably related to God's love for—and so vulnerability to—creation. Because everything that affects creatures affects God, every harm done to any creature, including oneself, is also a source of suffering for God.[1] God is the ultimate victim whenever we do anything wrong. Given that God is sensitive to anything that occurs in the created order, God feels the frustration of creational possibilities and the wrenching that results when creatures harm one another. The primary reason not to harm another creature is its own inherent value and vulnerability. But the recognition that, when we harm creation, we harm God as well provides a further reason, and motive, to behave lovingly toward creation.

In addition, sin is often rooted in, and often reinforces, a loss of freedom consequent on our failure to love God appropriately.[2] Sin is rightly characterized as rooted in mistrust of God and issues in alienation from God.[3] In sin, we are unfree: we are dominated by some aspect of the created order.

The loss of freedom associated with sin thus involves *idolatry*. That is to say, it involves treating something finite and created as absolute rather than relative, as possessing the right to trump the legitimate claims exerted by the parts of reality one has *not* idolized, as able on its own to provide us with absolute security. Idolatry is the denial, practical even if not theoretical, that God is God, that God love us, that we are grounded in God's love, that only God merits unqualified confidence and loyalty.

It is, of course, possible for us to love *ourselves* idolatrously. We can rely on our own characteristics and achievements and relationships to shore up our identities. But it is also possible for us to love *other creatures* in this way. We can ask of institutions or social movements or relationships or other persons that *they* give us absolute confidence and total love, and submit ourselves to them to gain the

---

1. Marjorie Suchocki, *The Fall to Violence: Original Sin in Relational Theology* (New York: Continuum 1995).
2. I am dependent throughout on insights into the dynamics of idolatry offered by Edward Farley, *Good and Evil: Interpreting a Human Condition* (Minneapolis: Fortress 1990).
3. Farley 152. Farley also identifies unbelief and disobedience, properly understood, as features of a sinful relationship with God. I think what Farley intends by unbelief (looking to finite goods for security) can be captured by talk of mistrust, and I avoid talk of disobedience for the reasons I outlined in the previous chapter.

security we seek.[1] Because both broad varieties of sin can be understood as varieties of idolatry, both have something to do with God. Both involve expecting creatures—ourselves or others—to provide a kind of security only God is capable of offering: a perfect, all-embracing love, a home where we are safe from all "the slings and arrows of outrageous fortune."

Thus, sin is what happens when our—natural and otherwise quite appropriate—love for created goods is disordered. It is *not* against God in the sense that it is a violation of some arbitrary divine command. But it *is* against God in that it causes God to suffer and in that it represents a failure to love God aright.

Why Sin Need Not Involve Explicit Awareness of God

Obviously, many people have never heard the Christian story. And many of those who have heard it have really only heard distorted—and distorting—versions. Does it make sense to talk about the sin of such people as rooted in disordered relationships with God?

If God is *God*, then God is present as creator and sustainer in all of our experience, whether we recognize it or not. As a result, whatever we do, we are shaping responses to our creator. The fundamental stance one adopts toward reality as a whole is really one's stance vis-à-vis God, whether one knows it or not.

When I assert, then, that idolatry—treating something finite as if it were God—lies at the root of all sin, I'm not saying that everyone has heard the Christian story and has reached decided to opt for some source of meaning and value alternative to the God that story identifies. I'm saying that they look to various finite goods for security and meaning, and sometimes do so in ways that lead them to disregard the reality and value of other creatures.

An important aspect of the problem of idolatry is lack of *basic trust*. People are profoundly doubtful, in various ways, that the universe can be experienced as, at root, a friendly place. The absence of basic trust makes overt, healthy belief in God very difficult. But it does more. It fractures people's relationships with each other and with themselves, as well as leading to a variety of distortions in social and cultural life.[2] Like the other features of human existence associated with idolatry, basic trust can be present or absent in people's lives whether or not they are aware of God's presence and God's love in an explicit, thematized way.

SIN AND HARM

An act which is not unfair and which is not a purposeful or instrumental infliction of harm cannot be a sin. But an act which *would* be a sin if performed in

---

1. Paul Tillich, *Systematic Theology*, 3 vols. (Chicago, IL: U of Chicago P 1951-63), describes a similar polarity. "Disintegration means failure to reach or to preserve self-integration. This failure can occur in one of two directions. Either it is the inability to overcome a limited, stabilized, and immovable centeredness, in which case there is a center, but a center which does not have a life process whose content is changed and increased; thus it approaches the death of mere self-identity. Or it is the inability to return because of the dispersing power of the manifoldness, in which case there is life, but it is dispersed and weak in centeredness, and it faces the danger of losing its center altogether—the death of mere self-alteration" (3: 33).

2. Jack Provonsha offers a helpful diagnosis of the consequences of basic mistrust in *God Is With Us* (Washington, DC: Review 1968) 114-25; see also *You Can Go Home Again: An Untheology of the Atonement* (Washington, DC: Review 1982) 60-84; Ellen G. White, *Christ's Object Lessons* (Oakland, CA: Pacific 1900) 415; Reinhold Niebuhr, *The Nature and Destiny of Man: A Christian Interpretation*, 2 vols. (New York: Scribner 1948): "The sin of the inordinate self-love . . . points to the prior sin of lack of trust in God" (1: 252).

awareness of the relevant facts and norms might not, in a given case, be blameworthy.[1]

Objective Harm and Subjective Sin

Rightly understood, some things—acts and character states—are inconsistent with love for God's good creation. They represent unfair disregard for the interests of others, or involve the purposeful or instrumental infliction of harm. Denying one's own potential by contracting oneself into a tight, loveless little ball; denying another's dignity; denying the goodness of creation by recklessly polluting and destroying it—these are *objectively* harmful. A loving person fully aware of the circumstances and consequences of her acts would never intend harm to another.[2]

But sin and harm cannot simply be identified; sin has a *subjective* dimension. A sinful choice is one that *loves* disorderedly. A sinful character state is one that disposes a person not to *love* appropriately. Sin has to do with the meaning a person's acts and character traits have for the person herself. Even if a person's act or character state is objectively harmful, that's no guarantee that the person herself has intentionally refused to love God's good creation. I may, for instance, say something that hurts you tremendously because it raises the specter of a long-buried and forgotten pain. But I may have no idea that I have hurt you. And if so, despite the destructive effects of my act—which may require reparation on my part—I haven't *sinned*. My character and my choices may well not reflect a disregard for the claim God's good creation exerts on me, its call to love.

Those who engage in harmful behavior may need to be restrained; they certainly will need to compensate those they have harmed. It is in connection with *sin*, rather than *harm*, that considerations of freedom become relevant. Subjective assessment is important as a way of understanding a person and determining her responsibility for her acts. But one can hardly be responsible for one's acts if one did not freely choose them, if they are simply the outworkings of inexorable natural processes of which one is part, or the products of psychological battles among various instincts and ideas. Christians believe that human freedom is *situated* freedom—that my character and circumstances constrain my freedom, that they limit the options available to me and incline me to favor some over others. But implicit in the idea of creation is the conviction that freedom is nonetheless real, that I am not simply a function of my history or my genes or my environment. If creatures lacked this sort of freedom, then there would be no difference, from God's point of view, between creating a world and just imagining one; and there would, therefore, have been no point in creating a world at all. A sinful act or character-state reflects, therefore, a *freely-chosen* denial that one is part of God's good creation.

The Significance of the Distinction

The distinction between harmful and sinful acts and dispositions matters, first of all, because persons have limited knowledge. Their intentions need to be taken into account if we want not merely to understand the consequences of their actions but rather to comprehend *them*, as persons. Institutionally—through our govern-

---

1. The meaning of *fairness* and *harm* will obviously vary depending on the creature or creatures affected by one's actions. One may engage in culpable, purposeful harm by destroying an insentient object of great beauty, but one has not acted unfairly toward it, and need not have acted unfairly toward any sentient. Fairness, in turn, is possible between different kinds of creatures, but it will obviously have a different meaning as a predicate of relationships between, say, a human being and a dog than as a characteristic of a relationship between two human beings.

2. Though harm might be a foreseen but unintended by-product of something she does, provided bringing it about proved consistent with fairness.

ments or corporations or churches or schools—we may need to take action to prevent harmful events and to promote the formation of traits of character reflective of personal sensitivity to the importance of creational flourishing. But as we do so, we need to be aware that not every objectively destructive act reflects an intentional, free choice on the part of the person involved to frustrate the flourishing of creation, a responsible decision to deny that she is part of God's good creation.

Its easy to see why this distinction is helpful when a destructive act derives from someone's lack of awareness of the *empirical* context or consequences of her actions. Suppose, for instance, she has *good reason* to believe that a loaded gun is unloaded (perhaps she has been intentionally deceived), and kills another person as a result. It's clear that, despite the awful consequences of what she has done, her character is not that of a murderer. She is not responsible, except in a very attenuated sense, for the death that happened as a consequence of what she did with a gun she was justified in believing was unloaded.

The harm-sin distinction also matters because people have limited freedom. Biological, psychological, or sociological pressure may minimize responsibility for an act or character-state—or even, in very extreme cases, eliminate it. (The effects of hypnosis and some kinds of drugs could, for instance, completely suspend the capacity for free, conscious volition.) None of us chooses in a vacuum. So our freedom is always constrained. And recognizing the constraints on our freedom can help us to understand, when it is necessary to do so, how to determine and distribute moral responsibility.

Sin and Conflicting Visions of Love

More difficult is the case where a person is unaware of the applicable *moral* norms, where someone does not see what it truly *means* to love God's good creation rightly. Some people believe that everyone instinctively knows what is morally right in any given situation, and that any immoral act represents a deliberate violation of naturally intuited norms of moral rightness. If this were true, then anyone who did something wrong would always be culpable. For, given all the relevant non-moral information, she should be able to assess any act or state in light of her built-in moral sense.

But, whether or not there is a moral sense,[1] it is clearly not infallible. Our responses to the objectively given reality of the good created world are shaped by traditions and cultural contexts that facilitate—or inhibit—our apprehension of creation's value and our place within it, as well as our response to the reality we have thus discerned. That reality applies an insistent pressure that continually nudges us to see it more clearly and respond to it more aptly. But we apprehend it in ways affected by our cultures and subcultures. It is perfectly possible, then, for us to be mistaken about the inherent worth of things and actions and traits as well as about their empirical characteristics.

Assessing responsibility when this occurs—in respect of our own lives or where the actions or characters of others are concerned—is obviously a difficult business. The typical response of the Christian church throughout its history has been that motivation and intention are decisive in determining the moral quality of our acts. If I believe I am responding correctly to creation's claim upon me, then I am forming the right sort of character whether or not the action or actions prompted by my motivation or intention can be seen to be destructive. And, conversely, if I believe I am acting destructively, I am warping my character, whether or not I actually *am* acting destructively.

---

1. Cp. James Q. Wilson, *The Moral Sense* (New York: Free 1995).

This is position needs to be qualified in two ways. First, all of our motives are mixed. We don't bring perfect motives to any situation. We can spend innumerable hours attempting fruitlessly to dissect our own motives. But whatever our motives and intentions, there will be times when we need to act. At those times, we cannot allow concern about our motives to prevent us from responding appropriately to the situations that confront us. Perhaps I am rushing into the burning building to save a trapped child in order to humiliate my ex-spouse's lover who is standing idly on the sidelines. But despite my problematic motive, my action remains an appropriate one.

Second, people are sometimes, perhaps often, caught between the good creation's demand to be taken seriously and the demands of their traditions or their hyperactive consciences.

> ... I may wrongly think I have an obligation that I do not have. In the past it was widely held that my believing, even misguidedly, that I have an obligation morally obliges me to fulfill it. To many of us today, however, it seems that if a person who takes too narrow a view of her own rights rebels against a falsely assumed burden of obligations, the moral gain in throwing off some of the shackles of servility may be more important than the damage to her conscientiousness.[1]

The Case of Huckleberry Finn

Mark Twain's *Huckleberry Finn* explores with great sensitivity the problem of an inner conflict created by a false demand imposed by one's conscience. Huck and the escaped slave, Jim, are traveling along the Mississippi on a raft. Slowly, it begins to dawn on Huck that he's helping Jim find freedom. And, even though he's promised Jim not to betray him, he doesn't like the thought of assisting an escaped slave very much.

> Jim said it made him all over trembly and feverish to be so close to freedom. Well, I can tell you it made me all over trembly and feverish, too, to hear him, because I begun to get it through my head that he *was* most free—and who was to blame for it? Why, *me*. I couldn't get that out of my conscience, not how nor no way. It got to troubling me so I couldn't rest; I couldn't stay still in one place. It hadn't ever come home to me before, what this thing was that I was doing. But now it did; and it stayed with me, and scorched me more and more. I tried to make out to myself that *I* warn't to blame, because *I* didn't run Jim off from his rightful owner; but it warn't no use, conscience up and says, every time, "But you knowed he was running for his freedom, and you could 'a' paddled ashore and told somebody." That was so—I couldn't get around that no way. That was where it pinched. Conscience says to me, "What had poor Miss Watson done to you that you could see her ... [slave] go off right under your eyes and never say one single word? What did that poor old woman do to you that you could treat her so mean? ..."
>
> Jim talked out loud all the time while I was talking to myself. He was saying how the first thing he would do when he got to a free state he would go to saving up money and never spend a single cent, and when he got enough he would buy his wife, which was owned on a farm close to where Miss Watson lived; and then they would both work to buy the two children, and if their masters wouldn't sell them, they'd get an Ab'litionist to go and steal them.
>
> ... Thinks I, this is what comes of my not thinking. Here was this ... [slave], which I had as good as helped to run away, coming right out flat-

---

1. Robert Merrihew Adams, *Finite and Infinite Goods: A Framework for Ethics* (New York: OUP 1999) 247.

footed and saying he would steal his children—children that belonged to a man I didn't even know; a man that hadn't ever done me no harm.
... My conscience got to stirring me up hotter than ever, until at last I says to it, "Let up on me—it ain't too late yet—I'll paddle ashore at the first light and tell." I felt easy and happy and light as a feather right off. All my troubles was gone. I went to looking out sharp for a light, and sort of singing to myself.[1]

When Huck and Jim see lights, Huck paddles off—telling Jim he's going to investigate, but really planning to turn the escaped slave in to the authorities. But when Jim tells him he's the best friend he's ever had, and the only white man who's ever kept a promise to him, Huck begins to have second thoughts. "Well, I just felt sick," he tells us. "But I says, I *got* to do it—I can't get *out* of it." When two men appear in a boat, Huck lies to keep them from investigating the raft. Still feeling guilty, he resigns himself to his fate as a moral failure.[2] But when Jim is later captured, Huck finds himself faced with his moral dilemma once again. Should he tell Jim's "owner" the location of her escaped slave? At first, he resists the urge to do so because of the risk of embarrassment. Quickly, however, another reason occurs to him.

> The more I studied about this the more my conscience went to grinding me, and the more wicked and low-down and ornery I got to feeling. And at last, when it hit me all of a sudden that here was the plain hand of Providence slapping me in the face and letting me know my wickedness was being watched all the time from up there in heaven, whilst I was stealin a poor old woman's ... [slave] that hadn't ever done me no harm, and now was showing me there's One that's always on the lookout, and ain't a-going to allow no such miserable doings to go only just so fur and no further, I most dropped in my tracks I was so scared. Well, I tried the best I could to kinder soften it up somehow for myself by saying I was brung up wicked, and so I warn't so much to blame; but something inside of my kept saying, "There was the Sunday school, you could 'a' gone to it; and if you'd 'a' done it they'd 'a' learnt you there that people that acts as I'd been acting about that ... [slave] goes to everlasting fire."
> It made me shiver. And I about made up my mind to pray, and see if I couldn't try to quit being the kind of a boy I was and be better. So I kneeled down. But the words wouldn't come. Why wouldn't they? It warn't no use to try and hide it from Him. Nor from *me*, neither. I knowed very well why they wouldn't come. It was because my heart warn't right; it was because I warn't square; it was because I was playing double. I was letting *on* to give up sin, but away in side of me I was holding on to the biggest one of all. I was trying to make my mouth *say* I would do the right thing and the clean thing, and go and write to that ... [slave's] owner and tell where he was; but deep down in me I knowed it was a lie, and He knowed it. You can't pray a lie—I found that out.[3]

So Huck writes to Jim's "owner," telling her that Jim has been captured and where he can be found. For a moment at least, he feels spiritually refreshed.

> I felt good and all washed clean of sin for the first time I had ever felt so in my life, and I knowed I could pray now. But I didn't do it straight off, but laid the paper down and set there thinking—thinking how good it was all this happened so, and how near I come to being lost and going to hell.[4]

1. Mark Twain, *The Adventures of Huckleberry Finn, Tom Sawyer's Comrade* (New York: Harper 1912) 117-9 (available at http://etext.virginia.edu/; last visited Jan. 31, 2007).
2. Twain 119-21.
3. Twain 282-3.
4. Twain 284.

But then he starts to remember the good times he's had with Jim, and the value of Jim's friendship.

> ... somehow I couldn't seem to strike no places to harden me against him, but only the other kind. I'd see him standing my watch on top of his'n, 'stead of calling me, so I could go on sleeping; and see him how glad he was when I come back out of the fog; and when I come to him again in the swamp ...; and ... would always ... do everything he could think of for me, and how good he always was; ... and said I was the best friend old Jim ever had in the world, and the *only* one he's got now; and then I happened to look around and see that paper.
> ... I took it up, and held it in my hand. I was a-trembling, because I'd got to decide, forever, betwixt two things, and I knowed it. I studied a minute, sort of holding my breath, and then says to myself:
> "All right, then, I'll *go* to hell"—and tore it up.[1]

Huck Finn has been taught that slavery is God's will. But Jim is still his friend. Should he follow the demands of his conscience, which dictate that he permit Jim's enslavement? Or should he accept the claim of Jim's friendship and his vulnerable creatureliness? Should he love God's good creation? Surely Huck is right to make the choice he does. But we have to recognize that, before he can help Jim escape, must overcome a great deal of guilt. We may judge him objectively innocent: God does not really endorse slavery. But he may also, perhaps, have been rationally justified in accepting his tradition's claim to mediate God's will to him regarding this matter, at least until he felt the force of Jim's humanity and friendship. Is he sinning when he chooses to help his friend?

We don't want, I think, to condemn Huck Finn as warping his character by opting against what he had reason to believe was the revealed will of God. We can make sense of Huck's choice, and discern its moral legitimacy, using the model I offered in Chapter 2 as an account of the way in which we form and justify our beliefs. His perception of Jim's value—as a human being and as a friend—became a source of tension within his web of belief. He could resolve this tension by denying Jim's claim on him. Or he could see this claim as a pointer to the inadequacy of the traditional convictions that had led him to believe slavery was appropriate, and revise those convictions accordingly.

He chose the latter, of course, though not without a lot of inner tension. He surely felt considerable guilt even after reaching his initial decision. In retrospect, it no doubt looked like the right one. That's certainly how it appears to us. But it didn't seem *unambiguously* correct. Huck had to sort out the legitimacy of competing claims about moral goodness. And so do we.

Sometimes our tradition will highlight features of reality we've ignored, or lead us to reinterpret the good created world and the nature of the claim it imposes on us. Sometimes, by contrast, our experience, even though it is shaped by our tradition, will highlight neglected aspects or even inadequacies of that tradition. In any case, at least initially, it is unlikely that we will be able to eliminate tension and ambiguity. There may well be times when we are torn in quite different directions.

At such times, we can only pray for self-understanding and insight, and proceed sensitively. We can still act in destructive ways. We can still warp our characters as we shape our histories under ambiguous circumstances. But the presence of tension, the fact that one may make conflicting judgments about moral appropriateness, is no sign that one is acting in a morally irresponsible way, provided that one is honest and sensitive to the claims of God's good creation. And throughout, we need to remember that "people are [not] under any valid

---

1. Twain 284.

obligation to perform duties they mistakenly believe they have, except insofar as . . . the erring views" are valid.[1]

Disordered Love as a Condition

In addition to the distinction between harm and sin, another distinction may also be useful in making sense of Christian talk about sin. This is the distinction between sin as an act or a developed character-state, on the one hand, and sin as a condition on the other. The traditional Christian way of making this distinction has been to contrast actual or personal sin with *original* sin.

The idea of original sin can be confusing. It has sometimes included all of the following elements: a conception of sin's pervasiveness, an account of its source, and the notion that moral responsibility follows from being in a condition in which sin is pervasive and endemic—the idea of inherited *guilt*.[2]

The Universality of Disordered Love

Implicit in the idea of original sin is the idea that human moral failure is universal part of human experience. And there is no real doubt about its universality. We do not know any perfect people.

There is an immediate practical reason for this affirmation: it calls into question any pretension I or any group of which I am a part might make to authoritative finality. Our actions are colored by sin; and we find it all too easy to make our intellects serve our desire to refuse to be parts of God's good creation. This recognition can help to keep us from being over-confident about our own capacities or those of the institutions in the lives of which we participate.[3]

Belief in sin's universality also calls into question any black-and-white distinctions between people. If sin is universal, then the moral differences between people will always be qualitative, not quantitative. Even the most faithful Christians have confessed their continuing proneness to moral failure, and even those who appear to be most flagrantly in violation of the moral order still exhibit traces of goodness. All of our lives are too morally ambiguous to justify any tidy categorization of human beings into "the good" and "the bad."

We all likely know the expression, "There, but for the grace of God, go I"—voiced under her breath, perhaps, by a Christian as she encounters a "sinner." It sounds humble, but it really reflects the familiar self-righteousness of the man in Jesus' story who begins a prayer by thanking God that he is not like other people. The love of God does not justify self-satisfied distinctions between "us" and "them." Indeed, such self-righteousness is itself a failure truly to love other people—themselves parts of the good creation—with the attentive care they deserve.

Of course, God is always seeking to make us better people. But we can have no idea what genetic or environmental constraints may affect God's activity in someone else's life, and certainly no right to declare that life off-limits to God's love. Nor can one use the state of someone else's moral and spiritual development as a justification for distancing oneself from her or him. A key part of accepting God's loving acceptance of us is recognizing the absurdity of the barriers that separate us from others. To erect such barriers—especially ones based on the pretense that God's love is one's own *possession*, and at the same time not someone else's—is

---

1. Adams 247.
2. Cp. Richard Swinburne, *Responsibility and Atonement* (Oxford: Clarendon-OUP 1989) 110-7, 137-47.
3. See Charles Scriven, *The Demons Have Had It: A Theological ABC* (Nashville: Southern 1976) 94.

simply evidence that one needs to be more open to the very love one claims to own. Belief in the universality of sin works together with belief in God's universal love to undermine barriers between persons wherever they might occur.

The Origin of Disordered Love in Human Freedom and History

If human beings are essentially free, then human sinning must have its origins in time. That is, there must have been a first sin. Thus, the traditional doctrine of original sin is correct to imply that human sin has historical roots. Christians have always asserted that the first human beings were the first sinners. So sin must have been here from the start. And if human actions are free, then it must have begun with the free actions of the first human beings.[1]

The Propagation of Disordered Love

Inappropriate behavior characteristically seems or feels attractive or even necessary to us because of messages communicated by our social contexts; from genetically transmitted impulses—to aggression, for instance—which, while not inherently evil, nonetheless provide the occasion for self- or other-destructive behavior; and from habits and perspectives unavoidably formed before the advent of moral responsibility because of various developmental processes.[2] These drives, processes, and dispositions are not themselves evil. They may have survival value, and they may be useful constituents of our growth as human beings. But they sometimes incline us, nonetheless, to do things that are inconsistent with accepting ourselves as parts of God's good creation.

Having come into existence, sin feeds on itself; it has become self-propagating.[3] And the effects not only of *one's own* past sins but also of the sins of *others* all the way back to the very first human sin combine to make it harder for one to live as a part of God's good creation.[4]

Social structures and institutions—educational, cultural, financial, governmental—perpetuate distorted values. They constrain people's perceptions, making it difficult for those who participate in them to see alternatives as live options.

---

1. Cp. Paul R. Sponheim, "Sin and Evil," *Christian Dogmatics*, ed. Carl E. Braaten and Robert W. Jenson, 2 vols. (Philadelphia: Fortress 1984) 1: 385-407.

2. See Wolfhart Pannenberg, *Anthropology in Theological Perspective*, trans. Matthew J. O'Connell (Philadelphia: Westminster 1985) 80-138.

3. Langdon Gilkey, *Message and Existence: An Introduction to Christian Theology* (New York: Crossroad-Seabury 1979) 142-3.

4. It may be that the morphogenetic fields to which Rupert Sheldrake, *A New Science of Life: The Hypothesis of Formative Causation* (London: Paladin-Granada 1983) has called our attention may help to explain the propagation of sin. For if Sheldrake is correct, it is possible, by engaging in a certain behavior, for one or more members of a species to render it easier or perhaps more likely for other members of the species to exhibit the behavior. The sin of the first human beings would therefore render it more probable that other human beings would sin. See also Rupert Sheldrake, *The Presence of the Past: Morphic Resonance and the Habits of Nature* (New York: Vintage 1988); Rupert Sheldrake, "The Laws of Nature as Habits: A Postmodern Basis for Science," *The Reenchantment of Science: Postmodern Proposals*, ed. David Ray Griffin, SUNY Series in Constructive Postmodern Thought (Albany: SUNY 1988) 79-86; Rupert Sheldrake, *The Rebirth of Nature: The Greening of Science and God* (London: Century 1990). Issue 12.6 (2005) of the *Journal of Consciousness Studies* was devoted to Sheldrake's work; see *Sheldrake and His Critics: The Sense of Being Glared At*, ed. Anthony Freeman (Exeter: Imprint 2005). This kind of understanding of the propagation of sin would complement the proposal I offer in Chapter 10 for a Sheldrake-inspired account of an aspect of Jesus' mediation of divine healing to humanity. Provonsha discusses some physiological processes that might make the transmission of sin possible in *You* 70, 75-6n19.

They find it hard to encourage self-criticism or even to make it possible. They multiply the human capacity for harm by ensuring that a sinful policy, perhaps adopted by a few people, will be carried out by many more people, drawing on far more resources than an individual would likely possess and operating in far more contexts than an individual would be likely to do. And they become the foci of loyalties that far exceed their inherent significance; an "inordinate, all-encompassing love of the self is redirected towards our group, our nation, our race, our cause . . . ."[1] The result can be that people feel licensed in causing unjust harms on behalf of causes or groups that they would never regard as appropriate if undertaken for their own benefit.

These structures insulate people from the results of their actions, and thus make these actions seem less like *theirs*. Thus, they shield individual persons from responsibility. And they help people to avoid occasions when they might be challenged to empathize with those they hurt, and ensure that they typically need not confront the full emotional impact of any harm they perpetrate. The behavior of structures and institutions is characteristically marked by a drive for self-preservation: the survival of a structure becomes more important than the people it comprises—or anyone else, for that matter. In fact, we often implicitly—and, I would maintain, unnecessarily—*expect* the behavior of structures to be governed by rules different from those that we expect to guide the lives of persons. Persons making choices in structural settings are still moral actors, to whom the Golden Rule and the Pauline Principle still apply. But structures tend to discourage people from thinking about their individual moral accountability for actions they perform in official capacities. Further, so many people are involved in corporate structures of one sort of another that a single individual rarely has much influence over decision-making; this fact, too, helps to make it easy for corporations and the individuals involved in them to be irresponsible.[2]

Institutional injustice becomes a self-perpetuating cycle. For it victimizes entire groups and classes of people. Only an institution can really damage a community. But, in so doing, it creates a fractured and broken collection of people who are themselves tempted to create new cycles and patterns of destruction. And there is another kind of cycle at work here as well. A self-aggrandizing group sets itself up for calamity. Either by over-extending itself or by arousing the resentment of other groups, a corporate entity that grows too convinced of its own status, too inclined to treat itself as the center of value, will likely suffer considerable loss. But in reacting to this loss, a devastated institution may in fact come to adopt an even more inflated communal self-concept.[3]

Individuals come and go, but structures and institutions continue to exhibit similar patterns of behavior. A structure takes on a life of its own, striving to perpetuate itself without regard for the consequences. People, in turn, become trapped in habitual ways of doing things by the structures that provide the settings for their actions. Without choosing to do so, people are caught up in practices that presuppose attitudes and serve values inconsistent with appropriate love for creation—racism, for instance, or militarism, or sexual exploitation. Victims

---

1. Gilkey 148. Such identification is also possible as a result of the other kind of sin—the self-effacing sort. The idolization of a corporate structure *may* be a way of redirecting idolatrous energies that would otherwise be focused on the self. But it may also reflect a valuation of the self as worthless, deserving only to be sacrificed to some larger good or goods.

2. These themes are powerfully elaborated in Niebuhr 1: 208-40, on which I am dependent—directly and indirectly—for much of what follows on corporate sin.

3. Cp. Gilkey 155; Marcus J. Borg, *Jesus: A New Vision—Spirit, Culture, and the Life of Discipleship* (San Francisco: Harper 1987) 86-91; Marcus J. Borg, *Conflict, Holiness, and Politics in the Teaching of Jesus* (Harrisburg, PA: TPI 1998) 66-87.

and their oppressors are both trapped by the ongoing operations of large organizations and complex social situations that seem to be operating according to inner dynamics of their own.

Social structures are a necessary part of human life together, and thus of God's good creation. But though structures are, in principle, good, they provide people with innumerable opportunities to harm creation. And they enmesh even more people in existing patterns of domination and exploitation. Thus, they contribute to the backdrop against which human sin takes place; they help to corrupt the circumstances within which we act. They are among the factors that make talk of humanity's sinful *condition* meaningful.

Does Guilt Precede Freedom?

None of this means that we need to accept the notion of inheritable *responsibility*, of original *guilt*, which is what some people have come to understand the idea of original sin to imply. On this view, we become responsible for sinful acts and character-traits just because sin is the human condition. Guilt is transmitted from generation to generation. Before we ever choose freely, we are already guilty.

There is clearly something wrong with this view as it stands. For we can be morally responsible only for what we ourselves do, what we personally contribute to the course of history. That is just what responsibility means. If my genes or my environment are the cause of an event, then I am a kind of innocent bystander at the event. A natural process—psychic or social or biological—over which I have no control has brought the event about, and it is the *process* that is therefore responsible for the event, a process of which I am only an inseparable part. If my genes or my environment or my upbringing are the cause of all that would ordinarily be attributed to me, then in an important sense *I* do not exist at all as a separate self. We are not and cannot be *guilty* for circumstances into which we are born or for situations over which we have no control.[1]

Despite its continuing value as a pointer to the fact that a sinful condition precedes my sinful choices and my acquisition of sinful character states, it may be that the *language* of original sin is inseparable from a history in which it has acquired unfortunate connotations. If using the phrase "original sin" unavoidably implies belief in original guilt or in the necessity of evil choices, then perhaps we need another expression to use in its place. We might, for instance, speak of *endemic* sin. But, whatever the label we use, key ideas embedded in the traditional notion of original sin are worth affirming.

Gender and Disordered Love

One of the many disorders of human love caused by endemic sin is the subordination and exclusion of people in virtue of their sex.[2] Such subordination and

---

1. Cp. Swinburne 144-6. Given the importance Augustine's view of original guilt has had for Catholicism over the course of its history, it is important to note the clear denial of this view by Karl Rahner, *Foundations of Christian Faith: An Introduction to the Idea of Christianity*, trans. William V. Dych (New York: Crossroad-Seabury 1978): "'original sin' in no way means that the moral quality of the actions of the first person or persons is transmitted to us, whether this by through a juridical imputation by God or through some kind of biological heredity, however conceived." (111).

2. Among the disorders of love involved here are ones that misshape intimate erotic relationships in our society: erotic love itself is a victim of the disordering of love that is sin. See Sandra Lee Bartky, "Feminine Masochism and the Politics of Personal Transformation," *Femininity and Domination: Studies in the Phenomenology of Oppression*

exclusion are themselves sinful; but they can also influence people's inclinations to sin in particular ways.

In our culture, at least, according to much recent criticism, men and women have quite different characteristic sins.[1] Critics maintain that men have defined "pride"—giving oneself the absoluteness only the infinite creator deserves—as the primordial sin because it is in fact *their* primordial sin. But where men's sense of self may be too pronounced, women's tends not to be pronounced enough: their temptation may be to give *other* kinds of reality absolute status.

Women's ego boundaries in our culture may be insufficiently defined. Women may tend to have trouble distinguishing their own inner voices—what *they* really want—from the voices of others—spouses, parents, authority figures of all sorts—who want them to behave in particular ways.[2] They may be susceptible to fragmentation, as competing claims tug them in different directions. Telling women not to be prideful is implicitly telling them to make room in their lives for God and others, to be more flexible and responsive, more mutual and open. These are messages *men* need to hear. And doubtless *some* women need to hear them, too. But their effect on many women may be to reinforce the submissiveness, self-dissolution, and lack of personal initiative they are already socialized to exhibit.

The definition of sin I've developed takes account of what have been identified as the distinctly different kinds of moral failure exhibited by men and women. On this view, the typically masculine problem is the tendency to take oneself and one's own projects too seriously. This kind of sin reflects an inappropriate form of love of the *self*. It involves, in effect, the denial that I am a *part* of God's good creation, a creation much larger and grander and richer than I am.

If I deny my contingency, if I refuse to allow myself and my projects to be relativized by others, or if I seek to secure my freedom from the vicissitudes of creaturely life by dominating others, then I am rejecting my creaturely status. Even if I deny the possibility verbally, I am, in effect, treating myself as able on my own to secure the meaning and value of my existence.[3] For that is the only alternative to seeing myself as part of God's creation, and thus finite and contingent. And I cannot relate properly with God if I deny in practical terms that I am a creature. If I sin in this way, I fundamentally misconstrue the character of reality, wrongly treating my own finite life as if it had the capacity to serve as the center of reality.[4] Implicitly or explicitly, therefore, I mistrust God's capacity to be God—to provide an anchor point for the universe so that I don't need to pretend to do so. Thus, to sin in this way is to alienate myself from God.[5]

To deal with this sort of sin, one will need to learn to appreciate the gifted quality of one's existence a lot more. One will need to learn to relativize oneself, one's plans, and one's projects. One will need to learn to be less assertive, to live

---

(New York: Routledge 1990) 45-62; Anna G. Jónasdóttir, *Why Women Are Oppressed* (Philadelphia: Temple UP 1994).

1. See Valerie Saiving Goldstein, "The Human Situation: A Feminine View," *Womanspirit Rising: A Feminist Reader in Religion*, ed. Carol P. Christ and Judith Plaskow (San Francisco: Harper 1979) 25-35; Judith Plaskow, *Sex, Sin, and Grace: Women's Experience and the Theologies of Reinhold Niebuhr and Paul Tillich* (Washington, DC: UP of America 1980).

2. See Dana Crowley Jack, *Silencing the Self: Women and Depression* (New York: Harper 1993). Thanks to Aimi Saunders for a conversation that contributed to my understanding of this problem.

3. This sort of sin is diagnosed and described in excruciating and helpful detail in Niebuhr 1: 178-264.

4. Cp. Niebuhr's suggestion that the deception of others is rooted in the attempt to solidify one's own self-deception (1: 207).

5. Farley 152.

out of life's giftedness more fully by accepting divine love, by receiving God's gifts—mediated through nature and other people—ungrudgingly, and by refraining from the constant need to secure their value by achieving and producing.

On the view I am considering, the typically feminine sin, by contrast, will consist in inappropriate love for the *other*, the denial, in effect, that one is oneself part of God's *good* creation—and that the other is simply a *part* of God's good creation. This kind of sin manifests itself in the tendency to frustrate creational flourishing by refusing to take oneself and one's projects seriously enough as distinct and valuable elements of creation. It may involve asking the other to serve as the ground of meaning and value in one's life, something she or he is just as incapable doing as one is oneself.

If one denies one's own value or submits willingly to domination or fragmentation, one is not pretending to transcend the good creation; one is behaving as if one isn't an inherently valuable part of it at all. One is denying the fact that, in one's unique and distinct way, one has an integrity and a value of one's own.

This kind of sin, too, has implications regarding one's relationship with God. It can be seen as reflecting a fundamental misunderstanding of God, as a demanding, authoritarian, alien despot whose impositions are mirrored in the claims of all those other voices which demand one's attention—voices that tell one that one has no inherent value, or that one must accept their diverse agendas even if doing so fragments one beyond repair. It can involve the mistaken conviction that God is primarily interested in securing obedience from one as a testament to arbitrary divine power. And it represents, in any case, a fundamental mistrust of and alienation from God insofar as it involves the expectation that something other than God can provide one with ultimate meaning and security.

In committing this kind of sin, one deprives God of a self with which to interact—one's own.[1] In our culture, at least, the way for people to fight this kind of sin will be for them to take themselves and their projects more seriously.

Men and women both fail to love God's good creation rightly. The typical man does so by treating himself as the center of meaning and value. The typical woman does so by subordinating herself and her projects to others and to the fragmenting effects of fate, while expecting others to provide her with meaning and value.[2] And both kinds of sin lead ultimately to self-disintegration.

Of course, it is not the case that either men or women are afflicted exclusively by certain sorts of sins. The critics who have suggested that our understanding of sin should be seen as gendered are best understood as elaborating ideal types. The distinction *does*, however, reflect the different ways in which women and men are socialized in our culture. Those differences can sometimes make the moral challenges faced by women and men quite different. Many men know far too little about dependence; others, especially women, need the freedom to practice *in*dependence. The goal, of course, is for members of both genders to reach a balanced state of *interdependence*.

Whether ours is the kind of sinfulness typical of men or that typical of women, our loves are too often disordered. We ask too much of ourselves or of others. We expect something finite and created to give us complete and absolute confidence. Distorted love prevents creation from reaching its full potential—and prevents creatures from giving each element of the good creation the love it merits. And it leads to suffering not only for creatures but for God. Not all distortions of

---

1. Cp. Wanda Warren Berry, "Images of Sin and Salvation in Feminist Theology," *Anglican Theological Review* 60 (Jan. 1978): "[o]ne can lose the relationship either by negating God in defiant 'strength' or by negating the self in weakly refusing to constitute a gathered will" (46; qtd. Sponheim 374).

2. Cp. Sponheim 374-5.

love are deliberate; and all are, indeed, conditioned by features of the human situation that precede our free choices. But all are occasions for God's healing love.

Because God loves the creation, God responds to its brokenness, including the brokenness resulting from disordered love—revealing, guiding, healing. And God's presence and activity in the world not only answer our need for healing but also foster the ongoing growth of the good creation. Acting out of love, and seeking our love for God and for each other, God's Spirit is at work in nature, in history, and in our individual lives. For Christians, the decisive moment of God's loving activity in our world is the life of Jesus of Nazareth. It is to Jesus and his significance that I turn in Chapter 7.

7

Love Takes Flesh

The Christian vision of God as love is profoundly indebted to a single human life.¹ Almost two thousand years ago, a Jew whose Aramaic name we Anglicize as "Jesus" died on a Roman cross outside of Jerusalem. Only a few decades later, Christians were according him the kind of devoted love ordinarily reserved for God, and talking about him in language they might have been expected to reserve for God.² Christianity is grounded on the events that gave rise to this re-

---

1. Cp. Lionel S. Thornton, *The Incarnate Lord: An Essay Concerning the Doctrine of the Incarnation in Its Relation to Organic Conceptions* (London: Longmans 1928); Stephen R. L. Clark, *God, Religion, and Reality* (London: SPCK 1998) 108, 116-9; Stephen R. L. Clark, *God's World and the Great Awakening*, Limits and Renewals 3 (Oxford: Clarendon-OUP 1991) 117-44; John B. Cobb, Jr., *Christ in a Pluralistic Age* (Philadelphia: Westminster 1975); David Ray Griffin, *A Process Christology* (Lanham, MD: UP of America 1990); Brian Hebblethwaite, *The Essence of Christianity: A Fresh Look at the Nicene Creed* (London: SPCK 1996) 84-99; Edward Farley, *Divine Empathy: A Theology of God* (Minneapolis: Fortress 1996) 278-85; Keith Ward, *Religion and Revelation: A Theology of Revelation in the World's Religions* (Oxford: Clarendon-OUP 1994) 258-82; Keith Ward, *The Concept of God* (Oxford: Blackwell 1974) 180-96; Wolfhart Pannenberg, *Systematic Theology*, 3 vols., trans. Geoffrey Bromiley (Grand Rapids: Eerdmans 1989-93) 2: 277-396; Thomas V. Morris, *The Logic of God Incarnate* (Ithaca, NY: Cornell UP 1986); Thomas V. Morris, "The Metaphysics of God Incarnate," *Trinity, Incarnation, and Atonement: Philosophical and Theological Essays*, ed. Ronald J. Feenstra and Cornelius Plantinga, Jr., Library of Religious Philosophy 1 (Notre Dame, IN: U of Notre Dame P 1989) 110-27; Ronald J. Feenstra, "Reconsidering Kenotic Christology," Feenstra and Plantinga 128-52; David Brown, *The Divine Trinity* (London: Duckworth 1985) 219-39, 245-71; Richard Sturch, *The Word and the Christ: An Essay in Analytic Christology* (Oxford: Clarendon-OUP 1991); Daniel Helminiak, *The Same Jesus: A Contemporary Christology* (Chicago, IL: Loyola UP 1986); Richard Swinburne, *The Christian God* (Oxford: Clarendon-OUP 1994) 192-215; C. Norman Kraus, *Jesus Christ Our Lord: Christology from a Disciple's Perspective* (Scottdale, PA: Herald 1987) 63-120; Adrian Thatcher, *Truly a Person, Truly God* (London: SPCK 1990).

2. See Larry W. Hurtado, *Lord Jesus Christ: Devotion to Jesus in Earliest Christianity* (Grand Rapids: Eerdmans 2005); Richard J. Bauckham, *God Crucified: Monotheism and Christology in the New Testament* (Grand Rapids: Eerdmans 1999); Murray J. Harris, *Jesus as God: The New Testament Use of Theos in Reference to Jesus* (Grand Rapids: Baker 1992); Oscar Cullmann, *The Christology of the New Testament*, trans. Shirley C. Guthrie and Charles A. M. Hall, rev. ed. (Philadelphia: Westminster 1963) 306-14; Raymond E. Brown, *Jesus: God and Man* (New York: Macmillan 1967) 1-38. While noting that "on the basis of the designation *Kyrios* early Christianity does not hesitate to transfer to Jesus everything the Old Testament says about God" (307) Cullmann goes on to assert that there are a number of instances in which Jesus is actually referred to as *theos*: John 1:1 (308-9; cp. 265-6), 1:18 (309-10), and 20:28 (308); 1 Jn. 5:20 (310); Heb. 1:8-9 (310-11); Rom. 9:5 (312-3; on this passage, cp. Bruce M. Metzger, "The Punctuation of Rom. 9:5," *Christ and Spirit in the New Testament*, FS C. F. D. Moule, ed. Barnabas

markable fact, that occasioned the identification of a crucified Jewish carpenter as embodying God's love in our world. The Christian understanding of Jesus is rooted in part in the way he expressed God's love. It can be seen as a decisive disclosure of that love. And it serves as a means of mediating that love to the world.

At the heart of the gospel is the conviction that Jesus is our best available clue to what God is doing for us behalf.[1] His life tells us where to look if we want to understand what God is doing in the world, and thus—implicitly—if we want to understand our place in the world.[2] Identifying Jesus in this way is the result of a complex process of judgment. We may rightly make the memory of the corporate Christian church over time our own in seeing Jesus as God's revelation. But we may also find evidence for the view that Jesus decisively reveals God in the support provided it by the inner logic of Christian belief, in the remarkable fact of the early Christians' worship of Jesus after his death, in the rapid growth of highly exalted views of his identity in the years immediately after his crucifixion, and in the evident challenge embodied in his implicit self-understanding.

God's revelation in Jesus shapes our understanding of God. It initiated a new phase of history. It underscores divine vulnerability and the goodness of creation. And it enriches our insight into the meaning of the Sabbath. A view of God as constantly present and active in creation helps us understand the belief that Jesus embodies God's love. The belief that he does so does not, however, imply that his maleness has any privileged status as a window on God's nature or character.

Jesus, the Remembered Lover

The belief that we meet God in Jesus, that we see God's love enacted in his life, is a remarkable and potentially powerful one. There are good reasons for taking this belief seriously.

The Rightness of Remembering

A crucial element of what I have called an epistemology of love is *piety*; and an important aspect of piety is respect for what we have learned from those who have preceded us. Acknowledging the value of piety means that, while gaining greater insight into the history of Jesus is important, each of us doesn't have to engage in careful historical reconstruction to answer the question of Jesus' identity.

There are innumerable personal paths to belief in Jesus as God's decisive self-disclosure. Some people do work painstakingly through the relevant historical and theological arguments and conclude that the probabilities weigh in favor of some

Lindars and Stephen S. Smalley [Cambridge: CUP 1973] 95); Col. 2:2 (313); Tit. 2:13 (313-4); and 2 Pet. 1:1 (314). Brown's somewhat shorter list is as follows: John 1:18 (12-3); Tit 2:13 (16-8); 1 Jn 5:20 (18-9); Rom. 9:5 (20-2); 2 Pet. 1:1 (22); Heb. 1:8-9 (23-5); and John 1:1 (25-7). Among Newer Testament passages that seem to "*imply* that Jesus is divine," Brown suggests, are John 8:24, 28, and 58; 10:30; 13:19; and 14:9 (23n38). He later proposes adding to this list Phil. 2:6-7 and Col. 1:19; the implications of these passages seem somewhat less clear. J. C. Fenton, "Matthew and the Divinity of Jesus," *Studia Biblica 1978*, ed. Elizabeth A. Livingstone, JSOT Supp. Ser. 11 (Sheffield: Sheffield 1980), notes that the reference to Jesus as *Emmanuel*, God-with-us, in Matt. 1:23 should be added to the list of Newer Testament passages characterizing Christ as in some way divine. On Matthew, see also James D. G. Dunn, *The Christ and the Spirit* 1: *Christology* (Grand Rapids: Eerdmans 1998) 44; cp. p. 382-3.

  1. See Fritz Guy, "Confidence in Salvation: The Meaning of the Sanctuary," *Spectrum* 11.2 (1980): 44-53; Fritz Guy, "Good News from the Sanctuary in Heaven: God's Continuing Initiative," *Spectrum* 14.1 (1983): 39-46.

  2. Cp. James Wm. McClendon, Jr., *Systematic Theology* 1: *Ethics* (Nashville: Abingdon 1986) 248-9.

version of Christian belief in Jesus as God's revelation. Others, perhaps, simply read the stories of Jesus and find themselves struck by their compelling power. And no doubt there are various other avenues to a Christian understanding Jesus. But the path of piety, in which we make the memory of the whole church our own, will probably the most common.¹ As we identify with the Christian community, we are taught the story of God-with-us by parents and teachers and pastors. We come to read the past through Christian eyes. We learn the church's recollection of Jesus—including the broad outlines of its theological interpretation of his identity and the nature of his ministry—as an accurate reflection of the impact he made on history, whatever the precise details may have been.

The process of evaluating Christian belief is an *ad hoc* one. As our convictions are challenged, we reformulate them if we find that we cannot integrate them successfully into our webs of belief. We need not follow some predetermined course to a belief in order for that belief to be valid. All that is necessary is that we take adequate account of reasonable objections.² So, whatever the origin of a person's beliefs about Jesus, she may rationally retain those beliefs unless they are shown to be invalid, provided she has ascertained that they can be successfully defended.

In the absence of a substantial challenge to belief in Jesus as God's revelation, there is no need to come up with arguments to defend this belief. But that doesn't mean there aren't positive reasons for the church's understanding of Jesus.

The Worship of Jesus

One way to get at the historical events that lie behind the development of Christian belief in Jesus as God's revelation is to begin with a man we call Pliny the Younger. Pliny was a Roman official in the region of Bithynia during the early part of the second century. Concerned about the growing influence of the Christian church, he investigated the nature of Christianity—and sought to suppress it. In about AD 112, he wrote a letter to the Roman Emperor, Trajan, explaining what he had discovered. Using torture where necessary, he had learned a variety of things about Christian belief and practice. One of the things he had studied was Christian worship. The Christians, he informed the Emperor, "were in the habit of meeting on a certain fixed day before it was light, when they sang in alternate verses a hymn to Christ, as to a god . . . ."³

What is so striking is that the early Christians were singing hymns to a man who had been crucified some eighty years earlier. Sometimes, historical heroes become gods long after their lives are over and they've become the stuff of legend.

---

1. This way of putting the matter reflects the influence of John Knox. See, *e.g.*, *Christ the Lord: The Meaning of Jesus in the Early Church* (Chicago: Willett 1945) 1-56. I believe that the church's corporate memory of Jesus—including the Jesus alive beyond death—is the basis for its contemporary acclamation of him. But I differ from Knox in my assessment of the Newer Testament evidence and its relation to that corporate memory and in my evaluation of the theological interpretations of Jesus formulated in and by the early church. See also Karl Rahner, *Foundations of Christian Faith: An Introduction to the Idea of Christianity*, trans. William V. Dych (New York: Crossroad 1978) 230-2; Peter Hinchliff, "Christology and Tradition," *God Incarnate: Story and Belief*, ed. A. E. Harvey (London: SPCK 1981).

2. As Morris rightly observes, many people reasonably adopt belief in Jesus on the basis of testimony, experience, or insight unmediated by argument (*Logic* 201-2).

3. Pliny the Younger, *Letters*, trans. William Melmoth (Cambridge: Harvard UP 1935) 10.96.7, qtd. Gary R. Habermas, *Ancient Evidence for the Life of Jesus: Historical Records of His Death and Resurrection* (Nashville: Nelson 1984) 95. On the hymn or hymns to which Pliny refers, Raymond Brown (*Jesus* 27) cites D. M. Stanley, "Carmenque Christo quasi Deo dicere," *Catholic Biblical Quarterly* 20 (1958): 173-91.

But these people were worshipping Jesus of Nazareth, who had walked and talked within living memory in a place to which it was possible to point on a map.

Much earlier than Pliny's investigation, in fact, the writers of what is now the Newer Testament seem to have referred to Jesus of Nazareth as divine.[1] There's something really remarkable about the fact that, not long after his death, a crucified Jewish carpenter, evidently part of the fabric of ordinary human experience, was apparently being described as divine.[2] No more than two decades or so following his crucifixion he was being venerated as a divine being: he was being acclaimed as Sovereign (*kyrios*), a title used in Greek-speaking Jewish communities for God; and he was being invoked in prayers that included the call, "Come, Sovereign" (*maranatha*).[3] Around the end of the first century, the Fourth Gospel identified him as God's Word made flesh.[4]

These developments imply that, not only after his death but during his public ministry, Jesus was identified as the kind of person regarding whom claims like those subsequently made about him by the church were (and are) appropriate. In trying to understand Jesus—who he was, what he did, what happened to him— we need to arrive at an answer that makes sense of these surprising developments. A Jesus whose career could justify them would rightly be confessed as the Jesus acclaimed by the Christian community.

God's Revelation in Jesus and the Inner Logic of Christian Doctrine

Belief in Jesus as God's revelation occupies a central position in the web of Christian belief. It does not follow *a priori* from any set of obvious premises that God should have become revealed in a human life. But that God did so can be seen to make sense given the trajectory of God's self-communication to humankind. This revelation can be seen as offering, not bare information, but a healing disclosure that the universe is at root a friendly place. God's activity in the life of Jesus appears, further, as the means by which God could reveal a solidarity with humankind in its creaturely condition of limitation and vulnerability that is plausibly interpreted as a corollary of divine love.

The sense of the doctrine's appropriateness increases in light of the perception of the relationship between Jesus the Jew and the heritage of Israel: this distinctive history can be discerned in retrospect as a uniquely fitting source for the images, concepts, practices, and ideas that formed the basis for Jesus' thinking, his ministry, and his message. That God's revelation in Jesus should have taken place at a point in the history of Israel when Judaism and Græco-Roman culture could interact productively, and thus provide the basis for a universalization of the Jesus message, also has a noteworthy air of appropriateness about it.

---

1. See above for relevant references to Harris; Hurtado, *Christ*; Brown; Cullmann; *et al.* I focus in the text on some of the more assured and less dramatic judgments of history regarding the early church's characterization of Jesus. The sources I cite at the beginning of the chapter suggest that the first Christians spoke in even more unequivocal terms of Jesus as divine.

2. I have come to see the problem of the rise of early Christology as the proper way into a discussion of contemporary Christological concerns as a result of my opportunity to learn from Martin Hengel, "The Son of God," *The Cross of the Son of God* (London: SCM 1986); C. F. D. Moule, *The Phenomenon of the New Testament: An Inquiry into the Implications of Certain Features of the New Testament*, Studies in Biblical Theology— 2d. ser., 1 (Naperville, IL: Allenson 1967); C. F. D. Moule, *The Origin of Christology* (Cambridge: CUP 1977).

3. See Cullmann 195-237; Moule, *Origin* 35-46; Eduard Schweizer, *Lordship and Discipleship*, Studies in Biblical Theology (Naperville, IL: Allenson 1960) 56-60.

4. Jn. 1:14.

Belief in Jesus as God's revelation is intimately related in a number of ways to various other Christian convictions. It helps to sustain a particular view of God as personal, loving, and valuing human nature and history. These and many other central things that Christians want to say make sense as elements in a relatively coherent whole of which belief in God's self-communication in Jesus is an integral part. To assess such a belief requires one to consider not only its relationship to particular historical facts and philosophical theories but to the network of convictions within which it finds its place. The doctrine of Jesus as God's revelation can be seen, then, to be justified by the "fittingness" of interpreting Jesus in this way within the framework provided by Christian belief as a whole. It is defensible in light of the inner logic of the Christian tradition.[1]

The Challenge of Jesus' Words and Actions

We can reasonably appeal directly to the information we have about Jesus, especially about his behavior during his public ministry, in support of the church's confession of him as God's revelation.

What Jesus said and implied about himself challenged his contemporaries, and challenges us, to ask about his identity. His words and actions seem to have implied a truly remarkable self-conception.[2] His assumption of authority is sufficiently dramatic that he can arguably be said to have dared to "put his own 'I' in the place of God's,"[3] speaking decisively in ways that seemed to suggest that his words needed the backing only of his own authority. He grounded "the truth of his proclamation" in "his person," speaking "as with God's authority" rather than merely *reporting* God's word.[4] He evidently believed that, in him, "God was acting

---

1. See Brian Hebblethwaite, "The Appeal to Experience in Christology," *Christ, Faith and History: Cambridge Studies in Christology*, ed. Stephen W. Sykes and John Powell Clayton (Cambridge: CUP 1971) 268-75. Ward, *Religion*, defends "a basic attitude of trust in the general reliability of the witnesses to that original historical person in whom one's faith is grounded" (242). John Milbank argues to the doctrine of the Incarnation from the inner logic of ecclesiology in *The Word Made Strange: Theology, Language, Culture* (Oxford: Blackwell 1997) 145-68. Cp. Ronald F. Thiemann, *Revelation and Theology: The Gospel as Narrated Promise* (Notre Dame, IN: U of Notre Dame P 1985); Hans Frei, *The Identity of Jesus Christ: The Hermeneutic Basis of Dogmatic Theology* (Philadelphia: Fortress 1975). Thiemann's purpose is to establish a doctrine of revelation; he argues that it would be inconsistent with the character of the triune God known in Jesus *not* to be self-revelatory. If the God thus disclosed *is* God, then our knowing so must be the result of divine action. Frei argues that, within the Gospel narratives, Jesus is identified decisively through the events of his passion and life beyond death, and that if that identification is correct then Jesus cannot but be alive and present. Both strategies are intriguing, but they seem less open-textured than Hebblethwaite's.

2. See James D. G. Dunn, *Christology in the Making: A New Testament Inquiry into the Origins of the Doctrine of the Incarnation*, 2d. ed. (Grand Rapids: Eerdmans 1996) 253-4; Dunn, *Christ* 3-54, 377-423; Bruce Vawter, *This Man Jesus* (Garden City, NY: Doubleday 1973); Wilckens 62-4; Turner; Cullmann; H. P. Owen, *Christian Theism: A Study in Its Basic Principles* (Edinburgh: Clark 1984) 36-7; Christopher Rowland, *Christian Origins: From Messianic Movement to Christian Religion* (Minneapolis: Augsburg 1985) 174-87; David Abernathy, *Understanding the Teaching of Jesus* (New York: Seabury 1983) 155-67.

3. The language is that of Ernst Fuchs; see Ernst Fuchs, *Studies of the Historical Jesus*, Studies in Biblical Theology 42 (London: SCM 1964) 20-5. See also Joachim Jeremias, *New Testament Theology: The Proclamation of Jesus*, trans. John Bowden (New York: Scribner 1971) 249-55; Ben F. Meyer, *The Aims of Jesus* (London: SCM 1979) 152. I believe one or more of the historians I have read on this point deserve credit for calling my attention to Fuchs and providing bibliographic information.

4. Brown, *Introduction* 70n94.

directly and immediately" and "regarded himself as having full authority to speak and act on behalf of God."[1] He affirmed and proclaimed *God's* sovereignty, but he understood himself as representing God and anticipated doing so in the future.[2] He

> combined and transcended the options normally available to a religious teacher and leader in his own culture. He assumed an authority to declare the will of God for . . . [human beings], and to act in accordance with that will, such as had not been claimed by any previous figure in the religious history of the Jews. "By what authority?" was the question raised again and again by his teaching, his healing acts and his prophetic stance . . . .[3]

Jesus' behavior suggested a claim to authority consistent with his understanding himself as the Messiah, the deliverer God would send to Israel.[4] But his evident sense of the identity between *his* words and actions and *God's* words and actions surpassed what his contemporaries would ordinarily have expected in the case of the Messiah. He seems to have characterized John the Baptist—whose ministry had preceded and prepared the way for his, and who had baptized him—as "the Elijah who is to come." In doing so, he called to mind Mal. 4:5, in which the prophet Elijah is described as the one "who ushers in the Day of the Lord"—God's decisive intervention in and transformation of history at the end of time. The implication seems to be that if "Jesus' herald, John the Baptist, is Elijah, then the coming of Jesus himself is tantamount to the coming of the Day of the Lord."[5]

Jesus declared that people's response to him and his message would determine their ultimate destiny.[6] He evidently assumed he possessed the authority "to assign his disciples roles in heaven . . . ." He indicated that death for his sake brought salvation.[7] He may have identified himself with God's Wisdom.[8] Depending on how it was understood at the time, his well attested if ambiguous reference to himself as "son of man" might also have represented a dramatic claim to authority.[9]

---

1. E. P. Sanders, *The Historical Figure of Jesus* (London: Lane-Penguin 1993) 236, 238.
2. Sanders, *Figure* 248. According to Sanders, "God was king, but Jesus represented him and would represent him in the coming kingdom."
3. Harvey 168.
4. See Marinus de Jonge, *Jesus, the Servant Messiah* (New Haven: Yale UP 1991) 68-72; Raymond E. Brown, *An Introduction to New Testament Christology* (New York: Paulist 1994) 73-80.
5. Moule, *Phenomenon* 71-2.
6. See, *e.g.*, Reginald H. Fuller, "The Clue to Jesus' Self-Understanding," *Christ and Christianity: Studies in the Formation of Christology*, comp., ed., and intro. Robert Kahl (Valley Forge, PA: TPI 1994) 37-46.
7. Brown, *Introduction* 69, citing Matt. 19:28, Lk. 22:28-30, and Lk. 9:24.
8. See Ben Witherington, *The Christology of Jesus* (Minneapolis: Augsburg/Fortress 1990) 51-3, 55, 222-3, 227, 232-3, 248, 274-5; and, rather hesitantly, Turner 231-2. Seeyoon Kim, *"The 'Son of Man'" as the Son of God* (Grand Rapids: Eerdmans 1985) 91-3 connects Jesus' self-identification with Wisdom with his self-designation as Son of Man. For the Christian availability of wisdom language to describe Jesus, see Rebecca Pentz, "Jesus as Sophia," *Reformed Journal* 38.12 (Dec. 1988): 17-22.
9. The expression "son of man" has been interpreted in a variety of ways. On the view that the expression referred in the minds of Jesus' contemporaries to a divine or semi-divine figure who would inaugurate God's Realm, see Jeremias 257-76; cp. Witherington 233-62; Kim, *Son*; Stein 132-48; Cullmann 152-64; Brown, *Introduction* 89-100; Werner Georg Kümmel, *The Theology of the New Testament According to Its Major Witnesses: Jesus–Paul–John*, trans. John E. Steely (Nashville: Abingdon 1973) 76-85; Rowland 185-7. In "Jesus, the Man of Universal Destiny," *The Myth of God Incarnate*, ed. John Hick (Philadelphia: Westminster 1977) 52-3, Michael Goulder defends the claim that Jesus believed himself to be the apocalyptic Son of Man. Goulder also asserts that Jesus performed "a large number of healings," "saw himself as the one through whom God's . . . [Realm] was being inaugurated," "likely . . . saw himself as (Davidic) Mes-

Jesus implied that God's coming realm, which Israel was anticipating, had actually arrived in and through his ministry, in and through him.[1] And he chose twelve disciples, as the symbolic core of a new Israel.

> It might not ... have been altogether surprising if he had chosen not twelve but eleven associates, so as to make up, with himself, the symbolical true Israel. ... But he chose twelve. Can this mean anything else than that he saw himself above and outside the true Israel, even when he identified his own mission with the mission of Israel? Is Jesus tacitly assuming toward the nucleus of the reformed and re-created Israel the position of God himself *vis-à-vis* his People?[2]

Israel's rulers, and Israel itself, had earlier been described as God's children; but Jesus implied that he was God's "son" in a distinctive sense.[3] He began, rather than concluded, important pronouncements with the formula "Amen, Amen."[4] What he said and implied about himself was, in short, remarkable.[5]

So Jesus presented people with a challenge.[6] They had to accept or reject his evident claim to authority.[7] And they might, if they thought about it, have to

---

siah," and "likely ... interpreted the term Messiah/Christ to imply a unique personal relationship of Sonship to God" (51-2). George R. Beasley-Murray, *Jesus and the Kingdom of God* (Grand Rapids: Eerdmans 1986) devotes almost a hundred pages (219-312) to an analysis if the Son of Man material, finding substantial justification for the claim that Jesus used the term "son of man" regularly, and that in doing so he implied an exalted status for himself, *but* that the expression is not the title of a mysterious heavenly figure but a means of veiled self-reference.

1. Marinus de Jonge speaks of "Jesus' message concerning God's Kingdom ... manifesting itself in his own words and deeds ..." (66). Cp. Beasley-Murray, *Jesus* and, more recently, "The Kingdom of God and Christology in the Gospels," *Jesus of Nazareth: Lord and Christ: Essays on the Historical Jesus and New Testament Christology*, FS I. Howard Marshall, ed. Joel B. Green and Max Turner (Grand Rapids, MI: Eerdmans; Carlisle: Paternoster 1994) 22-9; Brown, *Introduction* 67-8. E. P. Sanders, *Jesus and Judaism* (London: SCM 1985) 326, is rather more skeptical.

2. Moule, *Phenomenon* 69. Cp. Sanders, *Figure*: "Jesus thought that the twelve disciples represented the tribes of Israel, but also that they would judge them. Jesus was clearly above the disciples; a person who is above the judges of Israel is very high indeed" (248).

3. See, *e.g.*, Matt 11:27. Cp. Moule, *Origin* 22-31; de Jonge 68-75; Hengel; Jeremias 61-8; Anthony E. Harvey, *Jesus and the Constraints of History* (Philadelphia: Westminster 1982) 154-73; Richard Bauckham, "The Sonship of the Historical Jesus in Christology," *Scottish Journal of Theology* 31 (1978): 245-60; I. Howard Marshall, "The Divine Sonship of Jesus," *Interpretation* 21.1 (Jan. 1967): 87-103; Brown, *Introduction* 87-9; Robert H. Stein, *The Method and Message of Jesus' Teachings* (Philadelphia: Westminster 1978) 127-32.

4. See Moule, *Phenomenon* 67-8, Stein 117-8.

5. See Gerald O'Collins, *Christology: A Biblical, Historical, and Systematic Study of Jesus Christ* (Oxford: Clarendon-OUP 1995) 47-81.

6. Cp. Eduard Schweizer, *Jesus Christ—The Man from Nazareth and the Exalted Lord*, ed. Hulitt Gloer (London: SCM 1987). Cp. Walter Kasper, *Jesus the Christ*, trans. V. Green (London: Burns 1976) 103. John Riches, *Jesus and the Transformation of Judaism* (New York: Seabury 1982) maintains that "Jesus in thus embodying or symbolizing the way of forgiving love, pointed to himself not simply as an example for men to follow, or as a source of inspiration for them, but as the very point where God's love meets them" (188).

7. On Jesus' claim, see Wolfhart Pannenberg, *Jesus—God and Man*, trans. Duane A. Priebe (London: SCM 1967) 53-66. De Jonge asserts: "Jesus inspired the early Christian kerygma centering around his death and resurrection not only by what he did and how he died but also by what he said about what was about to happen. The Proclaimer became the Proclaimed because of the very nature of his own proclamation. Jesus was the one with whom it all began" (81).

reflect on what that claim implied. So do we. The alternative to accepting Jesus' implicit claims to authority—presuming they do go back to the historical Jesus—is dismissing Jesus as either flagrantly deceptive or deeply, insanely, self-deceived.[1] So his seemingly serene, confident authority (not that, evidently, of a maniac) provides—given his apparent honesty, decency, and compassion—is a striking pointer to his identity.[2] His "performance of 'wondrous events'" and his postmortem appearances give added weight to his claim to authority,[3] but it is his implicit self-understanding that presents the most powerful challenge to us, as it evidently did to his contemporaries.

Jesus' Disclosure and Demonstration of God's Love

Love is the motive and effect of God's self-disclosure in Jesus. This self-disclosure seems to highlight God's desire to touch human lives with love and deepen their loving connection with their creator. And Jesus' ministry, death, and life beyond death have served to make God's love effective in the world in new and powerful ways.

Jesus Affects Our Definition of "God"

We can talk about God only using human language. And when we talk about God, we necessarily privilege some kinds of language over others. We believe, in accordance with the doctrine of creation, that God can be encountered everywhere. But we find some districts of experience more fruitful than others as regions within which to find our pictures of who God is. God is not a generic deity. Our identification of God is unavoidably and intimately wrapped up with our understanding of Jesus.[4]

---

1. This classic argument has received contemporary currency through the work of C. S. Lewis; see *Mere Christianity* (New York: Macmillan 1952) 55-6. See also Richard Sturch, "Can One Say 'Jesus is God'?" *Christ the Lord: Studies in Christology Presented to Donald Guthrie*, ed. Harold Rowden (Leicester: IVP 1982) 337; Charles Gore, *The Incarnation of the Son of God* (London: Murray 1896) 238. Gore attributes the argument to Victorinus Afer, writing against Candidus the Arian.
   Some scholars regard the apparent incompatibility between Jesus' sanity and his reported claim to authority as good reason for doubting the authenticity of the reports of at least some of his claims, notably those implying his self-identification with the apocalyptic Son of Man (if, indeed, there was such a figure). These include Knox 39-40; Marcus Borg, *Conflict, Holiness, and Politics in the Teaching of Jesus* (Harrisburg, PA: TPI 1998) 231-3; Howard M. Teeple, "The Origin of the Son of Man Christology," *Journal of Biblical Literature* 84.3 (Sept. 1965): 221. In support of his view, Teeple cites Morton Scott Enslin, *Christian Beginnings* (New York: Harper 1938) 163; Morton Scott Enslin, *The Prophet from Nazareth* (New York: McGraw-Hill 1961) 146-7.

2. Cp. James P. Mackey, *Jesus: The Man and the Myth. A Contemporary Christology* (New York: Paulist 1979) 232-3. Mackey suggests that Jesus lived out of an intimate awareness of God's love and conveyed that experience to others; his role as the catalyst in their experience of love prompted and prompts his followers to conclude that in him they met God's love enacted, that his actions were the actions of God.

3. Griffin 6; cp. Pannenberg, *Jesus*; Rahner 245-6; Larry W. Hurtado, *One God, One Lord: Early Christian Devotion and Ancient Jewish Monotheism* (London: SCM 1988) 114-22; Brown, *Trinity* 144-154; Seeyoon Kim, *The Origin of Paul's Gospel*, WUNT (Tübingen: Mohr 1981); Helminiak 97-108.

4. Cp. Gordon D. Kaufman, *Systematic Theology: A Historicist Perspective* (New York: Scribner 1968) 177-89; Jon Sobrino, *Christology at the Crossroads: A Latin American View*, trans. John Drury (London: SCM 1978) 376-7.

"Of course," we say, "God is love, God forgives, God rescues the lost, god is victorious—of course." But where does that "of course" come from?—an "of course" assumed throughout the modern mythologies from evolutionism and process thought to Marxism and humanism. Ordinary life experience? *Time* magazine? the six o'clock news? "reason"? a well equipped laboratory?[1]

Understanding Jesus as God's revelation provides the answer to this query. It is the basis and expression of the Christian conviction that we ought to look at the Jesus if we want to identify God.[2] "It is the whole man Jesus, so far as historically recoverable, who is the ... communication of God to" humankind:[3] to say that Jesus reveals God shouldn't be read as implying that Jesus was in the business of passing on interesting information about God in a way that can be detached from Jesus himself and his activity.[4] It is not simply in Jesus' *ideas* that we meet God, but in Jesus' *life*.

That there might be a self-communication of God to humankind at all is not self-evident. A fundamental implication of the belief that God meets us in Jesus is that divine self-communication does, in fact, take place.[5] Consequently, it tells us that God is self-disclosing, not hidden—God-with-us. And God's self-communication seeks to draw us into communion with God and with each other, and to foster our healing and growth. God's choice to communicate is thus a sign of divine love. The divine love revealed in the life of Jesus underscores the conviction suggested by the fact of God's active self-disclosure: that the creator is graciously disposed toward the creation.[6]

It also underscores the nature of divine providence. God's self-revelation in Jesus builds upon a history. God does not fake or force the natural story.[7] Rather, God works within the natural structures and processes of the created world. In this way, God's presence and activity in the life of Jesus point to the constraints that affect God's interaction with the world.[8] Given what the life of Jesus, and the nature of God's presence in our world in Jesus, tells us about God, we can see that God does not overpower a recalcitrant creation; instead, God persuades and lures with responsive, faithful love.

Being Surprised by Jesus

Taking Jesus as key to our understanding of God's character will make a significant difference for our theology. But two qualifications should be noted. God's self-disclosure in Jesus does not obviate God's presence and activity throughout the whole creation. We know God through all God's gifts to us— from the structure of the physical world, to the dynamics of society, to ourselves and our scientific and philosophical insights. Though Jesus provides us with crucial criteria for our discourse about God, we should not suppose that Jesus is the only source of such criteria. God still spoke—and speaks—to people through, for instance, the history of Israel.

---

1. Langdon Gilkey, *Message and Existence: An Introduction to Christian Theology* (New York: Crossroad-Seabury 1979) 193; cp. John K. Riches, "What is a 'Christocentric' Theology?" *Christ, Faith and History: Cambridge Studies in Christology*, ed. Stephen W. Sykes and John Powell Clayton (Cambridge: CUP 1971) 223-38.
2. See Kaufman 177-89.
3. Kaufman 184.
4. Mackey 232-3.
5. Cp. Kaufman 211.
6. Cp. Kaufman 214; Brown, *Trinity* 13-4.
7. I owe this phrase to Austin Farrer.
8. Brian Hebblethwaite, "The Jewishness of Jesus from the Perspective of Christian Doctrine," *Scottish Journal of Theology* 42.1 (1989): 30

Second, we should not equate the real Jesus with our *image* of Jesus. Pictures of Jesus have been reshaped time and time again as people have sought to find in him validation for their convictions and projects. Each generation brings its own questions and assumptions to its interpretation of his story. Our portraits of Jesus all too easily become little more than reflections of our own concerns, attempts to control Jesus by making him ratify our individual and corporate agendas.[1]

We need to engage in, or take advantage of, serious scholarship—archæology; anthropology; source, editorial, and literary analysis of the relevant texts; sociology; and history—if we are to avoid creating Jesus in our own image. In doing so, we will likely realize more than once that we have misunderstood him, or that we have asked him questions he made no attempt to answer. Sometimes, of course, the Jesus we discover may be more immediately relevant than we had supposed. In any case, though, if we wish to avoid misappropriating and domesticating God's self-disclosure to us, we should confront the evidence as directly as possible.[2]

Jesus and the Course of History

Jesus' ministry changed and has continued to change people's thinking about God, to be sure. But ideas about God dependent on the activity of Jesus have been embodied in an historical community. Those ideas have set off chain reactions that continue to affect us today. The point of God's self-disclosure in Jesus was not simply to *say* something, but to *do* something. At first, the ministry of Jesus seems to have involved the creation of a renewal movement within Judaism. But the historical movement initiated by Jesus within Judaism has gone on to encompass innumerable people beyond Israel's boundaries. Thus, the life of Jesus is the "beginning [of] a historical process which is transforming human existence . . . ."[3]

Jesus and Divine Vulnerability

It seems as if, were God incapable of suffering, Jesus' suffering could make no difference to God. On the other hand, if God experiences all of the suffering that occurs throughout creation, is there anything in particular to say about the suffering God undergoes when *Jesus*, in particular, suffers? I believe there is.[4]

God's revelation in Jesus underscores God's experience of vulnerability and powerlessness, God's capacity to suffer along with creation. The suffering of Jesus

---

1. George Tyrell once famously quipped: "The Christ that Harnack sees, looking back through nineteen centuries of . . . darkness, is only the reflection of a Liberal Protestant face, seen at the bottom of a dark well" (qtd. Gerald O'Collins, *Interpreting Jesus*, Introducing Catholic Theology [London: Chapman 1983] 35)

2. Austin Farrer, "Infallibility and Historical Revelation," *Interpretation and Belief*, ed. Charles C. Conti (London: SPCK 1976): "[i]t is my special concern, as a reformed Christian, to emphasize the necessity of a constant overhaul of dogmatic development by the standard of Christian origins; and 'Christian origins' can only mean in practice the *evidences we have* for Christian origins; and they come down pretty nearly to the New Testament writings, and the primitive sacramental usages" (158).

3. Kaufman 402; cp. 407. Cp. Rupert Sheldrake, *A New Science of Life: The Hypothesis of Formative Causation* (London: Paladin-Granada 1983); Rupert Sheldrake, *The Presence of the Past: Morphic Resonance and the Habits of Nature* (New York: Vintage 1988); Rupert Sheldrake, "The Laws of Nature as Habits: A Postmodern Basis for Science," *The Reenchantment of Science: Postmodern Proposals*, ed. David Ray Griffin, SUNY Series in Constructive Postmodern Thought (Albany: SUNY 1988) 79-86; Rupert Sheldrake, *The Rebirth of Nature: The Greening of Science and God* (London: Century 1990).

4. My observations in this section reflect the influence of Paul Fiddes. See *The Creative Suffering of God* (Oxford: Clarendon-OUP 1988).

represents God's universal presence "'in' the sufferings of others."[1] The image of Jesus suffering on the cross is a powerful evocation of divine suffering, a decisive revelation of God's self-subjection to the vulnerability, contingency, and evil of creaturely existence. To identify Jesus as God's revelation is to see the cross as a drawing back of the curtain separating divinity from humanity which reveals the suffering God has experienced from the beginning of creation.[2] Thus, Jesus' suffering makes an epistemic contribution to the task of addressing the problem of evil. Historically, it was the reality of Jesus' sufferings that drove many Christians to conceive of God as vulnerable to disappointment and pain. It was believing that Jesus suffered which prompted the conclusion that God suffers.

There is no point in trying to argue that God suffers *only* in Jesus, that God only "really" knows suffering when Jesus suffers. If God can suffer in Jesus' sufferings, it seems clear that God can suffer when you and I suffer as well. But it can be argued that Jesus' suffering *does*, nonetheless, contribute distinctively to the pain God experiences because of the world's contingencies and evils.

The life of Jesus plays a distinctive role in God's activity in the world. In it, God seeks to reveal the divine character and to unleash a revelatory and transformative dynamic in history. Thus, Jesus' rejection and the roadblocks placed in his way by nature and history constitute more substantial impediments to God's plans for the world than any rejection or suffering I might experience. Certainly, murdering Jesus frustrated and undermined God's project in the world more seriously than the many tragic judicial murders that occurred in the first-century world and which have happened since then. And, indeed, anything that impeded the fulfillment of Jesus' mission struck directly at the possibility that the objectives God sought to realize through his life would be achieved in the world. God suffers when Jesus suffers not only because Jesus experiences pain and loss but also because God knows that associated with Jesus' pain and loss are varied threats to the achievement of God's plans for history as a whole.

In addition, insofar as God's character is clearly expressed in Jesus' actions, rejection of *Jesus'* character represents rejection of *God's* character. While God experiences all of the suffering we experience, it is rare that God is personally the object of our attacks. But to the extent that Jesus is attacked precisely because of who he is, the values he embodies, the vision by which he lives, his *character*, then it is that aspect of his life which most clearly makes God present to us that is the focus of his opponents' assaults. And so, in an important sense, we can say that God is the direct, though unacknowledged, object of those assaults. Hostility toward—or violence undertaken in disregard of—the divine character might reasonably serve as further reason for divine suffering over and above that resulting from immediate creaturely suffering (if for no other reason that it likely portends further creaturely suffering).[3] To view Jesus' suffering, culminating in his crucifixion, as a consequence—at least in part—of an implicit attack on God's character is another reason to see God as suffering distinctively in Jesus' suffering.

---

1. Brian Hebblethwaite, *The Incarnation: Collected Essays in Christology* (Cambridge: CUP 1987) 36.

2. Thanks to Ellen White for this image.

3. I believe it is reasonable to affirm that Jesus suffered, and was finally arrested and crucified, in part because of what he did, and that some of the things that led to opposition to his ministry embodied God's character with particular clarity. At the same time, with two thousand years of Christian anti-Semitism in view, it is crucial to stress that the Roman and Jewish leaders who seem to have colluded in Jesus' death clearly did not likely think simultaneously that his character was exemplary and that, because of this, they should have him killed. They were doubtless pragmatic politicians, not motivated by any greater hostility toward the divine character than political leaders elsewhere—or ourselves.

Jesus and Creation

God's presence in the life of Jesus highlights the value of creation. And the divine care for creation that Jesus represents reflects God's unwillingness to let the created order fracture and fragment itself into meaninglessness or oblivion.[1]

Jesus' ministry to people's physical and societal needs also emphasizes God's care for creation, and thus its inherent worth. And the fact of God's presence and self-disclosure in Jesus reveals to us something important about the *material* aspect of the creation and about human nature in particular: it shows that they are appropriate media for God's self-disclosure; thus, it underscores their goodness. If God is revealed in human nature, then humanness must have some inherent worth. Some early opponents of belief that God was revealed and present in the life of Jesus argued that it would detract from God's majesty and honor to become sullied by direct involvement with human reality. God's self-disclosure in Jesus underscores what the doctrine of creation suggests: that these critics were wrong. There is nothing wrong with being material, with being human. That the human life of Jesus' reveals God's love reflects the value of what we essentially are (even while Jesus' revelation of God calls into question the pervasive distortion of humanness and acting to liberate us from it).

There is no new gospel that nullifies God's work in creation. The good news of and in Jesus is the good news that creation is inherently good; that God seeks to heal and renew the creation; and that the death which seems to inhibit creation's flourishing cannot defeat the divine love for creation revealed in Jesus. In the life of Jesus, God dramatically addresses the human problem. And so, in turn, God emphasizes the reality that the human problem is worth addressing. Thus, in the life of Jesus, God asserts that the world is God's good creation, and humankind with it,[2] and that God has not given up on the world divine love has made.

Jesus and the Sabbath

God's presence in the human life of Jesus underscores the value of Jesus' Jewish heritage and identity. In light of Jesus' practice and of Christianity's Jewish heritage—for which the Sabbath was the festival of creation—it made sense for the early Christians to continue worshipping on the seventh day of the week. It seems to have been Christianity's split with Judaism, and Christians' fear that they would be identified by the Romans with the Jewish people, whom the Romans saw as ever-troublesome Jews, that led to the abandonment of Saturday and its replacement by Sunday as the Christian Sabbath.[3]

Those Christians who have continued to observe the Sabbath on Saturday look back, with the Jewish people, to the creation as the foundation for everything else God has done and is doing in the world. In so doing, they affirm both the goodness of creation and the value of God's revelation in the history of Israel.

THE IDENTITY OF JESUS AND THE LOVE OF GOD

Despite the attractiveness of saying that Jesus embodies God's love, is the conviction that he does really coherent when we scrutinize it? Could Jesus, or

---

1. Cp. Jürgen Moltmann, *The Way of Jesus Christ: Christology in Messianic Dimensions*, trans. Margaret Kohl (London: SCM 1990) 262.
2. Cp. Oliver O'Donovan, *Resurrection and Moral Order: An Outline for Evangelical Ethics* (Grand Rapids: Eerdmans 1986) 14.
3. So Samuele Bacchiocchi, *From Sabbath to Sunday* (Rome: Pontifical Gregorian UP 1977).

anyone else, incarnate God's love? What might it mean to say that God's love takes flesh?[1]

It cannot, first of all, mean that Jesus was a good man who became God. God is not something you become. It is at best an absurd category mistake, at worst a piece of idolatrous blasphemy to claim that a creature could become the absolute, creative source of all being.

On the other hand, it cannot mean that God simply "dressed up" as a human being, as if Jesus' human life were a divine disguise. The life of Jesus as it is historically accessible to us is the life of a person afflicted, just like us, by vulnerability, contingency, and suffering. If Jesus experienced himself as omnipotent and omniscient, if he lacked a genuinely human center of consciousness, then the gospels are sorely mistaken. Further, to think of Jesus as a make-believe human being would require us to think of God's action in the world as coercive, as unilaterally determining at least one strand of creaturely history, and, as I have already argued, such a view of divine action makes it much harder for Christians to respond to the problem of evil.

Positively, we can begin by noting that, for Christians, God is universally present and active in the world. To speak of God as creator is to see God at the root of all creation. To call God "Holy Spirit" is to refer to God as involved in every creaturely experience. God is not a stranger. God is not an alien. God is with us. At every moment, we are interacting with God. At every moment, we are intimately related to God. It's not as if God were the absentee proprietor of the deists, showing up occasionally to maintain a property otherwise left unattended. The presence and activity of God are necessary conditions for every occurrence; and, without overriding creaturely freedom, divine providence contributes to the shaping of each event. To speak of God's presence and activity in Jesus need not, therefore, mean imagining a bizarre exception to God's ordinary mode of activity, but as a decisive instance of the immanence and omnipresence we must predicate of God all the time.

The finite creation is made, paradoxically, to contain the infinite creator. The idea of an independent world, a world to which God is a stranger and from which God's activity is absent, is ultimately an abstraction that obscures the integral relationship between God and creation. And God's love is the underlying pattern of a world that subsists, finally, by mutual relation. But not every creaturely reality discloses God to the same degree or in the same way. In part, this is a function of creaturely circumstances: what God does and reveals in a given situation depends on what creatures do and have done. Particular histories make it possible for some individuals and communities to understand and respond to God in ways that other individuals and communities, in virtue of their circumstances, do not. But to see God as loving in freedom is to see God as choosing some good ends in preference to others, as taking initiative, as exercising choice, as acting particularly.

God's providential work in the history of Israel had prepared a particular religious tradition that embodied a particular vision of God's nature and character and that had shaped a particular way of being human, marked by a sense of individual openness and accountability to God.[2] God's love could be most effectively revealed in the love of an individual person in an environment in which individual personhood was central. And that humanly expressed love could be effectively shaped by all that had gone before in the history of Israel.

1. Cp. Rahner 178-305.
2. Cp. Austin Farrer, *Saving Belief: A Discussion of Essentials* (London: Hodder 1964) 70-4; Lewis S. Ford, *The Lure of God: A Biblical Background for Process Theism* (Philadelphia: Fortress 1978) 15-28; John B. Cobb, Jr., *The Structure of Christian Existence* (Philadelphia: Westminster 1967) 94-106, 131-3.

Within this Jewish environment, God chose freely to initiate the mediation of the divine love through a particular human life from the very beginning of that life. To speak of Jesus as incarnating God's love is to recognize his life as decisively mediating God's love and to say that the immanent love of the omnipresent God shone through the thirty-some years of Jesus' life with vital clarity.[1] It is a way of saying, with appropriate clarifications and qualifications, that Jesus' love was God's own love.[2]

This characterization of incarnation as transparency to God's love doubtless does not give us a perfectly adequate account of things, and it does not by any means solve all the puzzles raised by belief in God's presence and activity in the life of Jesus. It does, however, give us a useful way of talking about what we see in Jesus that is consistent with what we know about him and with the vision of divine love we derive from his teaching and his way of being human.[3] In turn, it offers us good reason to treat that vision as definitive for our lives.[1]

---

1. Cp. Harvey Cox, *Common Prayers: Faith, Family, and a Christian's Journey through the Jewish Year* (Boston: Houghton 2001) 76: Jesus "became the complete human receptor of God's love, the one who, more than any other person we know, was so totally open to God's love that he became its bearer and its vehicle."

2. Cp. Farley, *Empathy* 282; John Hick, "Christology at the Cross Roads," *Prospect for Theology: Essays in Honour of H. H. Farmer*, ed. Francis G. Healey (London: Nisbit 1966) 137-66 (advancing an account of Jesus as *homoagape* with God); John A. T. Robinson, *Truth is Two-Eyed* (London: SCM 1979); Monika Hellwig, *Jesus the Compassion of God: New Perspectives on the Tradition of Christianity* (Wilmington, DE: Glazier 1983); Vernon White, *Atonement and Incarnation: An Essay in Universalism and Particularity* (Cambridge: CUP 1991) 83-4.

3. A related way of talking about the link between divine and human love in Jesus is to appeal to the idea of the *Logos*. (On the idea of the *Logos* generally, see Clark, *World* 59-87.) John 1 declares that it was God's Word that became flesh in Jesus. The idea of the Word, or *Logos*, in first-century Greek thought—like the parallel idea of divine Wisdom in Judaism, which is surely also in the background of John 1—is the idea of the divine order, pattern, reason, or structure that grounds created reality. For the early Christians, the *Logos* had become real, visible, tangible in Jesus. Thus John Milbank, "The End of Dialogue," *Christian Uniqueness Reconsidered: The Myth of a Pluralistic Theology of Religions*, ed. Gavin D'Costa (Maryknoll, NY: Orbis 1990) observes: "It is, in effect, because the [Gospel] narratives and metaphors [depicting a universal model for humanness] are fundamental for defining the new and universal pattern of life that Jesus was regarded by the early church as identical with the divine *Logos*, not because he had become the random object of a cultic attachment" (179; my italics). And this is an idea that can still be powerful, evocative, and meaningful for us today. But I suggest that it can and should be especially powerful for us to the extent that we recognize that the pattern that orders all things is divine love. See Stephen R. L. Clark, *The Mysteries of Religion: An Introduction to Philosophy through Religion*, Philosophical Introductions 3 (Oxford: Blackwell 1986): "the *Logos* was not created, but 'begotten' and 'of one substance with the Father'. What was meant by this was that the One could not ever have produced any other word but Love, that there could not ever have been another pattern to be our lode-star. That pattern, Christians believed, was embodied in the very human life and character of a Galilean holy man, but it was accessible to all, the very light that lights everyone" (98-9; my italics). It is *this* pattern that we meet in the life and ministry of Jesus. "If the 'I' who acted was coconstituted by the presence of the *Logos* in him, then God was indeed immediately active in the action" (Cobb 141; my italics).

According to Christopher Stead, *Philosophy in Christian Antiquity* (Cambridge: CUP 1994), "we may think of personality as a characteristic variety of dispositions. It is found ... in all normal human beings; but we may be making a category-mistake if we regard it as a component of them; just as it is a category-mistake to think that the layout of a garden, or indeed its beauty, is one of its *components*, like the various trees, lawns and shrubs. ... [W]e may think of the personality, not simply as the

Jesus and Maleness

The meaning of male metaphors like "fatherhood" and "sonship" are transformed in the story of Jesus' life. They are associated with mutuality, community, and vulnerability, rather than authoritarian control. But for some Christians, Jesus' maleness underwrites the continuing authority of men over women in church and society. One recent writer, for instance, maintains that the "male headship of Christ in the church becomes . . . the model for the headship of the husband in the home and the headship of male pastor/elder in the church."[2] Though the fact of God's self-revelation in a human life points us to the value of human nature, it does not necessitate any belief in the superiority of *male* human nature. Maleness is not essential to the disclosure of God's nature or the achievement of God's purposes in the world. God is not male, and being male is not an essential condition for being God's revelation.

Some people suggest that male metaphors are required because of the nature of our relationship to God. This relationship should, they suggest, more closely approximate our relationship with our fathers than with our mothers.[3] On this view, God is more distant, more demanding, than would be the case if motherhood were a model for divine love.

It's not clear why this is an argument *for* the use of male metaphors; it might well be thought an argument *against* their employment. The God of the gospel is precisely *not* a distant and detached dispenser of conditional love. Further, this view doesn't take seriously enough the decisive role that men have played in shaping our metaphors for God; if we believe God to be distant and demanding, perhaps this is as much as anything because our thinking about God has been shaped in and through relationships with males acculturated to be distant and demanding. And, in any case, the assignment of particular characteristics to women and men is hardly consistent within or across cultures. What it means to be a woman or a man is to a significant degree a societal construct. Even if, as there is not, there were some merit in saying that God is more like a male than a female, doing so wouldn't accomplish much, since what maleness and femaleness are is constantly in flux.

Arguments for using exclusively or primarily male language about God ignore the inadequacy of relationships with distant and demanding parents as sources of insight into our relationships with God. Further, this approach also doesn't take seriously enough an alternative biblical and post-biblical tradition that suggests the

---

characteristic pattern of our behavior, but as its directive principle . . . ; but it does not follow that the personality itself is organized by some further directive principle, the 'ultimate metaphysical subject'. Of course, if we take this view, we are bound to think of the *Logos* in Christ as displacing this subject from its position of authority. But if, as I am inclined to do, we regard the ego as analogous, not to a monarchy but to a democracy, as a complex of mutually supporting dispositions, then their control by the *Logos* can be viewed as a special case of the fact that we continually respond to suggestions coming from outside ourselves. A human friend can influence, or even dominate, us by the choice of suggestions that he makes, assuming that there is some basic agreement on projects and values; and if we share the Fathers' assumption that the divine *Logos* can act in this way, there is no theoretical difficulty in seeing a human mind becoming perfectly attuned to an influence accepted as divine, who thus becomes its directive principle" (215-6; some italics added).

1. Cp. Cobb 143-6.
2. Samuele Bacchiocchi, *Women in the Church: A Biblical Study on the Role of Women in the Church* (Berrien Springs, MI: Biblical Perspectives 1987) 208; cp. 198-210.
3. C. S. Lewis comes to mind here. See Sallie McFague's criticism of Lewis in *Models of God: Theology for an Ecological, Nuclear Age* (London: SCM 1987).

appropriateness of female metaphors.[1] By apparently denying the full humanity of women, it seems to suggest a curiously deficient understanding of human being, one in which only males, not females, are capable of imaging the divine.

An exclusively male conception of God is spiritually harmful. It tends to produce guilt, a sense of alienation from God, and a lack of appreciation for the created order, among other things. For our own good, and for the good of all people of both genders, we need to incorporate female metaphors into our God-language. We need a view of God which preserves the range of characteristics imperfectly captured by talk of God in both masculine and feminine terms.[2]

If one believes on other grounds that God is better represented using masculine than feminine metaphors, then one can treat Jesus' maleness as confirming one's belief that this is the case. But there is good reason to doubt that masculine metaphors should be used in preference to feminine metaphors for God. Suppose, then, that one acknowledges that subordination or exclusion on the basis of gender is irrational and unfair, and that many generalizations about the sexes are false. Suppose one has, perhaps, experienced the unfortunate consequences of conceiving of God in male terms. Then one need not find Jesus' maleness a barrier to a view of sexual relationships that stresses equality and mutuality and that recognizes the distortion which results when female images for God are underused and female characteristics underemphasized.

Maleness and the Constraints of History

Jesus struck a blow for gender equality by affirming women in a way that was certainly not common in the ancient Mediterranean world. But if God had been revealed in and through the life of a woman, it is unlikely that she would have received sufficient public recognition to make the same impact on the first-century world as Jesus did. A message that was wildly inconsistent with Israel's traditions and deep-seated conviction would have a hard time getting serious attention at all, much less being understood and accepted.[3] God's self-disclosure in the life of a male human being does not represent a divine seal of approval on maleness. Rather, Jesus' maleness is probably best understood as, first of all, a simple consequence of the fact that God's interaction with human beings and communities takes place in and through the structures and processes of the created world.

Jesus as Model for a New Maleness

Furthermore, Jesus' maleness overturns male power by offering an alternative paradigm of maleness. "Who but a man could credibly teach and model . . . a

---

1. See Sallie McFague, *Speaking in Parables: A Study in Metaphor and Theology* (Philadelphia: Fortress 1975) and *Models*.

2. On gender roles and identities, see Sandra Lipsitz Bem, *The Lenses of Gender: Transforming the Debate on Sexual Equality* (New Haven: Yale UP 1993); Nancy Chodorow, *The Reproduction of Mothering: Psychoanalysis and the Sociology of Gender* (Berkeley: U of California P 1978); Dorothy Dinnerstein, *The Mermaid and the Minotaur: Sexual Arrangements and Human Nature* (New York: Harper 1991); Phyllis Burke, *Gender Shock: Exploding the Myths of Male and Female* (New York: Anchor-Doubleday 1996); Emmanuel Reynaud, *Holy Virility: The Social Construction of Masculinity*, trans. Ros Schwartz (London: Pluto 1983); R. W. Connell, *Gender and Power: Society, the Person and Sexual Politics* (Cambridge: Polity 1987); Jessica Benjamin, *The Bonds of Love: Psychoanalysis, Feminism, and the Problem of Domination* (New York: Pantheon 1988); R. W. Connell, *Masculinities* (Cambridge: Polity; Berkeley: U of California P 1995) 67-86.

3. I owe this point in part to Dalton Baldwin. Cp. Brian Wren, *What Language Shall I Borrow? God Talk in Worship: A Male Response to Feminist Theology* (New York: Crossroad 1991) 173-4, 186.

revolution in relationships by giving up power? Only a man could do that, because only men had power."[1] Jesus provides males with a new model of behavior that stresses mutual empowerment rather than dominance, while providing women with the hope for a maleness that is not inherently linked with oppression and exploitation.[2]

Women in our culture are encouraged to suffer and be submissive. Indeed, the subtle or not-so-subtle demand for passivity from women is a principal means by which they are subordinated and oppressed. The truth of a suffering, vulnerable God would have been far less apparent had God been revealed in and through the life of a woman; our cultural stereotypes make it seem disturbingly natural for women to suffer. Men, by contrast, are expected to be strong and invulnerable. For a suffering God to be revealed to us in the person of a man makes it clear that this, like other masculine stereotypes, cannot be the basis for our understanding of God.[3] Thus, the fact that Jesus was a man is in no sense a justification for patriarchy. Indeed, the style of masculinity he exhibited undercuts patriarchal dominance.

Describing Jesus as "Son"

So Christian talk about Jesus as "the Father's" only "Son" should not be understood or intended as part of an attempt to divinize masculinity—though it has obviously sometimes functioned that way. It does not entail the conviction that sonship matters more than daughterhood. And it does not require us to believe that God is more clearly revealed in male than in female human nature.

Son-language stresses the dependence on God that is a consequence of Jesus' humanity, but also the intimacy with God, the capacity to reveal God, evident in the course of a historically particular human life (since particular human beings must be either female or male, Jesus' sonship highlights the fact that he was not an abstract human-being-in-general). Divine love embraces all of humanity, female and male. And it would be painfully ironic to use Jesus' revelation of inclusive divine love as a justification for excluding or subordinating half of humanity.

Living God's love in our world ultimately led Jesus to death on a Roman cross. In Chapter 8, I want to consider how and why he suffered on the cross—and before he ever reached it.

---

1. Diane Tennis, *Is God the Only Reliable Father?* (Philadelphia: Westminster 1985) 105, qtd. Wren 179.
2. Wren 178-82; cp. Rebecca Pentz, "Can Jesus Save Women?" *Encountering Jesus: A Debate on Christology*, ed. Stephen T. Davis (Atlanta: Knox 1988) 77-91.
3. I owe this point to Fritz Guy.

8

Love Suffers Long

Love suffers. That is simply part of what it means to love. If I love you, I am vulnerable to you; and so, directly or inadvertently, you can make me suffer. And if I love you, and you suffer, I will suffer too. It can hardly be surprising, then, that Jesus suffered. Vulnerable, human, he was affected by historical contingencies outside his control. Living out God's love in our world would have to mean suffering, because *we* suffer and because we have the capacity to make *others* suffer. Jesus suffered, too, precisely because the love he offered and embodied challenged the dominant powers and their understanding of reality with a new vision of God and a new vision of loving community.

Jesus' suffering—fundamentally, the fact that his life was not at his own disposal—is evident, first of all, in that he had a history: he was heir to a rich tradition of action and discernment without which God's revelation in his life would not have been possible. That history offered him distinctive possibilities and embodied distinctive constraints.

God's suffering love is revealed in Jesus' suffering, both in the broad sense of vulnerability and in the narrow sense of pain. That suffering was a consequence of being human. Jesus underwent the pain of disappointment and rejection, and, finally, gruesome physical pain not only as a human being, not only as a member of the oppressed Jewish people, but also as someone who challenged the dominant authorities of his society and their values. He created an inclusive community—marked by openness not only to women and the poor but also to foreigners and people who collaborated with the Roman occupation forces—that offered a dramatic alternative to the *status quo*.

Identification with Jesus' story can help to determine who we are and to shape our action in the world. But the story of Jesus reveals not only who we can be but also who God *is*. To see God revealed in the crucified Jesus undermines false beliefs about divine invulnerability and authoritarianism. It underscores the value of embracing life even when doing so means risking suffering. And it judges corrupt political power, calls attention to the suffering of subordinated groups like those to which Jesus belonged, and emphasizes the reality of death.

JESUS' BIRTH AND HIS HISTORY

To suffer means, at root, to be passive, to be affected, to allow rather than to do. That's why the King James translators had Jesus tell his disciples, "Suffer the little children, and forbid them not, to come unto me . . . ."[1] He meant: don't restrain them, don't hold them back, let them be. Don't try to be in control. So we can say Jesus suffered, first of all, just because he had a history, just because he

---

1. Matt. 19:14.

was part of a genetic and historical line of development. Jesus didn't simply appear one day, full-grown. His was a normal human body, ushered into the world in the usual way. And he developed in the fashion of ordinary human beings; he had a history, including a mother who was a Galilean peasant named Mary.

The fact that Christians remember a *particular* woman as Jesus' mother is significant. In confessing our belief in Jesus' birth of Mary, we note, first of all, the simple importance of parenthood. Jesus was who he was in part because he had *this* mother. He experienced dependence on a particular *woman* in the way that most of us do. He was trained by her, he bonded with her, he was vulnerable to her. By affirming that Jesus shared in this common human experience, we emphasize both the importance that a woman could—and did—have in the history of God's work in the world. Further, we underscore Jesus' embeddedness in the web of humanity.

Not only did Jesus *have* a history—he was *part of a history*. I think that's the most important thing entailed by his recorded genealogies. By saying that he was the son of a particular mother, and by identifying how his roots fit into Israel's history, the genealogies stress that Jesus was *situated*—that he took his place within a particular culture, heritage, and tradition. He didn't drop out of nowhere, as it were. Instead, God's self-disclosure in Jesus was conditioned, shaped, structured by years of history, by the activity of Mary and Joseph.

Mary and Joseph both contributed to Jesus' identity by acculturating him, by helping him to make the history of the Jewish people his own. The history of Jesus' community helped to make him who he was. And Jesus didn't just inherit some history-in-general: he inherited the history of Israel,[1] a history that played a decisive role in forming his identity.[2] Israel's heritage seems to have been an effective vehicle for God's self-disclosure, prepared through the lengthy and sometimes tortuous operation of divine providence. So we ought to take the history and convictions of Israel seriously indeed. It "is not just Jesus' *human* mind and personality that manifest God to us salvifically; it is Jesus *Jewish* mind and personality that manifest God to us salvifically."[3] That's why the First Testament matters to us: it is the rootedness of Jesus' story in Israel's that points us to the Sabbath, the Ten Commandments, the socially transformative message of the biblical jubilee, and the comforting and accusing words of the prophets. "Christian knowledge of God is of course no more than a development of Israel's knowledge of God . . . ."[4]

Discerning God's self-disclosure in Jesus means recognizing that the people Israel makes a difference for who we are. We can understand neither the meaning of Jesus' actions for us nor their significance for him without understanding Israel's history of messianic expectation. Because Jesus was who he was—born of a Jewish mother, raised in a Jewish home—Israel's story becomes our story (though of course it does not thereby cease to be the story of the Jewish people). Thus, Israel's heritage is implicitly identified as a matrix through which we can filter our own contemporary perceptions. We are encouraged to find in the biblical narrative of Israel's development an important resource for use in identifying the God revealed in Jesus of Nazareth.

---

1. See Brian Hebblethwaite, "The Jewishness of Jesus from the Perspective of Christian Doctrine," *Scottish Journal of Theology* 42.1 (1989): 27-44; Austin Farrer, *Saving Belief: A Discussion of Essentials* (London: Hodder 1964) 70-4; Lewis S. Ford, *The Lure of God: A Biblical Background for Process Theism* (Philadelphia: Fortress 1978) 15-28; Gordon Kaufman, *Systematic Theology: A Historicist Perspective* (New York: Scribner 1968) 85-93.
2. Hebblethwaite 38.
3. Hebblethwaite 36.
4. Hebblethwaite 29.

Not only should we take our Jewish heritage seriously, we need to take *contemporary* Judaism seriously. Sometimes, we think of Christianity as having transcended Judaism. On this view, Jesus spent the balance of his ministry correcting fundamental errors in Judaism, which was essentially a graceless religion of ritual and law. But the ministry of Jesus is good evidence that this view of things is wrong. That the history of Israel provided the setting for God's self-revelation in Jesus points to its value as a window on God's nature and purposes. Obviously, Jesus differed with the religious leaders of first-century Judaism; it is implausible that his execution could be explained without such disagreement. But this was an argument *within* Judaism, not an argument *about* the merits of Judaism. It needs to be understood against the backdrop of the implicit affirmation of Israel's heritage that must be presupposed if we are to make sense of God's self-communication in Jesus at all.

Much of the history of Jewish-Christian relations since the first century has been characterized by conflict. An appreciation for Judaism as a specially important vehicle for God's self-revelation should make it difficult for Christians to write it off as easily as they have done in the past. Of course, Christians believe they have something distinctive to contribute to others. But they must be willing to take a new look at Judaism that reflects their awareness of its value as *both* the context without which the divine self-disclosure in Jesus fails to make sense *and* its role as a continuing locus for God's love and self-revelation.

A key element of that cultural context was (and is), of course, the Sabbath. The value of this crucial part of the Jewish experience is becoming increasingly obvious to Christians.[1] If we were outsiders to the Jewish tradition, we might simply admire the Sabbath from afar, as a powerful and productive ritual. But the fact that Israel's history was Jesus' history makes it Christians' history as well. The Sabbath is therefore part of our heritage. It claims our attention because it is a central element in Israel's history and because Jesus did not attack the Sabbath as an institution, but, instead, affirmed it.[2]

---

1. See Lynne M. Baab, *Sabbath Keeping: Finding Freedom in the Rhythms of Rest* (Downers Grove, IL: IVP 2005); Donna Schaper, *Sabbath Keeping* (Cambridge, MA: Cowley 1999); Wayne Muller, *Sabbath: Restoring the Sacred Rhythm of Rest* (New York: Bantam 1999); Marva J. Dawn, *Keeping the Sabbath Wholly: Ceasing, Resting, Embracing, Feasting* (Grand Rapids: Eerdmans 1988); Tilden Edwards, *Sabbath Time: Understanding and Practice for Contemporary Christians* (New York: Seabury 1982); Charles Scriven, *Jubilee of the World: The Sabbath as a Day of Gladness* (Nashville: Southern 1978); Kenneth L. Strand, ed., *The Sabbath in Scripture and History* (Washington, DC: Review 1982); Sakae Kubo, *God Meets Man: A Theology of the Sabbath and Second Advent* (Nashville: Southern 1978); Roy Branson, ed., *Festival of the Sabbath* (Washington, DC: Association of Adventist Forums 1985); Karl Barth, *Church Dogmatics*, 4 vols. in 13, ed. Geoffrey W. Bromiley, Thomas F. Torrance, et al., trans. G. T. Thompson et al. (Edinburgh: Clark 1936-69) 3.1: 98-9, 313-38; 3.4: 47-72; Niels-Erik A. Andreasen, *The Christian Use of Time* (Nashville: Abingdon 1978), *The Old Testament Sabbath: A Tradition-Historical Investigation*, SBL Diss. Ser. 7 (Missoula, MT: Scholars 1972); Niels-Erik A. Andreasen, *Rest and Redemption*, Andrews U Monographs (Berrien Springs, MI: Andrews UP 1978); John Brunt, *A Day for Healing: The Meaning of Jesus' Sabbath Miracles* (Washington, DC: Review 1981); Herbert W. Richardson, *Toward an American Theology* (New York: Harper 1967) 108-60; Samuele Bacchiocchi, *Divine Rest for Human Restlessness: A Theological Study of the Good News of the Sabbath for Today*, Biblical Perspectives 2 (Berrien Springs, MI: Bacchiocchi 1980); Abraham J. Heschel, *The Sabbath: Its Meaning for Modern Man* (New York: Farrar 1951). Thanks to Roy Branson, Fritz Guy, Sakae Kubo, and Charles Sandefur for many of these sources.

2. On Jesus and the Sabbath, see, for instance, Herold Weiss, *A Day of Gladness: The Sabbath among Jews and Christians in Antiquity* (Columbia, SC: U of South Carolina P 2003); E. P. Sanders, *Jesus and Judaism* (London: SCM 1985) 264-7; Marcus J. Borg, *Con-

To recognize that Jesus was embedded in Israel's history is to acknowledge the constraints integral to his humanness. Those constraints reflect his rootedness in his Jewish heritage, and the importance for his thinking and acting of the other aspects of his cultural and social context and of the natural environment.[1] To be a human being is to occupy a distinctive place in space and time, with a particular perspective and a particular heritage.[2]

The things Jesus thought and said would have had to be intelligible to his contemporaries—and to himself. Even striking new insights would have had to be marked by *some* continuity with prior thinking. That *is* a limitation: like twentieth-century North Americans, first-century Jews didn't know everything. But it's a limitation that's an inherent part of being human. Thus, it's one of the costs associated with God's being revealed in and through a human life.[3] Jesus' subjection to the constraints of humanness is a sign of the fact that God's way with the world is the way of persuasion rather than coercion, not of force but of love.

Jesus and God's Suffering Love

Suffering, as I have said, was an unavoidable part of Jesus' immersion in history. The idea that Jesus was going to suffer got in the way of his disciples' recognition of and response to him. And the fact that he *had* suffered made identifying him as revealing God scandalous from the standpoints of some religious and philosophical views common in the ancient Mediterranean world. Even today, it challenges and undermines ideas of God as invulnerable and unconcerned.

Jesus suffered most obviously, of course, during his passion and crucifixion. But suffering, as I've already suggested, is the necessary consequence of living out of control, of being vulnerable in relation to someone else, or to natural forces—an experience which is an unavoidable constituent of creaturely existence. And Jesus had been living out of control all of his life. As St. Paul suggests in Phil 2, the relinquishment of dominance was central to Jesus' story. Living a human life is essentially one of vulnerability to other people and to natural processes. So Jesus' suffering under Pontius Pilate was only the extreme case of what he had been undergoing all along as a human being. It was a heightened, intensified version of the subjection to the constraints of history that marked Jesus' entire career. He had always been vulnerable to the power of others. Now, that vulnerability manifested itself in an especially striking and horrible way.

Like all other kinds of experience, suffering always takes a distinctive form, for it is shaped by our attitudes, values, memories, beliefs, and prior experiences, as well as the natural processes that shape our bodily lives in the world. Jesus experienced the suffering that a typical first-century Jewish male might have expected to undergo. But he clearly also suffered in very specific, direct, painful, personal

flict, Holiness, and Politics in the Teaching of Jesus (Harrisburg, PA: TPI 1998) 156-73; John Riches, *Jesus and the Transformation of Judaism* (New York: Seabury 1982) 131; Christopher Rowland, *Christian Origins: From Messianic Movement to Christian Religion* (Minneapolis: Augsburg 1985) 156-7.

1. On the relevant biblical evidence, see, *e.g.*, Raymond E. Brown, *Jesus: God and Man* (New York: Macmillan 1973) 39-102. Cp. David Brown, *The Divine Trinity* (London: Duckworth 1985) 58-60, 115-9, 172-6, and 258-60.

2. On the general issue of Jesus' humanity, see Stephen W. Sykes, "The Theology of the Humanity of Christ," *Christ, Faith and History: Cambridge Studies in Christology*, ed. Sykes and John Powell Clayton (Cambridge: CUP 1972) 53-72.

3. Cp. Brown, *Jesus* 93-102; H. R. Mackintosh, *The Doctrine of the Person of Jesus Christ*, 2d. ed. (Edinburgh: Clark 1913) 481; Karl Rahner, *Foundations of Christian Faith: An Introduction to the Idea of Christianity*, trans. William V. Dych (New York: Crossroad-Seabury 1978) 102-4; Ben F. Meyer, *The Aims of Jesus* (London: SCM 1979) 246-9.

ways. Why? People used to depict him as exemplifying the ideal of the virtuous person to which "all sensible people" adhered. But a Jesus who was the epitome of niceness wouldn't have gotten crucified. Jesus' crucifixion is evidence that there was something threatening about him. The Romans executed him as a political agitator. The question whether they were correct to do so has received a wide variety of answers. Some people believe that his message lacked any explicit political overtones, but this approach leaves us with no real reason for his death, and is insensitive to the actual political implications of any plausible account of his teaching. He was not innocuous. His ministry was a source of conflict.

Jesus and the Renewal of Israel

Many Jews of Jesus' day anticipated the renewal or restoration of Israel, though they differed about the ways in which this renewal was going to be accomplished. Jesus' contemporaries often evidently supposed that renewed fidelity to God might lead to restored divine favor, lost at the time of the Exile, and with it their nation's deliverance from foreign dominance. They hoped that God would restore their community to its independence and former greatness. Foreign occupation and cultural influence seemed to some people to threaten Israel's existence. Both the desire for divinely effected national restoration and concern for national survival prompted some people within first-century Judaism—like many people in subsequent communities—to define their community's boundaries in rigid ways.

On their view, devotion to national renewal was associated with the avoidance of anything that might break down those boundaries, that might render less clear the distinctions that seemed essential to preserving Israel's identity.[1] For some, the restoration of Israel thus entailed the violent expulsion of the occupying Romans, so that their nation's distinctive way of life could be followed without foreign interference. For others, it meant a rigorous attentiveness to the distinguishing features of Jewish identity within the confines of ordinary, day-to-day life. For still others, it entailed withdrawal from society into secluded enclaves where people could be free from distraction as they sought to be faithful to God.[2]

Jesus associated himself with efforts anticipating or promoting Israel's restoration in a variety of ways.[3] He proclaimed the coming of a renewed Israel when he collected a group of disciples who were called "the Twelve"—in a way that must have been suggestive of Israel's twelve tribes. The "number twelve itself . . . points to 'all Israel.'" If Jesus' disciples represented all Israel, then his call to them may have seemed like a foretaste of a divine restoration that would include the entire nation, with "the Twelve" as the nucleus of the new Israel.[4] God's restoring activity—toward which he called his followers to look, and which he implied was already present in and as a result of his ministry—he called the Realm of God.

The Jesus Community

However, Jesus challenged the view that fidelity to God required the maintenance of rigid communal boundaries. The pattern of his ministry may have re-

---

1. So Marcus J. Borg, *Jesus: A New Vision—Spirit, Culture, and the Life of Discipleship* (San Francisco: Harper 1987) 86-7; *Conflict* 66-87.
2. Borg, *Vision* 86-91. Sanders reacts skeptically to claims about the exclusion of various groups from first-century Jewish society on the basis of what Borg terms a concern for holiness on the part of such factions as those referred to here; thus, Sanders doubts the distinctiveness of Jesus as one who offered acceptance to the members of such groups; cp. Borg, *Vision* 174-211.
3. See Sanders 61-119; Borg, *Vision* 123-49; Rowland 131-64.
4. Sanders 104; cp. Borg, *Vision* 126-7; Rowland 152. See also Meyer 154, 219.

flected models derived from the Greek-speaking world, or shared with fellow Jews who sought enhanced ties with that world.¹ But, whatever his ministry's resemblance to other contemporary social phenomena, an important part of it was the creation of a movement within which people could experience a tangible foretaste of the new order he anticipated. This movement would be characterized by concern not for separation and distinction but for compassion and openness. It anticipated a renewal of Israel that would encompass not only Jews but Gentiles.² Including the male and female disciples who traveled with him, Jesus' movement also comprehended many local supporters.³ It embodied several distinctive features which help to explain the opposition it aroused.

Fundamentally, Jesus' community was "a Realm of nobodies."⁴ When Jesus pointed to the child as the model for believers, he was describing his movement as made up, not so much of humble, teachable innocents as of people excluded from social power. A child in the ancient Mediterranean lacked rights, significance, and value. By linking childhood and participation in God's project in history, Jesus overturned typical views of power and status.⁵

This feature of the movement was emphasized by the nature of Jesus' charge to the missionaries he sent out. If they followed his instructions not to carry bags or take any food, they would symbolically express their rootedness in the communities they were to serve. Not only were they not to take food, but—since they weren't to bring bags—they couldn't beg for it either. They could only share it in common meals with those who received them hospitably. Their links with these communities would prevent the development of social divisions which would permit them to become a new and powerful class.⁶ Jesus' directive thus reflected "a strategy for building or rebuilding peasant community on radically different principles from those of honor and shame, patronage and clientage. It was based on an egalitarian sharing of spiritual and material power at the most grass-roots level."⁷

A key characteristic of Jesus' new community was his gracious embrace of the "tax collectors and sinners" who lay outside the bounds of Israel's covenant as it was understood by power brokers in his society. Especially noteworthy was his willingness to eat together with various sorts of outcasts—among them people who collaborated with the occupying Roman authorities. A common meal is a symbol of fellowship and acceptance almost everywhere, and by joining people at the dinner table, Jesus let them know that they were included within the circle of his

---

1. John Dominic Crossan, *The Historical Jesus: The Life of a Mediterranean Jewish Peasant* (San Francisco: Harper 1991) 72-88, 421-2, suggests that the ministry of Jesus makes sense as a Jewish adaptation of Græco-Roman cynicism, and thus fits within the context of what Crossan terms "inclusive Judaism"—*viz.*, "a Judaism seeking to adapt its ancestral customs as liberally as possible with maximal association, combination, or collaboration with Hellenism on the ideological level" (418).

2. So Meyer 164, 167-8, 247,

3. Borg, *Vision* 128.

4. So Crossan 266 (Crossan's word is the familiar "Kingdom").

5. Crossan 266-9. According to Crossan, Jesus also highlighted in other ways the fact that God's Realm comprised people who were undesirables and characterized by features that made it at least an embarrassment, if not a threat, to those in power. When, for instance, he compared God's Realm to a sprouting mustard plant, Jewish peasants would naturally have thought of mustard sprouts that ran rampant through cultivated plots of land. God's Realm, then was not always welcome. It was something "you would want in only small and carefully controlled doses—if you could control it" (277-9). According to Crossan, the point of the parable of the weeds is similar (280). Given social attitudes toward both women and leaven, the parable of the leaven must also have seemed problematic to many of Jesus' contemporaries (281).

6. Crossan 338-44.

7. Crossan 344.

care—and, implicitly, of God's as well.[1] "Jesus offered the truly wicked—those beyond the pale and outside the common religion by virtue of their implicit or explicit rejection of the commandments of the God of Israel—admission to *his* group . . . *if* they accepted him."[2]

Such loving acceptance must have been irritating and offensive to the conventionally pious. They can hardly have appreciated the message that in God's Realm expected social roles would be turned on their head, with the last—the excluded—now first and the first now last,[3] and the morally suspect treated as, at least, on a part with the righteous. And Jesus' acceptance of collaborators implied a basic disloyalty to Israel's community boundaries that threatened "to break down the cohesiveness necessary to the survival of a society immersed in conflict." It underscored Jesus' vision of Israel as an inclusive community that flew in the face of exclusivist construals of the nation's distinct identity.[4]

To reject the view that achievement and performance are the criteria for satisfaction with oneself and others is to open up the possibility of a distinctive way of life, one marked by trust, rather than anxiety. As long as people constantly worry about their performance levels, and measure themselves against social expectations, a society's commonly accepted standards of behavior will continue to be accepted. But if people no longer feel bound by the need to achieve, then the defenders of social order may well feel threatened.[5] For what can serve to uphold social order if not the threat that the disorderly will be shunned and excluded?

"Sinners" were not the only ones excluded by rigid social boundary definitions from full participation in social life. Women were often marginalized in the ancient Mediterranean world, but Jesus' community included them, too. Not only accepting their hospitality—even permitting unheard of intimacy by letting an outcast woman wash his feet with her hair—but also traveling in their company and teaching them in the same way he taught men, Jesus empowered and affirmed women.[6] He did this, too, by undermining the authority of the patriarchal family structure. Jesus' community was a new family for his followers, replacing the rigidly defined families that kept women and children in subjugation. He preached equality,[7] and recognized that the dynamic he unleashed would lead to intra-family conflicts that would in turn challenge hierarchies of gender and generation.[8] And his teaching about divorce may have been intended to imply that women enjoyed the same status, honor, and value as men.[9] With this teaching, he may have not only protected women against the economic disfranchisement that was a likely consequence of divorce—a disgraced and divorced woman had few

---

1. On this point see, for instance, Borg, *Vision* 101-2, 131-3 and *Conflict* 88-155; Crossan 341; Meyer 158-62.
2. Sanders 210.
3. Sanders 288.
4. Borg, *Conflict* 100, 107-34; cp. 120-3.
5. See Borg, *Vision* 102-3.
6. See, *e.g.*, Borg, *Vision* 133-5; Allen Verhey, *The Great Reversal: Ethics and the New Testament* (Grand Rapids: Eerdmans 1984) 19-20 and 95-6; cp. Jürgen Moltmann, *The Way of Jesus Christ: Christology in Messianic Dimensions*, trans. Margaret Kohl (London: SCM 1990) 146-7. Verhey's work is an especially stimulating discussion of the significance of the Newer Testament for contemporary Christian ethics, and offers not only careful reflection the relevant biblical materials but also an extensive theological argument regarding the appropriate use of those materials (153-197).
7. See the discussion in Crossan 295-8.
8. Cp. Matt 10:34-7 and Luke 12:51-3 and 14:26. For the interpretation of these passages offered here, see Crossan 299-301.
9. Crossan 301-2.

options other than prostitution—but also highlighted their full personhood in a powerfully symbolic way.

Prosperity had traditionally been seen as a sign of God's favor. But by pointing out the liberality with which God loves creation, Jesus attacked the moral and religious stigma associated with being poor: God gives good gifts to all, and not merely the "good." In addition, by accepting them, Jesus "would have enabled the poor to see themselves differently."[1] He called for constant generosity on the part of his followers and warned of the dangers of wealth. He announced "in shocking paradox, not . . . a Realm of the Poor but . . . a Realm of the Destitute." In the beatitudes, he declares that God blesses "not the poor but the destitute, not poverty but beggary."[2] In dramatic language, he highlighted the fact that his movement was not intended to replicate the prevailing social order, marked by hierarchy, patronage, and oppressive dependence. He represented the things that made for conventional social power as absent from his community, emphasizing the possibility that an alternative way of structuring social relationships was possible. In proclaiming "good news to the poor," "release to the captives," "liberty to those who are oppressed," and "the acceptable year of the Eternal" he was using language which his hearers cannot have failed to associate with the jubilee described in Leviticus—when, every half-century, slaves were to be released, debts were to be canceled, and agricultural land was to be redistributed to families which had lost it through adversity.[3] Jesus' community, therefore, was clearly marked by care for people on the economic edges of society.[4]

Jesus' ministry seems to have been marked by the performance of extraordinary wonders. His reputation as a wonder worker is deeply embedded in our sources of information regarding his career, both Christian and non-Christian.[5] These wonders demonstrated that it was possible to transcend "those constraints and limitations—including even death—which were felt instinctively to stand as an intractable and inexplicable barrier in the way of mankind attaining to a better world."[6] Genuine hope was an option; there was no need to be satisfied with the way things were.

1. Borg, *Vision* 136.
2. Crossan 273 (again, I opt for "Realm" over "Kingdom").
3. On Jesus and the Jubilee, see Sharon Ringe, *Jesus, Liberation, and the Biblical Jubilee*, Overtures to Biblical Theology (Philadelphia: Fortress 1985) and John Howard Yoder, *The Politics of Jesus: Vicit Agnus Noster* (Grand Rapids: Eerdmans 1972) 34-40, 64-77. Yoder suggests that when "Jesus formulated the celebrated commandment, 'Sell what you possess and give it as alms' (a better translation would be, 'sell what you possess and put in practice compassion'), this was not a 'counsel of perfection,' but neither was it a constitutional law to found a utopian state of Israel. It was a jubilee ordinance which was to be put into practice here and now, once, in AD 26, as a 'refreshment,' prefiguring the 'reestablishment of all things'" (76-7). For his identification as Jesus as a proclaimer of the jubilee, Yoder relies on André Trocmé, *Jésus-Christ et la révolution non-violente* (Geneva: Labor et Fides 1961).
4. Borg, *Vision* 135-7. On Jesus and wealth, see also, *e.g.*, Crossan 274-6 and Verhey 17-9, 32, 42, 81, and 93-5.
5. On the miracle stories, see A. E. Harvey, *Jesus and the Constraints of History* (Philadelphia: Westminster 1982) 98-119; Rowland 146-8; John P. Meier, *A Marginal Jew: Rethinking the Historical Jesus* 2: *Mentor, Message, and Miracles*, Anchor Bible Reference Library (New York: Doubleday 1994) 509-1038. Meier believes that the stories of several exorcisms, a range of healings, the healing of Jairus's daughter (though not necessarily her raising from death), the raising of the son of the widow of Nain, the raising of Lazarus, and the feeding of the multitude all go back in some form to the ministry of the historical Jesus (661, 726-7, 784-8, 797-8, 831-3, 965-7). For Meier's summary of his results, see 969-70.
6. Harvey 117.

Jesus' wonders had evident social implications. An independent miracle-worker like Jesus was claiming authority and legitimacy that placed him outside the religious sphere dominated by the establishment.[1] This was particularly true in connection with Jesus' healing wonders, for excessive

> taxation could leave poor people physically malnourished or hysterically disabled. But since the religiopolitical ascendancy could not blame excessive taxation, it blamed sick people themselves by claiming that their sins had led to their illnesses. And the cure for sinful sickness was, ultimately, in the Temple. And that meant more fees, in a perfect circle of victimization. When, therefore, ... Jesus ... cured people of their sicknesses, ... [he] implicitly declared their sins forgiven or nonexistent. ... [Thus, he challenged] the religious monopoly of the priests. All of this was religiopolitically subversive.[2]

Similarly, because many people believed that demons were responsible as much for social oppression as for the phenomena associated with individual possession, an assault on demons would have been interpreted by the Jewish peasantry as a symbolic assault on those in power.[3]

In a society polarized against the Romans and committed to clearly defined communal boundaries, Jesus urged inclusiveness and reconciliation. When he encouraged love of enemies and pronounced God's blessing on the peacemakers, he was offering very practical proposals for effective responses to contemporary tensions.[4] Violence was not the way forward, he asserted. And even those who did not actively urge violent revolution against Rome may have been discomfited by his repudiation of war with the occupying power.

The movement Jesus founded was, in short, a kind of counter-culture.[5] It modeled a way of addressing the problems Israel was experiencing that differed from the options offered by other major groups within Jewish society.[6] And Jesus explicitly called attention to the problems created by these options, criticizing the attitudes and practices that preserved rigid social boundaries.[7] He suggested that the attempt to preserve communal identity at all costs was, ironically, the central threat to the community's survival. Catastrophe was unavoidable, he assured his contemporaries, in the absence of genuine, meaningful change.[8]

Not surprisingly, Jesus found himself in conflict with those who regarded communal boundaries as sacrosanct.[9] His claim to authority seems also to have

---

1. See Crossan 303-10. Jesus' cure of the leper in Mk 1:40-5/Matt 8:1-4/Lk 5:12-6 portrays him "precisely as an authoritative healing and purifying alternative to the Temple" (322). Cp. Rowland 148.

2. Crossan 324.

3. Crossan 313-20. Writing about the Gerasene demoniac, Crossan observes: "An individual is, of course, being cured, but the symbolism is also hard to miss or ignore. The demon is both one and many; is named Legion, that fact and sign of Roman power; is consigned to swine; and is cast into the sea. A brief performancial summary, in other words, of every Jewish revolutionary's dream! And it may be left open whether the exorcist is asked to depart because a cured demoniac is not worth a herd of swine or because the people see quite clearly the political implications of the action" (314-5).

4. Cp., e.g., Borg, *Conflict* 144-6.

5. Gerd Theissen, *Sociology of Early Palestinian Christianity*, trans. John Bowden (Philadelphia: Fortress 1978).

6. Borg, *Vision* 141-2. On the contemporary church as alternate community see, for instance, Stanley M. Hauerwas, *Character and Community: Toward a Constructive Christian Social Ethic* (Notre Dame, IN: U of Notre Dame P 1981).

7. Borg, *Vision* 150-60.

8. Borg, *Vision* 161-71, *Conflict* 201-21.

9. Borg, *Vision* 150-60.

aroused discontent. What he said about *himself* apparently threatened those in power, who evidently resented what they likely viewed as his pretentious claim to speak and act for God. Provoked by other aspects of Jesus' ministry, those in power doubtless found his apparent arrogance a further reason to see him silenced.[1]

Jesus' Challenge to the Status Quo

The dispute between Jesus and some of his contemporaries was not, of course, a debate about *the viability or appropriateness of* Judaism; it was a dispute *within* Judaism, a dispute about its appropriate contours. Jesus did not seek to transcend or eliminate Judaism. But the conflict he provoked with proponents of other construals of Jewish identity, and with those who held the reigns of social power, was nonetheless vigorous and intense.

The negative reactions to Jesus' ministry were presumably especially strong because of his explicit criticism of prevailing abuses. And his movement, providing as it did a kind of laboratory demonstration of the possibility that things could be other than they were, must have been especially threatening. It is one thing to talk about alternate ways of doing things. It is quite another to put them on display. When an option is actually *lived*, the possibility that it might really work, that it might really be worth trying, becomes harder to ignore. Seeing Jesus' way of life take form in the community of his followers, those who did not share his vision must have reacted with dismay.[2]

But the most dramatic expression of Jesus' dedication to renewal, and his openness to conflict with the *status quo*, was his disruption of regular activities in the Jerusalem temple. He temporarily expelled from it the merchants who bought sacrificial birds and "the pilgrims who brought them, as well as those who operated the *bureau de change* where pilgrims could exchange their diverse currencies for acceptable coinage with which to pay the Temple tax."[3] This striking action was a symbolic destruction of the focal point of Israel's worship, implying that it was about to be leveled.[4] It said that decisive divine action was imminent, that the old temple's days were numbered, that it must give way to a new temple. Jesus pointed to the coming of God's Realm by symbolically destroying the old temple to make way for the new.[5] Further, the temple was "the seat and symbol of all that was nonegalitarian, patronal, and even oppressive on the religious and the political level." Thus, a figurative assault on the temple "actualized what . . . [Jesus] had already said in his teachings, effected in his healings, and realized in his" practice of inclusive shared meals.[6] His "cleansing of the temple" hardly sent a message calculated to endear him to the guardians of the social and religious order the temple represented.[7]

---

1. See Sanders 287-8; Rowland 159, 171; Harvey 32-4.
2. Borg, *Vision* 182-4.
3. Borg, *Conflict* 181-2.
4. Borg, *Conflict*, argues that Jesus' expulsion of the merchants from the temple reflected his conviction that Israel's concern to maintain its distinct identity, symbolized by the temple, would ultimately lead to its destruction—which he symbolized via a mock destruction of the temple (181-6).
5. Cp. Meyer: "the temple cleansing signalled the dawn of a new era and a restoration of cult appropriate to it" (170). "It was at once a fulfilment event and a sign of the future, pledging the restoration of temple, Zion, and Jerusalem. Since these were symbol and synecdoche for the whole people of God, the cleansing of the temple pledged the perfect restoration of Israel" (198). This account need not be seen as an alternative to Borg's proposal that the destruction of the existing temple would follow from continued confrontation with Rome.
6. Crossan 360.
7. See Sanders 61-90; Borg, *Vision* 181; Rowland 162-4; Crossan 357-60.

Though Jesus was not leading a violent insurrection, his talk of God's Realm must have been disturbing to those in authority. Even if he envisioned a new order established through immediate divine action rather than by means of a providentially inspired popular uprising, public excitement could have been generated by any mention of change. Naturally, those in power wanted to avoid public unrest; if it encouraged Roman military intervention, it was to be avoided at all costs.[1] His attack on the temple would have been not only offensive to the supporters of the *status quo* but especially provocative and likely to cause unrest.[2]

After Jesus' assault on the temple, the opposition to his ministry that had been building for some time finally exploded. That explosion led finally to his judicial murder. But what he said and what he had done earlier must have played an important part in convincing people with power that he was a menace who needed to be eliminated. Persuaded of Jesus' kingly pretensions, the Jewish leaders arrested him; the Roman procurator, Pontius Pilate, sentenced him to be crucified on a charge of sedition.[3]

Our Story and Jesus' Story

To be part of that strand of history that centers in Jesus is a key element of what it means to live Christianly. Thus, it occupies a central place in Christian spirituality and ethics. It is not, in any straightforward sense, a pattern to be *imitated*.[4] The earlier strands of the church's story, including that of Jesus, are not simply to be *copied*. But Jesus' story *does* disclose something about the way reality really is. Identifying with that story is integral to Christian living.

God's Story and Our Identities

Owning Jesus' story will mean, by implication, that we recognize the story of the Christian church—the ongoing community founded by Jesus—as our own. We will find our ancestors in Karl Barth, Karl Rahner, and Dietrich Bonhoeffer; in Walter Rauschenbusch, Reinhold Niebuhr, and Martin Luther King, Jr.; in Thomas Cranmer, Thomas Aquinas, and Thomas Becket; in Martin Luther, John Calvin and Huldrych Zwingli; in Francis of Assisi, Dante Alighieri, and Bernard of Clairvaux; in Julian of Norwich, Hildegard of Bingen, and Peter Abelard; in Augustine, Origen, and Athanasius; in Basil of Caesarea, Gregory Nazianzen, and Theodore of Mopsuestia; in John Chrysostom, Irenæus of Lyons, and Polycarp of Smyrna; in Ignatius of Antioch, Justin Martyr, and St. Paul; and, of course, in innumerable others. It will mean that we own Israel's story and find in it resources that can inspire our moral reflection. Straightforward imitation of incidents in the stories we claim as ours is neither possible nor necessary. But our characters and choices as Christians should reflect the fact that we do claim these stories, instead of rejecting them or ignoring them as superfluous.

1. Sanders 288; cp. Borg, *Vision* 180.
2. Sanders 287, 293; cp. Crossan 360.
3. Sanders 294-318, Harvey 11-35.
4. Yoder observes that "the concept of imitation as a *general* pastoral or moral guideline" is absent from the Newer Testament. He maintains that it "is *not* applied by the New Testament at some of those points where Franciscan and romantic devotion has tried most piously to apply it . . . . Only at one point, only on one subject—but then consistently, universally—is Jesus our example: in his cross" (97). Similarly, there is only "one realm in which the concept of imitation holds . . . : this is at the point of the concrete social meaning of the cross in its relation to enmity and power. Servanthood replaces dominion, forgiveness absorbs hostility. Thus—and only thus—are we bound by New Testament thought to 'be like Jesus'" (134).

Story and Character

In getting to know other people, we often relate our stories. Understanding who we are requires understanding the trajectories that give direction to the current moment, the assumptions and experiences that ground present action. And Israel's story, and the church's, are our stories. Christians find the center of God's revelation in the story of Israel that culminates in the life of Jesus,[1] as well as in the story of the church that Jesus' story brings into being.[2] "Christian convictions take the form of a story, or perhaps better, a set of stories that constitutes a tradition, which in turn creates and forms a community."[3] God's identity is disclosed through the life of Jesus (and so through the histories of Israel and the church), and our own identities are story-dependent, too. Our individual stories can find their place within the narratives that highlight for us the character of God.[4]

Owning these narratives has consequences for how we understand ourselves, and self-understanding, in turn, is profoundly affected when one identifies with a community.[5] Our personal and communal practices acquire meaning in the context of the Christian story.[6] As we make that story our own, we acquire the skills required to negotiate the challenges of a complex world. The particular strategies Jesus used to inspire human beings to live out of the realization that community, mutuality, and empowerment are at the heart of the universe may or may not be ours.[7] But to own his story is, among other things, to find our identity as people who recognize the profound truth that they are.

Jesus' Story and the Golden Rule

Jesus' story highlights the meaning of the Golden Rule; and identifying with it helps us to embody this norm in our actions. It is one thing to be aware of a principle in the abstract, another to understand how it can and should be enacted concretely.

Thus, for instance, Jesus empowered women in ways that seem to have put him at odds with some of his contemporaries. His behavior underscores the value of gender inclusiveness. Equal respect for people without regard to their genders is a clear implication of the Golden Rule when it's properly understood, but it often isn't. Jesus' actions bring it powerfully into focus.

Similarly, Jesus' practice suggests the importance of an authentic concern for the poor—again, an implication of the Golden Rule—that should inform out voting and our other public commitments. This concern must also manifest itself especially in a style of church life that empowers and involves people whatever their socio-economic status and provides assistance to economically disadvantaged

---

1. Stanley M. Hauerwas, *The Peaceable Kingdom: A Primer in Christian Ethics* (London: SCM 1983) 28-9.
2. Cp. James Wm. McClendon, Jr., *Systematic Theology* 1: *Ethics* (Nashville: Abingdon 1986) 346.
3. Hauerwas, *Kingdom* 24.
4. Hauerwas, *Kingdom* 27.
5. Hauerwas, *Kingdom* 30.
6. Cp. McClendon 348.
7. Yoder appropriately distances himself from "the extreme application of particularly radical commitment, such as the argument that everything having to do with the structure of this world is impure or unworthy for the Christian because of the coercion or violence that governs society . . . ." He suggests that "power in itself . . . is the good creation of God. . . . [But the disciple] chooses not to exercise certain types of power because, in a given context, the rebellion of the structure of a given particular power is so incorrigible that at the time the most effective way to *take* responsibility is to refuse to collaborate, and by that refusal to take sides in favor of the [women and] men whom that power is oppressing" (157-8).

people inside and outside its boundaries. And it must also have a personal dimension—involving both personal relationships with economically vulnerable people and a pattern of sharing resources locally and globally.

The practice of Jesus also calls attention to another implication of the Golden Rule: the significance of accepting others. "Liberal" Christians need to be open to others they might otherwise dismiss as stuffy, closed-minded, and narrow—not, perhaps, agreeing with them but caring about them and accepting them anyway, avoiding the especially pernicious self-righteousness to which only those who think they are free of self-righteousness are prone. "Conservative" Christians need to be open to the people they might otherwise dismiss as "bad." They need to join in friendship and love with people on the fringes of the church and beyond—not encouraging self-destructive behavior, but sensitive to the beauty of God's good creation and the presence of God's love.

As illumined in Jesus' practice, the Golden Rule suggests the importance of a conception of *authority* to which the empowerment of everyone and the end of subordination and exclusion are central. And it calls us, as I argue in more detail in Chapter 10, to forgive our enemies. For some of us, these will be people who have devastated our lives with their stupidity or wanton destructiveness. And when people have hurt us in such ways, forgiveness may be harder than I can presume to talk about here. For many of us, though, forgiveness will involve surmounting our own pride in ways that enable us to invite others into our lives again after we have allowed ruptures of a more typical sort to occur in our relationships with them. In either case, Jesus' story calls and challenges us to love beyond retribution.

THE CROSS AND THE VULNERABLE GOD

Jesus' crucifixion was the most intense example of the suffering he experienced as a result of his loving conflict with the *status quo* in first-century Palestine. His suffering was and is a sign of his faithful love for God. And it is a paradigm case of human suffering. But it is also a decisive pointer to God's own suffering.

God's Vulnerability to Suffering

The claim that the cross powerfully depicts God's suffering is offensive to those who deny that God can suffer. The notion of a suffering God struck many people as nonsense in the past, and it arouses a similar reaction in some quarters today.[1] But if God loves, then God suffers. And a human life in which God is revealed would unavoidably be marked by a suffering that both represented the suffering endemic to humanness and provided a window on God's own suffering. The contingent, vulnerable life of Jesus "becomes the place where the divine word can speak and be heard by suffering humanity, itself doomed to live through time and chance, accident and disaster and defeat."[2]

The event of the divine suffering that is Jesus' cross is the most dramatic and decisive possible response to human suffering. The problem of reconciling God's goodness with evil in a positive way, of offering an explanation for the fact of evil in the world, always challenges our complacency. Too readily, we opt for approaches to justifying God's goodness that end up justifying our own wickedness: "God is responsible for everything, so my own selfishness is just part of a divine

---

1. Martin Hengel has noted the scandal which talk of Jesus' crucifixion provoked among Christianity's Gnostic opponents. See "Crucifixion," *The Cross of the Son of God*, trans. John Bowden (London: SCM 1986).

2. John Barton, *Love Unknown: Meditations on the Death and Resurrection of Jesus* (Louisville, KY: Westminster/Knox 1990) 17.

plan." By pointing to the constraints of history and nature within which divine activity takes place, the cross hints at a theoretical response to the problem of evil. But more important for day-to-day living is the fact that it demonstrates a practical response: it highlights the fact that God enters into our suffering with us.[1]

God suffers all the time, experiencing the losses undergone by all creatures, just as God shares creatures' joy and delight with them. It is not the case that God somehow does not or could not suffer apart from suffering of Jesus. But the suffering of Jesus highlights and underscores the divine suffering, including the suffering God must experience at the fact that divine power cannot simply erase evil, that goodness is not always rewarded.

Jesus' Vulnerability and the Valorization of Suffering

Jesus suffered throughout his life. He especially suffered during his public ministry. And his suffering under Pontius Pilate reached his climax with his crucifixion. The crucifixion was therefore an intensification of the suffering that already marked his ministry. But we have no reason to believe that Jesus *sought* this or any other kind of suffering.

Jesus did not attempt to model any sort of holy masochism either for his immediate followers or for us.[2] Suffering was simply an unwelcome but essential consequence of his actions. When he told his followers to shoulder their crosses and follow him, he wasn't telling them to bear their daily burdens gladly and to attempt to view these burdens as means of grace. Nor was he calling them any kind of mystical death to the created world, to selfhood, or to sin.[3] Rather, he meant that they were to face the consequences of identifying with him and his community. He knew that his behavior was bringing him into conflict with the authorities, he knew that a decisive confrontation with them would mean death, and he knew what kind of death the Romans meted out to those they saw as enemies. It was a death he was willing to face, and it was a death he wanted them to know that they, too, might have to suffer.[4]

Though Jesus reckoned with the possibility of crucifixion, his submission to the agony of the cross should never serve as a basis for the glorification of suffering. God is no masochist who seeks suffering nor a sadist who imposes it.[5] Divine suffering is simply the necessary consequence of God's identification with humankind in its finite existence, of which vulnerable is an unavoidable element—a suffering which human brokenness and evil intensify. You can't be human if you're incapable of suffering, but suffering is to be accepted, not pursued.[6]

---

1. Cp. Moltmann, *Way* 170-81.
2. This point is made very helpfully in Barton.
3. *Contra* Borg, *Vision* 112-5. Borg maintains that Jesus' call to accept death should be understood "metaphorically and not literally. . . . [It] was a metaphor for an internal process, as Luke made clear by adding the word 'daily' to the saying about taking up one's cross . . . ." (*Vision* 112). "That Jesus said 'daily' is unlikely, since it is clearly Luke's redactional addition; yet the addition seems accurately to state the sense of Jesus' saying" (122n70). But as others—*e.g.*, Crossan, below, and Yoder 132-3—see the matter, however, it is precisely the accuracy of this interpretation that is worth questioning.
4. For a characteristic treatment, see Crossan 353.
5. Cp. Moltmann, *Way* 175-8.
6. See Barton: "Jesus did not teach and heal and make friends in order to kill time, until it was time for the Romans to kill him. That is a dreadful trivialization of the life the Gospels record. He did all these things because there was no way of being God's love in our world caught in the web of accidental encounters, the constraints of daily physical life, and the need for social and domestic life that belong inseparably to the human condition" (14).

On the other hand, it *is* to be accepted, both as—to one degree or another—an unavoidable part of life and, on occasion, as a consequence of challenging social conventions and authority structures in the way Jesus did. Some societies ostracize deviants; others crucify them. But few are altogether enthusiastic about hearing those voices that call them to become more inclusive and less hierarchical.

Thus, claiming Jesus' story as our own may mean risking the possibility of the kind of suffering Jesus experienced during his public ministry. For we may have to risk the possibility of persecution—even execution. Again, this is not because ridicule and death are good things. It is because faithfulness and integrity, living as the kind of people we were made to be, may require us to live in ways that make suffering and death the only real option. If we have to face them, the suffering of Jesus reminds us that we can do so knowing that God suffers with us.

Divine Vulnerability and the End of Illusion

Jesus' suffering and death by crucifixion help to undermine those myths of divine power which have been used to uphold authoritarian societies and authoritarian families. They also help to dispel the myth that, if we are faithful, God will deliver us.

If God is vulnerable love, then divine power is no model for domination and oppression. The essential character of the universe is not raw power, but liberating empowerment; not detached domination but sympathetic compassion.[1] However, a child who grows up in a society dominated by men typically experiences a love-hate relationship with her or his father. The dominant father becomes the model for ultimate reality. And the assumed will of the father assumes an identity of its own as the moralistic super-ego. During adolescence, there is a natural reaction against external domination by the father and the super-ego. In Christian homes, this liberation from the (real or imagined) demands of the father often translates into hostility toward Christian belief. The child has naturally construed God in terms associated with her or his father, so rejecting the father can easily mean rejecting God as well. And the church has often allowed its thinking about God to be dominated by images derived from the pre-adolescent experience of fatherhood. It has portrayed God as arbitrary, distant, and demanding, and claimed to give divine sanction to the dictates of the super-ego. And it has taken advantage of the guilt feelings produced by the violation of those dictates.[2]

Even people who seem to have escaped from infantile relationships with their fathers may still be trapped in ongoing battles with them. They may devote themselves in various subtle and not-so-subtle ways to defeating their fathers long after adolescent rebellion should have ended. "The parricide and blasphemer . . . rebels against the restrictions laid down by the authority of the father, but his rebellion does not free him from being a mirror image of his adversary."[3] It's important, therefore, for people to be free not only from patriarchal authority but from the obsessive need to fight it.

In light of what the cross emphasizes about God, Christianity can refuse to underwrite paternal dominance or to sanction the idolatrous identification of God with the human father. And it can offer a new image of fatherhood as vulnerable, and so as compassionate and empowering—one which will bear fruit, ideally, in changed social structures that will not perpetuate the cycle of rebellion and patriarchal authority. It may also offer a perspective within which battles with one's

---

1. Cp. Moltmann, *Way* 178-81.
2. See Jürgen Moltmann, *The Crucified God: The Cross of Christ as the Foundation and Criticism of Christian Theology*, trans R. A. Wilson and John Bowden (New York: Harper 1974) 303-5.
3. Moltmann, *God* 307.

father can assume comic, rather than tragic, proportions, and can therefore cease (consciously or unconsciously) to dominate one's thinking and acting.[1]

Like the myth that God's power is paternal power, the myth that being good, being faithful, means being protected by God from suffering distorts our perceptions of and responses to reality. Jesus died the death that might have been expected of one who chose consistent fidelity to God in the way he did. On the other hand, he was faithful even in the dark night of his suffering to the God to whom he prayed for deliverance.[2] We sometimes suppose that, if we are faithful, God will deliver us from every conceivable harm. But the death of Jesus shows that this is a false hope. Despite his closeness to God, Jesus found himself given over to agonizing despair as he sought unsuccessfully to detect some sign of God's favor in his present experience. The sense of having been forsaken by God despite fidelity to God is no sign of spiritual weakness, Jesus' suffering suggests. And it provides convincing evidence that trust in God is no insurance against pain and loss.

The Vulnerable God and the Flight from Contingency

To be a creature is to be vulnerable. Every element of the created world is affected by every other element. Each is finite, relatively powerless, and subject to the vicissitudes of nature and history. The whole creation, human and non-human alike, is at the mercy of time and chance. Jesus' suffering and death highlight and exemplify the reality of the vulnerability that is a source of suffering throughout creation, and God's immersion in that vulnerability.[3] The God who is disclosed on the cross is not a detached god, but the God who models openness to the world's anguish, as also to its richness and vitality.[4]

The message that God is vulnerable, and that we should be willing to be vulnerable, too, has not always been received with open arms. Because human beings are finite and mortal and because they are not always dependable or loyal, some Christians have believed, it is better to avoid loving them at all. We should love God instead of other people, on this view, because God's love is the only love we can count on. "The love of created things is deceiving and unstable," said Thomas à Kempis, "but the love of Jesus is faithful and lasting. . . . Love Him and hold him for thy friend, for He will not forsake thee when all depart from thee . . . ."[5] Augustine articulated the same conviction when he said, speaking of his reaction to the death of a cherished companion, "Wretched I was; and wretched is every soul bound by the friendship of perishable things; he is torn asunder when he loses them . . . ."[6]

Undoubtedly, we accept vulnerability when we love. To allow a person, institution, or project to become part of myself is to subject myself to possibilities of torment and loss that I could otherwise have avoided. Adhering solely to God can therefore be a means of deliverance from the perils associated with creaturely loves. And, of course, these perils were much more real for the writers I've quoted than for most of us. Disease, distance, and political upheaval made it much more difficult to sustain close interpersonal relationships and important personal projects. It

---

1. Moltmann, *God* 306-7.
2. Cp. Wolfhart Pannenberg, *Jesus—God and Man*, trans. Duane A. Priebe (London: SCM 1967) 270-1.
3. Moltmann, *Way* 169-70.
4. See Barton; cp. Moltmann, *Way* 303
5. Thomas à Kempis, *The Imitation of Christ*, trans. William Benham, Harvard Classics 7 (New York: Collier 1909) 2.7.
6. St. Augustine, *Confessions*, trans. E. B. Pusey (New York: Modern 1999) 4.10 (http://ccat.sas.upenn.edu/jod/augustine/Pusey/book04; last visited Feb. 8, 2007).

was more likely when Thomas or Augustine wrote than it is today that one might lose a friend suddenly or be separated from her or him by unbridgeable distance.¹

Further, while the temptation to avoid the intimacy that can give rise to vulnerability is common in our society, for many of our predecessors the real challenge may have been to find individuality, to learn to hear their own voices more clearly. If so, differentiating oneself from others may have been a more spiritually significant task than it is now.² On balance, however, a cautious approach seems problematic as a general recommendation for all persons at any time. And it is certainly inappropriate for most people in our culture at present.

The most basic problem with the conservative, pragmatic call to avoid entangling ourselves in creaturely loves is, of course, that we can't find God by leaving creation behind. There is no experience of God that is not also experience of the created world. We don't get any "closer" to God by avoiding contact with and commitment to people, institutions, and things in the created world. Instead, we shut ourselves up in individualistic prisons. The alternative to being present to, with, and for other people is being present to, with, and for ourselves alone. Love requires us to be open; thus, it impels us to accept vulnerability and venture trust. As I argued in Chapter 5, doing so can play a central role in orienting us correctly toward God. And, if anything, isolation may render us more narcissistic, more turned in on ourselves—and thus less open to God—than participation in the social world, which may stimulate us to change and grow.

Even if it were strictly possible, which it isn't, to leave the creaturely world entirely to find an unsullied relationship with God free from the effects of contingency, it wouldn't make sense to do so. Such a strategy would represent a denial of the truth evident in the life of Jesus. Jesus' cross, and the events leading up to it, highlight the fact that *God* is vulnerable, too. If vulnerability isn't inappropriate for God, it likely isn't inappropriate for us, either.

Jesus was no detached ascetic. He accepted the vulnerability that all human beings experience; but, more than that, he entered passionately into the experience of being human—both of sorrow and of delight. The pattern of his life suggests that to be God-like is not to escape the flux of human experience, not to cultivate a calm reserve about what happens in the world, but enthusiastically to enter into the richness, drama, and passion of being human.

Owning Jesus' story will mean being open to vulnerability. At minimum, it will mean accepting ourselves as God's creatures, as contingent beings who cannot transcend vulnerability, both for good and for ill.³ It will mean entering joyously into the flux of human existence with all its surprises and possibilities—and pains.

Our loves for people and causes and institutions will die stillborn if we are unwilling to risk. We try in all sorts of ways to deny our contingency, to avoid identifying ourselves with people or projects because we cannot control them, cannot be sure that they will behave in unpredictable ways that may cause us tremendous confusion, anger, or pain. But this flight from contingency leads to an impoverished existence. By closing oneself off to risk, one also rules out the possibility of adventure and joy. There is no way to receive life's rich gifts while holding oneself in reserve. Refusing to be open and vulnerable will undoubtedly protect one from a lot of sorrow. But it may also protect one from joy.

There is no coercive proof in matters like this. There is, however, a very real choice. It is a choice between two kinds of lives. One kind of life is marked by a certain flatness, a secure sameness. It is one relatively unscarred by the sorrows that

---

1. See Margaret R. Miles, *Practicing Christianity: Critical Perspectives for an Embodied Spirituality* (New York: Crossroad 1988).
2. Cp. Miles.
3. Cp. Barton 36.

afflict people who risk themselves in love. But it is also one from which the most intense delights are absent. The other is topsy-turvy, varied, diverse. It includes disappointment, discouragement, and dismay. More importantly, though, it is filled with degrees of joy and pleasure to which the more conservative are strangers. To avoid vulnerability is surely an option; but to embrace the real but vulnerable goods available in human experience opens up immense vistas of possibility that cry out to be explored and that offer rich rewards to those willing to venture within them. Loss is real; and for some people the risks may not be worth the rewards. For most of us, though, opening ourselves to created loves can enrich our lives in ways too good to pass up.

Christian hope in life beyond death can help to justify running the risk of vulnerability. While we may suffer the loss of people we love in the present, we can hope that we may be reunited with them in God's final future. Because we can hope in this way, our interpersonal loves, at least, may be everlasting ones. Recognizing this may make us more willing to commit ourselves to them confidently in the present.[1]

Escaping from the world to God is impossible. To be sure, it can seem like a welcome alternative to the vulnerability we associate with Jesus' cross. But a fearful flight from the transitory is untrue to the character of reality itself—to the character of God. It prevents us from reaping the rich rewards of truly immersing ourselves in the good creation. And it is unnecessary, given our hope in a divine love that is stronger than death.

The Politics of the Cross

The crucifixion of Jesus tells us something important about divine and human vulnerability. But it also sends a clear and significant political message: it calls state power into question. Jesus was condemned by the Romans as a political offender. His crucifixion places a giant question mark next to all claims about state authority and power. It doesn't imply that all states are inherently evil, that crucifying someone who reveals God is just what political authorities *do* as a matter of course. But it does suggest that state power is fundamentally fallible. It implies that not everyone condemned by the state is really guilty.[2] And it reminds us that corporate authority, whether "private" or "public," the authority of churches and business enterprises and universities and all other organizations, can serve as a screen that divides people from those who are affected by their decisions and makes it easier for them unthinkingly to abuse and destroy.

Corporate authority helps to make the decision-making process impersonal, and thus to make people feel less individually invested in the actions of the organizations with which they are associated. Jesus' death on a Roman cross points us to the kinds of abuses that can result, in the nature of things, from this kind of power. It may be unavoidable—human life requires corporate organizations of various sorts, including governments—but it always rests precariously on the narrow boundary that separates effectiveness from tyranny.

---

1. Cp. George Dennis O'Brien, *God and the New Haven Railway and Why Neither One is Doing Very Well* (Boston: Beacon 1986).
2. Cp. Pannenberg 263.

The Representative Particularity of Jesus' Suffering

Jesus' death on the cross was not just the death of *any* vulnerable human being. All suffering is particular. All suffering, like all experience, acquires meaning in a particular context. And Jesus' suffering was particular in a number of ways.[1]

Jesus died the death of a *Jew*. He was crucified by an occupying power that oppressed and in many ways despised the Jews. And he experienced a fate shared not only by the Jews of his day but by so many since.[2] Despite the rift between Christianity and Judaism, *Jesus was a Jew*. It is unfortunate that Christians sometimes need reminding of this fact, but it's true nonetheless. And the Christian history of hostility to Jews means that it's worth saying again that Jesus died as a Jew. If he had lived in Germany during the Nazi era, "he would have been branded like other Jews," and he might have "died in the gas chambers of Auschwitz."[3] By identifying with the suffering of Jesus (and, of course, in other ways as well), God identifies with the suffering of Israel.

Similarly, Jesus died the death of a *slave*. Roman citizens could not be crucified. Only the disfranchised met their deaths in the way Jesus did. Jesus identified with these people as a Jew, but more particularly as one excluded from the power structure of his already weak nation. Ultimately, he met the fate anyone on the margins of the first-century world might expect at the hands of an arbitrary imperial authority. Throughout his life, but especially in his death, Jesus identified—and so highlighted God's identification with—with those excluded from full participation in political, social, and cultural decision-making.[4]

The Cross and the Reality of Death

The death of Jesus was a terrifying fate to him, so terrifying that he cried out to be delivered from it and experienced it as a sign that God had completely abandoned him. For Jesus, death was an enemy. And that tells us something about our own deaths.

We can't avoid death. It is pathological to deny that we will have to face it.[5] But that's no reason for us to welcome it. Death is terrifying because we have no experience of what lies beyond it. And the same was true for Jesus. While Jesus clearly hoped beyond death in God's love, it's one thing to preach a belief grounded in divine love when one experiences God's presence as consistently intimate and sustaining. It's another thing to hope and trust in God when everything seems to be falling down around one's ears, as it seems to have been for Jesus at the time of his death. He greeted the possibility of death with fear, and there is no evidence that, on the cross, he experienced any lessening of that fear.

The experience of Jesus is true to our own: death is not a friend to be greeted warmly. The death of Jesus gives us no reason not to see death as a mysterious darkness that envelopes and suffocates us, hiding the face of God so that we scream, "Why have you forsaken me?" However, just as Jesus' story does not permit us to ignore the threat death poses, so that story also offers a promise of hope beyond death.

---

1. I am largely dependent for what follows on Moltmann, *Way* 167-9.
2. Moltmann, *Way* 167.
3. Moltmann, *Way* 168.
4. Moltmann, *Way* 168-9.
5. So Ernest Becker, *The Denial of Death* (New York: Free 1973).

Jesus' Descent to the Grave

Like all human beings, Jesus died. For Jesus, trustfully aware of God's presence and love, the fear that God had abandoned him to death in his hour of need must have been a source of tremendous anguish. "To be excluded from God's nearness in spite of clear consciousness of it would be hell."[1]

Traditionally, Christians viewed Jesus' death as providing him with an opportunity for him to preach the gospel to the dead. Those who had died without any contact with him were supposed to have been offered divine acceptance in this way. Even if the image of Jesus' preaching in the netherworld strikes one as mythological, it is still possible to see the importance of the concern that prompted Christians to think and talk in this way. God would not be God if anyone were beyond the pale of God's love and renewing activity.[2] That's part of what it means to speak of God as love. It is arguably highlighted, in particular, by God's identification with the suffering Jesus on the cross. Jesus experienced the human condition at its nadir.[3] It would be odd indeed if God, willing to suffer in for creatures in the way Jesus' cross depicts, were to leave any beyond the pale of divine love.

For us, Jesus' death is a symbol of hope—God suffers with us. We would find it vastly harder to view it in this way if Jesus' disciples had never encountered him alive again. But they did. In the following chapter, I want to discuss this remarkable fact and its implications.

---

1. Pannenberg 271.
2. Cp. Moltmann, *Way* 189-92.
3. Cp. Pannenberg 272.

9

Love Is Alive

The ministry of Jesus put God's suffering love on display. His death seemed to put an end to that ministry. But his disciples encountered him alive after his death. At first demoralized and dejected, they were reunited with their loving friend. And amazed by their rediscovery of God's love in Jesus, in Jesus who was alive beyond death, they changed their world.

Jesus had challenged people. He had called them to respond to his message (and, implicitly, his person) in decisive ways. His charisma had inspired many people and angered many others. For a brief period, during his public ministry, he was a force to be reckoned with in Palestine. But then all that changed. He died on a Roman cross, crying out "My God, my God, why have you forsaken me?" Joseph of Arimathea, a Jewish leader, arranged for Jesus' "private burial, thus rescuing . . . [his body] from the two common burial grounds reserved for executed criminals. . . ."[1]

His disciples seem at first to have been overwhelmed by despair. But then they began to hear that Jesus was alive: some women had gone to the borrowed tomb where he had been buried only to find it empty. What followed was a set of diverse encounters between Jesus and a variety of people—the last of whom was evidently Saul the Pharisee, until then a persecutor of the fledgling Christian movement. And those who had encountered Jesus alive after his crucifixion (including the previously skeptical James, Jesus' brother), and those who believed their testimony, began to preach that God had been decisively revealed in Jesus. They began their preaching in Jerusalem, the site of Jesus' crucifixion, but their message spread with dramatic rapidity throughout the first-century Mediterranean world.[2]

---

1. Michael Grant, *Jesus: An Historian's Review of the Gospels* (New York: Scribner 1977) 176.
2. See Wolfhart Pannenberg, *Jesus—God and Man*, trans. Duane A. Priebe (London: SCM 1968) 88-105; Gerald O'Collins, *The Easter Jesus* (London: Darton 1980); Gerald O'Collins, *Jesus Risen: An Historical, Fundamental, and Systematic Examination of Christ's Resurrection* (New York: Paulist 1987); David Brown, *The Divine Trinity* (London: Duckworth 1985) 126-45; Bruce Vawter, *This Man Jesus: An Essay Toward a New Testament Christology* (Garden City, NY: Doubleday 1973) 33-51; Pheme Perkins, *Resurrection: New Testament Witness and Contemporary Reflection* (Garden City, NY: Doubleday 1984); Ethelbert Stauffer, *Jesus and His Story*, trans. Richard and Clara Winston (New York: Knopf 1967) 143-53; John C. O'Neill, "On the Resurrection as an Historical Question," *Christ, Faith and History: Cambridge Studies in Christology* (Cambridge: CUP 1971) 205-19; William Lane Craig, *The Historical Argument for the Resurrection of Jesus during the Deist Controversy*, Texts and Studies in Religion 23 (Lewistown, NY: Mellen 1985) 528-46; N. T. Wright, *The Resurrection of the Son of God*, Christian Origins and the Question of God 3 (London: SPCK 2003); William Lane Craig, *Assessing the New Testament Evidence for the Historicity of the Resurrection of Jesus*, Studies in the Bible and Early Christianity 16 (Lewiston, NY: Mellen 1989). My initial framing of the issues parallels

Belief in Jesus' life beyond death offers reason for hope. It calls into question the finality of death. And it underscores the divine love revealed in Jesus. The evidence that Jesus' disciples really did encounter him alive after his death is very convincing. That they did is strongly suggested by experiences they reported and by the fact that Jesus' grave was empty.

The Difference Jesus' New Life Makes

The announcement of Jesus' life beyond death is a source of hope—that death need not be final and that love need not be defeated.

Jesus' Life Beyond Death and God's Final Future

Jesus' life beyond death calls death into question as the future of humankind. At the same time, it cannot be understood in abstraction from Jesus' cross. The cross stresses that God's goals are achieved as God works in and through the structures of the created order, that God's will is often not done. Jesus' life beyond death offers hope; but it offers no easy assurance.

There are genuine impediments to God's work in the world, notably "the death that is caused by *injustice* and *evil*." And God "does not exercises power over these two realities from somewhere outside," in the manner of a mediæval potentate lording it over his subjects, but suffers with us. The cross underscores God's solidarity with us in suffering.[1] There is a two-way relationship between the cross and Jesus' life beyond death. On the one hand, Jesus' life beyond death confirms that death need not be victorious. On the other hand, God's suffering identification with humanity on the cross makes clear that God's power in the world is the power of love. Jesus' life beyond death indicates that God's love *has the last word*. The cross underlines the fact that what has the last word is precisely the word of the God who is *vulnerable love*.[2]

Gary R. Habermas, "Affirmative Statement," *Did Jesus Rise from the Dead? The Resurrection Debate*, by Habermas and Antony G. N. Flew, ed. Terry L. Miethe (San Francisco: Harper 1987) 19-20. I do not discuss here the complex and fascinating argument offered in Richard Swinburne, *The Resurrection of God Incarnate* (Oxford: Clarendon-OUP 2003); I have examined this book in an essay review, ["Reason and the Resurrection,"] *Conversations in Religion and Theology* 2.1 (May 2004): 11-28.

Jesus' disciples' encounters with him beyond death seem likely to have given decisive impetus to subsequent Christological development. See, *e.g.*, Hurtado, *God*; Pannenberg 66-73; Eduard Schweizer, *Jesus*, trans. David E. Green (Atlanta: Knox 1971) 52-90 and *Lordship and Discipleship*, Studies in Biblical Theology (Naperville, IL: Allenson 1960) 32-76; Moule, *Significance*; Petr Pokorny, *The Genesis of Christology: Foundations for a Theology of the New Testament*, trans. Marcus Lefébure (Edinburgh: Clark 1987) 63-179. St. Paul's encounter with Jesus after his death, to which he refers obliquely on a number of occasions, is especially noteworthy here. This encounter could also have made clear to him that Jesus was in fact the "Son of Man" who may have been expected within some quarters of first-century Judaism (see Seeyoon Kim, *The Origin of Paul's Gospel*, 2d. ed., WUNT [Tübingen: Mohr 1984] for an extended defense of this claim; cp. Hurtado 118-9).

1. Jon Sobrino, *Christology at the Crossroads: A Latin American View*, trans. John Drury (London: SCM 1978) 261.

2. Sobrino 261-2.

The Politics of Hope

Jesus' life beyond death is a promise that something new remains possible.[1] As a result, it is also a reminder that the way things are now isn't always the way they're going to be. There is the possibility of real—and dramatic—change. The present order is fragile and contingent. Jesus' life beyond death calls into question any attitude or behavior that presupposes that it isn't—that it is incapable of improvement or impervious to change. Thus, it gives a new freedom over against the structures of our world. If they are good, we are quite free to affirm them. But to the extent that the structures of our world are problematic, Jesus' life beyond death tells us that we do not need to take them seriously. We can laugh at them instead of cowering before them. And, free *from* the constraining assumption that they are necessary and unchangeable, we are free *to* work for their transformation.[2]

Corrupt political power brought about the crucifixion of Jesus. But his life beyond death shows that oppressive authorities don't and can't win in the end. The arena in which they exercise their power isn't ultimate. Their power does not reach beyond the grave. The power of the oppressor depends most fundamentally on her ability to evoke the fear of death—one's own death, or the death of others one cares about. But in the light of Jesus' life beyond death, we know, therefore, that whatever pretensions to ultimacy any political authority may make, we can keep hoping whatever life oppressors may deprive us of. For those who know and celebrate the story of Jesus, there is no need to fear the tyrants. And without fear, the tyrants have no power; they have already been defeated.

Jesus' Life Beyond Death and God's Love

An important reason for Jesus' appearances after his death seems to have been to display God's love. The disciples had betrayed and forsaken him. But by appearing to them after his death, drawing them into fellowship with himself, and energizing them for service, he extended God's love to them. He accepted them again, despite their failings.[3] And when he showed himself to Saul the Pharisee and to the previously skeptical James, each the opportunity to discern and participate in new trajectories of divine action. In Jesus, God was offering them the possibility of a transformed identity through identification with the strand of history Jesus had initiated. And this offer of new possibilities, too, was an act of love.

Jesus' encounters with his disciples after his death underscore God's love. Jesus could have responded with anger and rejection those who betrayed him—and on those who condemned him to death. But on Calvary, he is reported to have prayed, "Father, forgive them, for they do not know what they are doing." And in his encounters with his disciples after his death, he came bearing the good news of God's acceptance. God's revelation in Jesus was "a salvific action of pardon and revitalization rather than of retribution."[4] To tell the story of his life beyond death is thus to underscore the significance of divine love.

---

1. Cp. Ulrich Wilckens, "The Tradition-History of the Resurrection of Jesus," *The Significance of the Message of the Resurrection for Faith in Jesus Christ*, Studies in Biblical Theology—2d. ser., 8, ed. C. F. D. Moule (London: SCM 1968) 61.
2. Cp. James Wm. McClendon, Jr., *Systematic Theology 2: Doctrine* (Nashville: Abingdon 1994) 249-53.
3. That the experience of God's love was at the center of the disciples' encounters with Jesus after his death is the thesis of Edward Schillebeeckx, *Jesus: An Experiment in Christology*, trans. Hubert Hoskins (New York: Crossroad-Seabury 1979) 379-97.
4. Sobrino 377.

Why Love Affirms Jesus' Life beyond Death

The Christian community today does not need to be embarrassed by asserting its belief in Jesus' life beyond death. That belief is grounded in the church's memory of the reliable witness of those who first met Jesus alive after his death.

People Encountered Jesus Alive after His Death

When St. Paul lays out the grounds of his belief that Jesus is alive in 1 Corinthians 15, he declares that Jesus appeared to numerous people, several of whom he names. He writes:

> For I handed on to you as of first importance what I in turn had received: that Christ died for our sins in accordance with the scriptures, and that he was buried, and that he was raised on the third day in accordance with the scriptures, and that he appeared to Cephas, then to the twelve. Then he appeared to more than five hundred brothers and sisters at one time, most of whom are still alive, though some have died. Then he appeared to James, then to all the apostles. Last of all, as to one untimely born, he appeared also to me.[1]

For St. Paul, the conviction that Jesus was alive rested on solid historical ground.[2] Of course, he did not rely simply on memory: there was his own vision of Jesus to reckon with. But his own experience could be crosschecked against those of others. He likely met with the leaders of the Christian community in Jerusalem—a community which would have included other people who had seen Jesus after his death—no more than eight years after Jesus' crucifixion. His testimony about Jesus' life beyond death gives us access not only to his own memory but to the recollections of other witnesses as well.[3]

It is profoundly difficult plausibly to explain the rise of Christianity without referring to the disciples' visions of Jesus[4] and their resultant conviction that he was alive. Their willingness to risk and sometimes sacrifice their own lives testifies to the firmness of that conviction.[5]

The stories of Jesus' appearances after his death emerged quickly—too quickly to have become wildly distorted by legendary accretions. They were stories involving people, many of them authoritative figures in the early Christian community, who would in some cases have been alive when they began to circulate, and who could therefore have challenged and corrected significant inaccuracies.[6] Indeed, when accounts with obviously legendary features circulated in the second century, "they were universally rejected by the early church,"[7] which suggests that the first Christians were willing to correct distortions of the appearance stories even when those distortions might have made them more impressive and dramatic.

Some of the appearance stories seem especially likely to be accurate recollections of exceptional experiences. Because women's testimony wasn't legally valid

---

1. 1 Cor. 15:3-8.
2. On St. Paul's discussion of encounters with Jesus after his death in 1 Cor. 15, see Vawter 35-9; Pannenberg 89-93; Christopher Rowland, *Christian Origins: From Messianic Movement to Christian Religion* (Minneapolis: Augsburg 1985) 189-91; Stauffer 147-53. Stauffer notes helpfully in this connection that, while "Christian dogmatists" have argued "that Jesus . . . appeared only to his followers," this claim is invalidated "by 1 Corinthians 15:7f. For before the resurrected Christ showed himself, James was neutral or skeptical, and Paul a fanatical opponent of Jesus" (153).
3. Pannenberg 90; cp. Grant 177.
4. So Pannenberg 91; Craig, *Assessing* 405-20.
5. See, e.g., Craig, *Assessing* 379.
6. Craig, *Assessing* 381-9.
7. Craig, *Assessing* 389.

and their social status was low, it's hard to see why women would have been identified as testifying that Jesus was alive if the early Christians didn't, in fact, remember clearly that women *were* among the first to see him after his crucifixion. Paul personally testifies to Jesus' appearances to Peter and other disciples, and we know from his own writings that he had met at least Peter, and probably others, personally. In short, early Christians almost certainly had experiences that seemed to them to be experiences of Jesus after his death.[1] The crucial question is: were they hallucinating, or did they really encounter Jesus?

One thing that makes it hard to believe that the stories of Jesus' appearances can all be dismissed as hallucinations is that there were so many of them, involving different people and occurring in different locations.[2] A large number of people seem to have seen Jesus over an extended period of time, in different places. It is unlikely that a hallucination could have been repeated in this way.[3] One person might hallucinate, but it's much more difficult to imagine geographically and temporally separated individuals and groups all experiencing basically similar hallucinations. Further, a number of the appearance stories involve encounters between the living Jesus and *groups* of people (the women at the Tomb, as well as "the Twelve" and the "five hundred" people in St. Paul's list in 1 Corinthians 15). It's not clear that a group of people can share a hallucination. If they can't, then it would be impossible to explain these group appearances of Jesus as hallucinatory.[4]

Another problem with viewing the appearances as hallucinatory is the difficulty of explaining what triggered them. Some people have argued that St. Paul imagined he saw Jesus on the road to Damascus because he felt so guilty either about his failure to keep the Jewish law or about his persecution of the early Christians. On this view, seeing Jesus gave him a way past his inner struggles. But seeing Jesus alone wouldn't have helped resolve the struggles with his sense of guilt with which people who advance this view suggest Paul was dealing. He would have needed a particular view of divine love, something which wasn't really part of the vision itself.[5] If he *had* been wrestling with his conscience, there's no obvious reason he should have sought relief from his purported struggles with the law from the condemned and rejected Jesus of Nazareth. And, in any case, the whole idea that Paul was wrestling with his conscience doesn't square with his own account of his life as a Pharisee.[6] He simply doesn't record any titanic struggles with guilt, either over the law or over his persecution of the early Christians,

---

1. Craig, *Assessing* 389-90.
2. Craig, *Assessing* 399.
3. So Brown 137.
4. In support of this position, Gary Habermas cites J. P. Brady, "The Veridicality of Hypnotic, Visual Hallucinations," *Origin and Mechanisms of Hallucinations: Proceedings of the 14th Annual Meeting of the Eastern Psychiatric Research Association Held in New York City, November 14-15, 1969*, ed. Wolfram Keup (New York: Plenum 1970) 181 and Weston LaBarre, "Anthropological Perspectives on Hallucination and Hallucinogens," *Hallucinations: Behavior, Experience and Theory*, ed. R. Kiegel and L. J. West (New York: Wiley 1975) 9-10. He also quotes from a personal letter written to him by "well-published clinical psychologist" Gary Collins (dated February 21, 1977) in which Collins asserts that hallucinations "are individual occurrences. By their very nature only one person can see a given hallucination at a time. They certainly are not something which can be seen by a group of people. Neither is it possible that one person could somehow induce an hallucination in somebody else. Since an hallucination exists only in this subjective, personal sense, it is obvious that others cannot witness it." ("Head to Head: Habermas-Flew," Habermas and Flew 50-1, 60).
5. Though Seyoon Kim, *The Origin of Paul's Gospel*, WUNT (Tübingen: Mohr 1981) argues otherwise, suggesting that Paul's theology of justification was implicit in his vision of Jesus.
6. Craig, *Assessing* 399.

even though it might have made sense for him to do so as a way of emphasizing Jesus' accepting love.

Jesus' followers didn't expect to see him after his crucifixion, so they weren't psychologically primed to interpret ambiguous experiences as encounters with him.[1] They had little reason for hope when they began to see him. His death had severely tested their trust in God. They were disheartened, in a state of emotional disarray. Their transformation into enthusiastic proclaimers that Jesus was alive becomes difficult to explain if it is supposed to depend on their emotional states prior to their reported encounters with Jesus. Their encounters with Jesus after his death make sense as an account of their passage from despair to hope; it is hard to see how the belief that Jesus was alive could be a by-product of that passage, rather than its cause.[2]

Some people have argued that the need to transcend their disappointment at Jesus' death led his followers to imagine that he had come back from the grave; wish-fulfillment could have led them to hallucinate.[3] But the fact that first-century Judaism seems to have lacked a clearly defined understanding of life after death also makes it difficult to accept this view.[4] In the absence of such an understanding, there was no predisposition to envision the future of humanity generally or that of Jesus particularly in the way his followers ultimately did.[5] Among contemporary Jews who *did* expect that human beings would live after death at the end of the age, there was no expectation of any *individual's* being encountered after death *in the present*. Jesus' disciples wouldn't have been primed to look for encounters with Jesus after his death.[6] There was no reason for his disciples to have expected that he would meet them after his death.[7] In short, the raw material for a hallucination of Jesus as presently alive wasn't readily available.

The diversity of the stories the early Christians told about encounters with the living Jesus after his death and the theological conclusions drawn from them also renders it unlikely that the disciples' expectations, shaped by their cultural context, *generated* their experiences of Jesus as alive. If that had happened, it would be reasonable to suppose that the experiences and the conclusions drawn from

---

1. Craig, *Assessing* 399.
2. Pannenberg 96. Among the results of these encounters, Stauffer proposes, was the Christian commitment to baptism. While John the Baptist and his followers had baptized, Jesus and the members of his community do not seem to have done so. But after the resurrection, baptism became an important Christian ritual. According to Stauffer, the renewed practice of baptism can best be explained as the result of "a command given by the Risen Christ" (153).
3. Maintaining a tolerant agnosticism regarding the nature of the events which gave rise to belief in Jesus' aliveness beyond death, and granting that the conviction that he was alive was unexpected, Paula Frederiksen, *From Jesus to Christ: The Origins of the New Testament Images of Jesus* (New Haven: Yale UP 1988) nonetheless implies that the disciples' experiences were created by their attempt to resolve their own cognitive dissonance (134). She refers the reader to Leon Festinger, Henry W. Reicken, and Solomon Schachter, *When Prophecy Fails: A Social and Psychological Study of a Modern Group that Predicted the Destruction of the World* (New York: Harper 1956), for a general account of the notion of cognitive dissonance; and John G. Gager, *Kingdom and Community: The Social World of Early Christianity* (Englewood Cliffs, NJ: Prentice-Hall 1975) 40-4, for an application of that theory to the rise of Christianity. See also Leon Festinger, *A Theory of Cognitive Dissonance* (Stanford, CA: Stanford UP 1957).
4. See Christopher Evans, *Resurrection and the New Testament*, Studies in Biblical Theology—2d. ser., 12 (London: SCM 1970) 39-40. The same passage is referenced both by Brown 137-8 and (apparently) Vawter 38.
5. Vawter 46.
6. So Wilckens 61; Craig, *Assessing* 409-10.
7. Brown 137-8.

them would have been much more alike than they seem to have been.¹ It makes more sense, therefore, to see Jesus' life beyond death as responsible for the idea of hope beyond death in Christianity, rather than supposing that it was Jewish beliefs about life after death which gave rise to hallucinations of Jesus as alive after his crucifixion.

The hallucination objection to the authenticity of the reports of Jesus' appearances after his death centers on the claim that his followers were driven to imagine that he was alive. According to this objection, their hallucinations gave them a way of dealing with the surprise and shock created by Jesus' death on a Roman cross. But the available evidence suggests that the reappearance of Jesus *itself* was a surprise. It was a *source* of dissonance in their thinking as much as a response to it. And apparently it did not eliminate their confusion immediately, as one might expect it to have done if it had been unconsciously generated as a way of eliminating that confusion. Certainly it led, as they must have known it would, to increased tension with the surrounding culture: a martyred—and thus safely dead—prophet is a reasonable object of veneration, but a crucified Messiah is another story entirely.² Both the background to the discovery of Jesus' empty grave and the appearances of Jesus after his death on the one hand and the consequences of these events on the other don't fit the view that self-suggestion on the part of Jesus' followers led to hallucinations of Jesus as a way of resolving tension in their thinking.

Imagining Jesus' reappearance after death would not have been the easiest way for his followers to rationalize his death and deal with their disappointment, either. They could have understood him as one in the long line of martyred prophets remembered by the Jewish people. That would have made sense both of their awareness of Jesus' closeness to God and his murder by the authorities—his story would have paralleled various others they would have known. Nothing would have predisposed them to expect that they would encounter him alive beyond death, and a simpler way of resolving their cognitive dissonance was readily available to them.³ The founders of other first-century Jewish groups were martyred, but no one seems to have believed that these founders were alive beyond death. If belief in Jesus' life beyond death was a rationalization, it is odd that a similar rationalization evidently wasn't employed by any of the disciples' contemporaries.⁴

Jesus' Grave Was Empty

The absence of Jesus' body from his grave⁵ provides a further reason to doubt the hallucination theory.⁶ For such a theory leaves the absence of Jesus' body from the grave unexplained.⁷ The empty tomb highlights the incompleteness of the

---

1. Brown 138.
2. I am elaborating here on the remarks of Gager (42-3). He maintains: "... the death of Jesus created a sense of cognitive dissonance, in that it seemed to disconfirm the belief that Jesus was the Messiah. Even the event of the resurrection, which the Gospels present as having surprised the disciples every bit as much as the death, seems not to have eradicated these doubts. Thus according to the theory [of cognitive dissonance], we may understand the zeal to reduce dissonance, not just in the early years but for a considerable time thereafter" (43).
3. Gerald O'Collins, *Interpreting Jesus* (London: Chapman 1983) 117-8.
4. Wright 700.
5. On the general question of Jesus' empty grave, see Craig, *Assessing* 351-78; O'Neill.
6. Cp. John A. T. Robinson, *The Human Face of God* (London: SCM; Philadelphia: Westminster 1973) 138-40; Chögyam Trungpa, *Born in Tibet* (London: Allen 1966) 95 (cited by Robinson).
7. Cp. Craig, *Assessing* 400.

hallucination theory as a reinterpretation of the phenomena that led the early Christians to say that Jesus was alive.

The empty tomb story itself is plausible for several reasons. Jesus was buried—specifically, the church recalled, in a tomb provided by Joseph of Arimathea. It would have been embarrassing that none of the Twelve had taken responsibility for Jesus' burial; that the church recalled Joseph's involvement despite this suggests that he really did provide Jesus' tomb.[1] Adding support to the claim that Jesus was buried is the fact that St. Paul refers to Jesus' burial in his early references to Jesus' life beyond death.[2] And first-century Jews revered the graves of holy people, which makes it unlikely that Jesus' followers would have been unaware of his place of burial. Because Jesus was buried, it would have been natural for people to inquire about the fate of his body[3] when his disciples said they had seen him alive after his crucifixion. That there is no evidence that anyone ever produced or claimed to have produced his body makes it very likely that his grave really *was* empty.[4]

The early church remembered that Jesus' empty grave was discovered by women.[5] And it's not very likely that anyone in the first-century Mediterranean world would have made up a story which included the claim that women were the discoverers of Jesus' vacant grave—especially if one of them was "a woman with an immoral record . . . ."[6] As I've already noted, women were not legally acceptable witnesses, and their testimony would not have carried much weight.[7] If, despite this fact, they were identified as the ones who found the tomb empty, we have good reason to believe the reports that tell us they did.

It's hard to imagine that the message that Jesus was alive could have been proclaimed in Jerusalem if his tomb *hadn't* been empty.[8] Someone might argue, perhaps, that Jesus' burial site wasn't really known, and that no one could therefore be sure whether his grave was empty or not. But we have no evidence that there was doubt about the location of his tomb: neither Christian nor Jewish records preserve any stories about attempts to find it.[9] Further, there is no evidence

---

1. Grant 176. Grant notes that this "story is likely to be true since the absence, which it records, of any participation by Jesus' followers was too unfortunate, indeed disgraceful, to have been voluntarily invented by the evangelists at a later date."

2. Craig, *Assessing* 352-3.

3. Craig argues powerfully that, when Jesus was encountered alive after his death, he was embodied; see *Assessing* 117-59; cp. Rowland 190-1; Evans 50-2, O'Neill 208-9; O'Collins, *Interpreting* 124-6. To be sure, belief that Jesus is alive is not logically dependent on belief in the empty tomb. As Brown puts it, one "can quite easily imagine circumstances in which, say, the tomb was robbed of the corpse unknown to disciples and general public alike; . . . should evidence of this robbery come to light now in the twentieth century, we would still be justified in continuing to believe in the fact of Christ's continued existence precisely because such evidence would be conceptually irrelevant" (132).

4. Craig, *Assessing* 356, 352.

5. See Craig, *Assessing* 355-6, 366-8.

6. Grant 176.

7. In support of this claim, Grant (232n6) cites A. E. Harvey, *A Companion to the Gospels* (Oxford/Cambridge: OUP/CUP 1972) 220. He notes that the women who found the tomb are said (in Mk 16:8) to have been frightened "because the violation of burial was an offence." Further, he observes that the "apostles disbelieved the women at first," drawing attention to Luke 24:11. Rowland (191) identifies *M. Shebu.* 4.1; *Sif. Deut.* 19.17; *b. Bab. Kam* 88a; and *Ant.* 4.219. as Jewish sources which document the minimal value attached to women's testimony at the time of Jesus; he references Joachim Jeremias, *Jerusalem in the Time of Jesus* (London: SCM 1969) 374-5 in support of his view.

8. Cp. Craig, *Assessing* 369-71.

9. Pannenberg 100-3.

that the opponents of early Christianity disagreed with the Christians about the fact that the tomb had been found empty. They explained its emptiness differently, of course, but they did not dispute the fact that it was vacant.[1] The very fact that people who doubted that Jesus was alive spread the story that his disciples had stolen his body suggests they shared the view that his grave was empty.[2]

The behavior of Jesus' disciples is very hard to square with the assumption that they stole his body. Their conviction that he was alive is evident from their dedication to his cause and their willingness to give their own lives for it. If they had stolen the body, it is difficult to see how they could not have regarded themselves as frauds, since they proclaimed that Jesus was alive as an embodied person. And their willingness to take risks for Jesus' cause isn't consistent with their being frauds. Frauds don't die for their hoaxes.

Could someone else have stolen Jesus' body? It's not impossible, of course, but there's no reason to think anyone else had any reason to take it. The grave wouldn't have contained anything robbers would have wanted; and, if they had mistakenly entered it in search of valuables, they wouldn't have had any reason to abscond with Jesus' body. People hostile to Jesus might have desecrated the grave, but why would they have wanted to remove his body? And if others stole the body, it seems plausible that their actions would have come to light and that early critics of Christianity would have publicized the discovery enthusiastically.[3]

An early Christian writer provides a good example of the anti-Christian response to reports that Jesus was alive beyond death. According to Justin Martyr, a communication from the Jewish authorities asserts that, after Jesus' crucifixion, "his disciples stole him by night from the tomb in which he had been placed after his removal from the cross . . . ."[4] Though they didn't interpret it in the same way as the early Christians, these authorities apparently did not dispute the claim that Jesus' tomb was empty.

Venerating the tombs of holy people seems to have been relatively common in first-century Palestine. This veneration reflected the assumption that these tombs actually contained the remains of holy people. It is striking that there is no evidence of any pattern of worship or any other kind of religious ritual centered on Jesus' tomb. If the early Christians had believed it still contained his bones, they might have been expected to make it a place of worship and pilgrimage. That they didn't suggests, again, that it was empty.[5]

Some people have proposed that Jesus didn't really die on the cross, that he was still alive when he was buried and that he revived sufficiently while in the tomb to leave it, then either recovering or else dying soon after at some other location. But the subsequent seriousness with which the Twelve and their associates

---

1. Pannenberg 101; cp. Stauffer 144, and Rowland's comments (192) about the relevant narrative in Matthew.
2. Craig, *Assessing* 371.
3. Craig, *Assessing* 376-7.
4. Justin Martyr, *Dial.* 108, qtd. Stauffer 144-5. Stauffer also indicates that Eusebius (*Historia Ecclesiastica* 2.2.1) "also mentions a circular letter of this sort issued by the Great Sanhedrin." Further, he calls attention to the biblical (Jn. 20:15) and external evidence suggesting that there was a rumor that Jesus' body had been stolen by the gardener responsible for the grounds around Jesus' tomb (145). Like Eusebius, Tertullian (*Apologeticus* 21) also reports a Roman investigation of the empty tomb story (Stauffer 145-6). Finally, Stauffer remarks on "a summary of an imperial edict directed against the robbery of corpses and the desecration of graves." "Perhaps," he says, "it is based upon a rescript of Emperor Tiberius, and may possibly be the Emperor's reply to Pontius Pilate's report on Jesus, the empty tomb, and the rumors that the body had been stolen" (146; see 231 for Stauffer's sources).
5. Craig, *Assessing* 372-3.

proclaimed that Jesus had been raised—a seriousness that led some of them to martyrdom—makes it difficult to accept such explanations. Again, people are unlikely to sacrifice themselves for causes they know to be based on fraud. And, given Jesus' fate, the first Christians must have realized what theirs might be if they repeated his message, kept his community alive, and proclaimed that God was on his side rather than that of those who had executed him—and still had the power to do the same to them.

Despite the suffering they knew they might have to endure, they persevered in hope as they proclaimed the good news of God's love. It is to the meaning of the Christian understanding of how God addresses the problems inherent in the human situation, an understanding rooted in that proclamation, that I turn in Chapter 10.

10

Love Bears All Things

Love—not sin, not death—has the last word. In this chapter, I explore salvation—God's loving response to the problems that misshape the human condition. These problems include sin, at the individual, interpersonal, and social levels; existential insecurity; and meaninglessness. God's loving answer to these problems is correspondingly pluriform; among its overlapping components are individual acceptance; the assurance of meaning for individual lives; individual, interpersonal, and social healing; divine judgment; and the revelation of divine love and divine purpose in the world.

Salvation comprises both objective and subjective elements. If we ask "whether Christ rectifies erroneous views concerning an unchangeable fact, namely the love of God . . . or whether Christ is the author of a changed situation,"[1] the answer, I believe, must be *both*. God's saving work is comprehensible only if it is always already rooted in the unchanging and unchangeable love of God, and we can be securely confident in divine love only if we believe it is invariant. At the same time, we must also say that what God does in Jesus has tangible consequences for the healing of the world, that the world is meaningfully different because of Jesus.

To say that God is the God of love, who accepts and heals, is obviously important for our own experience; but it isn't the most fundamental thing we can say about God. God would be the God of love whether or not love needed to be manifest as salvation. The doctrine of creation is logically prior to beliefs about what God is doing to repair and heal the world's brokenness. Healing the brokenness of creation wouldn't make any difference if it were not at root God's *good creation*, but rather an inferior and inherently flawed reality, a failed divine experiment suitable only for discarding. The purpose of creation is not to make salvation possible, as some Christians seem, in effect, to have thought. Creation is inherently valuable. It is a source of novelty that is worthwhile in and of itself and that can give delight to God. It provides the opportunity for new selves to come into being, to take pleasure in each other, in their created environment, and in God. Salvation, by contrast, is the process by which God resolves the diverse problems we confront.

For Christianity, being human is not the problem. The solutions to the human predicament that God offers—acceptance, healing, revelation, social transformation, and life beyond death—involve the enhancement of human life, not the denial of its value. Christians don't confess, "I believe in absorption into the cosmic all," "I believe in transcending time and matter," or "I believe in the end of

---

1. Wolfhart Pannenberg, *Systematic Theology*, 3 vols., trans. Geoffrey Bromiley (Grand Rapids: Eerdmans 1989-93) 2: 410 (summarizing a query he attributes to Martin Kähler, *Zur Lehre von der Versöhnung*, 2d ed. [Gütersloh: Bertelsmann 1937] 268).

desire." Rather, we celebrate what is essentially human, while pointing to the possibility that, where humanity's flourishing has been impeded, it can be healed.[1]

The foundational element of God's response to the human problem is the constant divine love that accepts and secures us. Divine acceptance is unalterable, though *we* can change by accepting it. In addition to acceptance, God's salvific work includes a multi-layered response to the threat of meaninglessness. It also includes the continuing activity of God's Spirit on behalf of our healing and growth. God could not love us without at the same time seeking to heal our individual brokenness as well as our sin-ravaged circumstances. God's promotion of individual and social healing is itself a product of unchanging love, and the communication of such love is central and essential; but the progress of divine healing is contingent on the cooperation of free creatures.

God's work aims at our complete healing; but whether or not such healing occurs during this life, the fundamental ground of our relationship with God remains God's unalterable love, to which we appropriately respond and which we rightly reflect and mediate by forgiving others. And divine love, which is not extended or withdrawn on the basis of performance, is also evident in God's activity as judge. Divine judgment takes two forms—revelation and rectification—and forms an integral part of God's loving, salvific activity in the world.

God's love—disclosed and enacted by Jesus—cannot and should not be compromised by accounts of God's work in Jesus. Theories of atonement according to which God is *entitled* to love only in virtue of what divine love does in Jesus call that love itself into question. Jesus' life and death and life beyond death do not *enable* God to *love* more fully or more constantly; but, in them, God reveals divine love, highlights divine suffering, and powerfully addresses the human problem.

To say that God loves is to deny that God could will the everlasting torment of anyone. It is also to deny that God extends loving acceptance and healing love to people arbitrarily, selecting some for salvation and some for damnation. God's loving embrace is neither capricious nor exclusive.

Divine Acceptance

Divine love is not contingent on our performance. Divine acceptance is the form that unconditional love takes in light of moral wrongdoing and shame. Because God is love, divine love embraces all creatures. To say that divine *acceptance* embraces all creatures is just another way of saying the same thing. But, while the reality of divine acceptance does not depend on our being aware of it, the conscious awareness of that acceptance can be a source of confidence, hope, and a sense of self-worth.

Divine Acceptance as a Consequence of Divine Love

God's acceptance means God's gracious willingness to be involved in the healing of human fragmentation. To say that God accepts us means that God will not allow human failings to prevent divine-human interaction from taking place. God loves us and works for our good despite our harmful actions. God cherishes us, and we are at home in God's love, even though we have sinned. Despite the fact that God is hurt by actions which hurt creatures, God will continue to care for the offender despite her behavior. Thus, when one person wrongs another,

---

1. Cp. Reinhold Niebuhr, *The Nature and Destiny of Man: A Christian Interpretation*, 2 vols. (New York: Scribner 1948) 2: 292; Langdon Gilkey, *Message and Existence: An Introduction to Christian Theology* (New York: Crossroad-Seabury 1979) 121-5.

God's love is not withdrawn and withheld pending interpersonal healing and reconciliation, though God's Spirit seeks both whenever they are needed.

It is not the case that accepting divine love "annuls justice because the morally demanded punishment of the wicked is compromised or withheld."[1] For retributive punishment is not—as I will argue later in this chapter, in connection both with Jesus' death and with human forgiveness—a requirement of justice, but, rather a violation of justice. So God's accepting love does not need to be vindicated as an alternative to justice. It is, indeed, a kind of justice—creative, transformative justice.[2] It is an essential feature of God's character and identity and of the relationship between creation and the God who is love.[3] *If God is love, then God accepts creatures and embraces them with divine love.* The death of Jesus did not represent or effect a change in God's attitude toward human beings.

This doesn't, of course, tell us how God's love will be expressed in any given case. There are many ways in which God can be freely loving. In addition, circumstances differ, and therefore call for different sorts of responses, so that some general statement about the character of divine love will be unhelpful and imprecise. And we are, in any case, ignorant of the details of the many circumstances God's love confronts. Still, we must begin with the recognition that divine love, and therefore divine acceptance, is an ineradicable aspect of God's character.

This understanding of divine acceptance should be sharply distinguished from the view that God has arbitrarily created a set of moral rules, and can choose to behave lovingly toward us on an equally arbitrary basis. God can't say, in effect, "Let's not count this one." For the problem with moral failure is not that it violates an arbitrary divine rule but that it is inconsistent with the character of reality.

The Significance of Divine Acceptance

Sin has to do with the sinner's relationship with God in at least two ways. God suffers whenever we cause suffering in the creation. And sin involves mistrust of and alienation from God. Ending a particular instance of my sinful behavior ends the present divine suffering directly caused by that behavior and, as I change habits responsible for my bad actions, reduces the risk of future divine suffering caused by comparable behavior. Acknowledging sinful behavior and moving beyond it helps to address the problem of alienation from God. And responding to God in trust—whether or not I thematize my acceptance of God's acceptance aptly—helps to resolve the root problem that disposes me to sin in the first place.

It matters, therefore, that I attend to my relationship with God when I sin. At the same time, my moral failures are moral failures precisely because they affect other people, the non-human created world, and myself. Real moral failure is an attack on the health of creation. There are no sins that affect *only* God. There could not be an act that did not harm God's good creation but which caused divine suffering or embodied mistrust of or alienation from God. Nor could there be an act that furthered or reflected a healthy relationship with God but which hampered the flourishing of creation.[4]

Divine acceptance doesn't substitute for (nor is it contingent on) my repairing the damage I've done, the healing of the relationship with any person I've

---

1. Ronald M. Green, *Religious Reason: The Rational and Moral Basis of Religious Belief* (New York: OUP 1978) 183.
2. See Paul Tillich, *Love, Power, and Justice: Ontological Analyses and Ethical Applications* (New York: OUP 1954) 64-6.
3. See the arguments to this effect briefly canvassed in Chapter 1. More specifically, with reference to grace, see Robert Merrihew Adams, *Finite and Infinite Goods: A Framework for Ethics* (New York: OUP 1999) 175-6.
4. Thanks to Craig Svonkin for the opportunity to discuss these matters.

harmed, or my own growth past any bad habits that might have led me to engage in harmful conduct. And it doesn't change the fact that I've engaged in culpable wrongdoing. Therefore, when—to take the simplest case—I've done something that harms another person, I need to repair the damage I've done, either tangibly (if this is possible) or symbolically. My *relationship* with the person I've harmed needs healing. And my own *character*, presuming it predisposed me to engage in harmful conduct, needs healing, too. But consciousness of God's acceptance can provide the context within which healing takes place, and can free us to begin the healing process.

The Value of Conscious Awareness of Divine Acceptance

The experience of God's accepting love can underscore our inherent worth to us—if God love us, it must not be the case that we are valueless, despite our harmful conduct. And it can offer us a sense of security that may make it less likely that we will seek from finite goods a degree of security that they cannot, in fact, offer.

We are always already accepted by God. But the awareness that I am embraced by divine love can still be important.[1] For divine acceptance to shape one's identity and behavior, one needs, effectively, to recognize that it is there and live out of that recognition: one needs to accept that one is *accepted*,[2] with the implication, I think, that one is *acceptable*. One needs to accept the gifted quality of one's existence—to acknowledge that one has real but finite value; that one is not dependent on one's own efforts to secure the meaning of one's existence; that one's performance does not determine one's value; that one is a divine gift; that one is embraced by God. Because being is inherently beautiful and valuable, divine acceptance does not *confer* value on us; but *consciousness* of God's acceptance can help to *confirm* our value.

The conscious or unconscious *awareness* of prior divine acceptance may be an essential condition in some cases for healing within the creation. There is all the difference in the world between resolving a problem *within* a relationship and resolving a problem *in order* to make a relationship possible. So the knowledge—implicit or explicit—that one is acting within the sphere of God's love, rather than working to gain it, may be a source of hope and empowerment that makes confidence and ongoing action, and so personal and relational repair, possible.

Accepting God's acceptance is worth doing at any time. It is, for instance, particularly important to *reaffirm* that one is not only valuable but also limited, that one is God's *gift*, and so not one's own god, after one has done something that is unfair or that is purposefully or instrumentally harmful. Because sin involves the denial that one is a part of the good creation, acknowledging anew that one *is* a part of the good creation is an act of repentance. Thus, it is an important aspect of the process of healing and repair.

Acknowledgment of God's acceptance is not simply important, however, because of the brokenness that results from wrongdoing. Divine acceptance also answers to another human need, the need to know oneself as valuable. This need is independent of, though clearly related to, the need to know oneself as loved despite one's having engaged in harmful conduct. It is the need to see the beauty of one's being reflected in another's eyes. The awareness, whether or not thematic,

---

1. See Jack W. Provonsha, *You Can Go Home Again: An Untheology of the Atonement* (Washington, DC: Review 1982) 106-11.
2. A notion I gratefully derive from Paul Tillich.

that we are embraced by God's love can empower us with this vision of ourselves as inherently worthwhile.[1]

While the active acceptance of God's acceptance can play a key role in the process of healing human brokenness, there need not be a particular, conscious point at which one deliberately accepts God's acceptance in order to be accepted. And it is not necessary, either, that one *thematize* God's presence and activity accurately. While it is obviously valuable to understand who God is and what God is doing in one's life, God loves everyone, whether inside or outside the Christian community. And God is active in every event in the world—that is part of what it means that confess that God is creator—and therefore in every event in every life. This is true however adequately God's activity is acknowledged or understood.

Performance as a Condition for Acceptance

God's acceptance is unconditional. The belief that it is contingent on our growth in love—or at least our seriousness about such growth—reflects a misunderstanding of what growth in love is *for*. It's a misunderstanding that has consistently complicated the spiritual lives of Christians. Recently, evangelical Christians have struggled with this view as they have debated the idea of "lordship salvation"—the notion that being accepted by God is contingent on accepting God's authority.

We have already seen that God's power is persuasive and empowering power. It is not exercised to dominate, but to liberate. A picture of God as demanding and authoritarian isn't true to the love we see manifested in Jesus.

It also isn't true to a proper understanding of what God's purposes for human life. God's fundamental call to every constituent of the universe is to live out its destiny as God's good creation: *to be itself* (which includes being present to, with, and for others). God does not ask human beings—or other creatures—to do things that aren't fundamentally related to their well-being as God's creatures. Proponents of "lordship salvation" sometimes make it sound as if God were like a mother who says to her daughter, "If you'll stop eating mothballs, I'll take you to the amusement park." What's wrong with eating mothballs is that they're poisonous; going to an amusement park is a reward that doesn't have anything to do with the real reason the daughter shouldn't eat mothballs. But salvation, in its varied aspects, isn't like the amusement park. At the personal level, salvation is *living as a part of God's good creation*, which begins now and continues beyond death.

We are healed and renewed as we realize our own value, the value of others, indeed the value of the whole created order, and live out of that realization, accepting our own limited but still significant places within God's good creation. Healing and renewal, human fulfillment, begin now. God can accept me whether I flourish or not, but if I reject renewal and fulfillment, God can't force me to live a flourishing life.[2]

None of us lives a *completely* fulfilled and responsible life, however. Even if one did so, this wouldn't earn divine acceptance, which isn't earnable. But failing to live up to standards we acknowledge can undermine our sense of who we are; it may propel us toward destructive compensatory behavior, or lead us to abandon the quest for improvement entirely out of a sense of futility. It's important, then,

---

1. See Edward Farley, *Good and Evil: Interpreting a Human Condition* (Minneapolis: Fortress 1990) 144-53.
2. Cp. C. S. Lewis; see *Mere Christianity* (New York: Macmillan 1952) 60: "repentance . . . is not something God demands of you before He will take you back and which He could let you off if He chose: it is simply a description of what going back to Him is like. If you ask God to take you back without it, you are really asking Him to let you go back without going back."

to realize that personal flourishing doesn't just mean accepting oneself as God's *good* creation. It also means recognizing oneself as *part* of *God's* good *creation*—accepting oneself, one's life, one's world, as gifts. To accept that God is *God* is to accept the gifted quality of one's existence, and to live out of a stance of basic trust, a conviction that the universe is a fundamentally friendly place. Even when one botches one's life in any of the innumerable ways we have of messing ourselves and others up, one can recognize one's giftedness and reach out in trust to God, who offers us loving acceptance unconditionally.

Life beyond death will give us the opportunity more fully to realize the potential with which we were created; to live out of a basic conviction that we can be trusting people; and ever more profoundly to realize that our lives are God's good gifts. It will be an opportunity for us to realize the purposes inherent in our creation, a natural outgrowth of what God has sought for us here. The proponents of "lordship salvation," then, are wrong if they equate salvation with "going to heaven," and then construe "going to heaven" as an arbitrary reward for good behavior. Not only could our good behavior never merit any kind of reward from God, life beyond death isn't the sort of thing that could be offered as a reward. Our life beyond death will offer an intensification of our personal relationships with God. But that relationship is not a consequence of our merit. And the experiences God desires us to have beyond death are appropriate outgrowths of our prior choices and experiences; they are not extrinsically but intrinsically related to those choices and experiences.

The proponents of "lordship salvation" have a point, of course, which is that behavior matters. But the *reason* to live a good life is that such a life is marked by participation in the various aspects of human welfare and that it is appropriately respectful of other persons and the rest of creation, not that it is a condition for God's acceptance. Of course we should live flourishing, responsible lives; but we need to do so for the right reasons.

The Sabbath as Sacrament of Divine Acceptance

The Sabbath can provide a valuable opportunity to experience divine acceptance. On the Sabbath, we acknowledge God's creative and sustaining power through our rest. As we rest, we symbolically express our dependence on God. We acknowledge and celebrate our status as God's good gifts. In owning ourselves anew as parts of God's good creation, we can both repent and experience divine acceptance. On the Sabbath—and whenever else we accept God's accepting love—we do not *become* dependent on God. Rather, we recognize and accept the dependence that is in fact essential to being human, and to being any other sort of creature. But on the Sabbath, especially, as we rehearse and reenact God's story, we remind ourselves that this dependence neither leads to nor results from a dominating divine authoritarianism, but that it is the occasion for consistent expressions of divine love.

Receiving God's accepting love isn't easy, on the Sabbath or at any other time. We may believe that we don't need to be graciously embraced by God. Or we may believe that we are too unworthy to be loved.[1] Our own experiences of ourselves as vacillating and undependable lovers may make us doubt God's fidelity.[2] We may resist love because we sense that we will be unable to love God in return.[3] But on the Sabbath, we *rest*. And, in resting, we come to know ourselves cherished and accepted without regard to our performance. The gift of time comes

---

1. Douglas John Hall, *Professing the Faith: Christian Theology in a North American Context* (Minneapolis: Fortress 1993) 154.
2. Hall 466.
3. Hall 467.

to us however poorly or effectively we have worked on the preceding six days. It envelops us in love. At the same time, it empowers us, as rest always does, to love more thoughtfully and more effectively in the future—not as a condition of receiving God's love but as a consequence of the empowerment being loved offers.

Salvation and Meaning

In addition to the guilt, shame, low self-esteem, moral brokenness, and failure to grow that plague us—and to which God seeks to respond by, among other things, communicating divine acceptance—we confront a further problem: the threat of meaninglessness.[1] Thus, addressing this threat must also be part of God's saving activity.

The threat of meaninglessness is the sense that one's actions finally do not matter, that they do not make sense, that they do not make any significant or lasting contribution to the state of things, that death will mean the inevitable end of everything for which one has hoped and worked, that one's story does not fit meaningfully into any larger whole, that everything is ultimately a confusing muddle, and that there's finally no reason to make one choice rather than another. It is easy to see how this threat could be a source of depression, despair, and nihilistic destructiveness (targeting oneself or of others). God's love responds to this threat in at least five complementary ways.

Every event in the creaturely world makes a permanent contribution to the divine life, and is known perfectly and completely by God. Thus, every choice we make, however much we may feel that it is ignored by others, is given ultimate significance by its lasting inclusion in the experience and knowledge of God. Obviously, this does not mean that all choices are equally important, that we should agonize over trivia. Nor does it mean that we are forever branded as those who have engaged in harmful conduct. It does mean, however, that we need not feel that our actions vanish into nothingness.

In addition, we rightly look forward in hope to life beyond death. And if there is life beyond death, death will not bring an end to our dreams and our projects and our loves. Death will not render our own self-cultivation and our loving interactions with others pointless, and it will not preclude the healing and transformation our broken lives so often need.

God's will is not perfectly done within history. But God is nonetheless at work in history, seeking the flourishing of individual lives and of creation as a whole. This means that, while history does not exhibit a deterministic order, it is also not patternless. As our choices are caught up on God's providential activity—characteristically without our knowing that they are—they acquire significance in relation to the lives of other individual creatures and to the history of communities, nations, and the world. We can be confident that they are meaningful in this way, then, even when we cannot see how they are or might be.

Confusion and incomprehension add to our sense of meaninglessness. God's revelation—general and special—is a gift of love that helps us to understand the nature and dynamics of our world. The reality of divine revelation does not enable us to bypass the messy business of disciplined inquiry and reflection. But it does give us insight into God as well as ourselves and the rest of the created world.

---

1. John Macquarrie suggests that (subjective) guilt will be some people's central problem, while meaninglessness will be the principal difficulty confronted by others; he proposes that we identify as "justification" the divine acceptance that might be thought to answer to both. See Principles of Christian Theology, 2d ed. (New York: Scribner 1977) 342.

By fostering understanding, it addresses the problem of meaninglessness (and, at the same time, of course, helps us to navigate our world more effectively).

Morality isn't a matter of arbitrary divine commands. But that doesn't mean that God is irrelevant to morality. Moral norms *do* reflect the way God has made the world. And the norms themselves are apprehensible *as norms* because they are (necessary) aspects of the being of God (rather than products of the divine will).[1] Thus, there are objective reasons for action, reasons for action accessible to finite, creaturely actors (made accessible in various ways to them by God). And, therefore, we need not say that there is finally no reason to choose in one way or another. While we rightly choose, freely, among various actions, the moral norms that constrain our choices are real, and so make our actions meaningful.

Thus, there is salvation, too, from the problem of meaninglessness. Awareness of God's love, of hope beyond death, of divine action in history, of God's self-disclosure, and of the objectivity of moral norms in the being of God can give us the confidence that we, our lives, and our choices matter.

Love, Growth, and Healing

God's response to the human condition must include both unconditional *accepting* love and winsome, attractive, *transformative* love.[2] There is no point in arguing which matters more—our growth and healing or the unconditional divine love that undergirds our growth and healing. God's unconditional love is the ineradicable foundation of our spiritual lives; flourishing and healing are the objectives of God's work in our lives. Each can be viewed in relation to the other.

What is clear, however we understand the relative priority of acceptance and growth, is that God's response to the human condition involves more than loving acceptance. It requires concrete changes in the human situation, both individually and structurally. Acceptance is just one dimension of a complex process by which God saves—fostering basic trust, healing fractured human lives, shaping history, and offering insight, meaning, and hope. We never stop returning to God's love as the basis for our Christian living. Indeed, divine love is not something we need just because of our moral failures; rather, our moral failures reflect, in part, our inability to see ourselves as gifts of divine love. But God's *goal* is the healing of persons and communities, and thus our continued growth in love.

God's unconditionally accepting love is not contingent on the reality or extent of our growth any more than it is contingent on our awareness that God loves us. And we do not grow in order to be loved; we grow with the aid and inspiration of a love in which God envelops us. Working at personal development in order *to gain God's acceptance* frustrates the rectification of one's relationship with God. But seeking personal growth and healing *for their own sake*, within the freedom provided by divine acceptance, is an integral part of that rectification.

God's creational design for our lives would be frustrated if we failed to experience growth toward flourishing, as well as long-term, substantial healing from moral failure and the other flaws that mar our humanness. Sin is, by definition, destructive and hurtful. God could not truly love without seeking to heal human lives substantially. God could not be satisfied with a purely objective acceptance, disconnected from the healing of human beings, including the healing of their broken relationships and the healing of their habits and their inner lives (including

---

1. Cp. Keith Ward, *Ethics and Christianity* (London: Allen 1970); David Ray Griffin, *Reenchantment without Supernaturalism: A Process Philosophy of Religion* (Ithaca, NY: Cornell UP 2001) 299-301.

2. Cp. Provonsha's memorable quip: "Justification, in a way, means being better off. Sanctification implies being better" (106).

attitudes toward their creator). Divine love must seek our healing and growth, or it would not *be* love.

Growth and Healing as Fulfilling Our Created Potential

In fostering growth and healing, God's love seeks the fulfillment of humanity's divinely created potential. Healing removes barriers to the fulfillment of our potential, while growth involves positive movement toward realizing it. Thus, growth and healing both involve development toward happiness and health,[1] progress toward human wholeness.

Growth in love includes moral growth, of course, but it involves the ongoing development of every facet of personal existence—spiritual, relational, intellectual, social, cultural—and the flourishing of each unique, individual personality. It involves loving God and others more, but it also involves loving ourselves and the non-human world more fully as well.

One of the key insights of the Protestant Reformation was that sin and goodness are found alongside each other in every part of human life. Hiding away from the world outside the church doesn't bring one any closer to God, and entering fully into human life in culture and society doesn't make it any harder for one to live a flourishing human life. We are called, not to flee from our humanness, but to accept it.

Some early Christians tried to speed up their growth toward human maturity by depriving themselves of human comforts—living in isolation in the middle of the desert or on the tops of pillars. Later, many faithful believers imagined that if they could seclude themselves in religious houses, away from the corrupting influences they believed were exerted by contemporary culture, they would find it easier to realize their created potentials. The reality, though, is that human wholeness isn't about escaping from the world. It's about living *in* the world as part of God's good creation. Some people may well have vocations to live in seclusion, or as part of religious orders that foreswear ordinary life in the world. But this will be because these people's personalities and opportunities are such that they can benefit and serve by taking up special patterns of life, not because ordinary life in God's good creation is inherently deficient or dangerous.

Part of being fully human is understanding oneself, one's world, and God correctly. To they extent that they offer meaningful insights into the nature of the world, Christian beliefs can contribute to personal growth. And to the extent that it is grounded in an accurate understanding of the way the world is, the pattern of life fostered by the Christian community can contribute to the achievement of flourishing humanness.[2]

The Social Dimension of Healing

God is active in and through the structures and processes of the human and non-human worlds to redress creaturely wrongs and promote creation's good at all levels of reality. The problem of evil—the challenge of reconciling God's goodness and power with the reality of a fractured creation—can only be solved if God is able to effect the wholeness and flourishing of the entire creation. Because social structures contribute to and compound the effects of sin, healing these structures is

---

1. The root meaning of the English word *holiness* is *wholeness, soundness,* or *health.* This fact is reflected in the title of Leo R. Van Dolson and J. Robert Spangler, *Healthy, Happy, Holy* (Washington, DC: Review 1975).

2. Richard Swinburne, *Responsibility and Atonement* (Oxford: Clarendon-OUP 1989) 173.

part of God's renewing work. As participants in God's saving activity, we have good reason to join in the healing and enhancement of these structures.

Growth and Healing as the Result of God's Activity

Though they are not brought about in ways that bypass our freedom and integrity, our growth and healing result from God's work.

God's activity lies at the root our being and acting. An important part of achieving human wholeness is precisely our coming to learn—really learn—and live out of the realization of this fact.[1] God's self-disclosure provides us with the assurance of God's gracious acceptance. Apprehension of God's presence, of God's reality as the ground of our existence, however it is thematized, can help to give someone a sense that the meaning and value of her life are secure, a sense that can, in turn, foster responsible choices, healing, and growth. And the realization that the universe is a friendly place is a potentially empowering and liberating one that can enable and further our healing and our growth toward full humanity. It can help to liberate us from idolatry and assist us in apprehending and responding to the reality of God aright.[2]

Basic trust doesn't happen by magic. It results from the experience of love. A range of communities—including the intimate communities of friendship, family, and marriage—can help to nourish basic trust. But the church must take deliberate responsibility for nurturing a sense of basic trust in its members. It must shape its preaching, teaching, and practice in ways that will aid those whose lives it touches in experiencing basic trust. And it must be attentive to the ways in which it uses its power, recognizing that people will often find it hard to distinguish between how *it* behaves and how *God* behaves.

Divine action in history has brought about the formation of communities that facilitate growth and healing. Formation through the church's practices, ideas, metaphors, and symbols can facilitate the process of growth and healing. And the church can bring to bear distinctive perspectives on moral and spiritual issues. And the church can encourage responsible action by offering challenge and moral support.

Of course, God can foster growth and healing outside the church. The church does not have a monopoly on moral goodness. The kind of moral and spiritual formation the church seeks to foster can clearly occur outside its walls, as we all know from personal experience. Non-Christians clearly "do perform objective, spontaneous, and subjectively good actions."[3] And there is every reason to believe that these actions do not occur in isolation from God's healing work. God can not only *accept* and *love* people outside the church; God can encourage the growth and healing of those outside the church. A god who could be encountered only in the church would not be the creator Christians worship. Thus, participation in the life of a healthy church can be an aid to healing and growth. But, while the church can witness to that process, the church does not control or monopolize it.

God also fosters our healing and growth by encouraging us to experience Sabbath rest. The Sabbath is a *sign* of healing and growth, a *means of experiencing*

---

1. See Nicholas Lash, *Easter in Ordinary: Reflections on Human Experience and the Knowledge of God* (Notre Dame, IN: U of Notre Dame P 1988) 175; Swinburne 172-3. Basic trust fosters God's work on behalf of our growth and healing; at the same time, encouraging it is one of the *goals* of that work.

2. Cp. Lash "in the absence of that basic trust which is the precondition of relationship, it is the lack of human community which renders prayer impossible (rather than, as preachers sometimes suggest, the other way around)" (202; Lash here summarizes what he takes to be the view of Martin Buber).

3. Swinburne 173.

healing and growth, and a *spur* to healing and growth. For on the Sabbath, liberated from production and achievement, we can experience in miniature the kind of community that we seek to realize in the wider world. Thus, the experience of Sabbath highlights the possibility of communities consistently marked by the freedom and equality that we herald and celebrate each week. Those who observe Sabbath rest can be challenged to discern in it the potential for a style of life that rejects the tyranny of work and achievement in our lives.

Further, on the Sabbath we celebrate and delight in God's good creation, which provides the norm for Christian growth and healing. In Sabbath worship, we are reminded of the Christian story that can invigorate and inspire our growth and healing. And, resting from productivity and achievement, we learn to accept God's acceptance—an experience that must become more, not less integral to our identities as our growth continues.

Quite apart from the church, and on days other than the Sabbath, God is, of course, actively promoting our healing and growth. Thus, divine love can persuade us to make correct choices. Providentially, God can enable us to see the attractiveness of particular choices and ways of looking at things. God's activity may nudge to surmount moral and spiritual challenges appropriate to our level of personal development.

God can touch our lives through revelation, by nourishing our awareness of divine acceptance and our disposition to trust that the universe is a friendly place; by fostering our sense that life is meaningful and that we are secure; in the church; on the Sabbath; and by means of providential activity in the circumstances of our lives. In all these ways, God can foster our healing and growth.

The Possibility of Complete Healing

We must believe that is seeking to heal human lives completely of everything that fractures and fragments them. Of course, the absence of moral failure from a life doesn't guarantee that that life will be a rich and flourishing one. Not making morally wrong choices *on its own* doesn't ensure that one will have a rich and flourishing existence any more than avoiding disease guarantees that one will experience consistent physical pleasure. Thus, God's healing work in our lives seeks to foster the formation of a character that will ultimately be free of moral failure, but it also involves a lot more than that.

That's why personal growth is really an endless work extending into God's final future. It is an ongoing process in which the individuality of each personal life is developed, in which everyone continually finds new opportunities for fulfilled and flourishing human existence. Transcending moral failure is hardly the only thing that matters.

But of course it *does* matter. It's not surprising, then, Christians from the beginning of the church's history have disagreed about the extent to which people can expect to experience complete healing from moral brokenness before the arrival of God's final future. Frankly, I think this question is a lot less important than many people have thought it was.

Many of the people who have thought that the question of perfection was crucial seem to have shared a common premise: that *if* it were possible for people to live flawless human lives, God wouldn't accept them unless they managed to do so. This idea flies in the face of the self-disclosure of God's love in Jesus of Nazareth. But it is not entailed by the belief that complete healing is achievable before death.[1] Experiencing growth and healing is not a way to get God to love us. It is

---

1. I see no reason *in principle* why, before death, someone with the right genetic inheritance and environment—perhaps even without these advantages—couldn't form

the process by which we come to live the kinds of lives that God created us to live. God will not love us any more because we have grown more. But because God loves us, God wants us to experience human life in all its fullness. Some people really do reach a point at which they stop making subjectively wrong choices in this life (without, of course, coming to a point at which they don't need to keep growing).[1] But whether this is possible or not, God's gracious acceptance can and should remain foundational in our lives.

I do not know how to resolve the debate over the possibility freedom from subjectively wrong acts in this life, and I do not intend to do so here. But I that partisans of alternative positions in this debate can agree on the following points:

• Our healing and our growth toward fulfillment and flourishing *matter*. Their significance should not be downplayed. Instead, they should be encouraged by our preaching and teaching and the style of our community life.

• Avoiding moral lapses does not mean the end of personal growth. Shunning moral failure doesn't in and of itself guarantee one a rich and flourishing life. We may hope that opportunities for growth and development, for infinitely varied new experiences, will be ours forever.[2] Even now, we can continually find new opportunities for fulfilled and flourishing human existence. Personal growth is about lots of things besides moral flawlessness, and will continue even if we succeed in transcending all of our bad habits.

• Whatever degree of moral and spiritual maturity we experience, we experience as a result of *growth* in wholeness, maturity, and flourishing, not as the result of coercive divine activity that bypasses our natural intellectual, emotional, and conative structures and processes. There is no way to have growth without the messy, ongoing process of *growing*. Growth and healing cannot simply be created or infused. To alter a person's moral character by fiat, as it were, to change it miraculously, would be to violate her freedom and the integrity of her life, to interrupt the continuity of her identity over time. It would disrupt the continuity underlying a person's selfhood. So it makes no sense to imagine that meaningful character change could be accomplished by divine intervention in an instant. Such change would represent the creation of a new person rather than the transformation of an existing one. There would be no link, no continuity, between the two.[3] In facilitating our growth and healing, God does not bypass our personalities or violate our individuality.

• The level of healing possible at a given point for one person will differ from that possible for another person at a comparable point as the result of environmental, genetic, and developmental factors.

• Our growth and healing are neither sufficient nor necessary to secure God's acceptance.

• God's love is not something we need just because of our moral failures; rather, our moral failures reflect, in part, our inability to see ourselves as recipients of that love—both as creatures and as objects of God's providential care. If the essence of sin is denying that one is a part of God's good creation, then flourishing humanity must be marked by the joyous and unshakeable realization that one's

---

a character marked by the strength required to successfully resist moral failure. The fact is, though, that (*contra* Wesley) we have little reason to believe that anyone has ever managed to do so in the past.

1. The point of focusing on subjectively wrong choices is that people can only avoid wrong choices if they're aware of the wrongness of these choices.

2. Ellen G. White, *The Great Controversy between Christ and Satan: The Conflict of the Ages in the Christian Dispensation* (Mountain View, CA: Pacific 1911) 677-8.

3. See Huw Parri Owen, *Christian Theism: A Study in Its Basic Principles* (Edinburgh: Clark 1984) 114.

being derives from God's love. The more we grow and the more we are healed, the more we will affirm God's love. This is not just because we become more aware of our flaws. Nor is it simply because God's love has been the precondition for our growth and healing and the basis for God's work in out lives. Personal growth and healing are about the increasing affirmation of God's love because what we are growing toward is, among other things, complete acceptance of ourselves as parts of God's good creation, and thus as gifts of love—no matter how mature or morally healthy we might become.

The Dynamics of Human Forgiveness

God accepts us despite our brokenness. And God's accepting love provides a basis for our own. Accepting God's gracious acceptance is owning oneself a *part* of God's good creation. It is thus the recognition that one is not the whole of creation, that there are others who are distinct and valuable like oneself. It is also, therefore, a recognition of one's limitedness and interdependence. That is one way in which the acceptance of God's acceptance can prompt us to see the value of community and relationship.

But if community and relationship are important, then forgiveness must be important, too—for forgiveness is essential if close relationships are to be created, maintained, and restored. And not only does God's love prompt us to be gracious, it models acceptance for us. Our forgiveness of others can take as its pattern God's loving acceptance of us. Forgiving those who wrong us is a crucial way of expressing our awareness of the reality and value of divine love, and of embodying the same responsiveness to creaturely vulnerability and beauty, the same desire for communion, that elicits God's gracious activity. It thus not only mirrors God's acceptance but also furthers God's healing work in the world.

The Golden Rule enjoins forgiveness: because we would like to be forgiven when we harm others, it would be inconsistent, and so unfair, of us not to forgive those who have wronged us. And the Pauline Principle precludes nourishing the hostility that might make it difficult for us to forgive them.

Forgiveness is a fitting and even necessary response to the need and the intrinsic worth of those who have violated us. Angry or calloused or disturbed, cut off from others, they suffer the loss of vital aspects of well-being—inner peace and friendship, for example. Whether they know it or not, they need help to overcome these losses. And because they are inherently, infinitely valuable, their intrinsic beauty and worth claim our attention and direct it to their needs. Forgiveness is what happens when we choose empathy even for those who have harmed us, refusing to make arbitrary distinctions that deny their humanity, their capacity for suffering and growth and healing.

Forgiveness means foreswearing retributive or vengeful actions and letting go of the desire for retribution.[1] But it is nonetheless perfectly compatible with confronting and challenging what is wrong. It does not require the toleration of injustice. Opposing ongoing violations of justice need not be motivated by a desire for retribution. Confronting a friend who has harmed one with the reality of one's pain can be, not an exercise in revenge, but a crucial means of seeking rectification, putting her in touch with reality, and moving her to change course.

---

1. On the dynamics of forgiveness, see L. Gregory Jones, *Embodying Forgiveness: A Theological Analysis* (Grand Rapids: Eerdmans 1995); Marilyn McCord Adams, "Forgiveness: A Christian Model," *Christian Theism and Moral Philosophy*, ed. Michael Beaty, Carlton Fischer, and Mark Nelson (Macon, GA: Mercer UP 1998) 77-106; L. William Countryman, *Forgiven and Forgiving* (Harrisburg, PA: Morehouse 1998).

Distancing oneself from a potentially violent spouse need not be a matter of *punishing* her or him; it may rather be a crucial means of protecting oneself.

Forgiveness doesn't mean ignoring the need for *restitution*, either. To demand that the thief pay back what she has stolen or that the practical joker take responsibility for cleaning up after a harmful prank is not necessarily to seek to humiliate those who have hurt us and to declare ourselves victorious. While those who have hurt us do not owe us their pain, they do owe us help in overcoming the harm they have done us. Asking them for this help not only gives us what is our due but simultaneously confronts them with the reality of their offenses in ways that will help them to grow morally and spiritually and that will provide them with opportunities to take tangible steps to reintegrate themselves into community with us.

Similarly, it's important to distinguish forgiving from excusing. Sometimes we may, of course, excuse. *She really can't see why that's wrong. He couldn't help it.* But when we do, forgiveness isn't what's in order. We can usually view those we excuse with compassion. But it is much harder to accept those who bear some responsibility for their actions. *He should have known better. She couldn't possibly do that without seeing why it was wrong. What he did was* deliberate! Forgiving means accepting the challenge to reach out in love, even in cases like these; it doesn't mean pretending that responsible people couldn't have done otherwise.

Forgiveness doesn't necessarily mean *trusting*, either. Forgiveness doesn't require hiring child molesters to run day-care centers or putting embezzlers in charge of corporate finance departments. Love—and so forgiveness—doesn't have to be earned; trust may. Risking trust may sometimes be a deeply redemptive act. In some instances, it may be a uniquely appropriate way of helping someone recover self-respect and grow morally; and an unconditional commitment to personal communion, as in some marital or quasi-marital relationships, calls us to take such risks wherever they are possible. But whether trust *is* appropriate is something that can only be determined on a case-by-case basis. And even when it is not, we can still forgive.

Thus, forgiveness may not necessarily mean *reconciliation*. Reconciliation may be an important element of healing for victims and victimizers alike. But it may not always be possible. The Golden Rule entails that we undertake the quest for reconciliation *when it is safe*, but, under ordinary circumstances, it may not require more than that. And attempts at reconciliation may not be at all safe for victims. It is more than understandable, too, that many victims may lack the inner resources to reconnect with those who have harmed them, and it would be profoundly cruel and insensitive for any third party—much less their victimizers—to demand that they seek reconciliation. And even when reconciliation is possible, its form will be thoroughly situation-dependent. The nature of one's commitments, capacities, and circumstances—and those of the other—will make a substantial difference.

Objections to forgiveness often center on the moral attractiveness of retributive conceptions of justice. When people engage in callous, violative conduct, retributivists say, we need to even the scales of justice. A loss to the other comparable to the one she has inflicted on me is somehow supposed to make up for what she has done. But of course the problem with the retributivist view is that harm to the victimizer won't actually benefit the victim. The various harms and benefits we and others experience are, as I have emphasized throughout, strictly incommensurable. No harm the other could experience, no loss she or he could undergo, could cancel out what has happened to me. I am still scarred. I am still broken. I have still been violated. I can pretend to myself that, if the other has been harmed in some comparable (or not-so-comparable) way, justice has been served and I have been compensated. But I have not been, however subjectively satisfied I may be if some harm befalls my victimizer. My satisfaction is a product of the illusion that I am somehow made better by the other's loss. Absent that illusion, I have no reason to be satisfied and no justification for seeking retribution. Punishment does not even the scales of justice, whatever that deceptive metaphor really means. What it does is to add needlessly to the totality of harm in the world and to perpetuate the cycle of violence and loss.

Because it is a response to the need and intrinsic worth of the other, forgiveness need not and should not wait on her or his repentance. Forgiveness refuses punishment from the very beginning for multiple reasons. Retribution is pointless—indeed, harmful. Love as equal respect seems to require anyone who would want forgiveness herself in advance of repentance to forgive someone else who had not yet repented. And love, and thus forgiveness, may be a crucial moment in the transformation of the victimizer—a means of bathing her or him in the healing waters of love.

Of course, forgiveness isn't just for those who are forgiven: it liberates those who forgive. To let go of hatred and resentment is to open oneself to the possibility of moving on after one has been hurt. While I cling to my anger, my victimization continues. But when I forgive, I release the pain that binds me to the past and equip myself to meet the future with renewed vitality.

Forgiveness matters. It is not a means of condoning or ignoring evil. It should not be an occasion for foolish risk. But it has the potential to be a profound means of liberation, a route to the embrace of righteousness and peace, a participation in God's healing of the world's brokenness, in the embrace of love God offers the world.

Judgment as Love's Work

If we understand God's ongoing activity as judge as the prophets and psalmists of Israel understood it—*the judge is the one who fosters and achieves justice*—we can see divine judgment as love's work. There are at least two senses in which we can talk about judgment as an aspect of God's salvific response to the human condition: judgment as revelation, and judgment as rectification. As judge, God confronts us with and discloses to us our brokenness, not to overwhelm us with guilt but to help us to transcend our self-deception; this is a matter of *individual* healing. Also as judge, God vindicates and delivers: God effects justice; this is a matter of healing *interpersonal relationships, institutions, and societal conditions.*

Though distinct, these activities of God as judge are interrelated. Judgment as disclosure, as revelation, challenges us to change our behavior, and thus contributes to God's rectification of interpersonal, institutional, and societal injustice. And God's creative justice, which overturns wrong, helps wrongdoers to escape the insulation from the truth that power can offer and to discover the meaning and consequences of their actions, and so contributes to their personal healing.

Judgment as Revelation

If God is love, we can be confident that God will do whatever God *can* do to foster the well-being not only of the whole creation but also of every creature. Creatures are always free to say "no" to God. They can refuse to acknowledge the reality of who they are and what they have done. God's love—expressed in the goodness of creation and in the possibility of healing and growth—cannot be offered to a free creature without the possibility that it might be rejected or ignored.

That does not mean, of course, that God could authentically *be* love while giving up on anyone, could stop trying to woo her or him to wholeness. Whatever the chasm that separates them, a mother will "cast herself across . . . [it] to relieve the suffering of her child. If he calls her, she will respond. Even the wickedest, if he calls, she must meet as one-caring."[1] And surely a mother's love is only a faint analogue of God's. "God will never cease to desire and actively to work for the salvation of each created person. . . . However long an individual may reject his Maker, salvation will remain an open possibility to which God is ever trying to draw him."[2]

But part of God's drawing us into the divine embrace is precisely the work of judgment as revelation. Healing means, among other things, being confronted with the reality and implications of one's refusal to accept oneself as a part of God's good creation, and so to accept God's loving acceptance. Thus, God's accepting love always embodies the possibility of judgment.[3] Judgment *in this sense*—a continuing confrontation between what we are and what we could be—is a possibility given with creation and necessarily actualized when free creatures sin.

Jesus' cross, as I will suggest in more detail in the next section, judges sin by highlighting it for what it is. To say that it judges is to say that it confronts those who are aware of its reality and meaning with a powerful revelation of the character and extent of human brokenness. And God also judges by acting providentially in history to confront us in a variety of other ways—both individually and collectively—with the reality of our brokenness. God's persuasive action prompts us to see who we are and how we have chosen, and to face the question how we will respond to painful truths we would prefer to avoid. God seeks to bring us face-to-face with reality, to help us to see ourselves as we truly are, albeit in light of divine love. This is part of the process by which we discover the truth about ourselves, and thus experience growth and healing.

Judgment as Rectification

As judge, God fosters the *establishment of justice*.[4] In human societies, this will mean the establishment of consistent adherence to the Golden Rule and the Pauline Principle, with all of their ramifications.[5]

In early Christian and Jewish thought, judgment meant *vindication*.[6] To preserve this insight into the nature of justice, we must affirm that, in the context of a given situation of injustice, divine judgment will favor those who are the victims of the injustice.

This does not mean that God treats them as if they are more worthy, more valuable as persons, than others, or as if they cannot themselves perpetrate injustice. It does not mean that, with respect to issues other than the injustice in question, God takes their part against others, as if no one is anything but either a victim or a victimizer. It does not mean that those God vindicates in any particular case are *absolutely* in the right—either sinless, or more favored by God than others.

To say that God favors the victims of injustice in the circumstances of their victimization is simply to state the obvious: that if God's providence seeks to rectify an injustice, it must side *in this respect* against the unjust position and

---

1. Nel Noddings, *Caring: A Feminine Approach to Ethics and Moral Education* (Berkeley: U of California P 1984) 98.
2. John Hick, *Evil and the God of Love*, rev. ed. (San Francisco: Harper 1977) 343. Cp. John Hick, *Death and Eternal Life* (San Francisco: Harper 1976) 242-61; cp. David Brown, "No Heaven without Purgatory," *Religious Studies* 21.4 (1985): 427-56.
3. Thanks to Fritz Guy for this point.
4. On judgment as creating rather than disclosing justice, see Jürgen Moltmann, *The Way of Jesus Christ: Christology in Messianic Dimensions*, trans. Margaret Kohl (London: SCM 1990) 315, 336.
5. Cp. John Finnis, *Natural Law and Natural Rights*, Clarendon Law Series (Oxford: Clarendon-OUP 1980) 161-230.
6. Cp. Moltmann 334.

prerogatives of those who have victimized others. When God as judge does justice, God necessarily empowers those who have been denied justice, working to restore to them what has been misappropriated from them and to ensure that they move from the margins into full participation in the life of their community.

In Jesus' "person and words," people met "the love and mercy of God." Divine judgment as rectification presupposes and embodies "the unconditional love and forgiveness which God offers men through the words of Jesus. . . ."[1] Thus, the conviction that God engages in judgment as rectification cannot serve to license any "dream of revenge for people who 'have had a poor deal' here. Nor must it be turned into a dream of almighty power for people who are present powerless."[2] Divine judgment as rectification seeks to heal and vindicate the oppressed, not to turn them into oppressors.[3]

The Activity of Jesus and God's Healing Work

God's action in Jesus doesn't make God's acceptance or God's healing work in history and individual lives *possible*. God does not need permission to love and accept human beings. And God can work in every strand of history to heal and deliver and save. But Jesus' ministry, death, and life beyond death not only reveal God's love but also contribute in diverse ways to God's healing work in the world. In this section, I examine some possible Christian accounts of the relationship between God's healing activity and what God does in Jesus. Then, I identify several possible elements of what might prove a satisfactory understanding.

Jesus' Death as Substitute for Ours?

Jesus' death was a consequence of his life. Provoking conflict as he did, he exposed himself to the risk of violent death. There is no reason to think he welcomed death. Nonetheless, he chose to be faithful to the One to whom he prayed as "Father," and, as a result, he was nailed to a Roman cross. But many people want more justification for Jesus' death than this. They suggest that Jesus' death was an essential prerequisite to God's acceptance, and perhaps also God's healing activity in the world.

The *substitutionary* theory of the atonement is one way of giving content to this suggestion. According to this view, on the cross Jesus' suffered death under divine judgment and, as a result, made it unnecessary for us to have to do so. Why? Because sin requires punishment. The death of Jesus under God's judgment fulfilled this requirement, thus permitting God to forgive instead of punishing. Dorothy Sayers pillories this view with painful scorn: "God wanted to damn everybody, but his vindictive sadism was sated by the crucifixion of his own Son,

---

1. John K. Riches, *Jesus and the Transformation of Judaism* (New York: Seabury 1982) 162-3. The entire chapter, "Jesus' Theism" (146-67), from which this quote is excerpted is useful in understanding Jesus and judgment. On Jesus' teaching regarding rewards and punishments, Riches (219n16) cites Bo Reicke, "The New Testament Conception of Reward," *Aux sources de la tradition chrétienne: mélanges offerts à Maurice Goguel à l'occasion de son soixante-dixième anniversaire*, ed. Oscar Cullmann and Philippe H. Menoud (Neuchatel: Delachaux 1950) 195-206 and Günther Bornkamm, "Der Lohngedanke im Neuen Testament," *Studien zu Antike und Urchristentum* (Munich: Kaiser 1970) 69-92.
2. Moltmann 314.
3. Cp. Moltmann 314.

who was quite innocent, and, therefore, a particularly attractive victim. He now only damns people who don't follow Christ or who have never heard of him."[1]

The substitutionary view makes clear neither what justifies Jesus' substitution for humanity nor what this substitution accomplishes. How does Jesus' death facilitate God's gracious acceptance?[2] An air of unreality starts to attach to these discussions. It is sometimes said that, incarnating God, Jesus was of infinite value, and was therefore a "fair trade" for all human sinners. We are invited to envision a mathematical comparison in which the value of Jesus' perfection, multiplied by his infinite divine worth, is seen to exceed the sum of the products of our sins and our respective finite worths. But, even if we ignore the impersonal oddness of this balance-sheet approach, it's not clear why the imagined transaction would offer anything to God. On the envisioned view, God is responsible for bringing about the whole transaction in the first place. And God is not an arbitrary tyrant who can be placated with gifts.[3]

Punishment is essentially associated with vengeance. It is not redemptive; its point is simply to cause harm putatively equivalent to that for which the offender is responsible, whether or not this does any positive good for her or anyone else. The harm done to a punished person by the criminal justice system isn't commensurable with any harm she's done to any of her putative victims.

We sometimes speak this way, under the influence of bad philosophy, as when a convicted murderer is released from prison and is said to have "paid her debt to society." But it is false both that society has been paid in any meaningful way by her incarceration and that, if society *were* in some fashion benefited *as such* by her incarceration this would in any meaningful sense make up for the harms brought about by her commission of murder. Harms cannot, as I have said, be converted into some common measure, compared with each other, and exchanged as necessary. Strictly monetary harms—if there are such—are an exception, and there may be others. But as a general rule the notion of retributive punishment rests on a mistake, the mistaken conviction that there exists a bank of justice into which deposits of suffering can be made to compensate for the withdrawals caused by harmful acts.

Even if harm done to victimizers were commensurable with the harms done by her to her victims, inflicting harm on her doesn't, in and of itself, confer a benefit on any of them or constitute a benefit to any of them. Punishment imposed by humans is pointless. And the same things that make it pointless would make punishment imposed by God pointless. Certainly, for instance, God would not be benefited by the punishment of a sinner; indeed, because God would suffer with the sinner, punishing her would add to God's pain. So the notion of punishment, understood as the infliction of harm for harm's sake, is not a helpful

---

1. *Christian Letters to a Post Christian World* (Grand Rapids: Eerdmans 1969), qtd. Hall 424.
2. Cp. C. Norman Kraus, *Jesus Christ Our Lord: Christology from a Disciple's Perspective* (Scottdale, PA: Herald 1987) 148.
3. Cp. Provonsha: "Calvary also reveals that . . . [God's] acceptance is absolutely free. Nobody has to (or can) pay for it or work for it. The cross rejects salvation by works *in principle*. It was a demonstration, not a payment. Golgotha is not a question of *whose* merits *earn* our salvation, but a rejection of the merit-earning formula itself. 'The gift of God is eternal life through Jesus Christ our Lord' (Rom. 6:23), and by definition we never earn a gift. The favor was entirely *unmerited*. Even Christ's very real merits *demonstrate* God's grace to us who are in doubt. They do not *earn* it" (94).

model for the salvific work of the God of love,[1] and it does nothing to illuminate God's saving activity in Jesus.

Even if the notion of punishment were credible, however, the idea of *substituted* punishment would be bizarre. On the view that punishment is morally appropriate, it is precisely the guilty person who must suffer. Someone else's suffering in place of a guilty person, even voluntarily, would be *unjust*, not a way of fulfilling the demands of justice. Retributive punishment can't be substituted.

Once we move beyond the dubious logic of retribution, the notion of substitution as a way of dealing with guilt becomes even more implausible. My guilt (my objective responsibility for some wrong, not my subjective *feeling* of guilt) is a matter of what I've done (and perhaps of the kind of character I have or have developed). It's not like a debt someone else can assume. In any case, objective guilt isn't really our fundamental problem. My decision to eat too much of the wrong food may cause me to have a heart attack. In this sense, I am "guilty" of irresponsible behavior. But my concern, and that of my physicians, will be to ensure that my heart is restored to its proper state and that my eating patterns change. The fundamental human problem isn't guilt: it's people's failure to live as parts of God's good creation. Talk about guilt is just another way of indicating human responsibility for human brokenness; but that brokenness, in all its forms, is still the *real* problem.

God's pluriform salvific work must include both the healing of any person who engages in harmful behavior *and* the healing of the creaturely reality or realities she has harmed. Concern about guilt is basically a distraction from these central concerns. While one may be aware that one has disappointed God, as one might disappoint a cherished parent or spouse, one's having done so is *evidence* of the fundamental problem, a *by-product* of that problem, not the problem itself.[2]

Concern for the individual sinner includes concern that she shape a character marked by integrity and responsibility, that she become a person consistently disposed to act like a part of God's good creation. Recognizing the nature of what she has done, and acknowledging that she is responsible for having done it—that is, her guilt—will help her to do this. But her guilt does not require that God *punish* her—that is, cause her to suffer in some way that is not a necessary part of the process of healing and re-forming her. The substitutionary view, however, depends on the supposition that punishment *is* a necessary response to wrongdoing.

Sin is sinful precisely because of what it does to creation. When we deny our identities as parts of God's good creation, we're not somehow *offending* the divine sense of self-importance and eliciting a punitive response from God; we're refusing to recognize the way things *really are*. There is no such thing as a creature that isn't a part of God's good creation, that isn't both valuable and limited; that's simply what it means to be a creature. Talk of punishment obscures the fact that morality isn't about obeying arbitrary divine commands. It's about living out of an awareness of the way creation really is.

Sometimes we "punish" people to teach them lessons. (In this case, we're not really talking about *punishment* in the focal sense of the term—thus the quotes—but about causing harm as a means of facilitating *education* or *rehabilitation*.) But surely there would be no point in harming Jesus in order to avoid harming us if *education* or *rehabilitation* were the primary reason for inflicting harm on wrongdoers. God wouldn't be doing us any favors by depriving us of experiences that might educate

---

1. Vernon White offers a lucid critique of the idea of retribution in *Incarnation and Atonement: An Essay in Universalism and Particularity* (Cambridge: CUP 1991) 91-106. A contrasting view is defended in Swinburne.

2. And the divine love revealed in Jesus is evidence that God does not use these feelings of disappointment to manipulate us.

or rehabilitate us. One might say that Jesus suffers and dies as a kind of object lesson, to show us the (natural or imposed) consequences of sin. But if Jesus' suffering and death is supposed to *substitute* for ours in that it permits God to display the consequences of sin, then in this case God isn't really *substituting* Jesus' death for ours; the idea of exchange is absent. Instead, God is bringing about Jesus' death to convince us to behave in ways that will enable us to escape death.

Some proponents of the substitutionary view believe that human beings become guilty because they violate essentially arbitrary impositions of God's will. If they were correct, and if these arbitrary impositions were the only standards there were for human moral behavior, then there couldn't be any standard of justice that required God to take one route rather than another in restoring, renewing, and healing humanity. Whatever standard there was would be the product of God's will. There wouldn't even be any reason for God to be consistent. Any "rule" that said God had to be would, after all, have been created, and could thus be altered, by God. The whole, elaborate process would be unnecessary as a means of eliminating human guilt,[1] even if it were otherwise possible to explain how Jesus' substitutionary death could accomplish this.

In short, it is difficult to give plausible, coherent, and morally credible significance to talk of Jesus' death as substitutionary. The substitutionary view doesn't provide a useful way of understanding Jesus' death as playing a role in God's salvific activity.

Salvation by Good Influence?

The *moral influence* view, perhaps the most popular position today, suggests that salvation is accomplished through Jesus' demonstration that God is love, which transforms people's attitudes and leads them to respond to God in love and to change their behavior.[2]

The moral influence theory rightly highlights the disclosure of divine love in the life of Jesus, and emphasizes ways in which seeing this love put on display can be winsome and transformative. This revelation certainly has the potential to affect people's attitudes and values, and so to contribute to God's healing of their lives. Through its various cultural ramifications, it has been and is powerfully efficacious. But what it underscores is precisely that God is always and everywhere love. And this means, in turn, God is able to heal and transform people whether or not they have encountered the divine revelation in Jesus. But if only someone who knows what Jesus' life, death, and life beyond death is intended to reveal can experience a proper relationship with God, then most people are out of luck. And it is difficult to reconcile this conclusion with the divine love which, on the moral influence theory, Jesus is supposed to reveal in the first place.[3] The God who is love would not deny access to acceptance and healing to people unaware of divine love as revealed in Jesus.[4]

Thus, the moral influence theory is best read as calling attention to God's revelation in the life and death of Jesus of a divine love that is active everywhere. It should not be understood as providing a comprehensive account of how God accepts and heals everyone. It can, however, focus our attention on the way in which the disclosure of divine love in Jesus can change people's lives and change history

---

1. On the flaws of the "judicial" model of divine-human relations, see Farley 140-4. It should be clear that, when I affirm the salvific significance of divine judgment, I am not talking about the same kind of judicial activity with which Farley is concerned.
2. Jack Provonsha suggests the use of the expression "atonement by revelation" (95).
3. Cp. White 23.
4. On the implicit universality in Jesus' conception of God's love, see Wolfhart Pannenberg, *Jesus—God and Man*, trans. Duane A. Priebe (London: SCM 1967) 272-3.

The Cross and God's Saving Love

God is revealed in Jesus' life as a whole, and not just his death. But his death is the capstone of his life, the culmination of his career, and it is powerfully revelatory.[1] This is so both in virtue of what it says about sin and divine love, and in virtue of what it discloses about divine vulnerability.

His suffering discloses the destructive character of human brokenness, which leads human beings to attack God in the person of Jesus.[2] It is thus a sign of humanity's "judgedness." For it is not an atypical, but a representative set of choices that bring about Jesus' death. It is a dramatic depiction of what happens constantly as people decide whether or not to live as God's good creations.[3] The sinfulness of sin is evident precisely in the fact that it leads to the crucifixion of God's revelation. In virtue of Jesus' innocence, "evil is deprived of all reason and is shown to have its basis in a radical, if corrupt, employment of freedom."[4] And the fact that God does not condemn, but graciously accepts, even in the face of the crucifixion is both a further instance of judgment—since it contrastively underscores the distorted character of the human condition that leads to the crucifixion—and, simultaneously, a means of dramatically communicating divine love.

Thus, God can be loving without appearing to falsify the character of reality or the genuineness of the moral order, for the moral brokenness despite which God accepts and loves humankind is what sends Jesus to the cross. The cross leaves no doubt about the enormity of evil even as it expresses God's gracious acceptance.[5] Being aware of this demonstration is not a precondition for receiving divine acceptance. But for anyone who is aware of it, it can serve as a decisive revelation of both human brokenness and divine love.

The ministry, and especially the death, of Jesus also contribute to salvation by highlighting God's solidarity with creation in suffering. The God of love revealed in Jesus of Nazareth can heal broken human lives whether or not they have been overtly touched by the story of the cross. But what God cannot do, and still be the God of love, is remain aloof from human suffering.[6] The fate of Jesus highlights the fact that God *is being* crucified perpetually. Suffering with creation, God is unavoidably affected by the harms caused to creation by accident and malice; God is unavoidably involved in the fragility and contradiction of finite existence. This involvement is highlighted by Jesus' suffering and death.[7]

Saving Love and the Rejection of Victimization

The ministry, death, and life beyond death of Jesus changed history forever, and they continue to exert salvific—transformative, healing—efficacy on historical existence.[8] They unleashed a new historical dynamic, centered on the community

---

1. Cp. Kraus 156.
2. Thanks to Fritz Guy for this insight.
3. I owe this point to Fritz Guy, "Confidence in Salvation: The Meaning of the Sanctuary," *Spectrum* 11.2 (1980): 44-53; see also Kraus 151-2.
4. See Green 185.
5. See Green 186.
6. Cp. Kraus 157.
7. See White 39, 54-5.
8. Gordon Kaufman, *Systematic Theology: A Historicist Perspective* (New York: Scribner 1968) 404. Kaufman's entire constructive discussion of the atonement (396-410) is fascinating, but I think he has overstated his case somewhat. According to Kaufman, in Jesus' "death and resurrection God's love succeeded in breaking into human history, becoming a new element in the on-going historical process. And thus without him, men could not become at-one with God, reconciled with him" (408). Surely God's love was evident in human history before Jesus. Surely it was "an element in

that Jesus founded and that continued as the Christian church, through which God is able to realize novel and important possibilities.

Among the most important of the historical and cultural consequences of Jesus' death is that it gives rise to a dramatic transformation of attitudes toward victims and victimization.[1] Groups in conflict find it all too easy to end the violence that divides them by scapegoating. If a person or group can become the focus of other people's anger, that anger can be displaced onto the scapegoat, and those previously in conflict can experience temporary peace. Former opponents can unite in targeting the scapegoat. And the scapegoat can become a kind of substitute for those who kill and victimize it, since its death stops the cycle of social conflict that would otherwise destroy them. Of course, this kind of social strategy is likely to work well only if those who employ it can regard their treatment of the scapegoat as justified. So it becomes important to legitimate the process of scapegoating by characterizing the scapegoat as deserving of the violence to which it is subjected. The scapegoat must *deserve* death—otherwise, feelings of guilt, self-doubt, and self-criticism would short-circuit the scapegoating process.

It's easy to read the death of Jesus as part of this kind of pattern: while the Roman occupiers and the domestic power structure are often at odds, they can collaborate in executing Jesus. The Third Gospel declares that Pilate and Herod, formerly enemies, became allies in the wake of their shared participation in the death of Jesus.[2] But Jesus' death doesn't have the same outcome as the deaths of other scapegoated victims. For his disciples encountered him alive after his death. And they proclaimed him as God's Word to the world.

Here was a victim who was unequivocally innocent. He was, indeed, God's revelation. Where *his* death was concerned, the process of victimization and scapegoating couldn't be justified. And so, as a result, that process began to lose its cultural legitimacy. It became increasingly clear that "[h]umankind is never the victim of God; God is always the victim of humankind."[3] Scapegoating continued[4]—and, shamefully, all too many of its victims were Jews brutalized and killed by Christians.[5] Nonetheless, as Christianity, with the story of an innocent victim at its center, grew in its cultural influence, being a victim came increasingly to be a source of claims to care and respect, even a badge of honor, rather than something shameful. The acceptability of scapegoating persecution was undermined,

the historical process" prior to the life of Jesus. In light of God's self-revelation in Jesus, one wants to say distinctive things about the history of Israel and the church. But the stream of history that centers in Jesus is not hermetically isolated from its environment. In fact, it is almost inconceivable that God could have providentially shaped that history in the same way in a different environment. God's distinctive success in the history of Israel and the church is no reason to suppose God's loving action to have been absent elsewhere.

1. What I offer here is a brief and inadequate sketch of the complex social theory advanced by René Girard. See *Violence and the Sacred*, trans. Patrick Gregory (Baltimore, MD: Johns Hopkins UP 1979); *The Scapegoat*, trans. Yvonne Freccero (Baltimore, MD: Johns Hopkins UP 1986); *Things Hidden since the Foundation of the World*, trans. Stephen Bann and Michael Metteer (Stanford, CA: Stanford UP 1987); *I See Satan Fall Like Lightning*, trans. James G. Williams (Maryknoll, NY: Orbis 2001). For a popular exposition of Girard, see Gil Bailie, *Violence Unveiled: Humanity at the Crossroads* (New York: Crossroad 1997).

2. Luke 23:12.

3. Girard, *Satan* 191.

4. "Christianity triumphed at the level of the state and soon began to cloak with its authority persecutions similar to those in which the early Christians were victims.... Christianity suffered persecution while it was weak and became the persecutor as soon as it gained strength" (Girard, *Scapegoat* 204).

5. See Girard, *Scapegoat* 1-11; *Satan* 170-1.

and the perspective of victim gained increasing significance,[1] with the result that "concern for victims" now serves as "the secular mask of Christian love."[2]

An important consequence, then, of Jesus' death was a long-term transformation of the status of the victim, of the meaning of victimization.[3] Clearly, this transformation was not merely an outcome of the death of Jesus: after all, centuries before, Israel had emerged as a nation of freed slaves, with an ethos that made care for the marginal a central element of social justice. And the First Testament contained striking narratives of the victimization of innocents,[4] narratives But Jesus' death dramatically underscored the pervasiveness and unjustifiability of victimization.[5] It is by no means the case that victimization has ended, of course; but it has been deprived of credibility (so that, in fact, the allegation of victimization can in our culture become an effective *means* of victimization.[6])

> Everything changed very slowly at first, but the pace has been accelerating more and more. When viewed in terms of the large picture, this social and cultural evolution goes always in the same direction, toward the mitigation of punishment, greater protection for potential victims.[7]

Thus, God has used Jesus' death powerfully to undermine the violence against victims that is a key instance, consequence, expression, and further cause of sin in our world.[8]

The victimization of the innocent Jesus has functioned as a revelation of the violence at the root of social order, and so as a means of addressing the social reality of sin. It is at the same time a source of personal transformation. For the image of the crucified Jesus serves as a powerful revelation of and judgment on our own individual tendencies to exclude and victimize. Precisely because it does, there is a certain irony in the persistence of substitutionary theories of Jesus' death. For the powerfully evocative, unjust death of the innocent victim, Jesus, serves to dethrone the process of victimization—and so of substitution.

1. Girard, *Scapegoat* 200-2.
2. Girard, *Satan* 165.
3. Girard, *Satan* 161-9.
4. Girard, *Satan* 83-5, 107-20; *Scapegoat* 117.
5. Some critics have alleged that Christianity's concern for victims reflects the fact that it was founded largely by slaves and lower-class people who cunningly valorized their victimhood as an act of spiritual revenge against the powerful and the successful, completed when their oppressors internalized the victims' perspective. (Girard discusses Nietzsche's canonical exposition of this analysis; see *Satan* 172-3.) But this criticism not only undervalues the insight embodied in the victim's perspective (while treating the perspectives of the dominant classes with insufficient critical distance), it also appears increasingly to rest on an historical misconception. More of the earliest Christians seem to have been middle- and upper-class people than has previously been supposed; see Rodney Stark, *The Rise of Christianity: How the Obscure, Marginal Jesus Movement Became the Dominant Religious Force in the Western World in a Few Centuries* (Princeton: Princeton UP 1996); Rodney Stark, *Cities of God: The Real Story of How Christianity Became an Urban Movement and Conquered Rome* (San Francisco: Harper 2006).
6. "The victims most interesting to us are always those who allow us to condemn out neighbors" (Girard, *Satan* 164). Girard believes that the Christian concern for victims has been turned on itself, as victimization-based objections are leveled against the churches on various fronts. But where Girard is inclined to understand these objections as neo-pagan, anti-moral attacks on authentic Christianity (see *Satan* 181), I would be inclined to see at least some of them as embodying challenges to Christianity to be true to its own best insights.
7. Girard, *Satan* 166.
8. Girard acknowledges that, because the process of scapegoating has fostered social solidarity, its delegitimation can tend to release previously suppressed and destructive social forces (cp. *Scapegoat* 101).

Saving Love and the Loving and Beloved Community

A further objective, salvific consequence of the ministry, death, and life beyond death of Jesus was the formation of the community that subsequently became the Christian church. Jesus' historical activity is objectively important as the precondition for the proclamation, enactment, and experience of reconciliation, mutuality, interdependence, and inclusive community in and through the church.[1] The church is a distinctive historical community—one that is deliberately transcultural, transethnic, and transnational. Clearly, it has often taken sides in national, ethnic, or cultural conflicts. But it has nonetheless powerfully represented the ideal, and—imperfectly—demonstrated the possibility of a community that lies beyond such conflicts, rooted in a relationship with God predicated on nothing but God's love itself.[2] Through Jesus' creation of this community, God has exerted a powerful salvific influence.

Saving Love and Human Nature

In multiple ways, the ministry, death, and life beyond death of Jesus are salvifically efficacious: they contribute in tangible ways to the healing of the world that is a crucial part of God's salvific activity. At minimum, this is so because human solidarity—social and historical—allows the effects of Jesus' actions to ramify throughout human cultures and across our planet.

Many early Christian thinkers believed in another sort of solidarity—a kind of metaphysical unity that linked every member of a species. They believed that what God did in Jesus transformed human nature as a whole. Of course, on a characteristically modern view, human nature is an abstraction, a label for a set of features typically shared by the members of an interbreeding population.[3] And if that's what human nature is, then it doesn't seem to be the sort of thing that's capable of being healed *as such*. So the notion that, in Jesus, God redeemed human nature seems difficult for us to comprehend, given our assumptions.

A provocative contemporary proposal might, however, allow us to reappropriate a central insight of those who propounded this early Christian view. The proposal is the "hypothesis of formative causation" advanced by Rupert Sheldrake,[4] and centering on "morphogenetic" or "morphic" fields. Such fields, he

---

1. Cp. John Milbank, *The Word Made Strange: Theology, Language, Culture* (Oxford: Blackwell 1997) 145-68.
2. Cp. John Milbank, "The End of Dialogue," *Christian Uniqueness Reconsidered: The Myth of a Pluralistic Theology of Religions*, ed. Gavin D'Costa (Maryknoll, NY: Orbis 1990) 179; Edward Farley, *Divine Empathy: A Theology of God* (Minneapolis: Fortress 1996) 272-6. As Farley notes, "the very need to be a religion, that is, to develop social forms (doctrines, morals, organizational structures) enabling it to exist at all, tends to define and tame the universalization. When this happens, universalization becomes a not-so-masked form of religious imperialism, a new universal conformity to whatever the new community has developed" (*Empathy* 284-5).
3. Thanks to Stephen Clark for calling this understanding of species to my attention.
4. See Rupert Sheldrake, *A New Science of Life: The Hypothesis of Formative Causation* (London: Paladin-Granada 1983); Rupert Sheldrake, *The Presence of the Past: Morphic Resonance and the Habits of Nature* (New York: Vintage 1988); Rupert Sheldrake, "The Laws of Nature as Habits: A Postmodern Basis for Science," *The Reenchantment of Science: Postmodern Proposals*, ed. David Ray Griffin, SUNY Series in Constructive Postmodern Thought (Albany: SUNY 1988) 79-86; Rupert Sheldrake, *The Rebirth of Nature: The Greening of Science and God* (London: Century 1990). I characterize an account of the work of Jesus featuring morphic fields as an alternative to the Platonism of many early Christian thinkers, but Sheldrake (*Presence* 101-6; *Rebirth* 87-8) notes that some contemporary theorists have understood such fields themselves in Platonic terms.

suggests, obtain "within and around organisms" and species, comprehending "a nested hierarchy of fields within fields . . . ."[1] According to Sheldrake,

> the fields of a given species . . . are inherited by present . . . [members of a species] from . . . previous [members] . . . . They contain a kind of collective memory on which each member of the species draws, and to which it in turn contributes. The formative activity of the fields is . . . [determined] by the actual forms taken up by previous members of the species. The more often a pattern of development is repeated, the more probable it is that it will be followed again. The fields are the means by which the habits of the species are built up, maintained and inherited.[2]

"Morphic fields" structure "self-organizing systems at all levels of complexity, including molecules, crystals, cells, tissues, organisms, and societies of organisms . . . ."[3] Thus, Sheldrake maintains, "morphic resonance" among similar entities ensures that changes experienced by some of the entities will affect others, not only structurally but behaviorally.[4] A body of experimental evidence can be read as providing support for this hypothesis.[5]

If there are, in fact, morphogenetic fields that link the members of a species, then, *ex hypothesi*, the fact that one member of the species acquires a behavior pattern will make a difference for the efforts of contemporaries and successors to do the same. Thus, the ministry of Jesus, his love, and the way he faced his death will all have affected human history not only by way of example—culturally, socially, psychologically—but also biologically. It will be true, if Sheldrake is correct, that Jesus was responsible for a new phase in human history—not merely in that he birthed a movement whose activity has had dramatic historical consequences, but also in that he initiated a change in the morphic field or fields affecting human development and behavior. Sheldrake's hypothesis has evoked intense criticism.[6] If, however, it does turn out to provide an accurate picture of the way the world works, then it could point to a further way in which God heals and transforms in and through the work of Jesus.

---

1. Sheldrake, *Rebirth* 87.
2. Sheldrake, *Rebirth* 88. It is important to distinguish the hypothesis of formative causation from Lamarckian accounts of inheritance, which concern genetic transmission and are generally believed to be inconsistent with biological theory and experimental evidence. Sheldrake discusses such accounts in relation to his own position in *Presence* 140-2, 146, 275-9. His approach should also be distinguished from vitalism: it is organismic or holistic, not vitalistic; see Presence 69-70, 314; Rebirth 78-80, 97-8.
3. Sheldrake, *Rebirth* 88.
4. Sheldrake, *Presence* 149-57.
5. See Sheldrake, *Presence* 97-196; *Rebirth* 87-98. A significant pointer to the reality of formative causation, according to Sheldrake, is provided by an experiment in which the members of a rat population were taught to perform a simple task. While originally undertaken to investigate the Lamarckian hypothesis that acquired characteristics can be genetically transmitted, the experiment established that the learning rates for members of successive generations of rats improved whether or not they were genetically linked with rats that had mastered the assigned task. See Sheldrake, *Science* 186-91; *Presence* 174-7. Another interesting example involves the tendency of large numbers of unconnected blue tits to develop the habit of pecking through tinfoil tops to drink milk from bottles delivered to people's doorsteps, a habit reestablished after a significant hiatus following World War II (*Presence* 177-80).
6. Issue 12.6 (2005) of the *Journal of Consciousness Studies* was devoted to Sheldrake's work; see *Sheldrake and His Critics: The Sense of Being Glared At*, ed. Anthony Freeman (Exeter: Imprint 2005).

The God of Love and the God of Hell

That God is love means that we must deny validity to belief in what is somewhat quaintly, but still terrifyingly, called "everlasting torment."[1] For belief in hell imagines God as a cosmic sadist who prevents the damned from repenting or preserves them in being after they have somehow rendered themselves incapable of repenting—while torturing them forever because they have not repented. Belief in this kind of divine punishment is inconsistent with the belief that God is love.

The *prima facie* conflict between belief in divine love and belief in endless torment is obvious. For how could consigning anyone to endless punishment be for her good? And if it could not be, how could it be said to be loving?

The ultimate objection to hell is that it is pointless. As traditionally conceived, hell is permanent. Consignment to hell is irreversible. Thus, it does not and cannot serve the good of those interned there. Loving the damned, if such there be, is unequivocally incompatible with relegating them to permanent torture—of whatever sort—in hell.

A defender of hell might wish to maintain that hell is necessary to fulfill the demands of retributive justice. But the expression "retributive justice" here masks nothing more interesting than an institutionalized form of revenge.

To be sure, the notion that justice should be retributive clearly captures something of importance. It is a crucial part of justice that, for instance, people not be sanctioned by the criminal justice system for actions they did not perform. It is never just knowingly to sanction one person for another's behavior. But retributive justice, as understood here, involves an additional claim: that causing loss of freedom, loss of property, perhaps loss of life to a person who has harmed another is required as a means of somehow balancing "the scales of justice." This view is deficient on two counts.

It assumes that harms are, as a general rule, commensurable. And, for a theology rooted in love, there is a further problem: it should be apparent that even if the notion of retributive punishment could be rendered coherent, it would still be inappropriate to suppose that God engages in it. For retributive punishment is, by definition, not redemptive. It doesn't seek the good of anyone—as I've stressed, victims are not compensated by the imposition of harms on their victimizers—and it is obvious that those who engage in harmful behavior are not benefited by retribution as such. Love seeks wholeness, healing, reconciliation, and it is hard to see how retribution is compatible with these goals.

It is equally hard to see how, given the centrality of the Golden Rule to the Christian moral life, living as a Christian could be compatible with desiring or willing that anyone should be consigned to hell.[2] If God nonetheless *does* damn people to hell, it would seem to follow that in order to follow the Golden Rule, Christians would have to will that God not do what God does, not just as a matter of sentiment but as a matter of reason. They would have to conclude either that

---

1. Cp. Marilyn McCord Adams, "The Problem of Hell: A Problem of Evil for Christians," *Reasoned Faith: Essays in Philosophical Theology in Honor of Norman Kretzmann*, ed. Eleonore Stump (Ithaca, NY: Cornell UP 1993) 301-27; C. S. Lewis, *The Great Divorce* (New York: Macmillan 1946); Swinburne 180-200; Karl Rahner, *Foundations of Christian Faith: An Introduction to the Idea of Christianity*, trans. William V. Dych (New York: Crossroad-Seabury 1978) 97-106.

2. I owe this useful point to Thomas B. Talbott, "On Predestination, Reprobation, and the Love of God," *Reformed Journal* 33.2 (Feb. 1983): 11-5; cp. Thomas B. Talbott, "The Doctrine of Everlasting Punishment," *Faith and Philosophy* 7 (1990): 19-42; Thomas B. Talbott, "Providence, Freedom, and Human Destiny," *Religious Studies* 26 (1990): 227-45; Thomas B. Talbott, *The Inescapable Love of God* (Boca Raton, FL: Universal 1999).

God does not will that people adhere to Golden Rule or that God does, and so wills that people will that God not do what God does. The same would be true of the Pauline Principle, since, if the idea of retribution is incoherent, willing that people were in hell could only be a matter of retaliatory hostility or instrumentalized harm, both of which are ruled out by the Principle.

The person who believes in everlasting torment might maintain that consigning a person to hell could be seen an expression of God's love, not for the damned person, but for others. Hell would be understood, then, as a cosmic analogue to a modern prison. But this is simply incredible. If God can consign an irredeemably impenitent person to hell, God need not deal with the risk to others posed by this person's existence by subjecting her to endless punishment. On the imagined view, God would also have the power to isolate this person from the rest of the created world—or at least from the saved—in any number of ways without torturing her, or simply allow or cause her to drop out of existence entirely. So God would have no reason to relegate her to hell.

The believer in hell could respond that complete isolation, or removal to some cosmic "penal colony" with other damned persons, would be a profoundly painful experience. Even if this is so, however, it would not follow that the pain associated with this experience would be remotely as intense as that to which hell as traditionally conceived would give rise.

To reject hell as traditionally conceived is not to reject the notion that sinful behavior has destructive consequences for the self as well as for others. It is not to reject the conviction that people must accept responsibility for their harmful as well as their helpful actions. And it is not to deny that coming to grips with our own destructiveness can be profoundly painful—not because we must be *punished* retributively but because accepting, truly owning, the reality of what we do and who we are involves coming to grips with truly awful things about ourselves as well as the truly horrifying consequences of our actions in the lives of others. *Images* of flames and other terrors are not out of place as metaphors. But belief in the God of love rules them out as *means of retributive punishment*.

We cannot know for certain what the ultimate destiny of any person might be. We can be certain, though, that if God is love then, should there be any persons who finally and irrevocably reject divine acceptance, they will not punished for this rejection by being tortured endlessly in hell. Hell-as-everlasting-torment would be a permanent, running sore in the body of the universe, a constant testimony to God's vindictiveness. After all, the sufferings of the damned in hell would not—on this view—do them any good. These sufferings wouldn't do anyone else any good, either. Punishment for its own sake is valueless. Their only imaginable purpose would be to satisfy a desire for vengeance putatively experienced by God or by their fellow creatures. But a desire for vengeance is both irrational and incompatible with the love we see revealed in Jesus; God can hardly be thought to encourage it, and enjoying the sufferings of the damned can hardly be thought a sign of spiritual maturity on the part of sentient creatures. It is difficult to see how one could adhere to the Golden Rule and the Pauline Principle while willing that one's neighbor be subjected to everlasting torment. So Christians cannot credibly affirm the reality of hell,[1] even if they recognize the possibility that someone might so turn in upon herself that she would finally shrivel out of existence.[2]

---

1. Cp. Hick, *Evil* 341: "The sufferings of the damned in hell, since they are interminable, can never lead to any constructive end beyond themselves and are thus the very type of ultimately wasted and pointless anguish. Indeed misery which is eternal and therefore infinite would constitute the largest part of the problem of evil."

2. Cp. Swinburne, Lewis.

F. W. Faber expressed a vision of God's love that makes clear how deficient belief in hell really is in a familiar hymn some of whose words bear repeating:

> Was there ever kindest shepherd
>   Half so gentle, half so sweet
> As the Saviour who would have us
>   Come and gather round His Feet?
> It is God: His love looks mighty,
>   But is mightier than it seems:
> 'Tis our Father: and His fondness
>   Goes far out beyond our dreams.
> There's a wideness in God's mercy,
>   Like the wideness of the sea:
> There's a kindness in his justice,
>   Which is more than liberty.
> There is no place where earth's sorrows
>   Are more felt than up in heaven;
> There is no place where earth's failings
>   Have such kindly judgment given.
>
> . . . .
>
> There is grace enough for thousands
>   Of new worlds as great as this;
> There is room for fresh creations
>   In that upper home of bliss.
> For the love of God is broader
>   Than the measure of man's mind;
> And the Heart of the Eternal
>   Is most wonderfully kind.
> But we make His love too narrow
>   By the false limits of our own;
> And we magnify His strictness
>   With a zeal He will not own.
>
> . . . .
>
> If our love were but more simple,
>   We should take Him at His word;
> And our lives would be all sunshine
>   In the sweetness of our Lord.[1]

As saving love, love expressed in redemption and transformation, God's love "bears all things." As Faber observes, God's "love looks mighty, / But is mightier than it seems." The ultimate power is the power of love, for only this power can achieve its goals by bringing about a free response. God's victory is so inspiring because it is the victory, not of coercive power but of unconditional love.

Love and Double Predestination

In this chapter, I have attempted to articulate a consistent view of God's response to the human problem that takes seriously both the unconditional divine love that is the presupposition and center of this book and the reality of human brokenness. But the approach I take here obviously doesn't represent the only way to understand the implications of belief in divine love. Not all Christians, obviously, would agree that God's power is persuasive rather than coercive. I want briefly to consider one aspect of an alternative position.

---

1. Frederick William Faber, "Come to Jesus," *Hymns*, 1st. American ed. (Baltimore: Murphy 1880) 342-4.

This alternative position focuses on divine freedom and sovereignty. Like the one I have sought to work out, it stresses the complete graciousness of God's accepting love. But it roots that love in God's arbitrary will rather than, as here, God's essential goodness. The aspect of this position to which I want to attend is the doctrine of double predestination—the view that it is *completely a matter of God's free decision* that some people accept divine acceptance and others reject it; that some grow in love and others in depravity; that some experience everlasting life in heaven, others in hell.

It is important to stress that this view has its origins in the idea of divine love. Belief in predestination is a reflection of the conviction that divine love is sturdily objective in much the way I have suggested it is—not contingent on any aspect of our performance.

The believer in double predestination is convinced that she has been grasped by a love that precedes her own and which conditions, undergirds, and elicits her response. Love comes first. Building on the experience of being overwhelmed by love, the predestinarian goes on to deduce a set of conclusions. Given that she has been saved without her own involvement, everyone who is saved must be saved in the same way. But some people will not be saved, goes the argument. This cannot be because of their own choices, for our choices do not determine whether or not we are grasped by God's love—God's choices determine this. Thus, on this view, it is God who must determine who is and who is not ultimately saved. God's selection of both the saved and the damned is the substance of the doctrine of "double predestination."

A stress on divine sovereignty like that found in the doctrine of double predestination can be seen as a desire to affirm that God's love is undefeated. This doctrine expresses the confidence that we can depend on God's love.

But belief in double predestination may also seem troublingly inconsistent with the belief that God calls us to love others as ourselves. For it is hard to see how God could call us to love them equally with ourselves while destining some for damnation and some for endless bliss on the basis of an unfettered choice made by the divine will. And it is hard, too, to imagine how we could consistently love others as ourselves while willing that they be damned if God has decided that they should be.[1] It is also hard to believe in double predestination while loving God wholeheartedly: it will be difficult to avoid resenting God for choosing to damn oneself or others whom one loves simply because God wills to do so. In addition, the *implications* of this belief make it hard to square with belief in divine love. The very love that is said to lie at the heart of the believer's salvation seems also to be responsible for the unbeliever's damnation. Can God truly be said *lovingly* to will that someone spend an eternity apart from the divine love—in torment?

Christians who have stressed divine sovereignty have sensed the problem here, and have tended to respond in one of two ways. They have either maintained that God's status as creator and God's absolute authority make critical evaluation of divine action improper and impossible, or that predestining some people to damnation is justifiable because it serves God's glory.

Neither of these arguments seems to me to be persuasive. It is not on alien philosophical premises that many Christians have been driven to question belief in double predestination, but on the basis of the picture of divine love found in the Bible, the subsequent Christian tradition, and Christian experience. The inconsistency between the claim that God is love and the claim that God chooses to damn some persons is not the creation of rationalist critics. It is a tension generated by Christian belief itself. It is possible to refuse the challenge posed belief in God as love only at the cost of evacuating content from belief in divine love. The

---

1. Thanks, again, as above, to Thomas Talbott for helping me to see this point.

positive argument that the divine glory is served by predestining some persons to damnation fails to evoke conviction both because it is unclear *how* God's glory might be served in this way and because, even if it were, the pursuit of divine glory at the expense of creature's ultimate damnation seems to make God a cosmic narcissist unworthy of worship. Such defenses of double predestination do not effectively meet the obvious challenge posed to the doctrine by the conviction that God is love. They grant the apparent conflict while seeking to mitigate it by denying its relevance or offering a justification for God's unloving behavior. They do not render belief in double predestination plausible.

It is possible to offer at least two alternate accounts of the role of divine love in salvation that do not encounter the same difficulties as does belief in double predestination. The first is the *universalist* option.[1] Universalist Christians would simply deny the assumption that some persons will be damned. A universalist proponent of belief in absolute divine sovereignty could identify God as the sole source of salvation, but maintain that precisely for this reason God can and will save everyone. But this sort of *a priori* universalism seems at least open to question precisely from the perspective of divine love. Suppose someone's being saved involves that person's choosing to respond in trust and love to God. If God is to determine unilaterally that this person will be saved, God must be able to determine unilaterally what this person's choices will be. It is hard, in this case, not to escape the conclusion that God must be in the business of determining people's' choices generally. And this picture of God as all-determining seems to pose multiple problems.

If God were absolutely sovereign, as *a priori* universalism requires, God would be responsible in detail for all the evil choices, all the choices with harmful consequences, made by free creatures, even if not for the evil of some people's being damned (as well, presumably, as the physical accidents and disasters responsible for so much suffering). It is hard to square this kind of responsibility for evil with authentic love: a god who causes the world's evils does not seem very loving. Further, the possibility of love between God and creatures seems to presuppose the existence of genuine freedom on the part of creatures, and the kind of absolute sovereignty required to make *a priori* universalism work is evidently inconsistent with the existence of this kind of freedom. So *a priori* universalism is undercut precisely by the belief in divine love that prompts it in the first place.

The other option, the one I have taken here, seems the more consistent one: God's love *does* precede, shape, and elicit our own loving responses to God's acceptance and activity in our lives. But it does so without overriding our freedom and by making us more, not less, free. This means that God woos each of us passionately and unceasingly. It also means, however, that God cannot *guarantee* at any given time that any of us will respond as God desires. As long as we are free, we are free to disappoint our creator.

If this view is to be compatible with belief in unconditional divine love, however, it is important that it be freed from association with the assumption that there is or can be any arbitrary point at which divine love says "enough." God must be supposed to continue wooing any potentially or actually conscious, choosing subject who has not constructed a character permanently impervious to divine love (if, indeed, it is *possible* to construct such a character). If God simply elected to stop seeking to win a recalcitrant person while that person still had the capacity to repent, divine love would be called into question.

With this qualifier, belief in a loving divine work on our behalf that does not override creaturely freedom but that never gives up can do justice to the sense of

---

1. Paul Griffiths offers a useful analysis of universalism and restrictivism in *Problems of Religious Diversity*, Exploring the Philosophy of Religion 1 (Oxford: Blackwell 2001) 161-8. See also Fritz Guy, "How Inclusive is Our Hope" *Spectrum* 33 (Spring 2005): 16-25.

being grasped by God's love that so many Christians report without implying that their freedom is thereby suspended. Thus, it can affirm the universality of God's love against the double predestinarian insistence on its limited character. And it can avoid the *a priori* universalist assumption that God can *compel* even the resolutely impenitent to accept divine acceptance—an assumption that is arguably inconsistent with belief in divine love. At the same time, it can allow for the possibility than an ever-wooing divine love might successfully win the love of all created being without offering any guarantee of this obviously desirable outcome.

Ideally, at least, that divine love is put on display in the church. It is to this community that I turn in Chapter 11.

11

A Loving and Beloved Community

The Christian church is a community of love.[1] It is grounded in God's love, manifested in the love of Jesus. Its life as a community is characterized by a commitment to love. It acknowledges and celebrates God's love. And God calls it to mediate divine love not only to its members but to the whole world.

The church originated in the inclusive, loving community that surrounded Jesus during his ministry. While the church helps to convey God's love, it would be inconsistent with the original vision of that community and with the church's identity as universal and inclusive to regard the church as the exclusive mediator of God's love, or the truth about that love, to humanity. God's Spirit works in the church, but also challenges it and opposes it.

The church's calling is to proclaim and embody love. It does so in its teaching and in its worship. The sacraments it administers are best seen as mediating and embodying love. And, in modeling divine love, it constitutes a loving counter-culture that with the potential to offer a tangible alternative to the subordination and exploitation evident throughout society. Its institutional structure enables it to preserve, develop, and transmit Christianity as a cultural tradition. Though often derided, Christian subcultures can be nurturant and supportive environments in which people can learn that they are loved and in which they can learn to love. But the church is also called to mediate God's healing love to the rest of God's world.

Love in doctrine and practice is, or should be, the distinctive mark of the church. And this means, in particular, that—in continuity with the community founded by Jesus—the church must be inclusive. Though it is reasonable for the church to commend its beliefs in dialogue with others, it must do so in a manner consistent with the recognition that its inclusiveness represents and reflects a divine love that embraces all of humanity and is active throughout creation. Loving the church itself can be a challenge, albeit one that can be understood and accepted in light of the church's own convictions.

Rooted in Love

The Christian community originated with the community that surrounded Jesus during his teaching ministry. Jesus deliberately extended hospitality, signified by table fellowship, to people without regard to social status, ethnicity, or gender. He embraced people his peers regarded as "bad" as well as those they thought of as "good." And he made it clear that he was extending *God's* love to all these people.

---

1. Martin Luther King, Jr., famously articulated a powerful vision of the "beloved community" (he owed the term to Josiah Royce); see Kenneth L. Smith and Ira G. Zepp, Jr., *Search for the Beloved Community: The Thinking of Martin Luther King, Jr.* (Valley Forge, PA: Judson 1974).

Jesus rejected a politics of holiness—a politics of separation from non-Jews and from Jews who weren't properly observant.[1] He made it clear that insiders, good people, God's chosen, don't need to define who they are by identifying themselves over against bad people, outsiders, the reprobate. In place of a politics of holiness, he offered a politics of compassion: a vision of an inclusive community in which all are loved by God and by each other.

Jesus was not offering an alternative *to* Judaism, as if Jewish faith and the politics of holiness were somehow synonymous. A faithful Jew, he was staking a claim to a particular kind of position *within* Judaism, a position which emphasized the value of inclusion.

A vision of inclusive community seems to have played a significant role in the growth of the early church. For Jews and Gentiles alike, the notion of a community from which artificial barriers to friendship were being eradicated was immensely attractive. Breaking down barriers through God's love lay at the center of Paul's gospel. His concern for community is apparent not only in the practical advice that permeates his letters, but in his explicitly doctrinal writing as well. The humility of Jesus should serve as a model for relationships within his churches, relationships marked by compassion, sympathy, and unity.[2] Spiritual gifts are designed to serve the community, and no gift is more important than love.[3] Traditional dividing walls no longer matter: "There is no longer Jew or Greek, there is no longer slave or free, there is no longer male and female; for all of you are one in Christ Jesus. And if you belong to Christ, then you are Abraham's offspring, heirs according to the promise."[4]

The Epistle to the Ephesians contains one of the most dramatic claims about community in the Newer Testament: "the mystery of Christ" is precisely that "the Gentiles have become fellow heirs [with Jews], members of the same body, and sharers in the promise in Christ Jesus through the gospel."[5] Jesus "is our peace; in his flesh he has made both groups into one and has broken down the dividing wall, that is, the hostility between us."[6] His purpose was to "create in himself one new humanity in place of the two, thus making peace, and . . . [to] reconcile both groups to God in one body through the cross, thus putting to death that hostility through it."[7] Similarly concerned with community, James rejects class divisions among Christians.[8] And for 1 John, love within the Christian community mirrors God's love and is the decisive test of a Christian's sincerity.[9]

Early Christian communities were known for their acceptance of slaves and women—often scorned by the free males who dominated the ancient Mediterranean world. Their contemporaries observed—with varying kinds of reactions—their ability to sit light to traditional distinctions based on nationality and their commitment to caring for the poor and the sick inside and outside their community. The Newer Testament writings give direct and indirect evidence of ongoing conflicts within the early church, as do accounts of the church's first centuries by insiders and outsiders alike. But it was still possible for someone observing the behavior of the first Christians to marvel: "See how they love one another."

1. On the politics of holiness, see Marcus J. Borg, *Conflict, Holiness, and Politics in the Teachings of Jesus* (Harrisburg, PA: TPI 1998).
2. Phil. 2:1-11.
3. 1 Cor. 12-13.
4. Gal. 3:28-9.
5. Eph. 3:4, 6.
6. Eph. 2:14.
7. Eph. 2:15b-16.
8. Jas. 5:1-6; cp. Pedrito U. Maynard-Reid, *Poverty and Wealth in James* (Maryknoll, NY: Orbis 1987).
9. 1 Jn 1:4-5; 3:11-21; 4:7-21.

The establishment of Christianity in Europe under Constantine and his successors was a mixed blessing. It has reasonably been criticized as fostering the growth of an authoritarian hierarchy within the church and as involving Christians in the abuses of the Empire. But despite the obvious ambiguities associated with it, I believe the church's acceptance of official status can be seen as at least in part a reflection of its commitment to love. If living God's love means accepting people without barriers and boundaries, then it surely made sense to embrace as many people as possible within the Christian community, even if some of those people weren't yet as serious about the call to love God and each other as they should have been. At least, once within the church's orbit, they could be affected by the good news of God's love. The Christian community could nurture them as they grew into more loving persons. And official status also meant the opportunity to exert a direct effect on the policies and politics of the Empire, to see that it more fully answered the call to love.

Renewal movements during the course of the church's history can in many cases be understood as centered on the good news of love. Of course, monasticism sought to provide new opportunities for the focused, disciplined love of God. But some forms of monasticism also sought to create richer and deeper forms of Christian community; thus, it is hardly surprising that mediæval monks produced classic works on the theme of friendship.[1] And, of course, When the Franciscans challenged materialism and complacency and urged service to the poor they, too, were encouraging a recovery of a vision of love as central to the church's identity. Martin Luther's proclamation of divine acceptance was a reminder of what it means to take God's accepting love seriously. John Wesley's Methodists formed small groups for mutual correction and discipline, to be sure, but rich and intense experiences of community must also have made these groups attractive. Today's liberation theologies, in Latin America, South Africa, East Asia and elsewhere, can be seen as attempts to gain a new sense of what it might mean to envision and work for truly loving communities from which violence and domination are absent.

This kind of impressionistic survey is hardly serious historiography. But it highlights, I hope, the way in which love has played a key role in shaping the church and driving its development. The Christian community exists because Jesus' contemporaries and successors caught a vision of divine and human love.

The Church, Jesus, and God's Spirit

The church is rooted in God's love, but it is not the *custodian* of God's love. God's love for us is in no way dependent on what the church does. This is a key insight underlying Christian belief in "the priesthood of all believers."

Sometimes contemporary Christians, like the author of the Epistle to the Hebrews, speak of Jesus as our high priest. The language of priesthood may seem odd to us now, since we don't function from day to day in the context of a system of sacrifices in which specially selected people perform ritual acts that are perceived to shape our relationship with God. But to speak of Jesus in this way isn't meaningless. Indeed, the absence of priests from our lives points quite precisely to its meaning. To say that Jesus is our "high priest" is to say that ritual sacrifices are neither necessary nor sufficient to heal our broken relationships with God and each other and that *mediation* between God and humankind is pointless.[2]

---

1. See Aelred of Rievaulx, *Spiritual Friendship*, trans. Mary Eugenia Laker, intro. Douglass Roby (Kalamazoo, MI: Cistercian 1977); Brian Patrick McGuire, *Friendship and Community: The Monastic Experience, 350-1250* (Kalamazoo, MI: Cistercian 1988).
2. I owe this point to John R. Jones.

Jesus emphasized the love at the heart of the universe. He stressed God's concern for particular persons, each of whom is free to approach God in prayer. A key feature of Jesus' ministry was precisely his opposition to anyone's claim to serve as a "broker" of religious authority or truth.[1] God's love isn't anyone's possession. Thus, the acceptance and healing experienced in the church are God's acceptance and healing, not the church's. And the church owes its existence to the ministry of Jesus. It is an outgrowth of the community he founded during his ministry. And it lives daily by the gracious divine acceptance he offered and embodied. The church has no independent religious status or authority. It depends upon the loving activity of the God whose love we meet in Jesus of Nazareth.

To speak of Jesus as high priest is thus to emphasize these facts in contrast to any claim on behalf of the independent authority of a human priesthood or any other church authority.[2] We need the church, to be sure. But we do not need it as a source of brokered access to God. We need no mediators. God has shown us that decisively in Jesus. There is no dividing wall to be overcome. God is with us. God loves us.

While divine love is not the church's property, God's Spirit can mediate divine love to and through the church. The decisive event of divine revelation is Jesus of Nazareth. That revelation is remembered in the church, and it forms the center of the church's self-identifying narrative. Consequently, the church is a community in whose formation God's Spirit's work may be discerned, and whose ongoing life God's Spirit facilitates and undergirds.

It is therefore also true, however, that the church is a community constantly *in tension* with God's Spirit. God's Spirit is, we may suppose, constantly at work to enable the church to receive and transmit more and more of God's self-disclosure. It is the church's inherent limitations, not God's Spirit's, that prevent the church from appropriating God's self-communication more effectively. Revelation involves the impartation of something new; if it didn't, it wouldn't be revelation at all, but only rehearsal. Like most individual human beings, institutions are typically inclined to prefer the security offered by the *status quo*. They resist the new, opting for rehearsal over revelation. God's Spirit is thus the church's beloved Enemy, constantly challenging its assumptions, its patterns of belief and behavior, in order to grant it the grace-ful newness of God's ongoing self-disclosure, challenging it to accept and convey God's love in new ways.

Love as the Church's Calling

The church is brought into being through God's love. In turn, it is called to love.[3] The *chosenness* of the church does not mean that God has picked it to receive some divine self-disclosure that God has withheld from others, or that God loves Christians more than God loves anyone else. Rather, it means that the church is part of a stream of history that has provided God with distinctive opportunities for communicating with humankind. The church responds to this chosenness by embracing and communicating about God's love. The church can

---

1. So John Dominic Crossan, *The Historical Jesus: The Life of a Mediterranean Jewish Peasant* (San Francisco: Harper 1991) 225-426.
2. I owe this point to John R. Jones.
3. The notion of calling provides one way of making sense of traditional descriptions of the church as "holy" when it so obviously is not morally perfect. According to J. N. D. Kelly, *Early Christian Creeds*, 3d. ed. (London: Longman 1972), the "Church is described as holy in the creed because it has been chosen by God, because He has predestined it to a glorious inheritance, and because He dwells in it in the Person of the Holy Spirit" (159).

and should make no claims to perfection. What it says about God's love and the way it lives God's love are both far from faultless. But it believes that the good news that God is love and that we are called and enabled to love in the life of the church as a result of God's revelation in Jesus is worth sharing with its members and with the whole world.

The church's concrete response to God's call takes a variety of forms. For instance: by teaching people to read their experience of the world Christianly; by offering them a context within they can work out responses to moral challenges; and by supporting them in their efforts to live flourishing, responsible lives, the church can assist them in accepting God's acceptance, in loving God's good creation, and in loving themselves as finite but valuable parts of that creation.

The church loves God, all creation, and itself in part by being a community of memory. The church remembers God's action in creation and history, and thus responds to God in gratitude and delight. It remembers not only the good things about its own history but also the embarrassing ones: the abuses for which it has been responsible, and the ways in which God has forced it to hear what it did not want to hear by speaking to it through sensitive persons outside its boundaries who saw truths from which it wished to hide and who ventured into places from which it chose to absent itself. In this way, it learns to love better, finding insight to help guide the continuing lives of its members, and equipping and challenging them to love more thoroughly.

Worship as Love's Work

One of the ways it does this is in and through worship. In worship, we are not passive spectators. Worship is part of the corporate work of the church and the individual work of the Christian. In worship, we not only observe, we act.[1] We do not simply reflect on and celebrate God's love in the past; rather, we experience and participate in God's love now.

The fact that we choose to worship at all is a deeply significant act. It expresses our conviction that the world is bigger than our minuscule niche of the cosmos, that we cannot live fulfilled and flourishing human lives simply by attending to the everyday and the ordinary without placing them in the broadest possible context. It reflects our realization that our lives need not be fragmented collections of random elements, but that they can find a unifying, integrating center—and that this center is to be found as we attend to a Christian vision of God's love.

Within our worship, we act—and love—partly by remembering.[2] In preaching, the Christian story is re-told, and the Christian understanding of God and God's world is elaborated. Thus, worshippers are enabled to discern more clearly what God is up to in the world and what the remembering community *stands for*, in light of the remembered—and ongoing—history that gives meaning to the church's existence.

In worship, we "re-enter" the world depicted in the Christian story. Of course, if that story is true, we have in fact been there all along. But we need reminding of its contours. Worship provides us with language, symbols (including

---

1. Cp. Charles Teel, Jr., "What is Church?" *Scope* (Nov.-Dec. 1978): 12-7.
2. See Nicholas P. Wolterstorff, "The Remembrance of Things (Not) Past: Philosophical Reflections on Christian Liturgy," *Christian Philosophy*, ed. Thomas P. Flint, U of Notre Dame Studies in the Philosophy of Religion 6 (Notre Dame, IN: U of Notre Dame P 1990) 118-61; William H. Willimon, *Worship as Pastoral Care* (Nashville: Abingdon 1979); William H. Willimon, *The Service of God: How Worship and Ethics are Related*, illus. Bruce Sayre (Nashville: Abingdon 1983); Gwen Kennedy Neville and John H. Westerhoff, III, *Learning through Liturgy* (New York: Seabury 1978).

symbolic practices), and metaphors we can use to make sense of our world.[1] These symbols in turn expand our imaginations, enabling us to envision new possibilities. Worship is not simply a rich resource for Christian living, though it is that; worship itself is an integral part of Christian living.[2] In it, we experience God's love and the love of others, and we offer our love to God, our community, our friends, and our world.

Unless Christian convictions find expression in worship, the Christian community begins to lose its distinctive identity. Thus, "all Christian doctrinal belief is worshipping belief."[3] So worship must be among the formal concerns of the institutional church. Of course, differently situated groups of Christians can and must express their uniqueness in and through their choices regarding worship style. At the same time, however, Christianity is not infinitely pliable. Not every practice is compatible with Christian convictions. And Christianity is not simply an abstract set of ideas, capable of being embodied in any conceivable social form. It is essentially socially embodied; its social form is crucial to its identity. So forms of worship, while they can and should vary, are not simply matters of indifference.[4]

Love We Can Touch

The sermon is by no means the only way in which the good news of God's love is announced and enacted. It is simply one part of Christian worship—and for many people hardly the most important. Christian worship comprises a variety of ritual and symbolic acts. For someone who does not find in the operation of the discursive intellect the route to religious formation, these symbols may bring home the meaning of the Christian story in a way in which no sermon could.[5] And those who have heard that story repeatedly may find in Christian symbols and rituals a richness and evocative power that sustains them even in dry spells when the recital of the Christian narrative on its own fails to move them.

Love feels most real when we can touch it. The symbols and rituals and practices of the Christian community help us to sense God's love in our world more clearly by representing and mediating it *tangibly*. The Christian sacraments are centrally important ways in which we experience and convey God's love with our bodies.

In the broadest sense, a sacrament is a this-worldly reality that mediates, focuses, or brings to expression God's love. God can be encountered everywhere—not just in church, and certainly not just in the "official" sacraments of the church. Anything has the potential to be a sacrament, though some things will obviously tend to inhibit rather than facilitate our encounters with God through them. The sacraments explicitly acknowledged by the Christian churches are important because of their evocative power, their ability to confront us with our status as parts of God's good creation in especially effective ways.

It is not surprising that all the major Christian denominations have agreed on the importance of baptism and holy communion as Christian sacraments. More than any others, these sacraments serve to create and sustain the Christian

---

1. I quote almost directly here from Willimon, *Service* 56.
2. I am dependent for this paragraph on the insights afforded in Willimon, *Service* 38-72.
3. Stephen Sykes, *The Essence of Christianity: Theologians and the Essence of Christianity from Schleiermacher to Barth* (Philadelphia: Fortress 1984) 278.
4. Sykes 284.
5. See Stanley Hauerwas, *The Peaceable Kingdom: A Primer in Christian Ethics* (London: SCM 1983) 106-11; cp. 26: "Because the Christian story is an enacted story, liturgy is probably a much more important resource than are doctrines or creeds for helping us to hear, tell, and live the story of God."

community. In baptism, our bodies are bathed in God's loving acceptance. Baptism signals one's initiation into the community that is the universal church (it may also—though it need not—be associated coincidentally with one's decision to join a particular branch of the Christian church). In baptism, we are identified with Jesus, and so with the God who loves and to be people committed to love.[1] In the communion service, we unite in love through our shared meal with God and with each other. We seek to experience ourselves as a single, loving body. The communion service re-invigorates our awareness of the unity in God's love that makes us a community—and that unites us in community with those who cannot partake of this or any other food. It also recalls the importance of God's self-gift to and for us.[2]

Some Christians believe that other relationships, events, or activities—marriage, say, or Christian ministry—should be understood as sacraments. There's nothing wrong with this view. Ministry helps to keep the Christian community together, and ministerial service can be a powerful expression of love. Though it need not involve physical contact, ministry definitely makes God's love tangible. Marriage, too, both sustains the wider communities of church and society and represents God's love in each. And, like baptism and communion, marriage can be a thoroughly embodied, tactile experience of God's love. The marriage *ceremony* reminds the bride and groom of the meaning of love. The service inducts them into a community which, by participating in their wedding, commits itself to sustaining the marriage of the new couple and their integration into a network of relationships in which their love can grow and in which it can also become part of a wider love to which it can contribute.[3] An authentically marital *relationship*, marked by unconditional commitment through the ups and downs of life, can express God's unfailing love to us, prompt our spiritual growth, and help to heal our spiritual wounds.[4]

Things, events, relationships, and people can be sacramental whether or not they are parts of worship services, even though the communion service, the central Christian sacrament, is typically an element of worship. In any case, though, aspects of worship quite apart from the communion service are also sacramental. We experience God's love and the love of others more fully, and are opened more completely to others in love, as we engage our bodies in song and recitation. The offering plate reminds us of our status as persons entrusted with God's gifts, gifts that are in need of sharing. We offer our love, our trust, and our worship to God through our gifts as we give offerings,[5] and we give in order to love those whose lives are touched by the church's ministries. The simple business of standing to

---

1. See Willimon, *Service* 95-117.
2. See Willimon, *Service* 118-37.
3. See Willimon, *Service* 158-86.
4. So Judith S. Wallerstein and Sandra Blakeslee, *The Good Marriage: How and Why Love Lasts* (New York: Warner 1995) 91-149. According to Wallerstein and Blakeslee, "[e]very good marriage provides healing. We marry with the hope that our sadnesses will be comforted, that a loving partner will redress the loneliness, rejections, and disappointments of life." However, "the rescue marriage [in particular] fulfills the child's fantasy that the early miseries will be canceled by the happiness of adult life.... The people in successful rescue marriages experience the enormous relief and pleasure in acceptance that the ugly duckling felt; they feel grateful for their rescue every day of their lives" (92). And cp. 239-47; the discussion here of "emotional nurturance" occurs in the context of the authors' analysis of what they label "traditional marriage," but clearly applies to other forms as well. "A good marriage ... is transformative.... [M]en and women come to adulthood unfinished, and over the course of a marriage they change each other profoundly" (334).
5. See Willimon, *Service* 187-204.

sing or kneeling to pray helps to involve our whole bodies, and thus our whole selves, in our response to God. We are loved by God as embodied; our bodies matter to God. We are reminded, because our bodies are involved in worship, that God loves bodies—and that we should, too. Our physical actions in worship keep us in touch with our physical space and, more broadly, the material creation, a key context in which we encounter God.[1] "Christian worship is most alive when it is most fully embodied."[2] Not only the things we do and touch with our bodies, but our bodies themselves, can be sacramental—expressing and mediating God's love.

Emphasizing sacraments understandably makes some people nervous. If we stress ritual, if we emphasize the spiritual importance of what we do or experience, it's possible that we will treat our behavior, our willingness to "go through the motions" of baptism or communion or marriage as a way of getting God to love us or as a substitute for an authentic, personal response to God.

This nervousness is understandable, but unnecessary. We may be tempted to focus on our behavior as a precondition for God's acceptance, but the gospel makes clear that God's love for us isn't dependent on what we do. Properly understood, the sacraments give tangible expression to a divine love that is prior to all our attempts to be good. They should undercut any attempt to base God's acceptance on our behavior precisely because they are about love.

We can be tempted to treat ritual practice as a substitute for authentic personal relationship with God and others. But, again, the sacraments call us precisely to be persons who truly love God and others. We can love and know ourselves loved in their absence, of course. That doesn't change the fact, though, that human beings learn best when their senses are engaged, when their bodies move. When we engage in rituals, we run the risk of ritual*ism*, but that's a risk worth taking because of the way in which the sacraments can help bring God's love home to our hearts and imaginations.

None of the sacraments *enables* God to love us. God *can* encounter and love and heal us in and through ministry and marriage—and in a vast number of other ways. But none is necessary for us to experience God's love in our lives, even though all of them can help to make that love more real. What's important is to avoid turning disagreements over the sacraments into occasions for conflict. The sacraments are effective and powerful precisely as they help us to know ourselves loved and to love in turn. It would be a bitter irony if disputes over these media of divine love made the church less loving.

The Church as Loving Counter-Culture

The church can sometimes best love God's creation by being different. God's Spirit is sometimes able to work with particular effectiveness through the church because of the categories of understanding and the habits adopted by its members. God may be especially successful in nudging members of the church to see and behave in certain ways because of the story they own, the way of interpreting the world and living in it that arises from their corporate identity. At the same time, of course, there may be things God's Spirit wants to say which the church, for whatever reason, cannot hear, but which others can.

God works through the church as one way—not the only way—of loving *this* world. The church is not an alternative to the created world: it is a place in the created world where God has fashioned a history which helps to show the created world how to flourish and which helps to enable it to do so. But despite the

---

1. Marianne H. Micks, *The Future Present: The Phenomenon of Christian Worship* (New York: Seabury 1970) 22-3.
2. Micks 177.

fact that the world is God's creation, a place in which God continues to be present and active, it is a distorted creation. The world is good at root, in principle, potentially—but its goodness is obscured by fragmentation, brokenness, suffering, and self-destructiveness. Inspecting the created order provides us with a lot of insight into the nature of human flourishing and the ways in which God's healing work might proceed. On occasion, though, we can't see any alternatives to the way things seem to be right now. If real change is going to happen, sometimes our horizons will need to be expanded.

How we interpret our situation will depend on the ideas and images and metaphors available to us. Different visions of the world will yield different accounts of what is going on in our experience and how we might respond to it. And we often acquire our visions of the world from our communities. The language, practices, symbols, and concepts that we use to structure our worlds are not our own creations; they come to us from groups of people—often whole societies, though sometimes much smaller groups. They come to us, that is, through tradition—the process of handing things on from one generation to the next.

In addition to habits, attitudes, ideas, and ways of seeing things, a community can give us something else, too: it can put a particular style of life on display. If we want to know how to live good lives, we won't be benefited most by abstract descriptions. We can gain a lot from those, but a community's concrete actualization of a lifestyle arising out of its convictions and practices can help us to see much more clearly the meaning of those convictions and practices. The church can be a kind of laboratory in which the practical import of Christian convictions can be put on display, a place where our society and our whole world can see what it might really mean to love God and each other. What might it mean to relate these particular stories and articulate these particular beliefs? The concrete life of the church ought to help us discern an answer to this question.

Thus, the church serves to preserve the Christian vision of the world and to keep it alive by teaching Christian language, ideas, and practices to new generations of its members (including both those nurtured within it from birth and those who choose to identify with it later in life). And it shows its own members and other communities the significance of its convictions by giving them practical expression in its ongoing life. It communicates God's love, inviting the whole world to experience that love and live it out; thus, it loves not only the world but God as well, insofar as it shares God's love for creation and seeks to help other people love God more effectively. It loves itself, since the style of life it is called to exhibit is no sacrifice, but a better, richer, fuller alternative to the superficiality and materialism of so much of contemporary culture. And so it loves God again, since as its life is enriched, so, too, is that of God, who shares creation's joys.

There are many ways in which the church can love God, the whole world, and itself by being a counter-culture:

• It can model the kind of *respect for women* Christians would like to see exhibited in the world as a whole. Institutionally, this will mean empowering women through ordination. But it will also have subtler ramifications affecting everything from the content of worship services to the content of publications.

• The church can practice the kind of *economic justice* that should characterize each nation and the entire world. It can support the needs of poor people around the globe through income transfers, educational activity, and work for social, political, and cultural change. It can manifest openness about income differences and work to resolve the tensions they create,[1] through such strategies as tithing

---

1. Cp. Wesley Granberg-Michaelson, *A Worldly Spirituality: The Call to Redeem Life on Earth* (San Francisco: Harper 1984).

specifically designed to reduce income inequities in the church.¹ A congregation can offer aid to deprived people in its local community—and work to ensure that the conditions which have led to their deprivation are eliminated. The church at all levels can help its members explore the possibility of a lifestyle marked by a concern for rich experiences of relationship and beauty and truth instead of the addictive acquisition of possessions.

• The church can demonstrate an *inclusiveness* that puts to shame a divided world. It can ensure that Christians find opportunities for full involvement in its corporate life without regard to ethnicity, gender, nationality, class, or sexual orientation. While it may nurture different groups differently, and give them chances to share together with each other in ways that reflect their unique histories, in its worship it can unite its members across all the barriers that divide them.

• The church can be a counter-culture by celebrating the *Sabbath*. In the course of Sabbath worship, we own ourselves as loved and we offer love to others and to ourselves. By resting on the Sabbath, we reject the tyranny of work in our society. And if we celebrate the Sabbath on Saturday, we identify ourselves with not only the Christian community but also the Jewish community. We choose to show our solidarity with the often-oppressed Jewish people (often oppressed, sadly, by us) by worshipping on the day they, too, gather in praise of God.

By resting on the Sabbath, we can counteract our natural tendency to treat performance as the most important thing there is. We have deluded ourselves into believing that production and achievement are of ultimate value. But, on the Sabbath, we can let go of our obsession with accomplishment; we are free to accept our giftedness and that of the entire world.² On the Sabbath, we can rest in celebration of God's love and creation's goodness. We can choose to appreciate rather than to control, to *be* rather than to *have* or to *accomplish*.³

Thus, on the Sabbath we can avoid activities that destroy the good creation—a choice with immediate symbolic and practical significance.⁴ On the Sabbath we can ignore status distinctions based on achievement—and thus relativize their significance throughout the week.⁵ In fact, in Sabbath worship we experience our oneness with each other and our collective and individual equality before God in such a way that we can never take seriously our world's obsession with hierarchy as long as the Sabbath remains a key component of our lives.

• And, as a counter-cultural community, the church can show how *power* is used if the model for the use of human power is the God we see revealed in Jesus, the God of mutuality and equality. Thus, it can involve young people, poor people, women, alienated professionals—all sorts of people conventionally absent from church leadership—in making decisions. In so doing, it will show the wider world the real potential of God's good creation.

---

1. For a related proposal, see Joseph Mesar, "Income-Sharing: A Plan for Economic Justice in the Local Church," *Spectrum* 13.4 (1983): 22-9.

2. See Charles Scriven, *Jubilee of the World: The Sabbath as a Day of Gladness* (Nashville: Southern 1978).

3. Tilden Edwards, *Sabbath Time: Understanding and Practice for Contemporary Christians* (New York: Seabury 1982) 76-7.

4. Cp. Samuele Bacchiocchi, *Divine Rest for Human Restlessness: A Theological Study of the Good News of the Sabbath for Today*, Biblical Perspectives 2 (Berrien Springs, MI: Bacchiocchi 1980) 204-14.

5. So Niels-Erik Andreasen, "Jubilee of Freedom and Equality," *Festival of the Sabbath*, ed. Roy Branson (Takoma Park, MD: Association of Adventist Forums 1985) 97-105.

The Church as Institution

The church loves in part by being an institution. If it is going to continue over time, if it is going to pass on from generation to generation the traditions of belief and practice that shape Christian living, then it must assume a form that allows this transmission to take place. Isolated individuals are incapable, as a rule, of transmitting entire ways of life. Institutions are required if this transmission is to take place.[1] No one's religious experience arises in a vacuum. Even religious revolutionaries—Luther, say, or Wesley—depend on their cultures and contexts for the resources that enable them to understand and articulate their experiences. Cultural resources shape and condition the experiences of even the most innovative person.[2]

And there's nothing wrong with this. We can't begin by pretending that there is some neutral, tradition-free setting or perspective that would enable us to have "pure" religious experience, and then go on to try escaping to that setting or perspective.[3] *All* of our experience is tradition-laden. The right question focuses instead on the best ways to enhance the various tradition-rich contexts that shape Christian living.[4]

The institutional church matters because we are essentially social. I do not mean only that we are instinctively gregarious, that we like each other's company, though we are certainly that. We are social, too, in the sense that social relationships are part of the good life for creatures like us and that our identities overlap with those of others, so that others help to constitute who we are.

We are social, too, in that the ideas, practices, symbols, and metaphors with which we navigate our ways through life are acquired from our communities and cultures and contexts. Each one of us enters—usually at birth—a framework of words, images, and practices that already exists. She learns to understand herself by means of metaphors and analytical descriptions that are already available in her environment when she makes her appearance. We can suppose "that the individual is what he is in abstraction from his community only if we are thinking of him *qua* organism." But we cannot do this if we wish to speak of individuals who are also persons with distinct identities. "The life of a language and culture is one whose locus is larger than that of the individual. . . . The individual possesses . . . identity by participating in this larger life."[5] Our individual characteristics emerge in the course of interpersonal interactions. Indeed, a person's very sense of what it *means* to be a self is socially mediated to her.

The church is a key element in our social formation. It inducts us into the culture constituted by the Christian story and characterized by Christian practices, language, and symbols. This does not mean that it *dominates* us. It is a basic Christian conviction that persons are *agents*, that they exhibit a creativity and a moral freedom that evince an ability to transcend in some measure their histories and environments. The formation of a person's character in the church does not result in her character's taking a shape that strictly determines her choices. Nonetheless, it *qualifies* her agency. It limits and constrains the options available to her.

Thus, the church contributes to the process of moral formation. It fosters the cultivation of love by helping us to develop the habits, the character-traits, required to sustain a life rooted in God's love and oriented toward the love of God's creation. To live seriously within the community that is the church, telling and retelling particular stories, responding to them, and interpreting the world through

---

1. See Nicholas Lash, *Easter in Ordinary: Reflections on Human Experience and the Knowledge of God* (London: SCM 1988) 51-70.
2. Lash 56-7.
3. Cp. Lash 58.
4. Lash 57-8.
5. Charles Taylor, *Hegel and Modern Society* (Cambridge: CUP 1979) 87.

the lenses they provide, requires the formation of particular patterns of behavior—hope, trust, and patience, for instance.[1]

People sometimes maintain that engaging in religious ritual is an alternative to human encounter with God. But God is not an object in the world, a finite *thing* that could occupy a bit of one's field of vision or be crowded out by other things—like liturgical rituals or theological ideas or moral practices or anything else the church might offer. God and the church are not in competition, anymore than God is in competition with any other element of creaturely reality for our attention. We encounter God *in and through* creation, not *apart from* it. Religious practice is one way, and sometimes the most helpful way, of consciously experiencing the God we encounter everywhere. It does not and cannot obscure a tradition-free experience of God, because such an experience is inconceivable and impossible. We cannot pit a pure experience of God, a flight-of-the-alone-to-the-alone, against the experience shaped by our "traditioning" in and through the church.[2]

The church must love the truth, which means, in turn, that it must care about ideas. The systematic exploration and analysis of ideas is another important aspect of the church's institutional life. For some people, its concern with ideas is as problematic as its focus on worship. On the critics' view, religion has to do with feelings, or perhaps behavior. Thinking is very much a secondary phenomenon. But feelings and ideas are themselves *shaped* by ideas. The ways in which particular people feel, and the *meanings* of their feelings, are significantly affected by the ideas that provide the context and occasion for their feeling.[3] And ideas help us to construe the world. We cannot avoid rational discourse about the nature of humanness and the character of human well-being if we are to find out way around the world, if we are to act responsibly and appropriately. The fact that the church is concerned with ideas is a positive, not a negative aspect of its being. Its attention to ideas is essential if it is to facilitate our life in the world.

The church works corporately in ways that enact love. Traditionally, Christians have been enthusiastically involved in health-care, education, and other social service activities. Such activities can't be managed successfully by individuals; lots of people have to be involved, and they need to be organized. Thus, the church has created a wide variety of subsidiary institutions. Like the church itself, these institutions aren't necessary evils. They can do more harm than individuals—but they can also do more good. They expand human capacities for structured action tremendously. So it's only appropriate that the church is involved in the institution-making business.

The fact that there is a church at all is evidence that fulfilled and flourishing human life is not life lived alone. Human life is life together, life in love. But the contemporary West is in large measure bereft of community. Seeking to secure their freedom from oppressive structures, persons during the last three hundred years or so have progressively ensured the emancipation of the human individual from all constraints except "freely chosen" ones—and those imposed by markets and impersonal bureaucracies.

In some ways, this has been a positive development. The freedom enjoyed by so many people reflects their inherent status as parts of God's good creation, as particular objects of God's love. But it is increasingly apparent that this development has also had destructive consequences. Among these is the rootlessness it has engendered. In the quest for freedom, people have been stripped of the histories, the communities, the relationships that provided their ancestors with context, meaning, and support. Of course, some communities and relationships can be

1. Hauerwas 102-6.
2. Lash 60.
3. Lash 60-2.

oppressive. But that doesn't mean that we can get by without communities and relationships altogether. People can't exist for long without meaningful communities; the fact that our society has come to be organized on the assumption that such communities are unnecessary doesn't bode well for its future.

Our economic system discourages love. It fosters an essentially competitive attitude that pits people against each other in impersonal contests to see who can win the rat race. The private, affective life is supposed to be the refuge from the heartless, soulless world of the economy, the place where everyone can truly be herself.[1] But people have been encouraged to flee authentic intimacy because of the contingency and vulnerability we experience when we open ourselves to others in a rapidly changing social environment. And, in the absence of risk, intimacy withers. In fact, our economic system consistently discourages the formation of intimate relationships with individuals and communities. It places a premium on mobility. The smooth functioning of the economic machine depends on the capacity of each part to move wherever the machine demands. But if people are constantly on the move, it will be impossible for anyone to make long-term connections with other people or causes. As long as people obey the dictates of the economic system, accepting its incentives as their own, relationships and communities will be fragmented.[2]

Even when one manages to avoid moving constantly, the sense that one is part of a real community may still be absent. One works in a given place, lives in another, plays in yet another. The only familiar face that one sees from context to context may be one's own, briefly glimpsed in a mirror.

The church can provide people with a communal context that can sustain their identities throughout the rootless flux of contemporary society. It can do this, in part, by providing them with a cosmic context for their lives. By situating their experience within the Christian story, it can give them purpose, meaning, hope, and identity. But it needs to offer more than that. It needs to offer concrete, tangible communities where people can live together and support each other in love.

Concrete Love

Aristotle said that friends live together. There is good reason for some church communities to do so as well. A critical mass of people linked by common convictions, worksites, places of worship, and recreational opportunities can offer each other something truly remarkable, something most people haven't experienced in our culture since the demise of the small town. The Christian Reformed community in Grand Rapids, Michigan, for instance, is an example of the kind of cluster I'm talking about. Such clusters regularly get a bad press. According to their critics, they're inward looking, not socially responsible, restrictive, and sheltered. And these criticisms all have some justification. But I think such communities can be valuable constituents of the Christian response to contemporary rootlessness.

Consider, for instance, the one I know best, the Seventh-day Adventist community in Riverside, California. This community has a distinct identity of its own. It exists because there is, as it were, a center of Adventist gravity in Riverside. The presence of a local church administrative center, a church-run insurance agency, La Sierra University, La Sierra Academy and Elementary School, and a (formerly) church-operated vegetarian food company has meant that a highly concentrated Adventist community exists in the La Sierra region of Riverside. Many Adventists work in La Sierra. But many of them also live there and

---

1. Cp. Christopher Lasch, *Haven in a Heartless World: The Family Besieged* (New York: Norton 1995).
2. See Alvin Toffler, *Future Shock* (New York: Random 1970) 92-107.

worship there. Organizations like the Adventist Ball League, and the easy availability of university and conference office recreation facilities, make it possible for people to do some of their playing locally as well. It is not simply the case that these different aspects of life are integrated in the same place, but that each involves many of the same people as the others in a potentially rich community life. Thus, La Sierra offers Adventists the possibility of integrated community—that is, community that combines the diverse dimensions of human activity—work, play, worship, residence—within itself. It provides people with a context within the central aspects of their lives can be incorporated.

Of course, there's a downside. Like all tight-knit communities, this one has its share of gossip and backbiting. Sensitive souls sometimes feel as if they're living in a fishbowl. There may be inappropriate constraints on the development of genuine individuality. Paternalism may restrict individual freedom. Isolationism or lethargy may prevent some La Sierra Adventists from getting involved in activities that bring them into contact with the wider civic community. Undoubtedly the Riverside-area Adventist community, like all communities, needs improving. But the important thing to note is that it offers people the possibility of a rootedness that can counteract the tendency to personal fragmentation that is evident in the wider society.

Not every Christian congregation can be part of a community as extensive and intensive as the one I have described, nor will this model be appropriate for everyone. Not everyone can find work, for instance, in an environment in which she is proximate to her co-religionists. And adventuresome service is often the work of small groups that can't take large institutions with them when they seek to touch new places with God's love. Some fragmentation will be unavoidable for some people. And, of course, a situation that one person judges to be fragmenting will seem to another like an opportunity to experience greater freedom by insulating different aspects of her life from each other. So I'm not suggesting that the kind of integrated community I've described should be universally emulated. But it provides one model that may be helpful to some groups of Christians.

By creating businesses, educational institutions, and other settings in which people can work and play and learn together, churches create opportunities for bonding and make it possible to display alternate ways of organizing work life and school life. These institutions not only serve to build community, but also help to fulfill the church's countercultural task of displaying the new and exciting possibilities inherent in a style of life that rejects dominance, hierarchy, and aggression. In a variety of ways, then, Christian churches can foster a rich community life that includes residence, work, education, and play as well as worship. Of course, if this kind of community life is truly Christian, it will not be exclusive—it will not discourage those who participate from building relationships outside the church, nor will it deny opportunities for participation to those not otherwise connected with the church. And the very presence of vibrant community may be enough to encourage many of those outside the church to participate.

As it relates the Christian story, the church can also address the problem of community fragmentation by highlighting—in its own life and in its preaching and teaching—the possibility of alternatives to the values that drive people to accept rootlessness and mobility as necessities. The church can challenge the ideal of independence, offering a mutually empowering interdependence in its place. It can deny the unequivocal value of economic growth and movement up the socioeconomic ladder. Instead, it can point—in light of concern not only for personal freedom but also for the state of the environment and the welfare of the world's poor—to the value of "downward mobility." Thus, in addition to fostering community directly, it can challenge features of contemporary society that are inimical to community both inside and outside its own walls.

The Church in the Rest of God's World

The church loves the rest of the world by being the best church it can be. But it also loves the rest of the world by actively involving itself in social, cultural, and political change.

I've talked at some length about the value of community within the church as an alternative to an increasingly chaotic society. But the church is hardly the only community there is. Christians participate in many communities. As a body and through its members—acting in groups or individually—the church works to promote the flourishing of creation through these communities. The church need not—indeed, cannot—dictate to every business enterprise, school, or voluntary society how to do its job. But it can provide informed Christian perspectives on the activities of all such entities by drawing on the skills of Christians with appropriate competencies and assisting them in understanding their work in the light of the Christian story. These Christians can assist the church in articulating coherent responses to educational, industrial, or cultural problems. And they can represent the church in the thick of those problems. They can ensure a Christian presence in every part of contemporary society by being there themselves, and bringing along not only their skills but also their Christian convictions.

"Every part of contemporary society" includes not only private and semi-public institutions like universities and corporations, but also government. Here, too, individual Christians must be involved. The church can most effectively love the world if it touches its community as a whole. Thus, the church must actively seek to make a difference at every level of policy formulation.

The extent to which this is possible will depend on the features of the societies in which the church finds itself. Some societies will provide Christians with no opportunities for political participation. And others will be so committed to values inimical to those of the church that participation in some or all aspects of their political lives would involve Christians unavoidably in support for demonic values. In these cases, the church can model for others in their societies what a style of community life more appropriate to the character of God's good creation might look like. In other, more fortunate, circumstances, Christians will *be*, rather than merely *witnessing to*, policy-makers. In this case, they can appropriately use the opportunities with which they have been presented to promote human welfare in all its dimensions.

Not only individual Christians but also corporate church bodies will sometimes have political responsibilities. I have already referred to the powerful witness a church can present by displaying the possibility of a style of life in community that reflects convictions in stark contrast to those prevailing in the wider society. In addition to this sort of witness, though, there may be times when the church will be required to speak out decisively on some public issue or issues in a way that directly addresses those in power. The Barmen Declaration, framed by Christians in Germany to express their convictions about the Nazi regime, provides a good example. We cannot know in advance what they will be like, but there will certainly be times when the church must speak out decisively, in light of a commitment to love, about some matter of public policy.

LOVE AS THE MARK OF THE TRUE CHURCH

Love makes the church what it is. Not only is it the grateful recipient of God's love, but it is committed to conveying that love to its members and to the world. It is the real, even if imperfect, reality of this commitment that makes the church the church.

The church finds its origin in the community that gathered around Jesus during his ministry in first-century Palestine. Today's church is a direct descendant of that one. Contemporary Christians enact love as piety when they affirm their unity in love not only with their contemporaries but also with Christians past and future. The church is a community of memory that looks back on its history throughout the centuries and finds itself in continuity with people in all eras of history. It recites the Christian story. It repeats Christianity's central rites and practices. And it continues to worship the God decisively revealed in the life of Jesus. In this way, its members are bonded with all Christians from the first followers of Jesus to the present. And they look forward to God's final future when they will realize their union with those from past ages who have shared their hope (and people, of course, who have not, as well).

But in what does the church's continuity over time consist? One popular answer suggests that it consists in continuity of *authority*. On this view, a person has the right to exercise church authority if she or (as is, sadly, far more typical) he has been invested with it by someone else who possesses it legitimately in virtue of having received it from yet another appropriately authorized person, *ad infinitum*. Jesus is supposed to have invested his disciples with church authority, and it is assumed by proponents of this view that it should be possible to trace an unbroken line connecting any properly empowered church authority with Jesus through the apostles.

It is easy to see why continuity was important in the early Christian centuries, when the church was challenged by all sorts of divisions and heresies and continuity in ministry seemed like an important safeguard against chaos. But this view seems to misconstrue the kind of community the church *is*. It's not based on hierarchy or power. In fact, if it's really a continuation of the community founded by Jesus, then central to its self-definition will be a *rejection* of many traditional views of power.

In addition, continuity of ministry doesn't guarantee that the church will tell the Christian story correctly. Its beliefs and practices—the complex of convictions, habits, metaphors, and symbols that characterize the Christian "cultural-linguistic system"—can be sustained and defended by people who haven't been authorized as ministers by others with credentials that link them with the apostles. And it's clearly possible for those who *have* such credentials to forsake the essentials of the Christian heritage.

According to the advocates of another view, church happens wherever the good news of God's love is preached and the sacraments are administered. This view has more going for it. It points to distinct, specifiable practices and (implicitly, through its reference to the announcement of God's love) convictions that identify the church.

There's always the risk, though, that, in making a set of ritual practices into defining marks of the church, we might begin to treat them as if they were necessary and sufficient conditions for us to be loved by God. There's also the problem that different Christian denominations disagree about what the sacraments are. The sacraments *matter*, both as aspects of the church's corporate witness and as means by which it makes God's love tangible for people. But it's important that we recognize that God can act to heal, liberate, and nourish people where these signs are absent, and that we remember that they are rooted in God's unconditional love.

Christian communities differ, too, about how God's love is to be characterized. The church must proclaim that God is love. But it is not enough to assert, in the abstract, "God is love," without giving more content to both "God" and "love." A host of other things Christians want to say provide additional content. Rightly understood and confessed, the things Christians say about love unite today's Christians with Christians of the last two millennia in joyful celebration.

They tell us what it means to say, "God is love," in a Christian context, and they point to the contours of our life in a world that is—like our lives—the gift of a loving creator. Therefore, the proclamation that God is love will be an appropriate identity marker for the presence of the church provided that love is given appropriate content and specificity by means of the Christian convictions that support, clarify, and elaborate it.

There's certainly room for disagreement about what those convictions are. There are different ways in which we can understand God's love. But there also limits to what can count as authentically Christian belief. That's why the church is more than just a body of people who exist now as a result of Christianity's founding events two millennia ago. To identify ourselves as Christian, we need to do more than just make a coherent story out of the events linking the first-century Jesus movement with whatever we would like to count as the church today.[1] Christianity is about the good news of God's love, and there must be some appropriate reference to that good news in a community's convictions if it is to be recognizably Christian.

Of course, doctrinal development takes place. The church changes over time as it confronts new moral and intellectual challenges. But there seem intuitively to be limits that it could not cross without ceasing to be the church. It might be, of course, that it was rationally required to move beyond these boundaries. In that case, though, it would not follow that that the church was now importantly different in some respect than it had been before, but was still the church. Rather, what would follow would be that the community which had been the church was now compelled, for whatever reason, to cease being the church.

The church can remain a community identified by common convictions if it changes within certain parameters. It will face the question of its identity every time it confronts a theological, scientific, philosophical, historical, or moral question. At such a time, it can preserve its identity if it demonstrates that the answer it adopts does is consistent with the belief that God is love and that Jesus decisively discloses God's love.

This view of continuity provides us, in turn, with an understanding of what ought to count as a *doctrine*—that is, as a rule governing the church's confession or practice which serves to sustain its identity—for the Christian community.[2] An affirmation will count as a doctrine—instead of as, say, a moral or theological conviction contingently endorsed by many members of the community—if *denying* it would *falsify* the central conviction that God is love and that God's love is revealed in the life of Jesus.[3]

Of course, it is not enough for the church to *say* the right things. The church can falsify its central conviction *practically* as well as theoretically. When it fails to love in its common life—segregating people by race, or denying women the opportunity to serve as ministers—it denies that it really believes in God's love. When it collaborates with oppressive governments, or simply fails to respond to cultural decay or economic injustice, it denies that it really believes in God's love. A sustained practical denial of God's love by a given Christian group raises the question whether it makes sense to regard the group in question as

---

1. It is, of course, especially so because identity-claims often carry normative force. To say that such-and-such is really the church is usually (though not necessarily) to imply that it deserves a respect and affirmation that other entities that might claim to be the church but aren't do not merit. An insightful exploration of these matters, suggesting that identity resides ultimately in continuity of worship, is Sykes.

2. For this view of doctrine, see Lash 257-66.

3. I am drawing here on Alan Donagan, "Can Anybody in a Post-Christian Culture Rationally Believe the Nicene Creed?" Flint 94-9.

authentically Christian. This hardly means that God's love stops embracing those who deny it. God is faithful even when we are not. But authentic Christian community is a matter of affirming love not only in doctrine but also in practice.

If being a Christian community is incompatible with the effective denial that God is love and that God's love is revealed in Jesus, we have a working criterion for assessing the church's continuity over time. But this criterion can also be used to determine the extent of the Christian community at any given time.

There is, at root, one Christian church. It need not be institutionally united. But it can be identified, nonetheless. It comprises all of those communities that:
- endorse and teach convictions whose affirmation does not entail the denial that God is love and that this love is revealed in Jesus; *and*
- are committed to styles of life in the world that don't practically, effectively deny that God is love, whatever their official affirmations.

Just because the church's confession and practice are what make it authentically Christian doesn't mean that God's accepting love is bestowed only on authentically Christian communities, only where worship happens or certain practices are engaged in or certain beliefs are affirmed. The church believes what it does because it knows no better account of the way things really are, no more satisfactory way of life in the world. Its institutional existence serves to safeguard and propagate beliefs and practices it regards as important. But even where people are not consciously aware of responding in trust, love, worship, fidelity, and dependence to God as identified in the Christian story, God's love is still present and active, and God's Spirit continues to facilitate the reception of God's self-disclosure.

The Inclusiveness of the Loving and Beloved Community

Love seeks to embrace the whole world without borders or barriers. That is the fundamental point of talk about the Christian community as "catholic," or universal. At least potentially, the church includes all people.[1] No one can be excluded from a community rooted in and committed to love because of race, nationality, gender, socioeconomic class, ideological nonconformity, or sexual orientation. More than that, the boundaries of the church are not the same as those of any political community. Apart from the church,

> no other religious community comprehends itself (in theory) as an international society, independent of political regimes and legal codes, including as equal members (in some sense) men, women, and children, without regard to social class and committed to the realization, within this society, of perfect mutual acceptance and cooperative interaction. Even if this has only applied in theory, the sheer theoretical force of this project has had, historically, an immense "deterritorializing" effect in terms of disturbing existing political, social, and legal barriers . . . .[2]

The church's basic impetus toward universality, toward inclusiveness, has made a real difference in the life of the world. But the church is anything but universal in practice. Many people would disavow membership in the church, and others are quite unaware of its existence. Christianity is fragmented by confessional divisions. And, sadly, membership in the same Christian denomination doesn't stop people from subjecting each other to horrific violence—it didn't keep

---

1. Cp. Brian Hebblethwaite, *The Essence of Christianity: A Fresh Look at the Nicene Creed* (London: SPCK 1996) 155.

2. John Milbank, "The End of Dialogue," *Christian Uniqueness Reconsidered: The Myth of a Pluralistic Theology of Religions*, ed. Gavin D'Costa (Maryknoll, NY: Orbis 1990) 179.

Christian Rwandans from different ethnic groups from butchering each other,[1] for instance. So we can't announce the church's universality as an accomplished fact. The church already exists as an international society that has helped to break down many barriers. But many more still exist—too frequently within the church itself. Complete inclusiveness is the church's *hope*. It is the logical outcome of the church's commitment to embracing and embodying God's love.

Inclusive Membership

One practical way of expressing this commitment is through decisions about who is a member of the Christian community. That community is, I have argued, defined by its affirmation that God is love and that this love is revealed in the life of Jesus and by its commitment to living out that conviction in its common life. But one can choose to be a member of the Christian community while differing with the community about its convictions or practices.

The *proclamation* of certain basic convictions is one of the distinguishing marks of the Christian community. So is the *commendation* of certain beliefs and practices. A *group* that did not exhibit these identifying characteristics would not be an authentic part of the Christian community. Someone who taught in opposition to the conviction that God is love or that God's love is revealed in Jesus, or who urged unloving conduct, would not be an appropriate teacher for the community. But the church's expectations of its teaching officers and its members can and should be different. Precisely because the church is committed to being an inclusive community in virtue of the beliefs it affirms, it can and must welcome as members people who are doubtful about those convictions (or their implications) or the church's behavioral commitments, *provided that they nonetheless genuinely wish to identify themselves with the church, knowing that it believes as it does*. Its members must have the freedom to explore convictions and lifestyles within a nurturing spiritual home without fear of censure and reprisal. Precisely because the church is committed to love, it must resist challenges to love in its preaching and teaching, while declining to exclude anyone from membership.

This doesn't mean, of course, that the Christian community should be indifferent to people's beliefs or actions or to the ways in which they commend their beliefs. It can rightly ask of its members that they refrain from advocating their beliefs in combative or disruptive ways. And it can challenge their inappropriate behavior. Members who beat their children, underpay their employees, or betray their partners need the loving concern of their church communities, just like those their behavior has harmed. But the way to express the community's concern with its members' belief and behavior is not to threaten rejection or exclusion. Persistently disruptive behavior may make some limits on members' actions unavoidable (it may be necessary to restrain the member who attempts to commandeer the pulpit at a worship service in order to respond to a sermon, for instance). Nonetheless, the church will be true to its convictions as a community rooted in love only if, even in the midst of heated disagreement, it offers all those who want to belong to it the warmth of God's acceptance.

Universal Love and Denominationalism

Christians can be united in love despite denominational differences. Their common commitment to God's love and its disclosure in the life of Jesus can bond them together even when they disagree about many things. That commitment makes them part of a community serious about inclusiveness, about universality.

---

1. On the Rwanda tragedy, see Philip Gourevitch, *We Wish to Inform You that Tomorrow We Will Be Killed with Our Families: Stories from Rwanda* (New York: Farrar 1998).

But confessional divisions do hamper the effectiveness of the church's witness. They lead to wasteful duplications of effort and to competition between church bodies. And, more importantly, they seem to falsify the church's claim to be a distinctive kind of community in which differences are not canceled, but transcended.

The Jesus movement was an inclusive community. Of course, there was division and discord within the growing church, and factions were perhaps, as St. Paul grudgingly admitted, an unavoidable part of church life. But Christianity's distinction from the wider culture that was its context served up to a point to unify Christians in a mutually supportive defensiveness. Things have changed considerably since the first century. The debates that divide today's numberless Christian denominations are often acrimonious and painful. If the love of Christians for one another is supposed to be evidence for the truth of their convictions, denominational conflicts seem to support the view that those convictions are false.

Of course, differences matter. Ideas have consequences, and people who have ideas can be expected to disagree about them—in fact, they sometimes *ought* to do so. Differences about things like the appropriateness of slavery—which split a number of American churches in the nineteenth century—can't and shouldn't be swept under the rug. Nor am I suggesting that denominational differences are the most important ones the church faces. The "most painful divisions afflicting the church are those based on class, race, and nationality that we have sinfully accepted as written into the nature of things."[1] But, even with these qualifications, the communal barriers between Christians are a problem.

The way forward is not to ignore important differences about genuine questions. Christians need to dialogue—even perhaps to debate—openly about these matters. But they need to do so *within* the sphere of their common confession—that God is love and that this love has been revealed in the life of Jesus. Their disagreements are not wars to the death; they are quarrels among sisters and brothers who own themselves as members of a common family.

Adherence to a particular tradition within Christianity can mean something special even if that tradition is not God's only witness in the world. Recognizing God's work in the rest of the Christian world—not to mention the rest of God's world, *simpliciter*—doesn't mean that a given community doesn't have something unique and important to do. No single tradition can claim to be the sole agent of God's work in the world. But a given tradition within Christianity *can* claim that it has things to say and do that others are not saying or doing. A given tradition within Christianity is worth affirming insofar as its distinctive synthesis of Christian beliefs is important.

A given tradition matters, of course, not just as an abstract synthesis of belief but also as the community that embodies and enacts that synthesis. This community is the context in which the meaning of its distinctive array of beliefs becomes clear. And it can serve as a catalyst for the recognition of the value of this synthesis throughout the Christian community and the wider world. Given the value of a tradition's proposed account of Christian practice and belief, it is responsible for articulating the meaning of that synthesis in relation to the challenges that face human beings today. Without any arrogant assumption of superiority, it can collectively exercise a prophetic ministry that enables it to serve, at least in some instances, as a kind of conscience for the wider communities of which it is a part,[2] with respect to the particular insights it emphasizes.

---

1. Hauerwas 100. See also H. Richard Niebuhr, *The Social Sources of Denominationalism* (New York: Holt 1929).

2. See Jack W. Provonsha, "The Church as a Prophetic Minority," *Pilgrimage of Hope*, ed. Roy Branson (Washington, DC: Association of Adventist Forums 1986) 98-

The flesh-and-blood confessional communities we know may not always seem very well equipped to play this role. The moral ambiguity of their own practice may call into question what they have to say to others. But, insofar as they have valuable insights to offer, they can and should touch the wider world with their unique visions of God's love.

Universal Love and Dialogue across Traditions

God's love embraces the whole world. To the extent that they see identifying with their community as fruitful, productive of healing and wholeness, Christians have reason to commend their beliefs to others;[1] doing so is an appropriate expression of love. On the other hand, the conviction that God's love already embraces the whole world should make Christians confident that God loves and embraces those who are not Christians and that God is present and active in their lives and religious communities.

Thus, commending Christian beliefs is not a way of ensuring that people are accepted by God; it is a way of seeking to enhance the quality of life in God's world. And, even as love for their own heritage must encourage them to affirm and celebrate it, love for otherness must enable Christians to be surprised by the insights others offer. The process of communicating with others about God and the character of God's world can and should result in conversations in which Christians find that they receive new insights from those with whom they are engaged in dialogue. Similarly, appropriate love for themselves must dispose Christians to welcome new insights from others that will enrich their lives.

In this section, I seek to spell out some of my reasons for advancing these claims. I do so in the course of consider a number of questions that naturally arise regarding the enterprise of commending Christian beliefs to others.[2]

- Should we commend Christian convictions to others?
- What is the link between commending Christian beliefs and fostering positive social change?

107; Jack W. Provonsha, *A Remnant in Crisis* (Hagerstown, MD: Review 1993). Cp. Charles Scriven, "The Real Truth about the Remnant," *Spectrum* 17.1 (Oct. 1986): 6-13.

1. Cp. Lash: "... even if all decisions as to how the word 'God' is to be used are decisions taken in respect of particular traditions, is it not arrogant to claim, for any one such tradition, comprehensive or universal validity? ... [T]his may be, and often has been, the case. But I cannot see that it need necessarily be so. We do not, as Christians, own or possess our own rules of discourse and behavior. But in the measure that we are brought, through experience and reflection, to endorse those rules, to acknowledge their use to be authorized and thus, in fact, required, we are thereby brought to acknowledge our responsibility to recommend them to others ..." (264).

2. See Paul Knitter, *No Other Name? A Critical Study of Christian Attitudes toward the Other Religions*, Faith Meets Faith Series (Maryknoll, NY: Orbis 1985); John Hick and Paul Knitter, ed., *The Myth of Christian Uniqueness*, Faith Meets Faith Series (Maryknoll, NY: Orbis 1987); Gavin D'Costa, *Theology and Religious Pluralism*, Signposts in Theology (Oxford: Blackwell 1986); D'Costa, *Uniqueness*; S. Mark Heim, *Salvations: Truth and Difference in Religion* (Maryknoll, NY: Orbis 1995); S. Mark Heim, *The Depth of the Riches: A Trinitarian Theology of Religious Ends* (Grand Rapids: Eerdmans 2001); Marjorie Suchocki, *Divinity and Diversity: A Christian Affirmation of Religious Pluralism* (Nashville, TN: Abingdon 2003); Schubert M. Ogden, *Is There Only One True Religion or Are There Many?* (Dallas, TX: Southern Methodist UP 1995); Paul J. Griffiths, *Problems of Religious Diversity*, Exploring the Philosophy of Religion 1 (Oxford: Blackwell 2001); John Hick, *A Christian Theology of Religions: The Rainbow of Faiths* (Louisville, KY: Westminster/Knox 1995); Joseph A. DiNoia, *The Diversity of Religions: A Christian Perspective* (Washington, DC: Catholic U of America P 1992).

- Does commending Christian convictions mean we should commend not only those convictions but also identification with the church?
- If commending Christian convictions to those outside the Christian community is useful, does this mean that their accepting our beliefs is necessary to their being accepted and healed by God?
- Can we converse meaningfully across the boundaries between traditions? Can we articulate our convictions in ways that can be convincing to those who do not share our assumptions?
- Can we expect to learn anything from conversations across the boundaries between traditions?
- Spiritually and theologically, how should we understand close personal relationships with people who don't share our religious beliefs?

Should We Commend Christian Convictions to Others?

It may seem that we should dialogue with others about our beliefs out of love. Christian beliefs shape love in particular ways that we may regard as important. Piety—love of our tradition—often lies in back of our believing and may incline us to encourage others to accept our convictions. We can love others who differ from us by learning from them, by learning to live with them and love them even when we disagree, and by offering them insights we hope will enrich their lives. But we may also wonder whether it is finally consistent with love to commend Christian beliefs. Doing so may seem paternalistic, intrusive, arrogant, domineering—anything but loving, while love may seem to point toward peaceful coexistence.

So being loving people means being tugged in different directions when we reflect on the possibility of communicating about our beliefs with others. I suggest, however, that while we should recognize that people don't need to accept our beliefs to be embraced by God's love, we should be willing confidently to commend our convictions to them when doing so seems likely to be useful and doesn't appear as if it will be intrusive.

Some people don't believe commending Christian convictions is appropriate because they believe others should be free to make up their own minds without pressure from us. If they adopt Christian convictions, well and good, but, if they don't, their freedom needs to be respected. This position is attractive because freedom matters. And most of us know too much about dogmatic and manipulative evangelistic strategies to deny that sometimes dialoguing about religious issues can take on an ugly color as people are browbeaten into Christian belief. But no one ever makes up her mind in a vacuum.[1] No one starts out with a blank slate and creates her own beliefs from scratch. Community matters. Conversation matters. And no one can avoid depending on others, trusting others, for assistance in making up her mind. That's what, at its best, Christians' engaging in dialogue about their convictions with others can offer: not dogmatic pronouncements, but the opportunity to explore what reading the world through Christian eyes is like and why it is attractive.

Some people may suggest that disagreements about most religious convictions are ultimately insignificant, and that there is therefore no real value in commending Christian convictions to others. In comparison with the similarities between traditions, their disagreements don't matter very much.

---

1. On this, see Charles Scriven, "When the Jailhouse Rocks: A Defense of Evangelism for the Church of Today," *Spectrum* 18.3 (Feb. 1988): 22-8, on which I rely throughout much of what follows.

But this view isn't, finally, persuasive. It's not clear that the major religious traditions of the world *do* in fact center on the same kind of experience, that they *are* all concerned to foster the same kind of behavior, or that they agree about the trajectories and goals of human life. We have good reason to doubt that their differences are as unreal or insignificant as people sometimes seem to suppose.[1]

There are genuine overlaps among traditions, of course. And by no means are all of the different positions taken by various religious traditions contradictory if properly understood. Sometimes, when they seem to conflict, we can conclude that they are actually concerned with different things—about different kinds of experiences, different aspects of reality. Members of different religious communities have a great deal to learn from each other, and it may sometimes be possible to synthesize insights drawn from what may seem initially like wholly alien perspectives in a way that preserves the valuable insights of different traditions.

Sometimes, though, there may be serious disagreements that can't be overcome in this way, and it is this fact which facile, relativistic views may ignore. Where such disagreements are concerned, we have good reason to commend Christian convictions to others if we believe that they are true, that endorsing them can have a significant, positive impact on people's lives, and that people are open to dialogue about them.

I have already argued that we can reasonably judge our beliefs to be true even though we cannot assess them from a standpoint beyond all human experience and tradition. We are free to accept the convictions we inherit from our tradition provided we assess them critically and engage responsibly with challenges to them. And I seek throughout this book to offer reasons for accepting particular Christian beliefs. So I assume here that we can reasonably regard the Christian beliefs I defend in this book as true.

Endorsing Christian beliefs can make a positive difference in the life of a person or community for several reasons. It can enrich understanding; it can transform experience, identity, and self-understanding; it can foster personal healing; it can offer meaning; it can enhance moral and political practice, both individual and societal; and it can commend distinctive goals for human life. That is why engaging in conversation about the claims of different traditions is important (though of course it's not the case that we will always find in the course of dialogue that we've got everything right).

The church can love those who identify with other communities, or with none, by attempting to enrich their understanding of the world and of human life. Understanding our world is inherently valuable. Seeking greater understanding is certainly not the only important human activity, and it need not be the most important. But it *is* meaningful and worthwhile. Thus, offering people insights that help them grasp the character of the world and what is going on in it more clearly can improve their lives. As the church communicates about its beliefs, it can show how convictions Christians and non-Christians share might make sense in light of a Christian vision of the world. It can offer accounts of God, humanity, and the world that show how Christian convictions can effectively integrate data from multiple sources into a persuasive and coherent account of important aspects of human experience and understanding. To the extent that commending Christian convictions improves people's lives, then, it is a worthwhile activity.

Altering one's religious convictions can be disruptive. Engaging in dialogue with others and learning from them can cause changes in one's life that can be

---

1. See William A. Christian, Sr., *Oppositions of Religious Doctrines* (London: Macmillan 1972); William A. Christian, Sr., *Doctrines of Religious Communities* (New Haven: Yale UP 1987) 125-218; Paul J. Griffiths, *An Apology for Apologetics: A Study in the Logic of Interreligious Dialogue*, Faith Meets Faith Series (Maryknoll, NY: Orbis 1991) 45-59.

disturbing, that can unsettle one's identity and fracture important interpersonal and communal relationships. If the only reason for doing so, then, were to increase understanding, dialogue about Christian convictions might be a relatively low priority, something the church might often choose to avoid. But religious convictions matter for experience, identity, healing, meaning, moral and political practice, and the ultimate trajectory of human life in ways that makes dialogue about religious issues a more pressing matter.

The language, images, ritual practices, ideas, metaphors, and symbols that constitute a religious tradition shape a distinctive kind of experience for the members of that tradition. There is no neutral reality called "human experience" that is simply interpreted in different ways by different people. "Christian experience is not the *same* experience as Jewish, or Muslim, or secular experience, differently described, because—in every case—experience is *modified* by the interpretations that we offer, the memories to which we appeal in the stories we tell."[1] The Christian interpretation of existence and the convictions, habits, and symbols that attend this interpretation serve to create a particular kind of experience that is distinctively Christian.

Identification with Christianity (like identification with any other cultural tradition) shapes and reshapes a person's experiences. But it also affects the structure of the person's existence itself—her "intrapsychic structure," the character of "the center from which . . . human experience is organized and unified."[2] Different cultural traditions form different patterns of being—affecting the relationship between conscious and unconscious elements in the mind; the relative significance of various kinds of inputs; the link between reason and emotion, and the tie between agency and both of these features of selfhood; the degree to which the self is an object as well as an agent of reflection; the relative weight given to instinct and reflection; the significance of the past and the future, of memory and anticipation; the degree to which self-transcendence is sought and encouraged; the role of other persons, one's own body, and God;[3] and an indefinite variety of other aspects of the character of experienced selfhood.[4] The great traditions of the so-called axial era—including Hinduism, Buddhism, classical Greek thought, Judaism, and Christianity—all generated distinctive conceptions of the status of the self and of the relationships among the constituents of the self and between the self and the world.

The faith of Israel nourished a sense of individuality marked by moral responsibility to the other and for oneself, with the will understood as the center of existence.[5] Hinduism fostered disidentification of the self with the rational consciousness. Buddhism encouraged the development of a pattern of existence in which what might otherwise be thought of as successive moments of selfhood were not to be identified as elements of a substantial, continuous self and the links between these putative moments were "trivialized."[6] In classical Greece, an ideal emerged in which reason dominated the other elements of the self: the self is identified with its rational aspect, but not, arguably, the others.[7] Christianity generated a model in which "[t]he self became responsible for the choice of the center from which it organized itself and not only for what it chose from a given center." Stepping outside its various elements, this self is "capable of retaining its

---

1. Lash 248-9.
2. John B. Cobb, Jr., *The Structure of Christian Existence* (Philadelphia: Westminster 1967) 143.
3. Cobb, *Structure* 143.
4. Cobb, *Structure* 7-34.
5. Cobb, *Structure* 94-106, 131-3.
6. Cobb, *Structure* 70-2.
7. Cobb, *Structure* 85-93.

transcendent identity and of refusing to identify itself with any other aspect of the psyche." It "is responsible both for what it is and for what it is not, both for what lies in its power and for what lies beyond its power."[1]

The structure of Christian existence I have just outlined is an ideal type, evident in different degrees in different people's lives and certainly not limited to those inside the church.[2] But this structure is, in any case, identifiable as a product of Christian spirituality, teaching, and community. It is, in the nature of the case, unsurpassable by alternatives along the same trajectory, since integral to it is the transcendence by the self of all of the potential elements of selfhood.[3] It can incorporate, while moving beyond, the values of the Socratic selfhood of classical Greece. Reason is crucial, but not the only element appropriately determinative of selfhood: there is more to self-transcending freedom than reason.[4] And the self-transcending freedom Christianity seeks to cultivate is a powerful alternative to the elimination of substantial selfhood encouraged by Buddhism,[5] as well as to the "posthistoric" pattern of existence marked by the dissolution of identity but lacking "the serenity of Buddhist selflessness."[6]

Thus, commending Christian beliefs isn't just a matter of presenting some vaguely interesting theoretical construal of reality; it has the potential to reshape people's experiences, identities, and self-understandings. If Christian convictions are true, it will be important to foster the kind of experience to which those convictions give rise, so commending them will be important and valuable.

Adopting Christian convictions can be a source of personal healing. The good news that God is love; that God is at work in the world, responsive to the needs and circumstances of each creature; that there is hope beyond death—this good news can prove liberating and transformative. Of course, accepting other construals of the world may be pragmatically effective, too. But the healing potential of Christian beliefs certainly gives Christians good reason to commend them to others.

Similarly, Christian convictions can offer people a sense of meaning—a sense that their lives fit coherently into the order of things, that their stories fit intelligibly into an historical narrative, as well as a cosmic narrative within which the historical narrative nests. Commending these beliefs can help people see that their lives make sense, that they're not absurd. The awareness that one has a meaningful life is of great value. There are other narratives, other accounts of terrestrial or cosmic order, which offer that awareness as well. But it is reasonable for Christians to articulate their own vision. Even though there are alternatives to it, some people have embraced none of those alternatives; and, in any case, Christians believe in the truth of their vision and its practical and existential significance, and so in the value of commending it to others.

Commending Christian convictions matters because of their impact on ethics and politics.[7] Moral goodness is not just a matter of preference. So we have to care about moral differences if we take our own moral stance seriously. And there *are* real differences. All major traditions may proscribe murder or theft, for instance, but *what counts* as murder or as theft can vary from tradition to tradition:

---

1. Cobb, *Structure* 123-4.
2. Cobb, *Structure* 139, 142.
3. Cobb, *Structure* 143-4.
4. Cobb, *Structure* 147.
5. See Cobb, *Structure* 148-50; cp. Griffiths, *Apology* 85-108, for an exploration of how inter-faith apologetics might proceed with respect to issues related to selfhood that divide Christians and Buddhists).
6. Cobb, *Structure* 150.
7. See Scriven, "Jailhouse."

Is abortion murder? Is assassination in the service of the revolution murder? Is it tantamount to murder when systemic hunger and high death-rates for certain groups of outcastes are viewed as results of the inevitable and moral laws of the cosmos? Is capitalist profit, the expropriation of private property during collectivization, or uncontrolled usury . . . stealing?[1]

Of course, Judaism and Christianity share a commitment to privileging the perspective of the victim over that of the victimizer,[2] and there are pronounced differences between mainstream Judaism, Christianity, and Buddhism on the one hand and such religious movements as Jim Jones's People's Temple, Aum Shinrikyo, or Heaven's Gate.[3] But, as contemporary Jewish theologian Michael Goldberg notes, even Jews and Christians—with such similar roots and values—don't endorse identical visions of life in the world.[4] And the differences between the Judaism and Christianity and other traditions are more pronounced. Buddhist practice clearly aims at forming a different *kind of life* than that which Christianity seeks to foster.[5] And Islam and Hinduism differ from Christianity and Judaism at key points.

> Only by significantly altering its traditional attitude to sacred law, and therefore its entire received character as a social product, can Islam, for example, bring its treatment of women into line with modern Western, never mind feminist, assumptions . . . . Or again, the abandonment of earlier pro-aristocratic sentiments and the traditional Indian sacralization of untrammeled royal power by modern Hindus has always been accompanied by a significant "ethicization" of their received philosophy under Islamic and Christian influence.[6]

The metaphysical convictions of traditional Hinduism lead to moral beliefs significantly at odds with those affirmed by Christians. The Law of Karma, for instance, which suggests that behavior in past lives causes present circumstances, has obvious consequences for beliefs about the social order: it is easy to see caste position as a product of metaphysical necessity rather than of sedimented social injustice.[7] Hindu thought seems to entail that there is an important sense in which the world of phenomenal experience is illusory and distinctions within it

---

1. Max L. Stackhouse, *Creeds, Society, and Human Rights: A Study in Three Cultures* (Grand Rapids: Eerdmans 1984) 269.
2. See René Girard, *I See Satan Fall Like Lightning*, trans. James G. Williams (Maryknoll, NY: Orbis 2001) 123.
3. Griffiths discusses the latter two movements in *Problems* 146-7.
4. See his *Jews and Christians: Getting Our Stories Straight—The Exodus and the Passion-Resurrection* (Nashville: Abingdon 1985). Goldberg argues plausibly that Judaism tells a particular story to identify God, and Christianity tells another. It's true that the Christian story *includes* the Jewish one. But Christians interpret that story differently than Jews. A Christian identification of God depends on the integration of the Exodus narrative—the preeminent means by which Jews ascertain who God is—and the story of Jesus. For Christians, each narrative will shape the interpretation of the other. For Jews, by contrast, the story of Jesus as understood by Christians appears as a fundamental *misidentification* of God, leading sometimes to alternative personal practices and social strategies.
5. See D'Costa, *Uniqueness*; Heim, *Salvations*; Heim, *Depth*; DiNoia, *Diversity*; Griffiths, *Problems*.
6. Milbank 184. In support of his claim about the modern reshaping of Hinduism, Milbank cites Nirad C. Chaudhuri, *Hinduism* (London: Chatto 1979) 95-8 and Karl H. Potter, *Presuppositions of India's Philosophies* (Westport, CT: Greenwood 1963) 3. He notes that he does "not assume that all traditional Islamic attitudes are necessarily further from feminist goals than some modern Western stances" (184).
7. See Arthur C. Danto, *Mysticism and Morality: Oriental Thought and Moral Philosophy* (New York: Columbia UP 1988 [1972[) 22-45.

ultimately insignificant[1]—a belief that obviously has the potential to cut the nerve of moral action. Thus, in different ways, arguably, a variety of religious and philosophical positions undermine the attempt to take up a morally critical perspective on one's own actions and on social phenomena.[2] Christian convictions, by contrast, can foster the development of this kind of perspective, and are worth commending for this reason.

That we ought to try to change people's beliefs is hard to deny when those beliefs lead to death camps and gas chambers. But we also need to care about beliefs that lead people to devalue women and persons who are ethnically or culturally different from themselves.[3] We need to care about beliefs that lead people to deny that they are parts of God's good creation. If I conceive of the world of sense-experience as ephemeral and deceptive, I may conclude that I need to escape from it to some kind of life beyond time and the senses. My valuation of the world and what happens in it will likely be relatively low. On the other hand, if I judge the world to be God's good creation, and my own temporality and vulnerability as essential to my creaturely experience of a variety of distinctive and important values, then the kind of life I seek to lead will be quite different.

Caring about disagreements regarding these sorts of issues can mean trying, when we judge them important, to change the beliefs with which we disagree. If we don't, "everything will remain the same, and we'll be stuck with the spiritual leadership of the Hollywood producers, the Wall Street brokers, the Pentagon bureaucrats—and all their counterparts across the bleeding earth." But if we do, "we will be able to share with others . . . instead of greed, servanthood; instead of unfairness, justice; instead of infidelity, faithfulness; instead of violence, peace; instead of partnership with the powers that be, partnership with God's power."[4]

There is obviously substantial overlap in the moral and political views of various religious and (overtly) non-religious traditions, and there are many opportunities for building coalitions and occupying common ground. People who more or less identify with various non-Christian traditions—Islam, Judaism, liberalism, Hinduism, Marxism, Buddhism—will often share Christians' discomfort with the Wall Street brokers and the Pentagon bureaucrats. But accepting any tradition characteristically involves both immediate and long-term consequences for our personal and social existence, consequences that distinguish its moral and political vision from those advanced by other traditions.[5] This makes it unlikely that serious representatives of different traditions could adopt *consistently* common positions regarding ethics and politics while retaining their divergent views of reality. The differences between traditions do *not* reduce to the abstractly metaphysical, the irrelevantly historical, or the superficially ritual.

This doesn't mean that Christians have any reason to think that those who disagree with them about moral or political issues are therefore wicked or perverse. It just means that different convictions about the nature of the world and the nature of the self may often have different behavioral implications.

The fact that Christian convictions have behavioral implications which differ from those of the beliefs of other traditions doesn't entail the conclusion that

1. Danto 50-64.
2. So Danto: ". . . [T]he very possibility of morality presupposes the mechanism of the will and the possibility of acting contrary to or deliberately in what takes to be conformity with the world. Exactly that space that Taoism intends to collapse is what makes morality possible at all" (119).
3. Conversations about these matters will doubtless occur within Christian communities as well as between Christians and others.
4. Scriven, "Jailhouse" 27.
5. Stackhouse offers a penetrating analysis of concrete social-ethical differences among religious traditions.

Christians have always been right when they have disagreed with others. Nor does it mean that, if Christians are right about one issue, they must be right about all the others. Christians surely have things to learn from others about moral questions. But where Christians do believe in the correctness of their judgments regarding their convictions, and the significance of these convictions for personal or social life, they have good reason to commend those convictions to others.

To be sure, the church's moral record has been spotty at best. Christians sometimes support the Pentagon bureaucrats. And—since we're focusing here on the activity of commending Christian convictions—offering Christian beliefs to others has sometimes provided cover for colonialism. We can find examples both in Spanish and Portuguese colonial activity in the New World and in the growth of the British empire during the nineteenth century. Christians have too often underwritten exploitative and oppressive colonial policies in the name of encouraging people to identify with the Christian community.

There is, however, no need for the activity of commending Christian convictions to be associated with exploitation and oppression.[1] The Christian story itself contains resources that can ground a Christian response to and rejection of oppressive power. The doctrine of creation implies that human beings are parts of God's good creation, and not simply instruments to be used for the achievement of the ends of others. Jesus modeled an unequivocal rejection of oppressive power. The Golden Rule and the Pauline Principle rule out various kinds of oppressive and abusive acts.

And, of course, Christians who seek to commend their tradition to others have not always supported oppressive powers; clearly, they have also confronted them. Bartolomé de las Casas, who spoke out for Indian rights in Spanish colonial America, is one example.[2] David Livingstone, who fought sickness and the slave trade, is another. And the role of Ana and Fernando Stahl in the empowerment of the Aymara people of Peru's highland has been lauded by anthropologists, sociologists, social activists, politicians, theologians, historians, and others.[3] Inviting people to identify with the Christian community can be associated positively with social change.

Commending Christian convictions may also, in the long run, play an even more fundamental role in fostering resistance against imperialism in at least some settings. For the whole notion that arbitrary power cannot be allowed to expand at will is not one that is universally endorsed. Violent revolution will always be possible, whether or not it is viewed a legitimate in the abstract. But a protest in the name of *justice* depends on the notion that power can, in fact, be limited in a way that transcends its arbitrary exercise. And the notion that power can rightly be constrained in this way is one for which not all cultural traditions provide equal support. Thus, commending Christian beliefs may sometimes bring to oppressed people convictions that enable them to challenge the fundamental legitimacy of their oppressors' actions, convictions which may otherwise be unavailable. For

> the East has no resources within itself to contest[,] as a matter of justice, Western imperial incursions upon its terrain. On the contrary, justice and

---

1. Rodney Stark offers a pointed critique of the notion that mission has been primarily a means of imperialism in *One True God: Historical Consequences of Monotheism* (Princeton: Princeton UP 2001) 104-5.
2. See Gustavo Gutierrez, *Las Casas: In Search of the Poor of Jesus Christ*, trans. Robert Barr (Maryknoll, NY: Orbis 1993).
3. See Charles W. Teel, Jr., "Lake Titicaca to the National Congress," *Spectrum* 25 (Sept. 1995): 3-7; "Revolutionary Missionaries in Peru: Fernando and Ana Stahl," *Spectrum* 18.3 (1988): 50-2; "Missionaries, Visionaries, and Revolutionaries: Logging a Passage in Search of Fernando and Ana Stahl," *Adventist Heritage* 12 (Sum. 1988): 3-14.

the Good are themselves the vehicles of western imperialism, and while this means that they may sometimes, or even always, be construed as the masks of dominant power, ... they can always be invoked against that which is exposed as having no legitimating grounds other than its own arbitrariness. Thus if the West is the great modern poison, it is also the only available cure; nearly all the revolts against the West have been in the name of the West—even Islamic revolution finds this hard to avoid, and Islam is, in any case, strictly speaking, Western. And if this consideration applies to the East, then it applies still more strongly to local societies, which have still fewer inner resources for arriving at norms for relations among cultures.[1]

Religious convictions have differing implications for ethics and politics. Conceptions of the goal or goals of human life vary from religious community to religious community.[2] So it doesn't seem accurate to say that religions share a common goal that can usefully be labeled *human salvation*.[3] Even if Christianity and Buddhism clearly sought an identical ultimate goal for their adherents, the Christian understanding of that goal's meaning and underpinnings would be significantly different from the Buddhist view. Christian beliefs would provide a different setting for it than would Buddhist convictions, and that would make these beliefs worth commending. In fact, however, it is not the case that Christians agree with Buddhists about what *constitutes* salvation, while disagreeing about how to achieve it. Rather, they disagree fundamentally about what the proper trajectory of human life *is*.

Westerners often view Eastern religions as exhibiting uncritical, tolerant, live-and-let-live attitudes. But Buddhists are as clear as Christians that Buddhism and Christianity are not making identical claims and that they direct their adherents along different trajectories. Enryo Inoue is unequivocal in explaining why he "uphold[s] Buddhism and reject[s] Christianity": "I love truth and hate untruth."[4] Phra Khantipalo maintains that "the Buddha's teaching cannot be diluted with others having different goals, or they will be tainted and their value destroyed." While "within Buddhism all other religions can be contained accurately," he maintains, one cannot "fit Buddhism into the range of thought of others without distortions, prunings, abuse or persecution." Non-Buddhist religions point "either in directions opposed [to] Nirvana (materialism, Communism), or, at most, only to the lower heavens gained by good works (and open therefore to the laymen of all religions) or to the higher states of bliss (attainable by the saints of, for instance, Christianity, Hinduism, and Islam."[5] According to a Zen master called Dögen, "the phrase 'the identity of the three religions' [*i.e.*, Buddhism, Taoism, Confucianism] is inferior to the babble of babies. Those who use it are destroyers of Buddhism."[6]

Religious traditions foster movement toward different goals—they're not all designed to equip people for "salvation." "Salvation" is a relatively formal label

---

1. Milbank 186-7.
2. Cp. the helpful discussion of universal religious ends in Griffiths, *Problems* 138-69.
3. See DiNoia, *Diversity* 43-7 and Heim, *Salvations* 71-98 for critiques of the "soteriocentric principle," which treats salvation as the common goal of different religious traditions. Milbank's "The End of Dialogue" is a pointed assessment of the view that different religious traditions share a commitment to particular kinds of social *praxis*.
4. Enryo Inoue, qtd. Masao Abe, "Buddhism and Christianity as a Problem of Today," *Japanese Religion* 3.2 (1963): 21, qtd. DiNoia, *Diversity* 109.
5. Phra Khantipalo, *Tolerance: A Study from Buddhist Sources* (London: Rider 1964) 114-5, qtd. Joseph A. DiNoia, "Pluralist Theology of Religions: Pluralistic or Non-Pluralistic?" D'Costa 122.
6. Dögen, *Shobo-Genzo*, qtd. Khantipalo 36, qtd. DiNoia, "Theology" 120.

for whatever it is that is sought by a particular religious community.[1] Salvation can be conceived of as denoting the dissolution of the self, acceptance in the face of sin, or the conquest of capitalism. It makes no sense to say that different traditions all offer appropriate ways of reaching the same goal if they're not seeking the same goal in the first place. Convinced of the worth of the particular goals their tradition can help people to reach, Christians have good reason to commend beliefs that foster the achievement of these goals. (Again, it needs to be emphasized that this does not imply that people in other traditions cannot be loved, accepted, and healed by God.)

Adopting Christian convictions can make a positive difference in people's lives. Thus commending those convictions can be both an expression of love and a call to love.

Commending Christian Convictions and Fostering Social Change

If Christian convictions matter in significant part because of their social impact, it seems natural to ask about the relationship between commending Christian convictions and fostering social change. Are these activities meaningfully distinguishable aspects of what the church should be doing? Is social change best understood as an adjunct to the really important work of commending Christian beliefs? Is commending Christian convictions just valuable instrumentally because of its contribution to social change?

Explicitly commending Christian beliefs and working directly for positive social change are both clearly appropriate, independently valuable, Christian activities, and they're obviously related. Commending Christian beliefs with others can help to make social change happen in a variety of ways. And since Christian convictions can foster positive social change, bringing about such change clearly provides good reason for commending such beliefs. Similarly, health care, political empowerment, education, and social, economic, and cultural development are all important. And fostering social change in these ways can provide an effective opportunity for commending a Christian vision of God and the world.

While the church should foster social change enthusiastically, it's important to remember the distinctive, specific value of Christian convictions. Of course, these convictions aren't valuable unless they are enacted, unless their significance is concretely displayed in the lives of persons and communities. The point, though, is that ideas matter, and the church cannot become so obsessed with pragmatically achieving certain kinds of results that it forgets the convictions that ground and its identity and give meaning and justification to its existence. If these convictions matter, then it makes sense to encourage others to share them, even if doing lots of other things is important, too.

But it also needs emphasizing that service activities are important in their own right. People deserve food, clothing, shelter, education, health care, transportation, communication, and culture whether or not they choose to identify with the church or not. People should not feel manipulated by Christians' assistance. Fostering human flourishing—whether by eliminating individual or social ills or by enriching human life and developing human culture—is an integral aspect of God's work in the world. Health care, education, musical composition, and political liberation are themselves valuable aspects of God's work in the world. Even though one need not endorse Christian convictions in order to be accepted and healed by God, human welfare can be served when people accept these

---

1. If we are to use the word "salvation" for the universal goals for human existence toward which different religious traditions point people, we will need to define it in formal terms; see Griffiths, *Problems* 138-9.

convictions. But whether or not people adopt Christian beliefs, their welfare is also served when they are educated and healthy.

There are good reasons for Christians to articulate and commend their distinctive convictions. And there are also good reasons for them to foster positive social change, whether or not their activities involve explicitly commending their beliefs or lead to the enlargement of the church.

Does Commending Christian Convictions Entail Inviting People to Join the Church?

Christian beliefs aren't just abstract ideas that people could endorse whatever their relationship with the church. Christian convictions are, in an important sense, *about* the church, and a key reason for Christian theological reflection is to guide the ongoing life of the church. One can hardly accept Christian convictions without taking the church seriously.

It is hard to see how one could come truly to understand Christian beliefs without participation in the Christian community. Christian community life embodies and enacts Christian convictions. Through involvement in the life of the church, people can determine what Christian convictions really mean.

It is harder still to see how, without being immersed in the church, one could develop the distinctive pattern of habits and interpretive skills that enable one to live Christianly. For it is only in the context of a community that one can really learn any set of moral habits or acquire the skills needed to negotiate life's challenges over time. The church does not simply commend a set of ideas or spiritual practices in the abstract. Rather, it embodies them, transmits them, interprets their meaning, and provides its members with the support they need to make Christian convictions and habits their own.

Further, living and working with others enables one to live out one's love more effectively—cooperation enhances one's ability to achieve one's goals. Thus, the church offers people the opportunity to participate in the strand of divine activity in history God initiated in and through the ministry of Jesus. Of course, God the world's transcendent creator, not a tribal deity; divine activity does not occur exclusively or primarily within the walls of the church. But the church does provide God with particular opportunities for action in history. And, where appropriate, it invites others to help make this particular sort of divine action possible by commending its convictions and working to achieve its vocation in the world.

Commending Christian convictions does seem, then, to involve asking people to identify with the Christian community. It can help people to internalize the Christian story, acquire Christian virtues, and participate in its work in the world—thus facilitating God's activity in human history in a distinctive manner.

Encountering God's Love Outside the Church

Engaging in dialogue about religious concerns can be a valuable expression of love. But it is not a means of providing those who do not endorse Christian beliefs with *access* to God's love.

God's love is *God's*, not ours. That means that, when it commends Christian convictions, the church is not *offering* people God's acceptance, even if it *witnesses* to this acceptance. If the life of Jesus is any guide at all to who God is, then human structures do not constrain God's love. It embraces all of creation. And God can love and accept people wherever and whoever they are, whatever their relationship with the church might be. They, in turn, can accept God's acceptance, and apprehend themselves as limited but valuable; thus, they can be "rightly related by faith to the God of Jesus Christ,"[1] whether or not they identify with the Christian church.[2]

Endorsing Christian convictions may enable someone to recognize more clearly God's healing work in her life, and to cooperate with it more effectively. And different settings will affect personal formation and individual choice, as well as societal structure and political ethics, in ways that will advance or retard God's work in people's lives. But having correct beliefs is not a necessary condition for God's healing work in people's lives or for their performance of good acts.

As the creator, whose activity lies at the root of every event and process in the world, God is at work everywhere and in every life.[3] So God can foster spiritual, moral, and personal growth and healing, and insight into the character of reality, outside the church. It is clear—indeed, I think it must be axiomatic—that non-Christians can acquire habits of mind and heart clearly reflective of God's loving influence. The lives of Hindus and Muslims, Jews and secular humanists, can reflect the inspiring, revealing, and transforming love of God. And Christian virtues may be *better* exemplified by non-Christians—Gandhi comes immediately to mind—than by Christians.[4]

What God does in the lives of individual people will obviously affect their communities in diverse ways. Their experiences of God will help to shape their traditions of belief and practice. These traditions will vary in adequacy; none of them—including our own—is flawless. Divine action is mediated action; creatures all too often do not do God's will. So religious communities rarely if ever apprehend flawlessly the truths God seeks to convey to them. But, despite their imperfections, God's Spirit can be present and active in and though them. Thus, we may reasonably speak of a "providential diversity of religions,"[5] of diverse religious traditions as shaped in ways that reflect God's providential activity.[6]

---

1. Griffiths, *Problems* 164; cp. 158.
2. Cp. Germain G. Grisez, *The Way of the Lord Jesus* 1: *Christian Moral Principles* (Chicago: Franciscan Herald 1983) 744.
3. Cp. Griffiths, *Problems* 61.
4. This fact is even admitted by as ardent a proponent of Christian particularity as Stanley Hauerwas. He asserts that "as Christians we may not only find that people who are not Christians manifest God's peace better than we ourselves, but we must demand that they exist. It is to be hoped that such people may provide the conditions for our ability to cooperate with others for securing justice in the world. Such cooperation . . . is a testimony to the fact that God's kingdom is wide indeed. As the church we have no right to determine the boundaries of God's kingdom, for it is our happy task to acknowledge God's power to make his kingdom present in the most surprising places and ways" (101).
5. DiNoia, *Diversity* 65-108. I think one can grant the value of DiNoia's insights here, and appreciate his recognition that religions do not intend to seek the same goals, while also acknowledging, in apparent contrast with his view, that God might be able to use religious communities that do not understand themselves as mediating grace or salvation as "channels of grace or means of salvation" (91).
6. The most plausible Christian theological proposals regarding the significance of non-Christian religious traditions are, it seems to me, the ones that take seriously the diversity of the experiences, beliefs, and practices associated with these traditions and of the goals they seek to help people realize. Two good examples, from very different theological perspectives, are Heim, *Depth* and David Ray Griffin, *Reenchantment without Supernaturalism: A Process Philosophy of Religion* (Ithaca, NY: Cornell UP 2001) 247-84. Each seeks to affirm the reality and value of the goals sought by different traditions and the differences between these traditions. Heim emphasizes more than Griffin the possibility that the quite different ends furthered by different traditions might all be realized, and maintains, as Griffin does not, that a trinitarian Christian vision can include and transcend other alternatives (without eliminating them or denying their value).

Commending Christian convictions can facilitate a deeper understanding of God and God's world and a sense of meaning linked with the way the world is. It can also offer habits, practices, and ideas with the potential to exert a positive affect on moral and political practice, and on the overall trajectories of people's lives. But there is no barrier to divine acceptance or to friendship with God beyond death for anyone, anywhere, because she hasn't managed to acquire the right set of beliefs. And, though cultural contexts can facilitate or impede God's activity, God can certainly be at work to heal the brokenness of people's individual lives, their relationships, and their societies, and to offer them meaning and understanding, whatever their traditions.

Can We Converse across the Boundaries between Traditions?

We validate our beliefs within the context of our distinctive traditions, rather than from some neutral standpoint outside all traditions.[1] But if this is so, even if we are rationally entitled to regard our beliefs as correct, we seem to have a problem. People are not, in general, *argued* into Christian belief.[2] But conversation about issues matters, nonetheless. The assumptions and categories of understanding of those who identify with other cultural traditions may be quite different from our own. So, given the absence of universal starting-points for conversation, it might appear that offering persuasive reasons to such people to accept Christian beliefs would be difficult or impossible.

We *can* offer such reasons, but we cannot appeal to some universal standard of rationality or some set of beliefs unavoidably accepted by "all rational people." Instead, we will have to build bridges in an *ad hoc*, tentative way. We will have to start with the common ground we happen to share with those whose views differ from our own, with the specific questions they confront, and with the particular challenges they offer to our own views.[3]

Individuals are shaped by diverse but overlapping traditions. Where different traditions compete for our loyalty, it is unlikely, whatever our explicit decisions, that any single one will win a decisive victory. We are educated by teachers whose thinking arises out of diverse perspectives; we read books and watch films and listen to music reflective of the standpoints of divergent cultural traditions; and we engage in practices which contribute to and are grounded in different forms of life. No one is simply and exclusively a member, much less a product, of a single tradition. People who identify with different traditions may share vocabularies and patterns of understanding not directly derived from those traditions but from some other shared experience.

Traditions intersect in piecemeal ways, and this makes mutual understanding and conversation much more feasible than they would be if religious traditions were hermetically sealed off from each other.[4] In the West, the major alternatives to Christianity are intimately related to it. The vocabulary of Greek philosophers and German psychologists has clearly influenced the way the Christian community speaks about God and salvation. Similarly, though many of its recent exponents have been atheists, existentialism developed from the stress on reflective

---

1. In this portion of Chapter 11, I draw on material which I also employed in "Righting Narrative: Robert Chang, Poststructuralism, and the Limits of Critique," *UCLA Asian Pacific American Law Journal* 7.1 (Spring 2001): 105-32.
2. Certainly, for instance, the experience of church plays an important role in determining whether people will want to identify themselves as Christians.
3. See DiNoia, *Diversity* 132, on some issues in a specifically Buddhist-Christian conversation about God.
4. See Terence Tilley, "Incommensurability, Intratextuality, and Fideism," *Modern Theology* 5.2 (Jan. 1989): 96.

individuality found in such Christian thinkers as Augustine and Kierkegaard. Thus, its analysis of the human situation has many parallels with a certain kind of Christian thinking, and its categories have provided Christians with useful tools for interpreting freedom, sin, and spirituality.

Buddhism emerged in the context of Hinduism. Christianity sprang from Judaism, and it identifies (more or less seriously) with a substantial part of the Jewish heritage, while, of course, it continues to accept the Bible of Judaism as significant for its own life. Islam was influenced by Christianity from its earliest years, and has, in turn, affected the development of Christian thought. Liberalism—the moral and political tradition centering on equal justice and private rights that unites such unlikely compatriots as Joseph Biden and Ronald Reagan, Margaret Thatcher and Tony Blair—grew out of basically Christian soil. Thus, many, though by no means all, of its central convictions about human life are similar to Christian ones. Marxism's vision of a universal community grounded in equality that emerges at the end of history is a transformed version of Christian hope.[1] And if liberalism and Marxism are, to some degree, Christian heresies, then they will include some categories which they share with (at least some varieties of) Christianity.

Most fundamentally, the world is God's good creation and the arena within which God's Spirit is ceaselessly active in love. There is nowhere from which God is absent. So we can expect that all people have an in-built need for and openness to God, whether they know it or not. In addition, the structure of God's good creation—the kind of world we inhabit and the kind of creatures we are—imposes limits on just how diverse people's ways of living and thinking can be, even though a lot of flexibility remains. The way the world is prompts people to adopt the right sorts of habits and attitudes (even if it doesn't necessitate that they do so).

Thus, there are clearly continuities as well as discontinuities between Christian and non-Christian experience. So someone who identifies with some non-Christian tradition may share sufficient common ground with a Christian that meaningful interchange about differences is possible. To be sure, the nature of the overlap between traditions (and segments of those traditions), and the capacity of people to understand and appreciate the positions of those who disagree with them, will differ from situation to situation. Conversations across religious boundaries will unavoidably be *ad hoc*, but that doesn't mean that we can't have these conversations—and so commend our beliefs to others—at all.

As a result, it may be possible in particular conversations to show "how particular features of Christian faith may contribute to sustaining and nurturing the particular identities" of non-Christians "with reference to a particular context of action or a particular contested question or belief." Someone might thus, for instance, seek to show that certain beliefs of a conversation partner with different beliefs make more sense if understood in the terms she proposes. She can point to the ways in which her convictions can provide an appropriate backdrop for commitments her conversation-partner has already made.[2] And she can suggest difficulties with her conversation-partner's assumptions which her own alternative might be able to resolve.[3]

Building on their common concern, people from different backgrounds can go on to examine their respective responses to the situation out of which their

---

1. Even self-conscious liberals or Marxists will experience God (even if they don't realize that's what they're doing) in ways shaped by Christian categories made available by the Christian influence on the context within which Marxism and liberalism function—and on Marxism and liberalism themselves.

2. William Werpehowski, "*Ad Hoc* Apologetics," *Journal of Religion* 66.3 (July 1986): 286, 287.

3. Cp. Griffiths, *Apology* 83-108.

dialogue arises. They can assess both the ability of these responses to provide understanding and the significance of these responses for future action. They may consider not merely whether they disagree about a given belief or practice, but about the relative adequacy of their respective justifications for shared beliefs and practices—and about the implications of accepting these differing warrants.[1]

Thus, genuine conversations across the boundaries between traditions can build, in *ad hoc* fashion, on shared commitments, understandings, and experiences. In the course of such conversations, representatives of alternative traditions—both alive and dead, present in person and through texts or artefacts—can confront each other with their diverse convictions, the justifications for those convictions, and the kinds of lives to which they give rise as they are embodied by their adherents.[2] The participants can—indeed, must—evaluate challenges to their own convictions and determine whether these challenges should be ignored, or whether they require the adoption of new convictions or even new practical and theoretical paradigms. If this kind of approach is in principle possible, even when significant disagreements are also evident, then it is reasonable to suppose that a non-Christian's experience *may* at least exhibit sufficient continuities with a Christian's to provide the basis for a meaningful cross-tradition exchange about religious belief.

Every individual or communal interchange about religious beliefs will follow a particular path shaped by the context in which it occurs; no one can create a universally valid approach to communication that will be effective everywhere and in all circumstances. But, beginning with our distinctiveness, we can dialogue with others in ways appropriate to their circumstances. It will be on that basis that we will be able to communicate about matters of ultimate concern. There would be no point in abandoning what makes us who we are in order to find such common ground, for it is precisely what we have that is distinctive which we seek to offer in dialogue with others.

I've said a lot here about conversation. But "conversation" needs to be understood as simply a metaphor for all the different sorts of interchange that enable the people to put their religious beliefs in display and commend them to others. In particular, the embodiment of Christian convictions by a living, vibrant community typically matters much more than the verbal articulation of those convictions.

Careful conversations, of whatever form, can result in change and growth and the resolution of disagreements. As we engage in dialogue, we may discover that we need to rethink some of what we are saying. The same may be true of our conversation-partners. But suppose there is no meeting of the minds in a given case. If we've carefully engaged with alternative positions, we may conclude a conversation justifiably confident in a position we've taken even if our conversation partners lack our confidence. Our reasons for adopting our position may be clearer and stronger as a result of an exchange with representatives of other views. And those with whom we converse may learn and benefit from our willingness to articulate and commend our convictions. If we communicate in the context of a loving search for truth, we and those with whom we communicate will be enabled more effectively to live together in a way that has the potential to foster flourishing, healing, hope, and love.

Can We Learn from Conversations across Boundaries between Traditions?

Just as the church doesn't control God's presence or provide people with necessary conditions for moral goodness, so, too, it doesn't control God's truth.

---

1. Werpehowski 292.
2. On the dynamics of such conversations more broadly, see DiNoia, *Diversity* 25-33, 109-54.

Christians have distinctive insights to offer, insights made possible by their unique historical location and by centuries of experience, practice, reflection, and analysis. They rightly believe they have something of distinctive value to offer others. But they also have reason to recognize that they are finite, fallible, and sinful, and that the unique historical location that helps them see things others may not see may also, on occasion, keep them from seeing truths others can discern. While they can offer their insights to others when doing so is appropriate, they must also acknowledge that they may have a tremendous amount to *learn* from others.[1]

It is perfectly reasonable to commend our own views in dialogue with participants in other cultural traditions. But it is also reasonable to seek understanding and to expect that God can surprise us with new insights gleaned through conversation with our dialogue partners. Benefiting us with such insights is a way in which they can offer us their love. And it is also a way in which God can love us in and through their actions. As we engage in dialogue, then, we must be prepared not only to offer love, but to receive it.[2]

Religious Disagreement with People We Love

Whether or not we engage in dialogue with them, religious disagreement with people to whom we are close can be painful. But recognizing that we love God in and through our love for creation can help us see more clearly how to deal with some of the challenges posed by our loving ties with those who don't share our religious convictions.[3]

A great deal of Christian preaching and teaching over the years has clearly answered, "Yes," to the question, "Does loving people who don't endorse our beliefs compromise our loyalty to God?" Contemporary Christians have not always echoed this negative assessment of close relationships across faith boundaries. But even the well intentioned can end up sounding rather stuffy and boundary-conscious. Discussing the "obligation to safeguard the faith," and problems arising from this obligation in connection with cooperation between Catholics and non-Catholics, Bernard Häring writes:

> A very sensitive area is that of close personal friendships between Catholics and unbelievers and people of other religions . . . . Such close friendships may be permitted for mature Catholics who are firmly grounded in their faith, provided the non-Catholic friend has a sincere respect for the faith of the Catholic party. Friendship of this kind is truly good and absolutely devoid of danger only when the Catholic is animated by prudent apostolic zeal for the salvation of his friend's soul. Much good can be effected by such a noble form of friendship.[4]

Häring is surely on the right track in suggesting that religious disagreement need not be a barrier to close ties with friends and family members. (For the sake of convenience, I will tend to speak here about friends and friendship, but my concern, in general, is with close relationships of all kinds.) But his remarks still reflect an exclusivism that is neither necessary nor appropriate.

---

1. What I offer here is a species of what Paul Griffiths terms "open inclusivism" with respect to religious truth claims; see *Problems* 56-65.

2. See DiNoia, *Diversity* 33. Of course, it is also a loving act to let someone else know that she has something of value to offer.

3. This issue is sensitively addressed, though with explicit reference only to family members, in Karl Rahner, "The Christian among Unbelieving Relations," *Theological Investigations* 3: *The Theology of the Spiritual Life*, trans. Karl-H. and Boniface Kruger (London: Darton; New York: Seabury 1974) 355-72.

4. *The Law of Christ: Moral Theology for Priests and Laity*, 3 vols., trans. Edwin G. Kaiser (Cork: Mercier 1961-5) 2: 46.

True friendship (and this includes the friendship of parents and children, of lovers and spouses) is, as I have argued, a sign and expression of implicit trust in and love for God. Thus—whatever his religious convictions—a genuine friend, in virtue of his friendship, has given evidence of his fruitful relationship with God. Indeed, that he *is* a friend is an *aspect* of his love for God. It doesn't seem, then, that his spiritual status is in question, at least not in the sense that it appears be for Häring. Because he is a friend, he has responded trustingly and lovingly, to God, owned himself as part of God's good creation, gratefully accepted God's acceptance. So it seems as if the burden of proof would rest on anyone who argued that he has not on some important level accepted God's acceptance or that God was not fostering healing and growth in his life.

Some Christian discomfort with close relationships across religious boundaries appears to be grounded in a concern with what we might label *purity*. Some Christians seem to feel as if close contact with non-Christians will defile them, make them unclean.[1] At its roots, the idea of purity has to do with maintaining social order and group identity. Categorizing and classifying people, places, practices, objects, and events imparts meaning and structure to a seemingly chaotic world. Establishing group boundary markers—we are the people who do this, who don't look like that, who don't go there—enables a community to feel secure and stable. Purity rules serve to maintain group identity.

Sometimes, of course, Christians worry about relationships with those outside the Christian community not only because of a vague fear of impurity but because they worry that their beliefs will be challenged, their perspectives altered, their habits changed. Of course, it's possible that a person might give up valuable convictions and practices because of a close relationship. But there's no reason for this possibility to make anyone fearful of intimacy and vulnerability with a family member or friend who doesn't share her religious beliefs.

Genuine friends will respect each other's differences. That's part of the affirmation of the other *as other* that makes friendship so spiritually significant. As a result, they will not seek to dominate each other. They will not seek to *force* each other to change.

The practice of friendship imposes moral constraints on people's behavior. Taken seriously, it inculcates a variety of character traits that reflect and contribute to growth and healing. That the practice of friendship requires the formation of at least some of these traits means that friends share some important moral ground. Because of this, there are limits not only on how real friends will consider it appropriate to treat each other but on how they will encourage each other to behave.

Still, few if any close relationships—and certainly no relationship between people whose religious or moral beliefs differ significantly—will be free of tension. Such tension is no reason to forsake a relationship. Instead, it can provide an opportunity for growth. People who disagree should be able to learn from each other. The respect they have for each other means that one won't force her beliefs on another. But each will still likely articulate her beliefs—sometimes verbally, but also (and more importantly) by embodying them.

Seeing what a particular vision of life looks like in practice can be a profound challenge to one's assumptions about what does and does not make for fulfilled, flourishing human existence. Obviously, that can be very unsettling. But unless one supposes that one already has everything figured out, that one has nothing to learn, one will seek to learn from a friend instead of ignoring, denying,

---

1. The standard discussion of purity is Mary Douglas, *Purity and Danger: An Analysis of Concepts of Pollution and Taboo* (London: Routledge 1966). Jeffrey Stout examines how Douglas's work might be appropriated by ethicists and theologians *Ethics after Babel: The Languages of Morals and Their Discontents* (Boston: Beacon 1988).

or rejecting out of hand the things that make her different from oneself. To close oneself off to a friend's challenge, even for supposedly religious reasons, would be to indulge in an excessive self-confidence that represented an implicit denial of one's creatureliness.

The conviction that God is the world's transcendent creator, that God's truth is infinitely greater than our beliefs, that God's world is far vaster than our particular communities, should make us question any attempt to keep our beliefs or lives pristine, unchallenged, and unchanged. The church, like any other community, has come to exercise demonic power in our lives if we refuse, whatever the price, to allow contact with those outside its boundaries to upset our orderly lives within it, if we seek to protect our identities at any cost.

Any community must be open to challenge and change if it is to avoid idolatry. But the Christian church has a particularly strong reason to reject purity rules that divide people. The ministry of Jesus and the teaching and preaching of Paul were clearly designed to create inclusive community. Christianity was founded on the premise that boundaries which separated people and communities ought to be broken down.[1]

Throughout his letters, we find Paul wrestling with the question of how Christianity, with distinctive, particular historical roots, could become a truly universal community. His solutions and prescriptions are, of course, carefully shaped—albeit pragmatic—responses to the particular challenges he confronted. But the consistency with which they exhibit his commitment to inclusivity in the face of prevailing purity rules is both obvious and noteworthy.[2]

Shunning those whose views might unsettle us or challenge the convictions of our communities is a manifestation of idolatry, and as such should be avoided, not embraced. Paul and Jesus were both committed to fighting the idolization of human communities and the consequent creation of boundaries designed to keep outsiders at arms' length. Thus, a central Christian belief and a fundamental trajectory of the Christian tradition both militate against Christian exclusivism.

Dialogue among friends with different religious beliefs can be an exceptional source of opportunities to learn. Someone with whom one differs about religious issues will usually have reasons for viewing things the way she does. If she holds her beliefs responsibly, if she has thought about them carefully and reflectively, then engaging with her will enrich one's own understanding. One undoubtedly has things to learn from her. One should expect to change in the course of sharing

---

1. See, *e.g.*, Marcus Borg, *Jesus: A New Vision—Spirit, Culture, and the Life of Discipleship* (San Francisco: Harper 1989) and E. P. Sanders, *Paul and Palestinian Judaism* (London: SCM 1983).

2. Paul addresses the question of community boundaries throughout his writings. The issue of eating with believing "gentiles" is addressed in Gal. 2:11-7 (cp. Acts 15). In 1 Cor. 10:27-30, he explicitly affirms the appropriateness of table fellowship with those outside the Christian community. The central importance in Pauline thought of the notion that the boundaries between the supposedly "pure" and "impure" are broken down is highlighted in Eph. 3:4-6, which asserts that "the mystery of Christ" is the fact that "the Gentiles are fellow heirs, members of the same body, and partakers of the promise in Christ Jesus through the gospel."

With its call not to be "mismatched with unbelievers" and its injunction, "touch nothing unclean," 2 Cor. 6:14-7:1 might appear to be an exception to Paul's general commitment to opposing purity distinctions. Read in context, however, it is perhaps best seen as representing a call to the Corinthian Christians to separate themselves in general from those outside the Christian community but as embodying a demand— making pragmatic use of traditional purity language—that they refuse to give their loyalty to the opponents whose views Paul implicitly critiques throughout the letter.

life with the people to whom one is close. Indeed, one should be disturbed if one does *not* change.¹

It is certainly possible that one may find one's own convictions essentially unaltered by a close relationship with someone who does not share them. But even then, one may well find that this relationship enables one to acquire a clearer understanding of just what it is one believes, what one's beliefs mean, and how important they are. Dialogue helps to clarify one's thinking whatever the outcome.²

A true friend is another self. And this means letting her into the inmost core of one's being, being vulnerable to her, accepting that one can and indeed likely will change in relationship with her. So respect for a friend's otherness cannot mean keeping her at a distance. The call to fidelity in friendship is a call to remain in relationship with another despite stresses and tensions. And the recognition of one's own creaturely finitude is a challenge to continue learning from a friend's disagreements.

Religious disagreements may, of course, tax people's love and fidelity. Religion is a principal cause of tension among friends.³ Painful conflict may teach some friends that they have no choice but to avoid certain activities or topics of conversation in each other's company. Some disagreements may prove unresolvable. But people who truly care about each other should usually be able to find creative, graceful ways of respecting each other's differences while remaining close. What is most important is that people whose religious convictions differ extend each other acceptance and understanding.

The Christian must avoid viewing her friends self-righteously.⁴ And she should recognize that accepting her differences may complicate life for them as much as accepting them does for her. She should credit the people to whom she is close with intellectual and moral responsibility when they disagree with her. She should never refuse to share *herself* with them; disagreements about appropriate behavior should never become excuses for emotional withdrawal. And she should always be ready to grow and change in and through her encounters with them.

At the same time, a non-Christian must accept the—seeming or real—peculiarities of a Christian friend. She must be aware that, at least in part because of Christian convictions, the friend acknowledges responsibilities—to other persons (a spouse, say), to institutions, to communities, to the world's poor—that may keep her from treating a friendship as her first priority. She must be sensitive to

---

1. Cp. Lorentz Gregory Jones, "Formation in Moral Judgment: An Essay on the Social Context of Christian Life" (PhD diss., Duke U 1988): "the good life inevitably entails friendship . . . because intimate friendships extend and redefine the boundaries of particular conceptions of the good life" (124).

2. Cp. Jones 121: a friend different from me can enable me "to learn who I am by contrasting myself with others." See also Stanley Hauerwas, "How My Mind Has Changed: The Testament of Friends," *The Christian Century* 107 (Feb. 28, 1990): "Unfortunately, I am unable to remember 'my position' or the arguments I use to support it. Without friends to remember my claims I am at a complete loss. But I discover that in their remembering, which is often expressed in disagreements, there is often more than I knew. I continue to be graced with graduate students who understand me better than I understand myself and can show me where I have got it wrong" (213). When Hauerwas says, ". . . many of my friends are churched" (214), he clearly implies that some are not. And there is no reason to suppose that he does not include them among the friends who help him to grow by challenging him and disagreeing with him. Cp. his *The Peaceable Kingdom: A Primer in Christian Ethics* (London: SCM 1983).

3. Rudy Arnold Haapanen, "Close Friendship: The Individualistic Community" (PhD diss., U of California, Davis 1976) 161.

4. Cp. Mary Elizabeth Hunt, *Fierce Tenderness: A Feminist Theology of Friendship* (New York: Crossroad 1990) 170: "[p]eople I want to be around do not subject their relationships to a standard of political correctness."

the fact that these loyalties may sometimes impose limits on her friend's actions. She must accept that while her friend can and should love her truly and deeply, she cannot be the only focus of the friend's care. Her claims will have to taken into account along with those of others.

Provided that each friend respects the other *as other*—exhibiting the regard for difference that is crucial to all true friendship—the challenges posed by the diversity of the moral claims to which each one must respond should be manageable.[1] Christians and non-Christians alike, sustained and lured by God's love, can resolve the challenges posed by friendship across religious boundaries as they learn to respect the otherness of those they love.

It is an implication of the doctrine of creation that people can love God implicitly in loving each other. Their friendship itself points to a moral disposition that is an expression of love for God, whether implicit or explicit.[2] People who disagree about religious matters can and should learn from each other; and, provided each truly respects the other, their disagreement should be no bar to a relationship in which both experience and enact God's love.

---

1. Cp. L. William Countryman, *Dirt, Greed, and Sex: Sexual Ethics in the New Testament and Their Implications for Today* (London: SCM 1988) 267: "The Christian will find it very difficult to live in an intimate relation with one who does not understand or accept the kind of demands which God's calling makes. While it is not impossible to live in such a relationship with a nonbeliever, the partner must at least be one who respects commitments that may seem unworldly and which do not place self or sexual partner first. The Christian must also retain a certain freedom to respond to God's call loyally in critical times."

Interestingly, the very conservative Catholic Germain Grisez takes a relatively more matter-of-fact approach to this question than the moderately liberal Episcopalian Countryman; see *Living a Christian Life, The Way of the Lord Jesus* 2 (Quincy: Franciscan 1993) 743-4. Grisez begins with a strong statement: "Since marriage should be a full communion of life suited to handing on that whole life to children, a Catholic should marry a Catholic who completely shares his or he faith and moral commitment. Differences in religion detract greatly from unity of mind and heart while impairing parental unity in a most important respect . . . ." He goes on, however, to acknowledge that "no . . . suitable partner [who completely shares one's Catholic faith] can be found. Then a Catholic's preference should be for baptized persons who firmly hold and faithfully practice Christian faith, even though in a church or ecclesial community not in full communion with the Catholic Church." Finally, "[l]acking a suitable potential Christian partner, a Catholic with marriage in prospect should try to find an upright non-Christian suitable in other respects, not least in beliefs and attitudes about marriage, its specific responsibilities, and the raising of children. Even if these criteria are met, such a marriage will involve serious difficulties, require greater efforts, and lack sacramentality. . . . However, it can truly realize the essential good of marital communion, which includes the natural holiness of marriage; it also provides a special apostolic opportunity for the Catholic who lives a faithful and exemplary life, since in this way his or her non-Christian spouse will receive a very effective communication of the gospel and a certain real link with Jesus and his Church."

2. This is not, in and of itself, an interpretation of non-Christian experience which Christians should expect non-Christians to find appealing. It is not a kind of "natural theology," an argument designed to convince non-Christians of anything. It is a Christian reading of experience, a theological interpretation of human existence that follows from basic Christian convictions about God and creation. Its function is not to convince anyone to join the Christian community, but to emphasize to fearful or arrogant Christians that God is present as accepting and transforming love throughout the entire creation.

Loving a Challenging Church

The church is a community of love. But sometimes it is itself quite hard to love. There is an ironic sense in which loving the church is harder for many people than accepting the seemingly more complicated and otherworldly aspects of Christianity.[1] It is far easier to believe in an unseen, hidden God than to suppose that a fallible, obnoxious, and sometimes oppressive community of human beings is an important context for God's loving activity in the world. Many people could echo the words of pastor and theologian William Willimon: "For me, the real scandal of the ordained ministry, the ultimate stumbling block, the thing I avoid and fear most, is the Church. . . . My problem . . . is that I am yoked to the Church." Willimon observes that like "many today, I love Jesus. I want to serve him. But he married beneath his station."[2]

This problem is often felt with particular acuteness by contemporary Christians, many of whom could agree with Jonathan Butler when he says that,

> as the good Christian Paul had a "wretched body" to contend with every day, so the . . . church has its wretched body. As a people . . . [we] mean as much as the Christian Paul meant in his great love-letters and general epistles. But as a people we also are weighed down with a body of death which we must fight daily. It pervades us with its languor, and discontent, and provincial grasp of mankind and systems, and cliché patterns of thought, and legalism, and PR faces, and materialism, and cliquish sociability. And we have sensed this flesh pervade our very selves, and well up within us—from we know not where—as a great current of darkness . . . . We wallow in the flesh of . . . [the church]—bored, frustrated, left-wingers or stragglers.[3]

The "scandal" of the church dilutes the impact of its efforts to touch the world in loving ways. It also presents a distinct pastoral problem that confronts those nurtured within the church itself. To be a Christian who senses the fallibility of the Christian community, who is all too aware of its sometimes obnoxious and abusive behavior, is to experience alienation. The alienation is only likely to deepen because the church itself finds it easy respond with hostility to doubts about its credibility or rectitude. The fact is, though, that dismay at the church's fallibility and sinfulness is thoroughly consistent with Christian convictions. Recognizing this should help those who feel alienated from the church to deal with their community of faith. Sensing the continuity between their concerns and its own theologically grounded self-understanding should help the church, in turn, to communicate more effectively—and lovingly—with them.

Loving a Sinful Church

Discomfort with the state of the church makes sense given the "in-between" character of Christian existence. The *identity* of the church and its members is

---

1. In this section, I draw on material appearing in my essay, "The Cynic and the Church: Some Theological Reflections," *Spectrum* 21.4 (Jan.-Mar 1993): 11-8. I would like to thank Heather Hessel, Charles Teel, Jr., Jon Hardt, Delmer Ross, Stephen Smith, and Paul Landa for comments that contributed to the development of this essay. Another version of this paper was presented at the October, 1990, Amersham Retreat in England; it has since appeared as "The Debate about Adventist Identity," *Opinion* 6.1 (May 1992): 4-9 (*Opinion* is an English journal published by the organizers of the Amersham Retreats).

2. William H. Willimon, *What's Right With the Church* (San Francisco: Harper 1985) 131.

3. Jonathan Butler, "ΙΧΘΥΣ" [3], La Sierra College *Criterion* 38.4 (Oct. 21, 1966): 2.

clear. That identity is shaped by the recognition of God's love, revealed in Jesus. But while a Christian's identity as a person who acknowledges her creation and unconditional acceptance by God as known in Jesus may be clear, her experience and behavior fail often enough to reflect that identity. Thus, St. Paul distances himself from enthusiasts who suppose that the Christian's new life eliminates the ambiguities inherent in sinful existence: "I do not claim that I have already succeeded or have already become perfect. I keep striving to win the prize for which Christ Jesus has already won me to himself. Of course, my brothers, I really do not think that I have already won it; the one thing I do, however, is to forget what is behind me and do my best to reach what is ahead."[1]

St. Paul makes the same point in a more general way in his Epistle to the Galatians: the sinful nature "sets its desires against the Spirit, while the Spirit fights against it. They are in conflict with one another so that what you will to do you cannot do."[2] And, while in no way condoning their behavior, Paul judges the Corinthian *believers* to be "infants in Christ," not ready for "solid food," and living in accordance with dictates of the "lower nature."[3]

What is true of individuals is also true of communities. *The Church always lives in need of God's accepting and healing love.* There is always cause for doubt, then, if the church presumes to be flawless.

That the church is a corporate entity renders it especially worthy of question. For corporate structures give ever-fresh opportunities to sinful people to cloak themselves and their actions in mantles of respectability. Even when people act from primarily good motives, the distance between them and the effects of corporate actions they encourage may render them irresponsible. Given the human tendency to self-deception, those involved in church structure may find it easy to allow this distance to hide from them the inappropriateness of their actions.

Freedom and Fallibility

Further, the fact that one is involved in *church* structure presents particular temptations. If one judges oneself to be legislating for God then the temptation to absolutize whatever one decides will be nigh irresistible. Since the church is doing God's work in the world, runs the argument, God's Spirit will ensure the church's infallibility.

The evidence against this view from ecclesiastical history is too strong to allow it to be taken seriously. The universal Christian church, like each of its particular manifestations, has strayed, wandered, exhibited inconsistencies in belief and practice. The Christian may believe that God is always at work in the church to bring good out of its evil or ineptitude. But she can hardly suppose that, human freedom, fallibility, and sinfulness being what they are, God manages always to *prevent* the church from making mistakes.

Not only human sin but also human finitude legitimizes questions and concerns. No creaturely performance can be based on completely adequate knowledge. No creaturely activity can be carried on with perfect effectiveness. It is not that creatures are necessarily evil, but that they are necessarily limited. They do not possess unlimited power or knowledge; and so, even under the best of circumstances, their actions and decisions can be faulty.

We can sensibly raise questions about the church's beliefs, the church's practice, the motives of the church's members (especially ourselves), because the church is a *human* community called by God. Doubts about the church are justi-

---

1. Phil. 3:12-3; cp. Ellen G. White, *The Acts of the Apostles in the Proclamation of the Gospel of Jesus Christ* (Mountain View, CA: Pacific 1911) 559-65.
2. Gal. 5:16-8.
3. 1 Cor. 3:1-4.

fied precisely because of the gospel the church preaches. If the church preached a cheerfully optimistic gospel, one characterized by belief in unwavering human goodness and the irresistibility of progress, then its own message would not make possible its ongoing self-criticism. But the gospel the church proclaims highlights not only human possibility but also human ambiguity, not only the goodness wrought by God's Spirit's work but also the sin and fallibility against which God's Spirit contends.

Doubt, Criticism, and Love

Love criticizes and challenges precisely because it cares. But, because its standards are so high, it can easily slide into a self-righteous superiority or a fashionable detachment that refuses to make commitments until all the problems are ironed out and all the questions answered. Of course, it can be tempting to cultivate tension as a sign of sophistication rather than accepting it as a sign of fallen and finite humanity. And Christian life is unlikely ever to be free of doubt. "The man that feareth, Lord, to doubt, / In that fear doubteth thee."[1]

Nonetheless—while one need not fear doubt—if one is to avoid self-righteousness, concern about the state of the church must go hand-in-hand with concern about oneself. One must recognize that the people whose actions prompt one's concern face challenges not dissimilar from one's own. One can recognize that one's own loyalties are often divided, that one's own love for God and others wavers, that one's own experience is pervaded by ambiguity. One may suspect others of different vices than one's own, but one cannot allow one's questions and doubts to blind one to one's own faults. Thus it seems to me that Butler is absolutely correct when, in the context of Christian collegiate life, but with a much broader application, he writes that we

> get off the subject when we place all our gripes on the head of a scapegoat ... [,] assuming that] if we can just rid ourselves of these goats everything will be alright. We are off the subject when it is always "their fault," Because even if we could drive out all these scapegoats from the camp, we would still be here (I would still be here), and now we're getting back on the subject.
>
> Because after I have exposed all the evils, and smashed all the idols, and burned all the tyrants in effigy, the real enemy still lurks. For the enemy is never the scapegoat we can send out of camp, the problem is never simply "their fault" (if we understand fully the problem), for it is part of me. The enemy must be met within me. I can gripe all I want through the day about the faculty, or the Commons, or the Dean's Council, but it's really only chit-chat until I turn out the lights and wait in the silence for sleep to take me.[2]

---

1. George McDonald, qtd. H. A. Williams, *Tensions: Necessary Conflicts in Life and Love* (London: Beazley 1976) 48. Williams argues that temporary conflict with God can foster intimacy with God: "When we find ourselves sneering at God-associated things we may be pretty certain that the God-associated things are only a cover for God Himself. We often find that too shocking an admission to make to ourselves— are we sneering at Absolute Goodness? Or if not too shocking, then too absurd. We might as well sneer at the Alps. Yet in fact that is precisely what we are doing, not because we are doomed and damned and totally depraved, but because here on earth our sneering and ridicule is a necessary stage or element in our love for the Creator, who is leading us towards that independence of Him by means of which alone we can finally give ourselves totally to Him. The acceptance of our inevitable ambiguity towards God—with all the tensions, conflicts and guilt-feelings it involves— is part of that cross through which alone we can enter into fullness of life" (34).

2. Jonathan Butler, "ΙΧΘΥΣ" [9], *La Sierra College Criterion* 38.10 (Jan. 20, 1967): 2.

Concern about the state of the church ceases to serve the church when it prevents the church from being a loving community. The recognition that God accepts us in spite of our failures ought to inspire us to treat each other with similar consideration. We must seek to differentiate between bad behavior and the people who engage in it, between bad ideas and people who are being made better by God's love. And because we must be wary of ourselves, we must be aware that our own suspicion of others *is itself suspicious*.

Responsible doubts and questions about the state of the church's doctrine and practice are always the doubts and concerns of a *participant*, not that of a (self-proclaimed) innocent by-stander. The church is worth getting mad about, but it only makes sense to get mad if the church can or does make some kind of difference in one's life, if one has some reason to care about it.

Criticism, Concern, and Community

We cannot expect to retreat from denominational to congregational Christianity and find ourselves free from the stresses occasioned by human sin and finitude; indeed, congregational churches may be more prey to certain kinds of authoritarianism because they lack the oversight of larger church bodies and because they are not accountable to traditions that demand inclusivity. At the same time, the universal church exists only in its various particular manifestations—in congregations and denominations and dioceses and house-groups and base Christian communities—and all of these, consisting as they do of sinful and limited human beings, will suffer from the same faults. The ideal church is a myth.

As I have suggested throughout this chapter, we must have community if we are to grow and heal. Spirituality is not nurtured in a vacuum, nor are the various worthwhile endeavors the church sponsors likely to be managed successfully by isolated individuals. Of course, our growth and healing and our active love of God can and should happen at least partly in communities that need not define themselves in explicitly or self-consciously religious ways. But to experience and respond to the world most adequately, I contend, we require the support of a community which helps to shape our interpretations of and responses to reality by means of the practices it inculcates, the language and images it employs, the stories it remembers, the self-discipline it fosters—in other words, a religious community.[1] Each of us will appropriate those communal gifts in different ways, and some of them are to be had elsewhere. But, as I have sought to show, some communal locus is important if our identities as Christians are to be nourished.

We do not start in a vacuum. One begins one's religious reflection with a heritage one cannot simply ignore. A

> man cannot do away with his parents once he is born. The very fact that we are and that we continue to exist assures us of the fact that they continue ceaselessly to be our parents. Hence we cannot be Christians . . . by quitting the Church which has been, and remains, once and for all the mother of this Christian existence of ours. . . . By way of analogy we may take our relationship to another man whom we have unreservedly accepted. In such a case even though there are elements in him which remain alien, so that we are constantly on the way to overcoming this alienation, nevertheless from the first we have accepted these alien elements in a spirit of trust, because we have already experienced in him that which

---

1. See George Lindbeck, *The Nature of Doctrine: Religion and Theology in a Post-Liberal Era* (Philadelphia: Westminster 1984); William C. Placher, *Unapologetic Theology: A Christian Voice in a Pluralistic Conversation* (Atlanta: Westminster/John Knox 1989).

we have at once understood and recognized as meaningful for us. It is the same with our relationship with the Church.[1]

Community is crucial for personal religious experience.[2] So there's no escaping communal fallibility. Though communities are flawed, they have the capacity dramatically to affect our lives in positive ways.

The Importance of Humor

Love for the church can and should find expression in humor. To the grimly serious and self-righteous pundits who take it upon themselves to call down divine judgment on the church, humor will seem flippant, a failure to take the measure of our responsibility to confront evil. To the church's sober defenders, humor will seem irreverent, even blasphemous. Issues of consequence are at stake, and the fate of the church is, both sides will tell us, no laughing matter.

But what could be more appropriate than humor in relation to religious matters? A key ingredient in humor is the sense of incongruity. And a sense of incongruity should always be very, very evident whenever religious issues are discussed by finite creatures. God so far exceeds our language and our imagery that we speak only to say something, not because what we say is adequate to the reality of God. The issues are important ones, and they must be addressed with whatever courage and clarity of thought we can bring to bear. Nonetheless, the division that separates our finite representations of ultimate reality from ultimate reality itself must be infinite—or else we wouldn't be talking about ultimate reality at all. And the tension obtains not only when we *speak*, but when we *act* Christianly. That is why you should "[t]hank God when you can take a delighted pleasure in the comic spectacle which is yourself, especially if it is yourself devoutly at prayer."[3] There is something more than faintly absurd about our religious performance and discourse, and when we or others speak in too-serious, too-ultimate terms about what we are doing, implying that we know, or could know, more than we do, laughter is surely the most fitting response.

Humor is also appropriate because it is necessarily related to justice. It "occurs when we are put in our place."[4] It happens when our pretense founders on the harsh shore of reality. It calls into question the illegitimate claims of the powerful and the self-righteous. Thus, it discloses us as we really are. It challenges our pretensions and so prepares us to acknowledge the worth of God's accepting love.[5]

Hope for the Cynic?

Is there a place, then, in the Christian community for the person who feels alienated from it? There must be—the church cannot do without her. The Christian is impelled to critical concern by the implications of the good news the church proclaims. And since the Christian's trust is always in God, and not in the church itself, that trust can continue despite her conflicts with her community.

> Why then does the Church remain alive as a community of faith? Not because there is no threat to life, no fatal illness, within it. But because God keeps it alive, *despite* all infirmities and weaknesses, and constantly endows it with a new continuity ....

---

1. Karl Rahner, *Theological Investigations* 12: *Confrontations* 2, trans. David Bourke (London: Darton 1974) 154.
2. See Lash.
3. Williams 113.
4. William H. Willimon, "Introduction," *And the Laugh Shall Be First: A Treasury of Religious Humor*, ed. Willimon (Nashville: Abingdon 1986) 9.
5. Cp. Willimon, "Introduction" 10-2.

> Why does the Church remain in grace? Not because it is itself steadfast and faithful. But because, *despite* all sin and guilt, God does not dismiss it from his favor and grace and constantly grants it a new indestructibility ....
> Why does the Church remain in truth? Not because there is in it no wavering or doubting, no deviation or going astray. But because God maintains it in truth, *despite* its doubts, misunderstandings, and errors ....[1]

Not everyone, perhaps, can play the role of engaged and loving critic *in* the church—for some people, leaving may be the only real option. And not every church, perhaps, can tolerate its critics. But individual Christians possess the capacity to continue their "lovers' quarrels" with the church,[2] and corporate Christianity possesses the resources to accommodate its questioning and sometimes alienated members and profit from their doubts and concerns. That is why even the cynics have cause to remain hopeful.

> We are critical in our attitude to the Church because this critique belongs to the very nature of our faith itself since in union with the faith of the Church it is on the way to eternal light. But this means that the critique itself derives its life from an assent to the Church as she exists in the concrete which is ever renewed in hope, causing our faith to rise above all temptations and constantly to renew itself.[3]

---

1. Hans Küng, *The Church—Maintained in Truth: A Theological Meditation*, trans. Edward Quinn (New York: Crossroad-Seabury 1980) 16.
2. I owe this metaphor to Dick Winn.
3. Rahner 159-60.

12

Love Hopes All Things

Love hopes, and love give us reason to hope. Because of God's love, we can have hope for love in history. Because of God's love, we can have hope—for loving relationships with other creatures and with God—beyond history. And that for which we hope is, among other things, a greater opportunity to love God, other creatures, and ourselves. Hope is not the same thing as unruffled optimism. We do not know just what we can expect in the future for ourselves or for our world. But to believe ourselves embraced by God's love is to believe that we need never give up our confidence—in God's presence with us, in the possibility of loving relationship with God, and in the security of the meaning of our lives in God—not only today but always.

God is active in history. Love is the motivation for this activity, and love—among creatures, and between creatures and God—is a central goal of divine providence. Because creation is free, God's love is not perfectly embodied in history. But it exerts a tangible influence, nonetheless. We are called to participate in enacting God's love historically; but, at the same time, we must avoid treating any actual or imagined historical formation as perfectly embodying that love.

The anticipation of life beyond death reflects the conviction that God loves creation and desires fellowship with creatures, the hope that the healing of our lives may reach its completion and that our growth may continue, and the belief that Jesus' life beyond death is a pointer to the possibility of our own. Hope beyond death can free us from the fear of death, and so free us for love—both personal and political—in the present. A vision of love beyond death can serve as both inspiration and norm for present action. And Sabbath rest can offer us a foretaste of the future beyond death for which we hope.

LOVE'S HOPE FOR HISTORY

Love hopes for a better world—a world in which love as care and love as respect are more clearly manifested, and a world that is more fully an appropriate object of love as delight. And love is confident that there can be such a world. The conviction that a better world is possible is a consequence of the conviction that God is no stranger to history. If God's Spirit is present and active in the world, then God can make a difference in history. I've already argued that God interacts with particular persons. But this means that God's action necessarily has effects that extend *beyond* particular persons to relationships, institutions, and social structures. It is impossible for a meaningful individual life to be lived in absolute isolation. To affect a person is thus to affect the relationships, institutions, and structures in which she participates. (Of course, to affect relationships, institutions, and structures will, in turn, have consequences for individuals. One way in which we must assume God touches individual lives is precisely through the influences on them of human relationships, cultures, and institutions.)

That the created world matters to God means that we can expect God to foster healing and development in history. Whatever we say about God's work in history cannot involve a denial that the world is God's good creation. Thus, Christian hope is not hope for the nullification of history. If history is valuable, if divine self-revelation takes place in history, if history is the context in which the human drama is played out as freedom and nature intersect, then history cannot be ignored by God's salvific work.

Given that God *can* make a difference in history, God's love means that God will *seek* to make a difference. Divine love will find expression both in the seeking and in the sought, for what God seeks in history will be, in significant part, the love of creatures for God and for each other. Love seeks the flourishing of the whole created order in relationships of mutuality and care and delight.

The degree to which God's love is actualized in history is, of course, affected by the reality of creation. But God is constantly present and active, persuading creation toward becoming a community of love.

That God's activity in the world is mediated in and through creaturely events does not mean that God is only to be encountered in smooth, slow, gradual developments. There will always be some connection between each moment of history and the ones that have preceded it, but this does not mean that God cannot draw persons and communities toward surprising goals and onto risky paths. The notion that God is continually present within history is sometimes understood as a complacent endorsement of the *status quo*. But human sin, fallibility, and ignorance mean that much that occurs in history is not God's will—indeed, that God's will actively opposes much that occurs in history. And this means, in turn, that we are as likely to discern God's intentions in decisions by persons and communities to challenge the existing order as in choices to maintain things as they are. Of course, dramatic change can be a reflection of sin just like complacency, but the present reality of sin, taken together with the reality of divine love, means that God's love will be felt as an incessant pressure toward flourishing and against injustice, a pressure which will sometimes have dramatic consequences.

Of course, hope is not always hope in the novel and the surprising. Sometimes we hope precisely that the good things we experience, the order that sustains our lives, will be nourished and enriched and preserved. We can discern God's presence and activity in institutions and structures, in experiences of order and stability, as well as in the revolutionary. Love's work includes maintaining as well as transforming the conditions of human life.[1] But it can never be content with complacency any more than it can sanction pointless change.

Human life is distorted on multiple levels. We can distinguish multiple interrelated problems as central to the human predicament: they include the problem of meaning, the problem of death, and the problem of sin. God's work in history does not eliminate these problems, but it addresses them in significant ways.

Our bodies are subject to deterioration because they are finite. They are physical systems unable to support themselves and subject to the effects of entropy. To be sure, historical transformation cannot abolish their mortality. Technological advance can extend our lives, but it cannot extend them limitlessly. Historical developments can address our vulnerability, our fragility, our subjection to harm and loss, in provisional and limited ways. They can ensure that we eat better and receive better medical care. None of these achievements is negligible, but none

---

1. Cp. Langdon Gilkey, *Reaping the Whirlwind: A Christian Interpretation of History* (New York: Crossroad-Seabury 1976) 246-7. I have benefited from Gilkey's insights throughout this chapter.

offers more than a temporary response to the cluster of problems centrally represented by our mortality.

Historical transformation can address our experience of meaninglessness. Historical communities can provide us with tasks, purposes, and identities. A smoothly functioning, orderly community can enable us to know who we are and how our lives are linked with and contribute to larger wholes. Through its symbols and practices and rituals it can even point us beyond itself toward God, toward the all-embracing context of meaning within which our lives can be seen to be truly significant.

But historical communities often fail miserably in providing us with order and meaning. Fragmented, chaotic, misshapen by power politics, they may lack the coherence to offer us meaningful niches or to employ the symbols and transmit the traditions we need to point us toward God. They can address the problem of meaning, but, again, they can at best give us partial solutions to this problem.

This is partly because of their finitude and fallibility. No creaturely community could possibly provide us with an ultimate and unshakeable source of meaning. Communities are made up of persons who do not know all that there is to know and do not fully understand what they do know. And every historical institution is finite and will ultimately disappear—and so cannot be a permanent repository of the significance of our lives. The very fact that these limitations obtain means that no community could *in principle* address our need for meaning perfectly. But quite apart from finitude and fallibility is the fact of our moral and spiritual brokenness: the fact of sin.

Sin distorts social and cultural structures, interpersonal relationships, and individual lives. Its roots lie ultimately in our inability to provide ourselves or each other with the complete security, the ultimate acceptance, the perfect love that we need if we are confidently to love other persons, the non-human world, and ourselves. But it can be occasioned, embodied, and rendered all the more awful in its hold on us and in its effects in our lives by social institutions, patterns of cultural life, and economic and political systems.

Political, economic, and cultural change cannot alter the fact that of our finitude and vulnerability. It cannot protect us from the fragility, isolation, and alienation that drive us toward idolatry. Indeed, for a movement or institution within history—a church or party or corporation or nation—to attempt to do this would be for it to seek idolatrous loyalty for itself. Social change can, however, address those structure and institutions that occasion, perpetuate, and deepen our moral and spiritual distortion.

The failure to make this distinction can lead some Christians to assume too optimistically that changing social structures will simply eliminate our moral and spiritual brokenness. The great temptation for those who take this overly optimistic route is to cut corners, to treat their goals in history as so overwhelmingly important that love can be sacrificed to achieve them. People who idolize agencies of social change can fail to criticize or challenge them. They can also fail to recognize the claims that a variety of relationships, institutions, and people can make on them—claims that may conflict with those of the movements with which they identify. And those who assume that social change has the potential to solve all human problems may lapse into pessimistic quietism when they discern the limits of movements in which they've placed their hopes.

It is all too possible, though, for some Christian groups to assume that, because some aspects of human sinfulness aren't produced by society, politics, and culture, social change is impossible or pointless. On this view, sin's embeddedness in our lives prevents real social change from happening, and its roots in our need for ultimate love and security make it impossible for social change to affect it.

The best we can do is to play along with the dominant order; seek small, ameliorative changes; and harness human selfishness in limited ways for the social good.

I think this view is overly pessimistic. It underestimates the reality of love's presence and work in human lives and relationships. Sin *is* embedded in our lives, and trusting in institutional and cultural transformation to eradicate it (especially given that everything we do in history is itself misshapen by sin) is naïve. But in virtue of both the created character of humanness and the historical activity of God's Spirit, people do sometimes opt for love instead of injustice. Sin is not so absolute and all-pervasive a phenomenon that all attempts to make social change happen will necessarily be halted or co-opted by sin.

The pessimistic view also misses the extent to which justice can restrain sinful *actions*—even if restraining such actions does not automatically heal sinful *hearts*. Though love may not be internalized, social justice can keep the effects of selfishness contained. The criminal justice system, for instance, is far from perfect, but it does make a positive difference in people's lives by keeping at least some of the violent and the dishonest at bay. Legal arrangements that protect the rights of workers to bargain collectively or that preclude employment discrimination based on religion, sex, or race don't eradicate sin from individuals or interpersonal relationships. They do, however, prevent some kinds of unfair behavior.

In addition, the pessimistic view ignores the ways in which culture, society, politics, and the economy not only *embody* but *perpetuate* sin. Structures of oppression and domination may be objects of idolatry, and they may arise or be maintained because of sinful motives and actions. In any event, however, they become vehicles and occasions for sin. Social structures and institutions extend people's ability to cause harm while simultaneously insulating them from the effects of the harm they do. It is much easier to refrain from being empathetic when one has no direct contact with someone who is harmed by one's actions. It is much easier to be unjust when one can justify one's actions as performed in the name of a cause greater than oneself. A person who would refuse to act unfairly or unkindly on her own behalf may feel justified in harming others in the name of an institution.

Further, problematic social structures can encourage destructive attitudes and may make it even less likely that people experience themselves as grounded in an ultimate love and security or learn habits of heart and mind marked by respectful love for other persons, the non-human world, or themselves.[1] By contrast, helpful social structures can reshape people's attitudes and beliefs, disposing them to be more fair-minded and compassionate. People may initially resent being required by law to behave fairly toward people who are, say, members of ethnic groups other than their own. But they may find over time that the experience of treating others fairly without regard to ethnicity becomes easier, that it comes to seem obviously like the right thing to do, that assumptions rooted in prejudice no longer seem plausible. Institutional change can foster personal change.

In short, social change can help to limit and moderate the effects of sin—or it can make them far worse. Even if it cannot touch the fundamental problem of idolatry, it can reduce the harm that people can do through unjust structures and help to create structures that will more effectively mediate God's securing and freeing love. Thus, social change matters. Things can and do improve. Even people convinced of the reality of sin can regard change—potentially dramatic change—in society, politics, culture, and the economy as worth hoping for, and so worth working for. And it will make sense to see history as an arena in which God's healing love is at work and in which that love makes a difference.

1. For instance: simply taking an introductory economics course can dispose people to be more selfish; cp. John Dupré, *Human Nature and the Limits of Science* (New York: OUP 2003).

The new is possible in history, and despite the continuation of sin within each novel form of history . . . life can in many ways become better. Because of these new possibilities for new social orders, history does ascend on one important level. The forms of historical life can progress—and have progressed—and thus represent higher, more humane structures of human social existence.[1]

Progress is rarely if ever unambiguous. The removal of an injustice may create new hazards and losses. Eliminating subsidies for tobacco may lead to painful economic dislocation for farmers whose livelihoods have depended on growing this deadly crop. A just international market that brought workers in the Two-Thirds World as equal partners into the global economy of design, production, and distribution couldn't help but create some tensions and challenges for First World citizens, at least in the short-term. Slavery was and is a great wrong, and its elimination is perhaps the most unequivocal instance of progress in human history, but there were, of course, goods that this great wrong offered to slave-owners, consumers, and others.[2]

At least sometimes, we can tell clearly when a given development constitutes genuine progress. But *genuine* progress isn't the same thing as *unambiguous* progress, unequivocal progress, a gain from *everyone's* point of view. What counts as progress from one perspective can seem like tragedy from another. That doesn't mean, though, that all perspectives are created equal. It doesn't mean that we can't determine whether or not, or in what ways, a given historical development really counts as progress. As I suggested when I examined the role of tradition in grounding our beliefs and at the problem posed for a view like mine by the existence of conflicting religious traditions, we necessarily make judgments from particular perspectives, from within particular traditions. But those traditions can be rationally assessed. They can change and grow. Their perspectives can be validated or invalidated. We assess particular claims about progress from within a tradition that is itself historical, developing and changing and particular. Insofar as that tradition survives the internal and external challenges it faces, however, it can rightly provide us with criteria for identifying progress when and where it occurs.

Inclusive love is a central criterion by which Christian faith will identify progress. This will mean a recognition of the infinite preciousness of each person, coupled with a bias in favor of those who, in any particular situation, are the victims of injustice. (Being a victim in one setting does not, obviously, preclude being an oppressor in another. Privileged women may be victims of sexism but agents of class oppression. Economically marginal people may suffer from class discrimination but discriminate against others on the basis of race.) Progress happens to the extent that communities of love are built and persons are both loved and enabled to love more fully. This does not mean that progress happens when people are treated uniformly; love demands attention to the particularity of each person. But it does entail giving each person the fullest possible opportunity to participate in loving interpersonal relationships and communal structures. Where such opportunities are evident, so is progress.

Hope in history is warranted by the conviction that God is love and by the reality of God's activity in history. But the countervailing realities of sin, finitude, and fallibility make any cheery optimism about inevitable and uninterrupted progress naïve at best. That God is the conserver of what is good and the One who calls us toward that which makes love more fully real in our lives does not mean that what God conserves cannot be shattered or that God's call cannot be ignored. Obviously, they are—all too frequently. Even presuming we can tell what does and

---

1. Gilkey 285-6.
2. Discussion with Alexander Lian helped to clarify my thinking on this point.

does not *count* as progress, we suppose that progress will consistently occur. We cannot envision history's course as consistently upward and linear. "We must insist . . . that there is no triumphal march of God in history, . . . but only a plurality of partial, fragmentary, ambiguous histories of love."[1] History is "an open-ended, never finished process of the formation and deformation of syntheses, harmonies, balances, on both macrohistorical and microhistorical scales."[2] God's Spirit "drives, shapes, lures" history, and history in turn embodies God's aims to a greater or lesser degree "in many distinct moments"; nonetheless, "it remains a process that is . . . always subject to demonic distortion,"[3] regress, and collapse.

During the heyday of optimistic Christianity in the nineteenth century, many people were confident that society and culture were almost inevitably improving. Because God was present and active in history, the historical world was becoming more and more clearly God's Realm. It is clear today that we have no license for this kind of optimism. To hope for God's love to become evident in history, to hope in turn that creaturely love will be more and more apparent, is not absurd. But to expect the divine Realm of love to appear in history untainted by sin and ambiguity is both unrealistic and dangerous. The challenge as we hope and work in history, as we recognize God's activity in and through our activity and that of others, is to acknowledge the ways in which sin distorts good motives and in which even the best movements become objects of idolatrous loyalty, while at the same time contributing to the development and healing of the world, and so to making it a place that more clearly embodies God's love. The presence and power of God's Spirit mean that we can not only work but truly hope for such a world.

Why Love Hopes Beyond Death

To hope as a Christian is to hope not only for history but for particular persons. It is to believe that one's short and not always edifying history is not all there is to one's life, that we can look forward to the possibility of a future beyond death of love for God and other creatures.[4]

We can and should hope for life beyond death for several reasons. It is an implication of the belief that God created a world in which creatures would be vulnerable to suffering, of the conviction that God creates persons intending their spiritual maturation, and of the belief that God desires the endless love of creatures. Further, Jesus' own life beyond death gives us reason for hope that death will not have the final verdict on our lives.

Love and Creation

Love takes risks, but not unwarranted ones. God's love must be, in part, an overflowing commitment to care for our well-being. But creation was and is for God an act of risk—love's risk. God could not be love and at the same time *desire* or *intend* the occurrence of physical accident or moral failure or any of the other sources of hurt that fill our world. Nonetheless, God evidently desired a world in which the suffering of sentient beings and the evil acts of persons do, in fact, take place, as by-products of creaturely freedom and natural regularity. Creaturely

---

1. Peter C. Hodgson, *God in History: Shapes of Freedom* (Nashville: Abingdon 1989) 233. The ellipsized phrase reads "no special history of salvation," which seems to me to push in a somewhat different direction. More ruthlessly, I have substituted "love" for "freedom."
2. Hodgson 243.
3. Hodgson 246.
4. My arguments in the next few paragraphs are paralleled in Huw Parri Own, *Christian Theism: A Study in Its Basic Principles* (Edinburgh: Clark 1984) 132-3.

freedom makes it possible for some of us to prey on others. Ignorance and confusion result from the fact that human knowledge is limited. Our capacity for action isn't great enough to permit us to address many of the problems we encounter. The order of the physical world leads to accident, injury, and disease. Life in such a world unavoidably gives rise to the challenge of reconciling confidence in God's love with the suffering and loss that plague creaturely existence.

A world in which creatures can suffer must be valuable at least in part because God desires the free love of creatures and because God wants to give real gifts to real persons, real persons who can further enrich the universe with their God-given creativity. It is obvious that God has taken a risk in creating this sort of world. The creation of a world in which people could be expected to experience pain, suffering, risk, vulnerability, and loss could only be a product of divine love if genuine hope were possible even for those whose lives have been stunted by evil and accident.

The problem of evil cannot adequately be addressed if the goods available in present experience are the only ones on offer. For many people have not experienced those goods in their fullness, or at all. Their availability is limited. And the fact that they can be experienced in this life hardly seems to compensate for the pain and disappointment that are the lot of so many people.

People lead stunted, meaningless lives for all sorts of reasons. Obviously, someone who dies of brain cancer can complain of terrible suffering. But someone who spends her life working at a pointless, unsatisfying job—as, say, a banana-picker in Central America—with little or no chance to experience the wider world, can also wonder whether her life has been a waste, or worse. And she would, I believe, have good reason to complain to God about her wasted life if she had no hope for a better life beyond death. People who have suffered from great pain or meaninglessness would be short-changed if this life were the end of their possibilities. Why should God have created them at all, if their lives were not, on balance, to prove worthwhile? The divine decision to create and nourish our world might seem like a cosmic joke or a needless source of pain were there no ultimate hope for people beyond death.

There must be some kind of life beyond death if all people are to have the chance to experience meaning and value. The problem of evil can be resolved, then, only if there is the possibility of a limitlessly good future.[1] Absent this possibility, many people would have good reason to judge the process of life and death in a world like ours—as it affected their own lives—to have been unjustifiably wasteful. From the premise that God is love, and would not, therefore, undertake a creative process that would leave many lives irremediably broken and meaningless, we can conclude that it is reasonable for us to hope for life beyond death.

The reality of life beyond death does not mean that other responses to the fact of evil are not important. The world's evil still doesn't make sense if we fail to take into account, for instance, the incompatibility of divine determination and human freedom—even with life beyond death in the picture, God would still be indictable for creaturely suffering in the absence of genuine creaturely freedom. But what justifies taking the risk involved in creating such a world in the first place? Creating the sort of world that is marked by characteristics which occasion our experiences of suffering and evil would be loving only if the end result of God's creation and work in the world were obviously good for created persons (and perhaps other creatures as well).[2] But unless God's aims for the world and its inhabitants are very low

---

1. I owe this phrase to John Hick.
2. Jay B. McDaniel, "Can Animal Suffering be Reconciled with Belief in an All-Loving God?" *Animals on the Agenda*, ed. Andrew Linzey and Dorothy Yamamoto (London: SCM 1998) 169-70.

indeed, it is apparent that they will not be achieved if death is allowed to say the last word. If, then, God's creative activity seeks the well-being of creatures, it must be that they can enjoy a life beyond death in which they can participate in the aspects of human welfare they were created to enjoy.[1]

Love and Spiritual Flourishing

For love's risk to be warranted, spiritual maturation must be a real possibility. Not only the creation of persons vulnerable to suffering but the creation of persons intended for spiritual maturity seems to imply the possibility of life beyond death. The spiritual development of most creatures can stand considerable improvement. There is no evidence that anyone's life concludes only after she has formed a flawless character. Even at death, people still seem to need to do a lot of growing spiritually. Only if life beyond death is possible will people have any hope of completing their healing and their growth to personal maturity.[2] If God's love means wanting to see free creatures reach spiritual maturity, it is difficult to see how that goal could be reached if death were the end for all of them. If God would create free persons only if real spiritual maturity were possible for them, then, since such maturity seems to require life beyond death for its realization, it follows that life beyond death must be a real possibility.[3]

God's Desire for Our Love

God's love desires the responsive love of creatures, not only their flourishing. Divine love is particular, concerned with each constituent of reality—and thus with each person. And if God loves each person, then God must desire to continue that love, to continue to experience the distinctive richness that each of us contributes to reality, to know our love in response to God's own. If life beyond death were impossible, then we would have to conceive of God's love as *essentially* tragic. We would have to envision God as bringing new persons into being *knowing* that their love for God would never truly be consummated. Perhaps God's love is tragic in this way, but surely it makes at least as much sense to see God's bringing into being of creatures whose love God desires as evidence that such creatures may, indeed, be capable of enjoying endless life in love with God.

Love and the Witness of Jesus' Life Beyond Death

Jesus' life beyond death provides further reason for belief in the possibility of our own. It serves as a witness to the truth that death need not be victorious. From the fact of Jesus' life beyond death, it seems to follow that life beyond death is a genuine possibility for human persons.

---

1. Cp. John Hick, *Evil and the God of Love*, rev. ed. (San Francisco: Harper 1977) 338-40; David Ray Griffin, *Reenchantment without Supernaturalism: A Process Philosophy of Religion* (Ithaca, NY: Cornell UP 2001) 233.

2. Cp. Immanuel Kant, "The Critique of Practical Reason," trans. Thomas Kingsmill Abbott, *Kant*, Great Books of the Western World 42 (Chicago: Encyclopædia Britannica 1952) 344: "the perfect accordance of the will with the moral law is *holiness*, a perfection of which no rational being of the sensible world is capable at any moment of his existence. Since, nevertheless, it is required as practically necessary, it can only be found in a *progress in infinitum* towards that perfect accordance .... Now, this endless progress is only possible on the supposition of an *endless* duration of the *existence* and personality of the same rational being...."

3. Cp. Hick 338.

The Significance of Personal Hope Beyond Death

Hopeful expectation of life beyond death is significant for Christian life in the present.

Hope Beyond Death and Love in the Present

Belief in the possibility of life beyond death is the basis for a hope that can inspire and inform our lives in the present.[1] For such hope, death is not the end. Thus, whatever our circumstances, we need not give in to despair. A future is always waiting for us, and it is God's future. However inadequate we may feel, there is still the possibility of a future in which the ambiguities of our lives are resolved. However excluded from power we may be, we can hope for a time when mutual empowerment is the rule rather than the exception. However fragmented our lives may be, we may anticipate an opportunity to knit together their pieces together. Life beyond death guarantees that we have the potential for unimaginable possibilities of flourishing and fulfillment yet to come.[2]

The future for which we hope is not *our own* future, however. Of course, it is ours in the sense that we will experience it. But that we will do so is the result of *God's* action.[3] On the one hand, this undercuts any arrogant expectation that we can guarantee our own life beyond death. That life is not something we effect or earn through our achievements. It will not be a reward for our virtuous individual or corporate behavior. We can afford to be honest about our own potential: we need not reproach ourselves for failing to achieve flawless individual or social lives, as if our participation in God's final future were dependent on our ability to do so. And we need not attempt in frustration to secure our destinies by imposing our wills on others in authoritarian fashion. That our final future with God lies beyond death points fundamentally, *not* to the valuelessness of everything we experience in this life (it is, after all, God's good creation), but to its *provisionality*. Thus, neither the church nor the political order can claim that its decisions deserve unqualified assent. Neither can control our participation in the life beyond death for which we hope. And no achievement of any human authority deserves to be treated as final, as if it were part of that life.

At the same time, because we are not responsible for the final future, we are free to enjoy life in the present. We need not feel the awesome responsibility for the universe that might be ours if the ultimate future had been entrusted to us. We can work confidently for creation's development and healing. But we need not be overcome with guilt as we ask ourselves whether we should have done more, or with despair as we realize that we have not done enough. We can take our work seriously without taking it ultimately. We can delight in God's good creation—in its inanimate, animal, human, social, and cultural dimensions. Hope frees us to play.[4]

Hope beyond death can also free us to love particular others and historical communities. It is easy to regard our loves as dangerous, since death can separate us from those persons and institutions and communities we love. But if we know

---

1. On the relationship between hope and Christian eschatology, see Jürgen Moltmann, *Theology of Hope: On the Ground and the Implications of a Christian Eschatology*, trans. James W. Leitch (New York: Harper 1967).

2. I owe this point to H. Maynard Lowry.

3. Cp. John B. Cobb, Jr., "The Resurrection of the Soul," *Harvard Theological Review* 80.2 (1987): 213-27; Griffin 236-46; Alfred North Whitehead, *Adventures of Ideas* (New York: Free 1933) 208 (thanks to Griffin for this reference).

4. Cp. Jürgen Moltmann, *Theology of Play*, trans. Reinhard Ulrich (New York: Harper 1972).

that our loves can continue beyond death, we will be free to let ourselves be vulnerable, to take risks, to care deeply.

In addition, belief in life beyond death can serve as the source of a potent critique of contemporary injustices, and as an inspiration for action designed to address them.[1]

That God's future is coming calls into question all human structures and decisions, including—and especially—our own. And if our vision of God's final future helps us to discern what a flourishing creation looks like, and if a flourishing creation is our goal in the present, then we can find in the character of Christian hope a source of insights that can contribute to the shaping of contemporary Christian moral, political, and cultural practice. We can, in short, "let our eschatology inform our ethics."[2]

God's final future will be one of genuine community with other creatures and with God. We cannot pretend to know its details. But we can draw on our basic convictions, and on the symbols and images God's self-revelation prompted apostles, prophets, seers, and mystics to employ in depicting God's glorious future. We can wait confidently for that future because of what God has already done on our behalf. We can work in the present to anticipate that future, using the numerous resources God has made available to us. And we can do so without fearing that the torturer and the executioner will triumph. Hope beyond death frees us to oppose them with the knowledge that they do not and cannot determine our ultimate destinies. Whatever losses they inflict need not be final.

Because we can consistently both work and hope, there is no conflict between, say, ecological concern, and Christian hope, provided that one works on behalf of our fragile ecosystem without believing that one is thus taking full, personal responsibility for humanity's future. Christian hope is thoroughly consistent with concern for the welfare of the material creation, including everything from our own bodies to the Brazilian rain-forests.

Hope Beyond Death and Sabbath Rest

On the Sabbath, we can enjoy, in part, the kind of life toward which we look in hope when we think about God's final future. We can rest from the demand that we produce and achieve. We can celebrate God's good creation, including ourselves and others, our communities, and the whole of the human and non-human worlds. We can realize the freedom and equality for which we were created.

Thus, Sabbath rest can serve as a foretaste of our life beyond death.[3] For the Sabbath offers time free from necessity, and celebrating the Sabbath is an implicit affirmation that one need not always be busy *doing*. The ultimate good is not always found in activity; sometimes, reflection and contemplation and conversation are the very things required. By providing us with freedom from the demand for achievement, the Sabbath liberates us for a playful humanness that anticipates the flourishing of our humanity beyond death.

In addition, the Sabbath can offer a very potent, and thus extremely practical critique of problematic features of contemporary experience. There is nothing more devastating to the status quo than the public display of an alternative to current ways of doing things, for such an alternative demonstrates that the way things are simply isn't necessary. Of course, the Sabbath is not the only way in

---

1. Cp. Hebblethwaite, *Hope* 202.
2. So Charles Teel, Jr.
3. I have been inspired here by the remarks of Stanley Hauerwas, "Taking Time for Peace: The Ethical Significance of the Trivial," *Religion and Intellectual Life* 3.3 (Spring 1986): 87-100.

which we realize God's final future in advance. Whenever we work to create and sustain personal or institutional community; whenever we work to transform unjust structures; whenever we envision and implement new possibilities for the created order; whenever we love, we anticipate God's final future. But the Sabbath can do so in a particularly striking way.

Our anticipation of God's final future is never flawless: neither our actions designed to foster the world's development and healing nor our efforts to understand the shape of God's future are perfect. Now, of course, we can only discern "through a glass, darkly," what the shape of that future might be. But, building on the clues present in our experience and in the witness of Christian voices from St. Paul to Julian of Norwich to Martin Luther King, Jr., we can begin to envision and experience it in advance. We act in the present with hope for the future, confident in the conviction that God is love.

Index

Abelard, Peter, 177
Abernathy, David, 153
abominations, 120
abortion, 254
Abraham, William J., 66, 68
absolutes, moral, 110, 111
Adams, Marilyn McCord, 39, 209, 222
Adams, Robert Merrihew, 9, 13, 28, 39, 54, 88, 90, 91, 96, 119, 138, 141, 199
Adventism, Seventh-day, 81, 128, 132, 169, 238, 241, 242, 248, 256, 269, 295
Aelred of Rievaulx, 231
Alighieri, Dante, 5, 177
Allen, Diogenes, 25, 28, 65, 89, 98
analogy, 1, 8, 10, 11, 12, 13, 39, 42, 56, 57, 64, 87, 96, 272
Anderson, Ray S., 37
Andreasen, Niels-Erik, 81, 128, 169, 238
Aristotle, 241
assassination, 254
Athanasius, St., 177
atonement
    substitutionary theory of, 213, 214, 215, 216, 219
Augustine, St., 4, 57, 144, 177, 182, 183, 262
autonomy, 117, 119
Baab, Lynne M., 81, 169
Bacchiocchi, Samuele, 81, 99, 160, 163, 169, 238
Baelz, Peter, 63, 65, 71
Bailie, Gil, 218
Baldwin, Dalton, 164
Balthasar, Hans Urs von, 57
Banks, Robert J., 112
Barr, James, 13, 28, 91, 256
Barth, Karl, 23, 54, 57, 81, 169, 177, 234
Bartky, Sandra Lee, 144
Barton, John, 68, 100, 115, 179, 180, 182, 183
Basinger, David, 36, 66, 69
Basinger, Randall, 36, 66, 69
Bauckham, Richard, 149, 155
Bauman, Zygmunt, 98

Beasley-Murray, George R., 155
Beaty, Michael D., 112, 209
Bem, Sandra Lipsitz, 164
Benjamin, Jessica, 164
Berger, Peter, 25, 28
Bernard, St., 5, 177
Berry, Wanda Warren, 146
Blakeselee, Sandra, 235
Borg, Marcus J., 143, 156, 169, 171, 172, 173, 174, 175, 176, 177, 180, 230, 266
Boros, Ladislaus, 94
Bowden, John, 153, 175, 179, 181
Boyle, Joseph, 65, 102, 106
Braaten, Carl E., 142
Bradcock, Gary D., 115
Brady, J. P., 191
Braine, David, 9, 52, 54
Branson, Roy, 81, 128, 169, 238, 248
Bromiley, Geoffrey, 24, 81, 84, 149, 169, 197
Brown, David, 22, 60, 69, 149, 170, 187, 191, 192, 194, 212
Brown, Raymond E., 149, 151, 152, 154, 155, 170
Brümmer, Vincent, 11, 65, 71, 73, 76
Brunner, Emil, 22, 59
Brunt, John C., 81, 169
Buber, Martin, 87, 206
Burke, Phyllis, 164
Butler, Jonathan, 269, 271
Cambridge, 11, 16, 26, 28, 32, 33, 44, 65, 69, 75, 78, 81, 89, 98, 103, 105, 106, 112, 117, 125, 127, 150, 151, 152, 153, 157, 158, 162, 164, 169, 170, 187, 194, 215, 239, 295
Caputo, John D., 98
Casas, Bartolomé de las, 256
change, social, 121, 249, 256, 258, 259, 277, 278
Chartier, Helen, 98, 133, 224
Chartier, Stanley, 131
Chaudhuri, Nirad C., 254
Chodorow, Nancy, 164
Christ, Carol P., 145

Christian Reformed Church, 241
Christian, William A., 251
Christianity, establishment of, 231
Clark, Stephen R. L., 27, 29, 30, 39, 96, 106, 113, 122, 123, 149, 162, 220
Clayton, John Powell, 32, 153, 157, 170
Clayton, Philip, 65
Clouser, Roy, 40, 41
Cobb, John B., 1, 65, 67, 77, 79, 149, 161, 162, 163, 252, 253, 283
co-housing, 126
colonialism, 256
Commandments, Ten, 3, 92, 168
commands, divine, 3, 82, 112, 113, 114, 115, 116, 117, 118, 119, 120, 121, 133, 135, 173, 204, 215
complacency, 15, 30, 276
Connell, R. W., 164
contingency, 2, 23, 34, 36, 52, 53, 72, 94, 95, 100, 112, 113, 115, 116, 118, 124, 145, 158, 161, 179, 183, 189, 198, 199, 201, 204, 225, 241
Countryman, L. William, 69, 100, 209, 268
Cox, Harvey, 162
Craig, William Lane, 187, 190, 191, 192, 193, 194, 195, 199
Crossan, John Dominic, 172, 173, 174, 175, 176, 177, 180, 232
Cullmann, Oscar, 149, 152, 153, 154, 213
Daily, Steven G., xi
Daly, Mary, 106
Dancy, Jonathan, 117
Danto, Arthur C., 254, 255
Davis, Stephen T., 13, 165
Dawn, Marva J., 81, 169
de Jonge, Marinus, 154, 155
denominations, 234, 244, 246, 248, 272
detachment, 81, 271
determinism, 53, 64, 65, 66, 203
development, doctrinal, 245
devotion, 15, 85, 89, 90, 91, 97, 171, 177
dialogue, 14, 25, 31, 32, 33, 55, 102, 145, 229, 248, 249, 250, 251, 259, 261, 262, 263, 264, 267, 284, 295
Dinnerstein, Dorothy, 164
DiNoia, Joseph A., 249, 254, 257, 260, 261, 263, 264
Dōgen, 257
Donagan, Alan, 105, 106, 117, 245
Dorrien, Gary, 127
Dunn, James D. G., 150, 153
Dupré, John, 278
economics, 56, 241, 278, 279
education, 100, 127, 215, 240, 242, 258
Edwards, Tilden, 81, 169, 238
ego, 30, 97, 145, 163

Elgin, Duane, 125
Ellis, George F. R., 64
Ellul, Jacques, 84, 126
emotion, 86, 94, 102, 115, 133, 143, 192, 208, 235, 252, 267
enjoyment, 102, 103, 123
Enslin, Morton Scott, 156
epistemology, 24, 26, 32, 33, 140, 151, 152, 153, 205
Epperly, Bruce, 79
ethics, 2, 3, 7, 13, 14, 16, 26, 28, 31, 35, 36, 40, 41, 45, 46, 51, 75, 81, 82, 85, 87-146, 173, 174, 177, 198, 199, 203-10, 215-7, 222, 233, 239, 240, 245, 249, 251-68, 277, 280, 282, 284, 295
   as rooted in gratitude, 114, 115
   consequentialist, 72, 82, 106, 107, 108, 109, 110
   moral judgment and, 121
   obligation, 28, 29, 40, 41, 98, 111, 115, 117, 119, 120, 138, 141, 264
   situation, 110
evangelicalism, 201
Evans, Christopher, 192
evil, problem of, 19, 44, 47, 49, 61, 64, 68, 159, 161, 179, 205, 223, 281
evolution, theory of, 28, 75, 82, 219
exclusivism, 173, 198, 229, 242, 264, 266
experience, religious, 19, 29, 35, 37, 38, 67, 85, 87, 90, 91, 132, 183, 189, 200, 235, 239, 240, 273
Faber, F. W., 224
fairness, 2, 14, 82, 102, 105-17, 125, 128, 143, 164, 173, 178, 179, 207-12, 222, 223, 238, 256, 262, 284
faith, 4, 6, 7, 10, 12, 19, 33, 34, 35, 49, 74, 121, 153, 230, 252, 260, 262, 264, 268, 269, 273, 274, 279
Farley, Edward, 47, 52, 82, 83, 84, 88, 134, 145, 149, 162, 201, 216, 220
Farley, Wendy, 24, 39, 98
Farmer, H. H., 63, 162
Farrer, Austin, 7, 34, 35, 36, 38, 39, 46, 63, 64, 65, 66, 68, 69, 71, 76, 157, 158, 161, 168
Feenstra, Ronald J., 149
feminism, 254
Fenn, Richard K., 132
Fenton, J. C., 150
Festinger, Leon, 192
Fiddes, Paul, 158
Finn, Huckleberry, 131, 138, 139, 140
Finnis, John M., 44, 72, 102, 103, 104, 105, 106, 107, 118, 125, 212
Fletcher, Joseph, 108, 109, 110
Flew, Antony, 27, 188, 191
food, 70, 78, 100, 123, 127, 172, 215, 235, 241, 258, 270, 295

forgiveness, 3, 4, 40, 177, 179, 189, 199, 209, 210, 211, 213
foundationalism, 25
Francis, St., 177
Franciscan order, 177, 231
Frederiksen, Paula, 192
freedom, 27, 43, 44, 45, 46, 47, 48, 52, 61, 65, 69, 70, 113, 137, 147, 161, 226, 280, 281
Freeman, Anthony, 142, 221
Frei, Hans, 153
Fried, Charles, 125
Friedman, Marilyn, 123
friendship, 2, 4, 11, 13, 43, 50, 54, 70, 72, 73, 74, 84, 86, 88, 89, 92-7, 100, 103, 109, 110, 115, 123, 124, 125, 139, 140, 163, 179, 180-7, 206, 209, 230, 231, 234, 241, 261, 264-8
Fuchs, Ernst, 153
Fuller, Daniel Payton, 10
Fuller, Reginald H., 154
Furrow, Dwight, 98
Gager, John, 192, 193
gender, gender relations, 31, 63, 86, 112, 128, 131, 139, 145, 146, 155, 163-73, 178, 181, 187, 190, 191, 194, 213, 217, 229, 230, 235, 237, 238, 245, 246, 254, 255, 279
Gewirth, Alan, 116
Gibbs, Robert, 98
gifts, spiritual, 60, 74, 75, 76, 77, 78, 79, 230
Gilkey, Langdon, 25, 28, 65, 83, 88, 97, 99, 101, 142, 143, 157, 198, 276, 279
Gillespie, Michael Allen, 113
Ginet, Carl, 65
giving, charitable, 124
God
    acceptance by, 3, 119, 182, 204, 213, 224
    activity of, 7, 8, 12, 19, 36, 39, 41, 44-73, 76-82, 84, 93, 153, 157, 161, 168, 174-80, 189, 204, 208, 212, 225, 259, 275
    apparent absence of, 19, 37
    arguments for the reality of, 28, 48, 49
    as Father, 15, 16, 56, 70, 78, 96, 162, 165, 189, 213, 224
    as judge, 197, 211, 212, 213, 216, 273
    as Trinity, 4, 5, 22, 50, 51, 55, 56, 57, 58, 60, 67, 69, 70, 74, 79, 149, 156, 157, 170, 187, 249, 260
    creative work of, 6, 9, 11, 19, 20, 23, 37, 38, 40, 48, 54-7, 62, 64, 71, 76, 79-97, 112, 115, 121, 128, 133, 135, 145, 156, 157, 161, 201, 205, 206, 225, 226, 245, 259, 260, 266, 271
    goodness of, 9, 39, 41, 47, 69, 95
    language about, 1, 8, 10, 11, 21, 22, 57, 86, 164
    love of, 5
    perfect knowledge of, 9, 43, 161
    perfection of, 11, 41, 72
    power of, 7, 26, 27, 39, 40, 44-8, 56-68, 71, 76, 79, 82, 112, 114, 116, 146, 161, 170, 180, 181, 183, 201, 208, 212, 224, 225, 251, 261, 280
    predestining activity of, 22, 94, 225, 226
    purposes of, 23, 53, 55, 67, 75, 197
    Realm of, 101, 155, 171, 173, 176, 177, 280
    self-revelation by, 4, 5, 9-12, 19, 22, 23, 24, 36, 50, 51, 54-70, 97, 99, 101, 121, 149-53, 157-69, 178, 189, 197, 198, 203, 207, 211, 212, 216-9, 232, 276, 284
    sovereignty of, 6, 7, 154, 225, 226
    Spirit of, 1, 16, 20, 22, 23, 24, 30, 38, 55-79, 92, 96, 143, 147, 149, 161, 171, 198, 199, 229, 231, 232, 236, 246, 260, 262, 266, 270, 271, 275, 278, 280
    suffering of, 131, 134, 158, 159, 179, 180, 181, 186, 198, 199
    will of, 154
Goetz, Ronald, 16
Goldberg, Michael, 254
Goldstein, Valerie Saiving, 145
Goodin, Robert L., 125
goods and harms, incommensurability of, 41, 71, 105, 106, 107, 108, 110, 116, 210, 214, 222
Gore, Charles, 156
Gorringe, Timothy, 65, 70, 71
Goulder, Michael, 38, 154
Gourevitch, Philip, 247
Granberg-Michaelson, Wesley, 237
Grant, Michael, 187
Green, Joel B., 155
Green, Ronald M., 119, 199, 217
Griffin, David Ray, 9, 26, 27, 39, 62, 65, 66, 68, 73, 122, 142, 149, 156, 158, 204, 220, 260, 282, 283
Griffiths, Paul, 33, 226, 249, 251, 264
Grisez, Germain, 65, 102, 103, 105, 106, 260, 268
Guernsey, Dennis, 37
guilt, 52, 87, 115, 131, 132, 140, 141, 144, 164, 181, 191, 203, 211, 215, 216, 218, 274, 283
Gustafson, James, 122
Gutierrez, Gustavo, 256

Guy, Fritz, 81, 83, 114, 128, 150, 165, 169, 212, 217, 226
Habermas, Gary R., 151, 188
Hall, Douglas John, 12, 16, 202
happiness, 42, 104, 106, 107, 205, 235
Hare, Peter H., 39
Häring, Bernard, 264, 265
Harnack, Adolf von, 158
Harris, Murray J., 149
Harrison, Jim, 30
Hart, Trevor, 11
Hartshorne, Charles, 47, 62, 82
Harvey, Anthony E., 151, 155, 174, 194
Hasker, William J., 43
Hauerwas, Stanley M., 85, 175, 178, 234, 240, 248, 260, 267, 284
health, 77, 101, 124, 126, 127, 135, 199, 205, 206, 209, 258
health-care, 77, 127, 258
Hebblethwaite, Brian, 10, 32, 39, 45, 65, 66, 69, 78, 149, 153, 157, 158, 168, 246, 284
Heim, S. Mark, 249, 254, 257, 260
hell, 139, 140, 186, 198, 213, 222, 223, 224, 225
Hellwig, Monika, 162
Helm, Paul, 41
Helminiak, Daniel, 149, 156
Henderson, Edward, 65
Hengel, Martin, 152, 155, 179
Heron, Alasdair I. C., 60
Heschel, Abraham Joshua, 81, 128, 169
Hessel, Heather, 49, 269
Hick, John H., 38, 39, 54, 154, 162, 212, 223, 249, 281, 282
Hinchliff, Peter, 151
Hinduism, 252, 254, 255, 257, 260, 262
Hodgson, Leonard, 70
Hodgson, Peter C., 280
holiness, politics of, 230
Holocaust, 185
Howard-Snyder, Daniel, 39, 44
Hübner, Hans, 112
Hume, David, 49
humor, 273
Hunt, Mary Elizabeth, 123, 267
Hurtado, Larry W., 149, 152, 156, 188
identity, corporate, 171, 175, 176, 178, 234, 236, 245, 265
identity, personal, 21, 25, 77, 189, 208, 239
idolatry, 10, 50, 55, 57, 81, 83, 85, 87, 88, 89, 90, 91, 134, 135, 206, 266, 277, 278
inclusion, 20, 127, 165, 167, 172, 173, 175, 176, 178, 181, 220, 229, 230, 238, 246, 247, 248, 264, 266
individualism, 20
individuality, 20, 56, 143, 161, 183, 205, 207, 208, 242, 252, 262

Inoue, Enryo, 257
inspiration, 68, 69
institutions, 2, 21, 24, 29, 77, 79, 90, 103, 108, 123, 132, 134, 141, 142, 143, 183, 211, 229, 232, 234, 239-46, 267, 275-8, 283, 285
Islam, 254, 255, 257, 262
Israel, renewal of, 158, 171, 176
Jack, Dana Crowley, 145
Jenson, Robert W., 142
Jeremias, Joachim, 153, 154, 155, 194
Jesus
   as God's son, 152, 154, 156, 179, 187
   as high priest, 232
   as kyrios, 149, 152
   as Logos, 113, 162, 163
   as Messiah, 154, 168, 193
   crucifixion of, 34, 62, 63, 115, 149, 150, 151, 152, 159, 165, 167, 170, 171, 177-95, 213, 217, 219
   disciples of, 4, 108, 154, 155, 167, 170, 171, 172, 186, 187, 188, 189, 190, 191, 192, 193, 194, 195, 218, 244
   identification of God by and through, 157
   identity of, 93, 150, 151, 153, 156, 168
   imitation of, 70, 177
   life beyond death of, 150, 155, 187, 194, 195
      empty tomb as evidence for, 193, 194, 195
      hallucination theory regarding, 191, 192, 193
      swoon theory regarding, 195
      wish-fulfillment theory regarding, 192
   worship of, 151, 152
Jews, Judaism, 3, 4, 8, 14, 23, 55, 56, 57, 58, 59, 60, 62, 83, 105, 112, 121, 128, 149-78, 185-95, 211-8, 219, 230, 232, 238, 252, 254, 255, 260, 262, 266
Johann, Robert, 2
John the Baptist, 154, 192
Johnson, John E., 4
Johnson, Luke T., 91, 125
Jónasdóttir, Anna G., 145
Jones, J. R., 98
Jones, John R., 231, 232
Jones, L. Gregory, 209
jubilee, 168, 174
justice, 3, 4, 9, 24, 36, 40, 60, 67, 68, 106, 126, 143, 188, 199, 209-16, 222, 224, 226, 237, 245, 254-62, 273, 276-9
   retributive, 17, 179, 189, 199, 209, 210, 214, 215, 222, 223
   social, 219, 278

INDEX

Kähler, Martin, 197
Kaiser, Christopher, 97
Kane, Robert, 65
Kang, Jerry, 26
Kant, Immanuel, 282
Karma, Law of, 254
Kasper, Walter, 22, 28, 54, 155
Kaufman, Gordon D., 23, 65, 66, 67, 156, 157, 158, 168, 217
Kelly, J. N. D., 232
Kempis, Thomas à, 86, 182
Keup, Wolfram, 191
Khantipalo, Phra, 257
Kim, Seeyoon, 154, 156, 188
King, Martin Luther, 177, 229, 285
Kinzer, Craig, xii
Knitter, Paul, 249
Knox, John, 25, 151, 272
Konstantine, Steven, 84
Kraus, C. Norman, 149, 214, 217
Kubo, Sakae, 81, 169
Kümmel, Werner Georg, 154
Küng, Hans, 274
LaBarre, Weston, 191
Lafargue, Paul, 128
Lakoff, George, 132
Langford, Michael, 65
Lasch, Christopher, 241
Lash, Nicholas, 29, 38, 50, 54, 55, 57, 59, 67, 76, 81, 85, 91, 92, 94, 95, 206, 239, 240, 245, 249, 252, 273
Latin America, 156, 188, 231
law, 4, 16, 26, 63, 78, 98, 102, 111, 112, 126, 133, 169, 174, 191, 246, 254, 278, 282, 295
legalism, 269
Levinas, Emmanuel, 98
Lewis, C. S., 2, 89, 156, 163, 201, 222
Lian, Alexander, 68, 279
liberation, 38, 61, 63, 128, 181, 211, 231, 258
life beyond death, 6, 99, 122, 153-6, 184-203, 213, 216, 217, 220, 275-84
Lindars, Barnabas, 150
Lindbeck, George A., 12, 33, 272
Lingis, Alphonso, 98
liturgy, 67, 234, 240
Livingstone, Elizabeth, 150
Løgstrup, Knud, 98
Longacre, Doris Jantzen, 125
Loughlin, Gerard, 33
love, criterion of, 14, 17
Lowry, H. Maynard, 283
lying, 19, 44, 62, 74, 139, 145, 151, 225, 277
MacIntyre, Alasdair, 33, 106, 117, 121
Mackey, James P., 156, 157
Mackintosh, H. R., 170
Madden, Edward H., 39
Marshall, I. Howard, 155

Martyr, Justin, 177, 195
Marx, Karl, 128
Marxism, 157, 255, 262
Mascall, Eric L., 82, 97
Maynard-Reid, Pedrito, 230
McClendon, James Wm., 32, 57, 150, 178, 189
McDaniel, Jay, 281
McFague, Sallie, 11, 163, 164
McGuire, Brian Patrick, 231
McIntyre, John, 1
McKelway, Alexander J., 63
McNaughton, David, 117
Meeks, M. Douglas, 124
Meier, John P., 174
Meilaender, Gilbert, 106, 123
Meilaender, Gilbert C., 125
memory, 66, 79, 150, 151, 152, 190, 221, 233, 244, 252
Mesar, Joseph, 238
Methodism, 231, 249
Metzger, Bruce M., 149
Meyer, Ben F., 153, 170
Micks, Marianne H., 236
Migliore, Daniel, 62
Milbank, John, 153, 162, 220, 246, 254, 257
Miles, Margaret R., 86, 183
militarism, 143
mission, Christian, 229, 247, 249, 250, 251, 253, 255, 256, 257, 258, 259, 262, 263, 264
mobility, geographic, 241
Moltmann, Jürgen, 83, 160, 173, 180, 181, 182, 185, 186, 212, 213, 283
Morris, Thomas V., 9, 149, 151
Moule, C. F. D., 60, 149, 152, 154, 155, 188, 189
Muller, Wayne, 81, 169
Munzer, Stephen R., x
Murdoch, Iris, 98, 119
Murphy, Liam, 125
Murphy, Nancey C., 27, 64, 65
mysticism, 38, 180
Nagel, Thomas, 26, 28, 116
narrative, 16, 66, 168, 195, 232, 234, 253, 254
Nazism, 36, 185, 243
Nelson, Mark, 209
Neville, Robert C., 82, 233
Newman, John Henry, 25
Niebuhr, H. Richard, 51, 88, 248
Niebuhr, Reinhold, 135, 143, 145, 177, 198
Noddings, Nel, 106, 114, 212
non-human world, 23, 64, 76, 82, 89, 102, 106, 121, 122, 123, 124, 126, 134, 182, 199, 205, 277, 278, 283, 284
Nove, Alec, 127

Nussbaum, Martha C., 103, 107, 117, 125
O'Collins, Gerald, 36, 155, 158, 187, 193, 194
O'Donovan, Oliver M. T., 88, 99, 112, 160
O'Neill, John C., 187, 193
O'Neill, Onora, 125
Oderberg, David S., 107
Oppenheimer, Helen, 97
oppression, 16, 31, 36, 50, 60, 94, 114, 119, 123, 132, 133, 165, 174, 175, 176, 181, 189, 240, 241, 245, 256, 269, 278, 279
orientation, sexual, 238, 246
Origen, 71, 177
otherness, 2, 16, 19, 25, 30, 31, 32, 33, 35, 83, 93, 95, 96, 98, 249, 267, 268
Owen, Huw Parri, 60, 153, 208
ownership, 127
Oxfam, 42, 78
Oxford, 2, 9, 13, 21, 27, 28, 29, 39, 44, 54, 65, 66, 68, 72, 74, 87, 88, 89, 92, 93, 96, 98, 102, 105, 107, 114, 116, 117, 119, 123, 125, 138, 141, 149, 153, 155, 158, 162, 188, 194, 199, 205, 212, 220, 226, 249, 278
Pailin, David A., 72
Pannenberg, Wolfhart, 5, 22, 23, 24, 49, 54, 132, 142, 149, 155, 156, 182, 184, 186, 187, 188, 190, 192, 194, 195, 197, 216
Pascal, Blaise, 34
Pateman, Carole, 127
patriarchy, 132, 133, 165, 173, 181
Paul, St., 3, 4, 28, 75, 79, 91, 105, 170, 177, 188, 190, 191, 194, 248, 269, 270, 285
Peacocke, Arthur, 65
Pentz, Rebecca, 154, 165
perfection, moral and spiritual, 207
Perkins, Pheme, 187
Pike, Nelson, 49
Pilate, Pontius, 170, 177, 180, 195, 218
Placher, William C., 25, 33, 61, 272
Plantinga, Alvin, 27, 39, 149
Plaskow, Judith, 145
Plé, Albert, 132
Pliny, 151, 152
pluralism, religious, 250
    Buddhist opposition to, 257
Pokorny, Petr, 188
politics, 6, 36, 50, 64, 88, 100, 124, 126, 127, 159, 167, 171-85, 189, 230, 231, 237, 243-67, 275-84, 295
Polkinghorne, John C., 28, 65, 82
Potter, Karl H., 254
poverty, 77, 123, 124, 125, 126, 127, 138, 139, 167, 174, 175, 178, 213, 230, 231, 237, 238, 242, 258, 267

Powell, John, 2, 111
power, economic, 127
Prather, Gayle, 2, 111
Prather, Hugh, 2, 111
prayer, 6, 21, 34, 38, 60, 64, 70, 71, 72, 73, 90, 91, 139, 140, 141, 206, 232, 236, 273
Price, Henry Habberly, 69, 73
priests, priesthood, 175, 231, 232
progress, 101, 198, 205, 271, 279, 282
promises, 3, 34, 40, 41, 47, 76, 105, 108, 109, 111, 139, 185, 189, 230, 266
Provonsha, Jack W., 11, 13, 34, 132, 135, 142, 200, 204, 214, 216, 248
punishment, 7, 87, 199, 211, 213, 214, 215, 219, 222, 223
Quine, Willard Van Orman, 32
racism, 143
Radin, Dean, 73
Rahner, Karl, 5, 23, 52, 54, 65, 70, 85, 87, 91, 92, 144, 151, 156, 161, 170, 177, 222, 264, 273, 274
Ramsey, Paul, 109
Rauschenbusch, Walter, 5, 177
reconciliation, 52, 70, 122, 123, 175, 199, 210, 220, 222
Regan, Tom, 123
relativism, 30, 33, 36
Reynaud, Emmanuel, 164
Richardson, Herbert W., 81, 169
Riches, John K., 62, 112, 155, 157, 170, 213, 249
Ringe, Sharon, 174
Riverside, California, 241, 295
Robinson, John A. T., 162, 193
Roemer, John, 127
Roman Empire, 4, 149, 151, 159, 160, 165, 167, 171, 172, 175, 176, 177, 180, 184, 185, 187, 193, 195, 213, 218, 219
Rowland, Christopher, 153, 154, 170, 171, 174, 175, 176, 190, 194, 195
Rowlands, Mark, 123
Royce, Josiah, 229
Runzo, Joseph, 36
Rwanda, 247
Sabbath, 81, 82, 84, 128, 150, 160, 168, 169, 202, 206, 207, 238, 275, 284
sacraments, 74, 158, 229, 234, 235, 236, 244
Sales, St. Francis de, 5, 86
salvation, 14, 22, 24, 154, 197-204, 212-7, 225, 226, 257-64, 280
    disagreements about meaning of, 257
    lordship, 201, 202
    personal growth and healing as dimensions of, 198, 204, 205, 207, 208, 209, 260
    universal, 226, 227
Sanders, E. P., 154, 155, 169, 266

Sapontzis, Stephen F., 123
Saunders, Aimi, 145
Sayers, Dorothy, 213, 214
Scanlon, Thomas M., 116
scapegoats, scapegoating, 218, 219, 271
Schaper, Donna, 81, 169
Schillebeeckx, Edward, 189
Schleiermacher, Friedrich, 38, 234
Schlesinger, George, 39
Schor, Juliet, 125, 128
Schweizer, Eduard, 60, 152, 155, 188
science, natural, 51, 64, 66, 82, 96, 97, 109, 123, 157, 245, 295
Scriven, Charles, 81, 141, 169, 238, 249, 250, 253, 255
Scruton, Roger, 106
Searle, John R., 21, 65
self-love, 133, 135
sexism, 143, 279
sexuality, 100, 111, 132, 133, 143, 144, 164, 238, 246, 268, 278
shalom, 106, 123
Shaw, Russell, 102, 105
Sheldrake, Rupert, 142, 158, 220, 221
Sheybany, Sarvenaz, 30
Shue, Henry, 125
Sider, Ronald J., 125
sin, original, 131, 141, 142, 144
slavery, 14, 119, 128, 138, 139, 140, 174, 185, 219, 230, 248, 256
Smalley, Stephen S., 150
Smart, Ninian, 84
Smith, Kenneth L., 229
Sobrino, Jon, 156, 188, 189
Son of Man, 154, 156, 188
South Africa, 231
Spangler, J. Robert, 205
spirituality, 3, 14, 15, 70, 81, 82, 85, 91, 96, 132, 177, 201, 204, 253, 262
Sponheim, Paul R., 142, 146
Stackhouse, Max L., 254, 255
Stanley, D. M., 151
Stark, Rodney, 219, 256
Stauffer, Ethelbert, 187, 190, 192, 195
Stead, Christopher, 162
Stein, Robert H., 155
Stout, Jeffrey, 26, 33, 120, 121, 265
Strand, Kenneth L., 81, 169
Sturch, Richard, 149, 156
Suchocki, Marjorie, 67, 70, 73, 79, 134, 249
Sutherland, Stewart, 13, 78
Svonkin, Craig, xi, 199
Swinburne, Richard, 9, 27, 39, 45, 65, 66, 141, 144, 149, 188, 205, 206, 215, 222, 223
Sykes, Stephen W., 32, 153, 157, 170, 234, 245
Talbott, Thomas B., 14, 222, 225
Taylor, Charles, 239

Teel, Charles W., 132, 233, 256, 269, 284
Teeple, Howard M., 156
Tennis, Diane, 165
Testament, First, 4, 60, 168, 219
Testament, Newer, 25, 100, 149, 152, 153, 154, 155, 158, 173, 177, 187, 188, 192, 213, 268
Thatcher, Adrian, 149
Theissen, Gerd, 175
theology, Christian, 1, 6, 8, 10, 11, 13, 14, 15, 16, 17, 25, 54, 56, 63, 97, 132, 157, 191, 222
theology, natural, 268
Thiemann, Ronald, 153
Thiselton, Anthony, 25, 31
Thomas, Owen C., 65
Thorp, John, 65
thrift shops, 126
Tilley, Terrence, 261
Tillich, Paul, 2, 65, 66, 67, 73, 88, 92, 93, 105, 135, 145, 199, 200
Toffler, Alvin, 241
Tollefsen, Olaf, 65
Torrance, Thomas F., 81, 169
Tracy, Thomas F., 65, 66
Trajan, 151
transit, public, 126
Trocmé, André, 174
Trungpa, Chögyam, 193
trust, basic, 24, 37, 49, 50, 51, 135, 202, 204, 206
truth, absolute, 80, 130, 148, 166, 228
Turner, H. E. W., 154
Turner, Max, 155
Twain, Mark, 138, 139, 140
Tyrell, George, 158
Van Dolson, Leo R., 205
Van Till, Howard J., 82
Vanauken, Jean, 90
Vanauken, Sheldon, 89, 90
Vanhoozer, Kevin J., 11, 115
Vawter, Bruce, 153, 187, 190, 192
vegetarianism, 126
Verhey, Allen, 173, 174
vocation, 6, 14, 39, 48, 57, 87, 118, 119, 133, 140, 153, 180, 216, 220, 229, 232, 259, 268
Wallerstein, Judith S., 235
Walzer, Michael, 127
Ward, Keith, 9, 27, 42, 63, 66, 71, 72, 92, 122, 149, 204
wealth, 41, 42, 75, 94, 105, 123, 124, 126, 127, 138, 174
Webb, Elenor, vi, ix, 1, 3, 4, 7, 11, 14, 15, 16, 17, 22, 28, 42, 50, 57, 59, 61, 86, 92, 93, 111, 116, 138, 145, 150, 197, 200, 202, 210, 215, 220, 229, 232, 246, 265, 267, 268, 274
Weil, Simone, 86, 93

Weiss, Herold, 169
Werpehowski, William, 32, 262, 263
Westerhoff, John H., 233
White, Ellen G., 135, 159, 208, 270
White, Vernon, 162, 215
Whitehead, Alfred North, 283
Whittier, John Greenleaf, 13
Wilckens, Ulrich, 153, 189, 192
Williams, Bernard, 16, 106
Williams, H. A., 271
Williams, Rowan, 96
Willimon, William H., 233, 234, 235, 269, 273
Winn, Dick, 274
Witherington, Ben, 154
Wolters, Albert M., 99, 100, 101, 103
Wolterstorff, Nicholas P., 27, 69, 102, 103, 106, 233
worship, 3, 20, 21, 30, 34, 52, 56, 62, 72, 82, 89, 90, 91, 129, 150, 151, 176, 195, 206, 207, 226-47
Wren, Brian, 164, 165
Wright, N. T., 187, 193
Wyschogrod, Edith, 98
Yandell, Keith, 13, 44
Yoder, John Howard, 174, 177, 178, 180
Young, Norman, 83
Yunker, James A., 127
Zepp, Ira G., 229

About the Author

GARY CHARTIER is Assistant Professor of Law and Business Ethics in the School of Business at La Sierra University, Riverside, California. A California native, he earned a BA from La Sierra (1987, history and political science) before studying religion and philosophy at Claremont Graduate School. He received a PhD in 1991 from the University of Cambridge, England, for a dissertation entitled "Toward a Theology and Ethics of Friendship." He holds a JD from the University of California at Los Angeles, from which he graduated in 2001 as a member of the Order of the Coif.

He has taught religion, philosophy, public policy, business ethics, and other subjects at La Sierra, Loma Linda, Brunel, and California Baptist Universities. His byline has appeared in publications including *Religious Studies*, *Legal Theory*, the *American Journal of Jurisprudence*, the *UCLA Law Review*, *Ratio Juris*, the *Annual Review of Law and Ethics*, the *Anglican Theological Review*, and *Conversations in Theology and Religious Studies*. He is at work on a variety of projects in the fields of law, philosophy, and religion.

Formerly the managing editor of La Sierra's *Adventist Heritage* journal and a member of the editorial staff of *Spectrum*, he is also a business consultant, serving as a member of the strategic consulting team of Thomas and Associates LLC. His hobbies include philosophy, film, writing, genre fiction, spicy food, and interminable conversation.

www.ingramcontent.com/pod-product-compliance
Lightning Source LLC
Chambersburg PA
CBHW021136230426
43667CB00005B/139